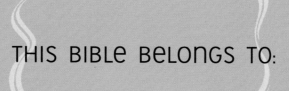

THIS BIBLE BELONGS TO:

_____

GIVEN BY:

_____

DATE:

_____

OCCASION:

_____

*"Charm can fool you, and beauty can trick you,*
*but a woman who respects the LORD should be praised."*
—PROVERBS 31:30

# revolve2™

## The Complete New Testament

### A Nelson BibleZine™

**NCV**™
NEW CENTURY VERSION®

**TRANSIT**®
www.TransitBooks.com
A Division of Thomas Nelson, Inc.
www.ThomasNelson.com

**NELSON BIBLES**
A Division of Thomas Nelson Publishers
*Since 1798*
www.thomasnelson.com

For media inquiries, contact Thomas Nelson, Inc., at:
P.O. Box 141000
Nashville, TN 37214-1000
1-800-251-4000

Managing Editor: Margaret Feinberg
Cover Design: Anderson Thomas Design, Inc.
Cover Photography: GettyOne
Interior Design: Heather Dryden
Contributors: Margaret Feinberg, Valerie Gibbs, Natalie Gillespie, Carrie Hagar, Lori Jones, Melissa Riddle

# TABLE OF CONTENTS

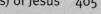

# INTRODUCTION

If life is a journey, then the Bible is your survival guide. It offers hope when you need a pick-me-up. It is filled with wisdom when you don't know what to do. And it provides direction when you feel like you've lost your way.

More importantly, the Bible holds the keys to living the God-infused life. The Bible reveals basic truths about God. Who he is. What he's like. And what he has done and is still doing today to express his love. It's designed to be one of the primary resources you use to connect your heart to God's heart.

The Bible is composed of chapters and broken down into verses. In the first four books of the New Testament—Matthew, Mark, Luke, and John—you'll learn about Jesus (God's Son) and his life on earth. You'll read about his death and resurrection, which was the greatest turning point in history. You'll learn about the grassroots movement that turned the world upside down. You'll read books that describe the birth of the church, the adventures of the first believers, and instructions to Christians of all generations.

## ALONG THE WAY, YOU'RE GOING TO READ ABOUT EVERYDAY PEOPLE.

You'll encounter doubting Thomas and die-hard Paul. You'll meet the overly ambitious Peter and the passionate Paul. You'll learn about how a renegade group of teens and twentysomethings, known as followers, or disciples, transformed the world with a simple message.

When you read the Bible, you need to have two sets of lenses. With one set of lenses, study the individuals, stories, and details. With the other set of lenses, look at the big picture. What does the entire book or series of books you're reading reveal about God? What themes appear again and again? How does what you read challenge you personally?

We've added some features to help you along the way. Every book has an **Introduction** that explores the background of the book you're reading. **Radical Faith** challenges you to trust God with everything you've got. **Promises** highlight all the commitments God has made to you. **Learn It and Live It** teaches you how to apply what you're reading to your life. **Bible Bios** tell the stories of real-life girls of the Bible. **Blabs** offer helpful answers to the questions you're asking every day. **Relationships** gives you tips on getting along with others. **Beauty Secrets** reveal ways to highlight both your inner and outer beauty. **Guys Speak Out** provides opinions from real-life teen guys. You'll also read about God's grace and power in **Changed Lives.** Plus, there's a ton of extra features to help you think, learn, and grow.

## LET THE JOURNEY BEGIN!

# a note about the *new century version*®

God never intended the Bible to be too difficult for his people. To make sure God's message was clear, the authors of the Bible recorded God's word in familiar everyday language. These books brought a message that the original readers could understand. These first readers knew that God spoke through these books. Down through the centuries, many people wanted a Bible so badly that they copied different Bible books by hand!

Today, now that the Bible is readily available, many Christians do not regularly read it. Many feel that the Bible is too hard to understand or irrelevant to life.

The *New Century Version* captures the clear and simple message that the very first readers understood. This version presents the Bible as God intended it: clear and dynamic.

A team of scholars from the World Bible Translation Center worked together with twenty-one other experienced Bible scholars from all over the world to translate the text directly from the best available Greek and Hebrew texts. You can trust that this Bible accurately presents God's Word as it came to us in the original languages.

Translators kept sentences short and simple. They avoided difficult words and worked to make the text easier to read. They used modern terms for places and measurements. And they put figures of speech and idiomatic expressions ("he was gathered to his people") in language that even children understand ("he died").

Following the tradition of other English versions, the *New Century Version* indicates the divine name, *Yahweh,* by putting LORD, and sometimes GOD, in capital letters. This distinguishes it from *Adonai,* another Hebrew word that is translated Lord.

We acknowledge the infallibility of God's Word and yet our own frailty. We pray that God will use this Bible to help you understand his rich truth for yourself. To God be the glory.

## FROM THE EDITORS OF *REVOLVE 2*

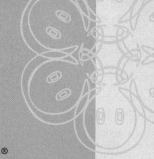

# THE NEW TESTAMENT

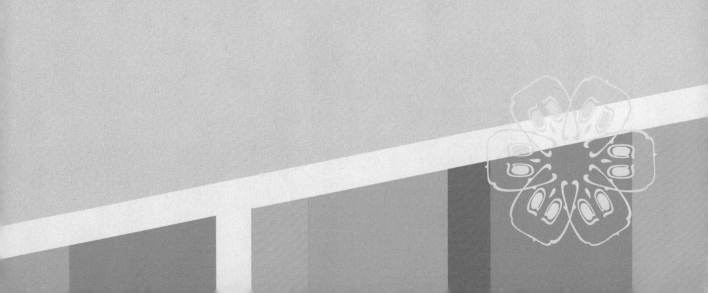

# Matthew (also called Levi)

was a tax collector when he first met Jesus. In biblical times, tax collectors were pretty much the most ruthless, corrupt professionals around. They regularly collected not only what was due the government, but also a little—or a lot—extra for themselves.

# Matthew

### Proclaims Jesus as the Long-Awaited Messiah

And yet, Jesus saw something in Matthew that the rest of us might have missed—a heart ready for change. When Matthew heard the call of Jesus, he followed and never looked back. He spent the rest of his life spreading the Good News as Christ's follower.

The Book of Matthew may seem to start a bit slowly (so-and-so was the father of so-and-so, etc.), but this genealogy lesson shows the royal lineage of Jesus and establishes King David as his ancestor.

Of the four Gospels—Matthew, Mark, Luke, and John—Matthew offers the most complete record of what Jesus taught. With four different authors telling basically the same stories, there are bound to be some differences among the four Gospels. Matthew's most distinguishable characteristic is that he never wavers from his central purpose: to show that Jesus is Israel's long-awaited Messiah. This book reads likes an encyclopedia of Christ—what he saw, what he did, and what he encountered. In this book, you will discover the teachings of Christ, lessons that have changed lives for more than two thousand years. Lessons that will change your life, too.

1

The Family History of Jesus

1 This is the family history of Jesus Christ. He came from the family of David, and David came from the family of Abraham.

2 Abraham was the father" of Isaac.

Isaac was the father of Jacob.

Jacob was the father of Judah and his brothers.

3 Judah was the father of Perez and Zerah.

(Their mother was Tamar.)

Perez was the father of Hezron.

Hezron was the father of Ram.

4 Ram was the father of Amminadab.

Amminadab was the father of Nahshon.

Nahshon was the father of Salmon.

5 Salmon was the father of Boaz.

(Boaz's mother was Rahab.)

Boaz was the father of Obed.

(Obed's mother was Ruth.)

Obed was the father of Jesse.

6 Jesse was the father of King David.

David was the father of Solomon.

(Solomon's mother had been Uriah's wife.)

7 Solomon was the father of Rehoboam.

Rehoboam was the father of Abijah.

Abijah was the father of Asa.

8 Asa was the father of Jehoshaphat.

Jehoshaphat was the father of Jehoram.

Jehoram was the ancestor of Uzziah.

Jehoiachin was the father of Shealtiel.

Shealtiel was the grandfather of Zerubbabel.

13 Zerubbabel was the father of Abiud.

Abiud was the father of Eliakim.

Eliakim was the father of Azor.

14 Azor was the father of Zadok.

Zadok was the father of Akim.

Akim was the father of Eliud.

15 Eliud was the father of Eleazar.

Eleazar was the father of Matthan.

## Bible Basics

The **Bible** is "alive and working" (Hebrews 4:12), which means that we can still use it today and it will speak into our lives. It has sixty-six books that were divinely inspired by God (which means that he controlled what the authors wrote) and was written by several different men a long time ago. God wrote it through these men, and Christians believe that it is 100 percent true and will always remain true. The Bible will last forever and will always have the power to change lives. It introduces people to the true story of creation and God's plan to offer salvation to humankind so that they can spend eternity with him. The Bible is a blueprint for the way to live a God-pleasing life on earth and a preview of what eternity holds. It's also a love letter from the best crush you'll ever have.

## DIDYA KNOW

MORE THAN HALF (53%) OF TEENS GO ONLINE EVERY DAY AND 73% ARE ONLINE FIVE OR MORE DAYS A WEEK. AOL TIME WARNER

9 Uzziah was the father of Jotham.

Jotham was the father of Ahaz.

Ahaz was the father of Hezekiah.

10 Hezekiah was the father of Manasseh.

Manasseh was the father of Amon.

Amon was the father of Josiah.

11 Josiah was the grandfather of Jehoiachin and his brothers.

(This was at the time that the people were taken to Babylon.)

12 After they were taken to Babylon:

Matthan was the father of Jacob.

16 Jacob was the father of Joseph.

Joseph was the husband of Mary, and Mary was the mother of Jesus.

Jesus is called the Christ.

17 So there were fourteen generations from Abraham to David. And there were fourteen generations from David until the people were taken to Babylon. And there were fourteen generations from the time when the people were taken to Babylon until Christ was born.

### THE BIRTH OF JESUS CHRIST

18 This is how the birth of Jesus Christ came about. His mother Mary was engaged" to marry Joseph, but before they married, she learned she was pregnant by the power of the Holy Spirit. 19 Because Mary's husband, Joseph, was a good man, he did not want to disgrace her in public, so he planned to divorce her secretly.

20 While Joseph thought about these things, an angel of the Lord came to him in a dream. The angel said, "Joseph, descendant of David, don't be afraid to take Mary as your wife, because the baby in her is from the Holy Spirit. 21 She will give birth to a son, and you will name him Jesus," because he will save his people from their sins."

22 All this happened to bring about what the Lord had said through the prophet: 23 "The virgin will be pregnant. She will have a son, and they will name him Immanuel,"" which means "God is with us."

24 When Joseph woke up, he did what the Lord's angel had told him to do. Joseph took Mary as his wife, 25 but he did not have sexual relations with her until she gave birth to the son. And Joseph named him Jesus.

### WISE MEN COME TO VISIT JESUS

2 Jesus was born in the town of Bethlehem in Judea during the time

notes 1:2 father "Father" in Jewish lists of ancestors can sometimes mean grandfather or more distant relative. 1:18 engaged For the Jewish people an engagement was a lasting agreement, which could only be broken by a divorce. If a bride-to-be was unfaithful, it was considered adultery, and she could be put to death. 1:21 Jesus The name "Jesus" means "salvation." 1:23 "The virgin . . . Immanuel" Quotation from Isaiah 7:14.

when Herod was king. When Jesus was born, some wise men from the east came to Jerusalem. [2]They asked, "Where is the baby who was born to be the king of the Jews? We saw his star in the east and have come to worship him."

[3]When King Herod heard this, he was troubled, as well as all the people in Jerusalem. [4]Herod called a meeting of all the leading priests and teachers of the law and asked them where the Christ would be born. [5]They answered, "In the town of Bethlehem in Judea. The prophet wrote about this in the Scriptures:

[6]'But you, Bethlehem, in the land of Judah,
 are important among the tribes of
  Judah.
A ruler will come from you
 who will be like a shepherd for my
  people Israel.' "

*Micah 5:2*

[7]Then Herod had a secret meeting with the wise men and learned from them the exact time they first saw the star. [8]He sent the wise men to Bethlehem, saying, "Look carefully for the child. When you find him, come tell me so I can worship him too."

[9]After the wise men heard the king, they left. The star that they had seen in the east went before them until it stopped above the place where the child was. [10]When the wise men saw the star, they were filled with joy. [11]They came to the house where the child was

and saw him with his mother, Mary, and they bowed down and worshiped him. They opened their gifts and gave him treasures of gold, frankincense, and myrrh. [12]But God warned the wise men in a dream not to go back to Herod, so they returned to their own country by a different way.

## Jesus' Parents Take Him to Egypt

[13]After they left, an angel of the Lord came to Joseph in a dream and said, "Get up! Take the child and his mother and escape to Egypt, because Herod is starting to look for the child so he can kill him. Stay in Egypt until I tell you to return."

[14]So Joseph got up and left for Egypt during the night with the child and his mother. [15]And Joseph stayed in Egypt until Herod died. This happened to bring about what the Lord had said through the prophet: "I called my son out of Egypt."[n]

## Herod Kills the Baby Boys

[16]When Herod saw that the wise men had tricked him, he was furious. So he gave an order to kill all the baby boys in Bethlehem and in the surrounding area who were two years old or younger. This was in keeping with the time he learned from the wise men. [17]So what God had said through the prophet Jeremiah came true:

[18]"A voice was heard in Ramah
 of painful crying and deep sadness:
Rachel crying for her children.
 She refused to be comforted,
 because her children are dead."

*Jeremiah 31:15*

## Joseph and Mary Return

[19]After Herod died, an angel of the Lord spoke to Joseph in a dream while he was in Egypt. [20]The angel said, "Get up! Take the child and his mother and go to the land of Israel, because the people who were trying to kill the child are now dead."

[21]So Joseph took the child and his mother and went to Israel. [22]But he heard that Archelaus was now king in Judea since his

Promises:

## Matthew 1:18-25

Have you ever noticed that the story of Jesus' birth—our traditional Christmas story—has some serious drama going on in it? Mary, a young virgin girl, is engaged to be married to Joseph when, suddenly, an angel appears and tells her that she is pregnant with the Son of God! Mary is obviously stunned and afraid, but accepts what the angel says as truth. And Joseph is just supposed to believe all that?

Even though everyone probably thought Joseph was crazy for still wanting to marry her, Joseph believed the angel that visited him in his dreams and told him not to be afraid to take Mary as his wife—that this baby was indeed from God. It was risky. But with their honor on the line, but both Mary and Joseph had tremendous faith in God in the midst of extreme circumstances. And God gifted them with the opportunity to be the earthly parents of Jesus. What a tremendous blessing! God keeps his promises to us and he does what he says he will do, even when his promises seem more than a little outrageous.

### GUYS SPEAK OUT

**Q:** What do you worry about the most?
**A:** "I think I worry the most about making a good first impression on people."

 2:15 "I called . . . Egypt." Quotation from Hosea 11:1.

3

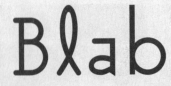

# Blab

father Herod had died. So Joseph was afraid to go there. After being warned in a dream, he went to the area of Galilee, 23to a town called Nazareth, and lived there. And so what God had said through the prophets came true: "He will be called a Nazarene.""

## THE WORK OF JOHN THE BAPTIST

3 About that time John the Baptist began preaching in the desert area of Judea. 2John said, "Change your hearts and lives because the kingdom of heaven is near." 3John the Baptist is the one Isaiah the prophet was talking about when he said:

"This is a voice of one
who calls out in the desert:
'Prepare the way for the Lord.
Make the road straight for him.' "

*Isaiah 40:3*

4John's clothes were made from camel's hair, and he wore a leather belt around his waist. For food, he ate locusts and wild honey. 5Many people came from Jerusalem and Judea and all the area around the Jordan River to hear John. 6They confessed their sins, and he baptized them in the Jordan River.

7Many of the Pharisees and Sadducees came to the place where John was baptizing people. When John saw them, he said, "You are all snakes! Who warned you to run away from God's coming punishment? 8Do the things that show you really have changed your hearts and lives. 9And don't think you can say to yourselves, 'Abraham is our father.' I tell you that God could make children for Abraham from these rocks. 10The ax is now ready to cut down the trees, and every tree that does not produce good fruit will be cut down and thrown into the fire."

11"I baptize you with water to show that your hearts and lives have changed. But there is one coming after me who is greater than I am, whose sandals I am not good enough to carry. He will baptize you with the Holy Spirit and fire. 12He will come ready to clean the grain, separating the good grain from the chaff. He will put the good part of the grain into his barn, but he will burn the chaff with a fire that cannot be put out.""

## JESUS IS BAPTIZED BY JOHN

13At that time Jesus came from Galilee to the Jordan River and wanted John to baptize him. 14But John tried to stop him, saying, "Why do you come to me to be baptized? I need to be baptized by you!"

15Jesus answered, "Let it be this way for now. We should do all things that are God's will." So John agreed to baptize Jesus.

16As soon as Jesus was baptized, he came up out of the water. Then heaven opened, and he saw God's Spirit coming down on him like a dove. 17And a voice from heaven said, "This is my Son, whom I love, and I am very pleased with him."

## THE TEMPTATION OF JESUS

4 Then the Spirit led Jesus into the desert to be tempted by the devil. 2Jesus ate nothing for forty days and nights. After this, he

# beautysecret

## Smiled Lately?

You're trapped in a room without access to any makeup, fresh clothes, or even a mirror. What's the quickest way to improve your personal appearance? Smile. A warm, friendly smile can go a long way to allowing the natural beauty that resides in you to express itself.

**notes** **2:23 Nazarene** A person from the city of Nazareth, a name probably meaning "branch" (see Isaiah 11:1). **3:10 The ax . . . fire.** This means that God is ready to punish his people who do not obey him. **3:12 He will . . . out.** This means that Jesus will come to separate good people from bad people, saving the good and punishing the bad.

was very hungry. ³The devil came to Jesus to tempt him, saying, "If you are the Son of God, tell these rocks to become bread."

⁴Jesus answered, "It is written in the Scriptures, 'A person does not live by eating only bread, but by everything God says.' "ⁿ

⁵Then the devil led Jesus to the holy city of Jerusalem and put him on a high place of the Temple. ⁶The devil said, "If you are the Son of God, jump down, because it is written in the Scriptures:

'He has put his angels in charge of you.
 They will catch you in their hands
so that you will not hit your foot on a rock.' "

*Psalm 91:11-12*

⁷Jesus answered him, "It also says in the Scriptures, 'Do not test the Lord your God.' "ⁿ

⁸Then the devil led Jesus to the top of a very high mountain and showed him all the kingdoms of the world and all their splendor. ⁹The devil said, "If you will bow down and worship me, I will give you all these things."

¹⁰Jesus said to the devil, "Go away from me, Satan! It is written in the Scriptures, 'You must worship the Lord your God and serve only him.' "ⁿ

¹¹So the devil left Jesus, and angels came and took care of him.

## Jesus Begins Work in Galilee

¹²When Jesus heard that John had been put in prison, he went back to Galilee. ¹³He left Nazareth and went to live in Capernaum, a town near Lake Galilee, in the area near Zebulun and Naphtali. ¹⁴Jesus did this to bring about what the prophet Isaiah had said:

¹⁵"Land of Zebulun and land of Naphtali
    along the sea,
 beyond the Jordan River.
    This is Galilee where the non-Jewish
       people live.
¹⁶These people who live in darkness
    will see a great light.
 They live in a place covered with the
       shadows of death,
    but a light will shine on them."

*Isaiah 9:1-2*

## BIBLE BIOS

# Abigail

**[1 SAMUEL 25]** Poor Abigail missed out when it came to getting a good man. Her foolish husband, Nabal, got into big trouble with David. In fact, if it weren't for Abigail, Nabal's arrogant rudeness would have cost him his life. But Abigail was quick on her feet, and her masterful negotiations squelched David's anger and saved her husband's neck. Abigail was one of those people who could look a challenge straight in the eye and bring the best out of a tough situation. She impressed David so much that, when Nabal died suddenly, David proposed to Abigail and she became his wife. Finally, a husband who appreciated her!

## Jesus Chooses Some Followers

¹⁷From that time Jesus began to preach, saying, "Change your hearts and lives, because the kingdom of heaven is near."

¹⁸As Jesus was walking by Lake Galilee, he saw two brothers, Simon (called Peter) and his brother Andrew. They were throwing a net into the lake because they were fishermen. ¹⁹Jesus said, "Come follow me, and I will make you fish for people." ²⁰So Simon and Andrew immediately left their nets and followed him.

²¹As Jesus continued walking by Lake Galilee, he saw two other brothers, James and John, the sons of Zebedee. They were in a boat with their father Zebedee, mending their nets. Jesus told them to come with him. ²²Immediately they left the boat and their father, and they followed Jesus.

## Jesus Teaches and Heals People

²³Jesus went everywhere in Galilee, teaching in the synagogues, preaching the Good News about the kingdom of heaven, and healing all the people's diseases and sicknesses. ²⁴The news about Jesus spread all over Syria, and people brought all the sick to him. They were suffering from different kinds of diseases. Some were in great pain, some had demons, some were epileptics,ⁿ and some were paralyzed. Jesus healed all of them. ²⁵Many people from Galilee, the Ten Towns,ⁿ Jerusalem, Judea, and the land across the Jordan River followed him.

## Jesus Teaches the People

5 When Jesus saw the crowds, he went up on a hill and sat down. His followers came to him, ²and he began to teach them, saying:

³"Those people who know they have great
    spiritual needs are happy,
 because the kingdom of heaven belongs
    to them.
⁴Those who are sad now are happy,
 because God will comfort them.
⁵Those who are humble are happy,
 because the earth will belong to them.
⁶Those who want to do right more than
    anything else are happy,
 because God will fully satisfy them.

4:4 **'A person . . . says.'** Quotation from Deuteronomy 8:3.   4:7 **'Do . . . God.'** Quotation from Deuteronomy 6:16.   4:10 **'You . . . him.'** Quotation from Deuteronomy 6:13.   4:24 **epileptics** People with a disease that causes them sometimes to lose control of their bodies and maybe faint, shake strongly, or not be able to move.   4:25 **Ten Towns** In Greek, called "Decapolis." It was an area east of Lake Galilee that once had ten main towns.

## Matthew 4:4

What do you live by? What do you "feed" your mind and your heart with? It could be an obsession with the way you look, an activity at school, a hope to be popular, drugs, alcohol, achievements, boys, or any number of things. Relationships, hobbies, and having fun are healthy, but if you only go to them for satisfaction and purpose, you'll wind up pretty miserable. Following your friends' ideas, dwelling on your own worries, or chasing after what impresses this world just won't cut it. All that stuff fades away (1 Peter 1:24-25). Here Jesus says that no one can really be living if they aren't continually hooked up to the life source—which is God. He says that humans can only live from "everything God says." When your heart, mind, spirit, and soul don't feed on the substance of his truth, it has the same effect as when your body doesn't get food. Without nourishment, your body doesn't operate like it should, and you'll eventually die. You are designed to depend on God in an extreme way. God will fill you up with what is true and meaningful when you spend time with him in his Word every day. Don't try to live by anything else.

7Those who show mercy to others are happy, because God will show mercy to them. 8Those who are pure in their thinking are happy,
because they will be with God. 9Those who work to bring peace are happy,
because God will call them his children. 10Those who are treated badly for doing good are happy,
because the kingdom of heaven belongs to them.

11"People will insult you and hurt you. They will lie and say all kinds of evil things about you because you follow me. But when they do, you will be happy. 12Rejoice and be glad, because you have a great reward waiting for you in heaven. People did the same evil things to the prophets who lived before you.

### You are Like Salt and Light

13"You are the salt of the earth. But if the salt loses its salty taste, it cannot be made salty again. It is good for nothing, except to be thrown out and walked on.

14"You are the light that gives light to the world. A city that is built on a hill cannot be hidden. 15And people don't hide a light under a bowl. They put it on a lampstand so the light shines for all the people in the house. 16In the same way, you should be a light for other people. Live so that they will see the good things you do and will praise your Father in heaven.

### The Importance of the Law

17"Don't think that I have come to destroy the law of Moses or the teaching of the prophets. I have not come to destroy them but to bring about what they said. 18I tell you the truth, nothing will disappear from the law until heaven and earth are gone. Not even the smallest letter or the smallest part of a letter will be lost until everything has happened. 19Whoever refuses to obey any command and teaches other people not to obey that command will be the least important in the kingdom of heaven. But whoever obeys the commands and teaches other people to obey them will be great in the kingdom of heaven. 20I tell

you that if you are no more obedient than the teachers of the law and the Pharisees, you will never enter the kingdom of heaven.

### Jesus Teaches About Anger

21"You have heard that it was said to our people long ago, 'You must not murder anyone.'" Anyone who murders another will be judged.' 22But I tell you, if you are angry with a brother or sister," you will be judged. If you say bad things to a brother or sister, you will be judged by the council. And if you call someone a fool, you will be in danger of the fire of hell.

> "THOSE WHO SHOW MERCY TO OTHERS ARE HAPPY, BECAUSE GOD WILL SHOW MERCY TO THEM."

23"So when you offer your gift to God at the altar, and you remember that your brother or sister has something against you, 24leave your gift there at the altar. Go and make peace with that person, and then come and offer your gift.

25"If your enemy is taking you to court, become friends quickly, before you go to court. Otherwise, your enemy might turn you over to the judge, and the judge might give you to a guard to put you in jail. 26I tell you the truth, you will not leave there until you have paid everything you owe.

### Jesus Teaches About Sexual Sin

27"You have heard that it was said, 'You must not be guilty of adultery.'" 28But I tell you that if anyone looks at a woman and wants to sin sexually with her, in his mind he has already done that sin with the woman. 29If your right eye causes you to sin, take it out and throw it away. It is better to lose one part of your body than to have your whole body thrown into hell. 30If your right hand causes you to sin, cut it off and throw it away. It is better to lose one part of your body than for your whole body to go into hell.

 **5:21 You . . . anyone.** Quotation from Exodus 20:13; Deuteronomy 5:17. **5:22 brother . . . sister** Although the Greek text reads "brother" here and throughout this book, Jesus' words were meant for the entire church, including men and women. **5:27 'You . . . adultery.'** Quotation from Exodus 20:14; Deuteronomy 5:18.

# January

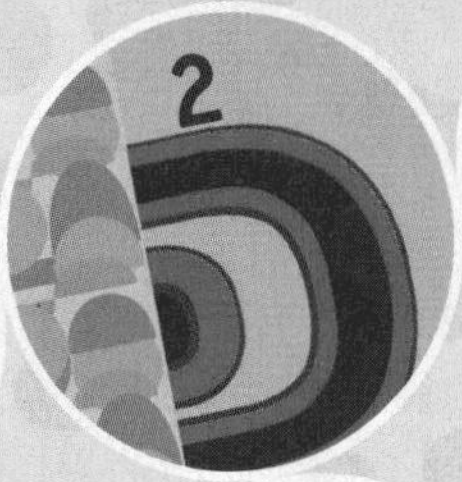

**1**
New Year's Day. Practice writing the new date a few times.

**2**

**3**

**4**
January is National Soup Month. Make some chicken noodle or vegetable beef soup and take it to a shut-in.

**5**

**6**
Write a thank-you note to a teacher.

**7**
Pray for a person of influence: It's Katie Couric's birthday.

**8**
Clean out your closet and give away your goodies to someone who needs them.

**9**

**10**
Read Genesis 1–3. Reflect on God's creativity.

**11**

**12**
Try to find God-themes in a movie you watch this weekend.

**13**

**14**

**15**
social

**16**

**17**
Tell your mom how much you love her.

**18**
Pray for a person of influence: It's Kevin Costner's birthday.

**19**

**20**

**21**

**22**
Memorize Mark 16:15 and look for one way to practice that verse today.

**23**

**24**
Organize a snowball fight with friends.

**25**
Pray for a person of influence: It's Alicia Keys's birthday.

**26**
Pray for a person of influence: It's Kirk Franklin's birthday.

**27**
Make a list of people you're mad at. One by one, spend time forgiving and praying for each person.

**28**

**29**

**30**

**31**
Pray for a person of influence: Today is Justin Timberlake's birthday.

> The thing you should want most is God's kingdom and doing what God wants.
> —Matthew 6:33

# Quiz

# are you a FLIRT?

**1. YOUR CRUSH RANDOMLY STOPS YOU IN THE HALL BETWEEN CLASSES AND TELLS YOU THAT YOU LOOK NICE TODAY. YOU:**

A. Giggle several times, put your arm through his, and insist he walk you to your next class.

B. Uncomfortably look at him like he just sprouted an extra head and quickly walk away.

C. Smile and say a genuine thanks. Chat with him for a few minutes and go on to your class.

**2. IT WAS JUST ANNOUNCED THAT A CUTE BOY IN YOUR CLASS WON AN IMPORTANT SWIM MEET. AS SOON AS YOU SEE HIM, YOU:**

A. Energetically say a congrats and ask what his winning time was.

B. Run up to him, squealing his name loudly. Give him a big hug and gush about how he must be the best swimmer in the *whole world*.

C. Mumble a few words of affirmation along with a pack of your friends as you pass by him in the hall.

**3. IT'S THE FIRST DAY OF SCHOOL AND YOU HAVEN'T SEEN YOUR CRUSH IN A WHILE. UPON SPOTTING HIM, YOU:**

A. Say hi in passing and meet up with a group your friends.

B. Duck into the nearest classroom before he sees you.

C. Corner him and insist that he tell you all about his summer vacation.

**4. DO YOUR FRIENDS TEASE YOU ABOUT FLIRTING WITH GUYS?**

A. Never.

B. Constantly.

C. Occasionally.

**5. YOU CONSIDER YOUR BEST SOCIAL SKILL TO BE:**

A. Friendliness.

B. Listening.

C. Conversation.

**SCORING:** 1. A=3, B=1, C=2    2. A=2, B=3, C=1    3. A=2, B=1, C=3    4. A=1, B=3, C=2    5. A=2, B=1, C=3

**IF YOU SCORED 12-15, YOU MAY BE A MAJOR FLIRT:**
All right, girl, we know how hard it can sometimes be to contain yourself around boys. The attention you get from them is nice, right? You are definitely outgoing and probably like being the center of attention—especially among boys. But honestly, a lot of guys consider flirting to be really annoying sometimes. Not to mention it may make you seem a little desperate. So just tone it down a bit.

**IF YOU SCORED 8-11, YOU ARE PROBABLY A GIRL NEXT DOOR:**
In the world of flirting, you are definitely middle-of-the-road. You're friendly and attentive without throwing yourself at any boy who walks by. That's good—guys like that about you. Besides, any boy who needs someone to gush over him all the time probably has an ego problem, right?

**IF YOU SCORED 5-7, YOU MAY BE A QUIET CUTIE:**
Okay, so maybe you're a little shy when guys are involved. And there's nothing wrong with that. Just be aware that others may think that your shyness indicates that you have no interest in them whatsoever or that you're avoiding them. You don't want to seem rude, so even though it may make you nervous, don't be afraid to offer up an occasional smile or hello.

# LEARN I+ & LIVE I+

**Matthew 2:10-11**
**Learn It:** Jesus is a king to be worshiped.
**Live It:** Give something important—your heart, your money, your time—to worship Jesus today.

**Matthew 5:6**
**Learn It:** Those who do right will be happy, because God will satisfy them.
**Live It:** Stand up for the right thing at school or with friends, even if you are the only one.

**Matthew 6:19-21**
**Learn It:** Too much stuff keeps you from having time to share Jesus with people. All that stuff has to be taken care of, leaving less time for relationships.
**Live It:** Clean out your drawers or closet today. Get rid of anything you don't use.

## Jesus Teaches About Divorce

³¹"It was also said, 'Anyone who divorces his wife must give her a written divorce paper.'" ³²But I tell you that anyone who divorces his wife forces her to be guilty of adultery. The only reason for a man to divorce his wife is if she has sexual relations with another man. And anyone who marries that divorced woman is guilty of adultery.

## Make Promises Carefully

³³"You have heard that it was said to our people long ago, 'Don't break your promises, but keep the promises you make to the Lord.'" ³⁴But I tell you, never swear an oath. Don't swear an oath using the name of heaven, because heaven is God's throne. ³⁵Don't swear an oath using the name of the earth, because the earth belongs to God. Don't swear an oath using the name of Jerusalem, because that is the city of the great King. ³⁶Don't even swear by your own head, because you cannot make one hair on your head become white or black. ³⁷Say only yes if you mean yes, and no if you mean no. If you say more than yes or no, it is from the Evil One.

## Don't Fight Back

³⁸"You have heard that it was said, 'An eye for an eye, and a tooth for a tooth.'" ³⁹But I tell you, don't stand up against an evil person. If someone slaps you on the right cheek, turn to him the other cheek also. ⁴⁰If someone wants to sue you in court and take your shirt, let him have your coat also. ⁴¹If someone forces you to go with him one mile, go with him two miles.

⁴²If a person asks you for something, give it to him. Don't refuse to give to someone who wants to borrow from you.

## Love All People

⁴³"You have heard that it was said, 'Love your neighbor' and hate your enemies.' ⁴⁴But I say to you, love your enemies. Pray for those who hurt you. ⁴⁵If you do this, you will be true children of your Father in heaven. He causes the sun to rise on good people and on evil people, and he sends rain to those who do right and to those who do wrong. ⁴⁶If you love only the people who love you, you will get no reward. Even the tax collectors do that. ⁴⁷And if you are nice only to your friends, you are no better than other people. Even those who don't know God are nice to their friends. ⁴⁸So you must be perfect, just as your Father in heaven is perfect.

## Jesus Teaches About Giving

6 "Be careful! When you do good things, don't do them in front of people to be seen by them. If you do that, you will have no reward from your Father in heaven.

²"When you give to the poor, don't be like the hypocrites. They blow trumpets in the synagogues and on the streets so that people will see them and honor them. I tell you the truth, those hypocrites already have their full reward. ³So when you give to the poor, don't let anyone know what you are doing. ⁴Your giving should be done in secret. Your Father can see what is done in secret, and he will reward you.

## Jesus Teaches About Prayer

⁵"When you pray, don't be like the hypocrites. They love to stand in the synagogues and on the street corners and pray so people will see them. I tell you the truth, they already have their full reward. ⁶When you pray, you should go into your room and close the door and pray to your Father who cannot be seen. Your Father can see what is done in secret, and he will reward you.

⁷"And when you pray, don't be like those people who don't know God. They continue saying things that mean nothing, thinking that God will hear them because of their many words. ⁸Don't be like them, because your Father knows the things you need before you ask him. ⁹So when you pray, you should pray like this:

'Our Father in heaven,
may your name always be kept holy.
¹⁰May your kingdom come
and what you want be done,
here on earth as it is in heaven.
¹¹Give us the food we need for each day.
¹²Forgive us for our sins,
just as we have forgiven those who
sinned against us.
¹³And do not cause us to be tempted,
but save us from the Evil One.'

¹⁴Yes, if you forgive others for their sins, your Father in heaven will also forgive you for your sins. ¹⁵But if you don't forgive others, your Father in heaven will not forgive your sins.

**notes**

**5:31** '**Anyone . . . divorce paper.**' Quotation from Deuteronomy 24:1.  **5:33** '**Don't . . . Lord.**' This refers to Leviticus 19:12; Numbers 30:2; Deuteronomy 23:21.  **5:38** '**An eye . . . tooth.**' Quotation from Exodus 21:24; Leviticus 24:20; Deuteronomy 19:21.  **5:43** '**Love your neighbor**' Quotation from Leviticus 19:18.

9

## Jesus Teaches about Worship

[16]"When you give up eating," don't put on a sad face like the hypocrites. They make their faces look sad to show people they are giving up eating. I tell you the truth, those hypocrites already have their full reward. [17]So when you give up eating, comb your hair and wash your face. [18]Then people will not know that you are giving up eating, but your Father, whom you cannot see, will see you. Your Father sees what is done in secret, and he will reward you.

## God Is More Important than Money

[19]"Don't store treasures for yourselves here on earth where moths and rust will destroy them and thieves can break in and steal them. [20]But store your treasures in heaven where they cannot be destroyed by moths or rust and where thieves cannot break in and steal them. [21]Your heart will be where your treasure is.

[22]"The eye is a light for the body. If your eyes are good, your whole body will be full of light. [23]But if your eyes are evil, your whole body will be full of darkness. And if the only light you have is really darkness, then you have the worst darkness.

[24]"No one can serve two masters. The person will hate one master and love the other, or will follow one master and refuse to follow the other. You cannot serve both God and worldly riches.

## Don't Worry

[25]"So I tell you, don't worry about the food or drink you need to live, or about the clothes you need for your body. Life is more than food, and the body is more than clothes. [26]Look at the birds in the air. They don't plant or harvest or store food in barns, but your heavenly Father feeds them. And you know that you are worth much more than the birds. [27]You cannot add any time to your life by worrying about it.

[28]"And why do you worry about clothes? Look at how the lilies in the field grow. They don't work or make clothes for themselves. [29]But I tell you that even Solomon with his riches was not dressed as beautifully as one of these flowers. [30]God clothes the grass in the field, which is alive today but tomorrow is thrown into the fire. So you can be even more sure that God will clothe you. Don't have so little faith! [31]Don't worry and say, 'What will we eat?' or 'What will we drink?' or 'What will we wear?' [32]The people who don't know God keep trying to get these things, and your Father in heaven knows you need them. [33]The thing you should want most is God's kingdom and doing what God wants. Then all these other things you need will be given to you. [34]So don't worry about tomorrow, because tomorrow will have its own worries. Each day has enough trouble of its own.

## Be Careful about Judging Others

7 "Don't judge other people, or you will be judged. [2]You will be judged in the same way that you judge others, and the amount you give to others will be given to you.

[3]"Why do you notice the little piece of dust in your friend's eye, but you don't notice the big piece of wood in your own eye? [4]How can you say to your friend, 'Let me take that little piece of dust out of your eye'? Look at yourself! You still have that big piece of wood in your own eye. [5]You hypocrite! First, take the wood out of your own eye. Then you will see clearly to take the dust out of your friend's eye.

[6]"Don't give holy things to dogs, and don't throw your pearls before pigs. Pigs will only trample on them, and dogs will turn to attack you.

## Ask God for What You Need

[7]"Ask, and God will give to you. Search, and you will find. Knock, and the door will open for you. [8]Yes, everyone who asks will receive. Everyone who searches will find. And everyone who knocks will have the door opened.

[9]"If your children ask for bread, which of

# Music Reviews

| GROUP: | ALBUM: |
|--------|--------|
| BEBO NORMAN | TRY |

Bebo Norman is a singer-songwriter with a witty, self-deprecating sense of humor whose lyrics tug at the heartstrings on past hits like "Great Light of the World" and "The Hammer Holds." On *Try,* Bebo is on his way to more hits with the first single "Disappear," which talks about how you can see God so much clearer when you take yourself out of the picture. Bebo's music has evolved from acoustic folk to catchy pop rock on this album, but the lyrics remain thoughtful and transparent. More hopeful than past releases, these songs—like "How You Love Me" and "Nothing Without You"—are squarely focused on God's love for us and our identity in him.

**WHY IT ROCKS: MUSICAL MATURITY AND AN UPBEAT OUTLOOK MAKE THIS ONE OF BEBO'S BEST.**

**6:16 give up eating** This is called "fasting." The people would give up eating for a special time of prayer and worship to God. It was also done to show sadness and disappointment.

you would give them a stone? ¹⁰Or if your children ask for a fish, would you give them a snake? ¹¹Even though you are bad, you know how to give good gifts to your children. How much more your heavenly Father will give good things to those who ask him!

### THE MOST IMPORTANT RULE

¹²"Do to others what you want them to do to you. This is the meaning of the law of Moses and the teaching of the prophets.

## "WHY DO YOU NOTICE THE LITTLE PIECE OF DUST IN YOUR FRIEND'S EYE, BUT YOU DON'T NOTICE THE BIG PIECE OF WOOD IN YOUR OWN EYE?"

### THE WAY TO HEAVEN IS HARD

¹³"Enter through the narrow gate. The gate is wide and the road is wide that leads to hell, and many people enter through that gate. ¹⁴But the gate is small and the road is narrow that leads to true life. Only a few people find that road.

### PEOPLE KNOW YOU BY YOUR ACTIONS

¹⁵"Be careful of false prophets. They come to you looking gentle like sheep, but they are really dangerous like wolves. ¹⁶You will know these people by what they do. Grapes don't come from thornbushes, and figs don't come from thorny weeds. ¹⁷In the same way, every good tree produces good fruit, but a bad tree produces bad fruit. ¹⁸A good tree cannot produce bad fruit, and a bad tree cannot produce good fruit. ¹⁹Every tree that does not produce good fruit is cut down and thrown into the fire. ²⁰In the same way, you will know these false prophets by what they do.

²¹"Not all those who say that I am their Lord will enter the kingdom of heaven. The only people who will enter the kingdom of heaven are those who do what my Father in heaven wants. ²²On the last day many people will say to me, 'Lord, Lord, we spoke for you, and through you we forced out demons and did many miracles.' ²³Then I will tell them clearly, 'Get away from me, you who do evil. I never knew you.'

### TWO KINDS OF PEOPLE

²⁴"Everyone who hears my words and obeys them is like a wise man who built his house on rock. ²⁵It rained hard, the floods came, and the winds blew and hit that house. But it did not fall, because it was built on rock. ²⁶Everyone who hears my words and does not obey them is like a foolish man who built his house on sand. ²⁷It rained hard, the floods came, and the winds blew and hit that house, and it fell with a big crash."

²⁸When Jesus finished saying these things, the people were amazed at his teaching, ²⁹because he did not teach like their teachers of the law. He taught like a person who had authority.

### JESUS HEALS A SICK MAN

**8** When Jesus came down from the hill, great crowds followed him. ²Then a man with a skin disease came to Jesus. The man bowed down before him and said, "Lord, you can heal me if you will."

³Jesus reached out his hand and touched the man and said, "I will. Be healed!" And immediately the man was healed from his disease. ⁴Then Jesus said to him, "Don't tell anyone about this. But go and show yourself to the priest" and offer the gift Moses commanded" for people who are made well. This will show the people what I have done."

### JESUS HEALS A SOLDIER'S SERVANT

⁵When Jesus entered the city of Capernaum, an army officer came to him, begging for help. ⁶The officer said, "Lord, my servant is at home in bed. He can't move his body and is in much pain."

⁷Jesus said to the officer, "I will go and heal him."

# Blab

**Q:** I am going to church with my friend this weekend. Do I have to take communion at a church I am only visiting?

**A:** Some churches prefer that you not take communion unless you are a member of that denomination or even that church. Ask your friend if she knows her church's policy. Taking communion is a beautiful sacrament, a celebration of the sacrifice Jesus made for our sins. If you pray about it and want to participate, go for it. If not, it is perfectly fine to pass the plate to the next person or remain seated.

**Q:** What is a "tithe"? Do I have to pay it?

**A:** The "tithe" is the firstfruit or part—often identified as ten percent—of any money you earn or receive, and the Bible says that money belongs to God. If you earn any money—through washing cars, babysitting, allowance, or a part-time job, it honors God and shows obedience to his Word if you give the first portion back to him.

**Q:** Is it okay to go to a church for youth group other than the one I attend with my parents on Sundays?

**A:** God wants you to get plugged in to a local church to spend time with other people who have the same beliefs you do, worship him, learn more of the Bible, and help others. If you feel that you get great teaching, worship, and fellowship at more than one church, then that can be a good thing. However, you also want to ask God for guidance so that you are not just taking from different churches but that you are also there enough to be able to serve and use your gifts for him.

**8:4 show . . . priest** The Law of Moses said a priest must say when a Jewish person with a skin disease was well. **8:4 Moses commanded** Read about this in Leviticus 14:1-32.

# CHECK IT OUT

## OPEN DOORS U.S.A.

Back in 1955, Brother Andrew began distributing Bibles in countries where it was forbidden to have one. Today, his Open Doors ministry continues to distribute millions of Bibles each year behind closed borders. Couriers distribute Bibles to persecuted Christians, while volunteer "Partners in Prayer" prayer teams meet on a monthly basis to cover the projects with prayer. The Underground program allows youth pastors and their youth groups to fundraise and raise awareness, and the Open Doors sister site www.donatebibles.org provides an opportunity for visitors to click a button and help send a free Bible to someone who needs one, as sponsors donate Bibles according to the number of hits the site gets.

To help Open Doors, you can forward emails to friends asking them to visit www.donate-bibles.org, pray for Christians who are being persecuted, buy a Bible to give away, sign up for newsletters to stay informed of what's happening in the local church, and donate time to a local chapter.

*Get involved by visiting* **www.opendoorsusa.com.**

8The officer answered, "Lord, I am not worthy for you to come into my house. You only need to command it, and my servant will be healed. 9I, too, am a man under the authority of others, and I have soldiers under my command. I tell one soldier, 'Go,' and he goes. I tell another soldier, 'Come,' and he comes. I say to my servant, 'Do this,' and my servant does it."

10When Jesus heard this, he was amazed. He said to those who were following him, "I tell you the truth, this is the greatest faith I have found, even in Israel. 11Many people will come from the east and from the west and will sit and eat with Abraham, Isaac, and Jacob in the kingdom of heaven. 12But those people who should be in the kingdom will be thrown outside into the darkness, where people will cry and grind their teeth with pain."

13Then Jesus said to the officer, "Go home. Your servant will be healed just as you believed he would." And his servant was healed that same hour.

## Jesus Heals Many People

14When Jesus went to Peter's house, he saw that Peter's mother-in-law was sick in bed with a fever. 15Jesus touched her hand, and the fever left her. Then she stood up and began to serve Jesus.

16That evening people brought to Jesus many who had demons. Jesus spoke and the demons left them, and he healed all the sick. 17He did these things to bring about what Isaiah the prophet had said:

"He took our suffering on him
and carried our diseases."      *Isaiah 53:4*

## People Want to Follow Jesus

18When Jesus saw the crowd around him, he told his followers to go to the other side of the lake. 19Then a teacher of the law came to Jesus and said, "Teacher, I will follow you any place you go."

20Jesus said to him, "The foxes have holes to live in, and the birds have nests, but the Son of Man has no place to rest his head."

21Another man, one of Jesus' followers, said to him, "Lord, first let me go and bury my father."

22But Jesus told him, "Follow me, and let the people who are dead bury their own dead."

## Jesus Calms a Storm

23Jesus got into a boat, and his followers went with him. 24A great storm arose on the lake so that waves covered the boat, but Jesus was sleeping. 25His followers went to him and woke him, saying, "Lord, save us! We will drown!"

26Jesus answered, "Why are you afraid? You don't have enough faith." Then Jesus got up and gave a command to the wind and the waves, and it became completely calm.

27The men were amazed and said, "What kind of man is this? Even the wind and the waves obey him!"

**DIDYA KNOW** **81% OF AMERICAN CHRISTIANS SAY UNMARRIED SEX IS MORALLY WRONG COMPARED WITH 33% OF OTHER AMERICANS.** WWW.KFF.ORG

## Jesus Heals Two Men with Demons

28When Jesus arrived at the other side of the lake in the area of the Gadarene[n] people, two men who had demons in them met him. These men lived in the burial caves and were so dangerous that people could not use the road by those caves. 29They shouted, "What do you want with us, Son of God? Did you come here to torture us before the right time?"

30Near that place there was a large herd of pigs feeding. 31The demons begged Jesus, "If

 **8:28 Gadarene** From Gadara, an area southeast of Lake Galilee.

you make us leave these men, please send us into that herd of pigs."

32Jesus said to them, "Go!" So the demons left the men and went into the pigs. Then the whole herd rushed down the hill into the lake and were drowned. 33The herdsmen ran away and went into town, where they told about all of this and what had happened to the men who had demons. 34Then the whole town went out to see Jesus. When they saw him, they begged him to leave their area.

## Jesus Heals a Paralyzed Man

9 Jesus got into a boat and went back across the lake to his own town. 2Some people brought to Jesus a man who was paralyzed and lying on a mat. When Jesus saw the faith of these people, he said to the paralyzed man, "Be encouraged, young man. Your sins are forgiven."

3Some of the teachers of the law said to themselves, "This man speaks as if he were God. That is blasphemy!"″

4Knowing their thoughts, Jesus said, "Why are you thinking evil thoughts? 5Which is easier: to say, 'Your sins are forgiven,' or to tell him, 'Stand up and walk'? 6But I will prove to you that the Son of Man has authority on earth to forgive sins." Then Jesus said to the paralyzed man, "Stand up, take your mat, and go home." 7And the man stood up and went

home. 8When the people saw this, they were amazed and praised God for giving power like this to human beings.

## Jesus Chooses Matthew

9When Jesus was leaving, he saw a man named Matthew sitting in the tax collector's booth. Jesus said to him, "Follow me," and he stood up and followed Jesus.

10As Jesus was having dinner at Matthew's house, many tax collectors and "sinners" came and ate with Jesus and his followers. 11When the Pharisees saw this, they asked Jesus' followers, "Why does your teacher eat with tax collectors and sinners?"

12When Jesus heard them, he said, "It is not the healthy people who need a doctor, but the sick. 13Go and learn what this means: 'I want kindness more than I want animal sacrifices.'″ I did not come to invite good people but to invite sinners."

## Jesus' Followers Are Criticized

14Then the followers of John″ came to Jesus and said, "Why do we and the Pharisees often give up eating for a certain time,″ but your followers don't?"

15Jesus answered, "The friends of the bridegroom are not sad while he is with them. But the time will come when the bridegroom will be taken from them, and then they will give up eating.

16"No one sews a patch of unshrunk cloth over a hole in an old coat. If he does, the patch will shrink and pull away from the coat, making the hole worse. 17Also, people never pour new wine into old leather bags. Otherwise, the bags will break, the wine will spill, and the wine bags will be ruined. But people always pour new wine into new wine bags. Then both will continue to be good."

## Jesus Gives Life to a Dead Girl and Heals a Sick Woman

18While Jesus was saying these things, a leader of the synagogue came to him. He bowed down before Jesus and said, "My daughter has just died. But if you come and lay your hand on her, she will live again." 19So Jesus and his followers stood up and went with the leader.

20Then a woman who had been bleeding for twelve years came behind Jesus and touched the edge of his coat. 21She was thinking, "If I can just touch his clothes, I will be healed."

22Jesus turned and saw the woman and said, "Be encouraged, dear woman. You are made well because you believed." And the woman was healed from that moment on.

23Jesus continued along with the leader and went into his house. There he saw the funeral musicians and many people crying. 24Jesus said, "Go away. The girl is not dead, only asleep." But the people laughed at him. 25After the crowd had been thrown out of the house, Jesus went into the girl's room and took hold of her hand, and she stood up. 26The news about this spread all around the area.

## Jesus Heals More People

27When Jesus was leaving there, two blind men followed him. They cried out, "Have mercy on us, Son of David!"

28After Jesus went inside, the blind men went with him. He asked the men, "Do you believe that I can make you see again?"

They answered, "Yes, Lord."

29Then Jesus touched their eyes and said, "Because you believe I can make you see again, it will happen." 30Then the men were able to see. But Jesus warned them strongly, saying, "Don't tell anyone about this." 31But the

### GUYS SPEAK OUT

**Q:** How do you show others your relationship with God?

**A:** "By making right choices and through kindness toward others."

9:3 blasphemy Saying things against God or not showing respect for God. 9:13 'I want . . . sacrifices.' Quotation from Hosea 6:6. 9:14 John John the Baptist, who preached to people about Christ's coming (Matthew 3, Luke 3). 9:14 give up . . . time This is called "fasting." The people would give up eating for a special time of prayer and worship to God. It was also done to show sadness and disappointment.

**13**

## RadicalFaith:

# Matthew 10:26, 28

Are you a people-pleaser? If your biggest concern is what people think of you, you'll wear yourself out trying to earn their approval. You can't live your life based on what will make other people happy, and you can't live in constant fear about what could go wrong on the social scene. Ultimately, that is not what's going to make or break you. In these verses, Jesus is saying that it's absurd for you to take relationships with people more seriously than your relationship with God. John talks about those who rejected Jesus in his day, saying, "They loved praise from people more than praise from God" (John 12:43). Afraid of being rejected by their friends, they rejected Christ. In 1 Thessalonians 2:4, the apostle Paul made it clear that he and the other followers of Christ had only one individual they wanted to please: "When we speak, we are not trying to please people, but God, who tests our hearts." God thinks you are incredible, and you should establish who you really are on that fact, regardless of what other people may think or say. Don't aim to please people. Seek to please God. Only his opinion lasts, and only what he thinks really matters.

blind men left and spread the news about Jesus all around that area.

³²When the two men were leaving, some people brought another man to Jesus. This man could not talk because he had a demon in him. ³³After Jesus forced the demon to leave the man, he was able to speak. The crowd was amazed and said, "We have never seen anything like this in Israel."

³⁴But the Pharisees said, "The prince of demons is the one that gives him power to force demons out."

³⁵Jesus traveled through all the towns and villages, teaching in their synagogues, preaching the Good News about the kingdom, and healing all kinds of diseases and sicknesses. ³⁶When he saw the crowds, he felt sorry for them because they were hurting and helpless, like sheep without a shepherd. ³⁷Jesus said to his followers, "There are many people to harvest but only a few workers to help harvest them. ³⁸Pray to the Lord, who owns the harvest, that he will send more workers to gather his harvest."

### Jesus Sends Out His Apostles

10 Jesus called his twelve followers together and gave them authority to drive out evil spirits and to heal every kind of disease and sickness. ²These are the names of the twelve apostles: Simon (also called Peter) and his brother Andrew; James son of Zebedee, and his brother John; ³Philip and Bartholomew; Thomas and Matthew, the tax collector; James son of Alphaeus, and Thaddaeus; ⁴Simon the Zealot and Judas Iscariot, who turned against Jesus.

⁵Jesus sent out these twelve men with the following order: "Don't go to the non-Jewish people or to any town where the Samaritans live. ⁶But go to the people of Israel, who are like lost sheep. ⁷When you go, preach this: 'The kingdom of heaven is near.' ⁸Heal the sick, raise the dead to life again, heal those who have skin diseases, and force demons out of people. I give you these powers freely, so help other people freely. ⁹Don't carry any money with you—gold or silver or copper. ¹⁰Don't

carry a bag or extra clothes or sandals or a walking stick. Workers should be given what they need.

¹¹"When you enter a city or town, find some worthy person there and stay in that home until you leave. ¹²When you enter that home, say, 'Peace be with you.' ¹³If the people there welcome you, let your peace stay there. But if they don't welcome you, take back the peace you wished for them. ¹⁴And if a home or town refuses to welcome you or listen to you, leave that place and shake its dust off your feet." ¹⁵I tell you the truth, on the Judgment Day it will be better for the towns of Sodom and Gomorrah" than for the people of that town.

### Jesus Warns His Apostles

¹⁶"Listen, I am sending you out like sheep among wolves. So be as smart as snakes and as

## relationships

"Some friends may ruin you, but a real friend will be more loyal than a brother" (Proverbs 18:24). It's easy to sign notes or IM "BFF" (Best Friends Forever), but do you really mean it? What kind of friend are you? Real friends do not turn on each other when things go wrong. They help each other in times of need, and they do not gossip behind each other's backs. Before you sign "BFF" the next time, make sure you really mean it.

**9:37-38** "There are . . . harvest." As a farmer sends workers to harvest the grain, Jesus sends his followers to bring people to God. **10:14 shake . . . feet.** A warning. It showed that they had rejected these people. **10:15 Sodom and Gomorrah** Two cities that God destroyed because the people were so evil.

14

innocent as doves. 17Be careful of people, because they will arrest you and take you to court and whip you in their synagogues. 18Because of me you will be taken to stand before governors and kings, and you will tell them and the non-Jewish people about me. 19When you are arrested, don't worry about what to say or how to say it. At that time you will be given the things to say. 20It will not really be you speaking but the Spirit of your Father speaking through you.

## "THE DEAF CAN HEAR, THE DEAD ARE RAISED TO LIFE, AND THE GOOD NEWS IS PREACHED TO THE POOR."

21"Brothers will give their own brothers to be killed, and fathers will give their own children to be killed. Children will fight against their own parents and have them put to death. 22All people will hate you because you follow me, but those people who keep their faith until the end will be saved. 23When you are treated badly in one city, run to another city. I tell you the truth, you will not finish going through all the cities of Israel before the Son of Man comes.

24"A student is not better than his teacher, and a servant is not better than his master. 25A student should be satisfied to become like his teacher; a servant should be satisfied to become like his master. If the head of the family is called Beelzebul, then the other members of the family will be called worse names!

### FEAR GOD, NOT PEOPLE

26"So don't be afraid of those people, because everything that is hidden will be shown. Everything that is secret will be made known. 27I tell you these things in the dark, but I want you to tell them in the light. What you hear whispered in your ear you should shout from the housetops. 28Don't be afraid of peo-

ple, who can kill the body but cannot kill the soul. The only one you should fear is the one who can destroy the soul and the body in hell. 29Two sparrows cost only a penny, but not even one of them can die without your Father's knowing it. 30God even knows how many hairs are on your head. 31So don't be afraid. You are worth much more than many sparrows.

### TELL PEOPLE ABOUT YOUR FAITH

32"All those who stand before others and say they believe in me, I will say before my Father in heaven that they belong to me. 33But all who stand before others and say they do not believe in me, I will say before my Father in heaven that they do not belong to me.

34"Don't think that I came to bring peace to the earth. I did not come to bring peace, but a sword. 35I have come so that

'a son will be against his father,
    a daughter will be against her mother,
a daughter-in-law will be against her
    mother-in-law.
36A person's enemies will be members of his
    own family.'          *Micah 7:6*

37"Those who love their father or mother more than they love me are not worthy to be my followers. Those who love their son or daughter more than they love me are not worthy to be my followers. 38Whoever is not willing to carry the cross and follow me is not worthy of me. 39Those who try to hold on to their lives will give up true life. Those who give up their lives for me will hold on to true life. 40Whoever accepts you also accepts me, and whoever accepts me also accepts the One who sent me. 41Whoever meets a prophet and accepts him will receive the reward of a prophet. And whoever accepts a good person because that person is good will receive the reward of a good person. 42Those who give one of these little ones a cup of cold water because they are my followers will truly get their reward."

### JESUS AND JOHN THE BAPTIST

11 After Jesus finished telling these things to his twelve followers, he left there and went to the towns in Galilee to teach and preach.

2John the Baptist was in prison, but he heard about what Christ was doing. So John sent some of his followers to Jesus. 3They asked him, "Are you the One who is to come, or should we wait for someone else?"

4Jesus answered them, "Go tell John what you hear and see: 5The blind can see, the crippled can walk, and people with skin diseases are healed. The deaf can hear, the dead are raised to life, and the Good News is preached to the poor. 6Those who do not stumble in their faith because of me are blessed."

7As John's followers were leaving, Jesus began talking to the people about John. Jesus said, "What did you go out into the desert to see? A reed*n* blown by the wind? 8What did you go out to see? A man dressed in fine clothes? No, those who wear fine clothes live in kings' palaces. 9So why did you go out? To see a

## beauty secret

### Long-Lasting Beauty

It's no secret that beautiful people generally get more attention. But the Bible says that beauty can be deceptive if you only look skin deep. Proverbs 31:30 says, "Charm can fool you, and beauty can trick you, but a woman who respects the LORD should be praised." What kind of woman are you?

**11:7 reed** It means that John was not ordinary or weak like grass blown by the wind.

# LEARN I+ & LIVE I+

**Matthew 6:25-34**
**Learn It:** God is in control.
**Live It:** Make a list of things that you worry about. Turn it into your prayer list.

**Matthew 7:1-5**
**Learn It:** Do not judge and criticize others.
**Live It:** Apologize to someone you have said something hurtful, negative, or critical to today.

**Matthew 11:28**
**Learn It:** Rest in Jesus.
**Live It:** When you get tired or worn down today, ask Jesus to carry your load and refresh you.

---

prophet? Yes, and I tell you, John is more than a prophet. ¹⁰This was written about him:

'I will send my messenger ahead of you,
who will prepare the way for you.'

*Malachi 3:1*

¹¹I tell you the truth, John the Baptist is greater than any other person ever born, but even the least important person in the kingdom of heaven is greater than John. ¹²Since the time John the Baptist came until now, the kingdom of heaven has been going forward in strength, and people have been trying to take it by force. ¹³All the prophets and the law of Moses told about what would happen until the time John came. ¹⁴And if you will believe what they said, you will believe that John is Elijah, whom they said would come. ¹⁵You people who can hear me, listen!

¹⁶"What can I say about the people of this time? What are they like? They are like children sitting in the marketplace, who call out to each other,

¹⁷'We played music for you, but you did not dance;

we sang a sad song, but you did not cry.'

¹⁸John came and did not eat or drink like other people. So people say, 'He has a demon.' ¹⁹The Son of Man came, eating and drinking, and people say, 'Look at him! He eats too much and drinks too much wine, and he is a friend of tax collectors and sinners.' But wisdom is proved to be right by what it does."

## JESUS WARNS UNBELIEVERS

²⁰Then Jesus criticized the cities where he did most of his miracles, because the people did not change their lives and stop sinning. ²¹He said, "How terrible for you, Korazin! How terrible for you, Bethsaida! If the same miracles I did in you had happened in Tyre and Sidon,ⁿ those people would have changed their lives a long time ago. They would have worn rough cloth and put ashes on themselves to show they had changed. ²²But I tell you, on the Judgment Day it will be better for Tyre and Sidon than for you. ²³And you, Capernaum,ⁿ will you be lifted up to heaven? No, you will be thrown down to the depths. If the miracles I did in you had happened in Sodom,ⁿ its people would have stopped sinning, and it would still be a city today. ²⁴But I tell you, on the Judgment Day it will be better for Sodom than for you."

## "COME TO ME, ALL OF YOU WHO ARE TIRED AND HAVE HEAVY LOADS, AND I WILL GIVE YOU REST."

## JESUS OFFERS REST TO PEOPLE

²⁵At that time Jesus said, "I praise you, Father, Lord of heaven and earth, because you have hidden these things from the people who are wise and smart. But you have shown them to those who are like little children. ²⁶Yes, Father, this is what you really wanted.

²⁷"My Father has given me all things. No one knows the Son, except the Father. And no one knows the Father, except the Son and those whom the Son chooses to tell.

²⁸"Come to me, all of you who are tired and have heavy loads, and I will give you rest. ²⁹Accept my teachings and learn from me, because I am gentle and humble in spirit, and you will find rest for your lives. ³⁰The teaching that I ask you to accept is easy; the load I give you to carry is light."

## JESUS IS LORD OF THE SABBATH

**12** At that time Jesus was walking through some fields of grain on a Sabbath day. His followers were hungry, so they began to pick the grain and eat it. ²When the Pharisees saw this, they said to Jesus, "Look! Your followers are doing what is unlawful to do on the Sabbath day."

³Jesus answered, "Have you not read what David did when he and the people with him were hungry? ⁴He went into God's house, and he and those with him ate the holy bread, which was lawful only for priests to eat. ⁵And have you not read in the law of Moses that on every Sabbath day the priests in the Temple break this law about the Sabbath day? But the priests are not wrong for doing that. ⁶I tell you that there is something here that is greater than the Temple. ⁷The Scripture says, 'I want kindness more than I want animal sacrifices.'ⁿ

---

**11:21 Tyre and Sidon** Towns where wicked people lived. **11:21, 23 Korazin . . . Bethsaida . . . Capernaum** Towns by Lake Galilee where Jesus preached to the people. **11:23 Sodom** A city that God destroyed because the people were so evil. **12:7 'I . . . sacrifices.'** Quotation from Hosea 6:6.

You don't really know what those words mean. If you understood them, you would not judge those who have done nothing wrong.

8"So the Son of Man is Lord of the Sabbath day."

### Jesus Heals a Man's Hand

9Jesus left there and went into their synagogue, 10where there was a man with a crippled hand. They were looking for a reason to accuse Jesus, so they asked him, "Is it right to heal on the Sabbath day?"[n]

11Jesus answered, "If any of you has a sheep, and it falls into a ditch on the Sabbath day, you will help it out of the ditch. 12Surely a human being is more important than a sheep. So it is lawful to do good things on the Sabbath day."

13Then Jesus said to the man with the crippled hand, "Hold out your hand." The man held out his hand, and it became well again, like the other hand. 14But the Pharisees left and made plans to kill Jesus.

### Jesus Is God's Chosen Servant

15Jesus knew what the Pharisees were doing, so he left that place. Many people followed him, and he healed all who were sick. 16But Jesus warned the people not to tell who he was. 17He did these things to bring about what Isaiah the prophet had said:

18"Here is my servant whom I have chosen.
    I love him, and I am pleased with him.
I will put my Spirit upon him,
    and he will tell of my justice to all people.
19He will not argue or cry out;
    no one will hear his voice in the streets.
20He will not break a crushed blade of grass
    or put out even a weak flame
until he makes justice win the victory.
21    In him will the non-Jewish people find
        hope."                    *Isaiah 42:1-4*

### Jesus' Power Is from God

22Then some people brought to Jesus a man who was blind and could not talk, because he had a demon. Jesus healed the man so that he could talk and see. 23All the people were amazed and said, "Perhaps this man is the Son of David!"

24When the Pharisees heard this, they said, "Jesus uses the power of Beelzebul, the ruler of demons, to force demons out of people."

# Changed Lives

### Candace's Story—Drug Addiction

I knew from the time I was a little girl that God was real and that he loved me, but by the time I hit my teens, I really didn't want him—or anybody else—telling me what to do. I was only 17 when I fell in love with Jake. Because he was a musician whose gigs were in bars and nightclubs, we had easy access to lots of drugs and alcohol. We got married and continued to party, and even though I was still in my teens, cocaine became my drug of choice. When I got pregnant with our daughter, Mandy, I managed to kick the drugs, but as soon as Mandy was born, I got hooked again. My habit was so expensive that I eventually left Jake and our little girl and hooked up with Ben, a rich guy who could better support my addiction. In less than a year, Ben and I spent one million dollars on drugs. What a waste! And all the time, Jake begged me to come home to him and Mandy. I tried rehab. I tried moving back home with Jake and Mandy. But nothing could keep me away from cocaine. I got pregnant again, but even that didn't stop me. Miraculously, Kinkade was born a healthy baby. I gave her up for adoption through a Christian agency that also specialized in helping young women. Not only did they help find Kinkade a family who could love her and take care of her, but also they began to take care of me. They saw potential in me, taught me about God's unconditional love, and helped me find hope. Even though I relapsed, they were still there for me. I was finally able to give up drugs completely, turn my life around, restore my relationship with Mandy, and become part of the staff at the facility that helped me heal. God poured out his blessings on me, and I want to help other girls understand that he is there for them, too.

*For help with drug addictions, check out www.christian-drug-alcohol-treatment.com. For information about residential care for females, visit www.mercyministries.com. (Names have been changed for the sake of privacy. Candace tells her story after going through biblically based counseling with Mercy Ministries.)*

**12:10** "Is it right . . . day?" It was against Jewish Law to work on the Sabbath day.

<sup>25</sup>Jesus knew what the Pharisees were thinking, so he said to them, "Every kingdom that is divided against itself will be destroyed. And any city or family that is divided against itself will not continue. <sup>26</sup>And if Satan forces out himself, then Satan is divided against himself, and his kingdom will not continue. <sup>27</sup>You say that I use the power of Beelzebul to force out demons. If that is true, then what power do your people use to force out demons? So they will be your judges. <sup>28</sup>But if I use the power of God's Spirit to force out demons, then the kingdom of God has come to you.

<sup>29</sup>"If anyone wants to enter a strong person's house and steal his things, he must first tie up the strong person. Then he can steal the things from the house.

<sup>30</sup>"Whoever is not with me is against me. Whoever does not work with me is working against me. <sup>31</sup>So I tell you, people can be forgiven for every sin and everything they say against God. But whoever speaks against the Holy Spirit will not be forgiven. <sup>32</sup>Anyone who speaks against the Son of Man can be forgiven, but anyone who speaks against the Holy Spirit will not be forgiven, now or in the future.

## "WHOEVER IS NOT WITH ME IS AGAINST ME. WHOEVER DOES NOT WORK WITH ME IS WORKING AGAINST ME."

### PEOPLE KNOW YOU BY YOUR WORDS

<sup>33</sup>"If you want good fruit, you must make the tree good. If your tree is not good, it will have bad fruit. A tree is known by the kind of fruit it produces. <sup>34</sup>You snakes! You are evil people, so how can you say anything good? The mouth speaks the things that are in the heart. <sup>35</sup>Good people have good things in their hearts, and so they say good things. But evil people have evil in their hearts, so they say evil things. <sup>36</sup>And I tell you that on the Judgment

## BIBLE BIOS

# Anna

[LUKE 2] Sometimes what we think is great simply isn't the best. Take Anna, for example. Married only seven years, Anna's husband died. The acceptable, traditional thing to do, back in the day, was to remarry as soon as possible. But Anna didn't go the traditional route. She took a risk. Instead, she chose to devote herself wholly to God, to serve him and live as a widow. And wouldn't you know it— God blessed Anna's decision. She became respected for her wisdom and leadership as a prophetess. God gave her a wondrous gift. Anna also got to be there, in the Temple, when the baby Jesus was brought in to receive the blessing. God knew what he was doing in Anna's life from the very beginning.

Day people will be responsible for every careless thing they have said. <sup>37</sup>The words you have said will be used to judge you. Some of your words will prove you right, but some of your words will prove you guilty."

### THE PEOPLE ASK FOR A MIRACLE

<sup>38</sup>Then some of the Pharisees and teachers of the law answered Jesus, saying, "Teacher, we want to see you work a miracle as a sign."

<sup>39</sup>Jesus answered, "Evil and sinful people are the ones who want to see a miracle for a sign. But no sign will be given to them, except the sign of the prophet Jonah. <sup>40</sup>Jonah was in the stomach of the big fish for three days and three nights. In the same way, the Son of Man will be in the grave three days and three nights. <sup>41</sup>On the Judgment Day the people from Nineveh" will stand up with you people who live now, and they will show that you are guilty. When Jonah preached to them, they were sorry and changed their lives. And I tell you that someone greater than Jonah is here. <sup>42</sup>On the Judgment Day, the Queen of the South" will stand up with you people who live today. She

will show that you are guilty, because she came from far away to listen to Solomon's wise teaching. And I tell you that someone greater than Solomon is here.

### PEOPLE TODAY ARE FULL OF EVIL

<sup>43</sup>"When an evil spirit comes out of a person, it travels through dry places, looking for a place to rest, but it doesn't find it. <sup>44</sup>So the spirit says, 'I will go back to the house I left.' When the spirit comes back, it finds the house still empty, swept clean, and made neat. <sup>45</sup>Then the evil spirit goes out and brings seven other spirits even more evil than it is, and they go in and live there. So the person has even more trouble than before. It is the same way with the evil people who live today."

### JESUS' TRUE FAMILY

<sup>46</sup>While Jesus was talking to the people, his mother and brothers stood outside, trying to find a way to talk to him. <sup>47</sup>Someone told Jesus, "Your mother and brothers are standing outside, and they want to talk to you."

<sup>48</sup>He answered, "Who is my mother? Who are my brothers?" <sup>49</sup>Then he pointed to his followers

**notes**    **12:41 Nineveh** The city where Jonah preached to warn the people. Read Jonah 3.    **12:42 Queen of the South** The Queen of Sheba. She traveled a thousand miles to learn God's wisdom from Solomon. Read 1 Kings 10:1-13.

and said, "Here are my mother and my brothers. 50My true brother and sister and mother are those who do what my Father in heaven wants."

## a story about planting seed

**13** That same day Jesus went out of the house and sat by the lake. 2Large crowds gathered around him, so he got into a boat and sat down, while the people stood on the shore. 3Then Jesus used stories to teach them many things. He said: "A farmer went out to plant his seed. 4While he was planting, some seed fell by the road, and the birds came and ate it all up. 5Some seed fell on rocky ground, where there wasn't much dirt. That seed grew very fast, because the ground was not deep. 6But when the sun rose, the plants dried up, because they did not have deep roots. 7Some other seed fell among thorny weeds, which grew and choked the good plants. 8Some other seed fell on good ground where it grew and produced a crop. Some plants made a hundred times more, some made sixty times more, and some made thirty times more. 9You people who can hear me, listen."

## why Jesus used stories to teach

10The followers came to Jesus and asked, "Why do you use stories to teach the people?"

11Jesus answered, "You have been chosen to know the secrets about the kingdom of heaven, but others cannot know these secrets. 12Those who have understanding will be given more, and they will have all they need. But those who do not have understanding, even what they have will be taken away from them. 13This is why I use stories to teach the people: They see, but they don't really see. They hear, but they don't really hear or understand. 14So they show that the things Isaiah said about them are true:

'You will listen and listen, but you will not understand.
You will look and look, but you will not learn.
15For the minds of these people have become stubborn.

They do not hear with their ears,
and they have closed their eyes.
Otherwise they might really understand
what they see with their eyes
and hear with their ears.
They might really understand in their minds
and come back to me and be healed.'

*Isaiah 6:9-10*

16But you are blessed, because you see with your eyes and hear with your ears. 17I tell you the truth, many prophets and good people wanted to see the things that you now see, but they did not see them. And they wanted to hear the things that you now hear, but they did not hear them.

## Jesus explains the seed story

18"So listen to the meaning of that story about the farmer. 19What is the seed that fell by the road? That seed is like the person who hears the message about the kingdom but does not understand it. The Evil One comes and takes away what was planted in that person's heart. 20And what is the seed that fell on rocky ground? That seed is like the person who hears the teaching and quickly accepts it with joy. 21But he does not let the teaching go deep into his life, so he keeps it only a short time. When trouble or persecution comes because of the teaching he accepted, he quickly gives up. 22And what is the seed that fell among the thorny weeds? That seed is like the person who hears the teaching but lets worries about this life and the temptation of wealth stop that teaching from growing. So the teaching does not produce fruit*n* in that person's life. 23But what is the seed that fell on the good ground? That seed is like the person who hears the teaching and understands it. That person grows and produces fruit, sometimes a hundred times more, sometimes sixty times more, and sometimes thirty times more."

## a story about wheat and weeds

24Then Jesus told them another story: "The kingdom of heaven is like a man who planted

# Blab

**Q:** I want to go to youth activities at my church to get closer to God, but there are so many cute guys that I start thinking more about them. What do I do?

**A:** It is normal to have lots of feelings for guys and to think that they look hot. God created you to want to have relationships and be intimate—but he also wants you to wait until the right time. Pray immediately whenever unwanted thoughts come into your head or when you begin to be distracted. God will help you redirect your thoughts toward him.

**Q:** My mom hates my stepmom and is always talking bad about her. She's really not that bad. What should I do?

**A:** You can't control your mom and telling parents what to do usually makes them mad. Ask God to soften your mom's heart toward your stepmother, and go out of your way to let your mom know that no one will ever take her place.

**Q:** For the first time in my life, I feel like I look sort of good and that guys are starting to notice me. Is it wrong to flirt?

**A:** When you flirt, you are definitely thinking only of yourself. Flirting can also make guys think you want a closer relationship with them than you do, which can hurt their feelings or make them angry. It is okay to feel good about yourself, but avoid the flirting.

**13:22 produce fruit** To produce fruit means to have in your life the good things God wants.

good seed in his field. ²⁵That night, when everyone was asleep, his enemy came and planted weeds among the wheat and then left. ²⁶Later, the wheat sprouted and the heads of grain grew, but the weeds also grew. ²⁷Then the man's servants came to him and said, 'You planted good seed in your field. Where did the weeds come from?' ²⁸The man answered, 'An enemy planted weeds.' The servants asked, 'Do you want us to pull up the weeds?' ²⁹The man answered, 'No, because when you pull up the weeds, you might also pull up the wheat. ³⁰Let the weeds and the wheat grow together until the harvest time. At harvest time I will tell the workers, "First gather the weeds and tie them together to be burned. Then gather the wheat and bring it to my barn." ' "

## STORIES OF MUSTARD SEED AND YEAST

³¹Then Jesus told another story: "The kingdom of heaven is like a mustard seed that a man planted in his field. ³²That seed is the smallest of all seeds, but when it grows, it is one of the largest garden plants. It becomes big enough for the wild birds to come and build nests in its branches."

³³Then Jesus told another story: "The kingdom of heaven is like yeast that a woman took and hid in a large tub of flour until it made all the dough rise."

³⁴Jesus used stories to tell all these things to the people; he always used stories to teach them. ³⁵This is as the prophet said:

"I will speak using stories;
I will tell things that have been secret
since the world was made."

*Psalm 78:2*

## JESUS EXPLAINS ABOUT THE WEEDS

³⁶Then Jesus left the crowd and went into the house. His followers came to him and said, "Explain to us the meaning of the story about the weeds in the field."

³⁷Jesus answered, "The man who planted the good seed in the field is the Son of Man. ³⁸The field is the world, and the good seed are all of God's children who belong to the kingdom. The weeds are those people who belong to the Evil One. ³⁹And the enemy who planted the bad seed is the devil. The harvest time is the end of the world, and the workers who gather are God's angels.

⁴⁰"Just as the weeds are pulled up and burned in the fire, so it will be at the end of the world. ⁴¹The Son of Man will send out his angels, and they will gather out of his kingdom all who cause sin and all who do evil. ⁴²The angels will throw them into the blazing furnace, where the people will cry and grind their teeth with pain. ⁴³Then the good people will shine like the sun in the kingdom of their Father. You people who can hear me, listen.

## STORIES OF A TREASURE AND A PEARL

⁴⁴"The kingdom of heaven is like a treasure hidden in a field. One day a man found the treasure, and then he hid it in the field again. He was so happy that he went and sold everything he owned to buy that field.

⁴⁵"Also, the kingdom of heaven is like a man looking for fine pearls. ⁴⁶When he found a very valuable pearl, he went and sold everything he had and bought it.

## A STORY OF A FISHING NET

⁴⁷"Also, the kingdom of heaven is like a net that was put into the lake and caught many different kinds of fish. ⁴⁸When it was full, the fishermen pulled the net to the shore. They sat down and put all the good fish in baskets and threw away the bad fish. ⁴⁹It will be this way at the end of the world. The angels will come and separate the evil people from the good people. ⁵⁰The angels will throw the evil people into the blazing furnace, where people will cry and grind their teeth with pain."

⁵¹Jesus asked his followers, "Do you understand all these things?"

They answered, "Yes, we understand."

⁵²Then Jesus said to them, "So every teacher of the law who has been taught about the kingdom of heaven is like the owner of a house. He brings out both new things and old things he has saved."

## JESUS GOES TO HIS HOMETOWN

⁵³When Jesus finished teaching with these stories, he left there. ⁵⁴He went to his hometown and taught the people in the synagogue, and they were amazed. They said, "Where did this man get this wisdom and this power to do miracles? ⁵⁵He is just the son of a carpenter. His mother is Mary, and his brothers are James, Joseph, Simon, and Judas. ⁵⁶And all his sisters are here with us. Where then does this man get all these things?" ⁵⁷So the people were upset with Jesus.

But Jesus said to them, "A prophet is honored everywhere except in his hometown and in his own home."

⁵⁸So he did not do many miracles there because they had no faith.

## HOW JOHN THE BAPTIST WAS KILLED

**14** At that time Herod, the ruler of Galilee, heard the reports about Jesus. ²So he said to his servants, "Jesus is John the Baptist, who has risen from the dead. That is why he can work these miracles."

³Sometime before this, Herod had arrested John, tied him up, and put him into prison. Herod did this because of Herodias, who had been the wife of Philip, Herod's brother. ⁴John had been telling Herod, "It is not lawful for you to be married to Herodias." ⁵Herod wanted to

# Music Reviews

**GROUP:** NICHOLE NORDEMAN

**ALBUM:** WIDE EYED (CLASSIC HIT)

Nichole Nordeman is another one of those singer-songwriters, like Sara Groves and Ginny Owens, who simply creates beautiful music. Nichole uses her music to express some of her struggles with faith, and listeners definitely benefit from her insightfulness. On this 1998 debut, Nichole describes the wonder of God on "Who You Are," wrestles with belief on "To Know You," and tackles her own shortsightedness on the title track, in which Nichole points out that the broken and destitute are also created in the image of God.

**WHY IT ROCKS: NICHOLE PAINTS POWERFUL WORD PICTURES THAT REMIND US OF THE MAGNITUDE AND MAGNIFICENCE OF GOD.**

kill John, but he was afraid of the people, because they believed John was a prophet.

⁶On Herod's birthday, the daughter of Herodias danced for Herod and his guests, and she pleased him. ⁷So he promised with an oath to give her anything she wanted. ⁸Herodias told her daughter what to ask for, so she said to Herod, "Give me the head of John the Baptist here on a platter." ⁹Although King Herod was very sad, he had made a promise, and his dinner guests had heard him. So Herod ordered that what she asked for be done. ¹⁰He sent soldiers to the prison to cut off John's head. ¹¹And they brought it on a platter and gave it to the girl, and she took it to her mother. ¹²John's followers came and got his body and buried it. Then they went and told Jesus.

## More Than Five Thousand Fed

¹³When Jesus heard what had happened to John, he left in a boat and went to a lonely place by himself. But the crowds heard about it and followed him on foot from the towns. ¹⁴When he arrived, he saw a great crowd waiting. He felt sorry for them and healed those who were sick.

¹⁵When it was evening, his followers came to him and said, "No one lives in this place, and it is already late. Send the people away so they can go to the towns and buy food for themselves."

¹⁶But Jesus answered, "They don't need to go away. You give them something to eat."

¹⁷They said to him, "But we have only five loaves of bread and two fish."

¹⁸Jesus said, "Bring the bread and the fish to me." ¹⁹Then he told the people to sit down on the grass. He took the five loaves and the two fish and, looking to heaven, he thanked God for the food. Jesus divided the bread and gave it to his followers, who gave it to the people. ²⁰All the people ate and were satisfied. Then the followers filled twelve baskets with the leftover pieces of food. ²¹There were about five thousand men there who ate, not counting women and children.

## Jesus Walks on the Water

²²Immediately Jesus told his followers to get into the boat and go ahead of him across the lake. He stayed there to send the people home. ²³After he had sent them away, he went by himself up into the hills to pray. It was late, and Jesus was there alone. ²⁴By this time, the boat was already far away from land. It was being hit by waves, because the wind was blowing against it.

²⁵Between three and six o'clock in the morning, Jesus came to them, walking on the water. ²⁶When his followers saw him walking on the water, they were afraid. They said, "It's a ghost!" and cried out in fear.

²⁷But Jesus quickly spoke to them, "Have courage! It is I. Do not be afraid."

²⁸Peter said, "Lord, if it is really you, then command me to come to you on the water."

²⁹Jesus said, "Come."

And Peter left the boat and walked on the water to Jesus. ³⁰But when Peter saw the wind and the waves, he became afraid and began to sink. He shouted, "Lord, save me!"

³¹Immediately Jesus reached out his hand and caught Peter. Jesus said, "Your faith is small. Why did you doubt?"

³²After they got into the boat, the wind became calm. ³³Then those who were in the boat worshiped Jesus and said, "Truly you are the Son of God!"

³⁴When they had crossed the lake, they came to shore at Gennesaret. ³⁵When the people there recognized Jesus, they told people all around there that Jesus had come, and they brought all their sick to him. ³⁶They begged Jesus to let them touch just the edge of his coat, and all who touched it were healed.

## Obey God's Law

**15** Then some Pharisees and teachers of the law came to Jesus from Jerusalem. They asked him, ²"Why don't your followers obey the unwritten laws which have been handed down to us? They don't wash their hands before they eat."

## Matthew 15:6-9

Sometimes people just miss the point. The Pharisees were playing games with God's instruction. They kept adding rules—which seemed righteous—that were really just loopholes they were using to avoid obeying the tougher commands. The Pharisees were playing the game of looking like God-pleasers, but really they were displeasing God by squirming out of taking care of their parents. They were offering their money to God to look holy, while ignoring the basic needs of their own parents. Honoring your mom and dad is a pretty big deal to God. After all, he did include it in the Ten Commandments. The actions of the Pharisees that looked like worship really had nothing to do with a genuine relationship with God. The truth is that you can't always tell just by looking at others what their motives are, and fortunately, it's not your place to decide anyway. That's God's job. The important thing is to keep your heart true. First Samuel 16:7 says, "God does not see the same way people see. People look at the outside of a person, but the LORD looks at the heart." God wants your heart to be all his and your love for him to drive all you do.

³Jesus answered, "And why do you refuse to obey God's command so that you can follow your own teachings? ⁴God said, 'Honor your father and your mother,'" and 'Anyone who says cruel things to his father or mother must be put to death.'" ⁵But you say a person can tell his father or mother, 'I have something I could use to help you, but I have given it to God already.' ⁶You teach that person not to honor his father or his mother. You rejected what God said for the sake of your own rules. ⁷You are hypocrites! Isaiah was right when he said about you:

⁸'These people show honor to me with words,

but their hearts are far from me.

⁹Their worship of me is worthless.

The things they teach are nothing but human rules.' "          *Isaiah 29:13*

¹⁰After Jesus called the crowd to him, he said, "Listen and understand what I am saying. ¹¹It is not what people put into their mouths that makes them unclean. It is what comes out of their mouths that makes them unclean."

¹²Then his followers came to him and asked, "Do you know that the Pharisees are angry because of what you said?"

¹³Jesus answered, "Every plant that my Father in heaven has not planted himself will be pulled up by the roots. ¹⁴Stay away from the Pharisees; they are blind leaders. And if a blind person leads a blind person, both will fall into a ditch."

¹⁵Peter said, "Explain the example to us."

¹⁶Jesus said, "Do you still not understand? ¹⁷Surely you know that all the food that enters the mouth goes into the stomach and then goes out of the body. ¹⁸But what people say with their mouths comes from the way they think; these are the things that make people unclean. ¹⁹Out of the mind come evil thoughts, murder, adultery, sexual sins, stealing, lying, and speaking evil of others. ²⁰These things make people unclean; eating with unwashed hands does not make them unclean."

### Jesus Helps a Non-Jewish Woman

²¹Jesus left that place and went to the area of Tyre and Sidon. ²²A Canaanite woman from that area came to Jesus and cried out, "Lord, Son of David, have mercy on me! My daughter has a demon, and she is suffering very much."

²³But Jesus did not answer the woman. So his followers came to Jesus and begged him, "Tell the woman to go away. She is following us and shouting."

²⁴Jesus answered, "God sent me only to the lost sheep, the people of Israel."

²⁵Then the woman came to Jesus again and bowed before him and said, "Lord, help me!"

²⁶Jesus answered, "It is not right to take the children's bread and give it to the dogs."

²⁷The woman said, "Yes, Lord, but even the dogs eat the crumbs that fall from their masters' table."

²⁸Then Jesus answered, "Woman, you have great faith! I will do what you asked." And at that moment the woman's daughter was healed.

## "HE TOOK THE SEVEN LOAVES OF BREAD AND THE FISH AND GAVE THANKS TO GOD."

### Jesus Heals Many People

²⁹After leaving there, Jesus went along the shore of Lake Galilee. He went up on a hill and sat there.

³⁰Great crowds came to Jesus, bringing with them the lame, the blind, the crippled, those who could not speak, and many others. They put them at Jesus' feet, and he healed them. ³¹The crowd was amazed when they saw that people who could not speak before were now able to speak. The crippled were made strong. The lame could walk, and the blind could see. And they praised the God of Israel for this.

### More Than Four Thousand Fed

³²Jesus called his followers to him and said, "I feel sorry for these people, because they

15:4 'Honor . . . mother.' Quotation from Exodus 20:12; Deuteronomy 5:16.   15:4 'Anyone . . . death.' Quotation from Exodus 21:17.

22

have already been with me three days, and they have nothing to eat. I don't want to send them away hungry. They might faint while going home."

33His followers asked him, "How can we get enough bread to feed all these people? We are far away from any town."

34Jesus asked, "How many loaves of bread do you have?"

They answered, "Seven, and a few small fish."

35Jesus told the people to sit on the ground. 36He took the seven loaves of bread and the fish and gave thanks to God. Then he divided the food and gave it to his followers, and they gave it to the people. 37All the people ate and were satisfied. Then his followers filled seven baskets with the leftover pieces of food. 38There were about four thousand men there who ate, besides women and children. 39After sending the people home, Jesus got into the boat and went to the area of Magadan.

## THE LEADERS ASK FOR A MIRACLE

**16** The Pharisees and Sadducees came to Jesus, wanting to trick him. So they asked him to show them a miracle from God.

2Jesus answered, "At sunset you say we will have good weather, because the sky is red. 3And in the morning you say that it will be a rainy day, because the sky is dark and red. You

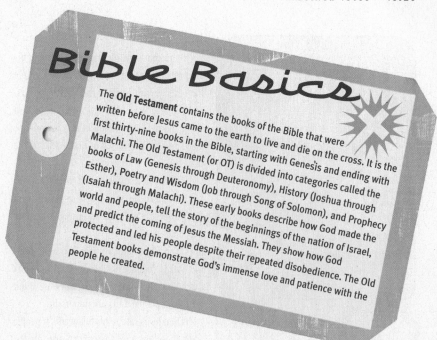

see these signs in the sky and know what they mean. In the same way, you see the things that I am doing now, but you don't know their meaning. 4Evil and sinful people ask for a miracle as a sign, but they will not be given any sign, except the sign of Jonah."n Then Jesus left them and went away.

## GUARD AGAINST WRONG TEACHINGS

5Jesus' followers went across the lake, but they had forgotten to bring bread. 6Jesus said to them, "Be careful! Beware of the yeast of the Pharisees and the Sadducees."

7His followers discussed the meaning of this, saying, "He said this because we forgot to bring bread."

8Knowing what they were talking about, Jesus asked them, "Why are you talking about not having bread? Your faith is small. 9Do you still not understand? Remember the five loaves of bread that fed the five thousand? And remember that you filled many baskets with the leftovers? 10Or the seven loaves of bread that fed the four thousand and the many baskets you filled then also? 11I was not talking to you about bread. Why don't you understand that? I am telling you to beware of the yeast of the Pharisees and the Sadducees." 12Then the

followers understood that Jesus was not telling them to beware of the yeast used in bread but to beware of the teaching of the Pharisees and the Sadducees.

## PETER SAYS JESUS IS THE CHRIST

13When Jesus came to the area of Caesarea Philippi, he asked his followers, "Who do people say the Son of Man is?"

14They answered, "Some say you are John the Baptist. Others say you are Elijah, and still others say you are Jeremiah or one of the prophets."

15Then Jesus asked them, "And who do you say I am?"

16Simon Peter answered, "You are the Christ, the Son of the living God."

17Jesus answered, "You are blessed, Simon son of Jonah, because no person taught you that. My Father in heaven showed you who I am. 18So I tell you, you are Peter.n On this rock I will build my church, and the power of death will not be able to defeat it. 19I will give you the keys of the kingdom of heaven; the things you don't allow on earth will be the things that God does not allow, and the things you allow on earth will be the things that God allows." 20Then Jesus warned his followers not to tell anyone he was the Christ.

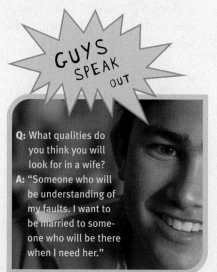

notes    **16:4 sign of Jonah** Jonah's three days in the fish are like Jesus' three days in the tomb. The story about Jonah is in the Book of Jonah.    **16:18 Peter** The Greek name "Peter," like the Aramaic name "Cephas," means "rock."

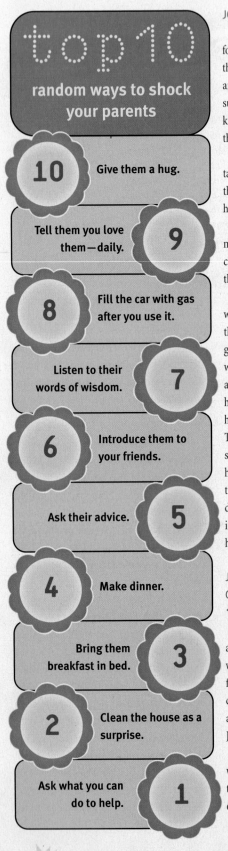

## top 10

### random ways to shock your parents

**10** Give them a hug.

**9** Tell them you love them—daily.

**8** Fill the car with gas after you use it.

**7** Listen to their words of wisdom.

**6** Introduce them to your friends.

**5** Ask their advice.

**4** Make dinner.

**3** Bring them breakfast in bed.

**2** Clean the house as a surprise.

**1** Ask what you can do to help.

## Jesus Says That He Must Die

21From that time on Jesus began telling his followers that he must go to Jerusalem, where the older Jewish leaders, the leading priests, and the teachers of the law would make him suffer many things. He told them he must be killed and then be raised from the dead on the third day.

22Peter took Jesus aside and told him not to talk like that. He said, "God save you from those things, Lord! Those things will never happen to you!"

23Then Jesus said to Peter, "Go away from me, Satan! You are not helping me! You don't care about the things of God, but only about the things people think are important."

24Then Jesus said to his followers, "If people want to follow me, they must give up the things they want. They must be willing even to give up their lives to follow me. 25Those who want to save their lives will give up true life, and those who give up their lives for me will have true life. 26It is worth nothing for them to have the whole world if they lose their souls. They could never pay enough to buy back their souls. 27The Son of Man will come again with his Father's glory and with his angels. At that time, he will reward them for what they have done. 28I tell you the truth, some people standing here will see the Son of Man coming with his kingdom before they die."

## Jesus Talks with Moses and Elijah

**17** Six days later, Jesus took Peter, James, and John, the brother of James, up on a high mountain by themselves. 2While they watched, Jesus' appearance was changed; his face became bright like the sun, and his clothes became white as light. 3Then Moses and Elijah appeared to them, talking with Jesus.

4Peter said to Jesus, "Lord, it is good that we are here. If you want, I will put up three tents here—one for you, one for Moses, and one for Elijah."

5While Peter was talking, a bright cloud covered them. A voice came from the cloud and said, "This is my Son, whom I love, and I am very pleased with him. Listen to him!"

6When his followers heard the voice, they were so frightened they fell to the ground. 7But Jesus went to them and touched them and said, "Stand up. Don't be afraid." 8When they looked up, they saw Jesus was now alone.

9As they were coming down the mountain, Jesus commanded them not to tell anyone about what they had seen until the Son of Man had risen from the dead.

10Then his followers asked him, "Why do the teachers of the law say that Elijah must come first?"

## "THOSE WHO GIVE UP THEIR LIVES FOR ME WILL HAVE TRUE LIFE."

11Jesus answered, "They are right to say that Elijah is coming and that he will make everything the way it should be. 12But I tell you that Elijah has already come, and they did not recognize him. They did to him whatever they wanted to do. It will be the same with the Son of Man; those same people will make the Son of Man suffer." 13Then the followers understood that Jesus was talking about John the Baptist.

## Jesus Heals a Sick Boy

14When Jesus and his followers came back to the crowd, a man came to Jesus and bowed before him. 15The man said, "Lord, have mercy on my son. He has epilepsy and is suffering very much, because he often falls into the fire or into the water. 16I brought him to your followers, but they could not cure him."

17Jesus answered, "You people have no faith, and your lives are all wrong. How long must I put up with you? How long must I continue to be patient with you? Bring the boy here."

 **16:23 Satan** Name for the devil, meaning "the enemy." Jesus means that Peter was talking like Satan. **17:3 Moses and Elijah** Two of the most important Jewish leaders in the past. God had given Moses the Law, and Elijah was an important prophet. **17:15 epilepsy** A disease that causes a person sometimes to lose control of his body and maybe faint, shake strongly, or not be able to move.

Promises!

# Matthew 17:20

Ever feel like you don't have "enough faith"? Maybe someone's told you that if you pray enough, believe in God really hard, and never doubt him that he will do great things in your life. The followers were trying really hard to walk in Jesus' footsteps and to be just like him in every way. But, to their disappointment, they weren't able to do all the things that Jesus could.

When they wanted to know what was wrong, Jesus told them that they only needed a tiny bit of faith to do great things. What? What about having huge, gargantuan amounts of faith? Nope. Jesus wanted us to know that our faith can be small because God is SO big. On its own, our faith can never be enough to do anything—it's God who makes it all happen. The important thing is to believe that Jesus is who he says he is and that he alone is salvation. God will do the rest. So put aside your fear, doubt, and belief that you have to be "enough," and let God do the rest. He can do great things with you!

18Jesus commanded the demon inside the boy. Then the demon came out, and the boy was healed from that time on.

19The followers came to Jesus when he was alone and asked, "Why couldn't we force the demon out?"

20Jesus answered, "Because your faith is too small. I tell you the truth, if your faith is as big as a mustard seed, you can say to this mountain, 'Move from here to there,' and it will move. All things will be possible for you." 21ⁿ

## Jesus Talks About His Death

22While Jesus' followers were gathering in Galilee, he said to them, "The Son of Man will be handed over to people, 23and they will kill him. But on the third day he will be raised from the dead." And the followers were filled with sadness.

## Jesus Talks About Paying Taxes

24When Jesus and his followers came to Capernaum, the men who collected the Temple tax came to Peter. They asked, "Does your teacher pay the Temple tax?"

25Peter answered, "Yes, Jesus pays the tax."

Peter went into the house, but before he could speak, Jesus said to him, "What do you think? The kings of the earth collect different kinds of taxes. But who pays the taxes—the king's children or others?"

26Peter answered, "Other people pay the taxes."

Jesus said to Peter, "Then the children of the king don't have to pay taxes. 27But we don't want to upset these tax collectors. So go to the lake and fish. After you catch the first fish, open its mouth and you will find a coin. Take that coin and give it to the tax collectors for you and me."

## Who Is the Greatest?

18 At that time the followers came to Jesus and asked, "Who is greatest in the kingdom of heaven?"

2Jesus called a little child to him and stood the child before his followers. 3Then he said, "I tell you the truth, you must change and become like little children. Otherwise, you will never enter the kingdom of heaven. 4The greatest person in the kingdom of heaven is the one who makes himself humble like this child.

5"Whoever accepts a child in my name accepts me. 6If one of these little children believes in me, and someone causes that child to sin, it would be better for that person to have a large stone tied around the neck and be drowned in the sea. 7How terrible for the people of the world because of the things that cause them to sin. Such things will happen, but how terrible for the one who causes them to happen! 8If your hand or your foot causes you to sin, cut it off and throw it away. It is better for you to lose part of your body and live forever than to have two hands and two feet and be thrown into the fire that burns forever. 9If

beauty secret

### Your Style

Do you have a defining style? Have you adopted a look that fits your personality? Building your life (and your look) on a truth from God's Word can not only change the way you see yourself; it can have a lasting impact on how others see you, too!

notes

17:21 Verse 21 Some Greek copies add verse 21: "That kind of spirit comes out only if you use prayer and give up eating."

your eye causes you to sin, take it out and throw it away. It is better for you to have only one eye and live forever than to have two eyes and be thrown into the fire of hell.

## a LOST SHeeP

10"Be careful. Don't think these little children are worth nothing. I tell you that they have angels in heaven who are always with my Father in heaven. 11"

12"If a man has a hundred sheep but one of the sheep gets lost, he will leave the other ninety-nine on the hill and go to look for the lost sheep. 13I tell you the truth, he is happier about that one sheep than about the ninety-nine that were never lost. 14In the same way, your Father in heaven does not want any of these little children to be lost.

## WHen a PeRSON SINS aGaINST YOU

15"If your fellow believer sins against you, go and tell him in private what he did wrong. If he listens to you, you have helped that person to be your brother or sister again. 16But if he refuses to listen, go to him again and take one or two other people with you. 'Every case may be proved by two or three witnesses.'" 17If he refuses to listen to them, tell the church. If he refuses to listen to the church, then treat him like a person who does not believe in God or like a tax collector.

18"I tell you the truth, the things you don't allow on earth will be the things God does not allow. And the things you allow on earth will be the things that God allows.

19"Also, I tell you that if two of you on earth agree about something and pray for it, it will be done for you by my Father in heaven. 20This is true because if two or three people come together in my name, I am there with them."

## an UNFORGIVING SeRVaNT

21Then Peter came to Jesus and asked, "Lord, when my fellow believer sins against me, how many times must I forgive him? Should I forgive him as many as seven times?"

22Jesus answered, "I tell you, you must forgive him more than seven times. You must for-give him even if he wrongs you seventy times seven.

23"The kingdom of heaven is like a king who decided to collect the money his servants owed him. 24When the king began to collect his money, a servant who owed him several million dollars was brought to him. 25But the servant did not have enough money to pay his master, the king. So the master ordered that everything the servant owned should be sold, even the servant's wife and children. Then the money would be used to pay the king what the servant owed.

26"But the servant fell on his knees and begged, 'Be patient with me, and I will pay you everything I owe.' 27The master felt sorry for his servant and told him he did not have to pay it back. Then he let the servant go free.

28"Later, that same servant found another servant who owed him a few dollars. The servant grabbed him around the neck and said, 'Pay me the money you owe me!'

29"The other servant fell on his knees and begged him, 'Be patient with me, and I will pay you everything I owe.'

30"But the first servant refused to be patient. He threw the other servant into prison until he could pay everything he owed. 31When the other servants saw what had happened, they were very sorry. So they went and told their master all that had happened.

32"Then the master called his servant in and said, 'You evil servant! Because you begged me to forget what you owed, I told you that you did not have to pay anything. 33You should have showed mercy to that other servant, just as I showed mercy to you.' 34The master was very angry and put the servant in prison to be punished until he could pay everything he owed.

35"This king did what my heavenly Father will do to you if you do not forgive your brother or sister from your heart."

## JeSUS TeacHeS aBOUT DIVORCe

**19** After Jesus said all these things, he left Galilee and went into the area of Judea on the other side of the Jordan River. 2Large crowds followed him, and he healed them there.

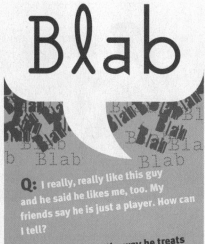

**18:11 Verse 11** Some Greek copies add verse 11: "The Son of Man came to save lost people." **18:16 'Every . . . witnesses.'** Quotation from Deuteronomy 19:15.

# LEARN I+ & LIVE I+

**Matthew 14:23**
**Learn It:** Jesus went off by himself to pray.
**Live It:** Find 10 minutes today to get by yourself and talk to God.

**Matthew 18:3**
**Learn It:** You must be like a child to enter into the kingdom of heaven.
**Live It:** Watch children play, and observe their joy and innocence. Ask Jesus to help you be like a child before him.

**Matthew 20:34**
**Learn It:** Jesus felt sorry for the blind men.
**Live It:** Look for someone around you who needs your help, and put yourself in their shoes. Offer to do what you can to help.

³Some Pharisees came to Jesus and tried to trick him. They asked, "Is it right for a man to divorce his wife for any reason he chooses?"

⁴Jesus answered, "Surely you have read in the Scriptures: When God made the world, 'he made them male and female.'" ⁵And God said, 'So a man will leave his father and mother and be united with his wife, and the two will become one body.'" ⁶So there are not two, but one. God has joined the two together, so no one should separate them."

⁷The Pharisees asked, "Why then did Moses give a command for a man to divorce his wife by giving her divorce papers?"

⁸Jesus answered, "Moses allowed you to divorce your wives because you refused to accept God's teaching, but divorce was not allowed in the beginning. ⁹I tell you that anyone who divorces his wife and marries another woman is guilty of adultery. The only reason for a man to divorce his wife is if his wife has sexual relations with another man."

¹⁰The followers said to him, "If that is the only reason a man can divorce his wife, it is better not to marry."

¹¹Jesus answered, "Not everyone can accept this teaching, but God has made some able to accept it. ¹²There are different reasons why some men cannot marry. Some men were born without the ability to become fathers. Others were made that way later in life by other people. And some men have given up marriage because of the kingdom of heaven. But the person who can marry should accept this teaching about marriage."

## JESUS WELCOMES CHILDREN

¹³Then the people brought their little children to Jesus so he could put his hands on them and pray for them. His followers told them to stop, ¹⁴but Jesus said, "Let the little children come to me. Don't stop them, because the kingdom of heaven belongs to people who are like these children." ¹⁵After Jesus put his hands on the children, he left there.

## A RICH YOUNG MAN'S QUESTION

¹⁶A man came to Jesus and asked, "Teacher, what good thing must I do to have life forever?"

# ◉➡ CHECK IT OUT

## PRESIDENTIAL PRAYER TEAM

The Presidential Prayer Team got started after the really close election in 2000, as American citizens came together and pledged to pray daily for the president, his cabinet, and other politicians and government officials. The Presidential Prayer Team is not affiliated with any political party or official. It gains no direction or support from the current administration, from any agency of the government, or from any political party.

The team's original goal was to sign up one percent of the American population—or 2.8 million people—to pray. That goal was reached in 600 days. There is no fee for joining, and members receive a window decal and email updates of prayer needs for the president. On September 1, 2002, the Presidential Prayer Team for Kids was also launched. The site provides historical facts, pictures of government leaders to pray for, a weekly list of national concerns to pray for, and more.

*Get involved by visiting* **www.presidentialprayerteam.org** *or* **www.pptkids.org**.

**19:4 'he made . . . female.'** Quotation from Genesis 1:27 or 5:2. **19:5 'So . . . body.'** Quotation from Genesis 2:24. **19:12 But . . . marriage.** This may also mean, "The person who can accept this teaching about not marrying should accept it." **19:13 put his hands on them** Showing that Jesus gave special blessings to these children.

17Jesus answered, "Why do you ask me about what is good? Only God is good. But if you want to have life forever, obey the commands."

18The man asked, "Which commands?"

Jesus answered, " 'You must not murder anyone; you must not be guilty of adultery; you must not steal; you must not tell lies about your neighbor; 19honor your father and mother;" and love your neighbor as you love yourself.' "ⁿ

20The young man said, "I have obeyed all these things. What else do I need to do?"

21Jesus answered, "If you want to be perfect, then go and sell your possessions and give the money to the poor. If you do this, you will have treasure in heaven. Then come and follow me."

22But when the young man heard this, he left sorrowfully, because he was rich.

23Then Jesus said to his followers, "I tell you the truth, it will be hard for a rich person to enter the kingdom of heaven. 24Yes, I tell you that it is easier for a camel to go through the eye of a needle than for a rich person to enter the kingdom of God."

25When Jesus' followers heard this, they were very surprised and asked, "Then who can be saved?"

26Jesus looked at them and said, "This is something people cannot do, but God can do all things."

27Peter said to Jesus, "Look, we have left everything and followed you. So what will we have?"

28Jesus said to them, "I tell you the truth, when the age to come has arrived, the Son of Man will sit on his great throne. All of you who followed me will also sit on twelve thrones, judging the twelve tribes of Israel. 29And all those who have left houses, brothers, sisters, father, mother, children, or farms to follow me will get much more than they left, and they will have life forever. 30Many who have the highest place now will have the lowest place in the future. And many who have the lowest place now will have the highest place in the future.

## A STORY ABOUT WORKERS

20 "The kingdom of heaven is like a person who owned some land. One morning, he went out very early to hire some people to work in his vineyard. 2The man agreed to pay the workers one coinⁿ for working that day. Then he sent them into the vineyard to work. 3About nine o'clock the man went to the marketplace and saw some other people standing there, doing nothing. 4So he said to them, 'If you go and work in my vineyard, I will pay you what your work is worth.' 5So they went to work in the vineyard. The man went out again about twelve o'clock and three o'clock and did the same thing. 6About five o'clock the man went to the marketplace again and saw others standing there. He asked them, 'Why did you stand here all day doing nothing?' 7They answered, 'No one gave us a job.' The man said to them, 'Then you can go and work in my vineyard.'

## "MANY WHO HAVE THE LOWEST PLACE NOW WILL HAVE THE HIGHEST PLACE IN THE FUTURE."

8"At the end of the day, the owner of the vineyard said to the boss of all the workers, 'Call the workers and pay them. Start with the last people I hired and end with those I hired first.'

9"When the workers who were hired at five o'clock came to get their pay, each received one coin. 10When the workers who were hired first came to get their pay, they thought they would be paid more than the others. But each one of them also received one coin. 11When they got their coin, they complained to the man who owned the land. 12They said, 'Those people were hired last and worked only one hour. But you paid them the same as you paid us who worked hard all day in the hot sun.' 13But the man who owned the vineyard said to one of those workers, 'Friend, I am being fair to you.

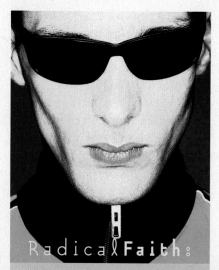

Radical Faith:

# Matthew 20:26-28

Ever find yourself wanting to be a "celebrity Christian"? You know, the one everyone looks at and listens to? Jesus says the top dog isn't necessarily the one in the spotlight. Rather, it's the person with a heart like his who pleases him most. It may be hard to understand, but being popular with everyone won't necessarily make you the greatest Christian. God isn't impressed with any of that. He is only concerned with your heart—what you really care about and why you do the things you do. In the work of God's kingdom, those held in the highest respect are the ones willing to be a slave to other people's needs and to give all they have to take care of others. So in God's eyes, what makes someone great is having a heart of love—full of genuine, selfless care—that is expressed in sacrificially serving other people. Whether you're in a role of leadership or busy behind the scenes, God loves it when you're interested in loving, serving, and sacrificing the way Jesus did. It's easy and normal to desire attention from people; but ask God to help you have pure, unselfish motives. Living like a slave isn't glamorous or easy, but God will recognize it as the most valuable kind of life.

notes 19:19 'You . . . mother.' Quotation from Exodus 20:12-16; Deuteronomy 5:16-20.  19:19 'love . . . yourself.' Quotation from Leviticus 19:18.  20:2 coin A Roman denarius. One coin was the average pay for one day's work.

29

You agreed to work for one coin. ¹⁴So take your pay and go. I want to give the man who was hired last the same pay that I gave you. ¹⁵I can do what I want with my own money. Are you jealous because I am good to those people?'

¹⁶"So those who have the last place now will have the first place in the future, and those who have the first place now will have the last place in the future."

## Jesus Talks about His Own Death

¹⁷While Jesus was going to Jerusalem, he took his twelve followers aside privately and said to them, ¹⁸"Look, we are going to Jerusalem. The Son of Man will be turned over to the leading priests and the teachers of the law, and they will say that he must die. ¹⁹They will give the Son of Man to the non-Jewish people to laugh at him and beat him with whips and crucify him. But on the third day, he will be raised to life again."

## A Mother Asks Jesus a Favor

²⁰Then the wife of Zebedee came to Jesus with her sons. She bowed before him and asked him to do something for her.

²¹Jesus asked, "What do you want?"

She said, "Promise that one of my sons will sit at your right side and the other will sit at your left side in your kingdom."

²²But Jesus said, "You don't understand what you are asking. Can you drink the cup that I am about to drink?"ⁿ

The sons answered, "Yes, we can."

²³Jesus said to them, "You will drink from my cup. But I cannot choose who will sit at my right or my left; those places belong to those for whom my Father has prepared them."

²⁴When the other ten followers heard this, they were angry with the two brothers.

²⁵Jesus called all the followers together and said, "You know that the rulers of the non-Jewish people love to show their power over the people. And their important leaders love to use all their authority. ²⁶But it should not be that way among you. Whoever wants to become great among you must serve the rest of you like a servant. ²⁷Whoever wants to become first among you must serve the rest of you like a slave. ²⁸In the same way, the Son of Man did not come to be served. He came to serve others and to give his life as a ransom for many people."

## Jesus Heals Two Blind Men

²⁹When Jesus and his followers were leaving Jericho, a great many people followed him. ³⁰Two blind men sitting by the road heard that Jesus was going by, so they shouted, "Lord, Son of David, have mercy on us!"

³¹The people warned the blind men to be quiet, but they shouted even more, "Lord, Son of David, have mercy on us!"

³²Jesus stopped and said to the blind men, "What do you want me to do for you?"

³³They answered, "Lord, we want to see."

³⁴Jesus felt sorry for the blind men and touched their eyes, and at once they could see. Then they followed Jesus.

## Jesus Enters Jerusalem as a King

**21** As Jesus and his followers were coming closer to Jerusalem, they stopped at Bethphage at the hill called the Mount of Olives. From there Jesus sent two of his followers ²and said to them, "Go to the town you can see there. When you enter it, you will quickly find a donkey tied there with its colt. Untie them and bring them to me. ³If anyone asks you why you are taking the donkeys, say that the Master needs them, and he will send them at once."

⁴This was to bring about what the prophet had said:

⁵"Tell the people of Jerusalem,
 'Your king is coming to you.
He is gentle and riding on a donkey,
 on the colt of a donkey.' "

*Isaiah 62:11; Zechariah 9:9*

⁶The followers went and did what Jesus told them to do. ⁷They brought the donkey and the colt to Jesus and laid their coats on them, and Jesus sat on them. ⁸Many people spread their coats on the road. Others cut branches from the trees and spread them on the road.

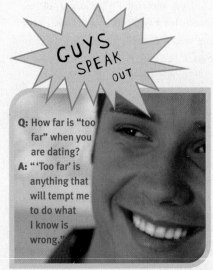

**GUYS SPEAK OUT**

**Q:** How far is "too far" when you are dating?
**A:** " 'Too far' is anything that will tempt me to do what I know is wrong."

## relationships

"Those who sin sexually sin against their own bodies" (1 Corinthians 6:18). When a relationship gets hot and heavy, and you *so* want to get closer to that fine guy, remember that getting too physical before marriage hurts not only your relationship with God, but it also hurts you! As a Christian, your body is where the Holy Spirit lives to guide, direct, and comfort you. Remember that your body is valuable, something to be respected and protected.

**notes** 20:22 **drink . . . drink** Jesus used the idea of drinking from a cup to ask if they could accept the same terrible things that would happen to him.

30

# LEARN I+ & LIVE I+

**Matthew 21:9**
**Learn It:** As Jesus entered Jerusalem, the people shouted praises to his name.
**Live It:** Spend time worshiping out loud. Sing, shout, and love God with your voice.

**Matthew 22:1**
**Learn It:** Jesus taught people by using stories.
**Live It:** Learn to tell others the story of your life and the difference Christ has made in it.

**Matthew 23:26**
**Learn It:** Make the inside of yourself clean before you worry about the outside.
**Live It:** Ask God to forgive you of the things you have done wrong this week. Make a list to remind yourself not to do them again.

⁹The people were walking ahead of Jesus and behind him, shouting,

"Praise" to the Son of David!

God bless the One who comes in the name of the Lord!          *Psalm 118:26*

Praise to God in heaven!"

¹⁰When Jesus entered Jerusalem, all the city was filled with excitement. The people asked, "Who is this man?"

¹¹The crowd said, "This man is Jesus, the prophet from the town of Nazareth in Galilee."

## JESUS GOES TO THE TEMPLE

¹²Jesus went into the Temple and threw out all the people who were buying and selling there. He turned over the tables of those who were exchanging different kinds of money, and he upset the benches of those who were selling doves. ¹³Jesus said to all the people there, "It is written in the Scriptures, 'My Temple will be called a house for prayer.'" But you are changing it into a 'hideout for robbers.' "

¹⁴The blind and crippled people came to Jesus in the Temple, and he healed them. ¹⁵The leading priests and the teachers of the law saw that Jesus was doing wonderful things and that the children were praising him in the Temple, saying, "Praise" to the Son of David." All these things made the priests and the teachers of the law very angry.

¹⁶They asked Jesus, "Do you hear the things these children are saying?"

Jesus answered, "Yes. Haven't you read in the Scriptures, 'You have taught children and babies to sing praises'?"

¹⁷Then Jesus left and went out of the city to Bethany, where he spent the night.

## THE POWER OF FAITH

¹⁸Early the next morning, as Jesus was going back to the city, he became hungry. ¹⁹Seeing a fig tree beside the road, Jesus went to it, but there were no figs on the tree, only leaves. So Jesus said to the tree, "You will never again have fruit." The tree immediately dried up.

## "IF YOU BELIEVE, YOU WILL GET ANYTHING YOU ASK FOR IN PRAYER."

²⁰When his followers saw this, they were amazed. They asked, "How did the fig tree dry up so quickly?"

²¹Jesus answered, "I tell you the truth, if you have faith and do not doubt, you will be able to do what I did to this tree and even more. You will be able to say to this mountain, 'Go, fall into the sea.' And if you have faith, it will happen. ²²If you believe, you will get anything you ask for in prayer."

## LEADERS DOUBT JESUS' AUTHORITY

²³Jesus went to the Temple, and while he was teaching there, the leading priests and the older leaders of the people came to him. They said, "What authority do you have to do these things? Who gave you this authority?"

²⁴Jesus answered, "I also will ask you a question. If you answer me, then I will tell you what authority I have to do these things. ²⁵Tell me: When John baptized people, did that come from God or just from other people?"

They argued about Jesus' question, saying, "If we answer, 'John's baptism was from God,' Jesus will say, 'Then why didn't you believe him?' ²⁶But if we say, 'It was from people,' we are afraid of what the crowd will do because they all believe that John was a prophet."

²⁷So they answered Jesus, "We don't know."

Jesus said to them, "Then I won't tell you what authority I have to do these things.

## A STORY ABOUT TWO SONS

²⁸"Tell me what you think about this: A man had two sons. He went to the first son and said, 'Son, go and work today in my vineyard.' ²⁹The son answered, 'I will not go.' But later the son changed his mind and went. ³⁰Then the father went to the other son and said, 'Son, go and work today in my vineyard.' The son answered, 'Yes, sir, I will go and work,' but he did not go. ³¹Which of the two sons obeyed his father?"

The priests and leaders answered, "The first son."

Jesus said to them, "I tell you the truth, the tax collectors and the prostitutes will enter the kingdom of God before you do. ³²John came to show you the right way to live. You did not believe him, but the tax collectors and prostitutes believed him. Even after seeing this, you

 **21:9 Praise** Literally, "Hosanna," a Hebrew word used at first in praying to God for help. At this time it was probably a shout of joy used in praising God or his Messiah. **21:13 'My Temple . . . prayer.'** Quotation from Isaiah 56:7. **21:13 'hideout for robbers.'** Quotation from Jeremiah 7:11. **21:15 Praise** Literally, "Hosanna," a Hebrew word used at first in praying to God for help. At this time it was probably a shout of joy used in praising God or his Messiah. **21:16 'You . . . praises'** Quotation from the Septuagint (Greek) version of Psalm 8:2.

still refused to change your ways and believe him.

## a STORY ABOUT GOD'S SON

33"Listen to this story: There was a man who owned a vineyard. He put a wall around it and dug a hole for a winepress and built a tower. Then he leased the land to some farmers and left for a trip. 34When it was time for the grapes to be picked, he sent his servants to the farmers to get his share of the grapes. 35But the farmers grabbed the servants, beat one, killed another, and then killed a third servant with stones. 36So the man sent some other servants to the farmers, even more than he sent the first time. But the farmers did the same thing to the servants that they had done before. 37So the man decided to send his son to the farmers. He said, 'They will respect my son.' 38But when the farmers saw the son, they said to each other, 'This son will inherit the vineyard. If we kill him, it will be ours!' 39Then the farmers grabbed the son, threw him out of the vineyard, and killed him. 40So what will the owner of the vineyard do to these farmers when he comes?"

41The priests and leaders said, "He will surely kill those evil men. Then he will lease the vineyard to some other farmers who will give him his share of the crop at harvest time."

42Jesus said to them, "Surely you have read this in the Scriptures:

'The stone that the builders rejected
    became the cornerstone.
The Lord did this,
    and it is wonderful to us.'    *Psalm 118:22-23*

43"So I tell you that the kingdom of God will be taken away from you and given to people who do the things God wants in his kingdom. 44The person who falls on this stone will be broken, and on whomever that stone falls, that person will be crushed."ⁿ

45When the leading priests and the Pharisees heard these stories, they knew Jesus was talking about them. 46They wanted to arrest him, but they were afraid of the people, because the people believed that Jesus was a prophet.

## a STORY ABOUT a WEDDING FEAST

22 Jesus again used stories to teach the people. He said, 2"The kingdom of heaven is like a king who prepared a wedding feast for his son. 3The king invited some people to the feast. When the feast was ready, the king sent his servants to tell the people, but they refused to come.

4"Then the king sent other servants, saying, 'Tell those who have been invited that my feast is ready. I have killed my best bulls and calves for the dinner, and everything is ready. Come to the wedding feast.'

5"But the people refused to listen to the servants and left to do other things. One went to work in his field, and another went to his business. 6Some of the other people grabbed the servants, beat them, and killed them. 7The king was furious and sent his army to kill the murderers and burn their city.

8"After that, the king said to his servants, 'The wedding feast is ready. I invited those people, but they were not worthy to come. 9So go to the street corners and invite everyone you find to come to my feast.' 10So the servants went into the streets and gathered all the people they could find, both good and bad. And the wedding hall was filled with guests.

11"When the king came in to see the guests, he saw a man who was not dressed for a wedding. 12The king said, 'Friend, how were you allowed to come in here? You are not dressed for a wedding.' But the man said nothing. 13So the king told some servants, 'Tie this man's hands and feet. Throw him out into the darkness, where people will cry and grind their teeth with pain.'

14"Yes, many people are invited, but only a few are chosen."

## Music Reviews

GROUP:  SARA GROVES

ALBUM:  CONVERSATIONS (CLASSIC HIT)

Sara Groves will knock your socks off, as she is hands-down one of the top singer/songwriters around. Her thought-provoking lyrics on this debut album will stay with you long after the songs end. The title track finds Sara longing to share Christ with a friend, while "Word" is a great reminder to us to open the Bible daily. "Pictures of Egypt" talks about how our human nature makes it hard for us to break out of doing things that aren't good for us sometimes. Every song makes an impact, so pick this one up and listen carefully.

**WHY IT ROCKS: SARA HOLDS UP A MIRROR TO OUR HEARTS AND MAKES US EXAMINE THE GOOD, THE BAD, AND THE GOD-FACTOR.**

21:44 **Verse 44** Some copies do not have verse 44.

**Q:** One of the guys in my class keeps touching himself. It totally grosses me out. What should I do?

**A:** Ask yourself if he is doing it on purpose or without even realizing it. If he doesn't know he is doing it, find a friend of his and ask the friend to speak to him discretely and tactfully. If he is purposely doing it and won't stop when you ask him to, then it can qualify as sexual harassment, which is against the law. Tell a teacher immediately.

**Q:** I'm bored out of my mind at my parents' church. All my friends go to another church, and it's so much better, but my parents won't let me go. What do I do?

**A:** You have to obey your parents. While you are praying that God will change their minds, ask God to change your attitude, as well. If you participate in your church with enthusiasm—whether you feel like it or not—God can change your perspective. When your parents see you trying, they might be more open to a change.

**Q:** My friend just had plastic surgery on her nose. It looks so cute and perfect now. Now I want to have my nose done. Is there anything wrong with that?

**A:** If you want a nose job to help your infected sinuses or remove a bump that is so big you can see it in front of you, then that kind of medical surgery won't displease God. But if you are doing it because you are focused on yourself and just want to look better, you are basically telling God he didn't get it right when he made you. Ask God to help you focus on the inside, and he'll let you know what's okay to change on the outside.

## IS IT RIGHT TO PAY TAXES OR NOT?

15Then the Pharisees left that place and made plans to trap Jesus in saying something wrong. 16They sent some of their own followers and some people from the group called Herodians." They said, "Teacher, we know that you are an honest man and that you teach the truth about God's way. You are not afraid of what other people think about you, because you pay no attention to who they are. 17So tell us what you think. Is it right to pay taxes to Caesar or not?"

18But knowing that these leaders were trying to trick him, Jesus said, "You hypocrites! Why are you trying to trap me? 19Show me a coin used for paying the tax." So the men showed him a coin." 20Then Jesus asked, "Whose image and name are on the coin?"

21The men answered, "Caesar's."

Then Jesus said to them, "Give to Caesar the things that are Caesar's, and give to God the things that are God's."

22When the men heard what Jesus said, they were amazed and left him and went away.

## SOME SADDUCEES TRY TO TRICK JESUS

23That same day some Sadducees came to Jesus and asked him a question. (Sadducees believed that people would not rise from the dead.) 24They said, "Teacher, Moses said if a married man dies without having children, his brother must marry the widow and have children for him. 25Once there were seven brothers among us. The first one married and died. Since he had no children, his brother married the widow. 26Then the second brother also died. The same thing happened to the third brother and all the other brothers. 27Finally, the woman died. 28Since all seven men had married her, when people rise from the dead, whose wife will she be?"

29Jesus answered, "You don't understand, because you don't know what the Scriptures say, and you don't know about the power of God. 30When people rise from the dead, they will not marry, nor will they be given to some-

one to marry. They will be like the angels in heaven. 31Surely you have read what God said to you about rising from the dead. 32God said, 'I am the God of Abraham, the God of Isaac, and the God of Jacob.'" God is the God of the living, not the dead."

33When the people heard this, they were amazed at Jesus' teaching.

## THE MOST IMPORTANT COMMAND

34When the Pharisees learned that the Sadducees could not argue with Jesus' answers to them, the Pharisees met together. 35One Pharisee, who was an expert on the law of Moses, asked Jesus this question to test him: 36"Teacher, which command in the law is the most important?"

37Jesus answered, " 'Love the Lord your God with all your heart, all your soul, and all your mind.'" 38This is the first and most important command. 39And the second command is like the first: 'Love your neighbor as you love yourself.'" 40All the law and the writings of the prophets depend on these two commands."

## JESUS QUESTIONS THE PHARISEES

41While the Pharisees were together, Jesus asked them, 42"What do you think about the Christ? Whose son is he?"

They answered, "The Christ is the Son of David."

43Then Jesus said to them, "Then why did David call him 'Lord'? David, speaking by the power of the Holy Spirit, said,

44'The Lord said to my Lord:
  Sit by me at my right side,
    until I put your enemies under your
      control.'           *Psalm 110:1*

45David calls the Christ 'Lord,' so how can the Christ be his son?"

46None of the Pharisees could answer Jesus' question, and after that day no one was brave enough to ask him any more questions.

## JESUS ACCUSES SOME LEADERS

**23** Then Jesus said to the crowds and to his followers, 2"The teachers of the law and the Pharisees have the authority to

22:16 **Herodians** A political group that followed Herod and his family.   22:19 **coin** A Roman denarius. One coin was the average pay for one day's work.   22:32 **'I am . . . Jacob.'** Quotation from Exodus 3:6.
22:37 **'Love . . . mind.'** Quotation from Deuteronomy 6:5.   22:39 **'Love . . . yourself.'** Quotation from Leviticus 19:18.

tell you what the law of Moses says. ³So you should obey and follow whatever they tell you, but their lives are not good examples for you to follow. They tell you to do things, but they themselves don't do them. ⁴They make strict rules and try to force people to obey them, but they are unwilling to help those who struggle under the weight of their rules.

⁵"They do good things so that other people will see them. They make the boxes" of Scriptures that they wear bigger, and they make their special prayer clothes very long. ⁶Those Pharisees and teachers of the law love to have the most important seats at feasts and in the synagogues. ⁷They love people to greet them with respect in the marketplaces, and they love to have people call them 'Teacher.'

⁸"But you must not be called 'Teacher,' because you have only one Teacher, and you are all brothers and sisters together. ⁹And don't call any person on earth 'Father,' because you have one Father, who is in heaven. ¹⁰And you should not be called 'Master,' because you have only one Master, the Christ. ¹¹Whoever is your servant is the greatest among you. ¹²Whoever makes himself great will be made humble. Whoever makes himself humble will be made great.

¹³"How terrible for you, teachers of the law and Pharisees! You are hypocrites! You close the door for people to enter the kingdom of heaven. You yourselves don't enter, and you stop others who are trying to enter. ¹⁴"

¹⁵"How terrible for you, teachers of the law and Pharisees! You are hypocrites! You travel across land and sea to find one person who will change to your ways. When you find that person, you make him more fit for hell than you are.

¹⁶"How terrible for you! You guide the people, but you are blind. You say, 'If people swear by the Temple when they make a promise, that means nothing. But if they swear by the gold that is in the Temple, they must keep that promise.' ¹⁷You are blind fools! Which is greater: the gold or the Temple that makes that gold holy? ¹⁸And you say, 'If people swear by

the altar when they make a promise, that means nothing. But if they swear by the gift on the altar, they must keep that promise.' ¹⁹You are blind! Which is greater: the gift or the altar that makes the gift holy? ²⁰The person who swears by the altar is really using the altar and also everything on the altar. ²¹And the person who swears by the Temple is really using the Temple and also everything in the Temple. ²²The person who swears by heaven is also using God's throne and the One who sits on that throne.

²³"How terrible for you, teachers of the law and Pharisees! You are hypocrites! You give to God one-tenth of everything you earn—even your mint, dill, and cumin." But you don't obey the really important teachings of the law—justice, mercy, and being loyal. These are the

things you should do, as well as those other things. ²⁴You guide the people, but you are blind! You are like a person who picks a fly out of a drink and then swallows a camel!"

²⁵"How terrible for you, teachers of the law and Pharisees! You are hypocrites! You wash the outside of your cups and dishes, but inside they are full of things you got by cheating others and by pleasing only yourselves. ²⁶Pharisees, you are blind! First make the inside of the cup clean, and then the outside of the cup can be truly clean.

²⁷"How terrible for you, teachers of the law and Pharisees! You are hypocrites! You are like tombs that are painted white. Outside, those tombs look fine, but inside, they are full of the bones of dead people and all kinds of unclean things. ²⁸It is the same with you. People look at

## BIBLE BIOS

### Bathsheba

[2 SAMUEL 11 AND 12] Bathsheba was on her back porch taking a bath when David spotted her from the roof of his palace. He could have respected her privacy, but David didn't turn away. And he certainly didn't have to send men to bring her to him, but he did. David got her pregnant. And when he couldn't get her husband, Uriah, to come home from the war to sleep with her and hide his sin, David had him killed in battle. Then he married Bathsheba. This woman lost a lot—her honor, her husband, the baby—and had a lot to forgive. Yet the Bible says that David and Bathsheba came to love each other and she eventually gave birth to a son, Solomon.

## DIDYA KNOW

84% OF TEENS LISTEN TO ONLINE MUSIC, 82% SEND EMAILS, 72% EXCHANGE INSTANT MESSAGES, 71% DO HOMEWORK OR RESEARCH FOR SCHOOL ONLINE, AND 65% PLAY ONLINE GAMES. AOL TIME WARNER

notes: 23:5 boxes Small leather boxes containing four important Scriptures. Some Jews tied these to their foreheads and left arms, probably to show they were very religious. 23:14 Verse 14 Some Greek copies add verse 14: "How terrible for you, teachers of the law and Pharisees. You are hypocrites. You take away widows' houses, and you say long prayers so that people will notice you. So you will have a worse punishment." 23:23 mint, dill, and cumin Small plants grown in gardens and used for spices. Only very religious people would be careful enough to give a tenth of these plants. 23:24 You . . . camel! Meaning, "You worry about the smallest mistakes but commit the biggest sin."

# LEARN I+ & LIVE I+

**Matthew 24:14**
**Learn It:** The Good News will be preached to every nation.
**Live It:** Ask God if he wants you to go on a short-term missions trip or become a missionary someday.

**Matthew 26:7**
**Learn It:** A woman poured expensive oil on Jesus' head.
**Live It:** Be willing to sacrifice something—your caffeine habit, your allowance, your TV or mall time for Christ.

**Matthew 26:42**
**Learn It:** Jesus prayed that what God wanted would be done, even though he knew his upcoming death would be painful.
**Live It:** Pray that you will be willing to do the difficult things God wants you to do.

you and think you are good, but on the inside you are full of hypocrisy and evil.

²⁹"How terrible for you, teachers of the law and Pharisees! You are hypocrites! You build tombs for the prophets, and you show honor to the graves of those who lived good lives. ³⁰You say, 'If we had lived during the time of our ancestors, we would not have helped them kill the prophets.' ³¹But you give proof that you are children of those who murdered the prophets. ³²And you will complete the sin that your ancestors started.

> "BE CAREFUL THAT NO ONE FOOLS YOU. MANY WILL COME IN MY NAME, SAYING, 'I AM THE CHRIST,' AND THEY WILL FOOL MANY PEOPLE. YOU WILL HEAR ABOUT WARS AND STORIES OF WARS THAT ARE COMING, BUT DON'T BE AFRAID."

³³"You are snakes! A family of poisonous snakes! How are you going to escape God's judgment? ³⁴So I tell you this: I am sending to you prophets and wise men and teachers. Some of them you will kill and crucify. Some of them you will beat in your synagogues and chase from town to town. ³⁵So you will be guilty for the death of all the good people who have been killed on earth—from the murder of that good man Abel to the murder of Zechariah" son of Berakiah, whom you murdered between the Temple and the altar. ³⁶I tell you the truth, all of these things will happen to you people who are living now.

## JESUS FEELS SORRY FOR JERUSALEM

³⁷"Jerusalem, Jerusalem! You kill the prophets and stone to death those who are sent to you. Many times I wanted to gather your people as a hen gathers her chicks under her wings, but you did not let me. ³⁸Now your house will be left completely empty. ³⁹I tell you, you will not see me again until that time when you will say, 'God bless the One who comes in the name of the Lord.' "

## THE TEMPLE WILL BE DESTROYED

**24** As Jesus left the Temple and was walking away, his followers came up to show him the Temple's buildings. ²Jesus asked, "Do you see all these buildings? I tell you the truth, not one stone will be left on another. Every stone will be thrown down to the ground."

³Later, as Jesus was sitting on the Mount of Olives, his followers came to be alone with him. They said, "Tell us, when will these things happen? And what will be the sign that it is time for you to come again and for this age to end?"

⁴Jesus answered, "Be careful that no one fools you. ⁵Many will come in my name, saying, 'I am the Christ,' and they will fool many people. ⁶You will hear about wars and stories of wars that are coming, but don't be afraid. These things must happen before the end comes. ⁷Nations will fight against other nations; kingdoms will fight against other kingdoms. There will be times when there is no food for people to eat, and there will be earthquakes in different places. ⁸These things are like the first pains when something new is about to be born.

⁹"Then people will arrest you, hand you over to be hurt, and kill you. They will hate you because you believe in me. ¹⁰At that time, many will lose their faith, and they will turn against each other and hate each other. ¹¹Many false prophets will come and cause many people to believe lies. ¹²There will be more and more evil in the world, so most people will stop showing their love for each other. ¹³But those people who keep their faith until the end will be saved. ¹⁴The Good News about God's kingdom will be preached in all the world, to every nation. Then the end will come.

¹⁵"Daniel the prophet spoke about 'the destroying terror.' You will see this standing in the holy place." (You who read this should understand what it means.) ¹⁶"At that time, the people in Judea should run away to the

**23:35 Abel . . . Zechariah** In the order of the books of the Hebrew Old Testament, the first and last men to be murdered. **23:39 'God . . . Lord.'** Quotation from Psalm 118:26. **24:15 'the destroying terror'** Mentioned in Daniel 9:27; 12:11 (see also Daniel 11:31).

# February

**1** February is Black History Month. Take time to read a book about Martin Luther King, Jr.

**2** Groundhog Day. Hopefully, it's time to look forward to spring.

**3**

**4** Call your grandparents and tell them how much you love them.

**5**

**6**

**7** Pray for a person of influence: It's Ashton Kutcher's birthday.

**8**

**9** Invite a friend to go to church with you this week.

**10**

**11** It's Make A New Friend Day. Celebrate by introducing yourself to someone new at school.

**12** It's Abraham Lincoln's birthday. Learn something new about this great president by doing some research on the Internet.

**13** Read 1 Corinthians 13. Pick a verse from this passage and memorize it. Look for ways to express God's love to at least two people today.

**14** Valentine's Day! Make a list of five ways God has demonstrated his love for you so far this year.

**15**

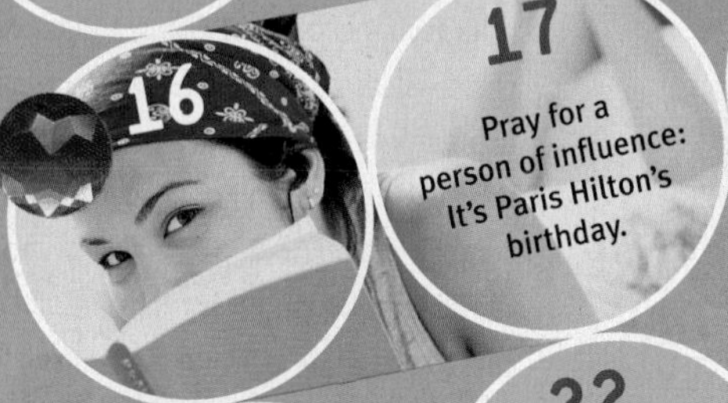

**16**

**17** Pray for a person of influence: It's Paris Hilton's birthday.

**18**

**19**

**20**

**21** Pray for a friend you know who is hurting.

**22**

**23** Volunteer to baby-sit for someone who can't afford to pay you.

**24**

**25** Buy a teddy bear today and donate it to an orphanage.

**26**

**27** Reality check: Are you keeping your New Year's resolutions?

**28** Eat at least two servings of fruit and three servings of vegetables today. They really are good for you!

What people say with their mouths comes from the way they think.
— Matthew 15:18

mountains. [17]If people are on the roofs" of their houses, they must not go down to get anything out of their houses. [18]If people are in the fields, they must not go back to get their coats. [19]At that time, how terrible it will be for women who are pregnant or have nursing babies! [20]Pray that it will not be winter or a Sabbath day when these things happen and you have to run away, [21]because at that time there will be much trouble. There will be more trouble than there has ever been since the beginning of the world until now, and nothing as bad will ever happen again. [22]God has decided to make that terrible time short. Otherwise, no one would go on living. But God will make that time short to help the people he has chosen. [23]At that time, someone might say to you, 'Look, there is the Christ!' Or another person might say, 'There he is!' But don't believe them. [24]False Christs and false prophets will come and perform great wonders and miracles. They will try to fool even the people God has chosen, if that is possible. [25]Now I have warned you about this before it happens.

[26]"If people tell you, 'The Christ is in the desert,' don't go there. If they say, 'The Christ is in the inner room,' don't believe it. [27]When the Son of Man comes, he will be seen by everyone, like lightning flashing from the east to the west. [28]Wherever the dead body is, there the vultures will gather.

[29]"Soon after the trouble of those days,

'the sun will grow dark,
and the moon will not give its light.
The stars will fall from the sky.
And the powers of the heavens will be shaken.'               *Isaiah 13:10; 34:4*

[30]"At that time, the sign of the Son of Man will appear in the sky. Then all the peoples of the world will cry. They will see the Son of Man coming on clouds in the sky with great power and glory. [31]He will use a loud trumpet to send his angels all around the earth, and they will gather his chosen people from every part of the world.

[32]"Learn a lesson from the fig tree: When its branches become green and soft and new

leaves appear, you know summer is near. [33]In the same way, when you see all these things happening, you will know that the time is near, ready to come. [34]I tell you the truth, all these things will happen while the people of this time are still living. [35]Earth and sky will be destroyed, but the words I have said will never be destroyed.

## when will Jesus come again?

[36]"No one knows when that day or time will be, not the angels in heaven, not even the Son. Only the Father knows. [37]When the Son of Man comes, it will be like what happened during Noah's time. [38]In those days before the flood, people were eating and drinking, marrying and giving their children to be married, until the day Noah entered the boat. [39]They knew nothing about what was happening until the flood came and destroyed them. It will be the same when the Son of Man comes. [40]Two men will be in the field. One will be taken, and the other will be left. [41]Two women will be grinding grain with a mill." One will be taken, and the other will be left.

> ## "SO ALWAYS BE READY, BECAUSE YOU DON'T KNOW THE DAY YOUR LORD WILL COME."

[42]"So always be ready, because you don't know the day your Lord will come. [43]Remember this: If the owner of the house knew what time of night a thief was coming, the owner would watch and not let the thief break in. [44]So you also must be ready, because the Son of Man will come at a time you don't expect him.

[45]"Who is the wise and loyal servant that the master trusts to give the other servants their food at the right time? [46]When the master comes and finds the servant doing his work, the servant will be blessed. [47]I tell you the truth, the

master will choose that servant to take care of everything he owns. [48]But suppose that evil servant thinks to himself, 'My master will not come back soon,' [49]and he begins to beat the other servants and eat and get drunk with others like him? [50]The master will come when that servant is not ready and is not expecting him. [51]Then the master will cut him in pieces and send him away to be with the hypocrites, where people will cry and grind their teeth with pain.

## a story about ten Bridesmaids

**25** "At that time the kingdom of heaven will be like ten bridesmaids who took their lamps and went to wait for the bridegroom. [2]Five of them were foolish and five were wise. [3]The five foolish bridesmaids took their lamps, but they did not take more oil for the lamps to burn. [4]The wise bridesmaids took their lamps and more oil in jars. [5]Because the bridegroom was late, they became sleepy and went to sleep.

[6]"At midnight someone cried out, 'The bridegroom is coming! Come and meet him!' [7]Then all the bridesmaids woke up and got their lamps ready. [8]But the foolish ones said to the wise, 'Give us some of your oil, because our lamps are going out.' [9]The wise bridesmaids answered, 'No, the oil we have might not be enough for all of us. Go to the people who sell oil and buy some for yourselves.'

[10]"So while the five foolish bridesmaids went to buy oil, the bridegroom came. The bridesmaids who were ready went in with the bridegroom to the wedding feast. Then the door was closed and locked.

[11]"Later the others came back and said, 'Sir, sir, open the door to let us in.' [12]But the bridegroom answered, 'I tell you the truth, I don't want to know you.'

[13]"So always be ready, because you don't know the day or the hour the Son of Man will come.

## a story about three servants

[14]"The kingdom of heaven is like a man who was going to another place for a visit.

---

**24:17 roofs** In Bible times houses were built with flat roofs. The roof was used for drying things such as flax and fruit. And it was used as an extra room, as a place for worship, and as a cool place to sleep in the summer.
**24:41 mill** Two large, round, flat rocks used for grinding grain to make flour.

Before he left, he called for his servants and told them to take care of his things while he was gone. ¹⁵He gave one servant five bags of gold, another servant two bags of gold, and a third servant one bag of gold, to each one as much as he could handle. Then he left. ¹⁶The servant who got five bags went quickly to invest the money and earned five more bags. ¹⁷In the same way, the servant who had two bags invested them and earned two more. ¹⁸But the servant who got one bag went out and dug a hole in the ground and hid the master's money.

¹⁹"After a long time the master came home and asked the servants what they did with his money. ²⁰The servant who was given five bags of gold brought five more bags to the master and said, 'Master, you trusted me to care for five bags of gold, so I used your five bags to earn five more.' ²¹The master answered, 'You did well. You are a good and loyal servant. Because you were loyal with small things, I will let you care for much greater things. Come and share my joy with me.'

**DIDYA KNOW**

## 41% OF TEENS REPORT PLANNING THEIR FIRST SEXUAL ENCOUNTER; 57% SAID IT WAS UNPLANNED.

WWW.KFF.ORG

²²"Then the servant who had been given two bags of gold came to the master and said, 'Master, you gave me two bags of gold to care for, so I used your two bags to earn two more.' ²³The master answered, 'You did well. You are a good and loyal servant. Because you were loyal with small things, I will let you care for much greater things. Come and share my joy with me.'

²⁴"Then the servant who had been given one bag of gold came to the master and said, 'Master, I knew that you were a hard man. You harvest things you did not plant. You gather crops where you did not sow any seed. ²⁵So I was afraid and went and hid your money in the ground. Here is your bag of gold.' ²⁶The master

answered, 'You are a wicked and lazy servant! You say you knew that I harvest things I did not plant and that I gather crops where I did not sow any seed. ²⁷So you should have put my gold in the bank. Then, when I came home, I would have received my gold back with interest.'

²⁸"So the master told his other servants, 'Take the bag of gold from that servant and give it to the servant who has ten bags of gold. ²⁹Those who have much will get more, and they will have much more than they need. But those who do not have much will have everything taken away from them.' ³⁰Then the master said, 'Throw that useless servant outside, into the darkness where people will cry and grind their teeth with pain.'

### THE KING WILL JUDGE ALL PEOPLE

³¹"The Son of Man will come again in his great glory, with all his angels. He will be King and sit on his great throne. ³²All the nations of the world will be gathered before him, and he will separate them into two groups as a shepherd separates the sheep from the goats. ³³The Son of Man will put the sheep on his right and the goats on his left.

³⁴"Then the King will say to the people on his right, 'Come, my Father has given you his blessing. Receive the kingdom God has prepared for you since the world was made. ³⁵I was hungry, and you gave me food. I was thirsty, and you gave me something to drink. I was alone and away from home, and you invited me into your house. ³⁶I was without clothes, and you gave me something to wear. I was sick, and you cared for me. I was in prison, and you visited me.'

³⁷"Then the good people will answer, 'Lord, when did we see you hungry and give you food, or thirsty and give you something to

**Radical Faith:**

# Matthew 25:35-40

When you recognize a need in someone, what do you do? Do you stay in your comfort zone, only concerned for yourself, or do you reach out to help them? Jesus is very clear that those with a loving heart will selflessly give their money, food, time, consideration, and love to people around them. Jesus is concerned with taking care of people, and it really matters to him when you meet other people's needs. He hurts when they hurt, and he knows joy when they know joy. First John 3:17 says, "Suppose someone has enough to live and sees a brother or sister in need, but does not help. Then God's love is not living in that person." Wow. That's a pretty strong statement. God's love in you motivates you to take care of others, even when it's uncomfortable or inconvenient. God gives you a chance to be a part of his ministry by putting people you can love in your world. Step into the lives of others and offer whatever you can—even small things can make a big difference. It could just be providing some food, a place to stay, a listening ear, or a warm hug. God will bless and welcome into his kingdom his true followers who radiate his heart in their daily behavior.

## beautysecret

### The Comparison Trap

Do you ever find yourself looking at other girls and comparing yourself to them? In Matthew 22:39, Jesus says, "Love your neighbor as you love yourself." That kind of love begins by accepting yourself the way God made you. So quit the comparisons and embrace the beauty God's given you.

drink? 38When did we see you alone and away from home and invite you into our house? When did we see you without clothes and give you something to wear? 39When did we see you sick or in prison and care for you?'

40"Then the King will answer, 'I tell you the truth, anything you did for even the least of my people here, you also did for me.'

41"Then the King will say to those on his left, 'Go away from me. You will be punished. Go into the fire that burns forever that was prepared for the devil and his angels. 42I was hungry, and you gave me nothing to eat. I was thirsty, and you gave me nothing to drink. 43I was alone and away from home, and you did not invite me into your house. I was without clothes, and you gave me nothing to wear. I was sick and in prison, and you did not care for me.'

44"Then those people will answer, 'Lord, when did we see you hungry or thirsty or alone and away from home or without clothes or sick or in prison? When did we see these things and not help you?'

45"Then the King will answer, 'I tell you the truth, anything you refused to do for even the least of my people here, you refused to do for me.'

46"These people will go off to be punished forever, but the good people will go to live forever."

### THE PLAN TO KILL JESUS

26 After Jesus finished saying all these things, he told his followers, 2"You know that the day after tomorrow is the day of the Passover Feast. On that day the Son of Man will be given to his enemies to be crucified."

3Then the leading priests and the older leaders had a meeting at the palace of the high priest, named Caiaphas. 4At the meeting, they planned to set a trap to arrest Jesus and kill him. 5But they said, "We must not do it during the feast, because the people might cause a riot."

### PERFUME FOR JESUS' BURIAL

6Jesus was in Bethany at the house of Simon, who had a skin disease. 7While Jesus was there, a woman approached him with an alabaster jar filled with expensive perfume. She poured this perfume on Jesus' head while he was eating.

8His followers were upset when they saw the woman do this. They asked, "Why waste that perfume? 9It could have been sold for a great deal of money and the money given to the poor."

10Knowing what had happened, Jesus said, "Why are you troubling this woman? She did an excellent thing for me. 11You will always have the poor with you, but you will not always have me. 12This woman poured perfume on my body to prepare me for burial. 13I tell you the truth, wherever the Good News is preached in all the world, what this woman has done will be told, and people will remember her."

### JUDAS BECOMES AN ENEMY OF JESUS

14Then one of the twelve apostles, Judas Iscariot, went to talk to the leading priests. 15He said, "What will you pay me for giving Jesus to you?" And they gave him thirty silver coins. 16After that, Judas watched for the best time to turn Jesus in.

### JESUS EATS THE PASSOVER MEAL

17On the first day of the Feast of Unleavened Bread, the followers came to Jesus. They said, "Where do you want us to prepare for you to eat the Passover meal?"

18Jesus answered, "Go into the city to a certain man and tell him, 'The Teacher says: The chosen time is near. I will have the Passover with my followers at your house.' " 19The followers did what Jesus told them to do, and they prepared the Passover meal.

20In the evening Jesus was sitting at the table with his twelve followers. 21As they were eating, Jesus said, "I tell you the truth, one of you will turn against me."

22This made the followers very sad. Each one began to say to Jesus, "Surely, Lord, I am not the one who will turn against you, am I?"

23Jesus answered, "The man who has dipped his hand with me into the bowl is the one who will turn against me. 24The Son of

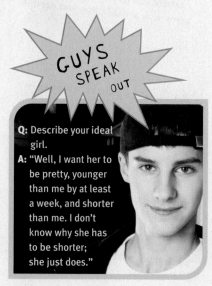

**GUYS SPEAK OUT**

**Q:** Describe your ideal girl.
**A:** "Well, I want her to be pretty, younger than me by at least a week, and shorter than me. I don't know why she has to be shorter; she just does."

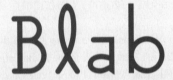

**Q:** I keep getting porn in my email inbox. I didn't ask for it or sign up for it. How do I get rid of it?

**A:** Delete suspicious emails without opening them. Buy software that can filter out unwanted messages, or download free filters. Turn on spam guards, and report those who send you porn to your email account provider (such as Yahoo, Hotmail, or AOL). Check your email only when other people are around, so you won't be tempted to look at images you shouldn't.

**Q:** I know my younger brother has some porn magazines under his bed. Is it my job to tell our parents?

**A:** Check your motivation first. Do you want to tell your parents because you are concerned for your brother or to get him in trouble? Have you taken it up with him first? If you truly want to see him do the right thing, gently confront him face-to-face. If he is not sorry, pray about telling your parents.

**Q:** I have a crush on one of my teachers. He's young, awesome, and so hot. What do I do?

**A:** Remember Song of Solomon 8:4, which warns young virgins not to awaken feelings of love too soon. Falling for someone in authority, who seems wise and experienced, is not unusual. But it can create a big mess. Ask God to redirect your thoughts away from seeing your teacher as a crush and back to seeing him as a guy who gives you homework. If God really wants you two to be together, it will be after you graduate.

Man will die, just as the Scriptures say. But how terrible it will be for the person who hands the Son of Man over to be killed. It would be better for him if he had never been born."

25Then Judas, who would give Jesus to his enemies, said to Jesus, "Teacher, surely I am not the one, am I?"

Jesus answered, "Yes, it is you."

## THE LORD'S SUPPER

26While they were eating, Jesus took some bread and thanked God for it and broke it. Then he gave it to his followers and said, "Take this bread and eat it; this is my body."

27Then Jesus took a cup and thanked God for it and gave it to the followers. He said, "Every one of you drink this. 28This is my blood which is the new agreement that God makes with his people. This blood is poured out for many to forgive their sins. 29I tell you this: I will not drink of this fruit of the vine" again until that day when I drink it new with you in my Father's kingdom."

30After singing a hymn, they went out to the Mount of Olives.

## JESUS' FOLLOWERS WILL LEAVE HIM

31Jesus told his followers, "Tonight you will all stumble in your faith on account of me, because it is written in the Scriptures:

'I will kill the shepherd,
  and the sheep will scatter.'   *Zechariah 13:7*
32But after I rise from the dead, I will go ahead of you into Galilee."

33Peter said, "Everyone else may stumble in their faith because of you, but I will not."

34Jesus said, "I tell you the truth, tonight before the rooster crows you will say three times that you don't know me."

35But Peter said, "I will never say that I don't know you! I will even die with you!" And all the other followers said the same thing.

## JESUS PRAYS ALONE

36Then Jesus went with his followers to a place called Gethsemane. He said to them, "Sit here while I go over there and pray." 37He took Peter and the two sons of Zebedee with him, and he began to be very sad and troubled. 38He said to them, "My heart is full of sorrow, to the point of death. Stay here and watch with me."

39After walking a little farther away from them, Jesus fell to the ground and prayed, "My Father, if it is possible, do not give me this cup" of suffering. But do what you want, not what I want." 40Then Jesus went back to his followers and found them asleep. He said to Peter, "You men could not stay awake with me for one hour? 41Stay awake and pray for strength against temptation. The spirit wants to do what is right, but the body is weak."

42Then Jesus went away a second time and prayed, "My Father, if it is not possible for this painful thing to be taken from me, and if I must do it, I pray that what you want will be done."

# "EVERYONE ELSE MAY STUMBLE IN THEIR FAITH BECAUSE OF YOU, BUT I WILL NOT."

43Then he went back to his followers, and again he found them asleep, because their eyes were heavy. 44So Jesus left them and went away and prayed a third time, saying the same thing.

45Then Jesus went back to his followers and said, "Are you still sleeping and resting? The time has come for the Son of Man to be handed over to sinful people. 46Get up, we must go. Look, here comes the man who has turned against me."

## JESUS IS ARRESTED

47While Jesus was still speaking, Judas, one of the twelve apostles, came up. With him were many people carrying swords and clubs who had been sent from the leading priests and the older Jewish leaders of the people. 48Judas had planned to give them a signal, saying, "The

**notes:** **26:29 fruit of the vine** Product of the grapevine; this may also be translated "wine." **26:39 cup** Jesus is talking about the terrible things that will happen to him. Accepting these things will be very hard, like drinking a cup of something bitter.

man I kiss is Jesus. Arrest him." 49At once Judas went to Jesus and said, "Greetings, Teacher!" and kissed him.

50Jesus answered, "Friend, do what you came to do."

Then the people came and grabbed Jesus and arrested him. 51When that happened, one of Jesus' followers reached for his sword and pulled it out. He struck the servant of the high priest and cut off his ear.

52Jesus said to the man, "Put your sword back in its place. All who use swords will be killed with swords. 53Surely you know I could ask my Father, and he would give me more than twelve armies of angels. 54But it must happen this way to bring about what the Scriptures say."

55Then Jesus said to the crowd, "You came to get me with swords and clubs as if I were a criminal. Every day I sat in the Temple teaching, and you did not arrest me there. 56But all these things have happened so that it will come about as the prophets wrote." Then all of Jesus' followers left him and ran away.

## JESUS BEFORE THE LEADERS

57Those people who arrested Jesus led him to the house of Caiaphas, the high priest, where the teachers of the law and the older leaders were gathered. 58Peter followed far behind to the courtyard of the high priest's house, and he sat down with the guards to see what would happen to Jesus.

59The leading priests and the whole Jewish council tried to find something false against Jesus so they could kill him. 60Many people came and told lies about him, but the council could find no real reason to kill him. Then two people came and said, 61"This man said, 'I can destroy the Temple of God and build it again in three days.'"

## "PUT YOUR SWORD BACK IN ITS PLACE. ALL WHO USE SWORDS WILL BE KILLED WITH SWORDS."

62Then the high priest stood up and said to Jesus, "Aren't you going to answer? Don't you have something to say about their charges against you?" 63But Jesus said nothing.

Again the high priest said to Jesus, "I command you by the power of the living God: Tell us if you are the Christ, the Son of God."

64Jesus answered, "Those are your words. But I tell you, in the future you will see the Son of Man sitting at the right hand of God, the Powerful One, and coming on clouds in the sky."

65When the high priest heard this, he tore his clothes and said, "This man has said things that are against God! We don't need any more witnesses; you all heard him say these things against God. 66What do you think?"

The people answered, "He should die."

67Then the people there spat in Jesus' face and beat him with their fists. Others slapped him. 68They said, "Prove to us that you are a prophet, you Christ! Tell us who hit you!"

## PETER SAYS HE DOESN'T KNOW JESUS

69At that time, as Peter was sitting in the courtyard, a servant girl came to him and said, "You also were with Jesus of Galilee."

70But Peter said to all the people there that he was never with Jesus. He said, "I don't know what you are talking about."

71When he left the courtyard and was at the gate, another girl saw him. She said to the people there, "This man was with Jesus of Nazareth."

72Again, Peter said he was never with him, saying, "I swear I don't know this man Jesus!"

73A short time later, some people standing there went to Peter and said, "Surely you are one of those who followed Jesus. The way you talk shows it."

74Then Peter began to place a curse on himself and swear, "I don't know the man." At once, a rooster crowed. 75And Peter remembered what Jesus had told him: "Before the rooster crows, you will say three times that you don't know me." Then Peter went outside and cried painfully.

Promises

## Matthew 27:51

Several of the greatest, most beautiful buildings around the world are majestic churches and cathedrals. Some are architecturally breathtaking, and some have the most beautiful stained-glass windows and painted murals you're ever seen. The builders and artists who created these places of worship wanted people to be able to meet God there and be reminded of his glory and majesty.

The Temple was one of the most important places for the Jews. Built to house the actual presence of God, the Temple was where Jews often came to offer sacrifices for their sins. However, only the priests were allowed into the presence of God in the Temple.

When Jesus died, the curtain in the Temple was torn into two pieces. It's interesting to note that the curtain was torn from the top to the bottom, rather than the bottom to the top. This signified that the one who tore the curtain was from above. In other words, man didn't tear the curtain—God did! Jesus came to earth to bridge the gap between God and people.

Because of what Jesus did for us, we don't need to find a religious leader or go to a certain building to be able to talk with God. And even though visiting beautiful places can help us remember the awesomeness of God, he is always with us and always ready to listen—wherever we are.

### JESUS IS TAKEN TO PILATE

**27** Early the next morning, all the leading priests and older leaders of the people decided that Jesus should die. ²They tied him, led him away, and turned him over to Pilate, the governor.

### JUDAS KILLS HIMSELF

³Judas, the one who had given Jesus to his enemies, saw that they had decided to kill Jesus. Then he was very sorry for what he had done. So he took the thirty silver coins back to the priests and the leaders, ⁴saying, "I sinned; I handed over to you an innocent man."

The leaders answered, "What is that to us? That's your problem, not ours."

⁵So Judas threw the money into the Temple. Then he went off and hanged himself.

⁶The leading priests picked up the silver coins in the Temple and said, "Our law does not allow us to keep this money with the Temple money, because it has paid for a man's death." ⁷So they decided to use the coins to buy Potter's Field as a place to bury strangers who died in Jerusalem. ⁸That is why that field is still called the Field of Blood. ⁹So what Jeremiah the prophet had said came true: "They took thirty silver coins. That is how little the Israelites thought he was worth. ¹⁰They used those thirty silver coins to buy the potter's field, as the Lord commanded me."ⁿ

### PILATE QUESTIONS JESUS

¹¹Jesus stood before Pilate the governor, and Pilate asked him, "Are you the king of the Jews?"

Jesus answered, "Those are your words."

¹²When the leading priests and the older leaders accused Jesus, he said nothing.

¹³So Pilate said to Jesus, "Don't you hear them accusing you of all these things?"

¹⁴But Jesus said nothing in answer to Pilate, and Pilate was very surprised at this.

### PILATE TRIES TO FREE JESUS

¹⁵Every year at the time of Passover the governor would free one prisoner whom the people chose. ¹⁶At that time there was a man in prison, named Barabbas, who was known to be very bad. ¹⁷When the people gathered at Pilate's house, Pilate said, "Whom do you want me to set free: Barabbas or Jesus who is called the Christ?" ¹⁸Pilate knew that the people turned Jesus in to him because they were jealous.

¹⁹While Pilate was sitting there on the judge's seat, his wife sent this message to him: "Don't do anything to that man, because he is innocent. Today I had a dream about him, and it troubled me very much."

²⁰But the leading priests and older leaders convinced the crowd to ask for Barabbas to be freed and for Jesus to be killed.

²¹Pilate said, "I have Barabbas and Jesus. Which do you want me to set free for you?"

The people answered, "Barabbas."

²²Pilate asked, "So what should I do with Jesus, the one called the Christ?"

They all answered, "Crucify him!"

²³Pilate asked, "Why? What wrong has he done?"

But they shouted louder, "Crucify him!"

²⁴When Pilate saw that he could do nothing about this and that a riot was starting, he took some water and washed his handsⁿ in front of the crowd. Then he said, "I am not guilty of this man's death. You are the ones who are causing it!"

²⁵All the people answered, "We and our children will be responsible for his death."

²⁶Then he set Barabbas free. But Jesus was beaten with whips and handed over to the soldiers to be crucified.

²⁷The governor's soldiers took Jesus into the governor's palace, and they all gathered around him. ²⁸They took off his clothes and put a red robe on him. ²⁹Using thorny branches, they made a crown, put it on his head, and put a stick in his right hand. Then the soldiers bowed before Jesus and made fun of him, saying, "Hail, King of the Jews!" ³⁰They spat on Jesus. Then they took his stick and began to beat him on the head. ³¹After they finished, the soldiers took off the robe and put his own clothes on him again. Then they led him away to be crucified.

notes

27:9-10 "They . . . commanded me." See Zechariah 11:12-13 and Jeremiah 32:6-9.   27:24 washed his hands He did this as a sign to show that he wanted no part in what the people did.

44

## Jesus is crucified

32As the soldiers were going out of the city with Jesus, they forced a man from Cyrene, named Simon, to carry the cross for Jesus. 33They all came to the place called Golgotha, which means the Place of the Skull. 34The soldiers gave Jesus wine mixed with gall" to drink. He tasted the wine but refused to drink it. 35When the soldiers had crucified him, they threw lots to decide who would get his clothes. 36The soldiers sat there and continued watching him. 37They put a sign above Jesus' head with a charge against him. It said: THIS IS JESUS, THE KING OF THE JEWS. 38Two robbers were crucified beside Jesus, one on the right and the other on the left. 39People walked by and insulted Jesus and shook their heads, 40saying, "You said you could destroy the Temple and build it again in three days. So save yourself! Come down from that cross if you are really the Son of God!"

41The leading priests, the teachers of the law, and the older Jewish leaders were also making fun of Jesus. 42They said, "He saved others, but he can't save himself! He says he is the king of Israel! If he is the king, let him come down now from the cross. Then we will believe in him. 43He trusts in God, so let God save him now, if God really wants him. He himself said, 'I am the Son of God.' " 44And in the same way, the robbers who were being crucified beside Jesus also insulted him.

## Jesus dies

45At noon the whole country became dark, and the darkness lasted for three hours. 46About three o'clock Jesus cried out in a loud voice, "Eli, Eli, lama sabachthani?" This means, "My God, my God, why have you rejected me?"

47Some of the people standing there who heard this said, "He is calling Elijah."

48Quickly one of them ran and got a sponge and filled it with vinegar and tied it to a stick and gave it to Jesus to drink. 49But the others said, "Don't bother him. We want to see if Elijah will come to save him."

50But Jesus cried out again in a loud voice and died.

51Then the curtain in the Temple" was torn into two pieces, from the top to the bottom. Also, the earth shook and rocks broke apart. 52The graves opened, and many of God's people who had died were raised from the dead. 53They came out of the graves after Jesus was raised from the dead and went into the holy city, where they appeared to many people.

54When the army officer and the soldiers guarding Jesus saw this earthquake and everything else that happened, they were very frightened and said, "He really was the Son of God!"

55Many women who had followed Jesus from Galilee to help him were standing at a distance from the cross, watching. 56Mary Magdalene, and Mary the mother of James and Joseph, and the mother of James and John were there.

> ## "THEY WERE VERY FRIGHTENED AND SAID, 'HE REALLY WAS THE SON OF GOD.' "

## Jesus is buried

57That evening a rich man named Joseph, a follower of Jesus from the town of Arimathea, came to Jerusalem. 58Joseph went to Pilate and asked to have Jesus' body. So Pilate gave orders for the soldiers to give it to Joseph. 59Then Joseph took the body and wrapped it in a clean linen cloth. 60He put Jesus' body in a new tomb that he had cut out of a wall of rock, and he rolled a very large stone to block the entrance of the tomb. Then Joseph went away. 61Mary Magdalene and the other woman named Mary were sitting near the tomb.

## The Tomb of Jesus is Guarded

62The next day, the day after Preparation Day, the leading priests and the Pharisees went

# Radical Faith:

## Matthew 28:1-7

Jesus endured excruciating torture on the cross and died. His body was placed in a grave. But it wasn't over. God proved that his power is greater than death and raised Jesus back to life. The scene sent shockwaves through the region. The angel who rolled away the stone caused quite a stir, too. The soldiers who saw him actually passed out and fell down. But the angel had comforting news for those at the scene—Christ was risen! It's a message that's still comforting, encouraging, and challenging to us today. Jesus said, "I am the resurrection and the life. Those who believe in me will have life even if they die" (John 11:25). It's an awesome promise that Jesus not only spoke about, but also demonstrated through his resurrection. In him, we have abundant life. The good news is that sin doesn't have to master you, heaven is your destination, and your role on earth is spreading God's truth. Live every day in a way that reflects what Jesus has done for you.

**notes**   **27:34 gall** Probably a drink of wine mixed with drugs to help a person feel less pain.   **27:51 curtain in the Temple** A curtain divided the Most Holy Place from the other part of the Temple. That was the special building in Jerusalem where God commanded the Jewish people to worship him.

to Pilate. [63]They said, "Sir, we remember that while that liar was still alive he said, 'After three days I will rise from the dead.' [64]So give the order for the tomb to be guarded closely till the third day. Otherwise, his followers might come and steal the body and tell people that he has risen from the dead. That lie would be even worse than the first one."

[65]Pilate said, "Take some soldiers and go guard the tomb the best way you know." [66]So they all went to the tomb and made it safe from thieves by sealing the stone in the entrance and putting soldiers there to guard it.

## JESUS RISES FROM THE DEAD

28 The day after the Sabbath day was the first day of the week. At dawn on the first day, Mary Magdalene and another woman named Mary went to look at the tomb.

[2]At that time there was a strong earthquake. An angel of the Lord came down from heaven, went to the tomb, and rolled the stone away from the entrance. Then he sat on the stone. [3]He was shining as bright as lightning, and his clothes were white as snow. [4]The soldiers guarding the tomb shook with fear because of the angel, and they became like dead men.

[5]The angel said to the women, "Don't be afraid. I know that you are looking for Jesus, who has been crucified. [6]He is not here. He has risen from the dead as he said he would. Come and see the place where his body was. [7]And go quickly and tell his followers, 'Jesus has risen from the dead. He is going into Galilee ahead of you, and you will see him there.' " Then the angel said, "Now I have told you."

[8]The women left the tomb quickly. They were afraid, but they were also very happy. They ran to tell Jesus' followers what had happened. [9]Suddenly, Jesus met them and said, "Greetings." The women came up to him, took hold of his feet, and worshiped him. [10]Then Jesus said to them, "Don't be afraid. Go and tell my followers to go on to Galilee, and they will see me there."

## THE SOLDIERS REPORT TO THE LEADERS

[11]While the women went to tell Jesus' followers, some of the soldiers who had been guarding the tomb went into the city to tell the leading priests everything that had happened. [12]Then the priests met with the older leaders and made a plan. They paid the soldiers a large amount of money [13]and said to them, "Tell the people that Jesus' followers came during the night and stole the body while you were asleep. [14]If the governor hears about this, we will satisfy him and save you from trouble." [15]So the soldiers kept the money and did as they were told. And that story is still spread among the people even today.

## JESUS TALKS TO HIS FOLLOWERS

[16]The eleven followers went to Galilee to the mountain where Jesus had told them to go. [17]On the mountain they saw Jesus and worshiped him, but some of them did not believe it was really Jesus. [18]Then Jesus came to them and said, "All power in heaven and on earth is given to me. [19]So go and make followers of all people in the world. Baptize them in the name of the Father and the Son and the Holy Spirit. [20]Teach them to obey everything that I have taught you, and I will be with you always, even until the end of this age."

## Bible Basics

The **New Testament** (or NT) contains twenty-seven books of the Bible that were written to tell people the story of Jesus coming to earth in order to save humankind. It also instructed the early Christians on how to live and work together and how to spread the story of Jesus. The first four books of the New Testament are called the Gospels: Matthew, Mark, Luke and John. Luke 2:1-20 is commonly referred to as the "Christmas story" and recounts the birth of Jesus. The New Testament contains the writings of the apostle Paul and ends with the Book of Revelation, which predicts the final triumph of Christ over evil.

# Mark, also called John Mark,

was a fairly young man when he authored this Gospel. Later, he would become a close companion of the apostle Peter and a recurring character in the Book of Acts.

# Mark
## The Suffering and Sacrifice of Jesus

If Matthew was written mostly for a Jewish audience, Mark seems to have targeted the Gentile (non-Jewish) Roman believers. The basis for this belief is rooted in the way Mark calculates the passage of time—according to the Roman system—and in the fact that he makes fewer references to the Old Testament than Matthew does. (Even today, most Jews study and believe only the Old Testament—something the Gentiles wouldn't have been too familiar with.)

The shortest of the four Gospels, Mark is packed with action, centering more on what Jesus *did* than what he *said*. You want miracles? Mark's got 'em! You want healing? Look no further! You wanna be amazed, astonished, wowed, or even flabbergasted? You've come to the right book!

But even more central to this book is the recurring theme of Jesus' humanity and his suffering for our sake. In fact, Mark was so overwhelmed by the supreme sacrifice of Christ that he devoted nearly half of his Gospel to the last week of Jesus' life—his trial, torture, cruel death by crucifixion, and, ultimately, his resurrection.

### JOHN PREPARES FOR JESUS

1 This is the beginning of the Good News about Jesus Christ, the Son of God," [2]as the prophet Isaiah wrote:

"I will send my messenger ahead of you,
who will prepare your way."     *Malachi 3:1*

[3]"This is a voice of one
who calls out in the desert:
'Prepare the way for the Lord.
Make the road straight for him.' "

*Isaiah 40:3*

[4]John was baptizing people in the desert and preaching a baptism of changed hearts and lives for the forgiveness of sins. [5]All the people from Judea and Jerusalem were going out to him. They confessed their sins and were baptized by him in the Jordan River. [6]John wore clothes made from camel's hair, had a leather belt around his waist, and ate locusts and wild honey. [7]This is what John preached to the people: "There is one coming after me who is greater than I; I am not good enough even to kneel down and untie his sandals. [8]I baptize you with water, but he will baptize you with the Holy Spirit."

### JESUS IS BAPTIZED

[9]At that time Jesus came from the town of Nazareth in Galilee and was baptized by John in the Jordan River. [10]Immediately, as Jesus was coming up out of the water, he saw heaven open. The Holy Spirit came down on him like a dove, [11]and a voice came from heaven: "You are my Son, whom I love, and I am very pleased with you."

[12]Then the Spirit sent Jesus into the desert. [13]He was in the desert forty days and was tempted by Satan. He was with the wild animals, and the angels came and took care of him.

### JESUS CHOOSES SOME FOLLOWERS

[14]After John was put in prison, Jesus went into Galilee, preaching the Good News from God. [15]He said, "The right time has come. The kingdom of God is near. Change your hearts and lives and believe the Good News!"

[16]When Jesus was walking by Lake Galilee, he saw Simon" and his brother Andrew throwing a net into the lake because they were fishermen. [17]Jesus said to them, "Come follow me, and I will make you fish for people." [18]So Simon and Andrew immediately left their nets and followed him.

[19]Going a little farther, Jesus saw two more brothers, James and John, the sons of Zebedee. They were in a boat, mending their nets. [20]Jesus immediately called them, and they left their father in the boat with the hired workers and followed Jesus.

### JESUS FORCES OUT AN EVIL SPIRIT

[21]Jesus and his followers went to Capernaum. On the Sabbath day He went to the synagogue and began to teach. [22]The people were amazed at his teaching, because he taught like a person who had authority, not like their teachers of the law. [23]Just then, a man was there in the synagogue who had an evil spirit in him. He shouted, [24]"Jesus of Nazareth! What do you want with us? Did you come to destroy us? I know who you are—God's Holy One!"

## "I BAPTIZE YOU WITH WATER, BUT HE WILL BAPTIZE YOU WITH THE HOLY SPIRIT."

[25]Jesus commanded the evil spirit, "Be quiet! Come out of the man!" [26]The evil spirit shook the man violently, gave a loud cry, and then came out of him.

[27]The people were so amazed they asked each other, "What is happening here? This man is teaching something new, and with authority. He even gives commands to evil

## CHECK IT OUT

### HANDS & FEET PROJECT

The Christian rock band Audio Adrenaline is committed to leaving a legacy of love for children in the country of Haiti. Imagine being five years old and not having any clothes, a bed to sleep in, or even a home. Imagine that you are also starving, with no hope of a meal today. You are five years old and don't have any parents, any family, or anywhere to go.

Those are the circumstances for many young children in Haiti, the poorest country in the western hemisphere. Audio Adrenaline wants to help by building a community of homes through the Hands & Feet Project, a nonprofit organization dedicated to the health, welfare, and education of the orphaned children of Haiti.

You can help by praying for the children's village project, volunteering to take a missions trip to Haiti, organizing a local team of volunteers to spread the word, or donating to the project by sending money. The website offers a number of opportunities to help the band help the kids.

*Get involved by visiting www.handsandfeetproject.org.*

1:1 **the Son of God** Some Greek copies omit these words.  1:16 **Simon** Simon's other name was Peter.

spirits, and they obey him." 28And the news about Jesus spread quickly everywhere in the area of Galilee.

## Jesus Heals Many People

29As soon as Jesus and his followers left the synagogue, they went with James and John to the home of Simon" and Andrew. 30Simon's mother-in-law was sick in bed with a fever, and the people told Jesus about her. 31So Jesus went to her bed, took her hand, and helped her up. The fever left her, and she began serving them.

32That evening, after the sun went down, the people brought to Jesus all who were sick and had demons in them. 33The whole town gathered at the door. 34Jesus healed many who had different kinds of sicknesses, and he forced many demons to leave people. But he would not allow the demons to speak, because they knew who he was.

35Early the next morning, while it was still dark, Jesus woke and left the house. He went to a lonely place, where he prayed. 36Simon and his friends went to look for Jesus. 37When they found him, they said, "Everyone is looking for you!"

38Jesus answered, "We should go to other towns around here so I can preach there too. That is the reason I came." 39So he went everywhere in Galilee, preaching in the synagogues and forcing out demons.

## Jesus Heals a Sick Man

40A man with a skin disease came to Jesus. He fell to his knees and begged Jesus, "You can heal me if you will."

41Jesus felt sorry for the man, so he reached out his hand and touched him and said, "I will. Be healed!" 42Immediately the disease left the man, and he was healed.

43Jesus told the man to go away at once, but he warned him strongly, 44"Don't tell anyone

about this. But go and show yourself to the priest. And offer the gift Moses commanded for people who are made well." This will show the people what I have done." 45The man left there, but he began to tell everyone that Jesus had healed him, and so he spread the news about Jesus. As a result, Jesus could not enter a town if people saw him. He stayed in places where nobody lived, but people came to him from everywhere.

## Jesus Heals a Paralyzed Man

2 A few days later, when Jesus came back to Capernaum, the news spread that he was at home. 2Many people gathered together so that there was no room in the house, not even outside the door. And Jesus was teaching them God's message. 3Four people came, carrying a paralyzed man. 4Since they could not get to Jesus because of the crowd, they dug a hole in the roof right above where he was speaking. When they got through, they lowered the mat with the paralyzed man on it. 5When Jesus saw the faith of these people, he said to the paralyzed man, "Young man, your sins are forgiven."

6Some of the teachers of the law were sitting there, thinking to themselves, 7"Why does this man say things like that? He is speaking as if he were God. Only God can forgive sins."

8Jesus knew immediately what these teachers of the law were thinking. So he said to them, "Why are you thinking these things? 9Which is easier: to tell this paralyzed man, 'Your sins are forgiven,' or to tell him, 'Stand up. Take your mat and walk'? 10But I will prove to you that the Son of Man has authority on earth to forgive sins." So Jesus said to the paralyzed man, 11"I tell you, stand up, take your mat, and go home." 12Immediately the paralyzed man stood up, took his mat, and walked out while everyone was watching him.

## Promises:

## Mark 2:17

Imagine this: You wake up for school one morning with a sore throat, killer headache, and raging fever. You feel terrible and realize that you probably have the flu. So you ask your mom to bring you some OJ and prepare to ride it out. After a week in bed, you're finally better, so you head off to the doctor. Kind of silly, right? The doctor's job is to help you start feeling better from Day 1 so you can get rid of that nasty flu. You need a doctor when you're sick, not well.

The Pharisees were all about being holy and pure as the Law dictated. So when Jesus showed up preaching and teaching and then hanging out with tax collectors and other shady characters, they were angry that he was eating with the "sinners." They thought the way to be close to God was to be pure and without sin, but Jesus was trying to show them that he accepted people as they were—and *then* he would help heal them of their sin.

What an awesome thing to know that we can come to Jesus as we are— sins and all—and that he loves us, accepts us, and is so excited to have a relationship with us.

1:29 **Simon** Simon's other name was Peter.  1:44 **Moses . . . well** Read about this in Leviticus 14:1-32.

# are you a good listener or a gabby friend?

**YOU KNOW YOUR BEST FRIEND'S FAVORITE FOOD AND/OR COLOR.**

A. Um, I could guess.
B. I think so.
C. Absolutely. (Pizza and green.)

**YOUR FRIEND JUST GOT DUMPED BY HER BOYFRIEND AND IS DEVASTATED. HOW DO YOU HELP HER GET THROUGH THIS HARD TIME?**

A. Tell her all about the time the same thing happened to you.
B. Offer any bits of advice you can think of to help her feel better.
C. Let her talk and ask questions when appropriate.

**YOU LIKE HAVING CONVERSATIONS WITH YOUR FRIENDS:**

A. While watching your favorite soap opera so you can talk about what's happening on the show.
B. At a coffee shop or at a small get-together.
C. On the phone or hanging out at each other's houses.

**YOUR FRIEND TELLS YOU A SECRET SHE DOESN'T WANT SHARED WITH ANYONE ELSE. DO YOU EVER SPILL IT?**

A. Only if in a situation where it becomes necessary information.
B. No. (Well, except maybe telling one other friend who swears she won't tell anyone.)
C. Never.

**YOU ARE HAVING A CONVERSATION WITH A FRIEND ON THE PHONE. HOW MANY TIMES DO YOU ANSWER YOUR CALL WAITING?**

A. More than once.
B. One time.
C. Not at all—you just ignore it.

**FRIENDS COME TO YOU WITH THEIR PROBLEMS:**

A. Sometimes.
B. Often.
C. All the time.

---

### IF YOU ANSWERED MOSTLY A's AND B's

## You may be a Gabby Friend!

It's obvious—you like to talk more than you like to listen. But that quality doesn't always make for the best friend. So next time you're listening to a friend discuss her latest problem, try to focus on what she's saying and try not to think about what you're going to say next. You are really fun to be around and always a great conversation-starter, but beware of getting caught up in a juicy gossip situation and spilling your friend's secrets.

### IF YOU ANSWERED MOSTLY B's AND C's

## You are a Good Listener!

People like to talk to you and to come to you for advice because they know you will really listen. Keep up the good work. Being a good listener is a great quality to have, especially in a friend.

The people were amazed and praised God. They said, "We have never seen anything like this!"

¹³Jesus went to the lake again. The whole crowd followed him there, and he taught them. ¹⁴While he was walking along, he saw a man named Levi son of Alphaeus, sitting in the tax collector's booth. Jesus said to him, "Follow me," and he stood up and followed Jesus.

¹⁵Later, as Jesus was having dinner at Levi's house, many tax collectors and "sinners" were eating there with Jesus and his followers. Many people like this followed Jesus. ¹⁶When the teachers of the law who were Pharisees saw Jesus eating with the tax collectors and "sinners," they asked his followers, "Why does he eat with tax collectors and sinners?"

¹⁷Jesus heard this and said to them, "It is not the healthy people who need a doctor, but the sick. I did not come to invite good people but to invite sinners."

### JESUS' FOLLOWERS ARE CRITICIZED

¹⁸Now the followers of John" and the Pharisees often gave up eating for a certain time." Some people came to Jesus and said, "Why do John's followers and the followers of the Pharisees often give up eating, but your followers don't?"

## "THE MAN HELD OUT HIS HAND AND IT WAS HEALED."

¹⁹Jesus answered, "The friends of the bridegroom do not give up eating while the bridegroom is still with them. As long as the bridegroom is with them, they cannot give up eating. ²⁰But the time will come when the bridegroom will be taken from them, and then they will give up eating.

²¹"No one sews a patch of unshrunk cloth over a hole in an old coat. Otherwise, the patch will shrink and pull away—the new patch will pull away from the old coat. Then the hole will be worse. ²²Also, no one ever pours new wine

## Deborah

[JUDGES 4 AND 5] Are you a big-picture person? Are you a natural leader to whom others look for ideas and enthusiasm? If you answered "yes," then you're probably a lot like Deborah. As a judge and a prophetess, she held a powerful position. She was a confident woman who had a strong, growing relationship with God that gave her an insight and an edge that many leaders lack. With this insight, she selected a valiant general, Barak, to lead Israel's army. Unafraid, Deborah rode with him into battle so he would know that God was with him. She was an incredible example of what God can do in our lives when we give him free reign. The sky's the limit!

into old leather bags. Otherwise, the new wine will break the bags, and the wine will be ruined along with the bags. But new wine should be put into new leather bags."

### JESUS IS LORD OF THE SABBATH

²³One Sabbath day, as Jesus was walking through some fields of grain, his followers began to pick some grain to eat. ²⁴The Pharisees said to Jesus, "Why are your followers doing what is not lawful on the Sabbath day?"

²⁵Jesus answered, "Have you never read what David did when he and those with him were hungry and needed food? ²⁶During the time of Abiathar the high priest, David went into God's house and ate the holy bread, which is lawful only for priests to eat. And David also gave some of the bread to those who were with him."

²⁷Then Jesus said to the Pharisees, "The Sabbath day was made to help people; they were not made to be ruled by the Sabbath day. ²⁸So then, the Son of Man is Lord even of the Sabbath day."

### JESUS HEALS A MAN'S HAND

3 Another time when Jesus went into a synagogue, a man with a crippled hand was there. ²Some people watched Jesus closely to see if he would heal the man on the Sabbath day so they could accuse him.

³Jesus said to the man with the crippled hand, "Stand up here in the middle of everyone."

⁴Then Jesus asked the people, "Which is lawful on the Sabbath day: to do good or to do evil, to save a life or to kill?" But they said nothing to answer him.

⁵Jesus was angry as he looked at the people, and he felt very sad because they were stubborn. Then he said to the man, "Hold out your hand." The man held out his hand and it was healed. ⁶Then the Pharisees left and began making plans with the Herodians" about a way to kill Jesus.

### MANY PEOPLE FOLLOW JESUS

⁷Jesus left with his followers for the lake, and a large crowd from Galilee followed him. ⁸Also many people came from Judea, from

2:18 **John** John the Baptist, who preached to the Jewish people about Christ's coming (Mark 1:4-8). 2:18 **gave . . . time** This is called "fasting." The people would give up eating for a special time of prayer and worship to God. It was also done to show sadness and disappointment. 3:6 **Herodians** A political group that followed Herod and his family.

# Mark 3:11

What really scares you? Besides snakes and spiders, are there more serious things that freak you out? Maybe there's a psycho movie you've watched recently or a scary experience you've had in the dark that has made you really afraid. Maybe you know people who call themselves witches or tell stories about people encountering dark spirits. If you ever think about what could hurt you or overpower you and become afraid, then consider this verse. When the evil spirits saw Jesus, they fell down before him. They didn't just back away or run away. Instead, they fell down because they recognized the holiness of Jesus. That was the effect of his mere presence on them. These spirits knew his power and his high position and they had to cry out that they were in the presence of the Son of God. No evil spirit can compete with Jesus' authority. When you feel weak or scared, know that you have a defender and no one can take him from you. The power that is in Jesus' name is mind-bogglingly intense—far greater than any power Satan possesses. Put all your faith in his name, and rely completely on his power.

Jerusalem, from Idumea, from the lands across the Jordan River, and from the area of Tyre and Sidon. When they heard what Jesus was doing, many people came to him. ⁹When Jesus saw the crowds, he told his followers to get a boat ready for him to keep people from crowding against him. ¹⁰He had healed many people, so all the sick were pushing toward him to touch him. ¹¹When evil spirits saw Jesus, they fell down before him and shouted, "You are the Son of God!" ¹²But Jesus strongly warned them not to tell who he was.

## JESUS CHOOSES HIS TWELVE APOSTLES

¹³Then Jesus went up on a mountain and called to him the men he wanted, and they came to him. ¹⁴Jesus chose twelve men and called them apostles. He wanted them to be with him, and he wanted to send them out to preach ¹⁵and to have the authority to force demons out of people. ¹⁶These are the twelve men he chose: Simon (Jesus named him Peter), ¹⁷James and John, the sons of Zebedee (Jesus named them Boanerges, which means "Sons of Thunder"), ¹⁸Andrew, Philip, Bartholomew, Matthew, Thomas, James the son of Alphaeus, Thaddaeus, Simon the Zealot, ¹⁹and Judas Iscariot, who later turned against Jesus.

## SOME PEOPLE SAY JESUS HAS A DEVIL

²⁰Then Jesus went home, but again a crowd gathered. There were so many people that Jesus and his followers could not eat. ²¹When his family heard this, they went to get him because they thought he was out of his mind. ²²But the teachers of the law from Jerusalem were saying, "Beelzebul is living inside him! He uses power from the ruler of demons to force demons out of people."

²³So Jesus called the people together and taught them with stories. He said, "Satan will not force himself out of people. ²⁴A kingdom that is divided cannot continue, ²⁵and a family that is divided cannot continue. ²⁶And if Satan is against himself and fights against his own

people, he cannot continue; that is the end of Satan. ²⁷No one can enter a strong person's house and steal his things unless he first ties up the strong person. Then he can steal things from the house. ²⁸I tell you the truth, all sins that people do and all the things people say against God can be forgiven. ²⁹But anyone who speaks against the Holy Spirit will never be forgiven; he is guilty of a sin that continues forever."

³⁰Jesus said this because the teachers of the law said that he had an evil spirit inside him.

## JESUS' TRUE FAMILY

³¹Then Jesus' mother and brothers arrived. Standing outside, they sent someone in to tell him to come out. ³²Many people were sitting around Jesus, and they said to him, "Your mother and brothers are waiting for you outside."

³³Jesus asked, "Who are my mother and my brothers?" ³⁴Then he looked at those sitting around him and said, "Here are my mother and my brothers! ³⁵My true brother and sister and mother are those who do what God wants."

## A STORY ABOUT PLANTING SEED

4 Again Jesus began teaching by the lake. A great crowd gathered around him, so he sat down in a boat near the shore. All the people stayed on the shore close to the water. ²Jesus taught them many things, using stories. He said, ³"Listen! A farmer went out to plant his seed. ⁴While he was planting, some seed fell by the road, and the birds came and ate it up. ⁵Some seed fell on rocky ground where there wasn't much dirt. That seed grew very fast, because the ground was not deep. ⁶But when the sun rose, the plants dried up because they did not have deep roots. ⁷Some other seed fell among thorny weeds, which grew and choked the good plants. So those plants did not produce a crop. ⁸Some other seed fell on good ground and began to grow. It got taller and produced a crop. Some plants made thirty times more, some made sixty times more, and some made a hundred times more."

⁹Then Jesus said, "You people who can hear me, listen!"

## Jesus Tells Why He Used Stories

¹⁰Later, when Jesus was alone, the twelve apostles and others around him asked him about the stories.

¹¹Jesus said, "You can know the secret about the kingdom of God. But to other people I tell everything by using stories ¹²so that:

'They will look and look, but they will not learn.

They will listen and listen, but they will not understand.

If they did learn and understand,

they would come back to me and be forgiven.' "                        *Isaiah 6:9-10*

## Jesus Explains The Seed Story

¹³Then Jesus said to his followers, "Don't you understand this story? If you don't, how will you understand any story? ¹⁴The farmer is like a person who plants God's message in people. ¹⁵Sometimes the teaching falls on the road. This is like the people who hear the teaching of God, but Satan quickly comes and takes away the teaching that was planted in them. ¹⁶Others are like the seed planted on rocky ground. They hear the teaching and quickly accept it with joy. ¹⁷But since they don't allow the teaching to go deep into their lives, they keep it only a short time. When trouble or persecution comes because of the teaching they accepted, they quickly give up. ¹⁸Others are like the seed planted among the thorny weeds. They hear the teaching, ¹⁹but the worries of this life, the temptation of wealth, and many other evil desires keep the teaching from growing and producing fruit" in their lives. ²⁰Others are like the seed planted in the good ground. They hear the teaching and accept it. Then they grow and produce fruit—sometimes thirty times more, sometimes sixty times more, and sometimes a hundred times more."

## Use What You Have

²¹Then Jesus said to them, "Do you hide a lamp under a bowl or under a bed? No! You put the lamp on a lampstand. ²²Everything that is hidden will be made clear and every secret thing will be made known. ²³You people who can hear me, listen!

²⁴"Think carefully about what you hear. The way you give to others is the way God will give to you, but God will give you even more. ²⁵Those who have understanding will be given more. But those who do not have understanding, even what they have will be taken away from them."

## Jesus Uses A Story About Seed

²⁶Then Jesus said, "The kingdom of God is like someone who plants seed in the ground. ²⁷Night and day, whether the person is asleep or awake, the seed still grows, but the person does not know how it grows. ²⁸By itself the earth produces grain. First the plant grows, then the head, and then all the grain in the head. ²⁹When the grain is ready, the farmer cuts it, because this is the harvest time."

## A Story About Mustard Seed

³⁰Then Jesus said, "How can I show you what the kingdom of God is like? What story can I use to explain it? ³¹The kingdom of God is like a mustard seed, the smallest seed you plant in the ground. ³²But when planted, this seed grows and becomes the largest of all garden plants. It produces large branches, and the wild birds can make nests in its shade."

# beauty secret

## Avoiding the Fashion Police

In order to avoid being a fashion victim, wear clothes that fit your figure. Psalm 139:13-16 says that God formed you in your mother's womb in an amazing way. Accept the shape God gave you and work with it. Find clothes that accentuate your best features.

³³Jesus used many stories like these to teach the crowd God's message—as much as they could understand. ³⁴He always used stories to teach them. But when he and his followers were alone, Jesus explained everything to them.

## Jesus Calms A Storm

³⁵That evening, Jesus said to his followers, "Let's go across the lake." ³⁶Leaving the crowd behind, they took him in the boat just as he was. There were also other boats with them. ³⁷A very strong wind came up on the lake. The waves came over the sides and into the boat so that it was already full of water. ³⁸Jesus was at the back of the boat, sleeping with his head on a cushion. His followers woke him and said, "Teacher, don't you care that we are drowning!"

³⁹Jesus stood up and commanded the wind and said to the waves, "Quiet! Be still!" Then

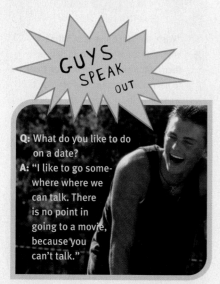

## GUYS SPEAK OUT

**Q:** What do you like to do on a date?
**A:** "I like to go somewhere where we can talk. There is no point in going to a movie, because you can't talk."

**notes**    **4:19 producing fruit** To produce fruit means to have in your life the good things God wants.

# Blab

the wind stopped, and it became completely calm.

40Jesus said to his followers, "Why are you afraid? Do you still have no faith?"

41The followers were very afraid and asked each other, "Who is this? Even the wind and the waves obey him!"

## a man with demons inside him

5 Jesus and his followers went to the other side of the lake to the area of the Gerasene people. 2When Jesus got out of the boat, instantly a man with an evil spirit came to him from the burial caves. 3This man lived in the caves, and no one could tie him up, not even with a chain. 4Many times people had used chains to tie the man's hands and feet, but he always broke them off. No one was strong enough to control him. 5Day and night he would wander around the burial caves and on the hills, screaming and cutting himself with stones. 6While Jesus was still far away, the man saw him, ran to him, and fell down before him.

7The man shouted in a loud voice, "What do you want with me, Jesus, Son of the Most High God? I command you in God's name not to torture me!" 8He said this because Jesus was saying to him, "You evil spirit, come out of the man."

9Then Jesus asked him, "What is your name?"

He answered, "My name is Legion,″ because we are many spirits." 10He begged Jesus again and again not to send them out of that area.

11A large herd of pigs was feeding on a hill near there. 12The demons begged Jesus, "Send us into the pigs; let us go into them." 13So Jesus allowed them to do this. The evil spirits left the man and went into the pigs. Then the herd of pigs—about two thousand of them—rushed down the hill into the lake and were drowned.

14The herdsmen ran away and went to the town and to the countryside, telling everyone about this. So people went out to see what had happened. 15They came to Jesus and saw the man who used to have the many evil spirits, sitting, clothed, and in his right mind. And they were frightened. 16The people who saw

this told the others what had happened to the man who had the demons living in him, and they told about the pigs. 17Then the people began to beg Jesus to leave their area.

18As Jesus was getting back into the boat, the man who was freed from the demons begged to go with him.

19But Jesus would not let him. He said, "Go home to your family and tell them how much the Lord has done for you and how he has had mercy on you." 20So the man left and began to tell the people in the Ten Towns″ about what Jesus had done for him. And everyone was amazed.

## Jesus gives life to a dead girl and heals a sick woman

21When Jesus went in the boat back to the other side of the lake, a large crowd gathered

# relationships

 **notes** 5:9 **Legion** Means very many. A legion was about five thousand men in the Roman army. 5:20 **Ten Towns** In Greek, called "Decapolis." It was an area east of Lake Galilee that once had ten main towns.

# LEARN I✝ & LIVE I✝

**Mark 4:19**
**Learn It:** Worrying can keep Christ's teachings from growing and producing fruit in your life.
**Live It:** Tell a trusted friend what is bothering you most; ask them to pray with you.

**Mark 5:28**
**Learn It:** A sick woman thought if she could just touch Jesus' clothes, she would be healed.
**Live It:** Ask God to allow you to get close enough to experience him in a new way.

**Mark 6:31-34**
**Learn It:** Even though Jesus wanted rest, he felt sorry for people and began to teach them.
**Live It:** When you are tired, make sure you still take time for people instead of getting grouchy with them.

around him there. <sup>22</sup>A leader of the synagogue, named Jairus, came there, saw Jesus, and fell at his feet. <sup>23</sup>He begged Jesus, saying again and again, "My daughter is dying. Please come and put your hands on her so she will be healed and will live." <sup>24</sup>So Jesus went with him.

A large crowd followed Jesus and pushed very close around him. <sup>25</sup>Among them was a woman who had been bleeding for twelve years. <sup>26</sup>She had suffered very much from many doctors and had spent all the money she had, but instead of improving, she was getting worse. <sup>27</sup>When the woman heard about Jesus, she came up behind him in the crowd and touched his coat. <sup>28</sup>She thought, "If I can just touch his clothes, I will be healed." <sup>29</sup>Instantly her bleeding stopped, and she felt in her body that she was healed from her disease.

<sup>30</sup>At once Jesus felt power go out from him. So he turned around in the crowd and asked, "Who touched my clothes?"

<sup>31</sup>His followers said, "Look at how many people are pushing against you! And you ask, 'Who touched me?' "

<sup>32</sup>But Jesus continued looking around to see who had touched him. <sup>33</sup>The woman, knowing that she was healed, came and fell at Jesus' feet. Shaking with fear, she told him the whole truth. <sup>34</sup>Jesus said to her, "Dear woman, you are made well because you believed. Go in peace; be healed of your disease."

<sup>35</sup>While Jesus was still speaking, some people came from the house of the synagogue leader. They said, "Your daughter is dead.

There is no need to bother the teacher anymore."

<sup>36</sup>But Jesus paid no attention to what they said. He told the synagogue leader, "Don't be afraid; just believe."

<sup>37</sup>Jesus let only Peter, James, and John the brother of James go with him. <sup>38</sup>When they came to the house of the synagogue leader, Jesus found many people there making lots of noise and crying loudly. <sup>39</sup>Jesus entered the house and said to them, "Why are you crying and making so much noise? The child is not dead, only asleep." <sup>40</sup>But they laughed at him. So, after throwing them out of the house, Jesus took the child's father and mother and his three followers into the room where the child was. <sup>41</sup>Taking hold of the girl's hand, he said to her, "Talitha, koum!" (This means, "Young girl, I tell you to stand up!") <sup>42</sup>At once the girl stood right up and began walking. (She was twelve years old.) Everyone was completely amazed. <sup>43</sup>Jesus gave them strict orders not to tell people about this. Then he told them to give the girl something to eat.

## JESUS GOES TO HIS HOMETOWN

**6** Jesus left there and went to his hometown, and his followers went with him. <sup>2</sup>On the Sabbath day he taught in the synagogue. Many people heard him and were amazed, saying, "Where did this man get these teachings? What is this wisdom that has been given to him? And where did he get the power to do miracles? <sup>3</sup>He is just the carpenter, the

son of Mary and the brother of James, Joseph, Judas, and Simon. And his sisters are here with us." So the people were upset with Jesus.

<sup>4</sup>Jesus said to them, "A prophet is honored everywhere except in his hometown and with his own people and in his own home." <sup>5</sup>So Jesus was not able to work any miracles there except to heal a few sick people by putting his hands on them. <sup>6</sup>He was amazed at how many people had no faith.

Then Jesus went to other villages in that area and taught. <sup>7</sup>He called his twelve followers together and got ready to send them out two by two and gave them authority over evil spirits. <sup>8</sup>This is what Jesus commanded them: "Take nothing for your trip except a walking stick. Take no bread, no bag, and no money in your pockets. <sup>9</sup>Wear sandals, but take only the clothes you are wearing. <sup>10</sup>When you enter a house, stay there until you leave that town. <sup>11</sup>If the people in a certain place refuse to welcome you or listen to you, leave that place. Shake its dust off your feet<sup>n</sup> as a warning to them."

<sup>12</sup>So the followers went out and preached that people should change their hearts and lives. <sup>13</sup>They forced many demons out and put olive oil on many sick people and healed them.

## HOW JOHN THE BAPTIST WAS KILLED

<sup>14</sup>King Herod heard about Jesus, because he was now well known. Some people said, "He is John the Baptist, who has risen from the dead. That is why he can work these miracles."

<sup>15</sup>Others said, "He is Elijah."<sup>n</sup>

**6:11 Shake . . . feet** A warning. It showed that they were rejecting these people.   **6:15 Elijah** A great prophet who spoke for God and who lived hundreds of years before Christ. See 1 Kings 17.

Other people said, "Jesus is a prophet, like the prophets who lived long ago."

[16]When Herod heard this, he said, "I killed John by cutting off his head. Now he has risen from the dead!"

[17]Herod himself had ordered his soldiers to arrest John and put him in prison in order to please his wife, Herodias. She had been the wife of Philip, Herod's brother, but then Herod had married her. [18]John had been telling Herod, "It is not lawful for you to be married to your brother's wife." [19]So Herodias hated John and wanted to kill him. But she couldn't, [20]because Herod was afraid of John and protected him. He knew John was a good and holy man. Also, though John's preaching always bothered him, he enjoyed listening to John.

[21]Then the perfect time came for Herodias to cause John's death. On Herod's birthday, he gave a dinner party for the most important government leaders, the commanders of his army, and the most important people in Galilee. [22]When the daughter of Herodias came in and danced, she pleased Herod and the people eating with him.

So King Herod said to the girl, "Ask me for anything you want, and I will give it to you." [23]He promised her, "Anything you ask for I will give to you—up to half of my kingdom."

**1.574 BILLION MOVIE TICKETS WERE SOLD IN THE U.S. IN 2003, AT AN AVERAGE PRICE OF $6.03 (UP 45.7% SINCE 1993).** NATIONAL ASSOCIATION OF THEATRE OWNERS

[24]The girl went to her mother and asked, "What should I ask for?"

Her mother answered, "Ask for the head of John the Baptist."

[25]At once the girl went back to the king and said to him, "I want the head of John the Baptist right now on a platter."

[26]Although the king was very sad, he had made a promise, and his dinner guests had heard it. So he did not want to refuse what she asked. [27]Immediately the king sent a soldier to bring John's head. The soldier went and cut off

John's head in the prison [28]and brought it back on a platter. He gave it to the girl, and the girl gave it to her mother. [29]When John's followers heard this, they came and got John's body and put it in a tomb.

## "THE APOSTLES GATHERED AROUND JESUS AND TOLD HIM ABOUT ALL THE THINGS THEY HAD DONE AND TAUGHT."

### More Than Five Thousand Fed

[30]The apostles gathered around Jesus and told him about all the things they had done and taught. [31]Crowds of people were coming and going so that Jesus and his followers did not even have time to eat. He said to them, "Come away by yourselves, and we will go to a lonely place to get some rest."

[32]So they went in a boat by themselves to a lonely place. [33]But many people saw them leave and recognized them. So from all the towns they ran to the place where Jesus was going, and they got there before him. [34]When

he arrived, he saw a great crowd waiting. He felt sorry for them, because they were like sheep without a shepherd. So he began to teach them many things.

[35]When it was late in the day, his followers came to him and said, "No one lives in this place, and it is already very late. [36]Send the people away so they can go to the countryside and towns around here to buy themselves something to eat."

[37]But Jesus answered, "You give them something to eat."

They said to him, "We would all have to work a month to earn enough money to buy that much bread!"

[38]Jesus asked them, "How many loaves of bread do you have? Go and see."

When they found out, they said, "Five loaves and two fish."

[39]Then Jesus told his followers to have the people sit in groups on the green grass. [40]So they sat in groups of fifty or a hundred. [41]Jesus took the five loaves and two fish and, looking up to heaven, he thanked God for the food. He divided the bread and gave it to his followers for them to give to the people. Then he divided the two fish among them all. [42]All the people ate and were satisfied. [43]The followers filled twelve baskets with the leftover pieces of bread and fish. [44]There were five thousand men who ate.

### Jesus Walks on the Water

[45]Immediately Jesus told his followers to get into the boat and go ahead of him to Bethsaida across the lake. He stayed there to send the people home. [46]After sending them away, he went into the hills to pray.

[47]That night, the boat was in the middle of the lake, and Jesus was alone on the land. [48]He saw his followers struggling hard to row the boat, because the wind was blowing against them. Between three and six o'clock in the morning, Jesus came to them, walking on the water, and he wanted to walk past the boat. [49]But when they saw him walking on the water, they thought he was a ghost and cried out. [50]They all saw him and were afraid. But quickly Jesus spoke to them and said, "Have courage! It is I. Do not be afraid." [51]Then he got into the boat with them, and the wind became calm. The followers were greatly amazed. [52]They did not understand about the miracle of the five loaves, because their minds were closed.

[53]When they had crossed the lake, they came to shore at Gennesaret and tied the boat there. [54]When they got out of the boat, people immediately recognized Jesus. [55]They ran everywhere in that area and began to bring

sick people on mats wherever they heard he was. ⁵⁶And everywhere he went—into towns, cities, or countryside—the people brought the sick to the marketplaces. They begged him to let them touch just the edge of his coat, and all who touched it were healed.

## OBEY GOD'S LAW

7 When some Pharisees and some teachers of the law came from Jerusalem, they gathered around Jesus. ²They saw that some of Jesus' followers ate food with hands that were not clean, that is, they hadn't washed them. ³(The Pharisees and all the Jews never eat before washing their hands in a special way according to their unwritten laws. ⁴And when they buy something in the market, they never eat it until they wash themselves in a special way. They also follow many other unwritten laws, such as the washing of cups, pitchers, and pots.)

⁵The Pharisees and the teachers of the law said to Jesus, "Why don't your followers obey the unwritten laws which have been handed down to us? Why do your followers eat their food with hands that are not clean?"

⁶Jesus answered, "Isaiah was right when he spoke about you hypocrites. He wrote,

'These people show honor to me with
        words,
    but their hearts are far from me.
⁷Their worship of me is worthless.
    The things they teach are nothing but
        human rules.'          *Isaiah 29:13*

⁸You have stopped following the commands of God, and you follow only human teachings."

⁹Then Jesus said to them, "You cleverly ignore the commands of God so you can follow your own teachings. ¹⁰Moses said, 'Honor your father and your mother,'ⁿ and 'Anyone who says cruel things to his father or mother must be put to death.'ⁿ ¹¹But you say a person can tell his father or mother, 'I have something I could use to help you, but it is Corban—a gift to God.' ¹²You no longer let that person use that money for his father or his mother. ¹³By your own rules, which you teach people, you are rejecting what God said. And you do many things like that."

¹⁴After Jesus called the crowd to him again, he said, "Every person should listen to me and understand what I am saying. ¹⁵There is nothing people put into their bodies that makes them unclean. People are made unclean by the things that come out of them."¹⁶ⁿ

¹⁷When Jesus left the people and went into the house, his followers asked him about this story. ¹⁸Jesus said, "Do you still not understand? Surely you know that nothing that enters someone from the outside can make that person unclean. ¹⁹It does not go into the mind, but into the stomach. Then it goes out of the body." (When Jesus said this, he meant that no longer was any food unclean for people to eat.)

²⁰And Jesus said, "The things that come out of people are the things that make them unclean. ²¹All these evil things begin inside people, in the mind: evil thoughts, sexual sins, stealing, murder, adultery, ²²greed, evil actions, lying, doing sinful things, jealousy, speaking evil of others, pride, and foolish living. ²³All these evil things come from inside and make people unclean."

## JESUS HELPS A NON-JEWISH WOMAN

²⁴Jesus left that place and went to the area around Tyre. When he went into a house, he did not want anyone to know he was there, but he could not stay hidden. ²⁵A woman whose daughter had an evil spirit in her heard that he was there. So she quickly came to Jesus and fell at his feet. ²⁶She was Greek, born in Phoenicia, in Syria. She begged Jesus to force the demon out of her daughter.

²⁷Jesus told the woman, "It is not right to take the children's bread and give it to the dogs. First let the children eat all they want."

²⁸But she answered, "Yes, Lord, but even the dogs under the table can eat the children's crumbs."

²⁹Then Jesus said, "Because of your answer, you may go. The demon has left your daughter."

**top10**

random ways to get along with your siblings

**10** Respect their privacy.

**9** Ask forgiveness for old hurts.

**8** Don't hog the bathroom.

**7** Give them a ride or let them use the car.

**6** Encourage instead of criticize.

**5** Meet their friends.

**4** Take an interest in their lives.

**3** Go shopping together.

**2** Wash your brother's car.

**1** Share your clothes with your sister.

**notes** 7:10 'Honor . . . mother' Quotation from Exodus 20:12; Deuteronomy 5:16. 7:10 'Anyone . . . death.' Quotation from Exodus 21:17. 7:16 Verse 16 Some Greek copies add verse 16: "You people who can hear me, listen!"

# *Music Reviews*

**GROUP:** TOBYMAC

**ALBUM:** WELCOME TO DIVERSE CITY

Throw a cup of funk, a dash of rock, a handful of rhymin' raps, and all the colors of the rainbow in a musical blender and you'd get tobyMac's second solo effort *Welcome to Diverse City*. The award-winning singer, songwriter, producer, and record label co-founder (and one-third of dc talk) believes that to fulfill Jesus' command to be the shining "city that is built on a hill" (Matthew 5:14), people need to be more accepting of diversity. The title track is a tribute to funk, while "Slam" rocks out with special guest T-Bone. Coffee of GRITS can be found on the hip "Hey Now," and tobyMac's five-year-old son Truett raps on "TruDog, the Return." Bonus: KMax and Tait team up with Toby for a dc talk reunion on "Atmosphere Remix."

**WHY IT ROCKS: TOBYMAC LIVES HIS MESSAGE OF DIVERSITY. HIS MUSIC BLENDS A VARIETY OF URBAN STYLES WITH STRAIGHT-UP ROCK 'N' ROLL.**

<sup>30</sup>The woman went home and found her daughter lying in bed; the demon was gone.

## Jesus Heals a Deaf Man

<sup>31</sup>Then Jesus left the area around Tyre and went through Sidon to Lake Galilee, to the area of the Ten Towns.<sup>*</sup> <sup>32</sup>While he was there, some people brought a man to him who was deaf and could not talk plainly. The people begged Jesus to put his hand on the man to heal him.

<sup>33</sup>Jesus led the man away from the crowd, by himself. He put his fingers in the man's ears and then spit and touched the man's tongue. <sup>34</sup>Looking up to heaven, he sighed and said to the man, "Ephphatha!" (This means, "Be opened.") <sup>35</sup>Instantly the man was able to hear and to use his tongue so that he spoke clearly.

<sup>36</sup>Jesus commanded the people not to tell anyone about what happened. But the more he commanded them, the more they told about it. <sup>37</sup>They were completely amazed and said, "Jesus does everything well. He makes the deaf hear! And those who can't talk he makes able to speak."

## More Than Four Thousand People Fed

**8** Another time there was a great crowd with Jesus that had nothing to eat. So Jesus called his followers and said, <sup>2</sup>"I feel sorry for these people, because they have already been with me for three days, and they have nothing to eat. <sup>3</sup>If I send them home hungry, they will faint on the way. Some of them live a long way from here."

<sup>4</sup>Jesus' followers answered, "How can we get enough bread to feed all these people? We are far away from any town."

<sup>5</sup>Jesus asked, "How many loaves of bread do you have?"

They answered, "Seven."

<sup>6</sup>Jesus told the people to sit on the ground. Then he took the seven loaves, gave thanks to God, and divided the bread. He gave the pieces to his followers to give to the people, and they did so. <sup>7</sup>The followers also had a few small fish. After Jesus gave thanks for the fish, he told his followers to give them to the people also. <sup>8</sup>All the people ate and were satisfied. Then his followers filled seven baskets with the leftover pieces of food. <sup>9</sup>There were about four thousand people who ate. After they had eaten, Jesus sent them home. <sup>10</sup>Then right away he got into a boat with his followers and went to the area of Dalmanutha.

## The Leaders Ask for a Miracle

<sup>11</sup>The Pharisees came to Jesus and began to ask him questions. Hoping to trap him, they asked Jesus for a miracle from God. <sup>12</sup>Jesus sighed deeply and said, "Why do you people ask for a miracle as a sign? I tell you the truth, no sign will be given to you." <sup>13</sup>Then Jesus left the Pharisees and went in the boat to the other side of the lake.

**DIDYA KNOW**

**SIX IN TEN AMERICAN TEENS WOULDN'T BEND DOWN TO PICK UP ANYTHING LESS THAN A DOLLAR FROM A SIDEWALK.** NUVEEN INVESTMENTS

## Guard Against Wrong Teachings

<sup>14</sup>His followers had only one loaf of bread with them in the boat; they had forgotten to bring more. <sup>15</sup>Jesus warned them, "Be careful! Beware of the yeast of the Pharisees and the yeast of Herod."

<sup>16</sup>His followers discussed the meaning of this, saying, "He said this because we have no bread."

<sup>17</sup>Knowing what they were talking about, Jesus asked them, "Why are you talking about

**notes**    **7:31 Ten Towns** In Greek, called "Decapolis." It was an area east of Lake Galilee that once had ten main towns.

**59**

Radical Faith:

# Mark 8:32-33

In these verses, Peter only seemed to be looking out for Jesus' best interests. But Jesus quickly corrected him and told him not to talk like that. Why? Peter might have been saying reasonable things, but he was thinking from an earthly perspective. He was thinking short-term. He didn't try to imagine that God could be at work—doing something big that could involve some unpleasant and difficult things. The idea of Jesus experiencing rejection, emotional and physical suffering, and death was horrible, but Peter needed to trust that what Jesus said was best in the long run. Jesus' response to Peter also shows that Satan will use anything—even a well-meaning act of a friend—to try to tempt you away from doing what God wants. He'll do whatever he can to get in the way of your obedience. Jesus knew right away that Satan was trying to put a roadblock in his way. Ask God to help you recognize Satan's schemes and to be quick to reject what's not from God. And learn from Peter that having only an earthly view is limiting. Ask God to help you understand more about his perspective and to have the things that are important to him guide your thoughts and actions.

not having bread? Do you still not see or understand? Are your minds closed? ¹⁸You have eyes, but you don't really see. You have ears, but you don't really listen. Remember when ¹⁹I divided five loaves of bread for the five thousand? How many baskets did you fill with leftover pieces of food?"

They answered, "Twelve."

²⁰"And when I divided seven loaves of bread for the four thousand, how many baskets did you fill with leftover pieces of food?"

They answered, "Seven."

²¹Then Jesus said to them, "Don't you understand yet?"

## JESUS HEALS A BLIND MAN

²²Jesus and his followers came to Bethsaida. There some people brought a blind man to Jesus and begged him to touch the man. ²³So Jesus took the blind man's hand and led him out of the village. Then he spit on the man's eyes and put his hands on the man and asked, "Can you see now?"

²⁴The man looked up and said, "Yes, I see people, but they look like trees walking around."

²⁵Again Jesus put his hands on the man's eyes. Then the man opened his eyes wide and they were healed, and he was able to see everything clearly. ²⁶Jesus told him to go home, saying, "Don't go into the town."

## PETER SAYS JESUS IS THE CHRIST

²⁷Jesus and his followers went to the towns around Caesarea Philippi. While they were traveling, Jesus asked them, "Who do people say I am?"

²⁸They answered, "Some say you are John the Baptist. Others say you are Elijah," and others say you are one of the prophets."

²⁹Then Jesus asked, "But who do you say I am?"

Peter answered, "You are the Christ."

³⁰Jesus warned his followers not to tell anyone who he was.

³¹Then Jesus began to teach them that the Son of Man must suffer many things and that he would be rejected by the older Jewish leaders,

the leading priests, and the teachers of the law. He told them that the Son of Man must be killed and then rise from the dead after three days. ³²Jesus told them plainly what would happen. Then Peter took Jesus aside and began to tell him not to talk like that. ³³But Jesus turned and looked at his followers. Then he told Peter not to talk that way. He said, "Go away from me, Satan!" You don't care about the things of God, but only about things people think are important."

³⁴Then Jesus called the crowd to him, along with his followers. He said, "If people want to follow me, they must give up the things they want. They must be willing even to give up their lives to follow me. ³⁵Those who want to save their lives will give up true life. But those who give up their lives for me and for the Good News will have true life. ³⁶It is worth nothing for them to have the whole world if they lose their souls. ³⁷They could never pay enough to buy back their souls. ³⁸The people who live now are living in a sinful and evil time. If people are ashamed of me and my teaching, the Son of Man will be ashamed of them when he comes with his Father's glory and with the holy angels."

9 Then Jesus said to the people, "I tell you the truth, some people standing here will see the kingdom of God come with power before they die."

## JESUS TALKS WITH MOSES AND ELIJAH

²Six days later, Jesus took Peter, James, and John up on a high mountain by themselves. While they watched, Jesus' appearance was changed. ³His clothes became shining white, whiter than any person could make them. ⁴Then Elijah and Moses" appeared to them, talking with Jesus.

⁵Peter said to Jesus, "Teacher, it is good that we are here. Let us make three tents—one for you, one for Moses, and one for Elijah." ⁶Peter did not know what to say, because he and the others were so frightened.

⁷Then a cloud came and covered them, and a voice came from the cloud, saying, "This is my Son, whom I love. Listen to him!"

**8:28 Elijah** A man who spoke for God and who lived hundreds of years before Christ. See 1 Kings 17. **8:33 Satan** Name for the devil meaning "the enemy." Jesus means that Peter was talking like Satan. **9:4 Elijah and Moses** Two of the most important Jewish leaders in the past. God had given Moses the Law, and Elijah was an important prophet.

## LEARN I+ & LIVE I+

**Mark 8:35**
**Learn It:** If you are willing to give up your life, you will get true life.
**Live It:** Talk to a spiritual mentor about what you need to let go of in your life. Turn it over fully to God.

**Mark 9:37**
**Learn It:** Anyone who accepts a child in Jesus' name accepts Jesus.
**Live It:** Spend time with a little sister or brother, baby-sit for a neighbor, or volunteer in the church nursery.

**Mark 10:45**
**Learn It:** Jesus set an example for us in the ways he served others.
**Live It:** Look for a way to serve your mom or dad today before they have to ask.

[8]Suddenly Peter, James, and John looked around, but they saw only Jesus there alone with them.

[9]As they were coming down the mountain, Jesus commanded them not to tell anyone about what they had seen until the Son of Man had risen from the dead.

[10]So the followers obeyed Jesus, but they discussed what he meant about rising from the dead.

[11]Then they asked Jesus, "Why do the teachers of the law say that Elijah must come first?"

[12]Jesus answered, "They are right to say that Elijah must come first and make everything the way it should be. But why does the Scripture say that the Son of Man will suffer much and that people will treat him as if he were nothing? [13]I tell you that Elijah has already come. And people did to him whatever they wanted to do, just as the Scriptures said it would happen."

### JESUS HEALS A SICK BOY

[14]When Jesus, Peter, James, and John came back to the other followers, they saw a great crowd around them and the teachers of the law arguing with them. [15]But as soon as the crowd saw Jesus, the people were surprised and ran to welcome him.

[16]Jesus asked, "What are you arguing about?"

[17]A man answered, "Teacher, I brought my son to you. He has an evil spirit in him that stops him from talking. [18]When the spirit attacks him, it throws him on the ground.

Then my son foams at the mouth, grinds his teeth, and becomes very stiff. I asked your followers to force the evil spirit out, but they couldn't."

[19]Jesus answered, "You people have no faith. How long must I stay with you? How long must I put up with you? Bring the boy to me."

[20]So the followers brought him to Jesus. As soon as the evil spirit saw Jesus, it made the boy lose control of himself, and he fell down and rolled on the ground, foaming at the mouth.

## "SO THE FOLLOWERS OBEYED JESUS, BUT THEY DISCUSSED WHAT HE MEANT ABOUT RISING FROM THE DEAD."

[21]Jesus asked the boy's father, "How long has this been happening?"

The father answered, "Since he was very young. [22]The spirit often throws him into a fire or into water to kill him. If you can do anything for him, please have pity on us and help us."

[23]Jesus said to the father, "You said, 'If you can!' All things are possible for the one who believes."

[24]Immediately the father cried out, "I do believe! Help me to believe more!"

[25]When Jesus saw that a crowd was quickly gathering, he ordered the evil spirit, saying, "You spirit that makes people unable to hear or speak, I command you to come out of this boy and never enter him again!"

[26]The evil spirit screamed and caused the boy to fall on the ground again. Then the spirit came out. The boy looked as if he were dead, and many people said, "He is dead!" [27]But Jesus took hold of the boy's hand and helped him to stand up.

[28]When Jesus went into the house, his followers began asking him privately, "Why couldn't we force that evil spirit out?"

[29]Jesus answered, "That kind of spirit can only be forced out by prayer."

### JESUS TALKS ABOUT HIS DEATH

[30]Then Jesus and his followers left that place and went through Galilee. He didn't want

**GUYS SPEAK OUT**

**Q:** How do you have fun with your family?
**A:** "We play football, and we go on vacation."

anyone to know where he was, 31because he was teaching his followers. He said to them, "The Son of Man will be handed over to people, and they will kill him. After three days, he will rise from the dead." 32But the followers did not understand what Jesus meant, and they were afraid to ask him.

### WHO IS THE GREATEST?

33Jesus and his followers went to Capernaum. When they went into a house there, he asked them, "What were you arguing about on the road?" 34But the followers did not answer, because their argument on the road was about which one of them was the greatest.

35Jesus sat down and called the twelve apostles to him. He said, "Whoever wants to be the most important must be last of all and servant of all."

36Then Jesus took a small child and had him stand among them. Taking the child in his arms, he said, 37"Whoever accepts a child like this in my name accepts me. And whoever accepts me accepts the One who sent me."

### ANYONE NOT AGAINST US IS FOR US

38Then John said, "Teacher, we saw someone using your name to force demons out of a person. We told him to stop, because he does not belong to our group."

39But Jesus said, "Don't stop him, because anyone who uses my name to do powerful things will not easily say evil things about me. 40Whoever is not against us is with us. 41I tell you the truth, whoever gives you a drink of water because you belong to the Christ will truly get his reward.

42"If one of these little children believes in me, and someone causes that child to sin, it would be better for that person to have a large stone tied around his neck and be drowned in the sea. 43If your hand causes you to sin, cut it off. It is better for you to lose part of your body and live forever than to have two hands and go to hell, where the fire never goes out. 44[n] 45If your foot causes you to sin, cut it off. It is better for you to lose part of your body and to live

forever than to have two feet and be thrown into hell. 46[n] 47If your eye causes you to sin, take it out. It is better for you to enter the kingdom of God with only one eye than to have two eyes and be thrown into hell. 48In hell the worm does not die; the fire is never put out. 49Every person will be salted with fire.

50"Salt is good, but if the salt loses its salty taste, you cannot make it salty again. So, be full of salt, and have peace with each other."

### JESUS TEACHES ABOUT DIVORCE

**10** Then Jesus left that place and went into the area of Judea and across the Jordan River. Again, crowds came to him, and he taught them as he usually did.

2Some Pharisees came to Jesus and tried to trick him. They asked, "Is it right for a man to divorce his wife?"

3Jesus answered, "What did Moses command you to do?"

4They said, "Moses allowed a man to write out divorce papers and send her away."[n]

5Jesus said, "Moses wrote that command for you because you were stubborn. 6But when God made the world, 'he made them male and female.'[n] 7"So a man will leave his father and mother and be united with his wife, 8and the two will become one body.'[n] So there are not two, but one. 9God has joined the two together, so no one should separate them."

> ## "AS JESUS STARTED TO LEAVE, A MAN RAN TO HIM AND FELL ON HIS KNEES BEFORE JESUS."

10Later, in the house, his followers asked Jesus again about the question of divorce. 11He answered, "Anyone who divorces his wife and marries another woman is guilty of adultery against her. 12And the woman who divorces her husband and marries another man is also guilty of adultery."

**9:44 Verse 44** Some Greek copies of Mark add verse 44, which is the same as verse 48. **9:46 Verse 46** Some Greek copies of Mark add verse 46, which is the same as verse 48. **10:4 "Moses . . . away."** Quotation from Deuteronomy 24:1. **10:6 'he made . . . female.'** Quotation from Genesis 1:27. **10:7-8 'So . . . body.'** Quotation from Genesis 2:24.

## Jesus accepts children

13Some people brought their little children to Jesus so he could touch them, but his followers told them to stop. 14When Jesus saw this, he was upset and said to them, "Let the little children come to me. Don't stop them, because the kingdom of God belongs to people who are like these children. 15I tell you the truth, you must accept the kingdom of God as if you were a little child, or you will never enter it." 16Then Jesus took the children in his arms, put his hands on them, and blessed them.

## A rich young man's question

17As Jesus started to leave, a man ran to him and fell on his knees before Jesus. The man asked, "Good teacher, what must I do to have life forever?"

18Jesus answered, "Why do you call me good? Only God is good. 19You know the commands: 'You must not murder anyone. You must not be guilty of adultery. You must not steal. You must not tell lies about your neighbor. You must not cheat. Honor your father and mother.' "ⁿ

20The man said, "Teacher, I have obeyed all these things since I was a boy."

21Jesus, looking at the man, loved him and said, "There is one more thing you need to do. Go and sell everything you have, and give the money to the poor, and you will have treasure in heaven. Then come and follow me."

22He was very sad to hear Jesus say this, and he left sorrowfully, because he was rich.

23Then Jesus looked at his followers and said, "How hard it will be for the rich to enter the kingdom of God!"

24The followers were amazed at what Jesus said. But he said again, "My children, it is very hard to enter the kingdom of God! 25It is easier for a camel to go through the eye of a needle than for a rich person to enter the kingdom of God."

26The followers were even more surprised and said to each other, "Then who can be saved?"

27Jesus looked at them and said, "This is something people cannot do, but God can. God can do all things."

28Peter said to Jesus, "Look, we have left everything and followed you."

29Jesus said, "I tell you the truth, all those who have left houses, brothers, sisters, mother, father, children, or farms for me and for the Good News 30will get more than they left. Here in this world they will have a hundred times

more homes, brothers, sisters, mothers, children, and fields. And with those things, they will also suffer for their belief. But in the age that is coming they will have life forever. 31Many who have the highest place now will have the lowest place in the future. And many who have the lowest place now will have the highest place in the future."

## Jesus talks about his death

32As Jesus and the people with him were on the road to Jerusalem, he was leading the way. His followers were amazed, but others in the crowd who followed were afraid. Again Jesus took the twelve apostles aside and began to tell them what was about to happen in Jerusalem. 33He said, "Look, we are going to Jerusalem. The Son of Man will be turned over to the leading priests and the teachers of the law. They will say that he must die, and they will turn him over to the non-Jewish people, 34who will laugh at him and spit on him. They will beat him with whips and crucify him. But on the third day, he will rise to life again."

## Two followers ask Jesus a favor

35Then James and John, sons of Zebedee, came to Jesus and said, "Teacher, we want to ask you to do something for us."

36Jesus asked, "What do you want me to do for you?"

37They answered, "Let one of us sit at your right side and one of us sit at your left side in your glory in your kingdom."

38Jesus said, "You don't understand what you are asking. Can you drink the cup that I must drink? And can you be baptized with the same kind of baptism that I must go through?"ⁿ

39They answered, "Yes, we can."

Jesus said to them, "You will drink the same cup that I will drink, and you will be baptized with the same baptism that I must go through. 40But I cannot choose who will sit at my right or my left; those places belong to those for whom they have been prepared."

41When the other ten followers heard this, they began to be angry with James and John.

42Jesus called them together and said, "The other nations have rulers. You know that those rulers love to show their power over the people, and their important leaders love to use all their authority. 43But it should not be that way among you. Whoever wants to become great among you must serve the rest of you like a servant. 44Whoever wants to become the first among you must serve all of you like a slave. 45In the same way, the Son of Man did not come to be served. He came to serve others and to give his life as a ransom for many people."

## Jesus heals a blind man

46Then they came to the town of Jericho. As Jesus was leaving there with his followers and a great many people, a blind beggar named Bartimaeus son of Timaeus was sitting by the road. 47When he heard that Jesus from Nazareth was walking by, he began to shout, "Jesus, Son of David, have mercy on me!"

48Many people warned the blind man to be quiet, but he shouted even more, "Son of David, have mercy on me!"

notes

10:19 'You . . . mother.' Quotation from Exodus 20:12-16; Deuteronomy 5:16-20.   10:38 Can you . . . through? Jesus was asking if they could suffer the same terrible things that would happen to him.

⁴⁹Jesus stopped and said, "Tell the man to come here."

So they called the blind man, saying, "Cheer up! Get to your feet. Jesus is calling you." ⁵⁰The blind man jumped up, left his coat there, and went to Jesus.

⁵¹Jesus asked him, "What do you want me to do for you?"

The blind man answered, "Teacher, I want to see."

⁵²Jesus said, "Go, you are healed because you believed." At once the man could see, and he followed Jesus on the road.

## Jesus enters Jerusalem as a king

11 As Jesus and his followers were coming closer to Jerusalem, they came to the towns of Bethphage and Bethany near the Mount of Olives. From there Jesus sent two of his followers ²and said to them, "Go to the town you can see there. When you enter it, you will quickly find a colt tied, which no one has ever ridden. Untie it and bring it here to me. ³If anyone asks you why you are doing this, tell him its Master needs the colt, and he will send it at once."

⁴The followers went into the town, found a colt tied in the street near the door of a house, and untied it. ⁵Some people were standing there and asked, "What are you doing? Why are you untying that colt?" ⁶The followers answered the way Jesus told them to answer, and the people let them take the colt.

⁷They brought the colt to Jesus and put their coats on it, and Jesus sat on it. ⁸Many people spread their coats on the road. Others cut branches in the fields and spread them on the road. ⁹The people were walking ahead of Jesus and behind him, shouting,

"Praise God!
God bless the One who comes in the name
    of the Lord!                    Psalm 118:26
¹⁰God bless the kingdom of our father David!
    That kingdom is coming!
Praise" to God in heaven!"

¹¹Jesus entered Jerusalem and went into the Temple. After he had looked at everything, since it was already late, he went out to Bethany with the twelve apostles.

¹²The next day as Jesus was leaving Bethany, he became hungry. ¹³Seeing a fig tree in leaf from far away, he went to see if it had any figs on it. But he found no figs, only leaves, because it was not the right season for figs. ¹⁴So Jesus said to the tree, "May no one ever eat fruit from you again." And Jesus' followers heard him say this.

## Jesus goes to the Temple

¹⁵When Jesus returned to Jerusalem, he went into the Temple and began to throw out those who were buying and selling there. He turned over the tables of those who were exchanging different kinds of money, and he upset the benches of those who were selling doves. ¹⁶Jesus refused to allow anyone to carry goods through the Temple courts. ¹⁷Then he taught the people, saying, "It is written in the

# Changed Lives

**MOLLIE'S STORY—SEXUAL ABUSE**

When I was only three years old, my 11-year-old adopted brother sexually molested me. My parents confronted him, and he promised it would not happen again, but it did. My brother abused and raped me for the next five years. My parents didn't know. They were too busy with my other five natural siblings and the foster children in their care. By the time they discovered the abuse, the damage had already been done. By junior high, I thought I could take control of my life by controlling my eating. I developed a severe eating disorder and began to experiment with alcohol and self-mutilation. By high school, I began running with a tough crowd and even attempted suicide. But nothing worked to fill the emptiness inside, heal the anger, or relieve my hatred. Then I went to a Christian youth camp the summer of my junior year. For the first time, I saw people who really lived out their faith, but that realization faded when school started again. A friend introduced me to a lot of New Age practices. I got into contacting the spirit world and projecting my soul out of my body. What I was doing bordered on Satanism—and it was scary. Spiritually confused, I started Bible college but my damaged emotions controlled my life. I became severely depressed, stayed in bed for days at a time, and became obsessed with death. Suicide seemed the only way out. I tried to kill myself again and again, but each time God intervened. At one point, I asked Jesus into my heart, but I still couldn't break free from my destructive habits and manipulation. Finally, I found a Christian girls' home where they didn't just put me on medications, but instead, they taught me about the Bible and how God works in our lives. They showed me how to have a relationship with him. God began to heal my bitter emotions. I was able to forgive my brother and parents. Now I have a job, have overcome my eating disorder, and am planning to go back to Bible school and finish my degree.

*If you or someone you know has been sexually abused, visit www.christianprogramsforteens.com or www.hoperanchmt.org. For information about residential care for females, visit mercyministries.com. (Names have been changed for the sake of privacy. Mollie tells her story after going through biblically based counseling with Mercy Ministries.)*

**11:10 Praise** Literally, "Hosanna," a Hebrew word used at first in praying to God for help, but at this time it was probably a shout of joy used in praising God or his Messiah.

## CHECK IT OUT

### COMPASSION INTERNATIONAL

Sponsoring a child through Compassion International means not only offering a child tutoring, nutritious meals, socialization, and other valuable skills, but also it means you gain a special place in that child's heart. The 600,000 children in Compassion projects around the world cherish letters and pictures from the people who sponsor them, and they write to their sponsors regularly, sharing details of their families, their countries, and their lives.

For less than $30 a month, you, your family, or a group of friends can change a child's life forever. Some Compassion children who graduate from high school are even being sponsored to attend universities, gain degrees, and make a positive difference in their own countries.

Compassion sets up projects through active churches in order to insure that the money you send gets put to the best possible use to change a child's life. The organization recently announced that it will dedicate more money to help children infected with the HIV/AIDS virus, especially in Africa.

*Get involved by visiting* **www.compassion.com**.

Scriptures, 'My Temple will be called a house for prayer for people from all nations.'" But you are changing God's house into a 'hideout for robbers.' "[n]

[18]The leading priests and the teachers of the law heard all this and began trying to find a way to kill Jesus. They were afraid of him, because all the people were amazed at his teaching. [19]That evening, Jesus and his followers left the city.

### THE POWER OF FAITH

[20]The next morning as Jesus was passing by with his followers, they saw the fig tree dry and dead, even to the roots. [21]Peter remembered the tree and said to Jesus, "Teacher, look! The fig tree you cursed is dry and dead!"

# "JESUS ANSWERED, 'HAVE FAITH IN GOD.' "

[22]Jesus answered, "Have faith in God. [23]I tell you the truth, you can say to this mountain, 'Go, fall into the sea.' And if you have no doubts in your mind and believe that what you say will happen, God will do it for you. [24]So I tell you to believe that you have received the things you ask for in prayer, and God will give them to you. [25]When you are praying, if you are angry

with someone, forgive him so that your Father in heaven will also forgive your sins." [26][n]

### LEADERS DOUBT JESUS' AUTHORITY

[27]Jesus and his followers went again to Jerusalem. As Jesus was walking in the Temple, the leading priests, the teachers of the law, and the older leaders came to him. [28]They said to him, "What authority do you have to do these things? Who gave you this authority?"

[29]Jesus answered, "I will ask you one question. If you answer me, I will tell you what authority I have to do these things. [30]Tell me: When John baptized people, was that authority from God or just from other people?"

[31]They argued about Jesus' question, saying, "If we answer, 'John's baptism was from God,' Jesus will say, 'Then why didn't you believe him?' [32]But if we say, 'It was from other people,' the crowd will be against us." (These leaders were afraid of the people, because all the people believed that John was a prophet.)

[33]So they answered Jesus, "We don't know."

Jesus said to them, "Then I won't tell you what authority I have to do these things."

### A STORY ABOUT GOD'S SON

**12** Jesus began to use stories to teach the people. He said, "A man planted a vineyard. He put a wall around it and dug a

hole for a winepress and built a tower. Then he leased the land to some farmers and left for a trip. [2]When it was time for the grapes to be picked, he sent a servant to the farmers to get his share of the grapes. [3]But the farmers grabbed the servant and beat him and sent him away empty-handed. [4]Then the man sent another servant. They hit him on the head and showed no respect for him. [5]So the man sent another servant, whom they killed. The man sent many other servants; the farmers beat some of them and killed others.

[6]"The man had one person left to send, his son whom he loved. He sent him last of all, saying, 'They will respect my son.'

[7]"But the farmers said to each other, 'This son will inherit the vineyard. If we kill him, it will be ours.' [8]So they took the son, killed him, and threw him out of the vineyard.

[9]"So what will the owner of the vineyard do? He will come and kill those farmers and will give the vineyard to other farmers. [10]Surely you have read this Scripture:

'The stone that the builders rejected
    became the cornerstone.
[11]The Lord did this,
    and it is wonderful to us.' "

*Psalm 118:22-23*

[12]The Jewish leaders knew that the story was about them. So they wanted to find a way

**11:17 'My Temple . . . nations.'** Quotation from Isaiah 56:7. **11:17 'hideout for robbers.'** Quotation from Jeremiah 7:11. **11:26 Verse 26** Some early Greek copies add verse 26: "But if you don't forgive other people, then your Father in heaven will not forgive your sins."

to arrest Jesus, but they were afraid of the people. So the leaders left him and went away.

## IS IT RIGHT TO PAY TAXES OR NOT?

[13]Later, the Jewish leaders sent some Pharisees and Herodians" to Jesus to trap him in saying something wrong. [14]They came to him and said, "Teacher, we know that you are an honest man. You are not afraid of what other people think about you, because you pay no attention to who they are. And you teach the truth about God's way. Tell us: Is it right to pay taxes to Caesar or not? [15]Should we pay them, or not?"

But knowing what these men were really trying to do, Jesus said to them, "Why are you trying to trap me? Bring me a coin to look at." [16]They gave Jesus a coin, and he asked, "Whose image and name are on the coin?"

They answered, "Caesar's."

[17]Then Jesus said to them, "Give to Caesar the things that are Caesar's, and give to God the things that are God's." The men were amazed at what Jesus said.

## "GIVE TO CAESAR THE THINGS THAT ARE CAESAR'S, AND GIVE TO GOD THE THINGS THAT ARE GOD'S."

### SOME SADDUCEES TRY TO TRICK JESUS

[18]Then some Sadducees came to Jesus and asked him a question. (Sadducees believed that people would not rise from the dead.) [19]They said, "Teacher, Moses wrote that if a man's brother dies, leaving a wife but no children, then that man must marry the widow and have children for his brother. [20]Once there were seven brothers. The first brother married and died, leaving no children. [21]So the second brother married the widow, but he also died and had no children. The same thing happened with the third brother. [22]All seven brothers married her and died, and none of the brothers had any children. Finally the woman died too. [23]Since all seven brothers had married her, when people rise from the dead, whose wife will she be?"

[24]Jesus answered, "Why don't you understand? Don't you know what the Scriptures say, and don't you know about the power of God? [25]When people rise from the dead, they will not marry, nor will they be given to someone to marry. They will be like the angels in heaven. [26]Surely you have read what God said about people rising from the dead. In the book in which Moses wrote about the burning bush," it says that God told Moses, 'I am the God of Abraham, the God of Isaac, and the God of Jacob.'" [27]God is the God of the living, not the dead. You Sadducees are wrong!"

### THE MOST IMPORTANT COMMAND

[28]One of the teachers of the law came and heard Jesus arguing with the Sadducees.

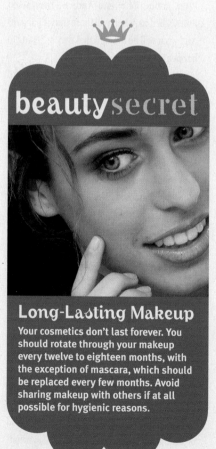

# beautysecret

## Long-Lasting Makeup

Your cosmetics don't last forever. You should rotate through your makeup every twelve to eighteen months, with the exception of mascara, which should be replaced every few months. Avoid sharing makeup with others if at all possible for hygienic reasons.

# Blab

**Q:** I asked Christ to forgive my sins and come into my life several years ago. I remember I used to feel so clean and excited about God. Now I am not that excited. I know he is there, but my friends seem like a lot more fun. Should I be concerned?

**A:** Revelation 3:16 says God prefers people who are hot or cold toward him, not those who are lukewarm. If your passion for him has dissolved, set aside time daily to pray that he will renew your fire. If you are disciplined about seeking it, he will. Otherwise, you are in danger of losing sight of God during your teen and early adult years, and the consequences can be disastrous.

**Q:** Does it really matter if I read the Bible?

**A:** Absolutely! The Bible is God's love letter to those who believe in him, with reminders of his love and a plan for the way to live to please him.

**Q:** I used to have a devotion time daily, but now it seems too hard. How can I get back into it?

**A:** Think of the time of day you are enthusiastic and the ways you learn best (by reading, hearing, trying things?). Mark out a specific time on your planner or calendar daily for six weeks that you will spend with God. Make it exciting to you, by walking and observing creation, listening to the Bible on CD instead of reading it, or trying a new Bible study guide or devotional book. After six weeks of doing it daily, your new habit should be in place.

 **notes** 12:13 **Herodians** A political group that followed Herod and his family. 12:26 **burning bush** Read Exodus 3:1-12 in the Old Testament. 12:26 **'I am . . . Jacob.'** Quotation from Exodus 3:6.

## RadicalFaith:

# Mark 13:13

If you love Jesus, you're going to face rejection and hostility sometime in your life. The world just doesn't get Jesus. It can't grasp or appreciate his high authority and value. Jesus said the world just can't accept God's Spirit of truth—it can't understand him (John 14:17). As a person who loves Jesus, you are going to face challenges, but you can stand firm. There are going to be tough times—when you're worn out and it's not easy to keep believing, serving, and being committed to him—but you can stay steady because you have Christ in your heart. He said, "I told you these things so that you can have peace in me. In this world you will have trouble, but be brave! I have defeated the world" (John 16:33). You can count on bad things happening just the way God says they will in his Word, but his kingdom will never end. He'll reign forever and you're going to be a part of it. Stay in the Word every day so God can keep fueling you with his perspective and power to persevere.

Seeing that Jesus gave good answers to their questions, he asked Jesus, "Which of the commands is most important?"

<sup>29</sup>Jesus answered, "The most important command is this: 'Listen, people of Israel! The Lord our God is the only Lord. <sup>30</sup>Love the Lord your God with all your heart, all your soul, all your mind, and all your strength.' <sup>31</sup>The second command is this: 'Love your neighbor as you love yourself.' There are no commands more important than these."

<sup>32</sup>The man answered, "That was a good answer, Teacher. You were right when you said God is the only Lord and there is no other God besides him. <sup>33</sup>One must love God with all his heart, all his mind, and all his strength. And one must love his neighbor as he loves himself. These commands are more important than all the animals and sacrifices we offer to God."

<sup>34</sup>When Jesus saw that the man answered him wisely, Jesus said to him, "You are close to the kingdom of God." And after that, no one was brave enough to ask Jesus any more questions.

<sup>35</sup>As Jesus was teaching in the Temple, he asked, "Why do the teachers of the law say that the Christ is the son of David? <sup>36</sup>David himself, speaking by the Holy Spirit, said:

'The Lord said to my Lord:
Sit by me at my right side,
until I put your enemies under your
control.'                    *Psalm 110:1*

<sup>37</sup>David himself calls the Christ 'Lord,' so how can the Christ be his son?" The large crowd listened to Jesus with pleasure.

<sup>38</sup>Jesus continued teaching and said, "Beware of the teachers of the law. They like to walk around wearing fancy clothes, and they love for people to greet them with respect in the marketplaces. <sup>39</sup>They love to have the most important seats in the synagogues and at feasts. <sup>40</sup>But they cheat widows and steal their houses and then try to make themselves look good by saying long prayers. They will receive a greater punishment."

## TRUE GIVING

<sup>41</sup>Jesus sat near the Temple money box and watched the people put in their money. Many rich people gave large sums of money. <sup>42</sup>Then a poor widow came and put in two small copper coins, which were only worth a few cents.

<sup>43</sup>Calling his followers to him, Jesus said, "I tell you the truth, this poor widow gave more than all those rich people. <sup>44</sup>They gave only what they did not need. This woman is very poor, but she gave all she had; she gave all she had to live on."

## THE TEMPLE WILL BE DESTROYED

**13** As Jesus was leaving the Temple, one of his followers said to him, "Look, Teacher! How beautiful the buildings are! How big the stones are!"

<sup>2</sup>Jesus said, "Do you see all these great buildings? Not one stone will be left on another. Every stone will be thrown down to the ground."

<sup>3</sup>Later, as Jesus was sitting on the Mount of Olives, opposite the Temple, he was alone with Peter, James, John, and Andrew. They asked Jesus, <sup>4</sup>"Tell us, when will these things happen? And what will be the sign that they are going to happen?"

<sup>5</sup>Jesus began to answer them, "Be careful that no one fools you. <sup>6</sup>Many people will come in my name, saying, 'I am the One,' and they will fool many people. <sup>7</sup>When you hear about wars and stories of wars that are coming, don't be afraid. These things must happen before the end comes. <sup>8</sup>Nations will fight against other nations, and kingdoms against other kingdoms. There will be earthquakes in different places, and there will be times when there is no food for people to eat. These things are like the first pains when something new is about to be born.

<sup>9</sup>"You must be careful. People will arrest you and take you to court and beat you in their synagogues. You will be forced to stand before kings and governors, to tell them about me. This will happen to you because you follow me. <sup>10</sup>But before these things happen, the Good News must be told to all people. <sup>11</sup>When you are arrested and judged, don't worry ahead of time about what you should say. Say whatever is given you to say at that time, because it

**12:30** 'Listen . . . strength.' Quotation from Deuteronomy 6:4-5. **12:31** 'Love . . . yourself.' Quotation from Leviticus 19:18.

will not really be you speaking; it will be the Holy Spirit.

¹²"Brothers will give their own brothers to be killed, and fathers will give their own children to be killed. Children will fight against their own parents and cause them to be put to death. ¹³All people will hate you because you follow me, but those people who keep their faith until the end will be saved.

¹⁴"You will see 'the destroying terror'ⁿ standing where it should not be." (You who read this should understand what it means.) "At that time, the people in Judea should run away to the mountains. ¹⁵If people are on the roofsⁿ of their houses, they must not go down or go inside to get anything out of their houses. ¹⁶If people are in the fields, they must not go back to get their coats. ¹⁷At that time, how terrible it will be for women who are pregnant or have nursing babies! ¹⁸Pray that these things will not happen in winter, ¹⁹because those days will be full of trouble. There will be more trouble than there has ever been since the beginning, when God made the world, until now, and nothing as bad will ever happen again. ²⁰God has decided to make that terrible time short. Otherwise, no one would go on living. But God will make that time short to help the people he has chosen. ²¹At that time, someone might say to you, 'Look, there is the Christ!' Or another person might say, 'There he is!' But don't believe them. ²²False Christs and false prophets will come and perform great wonders and miracles. They will try to fool even the people God has chosen, if that is possible. ²³So be careful. I have warned you about all this before it happens.

**BIBLE BIOS**

# Delilah

13:06

**[JUDGES 16]** In an evil scheme worthy of a soap opera plotline, Delilah agreed to seduce Samson into telling her the secret of his incomparable strength—which turned out to be his long hair. Then, for a nice, big wad of cash, she gave that information to the Philistines, allowing them to weaken Samson by cutting his hair as he slept so they could capture him. Cold and calculating, Delilah knew she could use Samson's weakness for women against him. She's the perfect example of how temptation, if acted upon, can ruin lives. People like Delilah still exist today. They would rather tear down and destroy the lives of others than be a force for good in the world. In the end, people like Delilah destroy more than the ones they deceive—they destroy their own souls.

## DIDYA KNOW

²⁴"During the days after this trouble comes,
  'the sun will grow dark,
    and the moon will not give its light.
²⁵The stars will fall from the sky.

And the powers of the heavens will be shaken.'        *Isaiah 13:10; 34:4*

²⁶"Then people will see the Son of Man coming in clouds with great power and glory. ²⁷Then he will send his angels all around the earth to gather his chosen people from every part of the earth and from every part of heaven.

²⁸"Learn a lesson from the fig tree: When its branches become green and soft and new leaves appear, you know summer is near. ²⁹In the same way, when you see these things happening, you will know that the time is near, ready to come. ³⁰I tell you the truth, all these things will happen while the people of this time are still living. ³¹Earth and sky will be destroyed, but the words I have said will never be destroyed.

## "NO ONE KNOWS WHEN THAT DAY OR TIME WILL BE, NOT THE ANGELS IN HEAVEN, NOT EVEN THE SON."

³²"No one knows when that day or time will be, not the angels in heaven, not even the Son. Only the Father knows. ³³Be careful! Always be ready, because you don't know when that time will be. ³⁴It is like a man who goes on a trip. He leaves his house and lets his servants take care of it, giving each one a special job to do. The man tells the servant guarding the door always to be watchful. ³⁵So always be ready, because you don't know when the owner of the house will come back. It might be in the evening, or at midnight, or in the morning while it is still dark, or when the sun rises. ³⁶Always be ready. Otherwise he might come back suddenly and find you sleeping. ³⁷I tell you this, and I say this to everyone: 'Be ready!' "

**notes**   **13:14 'the destroying terror'** Mentioned in Daniel 9:27; 12:11 (cf. Daniel 11:31).   **13:15 roofs** In Bible times houses were built with flat roofs. The roof was used for drying things such as flax and fruit. And it was used as an extra room, as a place for worship, and as a cool place to sleep in the summer.

### THE PLAN TO KILL JESUS

**14** It was now only two days before the Passover and the Feast of Unleavened Bread. The leading priests and teachers of the law were trying to find a trick to arrest Jesus and kill him. [2]But they said, "We must not do it during the feast, because the people might cause a riot."

### A WOMAN WITH PERFUME FOR JESUS

[3]Jesus was in Bethany at the house of Simon, who had a skin disease. While Jesus was eating there, a woman approached him with an alabaster jar filled with very expensive perfume, made of pure nard. She opened the jar and poured the perfume on Jesus' head.

[4]Some who were there became upset and said to each other, "Why waste that perfume? [5]It was worth a full year's work. It could have been sold and the money given to the poor." And they got very angry with the woman.

[6]Jesus said, "Leave her alone. Why are you troubling her? She did an excellent thing for me. [7]You will always have the poor with you, and you can help them anytime you want. But you will not always have me. [8]This woman did the only thing she could do for me; she poured perfume on my body to prepare me for burial. [9]I tell you the truth, wherever the Good News is preached in all the world, what this woman has done will be told, and people will remember her."

### JUDAS BECOMES AN ENEMY OF JESUS

[10]One of the twelve apostles, Judas Iscariot, went to talk to the leading priests to offer to hand Jesus over to them. [11]These priests were pleased about this and promised to pay Judas money. So he watched for the best time to turn Jesus in.

### JESUS EATS THE PASSOVER MEAL

[12]It was now the first day of the Feast of Unleavened Bread when the Passover lamb was sacrificed. Jesus' followers said to him, "Where do you want us to go and prepare for you to eat the Passover meal?"

[13]Jesus sent two of his followers and said to them, "Go into the city and a man carrying a jar of water will meet you. Follow him. [14]When he goes into a house, tell the owner of the house, 'The Teacher says: Where is my guest room in which I can eat the Passover meal with my followers?' [15]The owner will show you a large room upstairs that is furnished and ready. Prepare the food for us there."

[16]So the followers left and went into the city. Everything happened as Jesus had said, so they prepared the Passover meal.

[17]In the evening, Jesus went to that house with the twelve. [18]While they were all eating, Jesus said, "I tell you the truth, one of you will turn against me—one of you eating with me now."

[19]The followers were very sad to hear this. Each one began to say to Jesus, "I am not the one, am I?"

[20]Jesus answered, "It is one of the twelve—the one who dips his bread into the bowl with me. [21]The Son of Man will die, just as the Scriptures say. But how terrible it will be for the person who hands the Son of Man over to be killed. It would be better for him if he had never been born."

### THE LORD'S SUPPER

[22]While they were eating, Jesus took some bread and thanked God for it and broke it. Then he gave it to his followers and said, "Take it; this is my body."

[23]Then Jesus took a cup and thanked God for it and gave it to the followers, and they all drank from the cup.

[24]Then Jesus said, "This is my blood which is the new agreement that God makes with his people. This blood is poured out for many. [25]I tell you the truth, I will not drink of this fruit of the vine" again until that day when I drink it new in the kingdom of God."

---

## Music Reviews

**GROUP:** SWITCHFOOT

**ALBUM:** THE EARLY YEARS: 1997-2000 [CLASSIC HIT]

Switchfoot fans who love brothers Jon and Tim Foreman's brand of modern rock on *The Beautiful Meltdown* can rewind and get the band's early albums all for one price in this newly packaged triple-disc collection called *The Early Years: 1997-2000.* 1997's *The Legend of Chin,* 1999's *New Way to Be Human,* and 2000's *Learning to Breathe* are here, offering 32 songs, including the first recording of the hit "I Dare You to Move" plus radio faves "Chem 6A," "You," and "You Already Take Me There." Take a listen to "Only Hope" and "Under the Floor"; and in these early efforts, you can already hear the promise of great things to come.

**WHY IT ROCKS: THIS COLLECTION SHOWS OFF SWITCHFOOT'S TREMENDOUS POTENTIAL EARLY IN THEIR CAREER.**

---

**14:25 fruit of the vine** Product of the grapevine; this may also be translated "wine."

# LEARN I+ & LIVE I+

**Mark 11:25**
**Learn It:** Keep your faith life healthy and your prayer life successful by forgiving as God forgives.
**Live It:** When you are wronged, be quick to forgive the one who has hurt you.

**Mark 14:38**
**Learn It:** The spirit wants to do the right thing, but the body is weak.
**Live It:** While you work out this week, pray that you will build up your resistance to temptation, as well as your muscles.

**Luke 2:19**
**Learn It:** Mary treasured the miracles surrounding Jesus' birth and thought about them.
**Live It:** Write down the unusual ways God has worked in your life. Post the list where you will see it often.

26After singing a hymn, they went out to the Mount of Olives.

## JESUS' FOLLOWERS WILL LEAVE HIM

27Then Jesus told the followers, "You will all stumble in your faith, because it is written in the Scriptures:

'I will kill the shepherd,
and the sheep will scatter.'    *Zechariah 13:7*

28But after I rise from the dead, I will go ahead of you into Galilee."

29Peter said, "Everyone else may stumble in their faith, but I will not."

30Jesus answered, "I tell you the truth, tonight before the rooster crows twice you will say three times you don't know me."

31But Peter insisted, "I will never say that I don't know you! I will even die with you!" And all the other followers said the same thing.

## JESUS PRAYS ALONE

32Jesus and his followers went to a place called Gethsemane. He said to them, "Sit here while I pray." 33Jesus took Peter, James, and John with him, and he began to be very sad and troubled. 34He said to them, "My heart is full of sorrow, to the point of death. Stay here and watch."

35After walking a little farther away from them, Jesus fell to the ground and prayed that, if possible, he would not have this time of suffering. 36He prayed, "Abba,″ Father! You can do all things. Take away this cup″ of suffering. But do what you want, not what I want."

37Then Jesus went back to his followers and found them asleep. He said to Peter, "Simon, are you sleeping? Couldn't you stay awake with me for one hour? 38Stay awake and pray for strength against temptation. The spirit wants to do what is right, but the body is weak."

## "THE SPIRIT WANTS TO DO WHAT IS RIGHT, BUT THE BODY IS WEAK."

39Again Jesus went away and prayed the same thing. 40Then he went back to his followers, and again he found them asleep, because their eyes were very heavy. And they did not know what to say to him.

41After Jesus prayed a third time, he went back to his followers and said to them, "Are you still sleeping and resting? That's enough. The time has come for the Son of Man to be handed over to sinful people. 42Get up, we must go. Look, here comes the man who has turned against me."

## JESUS IS ARRESTED

43At once, while Jesus was still speaking, Judas, one of the twelve apostles, came up. With him were many people carrying swords and clubs who had been sent from the leading priests, the teachers of the law, and the older Jewish leaders.

44Judas had planned a signal for them, say-ing, "The man I kiss is Jesus. Arrest him and guard him while you lead him away." 45So Judas went straight to Jesus and said, "Teacher!" and kissed him. 46Then the people grabbed Jesus and arrested him. 47One of his followers standing nearby pulled out his sword and struck the servant of the high priest and cut off his ear.

48Then Jesus said, "You came to get me with swords and clubs as if I were a criminal. 49Every day I was with you teaching in the Temple, and you did not arrest me there. But all these things have happened to make the Scriptures come true." 50Then all of Jesus' followers left him and ran away.

51A young man, wearing only a linen cloth, was following Jesus, and the people also grabbed him. 52But the cloth he was wearing came off, and he ran away naked.

## JESUS BEFORE THE LEADERS

53The people who arrested Jesus led him to the house of the high priest, where all the leading priests, the older leaders, and the teachers of the law were gathered. 54Peter followed far behind and entered the courtyard of the high priest's house. There he sat with the guards, warming himself by the fire.

55The leading priests and the whole Jewish council tried to find something that Jesus had done wrong so they could kill him. But the council could find no proof of anything. 56Many people came and told false things about him, but all said different things—none of them agreed.

14:36 **Abba** Name that a Jewish child called his father.   14:36 **cup** Jesus is talking about the terrible things that will happen to him. Accepting these things will be very hard, like drinking a cup of something bitter.

⁵⁷Then some people stood up and lied about Jesus, saying, ⁵⁸"We heard this man say, 'I will destroy this Temple that people made. And three days later, I will build another Temple not made by people.'" ⁵⁹But even the things these people said did not agree.

⁶⁰Then the high priest stood before them and asked Jesus, "Aren't you going to answer? Don't you have something to say about their charges against you?" ⁶¹But Jesus said nothing; he did not answer.

The high priest asked Jesus another question: "Are you the Christ, the Son of the blessed God?"

⁶²Jesus answered, "I am. And in the future you will see the Son of Man sitting at the right hand of God, the Powerful One, and coming on clouds in the sky."

## relationships

"Love the Lord your God with all your heart, all your soul, and all your mind" (Matthew 22:37). You are probably always being warned about guys who are players—guys who use girls and just want to see what they can get from them. Any guy who loves himself more than he loves God has his priorities out of whack and isn't the kind who will build a solid relationship with you.

⁶³When the high priest heard this, he tore his clothes and said, "We don't need any more witnesses! ⁶⁴You all heard him say these things against God. What do you think?"

They all said that Jesus was guilty and should die. ⁶⁵Some of the people there began to spit at Jesus. They blindfolded him and beat him with their fists and said, "Prove you are a prophet!" Then the guards led Jesus away and beat him.

### PETER SAYS HE DOESN'T KNOW JESUS

⁶⁶While Peter was in the courtyard, a servant girl of the high priest came there. ⁶⁷She saw Peter warming himself at the fire and looked closely at him.

Then she said, "You also were with Jesus, that man from Nazareth."

⁶⁸But Peter said that he was never with Jesus. He said, "I don't know or understand what you are talking about." Then Peter left and went toward the entrance of the courtyard. And the rooster crowed."

⁶⁹The servant girl saw Peter there, and again she said to the people who were standing nearby, "This man is one of those who followed Jesus." ⁷⁰Again Peter said that it was not true.

A short time later, some people were standing near Peter saying, "Surely you are one of those who followed Jesus, because you are from Galilee, too."

⁷¹Then Peter began to place a curse on himself and swear, "I don't know this man you're talking about!"

⁷²At once, the rooster crowed the second time. Then Peter remembered what Jesus had told him: "Before the rooster crows twice, you will say three times that you don't know me." Then Peter lost control of himself and began to cry.

### PILATE QUESTIONS JESUS

15 Very early in the morning, the leading priests, the older leaders, the teachers of the law, and all the Jewish council decided what to do with Jesus. They tied him, led him away, and turned him over to Pilate, the governor.

²Pilate asked Jesus, "Are you the king of the Jews?"

Jesus answered, "Those are your words."

³The leading priests accused Jesus of many things. ⁴So Pilate asked Jesus another question, "You can see that they are accusing you of many things. Aren't you going to answer?"

⁵But Jesus still said nothing, so Pilate was very surprised.

### PILATE TRIES TO FREE JESUS

⁶Every year at the time of the Passover the governor would free one prisoner whom the people chose. ⁷At that time, there was a man named Barabbas in prison who was a rebel and had committed murder during a riot. ⁸The crowd came to Pilate and began to ask him to free a prisoner as he always did.

⁹So Pilate asked them, "Do you want me to free the king of the Jews?" ¹⁰Pilate knew that the leading priests had turned Jesus in to him because they were jealous. ¹¹But the leading priests had persuaded the people to ask Pilate to free Barabbas, not Jesus.

¹²Then Pilate asked the crowd again, "So what should I do with this man you call the king of the Jews?"

¹³They shouted, "Crucify him!"

¹⁴Pilate asked, "Why? What wrong has he done?"

But they shouted even louder, "Crucify him!"

¹⁵Pilate wanted to please the crowd, so he freed Barabbas for them. After having Jesus beaten with whips, he handed Jesus over to the soldiers to be crucified.

¹⁶The soldiers took Jesus into the governor's palace (called the Praetorium) and called all the other soldiers together. ¹⁷They put a purple robe on Jesus and used thorny branches to make a crown for his head. ¹⁸They began to call out to him, "Hail, King of the Jews!" ¹⁹The soldiers beat Jesus on the head many times with a stick. They spit on him and made fun of

notes  **14:68 And . . . crowed.** A few, early Greek copies leave out this phrase.

him by bowing on their knees and worshiping him. [20]After they finished, the soldiers took off the purple robe and put his own clothes on him again. Then they led him out of the palace to be crucified.

## JESUS IS CRUCIFIED

[21]A man named Simon from Cyrene, the father of Alexander and Rufus, was coming from the fields to the city. The soldiers forced Simon to carry the cross for Jesus. [22]They led Jesus to the place called Golgotha, which means the Place of the Skull. [23]The soldiers tried to give Jesus wine mixed with myrrh to drink, but he refused. [24]The soldiers crucified Jesus and divided his clothes among themselves, throwing lots to decide what each soldier would get.

[25]It was nine o'clock in the morning when they crucified Jesus. [26]There was a sign with this charge against Jesus written on it: THE KING OF THE JEWS. [27]They also put two robbers on crosses beside Jesus, one on the right, and the other on the left.[28] [29]People walked by and insulted Jesus and shook their heads, saying, "You said you could destroy the Temple and build it again in three days. [30]So save yourself! Come down from that cross!"

**Bible Basics**

God is known as the **"Trinity,"** three persons with three distinct personalities: God the Father, God the Son (Jesus), and God the Holy Spirit. That's not easy to understand, but think of it this way: Water can take on three forms. It can be solid, liquid, or gas—like ice, water, or steam. No matter what the form, it's all still water. That may not be a perfect example, but it's one way of trying to wrap our human minds around a great, big God. The Bible teaches that God the Father lives and reigns in heaven. Jesus came to earth, lived a perfect life, died on a cross for all sinful human beings, and was raised from the dead to return to heaven and sit on a throne at God's right hand. The Holy Spirit lives inside all who believe to guide, direct, and comfort.

[31]The leading priests and the teachers of the law were also making fun of Jesus. They said to each other, "He saved other people, but he can't save himself. [32]If he is really the Christ, the king of Israel, let him come down now from the cross. When we see this, we will believe in him." The robbers who were being crucified beside Jesus also insulted him.

## JESUS DIES

[33]At noon the whole country became dark, and the darkness lasted for three hours. [34]At three o'clock Jesus cried in a loud voice, "Eloi, Eloi, lama sabachthani." This means, "My God, my God, why have you rejected me?"

[35]When some of the people standing there heard this, they said, "Listen! He is calling Elijah."

[36]Someone there ran and got a sponge, filled it with vinegar, tied it to a stick, and gave it to Jesus to drink. He said, "We want to see if Elijah will come to take him down from the cross."

[37]Then Jesus cried in a loud voice and died. [38]The curtain in the Temple" was torn into two pieces, from the top to the bottom. [39]When the army officer who was standing in front of the cross saw what happened when Jesus died, he said, "This man really was the Son of God!"

[40]Some women were standing at a distance from the cross, watching; among them were Mary Magdalene, Salome, and Mary the mother of James and Joseph. (James was her youngest son.) [41]These women had followed Jesus in Galilee and helped him. Many other women were also there who had come with Jesus to Jerusalem.

## JESUS IS BURIED

[42]This was Preparation Day. (That means the day before the Sabbath day.) That evening, [43]Joseph from Arimathea was brave enough to go to Pilate and ask for Jesus' body. Joseph, an important member of the Jewish council, was one of the people who was waiting for the kingdom of God to come. [44]Pilate was amazed that Jesus would have already died, so he called the army officer who had guarded Jesus and asked him if Jesus had already died. [45]The officer told Pilate that he was dead, so Pilate told Joseph he could have the body. [46]Joseph bought some linen cloth, took the body down from the cross, and wrapped it in the linen. He put the body in a tomb that was cut out of a wall of rock. Then he rolled a very large stone to block the entrance of the tomb. [47]And Mary Magdalene and Mary the mother of Joseph saw the place where Jesus was laid.

## JESUS RISES FROM THE DEAD

16 The day after the Sabbath day, Mary Magdalene, Mary the mother of

**notes** 15:28 Verse 28 Some Greek copies add verse 28: "And the Scripture came true that says, 'They put him with criminals.'" 15:38 curtain in the Temple A curtain divided the Most Holy Place from the other part of the Temple. That was the special building in Jerusalem where God commanded the Jewish people to worship him.

# Blab

**Q:** I think I have a crush on my best friend (a girl), and I am so scared. She's just so smart, cute, and funny. Does this mean I am gay?

**A:** It is not unusual to be attracted to someone of the same sex who has all the qualities you want for yourself. It does not mean you are gay. Do not let your thoughts become sexual, however. The Bible says you can take sinful thoughts captive and turn them over to God before you act on them. Stand on that promise, and talk to an adult you can trust about your confusing feelings.

**Q:** I have major depression. I have accepted Christ, but I still think about killing myself a lot. Then I could be with him in heaven. Is it okay to kill myself now?

**A:** It is not okay to kill yourself. God has a purpose for you in this life, and he can use you even though you battle depression. Ask him to keep your thoughts under control, and make sure you call someone or go to someone else every time you think of killing yourself so that you have accountability and are not tempted to try it. Get into or continue Christian counseling and treatment.

**Q:** I like tube tops and low-rise jeans. My parents say I dress immodestly. I only wear what's in style. Are they right?

**A:** Keep in mind that guys are sexually stimulated by what they see (and even by imagining what they can't). The Bible says not to cause anyone else to sin. Are you putting sexual thoughts about your body into guys' heads? If you are showing a lot of skin, you probably are.

James, and Salome bought some sweet-smelling spices to put on Jesus' body. ²Very early on that day, the first day of the week, soon after sunrise, the women were on their way to the tomb. ³They said to each other, "Who will roll away for us the stone that covers the entrance of the tomb?"

⁴Then the women looked and saw that the stone had already been rolled away, even though it was very large. ⁵The women entered the tomb and saw a young man wearing a white robe and sitting on the right side, and they were afraid.

⁶But the man said, "Don't be afraid. You are looking for Jesus from Nazareth, who has been crucified. He has risen from the dead; he is not here. Look, here is the place they laid him. ⁷Now go and tell his followers and Peter, 'Jesus is going into Galilee ahead of you, and you will see him there as he told you before.' "

⁸The women were confused and shaking with fear, so they left the tomb and ran away. They did not tell anyone about what happened, because they were afraid.

---

Verses 9-20 are not included in two of the best and oldest Greek manuscripts of Mark.

## SOME FOLLOWERS SEE JESUS

[⁹After Jesus rose from the dead early on the first day of the week, he showed himself first to Mary Magdalene. One time in the past, he had forced seven demons out of her. ¹⁰After Mary saw Jesus, she went and told his followers, who were very sad and were crying. ¹¹But Mary told them that Jesus was alive. She said that she had seen him, but the followers did not believe her.

¹²Later, Jesus showed himself to two of his followers while they were walking in the country, but he did not look the same as before. ¹³These followers went back to the others and told them what had happened, but again, the followers did not believe them.

## JESUS TALKS TO THE APOSTLES

¹⁴Later Jesus showed himself to the eleven apostles while they were eating, and he criti-

cized them because they had no faith. They were stubborn and refused to believe those who had seen him after he had risen from the dead.

## "GO EVERYWHERE IN THE WORLD, AND TELL THE GOOD NEWS TO EVERYONE."

¹⁵Jesus said to his followers, "Go everywhere in the world, and tell the Good News to everyone. ¹⁶Anyone who believes and is baptized will be saved, but anyone who does not believe will be punished. ¹⁷And those who believe will be able to do these things as proof: They will use my name to force out demons. They will speak in new languages.ⁿ ¹⁸They will pick up snakes and drink poison without being hurt. They will touch the sick, and the sick will be healed."

¹⁹After the Lord Jesus said these things to his followers, he was carried up into heaven, and he sat at the right side of God. ²⁰The followers went everywhere in the world and told the Good News to people, and the Lord helped them. The Lord proved that the Good News they told was true by giving them power to work miracles.]

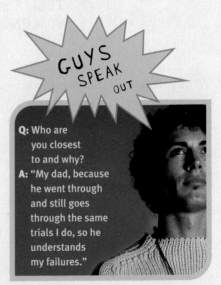

**GUYS SPEAK OUT**

**Q:** Who are you closest to and why?
**A:** "My dad, because he went through and still goes through the same trials I do, so he understands my failures."

**notes** 16:17 **languages** This can also be translated "tongues."

*i*t's fitting that a physician would give the most detailed and moving description of Jesus' birth. Luke, in polished literary style, tells us that he has "studied everything carefully from the beginning" and has "arranged it in order" (1:3). Today we benefit from his careful, deliberate research.

# Luke

### Detailed, Deliberate, Descriptive

It's cool to note that Luke was the only non-Jewish person to write a book in the Bible. In fact, he probably had Greek readers in mind when he wrote this. Luke used a lot of Greek terminology, and his style indicates that he was educated and sophisticated, as the Greeks were. Greece could be compared to Paris or New York today—a center of posh style, civilized culture, and forward thinking.

Maybe it had something to do with the fact that he himself was in the business of restoring health, but Luke gives special emphasis to the healing ministry of Jesus. You'll read about lepers who were healed and lots of other medical miracles that Jesus did. Luke also takes great care to show Jesus' compassion for those at the low end of the societal food chain—the outcasts and the sinners. Again and again, Jesus the Great Physician ministered to those who were most keenly aware of their need for him.

## LUKE WRITES ABOUT JESUS' LIFE

1 Many have tried to report on the things that happened among us. [2]They have written the same things that we learned from others—the people who saw those things from the beginning and served God by telling people his message. [3]Since I myself have studied everything carefully from the beginning, most excellent" Theophilus, it seemed good for me to write it out for you. I arranged it in order [4]to help you know that what you have been taught is true.

## ZECHARIAH AND ELIZABETH

[5]During the time Herod ruled Judea, there was a priest named Zechariah who belonged to Abijah's group." Zechariah's wife, Elizabeth, came from the family of Aaron. [6]Zechariah and Elizabeth truly did what God said was good. They did everything the Lord commanded and were without fault in keeping his law. [7]But they had no children, because Elizabeth could not have a baby, and both of them were very old.

[8]One day Zechariah was serving as a priest before God, because his group was on duty. [9]According to the custom of the priests, he was chosen by lot to go into the Temple of the Lord and burn incense. [10]There were a great many people outside praying at the time the incense was offered. [11]Then an angel of the Lord appeared to Zechariah, standing on the right side of the incense table. [12]When he saw the angel, Zechariah was startled and frightened. [13]But the angel said to him, "Zechariah, don't be afraid. God has heard your prayer. Your wife, Elizabeth, will give birth to a son, and you will name him John. [14]He will bring you joy and gladness, and many people will be happy because of his birth. [15]John will be a great man for the Lord. He will never drink wine or beer, and even from birth, he will be filled with the Holy Spirit. [16]He will help many people of Israel return to the Lord their God. [17]He will go before the Lord in spirit and power like Elijah. He will make peace between parents and their children and will bring those who are not obeying God back to the right way of thinking,

to make a people ready for the coming of the Lord."

[18]Zechariah said to the angel, "How can I know that what you say is true? I am an old man, and my wife is old, too."

[19]The angel answered him, "I am Gabriel. I stand before God, who sent me to talk to you and to tell you this good news. [20]Now, listen! You will not be able to speak until the day these things happen, because you did not believe what I told you. But they will really happen."

[21]Outside, the people were still waiting for Zechariah and were surprised that he was staying so long in the Temple. [22]When Zechariah came outside, he could not speak to them, and they knew he had seen a vision in the Temple. He could only make signs to them and remained unable to speak. [23]When his time of service at the Temple was finished, he went home.

> "LET US PRAISE THE LORD, THE GOD OF ISRAEL, BECAUSE HE HAS COME TO HELP HIS PEOPLE AND HAS GIVEN THEM FREEDOM."

[24]Later, Zechariah's wife, Elizabeth, became pregnant and did not go out of her house for five months. Elizabeth said, [25]"Look what the Lord has done for me! My people were ashamed" of me, but now the Lord has taken away that shame."

## AN ANGEL APPEARS TO MARY

[26]During Elizabeth's sixth month of pregnancy, God sent the angel Gabriel to Nazareth, a town in Galilee, [27]to a virgin. She was engaged to marry a man named Joseph from the family of David. Her name was Mary. [28]The angel came to her and said, "Greetings! The Lord has blessed you and is with you."

[29]But Mary was very startled by what the angel said and wondered what this greeting might mean.

[30]The angel said to her, "Don't be afraid, Mary; God has shown you his grace. [31]Listen! You will become pregnant and give birth to a son, and you will name him Jesus. [32]He will be great and will be called the Son of the Most High. The Lord God will give him the throne of King David, his ancestor. [33]He will rule over the people of Jacob forever, and his kingdom will never end."

[34]Mary said to the angel, "How will this happen since I am a virgin?"

[35]The angel said to Mary, "The Holy Spirit will come upon you, and the power of the Most High will cover you. For this reason the baby will be holy and will be called the Son of God. [36]Now Elizabeth, your relative, is also pregnant with a son though she is very old. Everyone thought she could not have a baby, but she has been pregnant for six months. [37]God can do anything!"

[38]Mary said, "I am the servant of the Lord. Let this happen to me as you say!" Then the angel went away.

## MARY VISITS ELIZABETH

[39]Mary got up and went quickly to a town in the hills of Judea. [40]She came to Zechariah's house and greeted Elizabeth. [41]When Elizabeth heard Mary's greeting, the unborn baby inside her jumped, and Elizabeth was filled with the Holy Spirit. [42]She cried out in a loud voice, "God has blessed you more than any other woman, and he has blessed the baby to which you will give birth. [43]Why has this good thing happened to me, that the mother of my Lord comes to me? [44]When I heard your voice, the baby inside me jumped with joy. [45]You are blessed because you believed that what the Lord said to you would really happen."

## MARY PRAISES GOD

[46]Then Mary said,

"My soul praises the Lord;
[47]      my heart rejoices in God my Savior,

**1:3 excellent** This word was used to show respect to an important person like a king or ruler.  **1:5 Abijah's group** The Jewish priests were divided into twenty-four groups. See 1 Chronicles 24.  **1:25 ashamed** The Jewish people thought it was a disgrace for women not to have children.

48because he has shown his concern for his humble servant girl.

From now on, all people will say that I am blessed,

49 because the Powerful One has done great things for me.

His name is holy.

50God will show his mercy forever and ever to those who worship and serve him.

51He has done mighty deeds by his power.

He has scattered the people who are proud and think great things about themselves.

52He has brought down rulers from their thrones

and raised up the humble.

53He has filled the hungry with good things and sent the rich away with nothing.

54He has helped his servant, the people of Israel,

remembering to show them mercy

55as he promised to our ancestors,

to Abraham and to his children forever."

56Mary stayed with Elizabeth for about three months and then returned home.

## THE BIRTH OF JOHN

57When it was time for Elizabeth to give birth, she had a boy. 58Her neighbors and relatives heard how good the Lord was to her, and they rejoiced with her.

59When the baby was eight days old, they came to circumcise him. They wanted to name him Zechariah because this was his father's name, 60but his mother said, "No! He will be named John."

61The people said to Elizabeth, "But no one in your family has this name." 62Then they made signs to his father to find out what he would like to name him.

63Zechariah asked for a writing tablet and wrote, "His name is John," and everyone was surprised. 64Immediately Zechariah could talk again, and he began praising God. 65All their neighbors became alarmed, and in all the mountains of Judea people continued talking about all these things. 66The people who heard about them wondered, saying, "What will this child be?" because the Lord was with him.

## ZECHARIAH PRAISES GOD

67Then Zechariah, John's father, was filled with the Holy Spirit and prophesied:

68"Let us praise the Lord, the God of Israel, because he has come to help his people and has given them freedom.

69He has given us a powerful Savior from the family of God's servant David.

70He said that he would do this through his holy prophets who lived long ago:

71He promised he would save us from our enemies

and from the power of all those who hate us.

72He said he would give mercy to our fathers and that he would remember his holy promise.

73God promised Abraham, our father,

74 that he would save us from the power of our enemies

so we could serve him without fear,

75being holy and good before God as long as we live.

76"Now you, child, will be called a prophet of the Most High God.

You will go before the Lord to prepare his way.

77You will make his people know that they will be saved

by having their sins forgiven.

78With the loving mercy of our God,

a new day from heaven will dawn upon us.

79It will shine on those who live in darkness, in the shadow of death.

It will guide us into the path of peace."

80And so the child grew up and became strong in spirit. John lived in the desert until the time when he came out to preach to Israel.

## THE BIRTH OF JESUS

2 At that time, Augustus Caesar sent an order that all people in the countries under Roman rule must list their names in a register. 2This was the first registration;" it was taken while Quirinius was governor of Syria.

R a d i c a l  Faith:

# Luke 1:68-75

If you have a day when you need a reminder of how awesome God is, read through Zechariah's description of what the Holy Spirit revealed to him about God's heart and character. Look at God's actions in these verses. He brings rescue to the ruined and protection from enemies. He gives loving mercy, life, and peace: everything we crave is found within him. He is always strong, good, and flawless. No wonder the true prize is walking with him. We serve an amazing God! God promises us the sweetest joy and gives us the most incredible gift when he asks us to get to know him more. Paul said his relationship with God surpassed any of the thrills or successes he experienced in life. He said, "I think that all things are worth nothing compared with the greatness of knowing Christ Jesus my Lord" (Philippians 3:8). How do you think of God? Do you ever think of God in that way? If you spend more time dwelling on who he is, you'll begin to know how exciting it is to know him deeply.

**notes** **2:2 registration** Census. A counting of all the people and the things they own.

3And all went to their own towns to be registered.

4So Joseph left Nazareth, a town in Galilee, and went to the town of Bethlehem in Judea, known as the town of David. Joseph went there because he was from the family of David. 5Joseph registered with Mary, to whom he was engaged" and who was now pregnant. 6While they were in Bethlehem, the time came for Mary to have the baby, 7and she gave birth to her first son. Because there were no rooms left in the inn, she wrapped the baby with pieces of cloth and laid him in a box where animals are fed.

## SHEPHERDS HEAR ABOUT JESUS

8That night, some shepherds were in the fields nearby watching their sheep. 9Then an angel of the Lord stood before them. The glory

of the Lord was shining around them, and they became very frightened. 10The angel said to them, "Do not be afraid. I am bringing you good news that will be a great joy to all the people. 11Today your Savior was born in the town of David. He is Christ, the Lord. 12This is how you will know him: You will find a baby wrapped in pieces of cloth and lying in a feeding box."

13Then a very large group of angels from heaven joined the first angel, praising God and saying:

14"Give glory to God in heaven,
    and on earth let there be peace among
        the people who please God."

15When the angels left them and went back to heaven, the shepherds said to each other, "Let's go to Bethlehem. Let's see this thing that has happened which the Lord has told us about."

16So the shepherds went quickly and found Mary and Joseph and the baby, who was lying in a feeding box. 17When they had seen him, they told what the angels had said about this

child. 18Everyone was amazed at what the shepherds said to them. 19But Mary treasured these things and continued to think about them. 20Then the shepherds went back to their sheep, praising God and thanking him for everything they had seen and heard. It had been just as the angel had told them.

21When the baby was eight days old, he was circumcised and was named Jesus, the name given by the angel before the baby began to grow inside Mary.

## JESUS IS PRESENTED IN THE TEMPLE

22When the time came for Mary and Joseph to do what the law of Moses taught about being made pure," they took Jesus to Jerusalem to present him to the Lord. 23(It is written in the law of the Lord: "Every firstborn male shall be given to the Lord.")" 24Mary and Joseph also went to offer a sacrifice, as the law of the Lord says: "You must sacrifice two doves or two young pigeons."

## SIMEON SEES JESUS

25In Jerusalem lived a man named Simeon who was a good man and godly. He was waiting for the time when God would take away Israel's sorrow, and the Holy Spirit was in him. 26Simeon had been told by the Holy Spirit that he would not die before he saw the Christ promised by the Lord. 27The Spirit led Simeon to the Temple. When Mary and Joseph brought the baby Jesus to the Temple to do what the law said they must do, 28Simeon took the baby in his arms and thanked God:

29"Now, Lord, you can let me, your servant,
    die in peace as you said.
30With my own eyes I have seen your
    salvation,
31    which you prepared before all people.
32It is a light for the non-Jewish people to see

and an honor for your people, the
    Israelites."

33Jesus' father and mother were amazed at what Simeon had said about him. 34Then Simeon blessed them and said to Mary, "God has chosen this child to cause the fall and rise of many in Israel. He will be a sign from God that many people will not accept 35so that the thoughts of many will be made known. And the things that will happen will make your heart sad, too."

## ANNA SEES JESUS

36There was a prophetess, Anna, from the family of Phanuel in the tribe of Asher. Anna was very old. She had once been married for seven years. 37Then her husband died, and she was a widow for eighty-four years. Anna never left the Temple but worshiped God, going without food and praying day and night. 38Standing there at that time, she thanked God and spoke about Jesus to all who were waiting for God to free Jerusalem.

## JOSEPH AND MARY RETURN HOME

39When Joseph and Mary had done everything the law of the Lord commanded, they went home to Nazareth, their own town in Galilee. 40The little child grew and became strong. He was filled with wisdom, and God's goodness was upon him.

# "EVERY YEAR JESUS' PARENTS WENT TO JERUSALEM FOR THE PASSOVER FEAST."

## JESUS AS A BOY

41Every year Jesus' parents went to Jerusalem for the Passover Feast. 42When he was twelve years old, they went to the feast as they always did. 43After the feast days were over, they started home. The boy Jesus stayed behind in Jerusalem, but his parents did not know it. 44Thinking that Jesus was with them

 2:5 engaged For the Jewish people, an engagement was a lasting agreement. It could only be broken by divorce. 2:22 pure The Law of Moses said that forty days after a Jewish woman gave birth to a son, she must be cleansed by a ceremony at the Temple. Read Leviticus 12:2-8. 2:23 "Every . . . Lord." Quotation from Exodus 13:2. 2:24 "You . . . pigeons." Quotation from Leviticus 12:8.

78

# March

**1** Make a calendar of your friends' birthdays.

**2**

**3** Pray for a person of influence: It's Stacie Orrico's birthday.

**4**

**5** Bake a treat for someone who needs a pick-me-up.

**6**

**7**

**8** Spend at least 10 minutes praying today.

**9** Send e-cards to three friends. Tell them what you love about them.

**10**

**11** Pray for persecuted Christians around the world.

**12** Spend time today with someone who doesn't have many friends.

**13**

**14** Impress your Algebra teacher. This is National Pi Day, because the first three digits of the date 3-14 correspond with the first three digits of the number pi.

**15**

**16**

**17** St. Patrick's Day. Don't forget to wear green!

**18** Read John 1. Tell a friend about what you learned.

**19**

**20** Tell God three things you love about him.

**21**

**22** Volunteer at a local soup kitchen.

**23** Make a prayer list at the back of this Bible and begin praying each day.

**24**

**25** Make a list of three specific ways God has shown he's faithful to you.

**26** It's Make Up Your Own Holiday Day. Pick someone or something to celebrate in your life.

**27**

**28** Try to form one new healthy habit today.

**29** Pray for your teachers and your school.

**30** It's Norah Jones's birthday. Celebrate with her by praying for her.

**31**

God is spirit, and those who worship him must worship in spirit and truth.
—John 4:24

## Blab

**Q:** How far can you go sexually before you are no longer pure?

**A:** Let's put it this way: How much dog poop stirred into your cookie batter does it take to ruin the whole batter? In sexual matters, it is much safer to see how far away from the line you can stay rather than ask how close you can get to it. Once you hug, you'll want to kiss. Once you kiss, you'll want to make out. Once you make out, you'll want to touch. And so on, and so on . . . you get the picture.

**Q:** What age should I be when I start dating?

**A:** If you think that you should only date someone you could marry, ideally you will wait for the one God has for you—and that's up to God when you will get together. If you want to practice being in social situations with a guy, try going out in groups and don't spend too much time alone. Getting too close, too soon, sets you up for a broken heart—or worse.

**Q:** Is it okay to think about sex?

**A:** God designed you to be curious, and your body in your teen years is doing all kinds of changing (and filling with all kinds of hormones), so naturally you will think about sex. God wants us to remain pure in our thoughts and our actions, however, so you shouldn't fantasize about *having* sex. Imaginary pornography (starring you) is not any better than looking at the real thing, and it will just make you want more.

in the group, they traveled for a whole day. Then they began to look for him among their family and friends. ⁴⁵When they did not find him, they went back to Jerusalem to look for him there. ⁴⁶After three days they found Jesus sitting in the Temple with the teachers, listening to them and asking them questions. ⁴⁷All who heard him were amazed at his understanding and answers. ⁴⁸When Jesus' parents saw him, they were astonished. His mother said to him, "Son, why did you do this to us? Your father and I were very worried about you and have been looking for you."

⁴⁹Jesus said to them, "Why were you looking for me? Didn't you know that I must be in my Father's house?" ⁵⁰But they did not understand the meaning of what he said.

⁵¹Jesus went with them to Nazareth and was obedient to them. But his mother kept in her mind all that had happened. ⁵²Jesus became wiser and grew physically. People liked him, and he pleased God.

### THE PREACHING OF JOHN

**3** It was the fifteenth year of the rule of Tiberius Caesar. These men were under Caesar: Pontius Pilate, the ruler of Judea; Herod, the ruler of Galilee; Philip, Herod's brother, the ruler of Iturea and Traconitis; and Lysanias, the ruler of Abilene. ²Annas and Caiaphas were the high priests. At this time, the word of God came to John son of Zechariah in the desert. ³He went all over the area around the Jordan River preaching a baptism of changed hearts and lives for the forgiveness of sins. ⁴As it is written in the book of Isaiah the prophet:

"This is a voice of one
who calls out in the desert:
'Prepare the way for the Lord.
Make the road straight for him.
⁵Every valley should be filled in,
and every mountain and hill should be
made flat.
Roads with turns should be made straight,
and rough roads should be made
smooth.
⁶And all people will know about the
salvation of God!'" *Isaiah 40:3-5*

⁷To the crowds of people who came to be baptized by John, he said, "You are all snakes! Who warned you to run away from God's coming punishment? ⁸Do the things that show you really have changed your hearts and lives. Don't begin to say to yourselves, 'Abraham is our father.' I tell you that God could make children for Abraham from these rocks. ⁹The ax is now ready to cut down the trees, and every tree that does not produce good fruit will be cut down and thrown into the fire."ⁿ

¹⁰The people asked John, "Then what should we do?"

¹¹John answered, "If you have two shirts, share with the person who does not have one. If you have food, share that also."

¹²Even tax collectors came to John to be baptized. They said to him, "Teacher, what should we do?"

¹³John said to them, "Don't take more taxes from people than you have been ordered to take."

## beauty secret

### Design

When you look in your closet, do you notice a dominant design or color of clothes filling your wardrobe? When you are deciding on the look you want, why not consider a Scripture verse? Memorizing a verse or two about who God says you are can go a long way.

**notes**  **3:9 The ax . . . fire.** This means that God is ready to punish his people who do not obey him.

¹⁴The soldiers asked John, "What about us? What should we do?"

John said to them, "Don't force people to give you money, and don't lie about them. Be satisfied with the pay you get."

¹⁵Since the people were hoping for the Christ to come, they wondered if John might be the one.

¹⁶John answered everyone, "I baptize you with water, but there is one coming who is greater than I am. I am not good enough to untie his sandals. He will baptize you with the Holy Spirit and fire. ¹⁷He will come ready to clean the grain, separating the good grain from the chaff. He will put the good part of the grain into his barn, but he will burn the chaff with a fire that cannot be put out."ⁿ ¹⁸And John continued to preach the Good News, saying many other things to encourage the people.

¹⁹But John spoke against Herod, the governor, because of his sin with Herodias, the wife of Herod's brother, and because of the many other evil things Herod did. ²⁰So Herod did something even worse: He put John in prison.

## JESUS IS BAPTIZED BY JOHN

²¹When all the people were being baptized by John, Jesus also was baptized. While Jesus was praying, heaven opened ²²and the Holy Spirit came down on him in the form of a dove. Then a voice came from heaven, saying, "You are my Son, whom I love, and I am very pleased with you."

## THE FAMILY HISTORY OF JESUS

²³When Jesus began his ministry, he was about thirty years old. People thought that Jesus was Joseph's son.

Joseph was the sonⁿ of Heli.
²⁴Heli was the son of Matthat.
Matthat was the son of Levi.
Levi was the son of Melki.
Melki was the son of Jannai.
Jannai was the son of Joseph.
²⁵Joseph was the son of Mattathias.
Mattathias was the son of Amos.
Amos was the son of Nahum.
Nahum was the son of Esli.

Esli was the son of Naggai.
²⁶Naggai was the son of Maath.
Maath was the son of Mattathias.
Mattathias was the son of Semein.
Semein was the son of Josech.
Josech was the son of Joda.
²⁷Joda was the son of Joanan.
Joanan was the son of Rhesa.
Rhesa was the son of Zerubbabel.
Zerubbabel was the grandson of Shealtiel.
Shealtiel was the son of Neri.
²⁸Neri was the son of Melki.
Melki was the son of Addi.
Addi was the son of Cosam.
Cosam was the son of Elmadam.
Elmadam was the son of Er.
²⁹Er was the son of Joshua.
Joshua was the son of Eliezer.
Eliezer was the son of Jorim.
Jorim was the son of Matthat.
Matthat was the son of Levi.
³⁰Levi was the son of Simeon.
Simeon was the son of Judah.
Judah was the son of Joseph.
Joseph was the son of Jonam.
Jonam was the son of Eliakim.
³¹Eliakim was the son of Melea.
Melea was the son of Menna.
Menna was the son of Mattatha.
Mattatha was the son of Nathan.
Nathan was the son of David.
³²David was the son of Jesse.
Jesse was the son of Obed.
Obed was the son of Boaz.
Boaz was the son of Salmon.
Salmon was the son of Nahshon.
³³Nahshon was the son of Amminadab.
Amminadab was the son of Admin.
Admin was the son of Arni.
Arni was the son of Hezron.
Hezron was the son of Perez.
Perez was the son of Judah.
³⁴Judah was the son of Jacob.
Jacob was the son of Isaac.
Isaac was the son of Abraham.
Abraham was the son of Terah.
Terah was the son of Nahor.

³⁵Nahor was the son of Serug.
Serug was the son of Reu.
Reu was the son of Peleg.
Peleg was the son of Eber.
Eber was the son of Shelah.
³⁶Shelah was the son of Cainan.
Cainan was the son of Arphaxad.
Arphaxad was the son of Shem.
Shem was the son of Noah.
Noah was the son of Lamech.
³⁷Lamech was the son of Methuselah.
Methuselah was the son of Enoch.
Enoch was the son of Jared.
Jared was the son of Mahalalel.
Mahalalel was the son of Kenan.
³⁸Kenan was the son of Enosh.
Enosh was the son of Seth.
Seth was the son of Adam.
Adam was the son of God.

## JESUS IS TEMPTED BY THE DEVIL

4 Jesus, filled with the Holy Spirit, returned from the Jordan River. The Spirit led Jesus into the desert ²where the devil tempted Jesus for forty days. Jesus ate nothing during that time, and when those days were ended, he was very hungry.

³The devil said to Jesus, "If you are the Son of God, tell this rock to become bread."

⁴Jesus answered, "It is written in the Scriptures: 'A person does not live by eating only bread.' "ⁿ

⁵Then the devil took Jesus and showed him all the kingdoms of the world in an instant. ⁶The devil said to Jesus, "I will give you all these kingdoms and all their power and glory. It has all been given to me, and I can give it to anyone I wish. ⁷If you worship me, then it will all be yours."

⁸Jesus answered, "It is written in the Scriptures: 'You must worship the Lord your God and serve only him.' "ⁿ

⁹Then the devil led Jesus to Jerusalem and put him on a high place of the Temple. He said to Jesus, "If you are the Son of God, jump down. ¹⁰It is written in the Scriptures:

'He has put his angels in charge of you
    to watch over you.'          *Psalm 91:11*

**3:17 He will . . . out.** This means that Jesus will come to separate good people from bad people, saving the good and punishing the bad.    **3:23 son** "Son" in Jewish lists of ancestors can sometimes mean grandson or more distant relative.    **4:4 'A person . . . bread.'** Quotation from Deuteronomy 8:3.    **4:8 'You . . . him.'** Quotation from Deuteronomy 6:13.

**81**

# Music Reviews

GROUP: EVERYDAY SUNDAY

ALBUM: ANTHEMS FOR THE IMPERFECT

*Anthems for the Imperfect* unfolds as a collection of twelve modern-rock songs backed by solid guitar work and the mournful pleadings of lead singer Trey Pearson. It's full of rich lyrics and downright great songs. The second album from Everyday Sunday swings from in-your-face rock like "Bring It On" and "Something" to worshipful ballads such as "The One" (with background vocals by Relient K's Matt Thiessen) and "I Won't Give Up."

**WHY IT ROCKS: IT'S SIMPLY GREAT MODERN ROCK WITH SOMETHING POSITIVE TO SAY.**

11It is also written:

'They will catch you in their hands
    so that you will not hit your foot on a
    rock.' "
                                    *Psalm 91:12*

12Jesus answered, "But it also says in the Scriptures: 'Do not test the Lord your God.' "*n*

13After the devil had tempted Jesus in every way, he left him to wait until a better time.

## Jesus Teaches the People

14Jesus returned to Galilee in the power of the Holy Spirit, and stories about him spread all through the area. 15He began to teach in their synagogues, and everyone praised him.

16Jesus traveled to Nazareth, where he had grown up. On the Sabbath day he went to the synagogue, as he always did, and stood up to read. 17The book of Isaiah the prophet was given to him. He opened the book and found the place where this is written:

18"The Lord has put his Spirit in me,
    because he appointed me to tell the
    Good News to the poor.
He has sent me to tell the captives they are
    free
    and to tell the blind that they can see
    again.
                                    *Isaiah 61:1*
God sent me to free those who have been
    treated unfairly
                                    *Isaiah 58:6*

19    and to announce the time when the
        Lord will show his kindness."
                                    *Isaiah 61:2*

20Jesus closed the book, gave it back to the assistant, and sat down. Everyone in the synagogue was watching Jesus closely. 21He began to say to them, "While you heard these words just now, they were coming true!"

22All the people spoke well of Jesus and were amazed at the words of grace he spoke. They asked, "Isn't this Joseph's son?"

23Jesus said to them, "I know that you will tell me the old saying: 'Doctor, heal yourself.' You want to say, 'We heard about the things you did in Capernaum. Do those things here in your own town!' " 24Then Jesus said, "I tell you the truth, a prophet is not accepted in his hometown. 25But I tell you the truth, there were many widows in Israel during the time of Elijah. It did not rain in Israel for three and one-half years, and there was no food anywhere in the whole country. 26But Elijah was sent to none of those widows, only to a widow in Zarephath, a town in Sidon. 27And there were many with skin diseases living in Israel during the time of the prophet Elisha. But none of them were healed, only Naaman, who was from the country of Syria."

28When all the people in the synagogue heard these things, they became very angry. 29They got up, forced Jesus out of town, and took him to the edge of the cliff on which the town was built. They planned to throw him off the edge, 30but Jesus walked through the crowd and went on his way.

## Jesus Forces Out an Evil Spirit

31Jesus went to Capernaum, a city in Galilee, and on the Sabbath day, he taught the people. 32They were amazed at his teaching, because he spoke with authority. 33In the synagogue a man who had within him an evil spirit shouted in a loud voice, 34"Jesus of Nazareth! What do you want with us? Did you come to destroy us? I know who you are—God's Holy One!"

35Jesus commanded the evil spirit, "Be quiet! Come out of the man!" The evil spirit threw the man down to the ground before all the people and then left the man without hurting him.

36The people were amazed and said to each other, "What does this mean? With authority and power he commands evil spirits, and they come out." 37And so the news about Jesus spread to every place in the whole area.

## Jesus Heals Many People

38Jesus left the synagogue and went to the home of Simon.*n* Simon's mother-in-law was sick with a high fever, and they asked Jesus to

 **notes** 4:12 'Do . . . God.' Quotation from Deuteronomy 6:16. 4:38 Simon Simon's other name was Peter.

help her. <sup>39</sup>He came to her side and commanded the fever to leave. It left her, and immediately she got up and began serving them.

<sup>40</sup>When the sun went down, the people brought those who were sick to Jesus. Putting his hands on each sick person, he healed every one of them. <sup>41</sup>Demons came out of many people, shouting, "You are the Son of God." But Jesus commanded the demons and would not allow them to speak, because they knew Jesus was the Christ.

<sup>42</sup>At daybreak, Jesus went to a lonely place, but the people looked for him. When they found him, they tried to keep him from leaving. <sup>43</sup>But Jesus said to them, "I must preach about God's kingdom to other towns, too. This is why I was sent."

<sup>44</sup>Then he kept on preaching in the synagogues of Judea.

## JESUS' FIRST FOLLOWERS

5 One day while Jesus was standing beside Lake Galilee, many people were pressing all around him to hear the word of God. <sup>2</sup>Jesus saw two boats at the shore of the lake. The fishermen had left them and were washing their nets. <sup>3</sup>Jesus got into one of the boats, the one that belonged to Simon,<sup>n</sup> and asked him to push off a little from the land. Then Jesus sat down and continued to teach the people from the boat.

<sup>4</sup>When Jesus had finished speaking, he said to Simon, "Take the boat into deep water, and put your nets in the water to catch some fish."

<sup>5</sup>Simon answered, "Master, we worked hard all night trying to catch fish, and we caught nothing. But you say to put the nets in the water, so I will." <sup>6</sup>When the fishermen did as Jesus told them, they caught so many fish that the nets began to break. <sup>7</sup>They called to their partners in the other boat to come and help them. They came and filled both boats so full that they were almost sinking.

<sup>8</sup>When Simon Peter saw what had happened, he bowed down before Jesus and said, "Go away from me, Lord. I am a sinful man!"

## Elizabeth

## BIBLE BIOS

**[LUKE 1]** When the angel Gabriel approached Zechariah and told him that Elizabeth would definitely have a baby after years of infertility, Zechariah couldn't help but question the news. But God was not amused by his lack of faith. The whole time Elizabeth was pregnant, God silenced Zech's voice. Elizabeth, on the other hand, believed the incredible news without question, confident that God had answered her prayer. She gave birth to John (the Baptist), the cousin of Jesus and the one who later baptized him. Elizabeth didn't really have a clue about how important her son would be in Jesus' life, but God rewarded her unwavering, childlike faith beyond her wildest dreams.

<sup>9</sup>He and the other fishermen were amazed at the many fish they caught, as were <sup>10</sup>James and John, the sons of Zebedee, Simon's partners.

Jesus said to Simon, "Don't be afraid. From now on you will fish for people." <sup>11</sup>When the men brought their boats to the shore, they left everything and followed Jesus.

## JESUS HEALS A SICK MAN

<sup>12</sup>When Jesus was in one of the towns, there was a man covered with a skin disease. When he saw Jesus, he bowed before him and begged him, "Lord, you can heal me if you will."

<sup>13</sup>Jesus reached out his hand and touched the man and said, "I will. Be healed!" Immediately the disease disappeared. <sup>14</sup>Then Jesus said, "Don't tell anyone about this, but go and show yourself to the priest<sup>n</sup> and offer a gift for your healing, as Moses commanded.<sup>n</sup> This will show the people what I have done."

<sup>15</sup>But the news about Jesus spread even more. Many people came to hear Jesus and to be healed of their sicknesses, <sup>16</sup>but Jesus often slipped away to be alone so he could pray.

## JESUS HEALS A PARALYZED MAN

<sup>17</sup>One day as Jesus was teaching the people, the Pharisees and teachers of the law from every town in Galilee and Judea and from Jerusalem were there. The Lord was giving Jesus the power to heal people. <sup>18</sup>Just then, some men were carrying on a mat a man who was paralyzed. They tried to bring him in and put him down before Jesus. <sup>19</sup>But because there were so many people there, they could not find a way in. So they went up on the roof and lowered the man on his mat through the ceiling into the middle of the crowd right before Jesus. <sup>20</sup>Seeing their faith, Jesus said, "Friend, your sins are forgiven."

<sup>21</sup>The Jewish teachers of the law and the Pharisees thought to themselves, "Who is this man who is speaking as if he were God? Only God can forgive sins."

<sup>22</sup>But Jesus knew what they were thinking and said, "Why are you thinking these things? <sup>23</sup>Which is easier: to say, 'Your sins are forgiven,' or to say, 'Stand up and walk'? <sup>24</sup>But I will prove to you that the Son of Man has

**5:3 Simon** Simon's other name was Peter. **5:14 show . . . priest** The Law of Moses said a priest must say when a Jewish person with a skin disease was well. **5:14 Moses commanded** Read about this in Leviticus 14:1-32.

authority on earth to forgive sins." So Jesus said to the paralyzed man, "I tell you, stand up, take your mat, and go home."

25At once the man stood up before them, picked up his mat, and went home, praising God. 26All the people were fully amazed and began to praise God. They were filled with much respect and said, "Today we have seen amazing things!"

## LEVI FOLLOWS JESUS

27After this, Jesus went out and saw a tax collector named Levi sitting in the tax collector's booth. Jesus said to him, "Follow me!" 28So Levi got up, left everything, and followed him.

29Then Levi gave a big dinner for Jesus at his house. Many tax collectors and other people were eating there, too. 30But the Pharisees and the men who taught the law for the Pharisees began to complain to Jesus' followers, "Why do you eat and drink with tax collectors and sinners?"

31Jesus answered them, "It is not the healthy people who need a doctor, but the sick. 32I have not come to invite good people but sinners to change their hearts and lives."

## JESUS ANSWERS A QUESTION

33They said to Jesus, "John's followers often give up eating" for a certain time and pray, just as the Pharisees do. But your followers eat and drink all the time."

34Jesus said to them, "You cannot make the friends of the bridegroom give up eating while he is still with them. 35But the time will come when the bridegroom will be taken away from them, and then they will give up eating."

36Jesus told them this story: "No one takes cloth off a new coat to cover a hole in an old coat. Otherwise, he ruins the new coat, and the cloth from the new coat will not be the same as the old cloth. 37Also, no one ever pours new wine into old leather bags. Otherwise, the new wine will break the bags, the wine will spill out, and the leather bags will be ruined. 38New wine must be put into new leather bags. 39No one after drinking old wine wants new wine, because he says, 'The old wine is better.' "

## JESUS IS LORD OVER THE SABBATH

6 One Sabbath day Jesus was walking through some fields of grain. His followers picked the heads of grain, rubbed them in their hands, and ate them. 2Some Pharisees said, "Why do you do what is not lawful on the Sabbath day?"

3Jesus answered, "Have you not read what David did when he and those with him were hungry? 4He went into God's house and took and ate the holy bread, which is lawful only for priests to eat. And he gave some to the people who were with him." 5Then Jesus said to the Pharisees, "The Son of Man is Lord of the Sabbath day."

## JESUS HEALS A MAN'S HAND

6On another Sabbath day Jesus went into the synagogue and was teaching, and a man with a crippled right hand was there. 7The teachers of the law and the Pharisees were watching closely to see if Jesus would heal on the Sabbath day so they could accuse him. 8But he knew what they were thinking, and he said to the man with the crippled hand, "Stand up here in the middle of everyone." The man got

notes | **5:33 give up eating** This is called "fasting." The people would give up eating for a special time of prayer and worship to God. It was also done to show sadness and disappointment.

up and stood there. [9]Then Jesus said to them, "I ask you, which is lawful on the Sabbath day: to do good or to do evil, to save a life or to destroy it?" [10]Jesus looked around at all of them and said to the man, "Hold out your hand." The man held out his hand, and it was healed.

[11]But the Pharisees and the teachers of the law were very angry and discussed with each other what they could do to Jesus.

## "AT THAT TIME JESUS WENT OFF TO A MOUNTAIN TO PRAY, AND HE SPENT THE NIGHT PRAYING TO GOD."

### Jesus Chooses His Apostles

[12]At that time Jesus went off to a mountain to pray, and he spent the night praying to God. [13]The next morning, Jesus called his followers to him and chose twelve of them, whom he named apostles: [14]Simon (Jesus named him Peter), his brother Andrew, James, John, Philip, Bartholomew, [15]Matthew, Thomas, James son of Alphaeus, Simon (called the Zealot), [16]Judas son of James, and Judas Iscariot, who later turned Jesus over to his enemies.

### Jesus Teaches and Heals

[17]Jesus and the apostles came down from the mountain, and he stood on level ground. A large group of his followers was there, as well as many people from all around Judea, Jerusalem, and the seacoast cities of Tyre and Sidon. [18]They all came to hear Jesus teach and to be healed of their sicknesses, and he healed those who were troubled by evil spirits. [19]All the people were trying to touch Jesus, because power was coming from him and healing them all.

[20]Jesus looked at his followers and said,

"You people who are poor are happy, because the kingdom of God belongs to you.

[21]You people who are now hungry are happy, because you will be satisfied.

You people who are now crying are happy, because you will laugh with joy.

[22]"People will hate you, shut you out, insult you, and say you are evil because you follow the Son of Man. But when they do, you will be happy. [23]Be full of joy at that time, because you have a great reward waiting for you in heaven. Their ancestors did the same things to the prophets.

[24]"But how terrible it will be for you who are rich,

because you have had your easy life.

[25]How terrible it will be for you who are full now,

because you will be hungry.

How terrible it will be for you who are laughing now,

because you will be sad and cry.

[26]"How terrible when everyone says only good things about you, because their ancestors said the same things about the false prophets.

### Love Your Enemies

[27]"But I say to you who are listening, love your enemies. Do good to those who hate you, [28]bless those who curse you, pray for those who are cruel to you. [29]If anyone slaps you on one cheek, offer him the other cheek, too. If someone takes your coat, do not stop him from taking your shirt. [30]Give to everyone who asks you, and when someone takes something that is yours, don't ask for it back. [31]Do to others what you would want them to do to you. [32]If you love only the people who love you, what praise should you get? Even sinners love the people who love them. [33]If you do good only to those who do good to you, what praise should you get? Even sinners do that! [34]If you lend things to people, always hoping to get something back, what praise should you get? Even sinners lend to other sinners so that they can get back the same amount! [35]But love your enemies, do good to them, and lend to them without hoping to get anything back. Then you will have a great reward, and you will be children of the Most High God, because he is kind

even to people who are ungrateful and full of sin. [36]Show mercy, just as your Father shows mercy.

### Look at Yourselves

[37]"Don't judge other people, and you will not be judged. Don't accuse others of being guilty, and you will not be accused of being guilty. Forgive, and you will be forgiven. [38]Give, and you will receive. You will be given much. Pressed down, shaken together, and running over, it will spill into your lap. The way you give to others is the way God will give to you."

[39]Jesus told them this story: "Can a blind person lead another blind person? No! Both of them will fall into a ditch. [40]A student is not better than the teacher, but the student who has been fully trained will be like the teacher.

[41]"Why do you notice the little piece of dust in your friend's eye, but you don't notice the big piece of wood in your own eye? [42]How can you say to your friend, 'Friend, let me take that little piece of dust out of your eye' when you cannot see that big piece of wood in your own eye! You hypocrite! First, take the wood out of your own eye. Then you will see clearly to take the dust out of your friend's eye.

### Two Kinds of Fruit

[43]"A good tree does not produce bad fruit, nor does a bad tree produce good fruit. [44]Each tree is known by its own fruit. People don't

top 10

random ways to fill
a lonely friday night

**10**    Visit a local coffee-house.

**9**    Take yourself to dinner.

**8**    Read a great book.

**7**    Spend some time with God.

**6**    Write letters to old friends.

**5**    Start a scrapbook.

**4**    Eat your favorite ice cream.

**3**    Watch funny movies (not romantic ones).

**2**    Get a head start on your homework.

**1**    Invite friends over.

gather figs from thornbushes, and they don't get grapes from bushes. ⁴⁵Good people bring good things out of the good they stored in their hearts. But evil people bring evil things out of the evil they stored in their hearts. People speak the things that are in their hearts.

## TWO KINDS OF PEOPLE

⁴⁶"Why do you call me, 'Lord, Lord,' but do not do what I say? ⁴⁷I will show you what everyone is like who comes to me and hears my words and obeys. ⁴⁸That person is like a man building a house who dug deep and laid the foundation on rock. When the floods came, the water tried to wash the house away, but it could not shake it, because the house was built well. ⁴⁹But the one who hears my words and does not obey is like a man who built his house on the ground without a foundation. When the floods came, the house quickly fell and was completely destroyed."

## JESUS HEALS A SOLDIER'S SERVANT

7 When Jesus finished saying all these things to the people, he went to Capernaum. ²There was an army officer who had a servant who was very important to him. The servant was so sick he was nearly dead. ³When the officer heard about Jesus, he sent some older Jewish leaders to him to ask Jesus to come and heal his servant. ⁴The men went to Jesus and begged him, saying, "This officer is worthy of your help. ⁵He loves our people, and he built us a synagogue."

⁶So Jesus went with the men. He was getting near the officer's house when the officer sent friends to say, "Lord, don't trouble yourself, because I am not worthy to have you come into my house. ⁷That is why I did not come to you myself. But you only need to command it, and my servant will be healed. ⁸I, too, am a man under the authority of others, and I have soldiers under my command. I tell one soldier, 'Go,' and he goes. I tell another soldier, 'Come,' and he comes. I say to my servant, 'Do this,' and my servant does it."

⁹When Jesus heard this, he was amazed. Turning to the crowd that was following him, he said, "I tell you, this is the greatest faith I have found anywhere, even in Israel."

¹⁰Those who had been sent to Jesus went back to the house where they found the servant in good health.

## JESUS BRINGS A MAN BACK TO LIFE

¹¹Soon afterwards Jesus went to a town called Nain, and his followers and a large crowd traveled with him. ¹²When he came near the town gate, he saw a funeral. A mother, who was a widow, had lost her only son. A large crowd from the town was with the mother while her son was being carried out. ¹³When the Lord saw her, he felt very sorry for her and said, "Don't cry." ¹⁴He went up and touched the coffin, and the people who were carrying it stopped. Jesus said, "Young man, I tell you, get up!" ¹⁵And the son sat up and began to talk. Then Jesus gave him back to his mother.

¹⁶All the people were amazed and began praising God, saying, "A great prophet has come to us! God has come to help his people."

¹⁷This news about Jesus spread through all Judea and into all the places around there.

## JOHN ASKS A QUESTION

¹⁸John's followers told him about all these things. He called for two of his followers ¹⁹and sent them to the Lord to ask, "Are you the One who is to come, or should we wait for someone else?"

²⁰When the men came to Jesus, they said, "John the Baptist sent us to you with this question: 'Are you the One who is to come, or should we wait for someone else?' "

²¹At that time, Jesus healed many people of their sicknesses, diseases, and evil spirits, and he gave sight to many blind people. ²²Then Jesus answered John's followers, "Go tell John what you saw and heard here. The blind can see, the crippled can walk, and people with skin diseases are healed. The deaf can hear, the dead are raised to life, and the Good News is preached to the poor. ²³Those who do not

stumble in their faith because of me are blessed!"

²⁴When John's followers left, Jesus began talking to the people about John: "What did you go out into the desert to see? A reed" blown by the wind? ²⁵What did you go out to see? A man dressed in fine clothes? No, people who have fine clothes and much wealth live in kings' palaces. ²⁶But what did you go out to see? A prophet? Yes, and I tell you, John is more than a prophet. ²⁷This was written about him:

'I will send my messenger ahead of you,
who will prepare the way for you.'

*Malachi 3:1*

²⁸I tell you, John is greater than any other person ever born, but even the least important person in the kingdom of God is greater than John."

²⁹(When the people, including the tax collectors, heard this, they all agreed that God's teaching was good, because they had been baptized by John. ³⁰But the Pharisees and experts on the law refused to accept God's plan for themselves; they did not let John baptize them.)

³¹Then Jesus said, "What shall I say about the people of this time? What are they like? ³²They are like children sitting in the marketplace, calling to one another and saying,

'We played music for you, but you did not dance;
we sang a sad song, but you did not cry.'

³³John the Baptist came and did not eat bread or drink wine, and you say, 'He has a demon in him.' ³⁴The Son of Man came eating and drinking, and you say, 'Look at him! He eats too much and drinks too much wine, and he is a friend of tax collectors and sinners!' ³⁵But wisdom is proved to be right by what it does."

## a woman washes Jesus' feet

³⁶One of the Pharisees asked Jesus to eat with him, so Jesus went into the Pharisee's house and sat at the table. ³⁷A sinful woman in the town learned that Jesus was eating at the Pharisee's house. So she brought an alabaster jar of perfume ³⁸and stood behind Jesus at his feet, crying. She began to wash his feet with her tears, and she dried them with her hair, kissing them many times and rubbing them with the perfume. ³⁹When the Pharisee who asked Jesus to come to his house saw this, he thought to himself, "If Jesus were a prophet, he would know that the woman touching him is a sinner!"

⁴⁰Jesus said to the Pharisee, "Simon, I have something to say to you."

Simon said, "Teacher, tell me."

⁴¹Jesus said, "Two people owed money to the same banker. One owed five hundred coins" and the other owed fifty. ⁴²They had no money to pay what they owed, but the banker told both of them they did not have to pay him. Which person will love the banker more?"

⁴³Simon, the Pharisee, answered, "I think it would be the one who owed him the most money."

Jesus said to Simon, "You are right." ⁴⁴Then Jesus turned toward the woman and said to Simon, "Do you see this woman? When I came into your house, you gave me no water for my feet, but she washed my feet with her tears and dried them with her hair. ⁴⁵You gave me no kiss of greeting, but she has been kissing my feet since I came in. ⁴⁶You did not put oil on my head, but she poured perfume on my feet. ⁴⁷I tell you that her many sins are forgiven, so she showed great love. But the person who is forgiven only a little will love only a little."

⁴⁸Then Jesus said to her, "Your sins are forgiven."

⁴⁹The people sitting at the table began to say among themselves, "Who is this who even forgives sins?"

⁵⁰Jesus said to the woman, "Because you believed, you are saved from your sins. Go in peace."

## THE GROUP WITH JESUS

**8** After this, while Jesus was traveling through some cities and small towns, he preached and told the Good News about God's kingdom. The twelve apostles were with

# Radical Faith:

## Luke 7:44-45

In this beautiful passage, a woman marked by mistakes, impurity, guilt, and ridicule received acceptance, affirmation, and grace in her encounter with Christ. Freed from the ugliness and shame of sin, she now had a new future, and she knew real love for the first time. The woman sat at Jesus' feet expressing gratitude, love, and humility. She believed his words, and they transformed her life. She couldn't help but be grateful. This woman poured out uninhibited worship, even in front of people who would mock her—like Simon, who cared a lot about his image among the religious people. Simon didn't seem to think of himself as needing any help to be good, but the woman sitting on the floor definitely knew she needed help. Simon was slow to grasp that he, along with this woman, could only be made pure before God by receiving forgiveness for sins through Christ. Jesus looked at this woman's heart, not at her past or her reputation. He saw her response to his truth. Would you tend to see the sinful woman the way Simon did or the way Jesus did? How do you express your gratitude to Jesus for what he has done in your life?

**7:24 reed** It means that John was not ordinary or weak like grass blown by the wind. **7:41 coins** Roman denarii. One coin was the average pay for one day's work.

him, [2]and also some women who had been healed of sicknesses and evil spirits: Mary, called Magdalene, from whom seven demons had gone out; [3]Joanna, the wife of Cuza (the manager of Herod's house); Susanna; and many others. These women used their own money to help Jesus and his apostles.

## a story about planting seed

[4]When a great crowd was gathered, and people were coming to Jesus from every town, he told them this story:

[5]"A farmer went out to plant his seed. While he was planting, some seed fell by the road. People walked on the seed, and the birds ate it up. [6]Some seed fell on rock, and when it began to grow, it died because it had no water.

[7]Some seed fell among thorny weeds, but the weeds grew up with it and choked the good plants. [8]And some seed fell on good ground and grew and made a hundred times more."

As Jesus finished the story, he called out, "You people who can hear me, listen!"

[9]Jesus' followers asked him what this story meant.

[10]Jesus said, "You have been chosen to know the secrets about the kingdom of God. But I use stories to speak to other people so that:

'They will look, but they may not see.
They will listen, but they may not understand.'        *Isaiah 6:9*

[11]"This is what the story means: The seed is God's message. [12]The seed that fell beside the road is like the people who hear God's teaching, but the devil comes and takes it away from them so they cannot believe it and be saved. [13]The seed that fell on rock is like those who hear God's teaching and accept it gladly, but they don't allow the teaching to go deep into their lives. They believe for a while, but when trouble comes, they give up. [14]The seed that fell among the thorny weeds is like those who hear God's teaching, but they let the worries, riches, and pleasures of this life keep them from growing and producing good fruit. [15]And the seed that fell on the good ground is like those who hear God's teaching with good, honest hearts and obey it and patiently produce good fruit.

## use what you have

[16]"No one after lighting a lamp covers it with a bowl or hides it under a bed. Instead, the person puts it on a lampstand so those who come in will see the light. [17]Everything that is hidden will become clear, and every secret thing will be made known. [18]So be careful how you listen. Those who have understanding will be given more. But those who do not have understanding, even what they think they have will be taken away from them."

## Jesus' True Family

[19]Jesus' mother and brothers came to see him, but there was such a crowd they could not get to him. [20]Someone said to Jesus, "Your mother and your brothers are standing outside, wanting to see you."

[21]Jesus answered them, "My mother and my brothers are those who listen to God's teaching and obey it!"

## Jesus Calms a Storm

[22]One day Jesus and his followers got into a boat, and he said to them, "Let's go across the lake." And so they started across. [23]While they were sailing, Jesus fell asleep. A very strong wind blew up on the lake, causing the boat to fill with water, and they were in danger.

[24]The followers went to Jesus and woke him, saying, "Master! Master! We will drown!"

Jesus got up and gave a command to the wind and the waves. They stopped, and it became calm. [25]Jesus said to his followers, "Where is your faith?"

The followers were afraid and amazed and said to each other, "Who is this that commands even the wind and the water, and they obey him?"

## a man with demons inside him

[26]Jesus and his followers sailed across the lake from Galilee to the area of the Gerasene

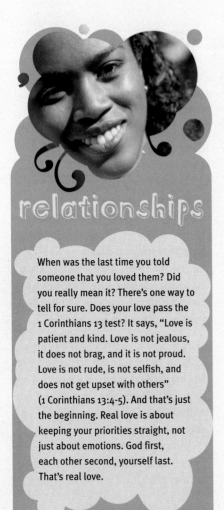

## relationships

When was the last time you told someone that you loved them? Did you really mean it? There's one way to tell for sure. Does your love pass the 1 Corinthians 13 test? It says, "Love is patient and kind. Love is not jealous, it does not brag, and it is not proud. Love is not rude, is not selfish, and does not get upset with others" (1 Corinthians 13:4-5). And that's just the beginning. Real love is about keeping your priorities straight, not just about emotions. God first, each other second, yourself last. That's real love.

people. ²⁷When Jesus got out on the land, a man from the town who had demons inside him came to Jesus. For a long time he had worn no clothes and had lived in the burial caves, not in a house. ²⁸When he saw Jesus, he cried out and fell down before him. He said with a loud voice, "What do you want with me, Jesus, Son of the Most High God? I beg you, don't torture me!" ²⁹He said this because Jesus was commanding the evil spirit to come out of the man. Many times it had taken hold of him. Though he had been kept under guard and chained hand and foot, he had broken his chains and had been forced by the demon out into a lonely place.

³⁰Jesus asked him, "What is your name?"

He answered, "Legion,"ⁿ because many demons were in him. ³¹The demons begged Jesus not to send them into eternal darkness." ³²A large herd of pigs was feeding on a hill, and the demons begged Jesus to allow them to go into the pigs. So Jesus allowed them to do this. ³³When the demons came out of the man, they went into the pigs, and the herd ran down the hill into the lake and was drowned.

³⁴When the herdsmen saw what had happened, they ran away and told about this in the town and the countryside. ³⁵And people went to see what had happened. When they came to Jesus, they found the man sitting at Jesus' feet, clothed and in his right mind, because the demons were gone. But the people were frightened. ³⁶The people who saw this happen told the others how Jesus had made the man well. ³⁷All the people of the Gerasene country asked Jesus to leave, because they were all very afraid. So Jesus got into the boat and went back to Galilee.

³⁸The man whom Jesus had healed begged to go with him, but Jesus sent him away, saying, ³⁹"Go back home and tell people how much God has done for you." So the man went all over town telling how much Jesus had done for him.

### Jesus Gives Life to a Dead Girl and Heals a Sick Woman

⁴⁰When Jesus got back to Galilee, a crowd welcomed him, because everyone was waiting for him. ⁴¹A man named Jairus, a leader of the synagogue, came to Jesus and fell at his feet, begging him to come to his house. ⁴²Jairus' only daughter, about twelve years old, was dying.

While Jesus was on his way to Jairus' house, the people were crowding all around him. ⁴³A woman was in the crowd who had been bleeding for twelve years, but no one was able to heal her. ⁴⁴She came up behind Jesus and touched the edge of his coat, and instantly her bleeding stopped. ⁴⁵Then Jesus said, "Who touched me?"

When all the people said they had not touched him, Peter said, "Master, the people are all around you and are pushing against you."

⁴⁶But Jesus said, "Someone did touch me, because I felt power go out from me." ⁴⁷When the woman saw she could not hide, she came forward, shaking, and fell down before Jesus. While all the people listened, she told why she had touched him and how she had been instantly healed. ⁴⁸Jesus said to her, "Dear woman, you are made well because you believed. Go in peace."

⁴⁹While Jesus was still speaking, someone came from the house of the synagogue leader and said to him, "Your daughter is dead. Don't bother the teacher anymore."

⁵⁰When Jesus heard this, he said to Jairus, "Don't be afraid. Just believe, and your daughter will be well."

⁵¹When Jesus went to the house, he let only Peter, John, James, and the girl's father and mother go inside with him. ⁵²All the people were crying and feeling sad because the girl was dead, but Jesus said, "Stop crying. She is not dead, only asleep."

> "JESUS TOOK HOLD OF HER HAND AND CALLED TO HER, 'MY CHILD, STAND UP!' HER SPIRIT CAME BACK INTO HER, AND SHE STOOD UP AT ONCE."

⁵³The people laughed at Jesus because they knew the girl was dead. ⁵⁴But Jesus took hold of her hand and called to her, "My child, stand up!" ⁵⁵Her spirit came back into her, and she stood up at once. Then Jesus ordered that she be given something to eat. ⁵⁶The girl's parents were amazed, but Jesus told them not to tell anyone what had happened.

### Jesus Sends Out the Apostles

9 Jesus called the twelve apostles together and gave them power and authority over all demons and the ability to

**8:30 "Legion"** Means very many. A legion was about five thousand men in the Roman army. **8:31 eternal darkness** Literally, "the abyss," something like a pit or a hole that has no end.

heal sicknesses. [2]He sent the apostles out to tell about God's kingdom and to heal the sick. [3]He said to them, "Take nothing for your trip, neither a walking stick, bag, bread, money, or extra clothes. [4]When you enter a house, stay there until it is time to leave. [5]If people do not welcome you, shake the dust off of your feet" as you leave the town, as a warning to them."

[6]So the apostles went out and traveled through all the towns, preaching the Good News and healing people everywhere.

## HEROD IS CONFUSED ABOUT JESUS

[7]Herod, the governor, heard about all the things that were happening and was confused, because some people said, "John the Baptist has risen from the dead." [8]Others said, "Elijah has come to us." And still others said, "One of the prophets who lived long ago has risen from the dead." [9]Herod said, "I cut off John's head, so who is this man I hear such things about?" And Herod kept trying to see Jesus.

## MORE THAN FIVE THOUSAND FED

[10]When the apostles returned, they told Jesus everything they had done. Then Jesus took them with him to a town called Bethsaida where they could be alone together. [11]But the people learned where Jesus went and followed him. He welcomed them and talked with them about God's kingdom and healed those who needed to be healed.

[12]Late in the afternoon, the twelve apostles came to Jesus and said, "Send the people away. They need to go to the towns and countryside around here and find places to sleep and something to eat, because no one lives in this place."

[13]But Jesus said to them, "You give them something to eat."

They said, "We have only five loaves of bread and two fish, unless we go buy food for all these people." [14](There were about five thousand men there.)

Jesus said to his followers, "Tell the people to sit in groups of about fifty people."

[15]So the followers did this, and all the people sat down. [16]Then Jesus took the five loaves of bread and two fish, and looking up to heaven, he thanked God for the food. Then he divided the food and gave it to the followers to give to the people. [17]They all ate and were satisfied, and what was left over was gathered up, filling twelve baskets.

## JESUS IS THE CHRIST

[18]One time when Jesus was praying alone, his followers were with him, and he asked them, "Who do the people say I am?"

[19]They answered, "Some say you are John the Baptist. Others say you are Elijah." And others say you are one of the prophets from long ago who has come back to life."

[20]Then Jesus asked, "But who do you say I am?"

Peter answered, "You are the Christ from God."

[21]Jesus warned them not to tell anyone, saying, [22]"The Son of Man must suffer many things. He will be rejected by the older Jewish leaders, the leading priests, and the teachers of the law. He will be killed and after three days will be raised from the dead."

[23]Jesus said to all of them, "If people want to follow me, they must give up the things they want. They must be willing to give up their lives daily to follow me. [24]Those who want to save their lives will give up true life. But those who give up their lives for me will have true life. [25]It is worth nothing for them to have the whole world if they themselves are destroyed or lost. [26]If people are ashamed of me and my teaching, then the Son of Man will be ashamed of them when he comes in his glory and with the glory of the Father and the holy angels. [27]I tell you the truth, some people standing here will see the kingdom of God before they die."

## JESUS TALKS WITH MOSES AND ELIJAH

[28]About eight days after Jesus said these things, he took Peter, John, and James and went up on a mountain to pray. [29]While Jesus was praying, the appearance of his face changed, and his clothes became shining white. [30]Then two men, Moses and Elijah,"

## Promises:

# Luke 9:18-22

There is no doubt that Jesus is one of the most controversial figures in all of history. Many people say that he was a good man—a great prophet, even. Various religions respect the good he did and even acknowledge that he was a perfect, sinless man. And those things about Jesus are true. But it is very different and supremely significant to believe that Jesus was the Son of God and that his death and resurrection are the basis for our redemption from sin.

Jesus anticipated the controversy that would surround him. The truths that he was revealing to his followers and the people of his day were extremely radical and very hard for some to believe. So Jesus asked his followers, "Who do the people say I am?" because he knew that many didn't understand exactly who he was. He then asked a much more important question: "But who do you say I am?" And he asks us that same question today, encouraging us in the midst of a multi-religion culture that he is the Son of God, and that fact is something no other religion or opinion can change.

9:5 **shake . . . feet** A warning. It showed that they had rejected these people.    9:19 **Elijah** A man who spoke for God and who lived hundreds of years before Christ. See 1 Kings 17.    9:30 **Moses and Elijah** Two of the most important Jewish leaders in the past. God had given Moses the Law, and Elijah was an important prophet.

# Blab

were talking with Jesus. ³¹They appeared in heavenly glory, talking about his departure which he would soon bring about in Jerusalem. ³²Peter and the others were very sleepy, but when they awoke fully, they saw the glory of Jesus and the two men standing with him. ³³When Moses and Elijah were about to leave, Peter said to Jesus, "Master, it is good that we are here. Let us make three tents—one for you, one for Moses, and one for Elijah." (Peter did not know what he was talking about.)

³⁴While he was saying these things, a cloud came and covered them, and they became afraid as the cloud covered them. ³⁵A voice came from the cloud, saying, "This is my Son, whom I have chosen. Listen to him!"

³⁶When the voice finished speaking, only Jesus was there. Peter, John, and James said nothing and told no one at that time what they had seen.

## Jesus Heals a Sick Boy

³⁷The next day, when they came down from the mountain, a large crowd met Jesus. ³⁸A man in the crowd shouted to him, "Teacher, please come and look at my son, because he is my only child. ³⁹An evil spirit seizes my son, and suddenly he screams. It causes him to lose control of himself and foam at the mouth. The evil spirit keeps on hurting him and almost never leaves him. ⁴⁰I begged your followers to force the evil spirit out, but they could not do it."

⁴¹Jesus answered, "You people have no faith, and your lives are all wrong. How long must I stay with you and put up with you? Bring your son here."

⁴²While the boy was coming, the demon threw him on the ground and made him lose control of himself. But Jesus gave a strong command to the evil spirit and healed the boy and gave him back to his father. ⁴³All the people were amazed at the great power of God.

## Jesus Talks About His Death

While everyone was wondering about all that Jesus did, he said to his followers, ⁴⁴"Don't forget what I tell you now: The Son of Man will be handed over to people." ⁴⁵But the followers did not understand what this meant; the meaning was hidden from them so they could not understand. But they were afraid to ask Jesus about it.

## Who Is the Greatest?

⁴⁶Jesus' followers began to have an argument about which one of them was the greatest. ⁴⁷Jesus knew what they were thinking, so he took a little child and stood the child beside him. ⁴⁸Then Jesus said, "Whoever accepts this little child in my name accepts me. And whoever accepts me accepts the One who sent me, because whoever is least among you all is really the greatest."

## Anyone Not Against Us Is For Us

⁴⁹John answered, "Master, we saw someone using your name to force demons out of people. We told him to stop, because he does not belong to our group."

⁵⁰But Jesus said to him, "Don't stop him, because whoever is not against you is for you."

## A Town Rejects Jesus

⁵¹When the time was coming near for Jesus to depart, he was determined to go to Jerusalem. ⁵²He sent some men ahead of him, who went into a town in Samaria to make everything ready for him. ⁵³But the people there would not welcome him, because he was set on going to Jerusalem. ⁵⁴When James and John, followers of Jesus, saw this, they said, "Lord, do you want us to call fire down from heaven and destroy those people?"ⁿ

⁵⁵But Jesus turned and scolded them. ⁵⁶Thenⁿ they went to another town.

## Following Jesus

⁵⁷As they were going along the road, someone said to Jesus, "I will follow you any place you go."

⁵⁸Jesus said to them, "The foxes have holes to live in, and the birds have nests, but the Son of Man has no place to rest his head."

⁵⁹Jesus said to another man, "Follow me!"

But he said, "Lord, first let me go and bury my father."

[60]But Jesus said to him, "Let the people who are dead bury their own dead. You must go and tell about the kingdom of God."

[61]Another man said, "I will follow you, Lord, but first let me go and say good-bye to my family."

[62]Jesus said, "Anyone who begins to plow a field but keeps looking back is of no use in the kingdom of God."

## JESUS SENDS OUT THE SEVENTY-TWO

**10** After this, the Lord chose seventy-two[n] others and sent them out in pairs ahead of him into every town and place where he planned to go. [2]He said to them, "There are a great many people to harvest, but there are only a few workers. So pray to God, who owns the harvest, that he will send more workers to help gather his harvest. [3]Go now, but listen! I am sending you out like sheep among wolves. [4]Don't carry a purse, a bag, or sandals, and don't waste time talking with people on the road. [5]Before you go into a house, say, 'Peace be with this house.' [6]If peaceful people live there, your blessing of peace will stay with them, but if not, then your blessing will come back to you.

[7]Stay in the peaceful house, eating and drinking what the people there give you. A worker should be given his pay. Don't move from house to house. [8]If you go into a town and the people welcome you, eat what they give you. [9]Heal the sick who live there, and tell them, 'The kingdom of God is near you.' [10]But if you go into a town, and the people don't welcome you, then go into the streets and say, [11]'Even the dirt from your town that sticks to our feet we wipe off against you.[n] But remember that the kingdom of God is near.' [12]I tell you, on the Judgment Day it will be better for the people of Sodom[n] than for the people of that town.

## JESUS WARNS UNBELIEVERS

[13]"How terrible for you, Korazin! How terrible for you, Bethsaida! If the miracles I did in you had happened in Tyre and Sidon,[n] those people would have changed their lives long ago. They would have worn rough cloth and put ashes on themselves to show they had changed. [14]But on the Judgment Day it will be better for Tyre and Sidon than for you. [15]And you, Capernaum,[n] will you be lifted up to heaven? No! You will be thrown down to the depths!

[16]"Whoever listens to you listens to me, and whoever refuses to accept you refuses to accept me. And whoever refuses to accept me refuses to accept the One who sent me."

## SATAN FALLS

[17]When the seventy-two[n] came back, they were very happy and said, "Lord, even the demons obeyed us when we used your name!"

[18]Jesus said, "I saw Satan fall like lightning from heaven. [19]Listen, I have given you power to walk on snakes and scorpions, power that is greater than the enemy has. So nothing will hurt you. [20]But you should not be happy because the spirits obey you but because your names are written in heaven."

## JESUS PRAYS TO THE FATHER

[21]Then Jesus rejoiced in the Holy Spirit and said, "I praise you, Father, Lord of heaven and earth, because you have hidden these things from the people who are wise and smart. But you have shown them to those who are like little children. Yes, Father, this is what you really wanted.

[22]"My Father has given me all things. No one knows who the Son is, except the Father. And no one knows who the Father is, except the Son and those whom the Son chooses to tell."

[23]Then Jesus turned to his followers and said privately, "You are blessed to see what you now see. [24]I tell you, many prophets and kings wanted to see what you now see, but they did not, and they wanted to hear what you now hear, but they did not."

## THE GOOD SAMARITAN

[25]Then an expert on the law stood up to test Jesus, saying, "Teacher, what must I do to get life forever?"

## Bible Basics

Some people think that **worship** only means singing to God or playing music to him, but worship is actually everything that you do to please God. Worship is reverent devotion, which means that praying, giving, singing, studying the Bible, loving your family, and thanking God are all forms of worshiping him. Every action that shows love and respect toward God and his creation is an act of worship. Many of the psalms command people to worship God by making joyful noises, being enthusiastic, playing instruments, even dancing before him. Worship is not a request; it is a duty. We were created by God to honor and revere him. We can do that by worshiping him in everything we do.

**DIDYA KNOW** 48% (9.1 MILLION) OF THE ESTIMATED 18.9 MILLION NEW CASES OF SEXUALLY TRANSMITTED DISEASES IN 2000 WERE IN 15- TO 24-YEAR-OLDS. WWW.AGI-USA.ORG

## beauty secret

### The Finest Fifteen Minutes

If beauty begins on the inside, then you need to take time to maintain your inner self. Take fifteen minutes a day to talk to God and read the Bible. You'll be surprised how much this changes your perspective about yourself and those around you.

[26]Jesus said, "What is written in the law? What do you read there?"

[27]The man answered, "Love the Lord your God with all your heart, all your soul, all your strength, and all your mind."[n] Also, "Love your neighbor as you love yourself."[n]

[28]Jesus said to him, "Your answer is right. Do this and you will live."

[29]But the man, wanting to show the importance of his question, said to Jesus, "And who is my neighbor?"

[30]Jesus answered, "As a man was going down from Jerusalem to Jericho, some robbers attacked him. They tore off his clothes, beat him, and left him lying there, almost dead. [31]It happened that a priest was going down that road. When he saw the man, he walked by on the other side. [32]Next, a Levite[n] came there, and after he went over and looked at the man, he walked by on the other side of the road. [33]Then a Samaritan[n] traveling down the road came to where the hurt man was. When he saw the man, he felt very sorry for him. [34]The Samaritan went to him, poured olive oil and wine[n] on his wounds, and bandaged them. Then he put the hurt man on his own donkey and took him to an inn where he cared for him. [35]The next day, the Samaritan brought out two coins,[n] gave them to the innkeeper, and said, 'Take care of this man. If you spend more money on him, I will pay it back to you when I come again.' "

[36]Then Jesus said, "Which one of these three men do you think was a neighbor to the man who was attacked by the robbers?"

[37]The expert on the law answered, "The one who showed him mercy."

Jesus said to him, "Then go and do what he did."

## MARY AND MARTHA

[38]While Jesus and his followers were traveling, Jesus went into a town. A woman named Martha let Jesus stay at her house. [39]Martha had a sister named Mary, who was sitting at Jesus' feet and listening to him teach. [40]But Martha was busy with all the work to be done. She went in and said, "Lord, don't you care that my sister has left me alone to do all the work? Tell her to help me."

[41]But the Lord answered her, "Martha, Martha, you are worried and upset about many things. [42]Only one thing is important. Mary has chosen the better thing, and it will never be taken away from her."

## JESUS TEACHES ABOUT PRAYER

11 One time Jesus was praying in a certain place. When he finished, one of his followers said to him, "Lord, teach us to pray as John taught his followers."

[2]Jesus said to them, "When you pray, say:

'Father, may your name always be kept holy.

May your kingdom come.

[3]Give us the food we need for each day.

[4]Forgive us for our sins,

because we forgive everyone who has done wrong to us.

And do not cause us to be tempted.' "

## CONTINUE TO ASK

[5]Then Jesus said to them, "Suppose one of you went to your friend's house at midnight and said to him, 'Friend, loan me three loaves of bread. [6]A friend of mine has come into town to visit me, but I have nothing for him to eat.' [7]Your friend inside the house answers, 'Don't bother me! The door is already locked, and my children and I are in bed. I cannot get up and give you anything.' [8]I tell you, if friendship is not enough to make him get up to give you the bread, your boldness will make him get up and give you whatever you need. [9]So I tell you, ask, and God will give to you. Search, and you will find. Knock, and the door will open for you. [10]Yes, everyone who asks will receive. The one who searches will find. And everyone who knocks will have the door opened. [11]If your children ask for a fish, which of you would give them a snake instead? [12]Or, if your children ask for an egg, would you give them a scorpion? [13]Even though you are bad, you know how to give good things to your children. How much more your heavenly Father will give the Holy Spirit to those who ask him!"

## JESUS' POWER IS FROM GOD

[14]One time Jesus was sending out a demon that could not talk. When the demon came out, the man who had been unable to speak, then spoke. The people were amazed. [15]But some of them said, "Jesus uses the power of Beelzebul, the ruler of demons, to force demons out of people."

[16]Other people, wanting to test Jesus, asked him to give them a sign from heaven. [17]But knowing their thoughts, he said to them, "Every kingdom that is divided against itself will be destroyed. And a family that is divided against itself will not continue. [18]So if Satan is divided against himself, his kingdom will not continue. You say that I use the power of Beelzebul to force out demons. [19]But if I use

 **notes** 10:27 "Love . . . mind." Quotation from Deuteronomy 6:5. 10:27 "Love . . . yourself." Quotation from Leviticus 19:18. 10:32 Levite Levites were members of the tribe of Levi who helped the Jewish priests with their work in the Temple. Read 1 Chronicles 23:24-32. 10:33 Samaritan Samaritans were people from Samaria. These people were part Jewish, but the Jews did not accept them as true Jews. Samaritans and Jews disliked each other. 10:34 olive oil and wine Oil and wine were used like medicine to soften and clean wounds. 10:35 coins Roman denarii. One coin was the average pay for one day's work.

the power of Beelzebul to force out demons, what power do your people use to force demons out? So they will be your judges. ²⁰But if I use the power of God to force out demons, then the kingdom of God has come to you.

²¹"When a strong person with many weapons guards his own house, his possessions are safe. ²²But when someone stronger comes and defeats him, the stronger one will take away the weapons the first man trusted and will give away the possessions.

²³"Anyone who is not with me is against me, and anyone who does not work with me is working against me.

> ## "ANYONE WHO IS NOT WITH ME IS AGAINST ME, AND ANYONE WHO DOES NOT WORK WITH ME IS WORKING AGAINST ME."

### THE EMPTY PERSON

²⁴"When an evil spirit comes out of a person, it travels through dry places, looking for a place to rest. But when it finds no place, it says, 'I will go back to the house I left.' ²⁵And when it comes back, it finds that house swept clean and made neat. ²⁶Then the evil spirit goes out and brings seven other spirits more evil than it is, and they go in and live there. So the person has even more trouble than before."

### PEOPLE WHO ARE TRULY HAPPY

²⁷As Jesus was saying these things, a woman in the crowd called out to Jesus, "Happy is the mother who gave birth to you and nursed you."

²⁸But Jesus said, "No, happy are those who hear the teaching of God and obey it."

### THE PEOPLE WANT A MIRACLE

²⁹As the crowd grew larger, Jesus said, "The people who live today are evil. They want to see a miracle for a sign, but no sign will be given them, except the sign of Jonah." ³⁰As Jonah was a sign for those people who lived in Nineveh, the Son of Man will be a sign for the people of this time. ³¹On the Judgment Day the Queen of the South" will stand up with the people who live now. She will show they are guilty, because she came from far away to listen to Solomon's wise teaching. And I tell you that someone greater than Solomon is here. ³²On the Judgment Day the people of Nineveh will stand up with the people who live now, and they will show that you are guilty. When Jonah preached to them, they were sorry and changed their lives. And I tell you that someone greater than Jonah is here.

### BE A LIGHT FOR THE WORLD

³³"No one lights a lamp and puts it in a secret place or under a bowl, but on a lampstand so the people who come in can see. ³⁴Your eye is a light for the body. When your eyes are good, your whole body will be full of light. But when your eyes are evil, your whole body will be full of darkness. ³⁵So be careful not to let the light in you become darkness. ³⁶If your whole body is full of light, and none of it is dark, then you will shine bright, as when a lamp shines on you."

### JESUS ACCUSES THE PHARISEES

³⁷After Jesus had finished speaking, a Pharisee asked Jesus to eat with him. So Jesus went in and sat at the table. ³⁸But the Pharisee was surprised when he saw that Jesus did not wash his hands" before the meal. ³⁹The Lord said to him, "You Pharisees clean the outside of the cup and the dish, but inside you are full of greed and evil. ⁴⁰You foolish people! The same one who made what is outside also made what is inside. ⁴¹So give what is in your dishes to the poor, and then you will be fully clean. ⁴²How terrible for you Pharisees! You give God one-tenth of even your mint, your rue, and every other plant in your garden. But you fail to be fair to others and to love God. These are the things you should do while continuing to do those other things. ⁴³How terrible for you Pharisees, because you love to have the most important seats in the

## Radical Faith

# Luke 11:1-4

When do you pray? Before meals or at bedtime? Whenever life seems hard? Those are all common times of prayer for a lot of Christians. But Jesus made it clear that we're supposed to pray a whole lot more than that. Why? Because you need God even more than you realize. During Jesus' life on earth, he insisted on spending time connecting with his Father through prayer. Jesus didn't just talk about prayer. He lived a life full of prayer. Even when things were out-of-control busy and people were counting on him to do lots of good things, Jesus would take off to have some quality time with his Father. There were times when people came long distances to hear Jesus teach. Many of them were sick, and some were even dying; but even with such important needs, Jesus still slipped away to be alone so he could pray. It was a matter of dependence; it was absolutely vital. In order to live the abundant life God wants you to live, you have to connect with God on a daily basis. You'll fall into sin if you're left to yourself. You *need* him. He is your resting place, your stronghold, your light, and your life source. Connect with him at every opportunity.

**11:29 sign of Jonah** Jonah's three days in the fish are like Jesus' three days in the tomb. See Matthew 12:40.   **11:31 Queen of the South** The Queen of Sheba. She traveled a thousand miles to learn God's wisdom from Solomon. Read 1 Kings 10:1-3.   **11:38 wash his hands** This was a Jewish religious custom that the Pharisees thought was very important.

# LEARN I+ & LIVE I+

**Luke 11:9**
**Learn It:** Ask and God will give to you.
**Live It:** Don't be afraid to ask God for your heart's desires, but first ask God to make your desires what he wants for you.

**Luke 11:28**
**Learn It:** People who hear God's teaching and obey it are happy.
**Live It:** Grab opportunities to hear God's Word being taught—at church, at conferences, and at youth group.

**Luke 14:34**
**Learn It:** As salt is only good if it has its salty taste, your faith is only good and effective if you stay true and committed to it.
**Live It:** Look for practical ways to demonstrate your faith as part of your lifestyle.

synagogues, and you love to be greeted with respect in the marketplaces. ⁴⁴How terrible for you, because you are like hidden graves, which people walk on without knowing."

## Jesus Talks to Experts on the Law

⁴⁵One of the experts on the law said to Jesus, "Teacher, when you say these things, you are insulting us, too."

⁴⁶Jesus answered, "How terrible for you, you experts on the law! You make strict rules that are very hard for people to obey, but you yourselves don't even try to follow those rules. ⁴⁷How terrible for you, because you build tombs for the prophets whom your ancestors killed! ⁴⁸And now you show that you approve of what your ancestors did. They killed the prophets, and you build tombs for them! ⁴⁹This is why in his wisdom God said, 'I will send prophets and apostles to them. They will kill some, and they will treat others cruelly.' ⁵⁰So you who live now will be punished for the deaths of all the prophets who were killed since the beginning of the world— ⁵¹from the killing of Abel to the killing of Zechariah,ⁿ who died between the altar and the Temple. Yes, I tell you that you who are alive now will be punished for them all.

⁵²"How terrible for you, you experts on the law. You have taken away the key to learning about God. You yourselves would not learn, and you stopped others from learning, too."

⁵³When Jesus left, the teachers of the law and the Pharisees began to give him trouble, asking him questions about many things, ⁵⁴trying to catch him saying something wrong.

## Don't Be Like the Pharisees

**12** So many thousands of people had gathered that they were stepping on each other. Jesus spoke first to his followers, saying, "Beware of the yeast of the Pharisees, because they are hypocrites. ²Everything that is hidden will be shown, and everything that is secret will be made known. ³What you have said in the dark will be heard in the light, and

# Music Reviews

| GROUP: | ALBUM: |
|---|---|
| BENJAMIN GATE | [UNTITLED] [CLASSIC HIT] |

Even though this band from South Africa is no longer together, this album is a must-have for rock fans. Adrienne Liesching's throaty vocals and high emotional intensity make this music sparkle. Check out the unforgettable "Lay It Down," the upbeat "All Over Me," and the pleading-for-Jesus "How Long," which begs for his return. The Benjamin Gate was one of Christian music's only female-fronted true rock bands and deserves to be added to your collection.

**WHY IT ROCKS: ADRIENNE LIESCHING SHOWS WITH PASSION AND PANACHE THAT GIRLS CAN ROCK 'N' ROLL WITH THE BEST OF THEM.**

 **notes**    **11:51 Abel . . . Zechariah** In the Hebrew Old Testament, the first and last men to be murdered.

what you have whispered in an inner room will be shouted from the housetops.

⁴"I tell you, my friends, don't be afraid of people who can kill the body but after that can do nothing more to hurt you. ⁵I will show you the one to fear. Fear the one who has the power to kill you and also to throw you into hell. Yes, this is the one you should fear.

⁶"Five sparrows are sold for only two pennies, and God does not forget any of them. ⁷But God even knows how many hairs you have on your head. Don't be afraid. You are worth much more than many sparrows.

## DON'T BE ASHAMED OF JESUS

⁸"I tell you, all those who stand before others and say they believe in me, I, the Son of Man, will say before the angels of God that they belong to me. ⁹But all who stand before others and say they do not believe in me, I will say before the angels of God that they do not belong to me.

¹⁰"Anyone who speaks against the Son of Man can be forgiven, but anyone who speaks against the Holy Spirit will not be forgiven.

¹¹"When you are brought into the synagogues before the leaders and other powerful people, don't worry about how to defend yourself or what to say. ¹²At that time the Holy Spirit will teach you what you must say."

## JESUS WARNS AGAINST SELFISHNESS

¹³Someone in the crowd said to Jesus, "Teacher, tell my brother to divide with me the property our father left us."

¹⁴But Jesus said to him, "Who said I should judge or decide between you?" ¹⁵Then Jesus said to them, "Be careful and guard against all kinds of greed. Life is not measured by how much one owns."

¹⁶Then Jesus told this story: "There was a rich man who had some land, which grew a good crop. ¹⁷He thought to himself, 'What will I do? I have no place to keep all my crops.' ¹⁸Then he said, 'This is what I will do: I will tear down my barns and build bigger ones, and there I will store all my grain and other goods. ¹⁹Then I can say to myself, "I have enough good things stored to last for many years. Rest, eat, drink, and enjoy life!"'

²⁰"But God said to him, 'Foolish man! Tonight your life will be taken from you. So who will get those things you have prepared for yourself?'

²¹"This is how it will be for those who store up things for themselves and are not rich toward God."

## DON'T WORRY

²²Jesus said to his followers, "So I tell you, don't worry about the food you need to live, or about the clothes you need for your body. ²³Life is more than food, and the body is more than clothes. ²⁴Look at the birds. They don't plant or harvest, they don't have storerooms or barns, but God feeds them. And you are worth much more than birds. ²⁵You cannot add any time to your life by worrying about it. ²⁶If you cannot do even the little things, then why worry about the big things? ²⁷Consider how the lilies grow; they don't work or make clothes for themselves. But I tell you that even Solomon with his riches was not dressed as beautifully as one of these flowers. ²⁸God clothes the grass in the field, which is alive today but tomorrow is thrown into the fire. So how much more will God clothe you? Don't have so little faith! ²⁹Don't always think about what you will eat or what you will drink, and don't keep worrying. ³⁰All the people in the world are trying to get these things, and your Father knows you need them. ³¹But seek God's kingdom, and all the other things you need will be given to you.

## DON'T TRUST IN MONEY

³²"Don't fear, little flock, because your Father wants to give you the kingdom. ³³Sell your possessions and give to the poor. Get for yourselves purses that will not wear out, the treasure in heaven that never runs out, where thieves can't steal and moths can't destroy. ³⁴Your heart will be where your treasure is.

## ALWAYS BE READY

³⁵"Be dressed, ready for service, and have your lamps shining. ³⁶Be like servants who are

## Luke 12:8

Ever felt left out? That you didn't fit into a certain clique at school or were alienated from something you wanted to be a part of? Remember the character of Elle Woods in the movie *Legally Blonde*? Moving from sunny California to Harvard Law School, Elle was a pair of bright-pink-stilettos in a sensible-black-pumps kind of world. She stood out because she was different. And the others made fun of her and were mean to her for not being like them instead of accepting her differences. She was pushed out of the group and forced to work extra hard to earn their acceptance and respect.

Does this sound familiar to you? It is really frustrating to be separated from a group of people you want to be a part of. It's hurtful. It's unfair. And, unfortunately, these types of cliques can happen all the time—even among Christians. It's not right, but it happens. So how cool is it to know that Jesus actually claims you as his own? You are chosen to be on the same team as the Son of God! He doesn't alienate or discriminate—he loves you, protects you, and delights in you.

# quiz

# are you OBSESSED WITH celebrity?

**1. QUICK: HOW MANY CELEBRITY COUPLES CAN YOU NAME RIGHT OFF THE TOP OF YOUR HEAD?**

A.  1.
B.  2 or 3.
C.  5 +.

**2. THE WALLS OF YOUR ROOM ARE COVERED WITH:**

A.  Original, funky art.
B.  Posters of Orlando Bloom and Chad Michael Murray.
C.  Pictures of you and your friends.

**3. DO YOU BASE YOUR OWN FASHION STYLE ON WHAT YOUR FAVE CELEBRITIES ARE WEARING?**

A.  Occasionally.
B.  Never.
C.  Often.

**4. IN THE LAST MONTH, HOW MANY CELEBRITY MAGAZINES (LIKE *US WEEKLY* OR *PEOPLE*) HAVE YOU PURCHASED?**

A.  Several.
B.  1 or 2.
C.  Never buy them.

**5. YOU HAVE A WEBSITE DEDICATED SOLELY TO YOUR FAVORITE MOVIE STAR:**

A.  True.
B.  False.

**6. WHEN WATCHING TV, YOU'RE MOST LIKELY TO FLIP ON:**

A.  *The O.C.*
B.  *7th Heaven.*
C.  *Newlyweds.*

**SCORING:**   1. A=2, B=3, C=4    2. A=2, B=4, C=3    3. A=3, B=2, C=4    4. A=4, B=3, C=2    5. A=4, B=0    6. A=3, B=2, C=4

**IF YOU SCORED BETWEEN 19 AND 24, YOU ARE TOTALLY OBSESSED:**

The lives of the rich and famous seem pretty great, right? Not necessarily. Celebrities do have a lot of great stuff, but that doesn't mean you should base your life on what they're doing or not doing. Stay out of stalker mode, please.

**IF YOU SCORED BETWEEN 15 AND 18, YOU HAVE A SLIGHT INFATUATION:**

Following the crazy lives of celebrities is usually interesting and sometimes fun, but you don't let yourself get too carried away by it all. Besides, remember how tired you got of hearing about Bennifer?

**IF YOU SCORED BETWEEN 10 AND 14, YOU ARE UNIMPRESSED:**

You are generally unimpressed with the life and loves of today's celebrities. Not a bad thing.

waiting for their master to come home from a wedding party. When he comes and knocks, the servants immediately open the door for him. ³⁷They will be blessed when their master comes home, because he sees that they were watching for him. I tell you the truth, the master will dress himself to serve and tell the servants to sit at the table, and he will serve them. ³⁸Those servants will be happy when he comes in and finds them still waiting, even if it is midnight or later.

³⁹"Remember this: If the owner of the house knew what time a thief was coming, he would not allow the thief to enter his house. ⁴⁰So you also must be ready, because the Son of Man will come at a time when you don't expect him!"

## WHO IS THE TRUSTED SERVANT?

⁴¹Peter said, "Lord, did you tell this story to us or to all people?"

⁴²The Lord said, "Who is the wise and trusted servant that the master trusts to give the other servants their food at the right time? ⁴³When the master comes and finds the servant doing his work, the servant will be blessed. ⁴⁴I tell you the truth, the master will choose that servant to take care of everything he owns. ⁴⁵But suppose the servant thinks to himself, 'My master will not come back soon,' and he begins to beat the other servants, men and women, and to eat and drink and get drunk. ⁴⁶The master will come when that servant is not ready and is not expecting him. Then the master will cut him in pieces and send him away to be with the others who don't obey.

⁴⁷"The servant who knows what his master wants but is not ready, or who does not do what the master wants, will be beaten with many blows! ⁴⁸But the servant who does not know what his master wants and does things that should be punished will be beaten with few blows. From everyone who has been given much, much will be demanded. And from the one trusted with much, much more will be expected.

## JESUS CAUSES DIVISION

⁴⁹"I came to set fire to the world, and I wish it were already burning! ⁵⁰I have a baptism" to

suffer through, and I feel very troubled until it is over. ⁵¹Do you think I came to give peace to the earth? No, I tell you, I came to divide it. ⁵²From now on, a family with five people will be divided, three against two, and two against three. ⁵³They will be divided: father against son and son against father, mother against daughter and daughter against mother, mother-in-law against daughter-in-law and daughter-in-law against mother-in-law."

## UNDERSTANDING THE TIMES

⁵⁴Then Jesus said to the people, "When you see clouds coming up in the west, you say, 'It's going to rain,' and it happens. ⁵⁵When you feel the wind begin to blow from the south, you say, 'It will be a hot day,' and it happens. ⁵⁶Hypocrites! You know how to understand the appearance of the earth and sky. Why don't you understand what is happening now?

## SETTLE YOUR PROBLEMS

⁵⁷"Why can't you decide for yourselves what is right? ⁵⁸If your enemy is taking you to court, try hard to settle it on the way. If you don't, your enemy might take you to the judge, and the judge might turn you over to the officer, and the officer might throw you into jail. ⁵⁹I tell you, you will not get out of there until you have paid everything you owe."

## CHANGE YOUR HEARTS

**13** At that time some people were there who told Jesus that Pilate" had killed some people from Galilee while they were worshiping. He mixed their blood with the blood of the animals they were sacrificing to God. ²Jesus answered, "Do you think this happened to them because they were more sinful than all others from Galilee? ³No, I tell you. But unless you change your hearts and lives, you will be destroyed as they were! ⁴What about those eighteen people who died when the tower of Siloam fell on them? Do you think they were more sinful than all the others who live in Jerusalem? ⁵No, I tell you. But unless you change your hearts and lives, you will all be destroyed too!"

**Q:** My mom is getting remarried, and I am going to have stepsisters. One of them will share my room when she visits. I want to get along, but I don't really want to share my space. Is that selfish?

**A:** It's great that you want to start off right, and it's okay to wish you could keep your own room. Why not make your stepsister a basket of gift soaps, candles, candy bars, and other cool stuff as a welcome gift? While you're at it, make one for yourself, too. Celebrate together when she comes over.

**Q:** My parents just said we are moving and I will have to change schools. I am so mad. I don't want to move. Can you help?

**A:** If your parents have decided to move, you have to go with them. Ask God to help you make the best of it. Keep in touch with your old friends (collect phone numbers and email addresses), and make new ones in your new school. Instead of dwelling on what you are losing, try to focus on what good things are ahead.

**Q:** I'm about to graduate, and my divorced parents do not get along. In fact, my mom said she won't come to graduation if my dad is there. I want both parents there. Help!

**A:** Ask your mom to give you her presence as your graduation gift, and pray for her. If your mom still refuses to come, remember that it is her loss. Ask God to comfort you and not let her absence ruin your big day. If you have a stepmom there, thank her for her support.

**12:50 I . . . baptism** Jesus was talking about the suffering he would soon go through. **13:1 Pilate** Pontius Pilate was the Roman governor of Judea from A.D. 26 to A.D. 36.

## Radical Faith:

# Luke 14:26-27

Jesus pretty much says, "You're either with me, or you're not. And if you're with me, you're in it all the way." God has given you lots of amazing things to enjoy on earth. Think about all the things you love in life. They're wonderful, but they are still created things that will never compare to the actual Creator. Jesus wants us to choose him above all else. In fact, in the Ten Commandments, God says we aren't supposed to have any other gods before him. In other words, God is supposed to be top priority in our lives. If you stick with Jesus and have first devotion to him, you have your priorities in order. You will care more about him than your comfort, your reputation, and always getting your own way. Putting God first means making a lot of sacrifices, but Jesus promises that it's totally worth it in the long run. Look at your daily life and do a reality check. Who or what do you give more attention to than God? What controls your decisions? What do your actions say about your real priorities? What's really getting top billing in your life?

## THE USELESS TREE

⁶Jesus told this story: "A man had a fig tree planted in his vineyard. He came looking for some fruit on the tree, but he found none. ⁷So the man said to his gardener, 'I have been looking for fruit on this tree for three years, but I never find any. Cut it down. Why should it waste the ground?' ⁸But the servant answered, 'Master, let the tree have one more year to produce fruit. Let me dig up the dirt around it and put on some fertilizer. ⁹If the tree produces fruit next year, good. But if not, you can cut it down.' "

## JESUS HEALS ON THE SABBATH

¹⁰Jesus was teaching in one of the synagogues on the Sabbath day. ¹¹A woman was there who, for eighteen years, had an evil spirit in her that made her crippled. Her back was always bent; she could not stand up straight. ¹²When Jesus saw her, he called her over and said, "Woman, you are free from your sickness." ¹³Jesus put his hands on her, and immediately she was able to stand up straight and began praising God.

¹⁴The synagogue leader was angry because Jesus healed on the Sabbath day. He said to the people, "There are six days when one has to work. So come to be healed on one of those days, and not on the Sabbath day."

¹⁵The Lord answered, "You hypocrites! Doesn't each of you untie your work animals and lead them to drink water every day—even on the Sabbath day? ¹⁶This woman that I healed, a daughter of Abraham, has been held by Satan for eighteen years. Surely it is not wrong for her to be freed from her sickness on a Sabbath day!" ¹⁷When Jesus said this, all of those who were criticizing him were ashamed, but the entire crowd rejoiced at all the wonderful things Jesus was doing.

## STORIES OF MUSTARD SEED AND YEAST

¹⁸Then Jesus said, "What is God's kingdom like? What can I compare it with? ¹⁹It is like a mustard seed that a man plants in his garden. The seed grows and becomes a tree, and the wild birds build nests in its branches."

²⁰Jesus said again, "What can I compare God's kingdom with? ²¹It is like yeast that a woman took and hid in a large tub of flour until it made all the dough rise."

## THE NARROW DOOR

²²Jesus was teaching in every town and village as he traveled toward Jerusalem. ²³Someone said to Jesus, "Lord, will only a few people be saved?"

Jesus said, ²⁴"Try hard to enter through the narrow door, because many people will try to enter there, but they will not be able. ²⁵When the owner of the house gets up and closes the door, you can stand outside and knock on the door and say, 'Sir, open the door for us.' But he will answer, 'I don't know you or where you come from.' ²⁶Then you will say, 'We ate and drank with you, and you taught in the streets of our town.' ²⁷But he will say to you, 'I don't know you or where you come from. Go away from me, all you who do evil!' ²⁸You will cry and grind your teeth with pain when you see Abraham, Isaac, Jacob, and all the prophets in God's kingdom, but you yourselves thrown outside. ²⁹People will come from the east, west, north, and south and will sit down at the table in the kingdom of God. ³⁰There are those who have the lowest place in life now who will have the highest place in the future. And there are those who have the highest place now who will have the lowest place in the future."

## JESUS WILL DIE IN JERUSALEM

³¹At that time some Pharisees came to Jesus and said, "Go away from here! Herod wants to kill you!"

³²Jesus said to them, "Go tell that fox Herod, 'Today and tomorrow I am forcing demons out and healing people. Then, on the third day, I will reach my goal.' ³³Yet I must be on my way today and tomorrow and the next day. Surely it cannot be right for a prophet to be killed anywhere except in Jerusalem.

³⁴"Jerusalem, Jerusalem! You kill the prophets and stone to death those who are sent to you. Many times I wanted to gather your people as a hen gathers her chicks under

her wings, but you would not let me. 35Now your house is left completely empty. I tell you, you will not see me until that time when you will say, 'God bless the One who comes in the name of the Lord.' "*n*

## Healing on the Sabbath

14 On a Sabbath day, when Jesus went to eat at the home of a leading Pharisee, the people were watching Jesus very closely. 2And in front of him was a man with dropsy.*n* 3Jesus said to the Pharisees and experts on the law, "Is it right or wrong to heal on the Sabbath day?" 4But they would not answer his question. So Jesus took the man, healed him, and sent him away. 5Jesus said to the Pharisees and teachers of the law, "If your child or ox falls into a well on the Sabbath day, will you not pull him out quickly?" 6And they could not answer him.

## Don't Make Yourself Important

7When Jesus noticed that some of the guests were choosing the best places to sit, he told this story: 8"When someone invites you to a wedding feast, don't take the most important seat, because someone more important than you may have been invited. 9The host, who invited both of you, will come to you and say, 'Give this person your seat.' Then you will be embarrassed and will have to move to the last place. 10So when you are invited, go sit in a seat that is not important. When the host comes to you, he may say, 'Friend, move up here to a more important place.' Then all the other guests will respect you. 11All who make themselves great will be made humble, but those who make themselves humble will be made great."

## You Will Be Rewarded

12Then Jesus said to the man who had invited him, "When you give a lunch or a dinner, don't invite only your friends, your family, your other relatives, and your rich neighbors. At another time they will invite you to eat with them, and you will be repaid. 13Instead, when you give a feast, invite the poor, the crippled, the lame, and the blind. 14Then you will be blessed, because they have nothing and cannot pay you back. But you will be repaid when the good people rise from the dead."

## A Story About a Big Banquet

15One of those at the table with Jesus heard these things and said to him, "Happy are the people who will share in the meal in God's kingdom."

16Jesus said to him, "A man gave a big banquet and invited many people. 17When it was time to eat, the man sent his servant to tell the guests, 'Come. Everything is ready.'

18"But all the guests made excuses. The first one said, 'I have just bought a field, and I must go look at it. Please excuse me.' 19Another said, 'I have just bought five pairs of oxen; I must go and try them. Please excuse me.' 20A third person said, 'I just got married; I can't come.' 21So the servant returned and told his master what had happened. Then the master became angry and said, 'Go at once into the streets and alleys of the town, and bring in the poor, the crippled, the blind, and the lame.' 22Later the servant said to him, 'Master, I did what you commanded, but we still have room.' 23The master said to the servant, 'Go out to the roads and country lanes, and urge the people there to come so my house will be full. 24I tell you, none of those whom I invited first will eat with me.' "

## Luke 15:10, 24

Picture this. It's a nice Saturday afternoon and your dad decides it's the perfect day for some much-needed yard work. You get the job of raking leaves while your younger sis is responsible for the weed pulling. At the end of the day, when the jobs are done, Dad promises you both a trip to the mall. So you work hard all afternoon, raking and raking, but when you look for your sis, she's gone and the weeds still peek out of the flowerbed.

Dad is disappointed that she didn't do her job, but when she comes home from her friend's house and apologizes, he hugs her and forgives her. In fact, she still gets to go the mall! This isn't fair, right? Well, that's exactly how the older brother in this chapter felt. But that's not the point Jesus was trying to make with this parable. He was trying to tell us that he doesn't expect us to be perfect—he knows we can't do it. So when we mess up and then run to him for forgiveness, he doesn't reject us for being sinful, but embraces and forgives us. In fact, when we come to God honestly wanting to get our heart back on track, it says the angels actually throw a party in excitement! Pretty cool, huh?

GUYS SPEAK OUT

**Q:** What hurts you the most?
**A:** "When people laugh at my mistakes. Especially girls, because they are the ones I'm trying to impress."

notes    **13:35** 'God . . . Lord.' Quotation from Psalm 118:26.   **14:2** dropsy A sickness that causes the body to swell larger and larger.

## THE COST OF BEING JESUS' FOLLOWER

25Large crowds were traveling with Jesus, and he turned and said to them, 26"If anyone comes to me but loves his father, mother, wife, children, brothers, or sisters—or even life—more than me, he cannot be my follower. 27Whoever is not willing to carry the cross and follow me cannot be my follower. 28If you want to build a tower, you first sit down and decide how much it will cost, to see if you have enough money to finish the job. 29If you don't, you might lay the foundation, but you would not be able to finish. Then all who would see it would make fun of you, 30saying, 'This person began to build but was not able to finish.'

31"If a king is going to fight another king, first he will sit down and plan. He will decide if he and his ten thousand soldiers can defeat the other king who has twenty thousand soldiers. 32If he can't, then while the other king is still far away, he will send some people to speak to him and ask for peace. 33In the same way, you must give up everything you have to be my follower.

## DON'T LOSE YOUR INFLUENCE

34"Salt is good, but if it loses its salty taste, you cannot make it salty again. 35It is no good for the soil or for manure; it is thrown away.

"You people who can hear me, listen."

## "THE TAX COLLECTORS AND SINNERS ALL CAME TO LISTEN TO JESUS."

## A LOST SHEEP, A LOST COIN

15 The tax collectors and sinners all came to listen to Jesus. 2But the Pharisees and the teachers of the law began to complain: "Look, this man welcomes sinners and even eats with them."

3Then Jesus told them this story: 4"Suppose one of you has a hundred sheep but loses one of them. Then he will leave the other ninety-nine sheep in the open field and go out and look for the lost sheep until he finds it. 5And when he finds it, he happily puts it on his shoulders 6and goes home. He calls to his friends and neighbors and says, 'Be happy with me because I found my lost sheep.' 7In the same way, I tell you there is more joy in heaven over one sinner who changes his heart and life, than over ninety-nine good people who don't need to change.

8"Suppose a woman has ten silver coins," but loses one. She will light a lamp, sweep the house, and look carefully for the coin until she finds it. 9And when she finds it, she will call her friends and neighbors and say, 'Be happy with me because I have found the coin that I lost.' 10In the same way, there is joy in the presence of the angels of God when one sinner changes his heart and life."

## THE SON WHO LEFT HOME

11Then Jesus said, "A man had two sons. 12The younger son said to his father, 'Give me my share of the property.' So the father divided the property between his two sons. 13Then the younger son gathered up all that was his and traveled far away to another country. There he wasted his money in foolish living. 14After he had spent everything, a time came when there was no food anywhere in the country, and the son was poor and hungry. 15So he got a job with one of the citizens there who sent the son into the fields to feed pigs. 16The son was so hungry that he wanted to eat the pods the pigs were eating, but no one gave him anything. 17When he realized what he was doing, he thought, 'All of my father's servants have plenty of food. But I am here, almost dying with hunger. 18I will leave and return to my father and say to him, "Father, I have sinned against God and have done wrong to you. 19I am no longer worthy to be called your son, but let me be like one of your servants."' 20So the son left and went to his father.

"While the son was still a long way off, his father saw him and felt sorry for his son. So the father ran to him and hugged and kissed him. 21The son said, 'Father, I have sinned against God and have done wrong to you. I am no longer worthy to be called your son.' 22But

## BIBLE BIOS

# Esther

[BOOK OF ESTHER] Once a government official named Haman planned to kill all the Jews in Persia. But God used a courageous woman to thwart Haman's evil plot. Esther was a Jewish virgin and had reached the perfect age for marriage, when the king of Persia, Xerxes, decided he wanted a new queen. So the most beautiful women in the kingdom became queens-in-training and received beauty treatments for a whole year before the big pageant in which Xerxes would pick his queen. Esther won, hands down. And once she was queen, she used her position to help save the Jewish people. Right place, right time, right girl.

notes    **15:8 silver coins** Roman denarii. One coin was the average pay for one day's work.

the father said to his servants, 'Hurry! Bring the best clothes and put them on him. Also, put a ring on his finger and sandals on his feet. 23And get our fat calf and kill it so we can have a feast and celebrate. 24My son was dead, but now he is alive again! He was lost, but now he is found!' So they began to celebrate.

25"The older son was in the field, and as he came closer to the house, he heard the sound of music and dancing. 26So he called to one of the servants and asked what all this meant. 27The servant said, 'Your brother has come back, and your father killed the fat calf, because your brother came home safely.' 28The older son was angry and would not go in to the feast. So his father went out and begged him to come in. 29But the older son said to his father, 'I have served you like a slave for many years and have always obeyed your commands. But you never gave me even a young goat to have at a feast with my friends. 30But your other son, who wasted all your money on prostitutes, comes home, and you kill the fat calf for him!' 31The father said to him, 'Son, you are always with me, and all that I have is yours. 32We had to celebrate and be happy because your brother was dead, but now he is alive. He was lost, but now he is found.' "

## TRUE WEALTH

**16** Jesus also said to his followers, "Once there was a rich man who had a manager to take care of his business. This manager was accused of cheating him. 2So he called the manager in and said to him, 'What is this I hear about you? Give me a report of what you have done with my money, because you can't be my manager any longer.' 3The manager thought to himself, 'What will I do since my master is taking my job away from me? I am not strong enough to dig ditches, and I am ashamed to beg. 4I know what I'll do so that when I lose my job people will welcome me into their homes.'

5"So the manager called in everyone who owed the master any money. He asked the first one, 'How much do you owe?' 6He answered, 'Eight hundred gallons of olive oil.' The manager said to him, 'Take your bill, sit down quickly, and write four hundred gallons.' 7Then the manager asked another one, 'How much do you owe?' He answered, 'One thousand bushels of wheat.' Then the manager said to him, 'Take your bill and write eight hundred bushels.' 8So, the master praised the dishonest manager for being smart. Yes, worldly people are smarter with their own kind than spiritual people are.

9"I tell you, make friends for yourselves using worldly riches so that when those riches are gone, you will be welcomed in those homes that continue forever. 10Whoever can be trusted with a little can also be trusted with a lot, and whoever is dishonest with a little is dishonest with a lot. 11If you cannot be trusted with worldly riches, then who will trust you with true riches? 12And if you cannot be trusted with things that belong to someone else, who will give you things of your own?

13"No servant can serve two masters. The servant will hate one master and love the other, or will follow one master and refuse to follow the other. You cannot serve both God and worldly riches."

## GOD'S LAW CANNOT BE CHANGED

14The Pharisees, who loved money, were listening to all these things and made fun of Jesus. 15He said to them, "You make yourselves look good in front of people, but God knows what is really in your hearts. What is important to people is hateful in God's sight.

16"The law of Moses and the writings of the prophets were preached until John" came. Since then the Good News about the kingdom of God is being told, and everyone tries to

**16:16 John** John the Baptist, who preached to people about Christ's coming (Matthew 3, Luke 3).

enter it by force. [17]It would be easier for heaven and earth to pass away than for the smallest part of a letter in the law to be changed.

## DIVORCE AND REMARRIAGE

[18]"If a man divorces his wife and marries another woman, he is guilty of adultery, and the man who marries a divorced woman is also guilty of adultery."

## THE RICH MAN AND LAZARUS

[19]Jesus said, "There was a rich man who always dressed in the finest clothes and lived in luxury every day. [20]And a very poor man named Lazarus, whose body was covered with sores, was laid at the rich man's gate. [21]He wanted to eat only the small pieces of food that fell from the rich man's table. And the dogs would come and lick his sores. [22]Later, Lazarus died, and the angels carried him to the arms of Abraham. The rich man died, too, and was buried. [23]In the place of the dead, he was in much pain. The rich man saw Abraham far away with Lazarus at his side. [24]He called, 'Father Abraham, have mercy on me! Send Lazarus to dip his finger in water and cool my tongue, because I am suffering in this fire!' [25]But Abraham said, 'Child, remember when you were alive you had the good things in life, but bad things happened to Lazarus. Now he is comforted here, and you are suffering. [26]Besides, there is a big pit between you and us, so no one can cross over to you, and no one can leave there and come here.' [27]The rich man said, 'Father, then please send Lazarus to my father's house. [28]I have five brothers, and

goes to them from the dead, they would believe and change their hearts and lives.' [31]But Abraham said to him, 'If they will not listen to Moses and the prophets, they will not listen to someone who comes back from the dead.' "

## SIN AND FORGIVENESS

**17** Jesus said to his followers, "Things that cause people to sin will happen, but how terrible for the person who causes them to happen! [2]It would be better for you to be thrown into the sea with a large stone around your neck than to cause one of these little ones to sin. [3]So be careful!

"If another follower sins, warn him, and if he is sorry and stops sinning, forgive him. [4]If he sins against you seven times in one day and says that he is sorry each time, forgive him."

## HOW BIG IS YOUR FAITH?

[5]The apostles said to the Lord, "Give us more faith!"

[6]The Lord said, "If your faith were the size of a mustard seed, you could say to this mulberry tree, 'Dig yourself up and plant yourself in the sea,' and it would obey you.

## BE GOOD SERVANTS

[7]"Suppose one of you has a servant who has been plowing the ground or caring for the sheep. When the servant comes in from working in the field, would you say, 'Come in and sit down to eat'? [8]No, you would say to him, 'Prepare something for me to eat. Then get yourself ready and serve me. After I finish eating and drinking, you can eat.' [9]The servant does not get any special

## relationships

Proverbs 31:30 says, "Charm can fool you, and beauty can trick you, but a woman who respects the LORD should be praised." Do you drop your friends like hot potatoes in order to flirt with the football players at the next table? Flirting can be fun, but it isn't always harmless. Flirting is exercising power over someone else, trying to get a reaction. Remember that you are probably going to be somebody's wife someday, and the guys you are flirting with will most likely be somebody else's husbands. Keep flirting to a minimum; just be yourself.

## BE THANKFUL

[11]While Jesus was on his way to Jerusalem, he was going through the area between Samaria and Galilee. [12]As he came into a small town, ten men who had a skin disease met him there. They did not come close to Jesus [13]but called to him, "Jesus! Master! Have mercy on us!"

[14]When Jesus saw the men, he said, "Go and show yourselves to the priests."[n]

As the ten men were going, they were healed. [15]When one of them saw that he was healed, he went back to Jesus, praising God in a loud voice. [16]Then he bowed down at Jesus' feet and thanked him. (And this man was a Samaritan.) [17]Jesus said, "Weren't ten men

**DIDYA KNOW** **ONLY ONE IN TEN 17-YEAR-OLDS HAS MORE THAN TWO HOURS OF HOMEWORK PER NIGHT.** UNIVERSITY OF MICHIGAN

Lazarus could warn them so that they will not come to this place of pain.' [29]But Abraham said, 'They have the law of Moses and the writings of the prophets; let them learn from them.' [30]The rich man said, 'No, father Abraham! If someone

thanks for doing what his master commanded. [10]It is the same with you. When you have done everything you are told to do, you should say, 'We are unworthy servants; we have only done the work we should do.' "

notes
17:14 show . . . priests The Law of Moses said a priest must say when a person with a skin disease became well.

# Blab

**Q:** What are spiritual gifts, and how do you get them?

**A:** Spiritual gifts are abilities people have in areas like teaching, being wise, leading, playing music, and more. They benefit the body of Christ and others. God gives them to you at birth, and it's your job to discover them and use them. Ask a pastor or youth leader to help you figure out yours.

**Q:** My parents like hymns, but I love modern worship. How can I convince them that I am worshiping God, even though it's to a rock 'n' roll beat?

**A:** Explain to them how it helps you draw close to God. Show them the words to the music. If this doesn't convince them, chalk it up to a difference in tastes, and just ask their permission to keep listening to what you like.

**Q:** I have a strong desire to make a difference in my community but don't know where to start. Got any ideas?

**A:** It's totally cool that you want to help out. Start with your church, and see if there is a homeless shelter or food kitchen where you can volunteer. Support a local charity with a portion of your allowance, or check out www.volunteermatch.org and click on your state for more ideas.

---

healed? Where are the other nine? [18]Is this Samaritan the only one who came back to thank God?" [19]Then Jesus said to him, "Stand up and go on your way. You were healed because you believed."

## GOD'S KINGDOM IS WITHIN YOU

[20]Some of the Pharisees asked Jesus, "When will the kingdom of God come?"

Jesus answered, "God's kingdom is coming, but not in a way that you will be able to see with your eyes. [21]People will not say, 'Look, here it is!' or, 'There it is!' because God's kingdom is within[n] you."

[22]Then Jesus said to his followers, "The time will come when you will want very much to see one of the days of the Son of Man. But you will not see it. [23]People will say to you, 'Look, there he is!' or, 'Look, here he is!' Stay where you are; don't go away and search.

## WHEN JESUS COMES AGAIN

[24]"When the Son of Man comes again, he will shine like lightning, which flashes across the sky and lights it up from one side to the other. [25]But first he must suffer many things and be rejected by the people of this time. [26]When the Son of Man comes again, it will be as it was when Noah lived. [27]People were eating, drinking, marrying, and giving their children to be married until the day Noah entered the boat. Then the flood came and killed them all. [28]It will be the same as during the time of Lot. People were eating, drinking, buying, selling, planting, and building. [29]But the day Lot left Sodom,[n] fire and sulfur rained down from the sky and killed them all. [30]This is how it will be when the Son of Man comes again.

[31]"On that day, a person who is on the roof and whose belongings are in the house should not go inside to get them. A person who is in the field should not go back home. [32]Remember Lot's wife.[n] [33]Those who try to keep their lives will lose them. But those who give up their lives will save them. [34]I tell you, on that night two people will be sleeping in one bed; one will be taken and the other will be left. [35]There will be two women grinding grain together; one will be taken, and the other will be left." [36][n]

[37]The followers asked Jesus, "Where will this be, Lord?"

Jesus answered, "Where there is a dead body, there the vultures will gather."

## GOD WILL ANSWER HIS PEOPLE

**18** Then Jesus used this story to teach his followers that they should always pray and never lose hope. [2]"In a certain town there was a judge who did not respect God or care about people. [3]In that same town there was a widow who kept coming to this judge, saying, 'Give me my rights against my enemy.' [4]For a while the judge refused to help her. But afterwards, he thought to himself, 'Even though I don't respect God or care about people, [5]I will see that she gets her rights. Otherwise she will continue to bother me until I am worn out.' "

> ## "THE BLIND MAN CRIED OUT, 'JESUS, SON OF DAVID, HAVE MERCY ON ME!' "

[6]The Lord said, "Listen to what the unfair judge said. [7]God will always give what is right to his people who cry to him night and day, and he will not be slow to answer them. [8]I tell you, God will help his people quickly. But when the Son of Man comes again, will he find those on earth who believe in him?"

## BEING RIGHT WITH GOD

[9]Jesus told this story to some people who thought they were very good and looked down on everyone else: [10]"A Pharisee and a tax collector both went to the Temple to pray. [11]The Pharisee stood alone and prayed, 'God, I thank you that I am not like other people who steal, cheat, or take part in adultery, or even like this tax collector. [12]I give up eating[n] twice a week, and I give one-tenth of everything I get!'

[13]"The tax collector, standing at a distance, would not even look up to heaven. But he beat on

---

**17:21 within** Or "among." **17:29 Sodom** City that God destroyed because the people were so evil. **17:32 Lot's wife** A story about what happened to Lot's wife is found in Genesis 19:15-17, 26. **17:36 Verse 36** A few Greek copies add verse 36: "Two people will be in the field. One will be taken, and the other will be left." **18:12 give up eating** This is called "fasting." The people would give up eating for a special time of prayer and worship to God. It was also done to show sadness and disappointment.

his chest because he was so sad. He said, 'God, have mercy on me, a sinner.' ¹⁴I tell you, when this man went home, he was right with God, but the Pharisee was not. All who make themselves great will be made humble, but all who make themselves humble will be made great."

## WHO WILL ENTER GOD'S KINGDOM?

¹⁵Some people brought even their babies to Jesus so he could touch them. When the followers saw this, they told them to stop. ¹⁶But Jesus called for the children, saying, "Let the little children come to me. Don't stop them, because the kingdom of God belongs to people who are like these children. ¹⁷I tell you the truth, you must accept the kingdom of God as if you were a child, or you will never enter it."

## A RICH MAN'S QUESTION

¹⁸A certain leader asked Jesus, "Good Teacher, what must I do to have life forever?"

¹⁹Jesus said to him, "Why do you call me good? Only God is good. ²⁰You know the commands: 'You must not be guilty of adultery. You must not murder anyone. You must not steal. You must not tell lies about your neighbor. Honor your father and mother.' "ⁿ

²¹But the leader said, "I have obeyed all these commands since I was a boy."

²²When Jesus heard this, he said to him, "There is still one more thing you need to do.

Sell everything you have and give it to the poor, and you will have treasure in heaven. Then come and follow me." ²³But when the man heard this, he became very sad, because he was very rich.

²⁴Jesus looked at him and said, "It is very hard for rich people to enter the kingdom of God. ²⁵It is easier for a camel to go through the eye of a needle than for a rich person to enter the kingdom of God."

## WHO CAN BE SAVED?

²⁶When the people heard this, they asked, "Then who can be saved?"

²⁷Jesus answered, "God can do things that are not possible for people to do."

²⁸Peter said, "Look, we have left everything and followed you."

²⁹Jesus said, "I tell you the truth, all those who have left houses, wives, brothers, parents, or children for the kingdom of God ³⁰will get much more in this life. And in the age that is coming, they will have life forever."

## JESUS WILL RISE FROM THE DEAD

³¹Then Jesus took the twelve apostles aside and said to them, "We are going to Jerusalem. Everything the prophets wrote about the Son of Man will happen. ³²He will be turned over to those who are evil. They will laugh at him, insult him, spit on him, ³³beat him with whips, and kill him. But on the third day, he will rise to life again." ³⁴The apostles did not understand this; the meaning was hidden from them, and they did not realize what was said.

## JESUS HEALS A BLIND MAN

³⁵As Jesus came near the city of Jericho, a blind man was sitting beside the road, begging. ³⁶When he heard the people coming down the road, he asked, "What is happening?"

³⁷They told him, "Jesus, from Nazareth, is going by."

³⁸The blind man cried out, "Jesus, Son of David, have mercy on me!"

³⁹The people leading the group warned the blind man to be quiet. But the blind man shouted even more, "Son of David, have mercy on me!"

## RadicalFaith:

# Luke 18:1-8

In this story, Jesus tells of a woman who was so determined to get justice that she kept going to the judge even after he continually refused to help her. She needed help, and she wasn't afraid to keep asking for it. She simply refused to give up. Jesus used this story to explain how much God wants you to persistently come to him with your needs and with your heart. God wants to see your faith expressed in prayer. Coming to him in prayer shows that you believe he's able to handle your needs, that he can do anything imaginable in your life, and that he cares about every issue and concern you have. God may not do what you suggest or ask, but he'll always do what's right. He is just—that's his character and that doesn't change. Even if you don't see him work in the way you expect or in the timing you'd like, he'll do good things through your prayers. He will honor your efforts. Persistence is key because you are living by faith, which means you're not going by what you can necessarily see, feel, or understand. You're trusting the Lord completely and depending on his perfect wisdom.

## GUYS SPEAK OUT

**Q:** What bugs you the most about girls?
**A:** "Well, I know this is, like, chemical, but the mood swings bug me the most. One minute they are happy and talking to you; the next they are mad and won't talk to you."

 notes 18:20 'You . . . mother.' Quotation from Exodus 20:12-16; Deuteronomy 5:16-20.

⁴⁰Jesus stopped and ordered the blind man to be brought to him. When he came near, Jesus asked him, ⁴¹"What do you want me to do for you?"

He said, "Lord, I want to see."

⁴²Jesus said to him, "Then see. You are healed because you believed."

⁴³At once the man was able to see, and he followed Jesus, thanking God. All the people who saw this praised God.

## zacchaeus meets Jesus

**19** Jesus was going through the city of Jericho. ²A man was there named Zacchaeus, who was a very important tax collector, and he was wealthy. ³He wanted to see who Jesus was, but he was not able because he was too short to see above the crowd. ⁴He ran ahead to a place where Jesus would come, and he climbed a sycamore tree so he could see him. ⁵When Jesus came to that place, he looked up and said to him, "Zacchaeus, hurry and come down! I must stay at your house today."

⁶Zacchaeus came down quickly and welcomed him gladly. ⁷All the people saw this and began to complain, "Jesus is staying with a sinner!"

⁸But Zacchaeus stood and said to the Lord, "I will give half of my possessions to the poor. And if I have cheated anyone, I will pay back four times more."

⁹Jesus said to him, "Salvation has come to this house today, because this man also belongs to the family of Abraham. ¹⁰The Son of Man came to find lost people and save them."

## a story about three servants

¹¹As the people were listening to this, Jesus told them a story because he was near Jerusalem and they thought God's kingdom would appear immediately. ¹²He said: "A very important man went to a country far away to be made a king and then to return home. ¹³So he called ten of his servants and gave a coin" to each servant. He said, 'Do business with this money until I get back.' ¹⁴But the people in the kingdom hated the man. So they sent a group to follow him and say, 'We don't want this man to be our king.'

¹⁵"But the man became king. When he returned home, he said, 'Call those servants who have my money so I can know how much they earned with it.'

¹⁶"The first servant came and said, 'Sir, I earned ten coins with the one you gave me.' ¹⁷The king said to the servant, 'Excellent! You are a good servant. Since I can trust you with small things, I will let you rule over ten of my cities.'

¹⁸"The second servant said, 'Sir, I earned five coins with your one.' ¹⁹The king said to this servant, 'You can rule over five cities.'

²⁰"Then another servant came in and said to the king, 'Sir, here is your coin which I wrapped in a piece of cloth and hid. ²¹I was afraid of you, because you are a hard man. You even take money that you didn't earn and gather food that you didn't plant.' ²²Then the king said to the servant, 'I will condemn you by your own words, you evil servant. You knew that I am a hard man, taking money that I didn't earn and gathering food that I didn't plant. ²³Why then didn't you put my money in the bank? Then when I came back, my money would have earned some interest.'

²⁴"The king said to the men who were standing by, 'Take the coin away from this servant and give it to the servant who earned ten coins.' ²⁵They said, 'But sir, that servant already has ten coins.' ²⁶The king said, 'Those who have will be given more, but those who do not have anything will have everything taken away from them. ²⁷Now where are my enemies who didn't want me to be king? Bring them here and kill them before me.' "

## Jesus enters Jerusalem as a king

²⁸After Jesus said this, he went on toward Jerusalem. ²⁹As Jesus came near Bethphage and Bethany, towns near the hill called the Mount of Olives, he sent out two of his followers. ³⁰He said, "Go to the town you can see there. When you enter it, you will find a colt tied there, which no one has ever ridden. Untie it and bring it here to me. ³¹If anyone asks you why you are untying it, say that the Master needs it."

³²The two followers went into town and found the colt just as Jesus had told them. ³³As they were untying it, its owners came out and asked the followers, "Why are you untying our colt?"

³⁴The followers answered, "The Master needs it." ³⁵So they brought it to Jesus, threw their coats on the colt's back, and put Jesus on

### DIDYA KNOW

**MORE THAN TWO-THIRDS OF TEENS AND KIDS LIVE IN A HOME WITH A VIDEO GAME SYSTEM.**

NATIONAL INSTITUTE ON MEDIA AND THE FAMILY

## beauty secret

### Split Ends

Do you have a problem with split ends? Are you ever tempted to pull off that part of the hair? Don't! This isn't healthy for your hair because it further destroys the hair shaft. Instead, make an appointment for a haircut and allow a professional to take care of any frayed ends.

19:13 **coin** A Greek "mina." One mina was enough money to pay a person for working three months.

it. ³⁶As Jesus rode toward Jerusalem, others spread their coats on the road before him.

³⁷As he was coming close to Jerusalem, on the way down the Mount of Olives, the whole crowd of followers began joyfully shouting praise to God for all the miracles they had seen. ³⁸They said,

"God bless the king who comes in the
name of the Lord! *Psalm 118:26*
There is peace in heaven and glory to God!"

³⁹Some of the Pharisees in the crowd said to Jesus, "Teacher, tell your followers not to say these things."

⁴⁰But Jesus answered, "I tell you, if my followers didn't say these things, then the stones would cry out."

## JESUS CRIES FOR JERUSALEM

⁴¹As Jesus came near Jerusalem, he saw the city and cried for it, ⁴²saying, "I wish you knew today what would bring you peace. But now it is hidden from you. ⁴³The time is coming when your enemies will build a wall around you and will hold you in on all sides. ⁴⁴They will destroy you and all your people, and not one stone will be left on another. All this will happen because you did not recognize the time when God came to save you."

## JESUS GOES TO THE TEMPLE

⁴⁵Jesus went into the Temple and began to throw out the people who were selling things there. ⁴⁶He said, "It is written in the Scriptures, 'My Temple will be a house for prayer.'ⁿ But you have changed it into a 'hideout for robbers'!'ⁿ"

⁴⁷Jesus taught in the Temple every day. The leading priests, the experts on the law, and some of the leaders of the people wanted to kill Jesus. ⁴⁸But they did not know how they could do it, because all the people were listening closely to him.

## JEWISH LEADERS QUESTION JESUS

**20** One day Jesus was in the Temple, teaching the people and telling them the Good News. The leading priests, teachers of the law, and older leaders came up to talk with him, ²saying, "Tell us what authority you have to do these things? Who gave you this authority?"

³Jesus answered, "I will also ask you a question. Tell me: ⁴When John baptized people, was that authority from God or just from other people?"

⁵They argued about this, saying, "If we answer, 'John's baptism was from God,' Jesus will say, 'Then why did you not believe him?' ⁶But if we say, 'It was from other people,' all the

people will stone us to death, because they believe John was a prophet." ⁷So they answered that they didn't know where it came from.

⁸Jesus said to them, "Then I won't tell you what authority I have to do these things."

## A STORY ABOUT GOD'S SON

⁹Then Jesus told the people this story: "A man planted a vineyard and leased it to some farmers. Then he went away for a long time. ¹⁰When it was time for the grapes to be picked, he sent a servant to the farmers to get some of the grapes. But they beat the servant and sent him away empty-handed. ¹¹Then he sent another servant. They beat this servant also, and showed no respect for him, and sent him away empty-handed. ¹²So the man sent a third servant. The farmers wounded him and threw him out. ¹³The owner of the vineyard said, 'What will I do now? I will send my son whom I love. Maybe they will respect him.' ¹⁴But when the farmers saw the son, they said to each other, 'This son will inherit the vineyard. If we kill him, it will be ours.' ¹⁵So the farmers threw the son out of the vineyard and killed him.

"What will the owner of this vineyard do to them? ¹⁶He will come and kill those farmers and will give the vineyard to other farmers."

# *Music Reviews*

| GROUP: | ALBUM: |
|--------|--------|
| GOTEE | 10 YEARS BRAND NEW |

Gotee Records was cofounded in the 1990s by dc talk's tobyMac to bring urban sounds to the forefront of Christian music, and it has succeeded in a big way. Some of the coolest Christian acts like Relient K, Jennifer Knapp, John Reuben, Verbs, Out of Eden, and other hip groups all call Gotee their label home. *Gotee: 10 Years Brand New* celebrates the label's first decade with twenty-one hits from their top bands, including "They All Fall Down" from GRITS, Jennifer Knapp's "Undo Me," Relient K's "Sadie Hawkins Dance," Paul Wright's "Your Love Never Changes," "Thank You" from The Katinas, and lots more.

**WHY IT ROCKS: 21 HIP HITS FOR AROUND TEN BUCKS—ENOUGH SAID.**

**notes** **19:46** '**My Temple . . . prayer.**' Quotation from Isaiah 56:7. **19:46** '**hideout for robbers**' Quotation from Jeremiah 7:11.

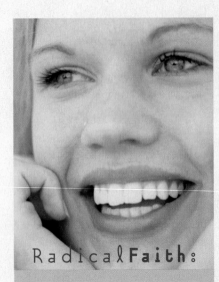

R a d i c a l **Faith**:

# Luke 21:1-4

While everyone else was dropping loads of cash into the offering box, one woman walked by and dropped in only two little coins. Jesus stopped in his tracks and directed everyone's attention her way. Why? She gave two coins, not two *crates* of coins. But Jesus said she gave more than all the rest of them. Jesus admired her generosity and surrender of resources. She gave all she had. She gave everything. Now that's sacrifice! This woman's offering expressed genuine love for and devotion to God. Other people gave and still had plenty left over. They may not have even noticed anything was gone from their bank account. Jesus praised her gift because it's not about what you have to offer, but what you're willing to give. Give from a willing heart as a way to honor God. Seek opportunities to offer your time, abilities, and resources for God's use. Give regardless of your comfort and convenience so God can work through you. A willing heart is about caring and taking action, not simply using lip service and a list of righteous acts to make you look good. Live with your heart in God's hands and give him all you've got.

When the people heard this story, they said, "Let this never happen!"

<sup>17</sup>But Jesus looked at them and said, "Then what does this verse mean:

'The stone that the builders rejected

became the cornerstone'? *Psalm 118:22*

<sup>18</sup>Everyone who falls on that stone will be broken, and the person on whom it falls, that person will be crushed!"

<sup>19</sup>The teachers of the law and the leading priests wanted to arrest Jesus at once, because they knew the story was about them. But they were afraid of what the people would do.

## IS IT RIGHT TO PAY TAXES OR NOT?

<sup>20</sup>So they watched Jesus and sent some spies who acted as if they were sincere. They wanted to trap Jesus in saying something wrong so they could hand him over to the authority and power of the governor. <sup>21</sup>So the spies asked Jesus, "Teacher, we know that what you say and teach is true. You pay no attention to who people are, and you always teach the truth about God's way. <sup>22</sup>Tell us, is it right for us to pay taxes to Caesar or not?"

<sup>23</sup>But Jesus, knowing they were trying to trick him, said, <sup>24</sup>"Show me a coin. Whose image and name are on it?"

They said, "Caesar's."

<sup>25</sup>Jesus said to them, "Then give to Caesar the things that are Caesar's, and give to God the things that are God's."

<sup>26</sup>So they were not able to trap Jesus in anything he said in the presence of the people. And being amazed at his answer, they became silent.

## SOME SADDUCEES TRY TO TRICK JESUS

<sup>27</sup>Some Sadducees, who believed people would not rise from the dead, came to Jesus. <sup>28</sup>They asked, "Teacher, Moses wrote that if a man's brother dies and leaves a wife but no children, then that man must marry the widow and have children for his brother. <sup>29</sup>Once there were seven brothers. The first brother married and died, but had no chil-

dren. <sup>30</sup>Then the second brother married the widow, and he died. <sup>31</sup>And the third brother married the widow, and he died. The same thing happened with all seven brothers; they died and had no children. <sup>32</sup>Finally, the woman died also. <sup>33</sup>Since all seven brothers had married her, whose wife will she be when people rise from the dead?"

# "GIVE TO CAESAR THE THINGS THAT ARE CAESAR'S, AND GIVE TO GOD THE THINGS THAT ARE GOD'S."

<sup>34</sup>Jesus said to them, "On earth, people marry and are given to someone to marry. <sup>35</sup>But those who will be worthy to be raised from the dead and live again will not marry, nor will they be given to someone to marry. <sup>36</sup>In that life they are like angels and cannot die. They are children of God, because they have been raised from the dead. <sup>37</sup>Even Moses clearly showed that the dead are raised to life. When he wrote about the burning bush," he said that the Lord is 'the God of Abraham, the God of Isaac, and the God of Jacob.'" <sup>38</sup>God is the God of the living, not the dead, because all people are alive to him."

<sup>39</sup>Some of the teachers of the law said, "Teacher, your answer was good." <sup>40</sup>No one was brave enough to ask him another question.

## IS THE CHRIST THE SON OF DAVID?

<sup>41</sup>Then Jesus said, "Why do people say that the Christ is the Son of David? <sup>42</sup>In the book of Psalms, David himself says:

'The Lord said to my Lord:

Sit by me at my right side,

<sup>43</sup>  until I put your enemies under your

control.'" *Psalm 110:1*

<sup>44</sup>David calls the Christ 'Lord,' so how can the Christ be his son?"

---

**20:37 burning bush** Read Exodus 3:1-12 in the Old Testament.  **20:37 'the God of . . . Jacob'** These words are taken from Exodus 3:6.  **20:43 until . . . control** Literally, "until I make your enemies a footstool for your feet."

## Jesus Accuses Some Leaders

⁴⁵While all the people were listening, Jesus said to his followers, ⁴⁶"Beware of the teachers of the law. They like to walk around wearing fancy clothes, and they love for people to greet them with respect in the marketplaces. They love to have the most important seats in the synagogues and at feasts. ⁴⁷But they cheat widows and steal their houses and then try to make themselves look good by saying long prayers. They will receive a greater punishment."

## True Giving

21 As Jesus looked up, he saw some rich people putting their gifts into the Temple money box.ⁿ ²Then he saw a poor widow putting two small copper coins into the box. ³He said, "I tell you the truth, this poor widow gave more than all those rich people. ⁴They gave only what they did not need. This woman is very poor, but she gave all she had to live on."

## The Temple Will Be Destroyed

⁵Some people were talking about the Temple and how it was decorated with beautiful stones and gifts offered to God.

But Jesus said, ⁶"As for these things you are looking at, the time will come when not one stone will be left on another. Every stone will be thrown down."

⁷They asked Jesus, "Teacher, when will these things happen? What will be the sign that they are about to take place?"

⁸Jesus said, "Be careful so you are not fooled. Many people will come in my name, saying, 'I am the One' and, 'The time has come!' But don't follow them. ⁹When you hear about wars and riots, don't be afraid, because these things must happen first, but the end will come later."

¹⁰Then he said to them, "Nations will fight against other nations, and kingdoms against other kingdoms. ¹¹In various places there will be great earthquakes, sicknesses, and a lack of food. Fearful events and great signs will come from heaven.

¹²"But before all these things happen, people will arrest you and treat you cruelly. They will judge you in their synagogues and put you in jail and force you to stand before kings and governors, because you follow me. ¹³But this will give you an opportunity to tell about me. ¹⁴Make up your minds not to worry ahead of time about what you will say. ¹⁵I will give you the wisdom to say things that none of your enemies will be able to stand against or prove wrong. ¹⁶Even your parents, brothers, relatives, and friends will turn against you, and they will kill some of you. ¹⁷All people will hate you because you follow me. ¹⁸But none of these things can really harm you. ¹⁹By continuing to have faith you will save your lives.

## Jerusalem Will Be Destroyed

²⁰"When you see armies all around Jerusalem, you will know it will soon be destroyed. ²¹At that time, the people in Judea should run away to the mountains. The people in Jerusalem must get out, and those who are

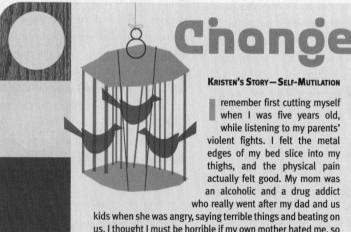

# Changed Lives

### Kristen's Story—Self-Mutilation

I remember first cutting myself when I was five years old, while listening to my parents' violent fights. I felt the metal edges of my bed slice into my thighs, and the physical pain actually felt good. My mom was an alcoholic and a drug addict who really went after my dad and us kids when she was angry, saying terrible things and beating on us. I thought I must be horrible if my own mother hated me, so I kept cutting myself and beating my arms and legs against walls. When I was 12, I asked Christ into my heart, but I didn't know how to deal with the pain inside of me. Through high school, I really led a double life—all together with good grades and everything on the outside—but unable to stop cutting on myself. I graduated and was accepted into college; but when I was 19, my double life finally fell apart. I just couldn't keep the mask in place anymore, and I began to lose track of time. My blackouts were eventually diagnosed as multiple personality disorder. Then I began to starve myself, as well as binge and purge. I also began drinking. My life was a mess. I tried to kill myself on more than one occasion. I was hospitalized several times and even landed in the county jail while they tried to find a bed for me in a state psychiatric hospital. After a final suicide attempt, I came to the conclusion that God was not going to let me die. I was out of options. Then a counselor got me an application to a Christian girls' home. I decided I wanted to change and began learning about the Bible. I heard for the first time that I could take authority over my suicidal thoughts. Kicking my bad habits was hard, and I left the program a couple of times. But God didn't give up on me. I quit drinking and no longer binged and purged. I was able to stop taking medications for mental illness, returned to college, and graduated with a degree in psychology. Now I get to work with other teen girls who struggle like I did. God has set me free.

*If you or someone you know needs help with cutting and self-harming behaviors, visit www.abundantlifeacademy.com. For information about residential care for females, visit www.mercyministries.com. (Names have been changed for the sake of privacy. Kristen tells her story after going through biblically based counseling with Mercy Ministries.)*

**21:1 money box** A special box in the Jewish place of worship where people put their gifts to God.

near the city should not go in. ²²These are the days of punishment to bring about all that is written in the Scriptures. ²³How terrible it will be for women who are pregnant or have nursing babies! Great trouble will come upon this land, and God will be angry with these people. ²⁴They will be killed by the sword and taken as prisoners to all nations. Jerusalem will be crushed by non-Jewish people until their time is over.

### DON'T FEAR

²⁵"There will be signs in the sun, moon, and stars. On earth, nations will be afraid and confused because of the roar and fury of the sea. ²⁶People will be so afraid they will faint, wondering what is happening to the world, because the powers of the heavens will be shaken. ²⁷Then people will see the Son of Man coming in a cloud with power and great glory. ²⁸When these things begin to happen, look up and hold your heads high, because the time when God will free you is near!"

### JESUS' WORDS WILL LIVE FOREVER

²⁹Then Jesus told this story: "Look at the fig tree and all the other trees. ³⁰When their leaves appear, you know that summer is near. ³¹In the same way, when you see these things happening, you will know that God's kingdom is near.

³²"I tell you the truth, all these things will happen while the people of this time are still living. ³³Earth and sky will be destroyed, but the words I have spoken will never be destroyed.

### BE READY ALL THE TIME

³⁴"Be careful not to spend your time feasting, drinking, or worrying about worldly things. If you do, that day might come on you suddenly, ³⁵like a trap on all people on earth. ³⁶So be ready all the time. Pray that you will be strong enough to escape all these things that will happen and that you will be able to stand before the Son of Man."

³⁷During the day, Jesus taught the people in the Temple, and at night he went out of the city and stayed on the Mount of Olives. ³⁸Every morning all the people got up early to go to the Temple to listen to him.

### JUDAS BECOMES AN ENEMY OF JESUS

**22** It was almost time for the Feast of Unleavened Bread, called the Passover Feast. ²The leading priests and teachers of the law were trying to find a way to kill Jesus, because they were afraid of the people.

³Satan entered Judas Iscariot, one of Jesus' twelve apostles. ⁴Judas went to the leading priests and some of the soldiers who guarded the Temple and talked to them about a way to hand Jesus over to them. ⁵They were pleased and agreed to give Judas money. ⁶He agreed and watched for the best time to hand Jesus over to them when he was away from the crowd.

### JESUS EATS THE PASSOVER MEAL

⁷The Day of Unleavened Bread came when the Passover lambs had to be sacrificed. ⁸Jesus said to Peter and John, "Go and prepare the Passover meal for us to eat."

⁹They asked, "Where do you want us to prepare it?" ¹⁰Jesus said to them, "After you go into the city, a man carrying a jar of water will meet you. Follow him into the house that he enters, ¹¹and tell the owner of the house, 'The Teacher says: Where is the guest room in which I may eat the Passover meal with my followers?' ¹²Then he will show you a large, furnished room upstairs. Prepare the Passover meal there."

¹³So Peter and John left and found everything as Jesus had said. And they prepared the Passover meal.

### THE LORD'S SUPPER

¹⁴When the time came, Jesus and the apostles were sitting at the table. ¹⁵He said to them, "I wanted very much to eat this Passover meal with you before I suffer. ¹⁶I will not eat another Passover meal until it is given its true meaning in the kingdom of God."

¹⁷Then Jesus took a cup, gave thanks, and said, "Take this cup and share it among yourselves. ¹⁸I will not drink again from the fruit of the vine" until God's kingdom comes."

¹⁹Then Jesus took some bread, gave thanks,

**notes**    **22:18 fruit of the vine** Product of the grapevine; this may also be translated "wine."

112

# April

**1** April Fools' Day! Play a funny joke on someone you love.

**2** Learn how to make chili. Share it with your family.

**3**

**4** Study hard. Take time to review your notes from your classes.

**5**

**6** Pray for your parents every night this week.

**7** April is National Frog Month. Rib-bet.

**8**

**9** Get honest with God in your prayer time. Tell him what is really on your mind.

**10** Pray for a person of influence: It's Mandy Moore's birthday.

**11**

**12** Read Ephesians 6. Tell a friend about what you learned.

**13** Ask your mom or dad how you can help them out today.

**14** Floss at least three times this week.

**15**

**16**

**17**

**18** Reach out to a person of a different race. Make a new friend.

**19** Pray for a person of influence: Kate Hudson is having a birthday.

**20**

**21**

**22** Earth Day. Get a group of friends to pick up trash in a nearby park.

**23**

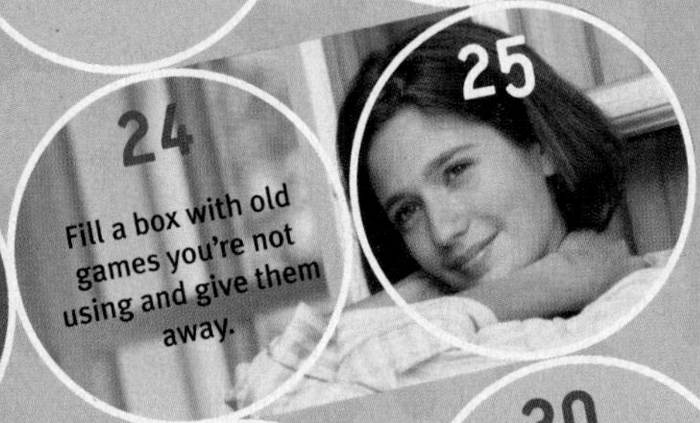

**24** Fill a box with old games you're not using and give them away.

**25**

**26**

**27**

**28** Go for a brisk walk or jog. Get your heart pumping.

**29** Pick a fresh bouquet of flowers. Give them to one of your neighbors.

**30** Pray for a person of influence: Kirsten Dunst is celebrating a birthday today.

Daylight Saving Time begins the first weekend in April. Turn your clocks foward one hour!

broke it, and gave it to the apostles, saying, "This is my body, which I am giving for you. Do this to remember me." [20]In the same way, after supper, Jesus took the cup and said, "This cup is the new agreement that God makes with his people. This new agreement begins with my blood which is poured out for you.

## WHO WILL TURN AGAINST JESUS?

[21]"But one of you will turn against me, and his hand is with mine on the table. [22]What God has planned for the Son of Man will happen, but how terrible it will be for that one who turns against the Son of Man."

[23]Then the apostles asked each other which one of them would do that.

## BE LIKE A SERVANT

[24]The apostles also began to argue about which one of them was the most important. [25]But Jesus said to them, "The kings of the non-Jewish people rule over them, and those who have authority over others like to be called 'friends of the people.' [26]But you must not be like that. Instead, the greatest among you should be like the youngest, and the leader should be like the servant. [27]Who is more important: the one sitting at the table or the one serving? You think the one at the table is more important, but I am like a servant among you.

[28]"You have stayed with me through my struggles. [29]Just as my Father has given me a kingdom, I also give you a kingdom [30]so you may eat and drink at my table in my kingdom. And you will sit on thrones, judging the twelve tribes of Israel.

## DON'T LOSE YOUR FAITH!

[31]"Simon, Simon, Satan has asked to test all of you as a farmer sifts his wheat. [32]I have prayed that you will not lose your faith! Help your brothers be stronger when you come back to me."

[33]But Peter said to Jesus, "Lord, I am ready to go with you to prison and even to die with you!"

[34]But Jesus said, "Peter, before the rooster crows this day, you will say three times that you don't know me."

## BE READY FOR TROUBLE

[35]Then Jesus said to the apostles, "When I sent you out without a purse, a bag, or sandals, did you need anything?"

They said, "No."

[36]He said to them, "But now if you have a purse or a bag, carry that with you. If you don't have a sword, sell your coat and buy one. [37]The Scripture says, 'He was treated like a criminal,' and I tell you this scripture must have its full meaning. It was written about me, and it is happening now."

[38]His followers said, "Look, Lord, here are two swords."

He said to them, "That is enough."

## JESUS PRAYS ALONE

[39]Jesus left the city and went to the Mount of Olives, as he often did, and his followers went with him. [40]When he reached the place, he said to them, "Pray for strength against temptation."

> "THEN AN ANGEL FROM HEAVEN APPEARED TO HIM TO STRENGTHEN HIM."

[41]Then Jesus went about a stone's throw away from them. He kneeled down and prayed, [42]"Father, if you are willing, take away this cup of suffering. But do what you want, not what I want." [43]Then an angel from heaven appeared to him to strengthen him. [44]Being full of pain, Jesus prayed even harder. His sweat was like drops of blood falling to the ground. [45]When he finished praying, he went to his followers and found them asleep because of their sadness. [46]Jesus said to them, "Why are you sleeping? Get up and pray for strength against temptation."

## JESUS IS ARRESTED

[47]While Jesus was speaking, a crowd came up, and Judas, one of the twelve apostles, was leading them. He came close to Jesus so he could kiss him.

[48]But Jesus said to him, "Judas, are you using the kiss to give the Son of Man to his enemies?"

[49]When those who were standing around him saw what was happening, they said, "Lord, should we strike them with our swords?" [50]And one of them struck the servant of the high priest and cut off his right ear.

[51]Jesus said, "Stop! No more of this." Then he touched the servant's ear and healed him.

[52]Those who came to arrest Jesus were the leading priests, the soldiers who guarded the Temple, and the older leaders. Jesus said to them, "You came out here with swords and clubs as though I were a criminal. [53]I was with you every day in the Temple, and you didn't arrest me there. But this is your time—the time when darkness rules."

## PETER SAYS HE DOESN'T KNOW JESUS

[54]They arrested Jesus, and led him away, and brought him into the house of the high priest. Peter followed far behind them. [55]After the soldiers started a fire in the middle of the courtyard and sat together, Peter sat with them. [56]A servant girl saw Peter sitting there in the firelight, and looking closely at him, she said, "This man was also with him."

[57]But Peter said this was not true; he said, "Woman, I don't know him."

[58]A short time later, another person saw Peter and said, "You are also one of them."

But Peter said, "Man, I am not!"

[59]About an hour later, another man insisted, "Certainly this man was with him, because he is from Galilee, too."

[60]But Peter said, "Man, I don't know what you are talking about!"

At once, while Peter was still speaking, a rooster crowed. [61]Then the Lord turned and looked straight at Peter. And Peter remembered what the Lord had said: "Before the rooster crows this day, you will say three times that you don't know me." [62]Then Peter went outside and cried painfully.

## THE PEOPLE MAKE FUN OF JESUS

[63]The men who were guarding Jesus began making fun of him and beating him.

22:37 'He . . . criminal' Quotation from Isaiah 53:12. 22:42 cup Jesus is talking about the painful things that will happen to him. Accepting these things will be hard, like drinking a cup of something bitter.

[64]They blindfolded him and said, "Prove that you are a prophet, and tell us who hit you." [65]They said many cruel things to Jesus.

## JESUS BEFORE THE LEADERS

[66]When day came, the council of the older leaders of the people, both the leading priests and the teachers of the law, came together and led Jesus to their highest court. [67]They said, "If you are the Christ, tell us."

Jesus said to them, "If I tell you, you will not believe me. [68]And if I ask you, you will not answer. [69]But from now on, the Son of Man will sit at the right hand of the powerful God."

[70]They all said, "Then are you the Son of God?"

Jesus said to them, "You say that I am."

[71]They said, "Why do we need witnesses now? We ourselves heard him say this."

## PILATE QUESTIONS JESUS

23 Then the whole group stood up and led Jesus to Pilate." [2]They began to accuse Jesus, saying, "We caught this man telling things that mislead our people. He says that we should not pay taxes to Caesar, and he calls himself the Christ, a king."

[3]Pilate asked Jesus, "Are you the king of the Jews?"

Jesus answered, "Those are your words."

[4]Pilate said to the leading priests and the people, "I find nothing against this man."

[5]They were insisting, saying, "But Jesus makes trouble with the people, teaching all around Judea. He began in Galilee, and now he is here."

## PILATE SENDS JESUS TO HEROD

[6]Pilate heard this and asked if Jesus was from Galilee. [7]Since Jesus was under Herod's authority, Pilate sent Jesus to Herod, who was in Jerusalem at that time. [8]When Herod saw Jesus, he was very glad, because he had heard about Jesus and had wanted to meet him for a long time. He was hoping to see Jesus work a miracle. [9]Herod asked Jesus many questions, but Jesus said nothing. [10]The leading priests and teachers of the law were standing there, strongly accusing Jesus. [11]After Herod and his soldiers

had made fun of Jesus, they dressed him in a kingly robe and sent him back to Pilate. [12]In the past, Pilate and Herod had always been enemies, but on that day they became friends.

## "AT ONCE, WHILE PETER WAS STILL SPEAKING, A ROOSTER CROWED."

## JESUS MUST DIE

[13]Pilate called the people together with the leading priests and the rulers. [14]He said to them, "You brought this man to me, saying he makes trouble among the people. But I have questioned him before you all, and I have not found him guilty of what you say. [15]Also, Herod found nothing wrong with him; he sent him back to us. Look, he has done nothing for which he should die. [16]So, after I punish him, I will let him go free." [17]"

[18]But the people shouted together, "Take this man away! Let Barabbas go free!" [19](Barabbas was a man who was in prison for his part in a riot in the city and for murder.)

[20]Pilate wanted to let Jesus go free and told this to the crowd. [21]But they shouted again, "Crucify him! Crucify him!"

[22]A third time Pilate said to them, "Why? What wrong has he done? I can find no reason to kill him. So I will have him punished and set him free."

[23]But they continued to shout, demanding that Jesus be crucified. Their yelling became so loud that [24]Pilate decided to give them what they wanted. [25]He set free the man who was in jail for rioting and murder, and he handed Jesus over to them to do with him as they wished.

## JESUS IS CRUCIFIED

[26]As they led Jesus away, Simon, a man from Cyrene, was coming in from the fields. They forced him to carry Jesus' cross and to walk behind him.

[27]A large crowd of people was following Jesus, including some women who were sad and crying for him. [28]But Jesus turned and said to them, "Women of Jerusalem, don't cry for me. Cry for yourselves and for your children. [29]The time is coming when people will say, 'Happy are the women who cannot have children and who have no babies to nurse.' [30]Then people will say to the mountains, 'Fall on us!' And they will say to the hills, 'Cover us!' [31]If they act like this now when life is good, what will happen when bad times come?'"

## Bible Basics

**Resurrection** means "a dead person's coming back to life." When Jesus came to earth as fully God and fully man and was put to death on the cross, he died a literal, physical death. The body of Jesus died on that cross, just like our bodies die. He was prepared for burial and laid in a tomb for three days. The tomb even had a huge stone in front of it to act as a door. After three days, an angel rolled the stone away, and Jesus walked out of the tomb alive again. He had come back to life, or been resurrected, because God has power over death. He was resurrected to prove that he has the power to offer eternal life in heaven for those who believe in him through faith.

 **23:1 Pilate** Pontius Pilate was the Roman governor of Judea from A.D. 26 to A.D. 36. **23:17 Verse 17** A few Greek copies add verse 17: "Every year at the Passover Feast, Pilate had to release one prisoner to the people." **23:31 If . . . come?** Literally, "If they do these things in the green tree, what will happen in the dry?"

# LEARN I+ & LIVE I+

**Luke 18:27**
**Learn It:** God can do things that are impossible for people.
**Live It:** In a journal, write the most impossible-seeming challenge in your life, and ask God to show you how to overcome it. Make a new entry when he does.

**Luke 23:56**
**Learn It:** On the Sabbath day, God's people rested.
**Live It:** Take time out one day each week to rest and reflect on Christ.

**John 3:7**
**Learn It:** Jesus said not to be surprised that all should be born again.
**Live It:** If you have not asked Jesus to forgive your sins, come into your heart, and guide your life, talk to him today.

³²There were also two criminals led out with Jesus to be put to death. ³³When they came to a place called the Skull, the soldiers crucified Jesus and the criminals—one on his right and the other on his left. ³⁴Jesus said, "Father, forgive them, because they don't know what they are doing."ⁿ

The soldiers threw lots to decide who would get his clothes. ³⁵The people stood there watching. And the leaders made fun of Jesus, saying, "He saved others. Let him save himself if he is God's Chosen One, the Christ."

³⁶The soldiers also made fun of him, coming to Jesus and offering him some vinegar. ³⁷They said, "If you are the king of the Jews, save yourself!" ³⁸At the top of the cross these words were written: THIS IS THE KING OF THE JEWS.

³⁹One of the criminals on a cross began to shout insults at Jesus: "Aren't you the Christ? Then save yourself and us."

⁴⁰But the other criminal stopped him and said, "You should fear God! You are getting the same punishment he is. ⁴¹We are punished justly, getting what we deserve for what we did. But this man has done nothing wrong." ⁴²Then he said, "Jesus, remember me when you come into your kingdom."

⁴³Jesus said to him, "I tell you the truth, today you will be with me in paradise."ⁿ

## JESUS DIES

⁴⁴It was about noon, and the whole land became dark until three o'clock in the after-noon, ⁴⁵because the sun did not shine. The curtain in the Templeⁿ was torn in two. ⁴⁶Jesus cried out in a loud voice, "Father, I give you my life." After Jesus said this, he died.

⁴⁷When the army officer there saw what happened, he praised God, saying, "Surely this was a good man!"

⁴⁸When all the people who had gathered there to watch saw what happened, they returned home, beating their chests because they were so sad. ⁴⁹But those who were close friends of Jesus, including the women who had followed him from Galilee, stood at a distance and watched.

> "WHY ARE YOU LOOKING FOR A LIVING PERSON IN THIS PLACE FOR THE DEAD? HE IS NOT HERE; HE HAS RISEN FROM THE DEAD."

## JOSEPH TAKES JESUS' BODY

⁵⁰There was a good and religious man named Joseph who was a member of the council. ⁵¹But he had not agreed to the other leaders' plans and actions against Jesus. He was from the town of Arimathea and was waiting for the kingdom of God to come. ⁵²Joseph went to Pilate to ask for the body of Jesus. ⁵³He took the body down from the cross, wrapped it in cloth, and put it in a tomb that was cut out of a wall of rock. This tomb had never been used before. ⁵⁴This was late on Preparation Day, and when the sun went down, the Sabbath day would begin.

⁵⁵The women who had come from Galilee with Jesus followed Joseph and saw the tomb and how Jesus' body was laid. ⁵⁶Then the women left to prepare spices and perfumes.

On the Sabbath day they rested, as the law of Moses commanded.

## JESUS RISES FROM THE DEAD

**24** Very early on the first day of the week, at dawn, the women came to the tomb, bringing the spices they had prepared. ²They found the stone rolled away from the entrance of the tomb, ³but when they went in, they did not find the body of the Lord Jesus. ⁴While they were wondering about this, two men in shining clothes suddenly stood beside them. ⁵The women were very afraid and bowed their heads to the ground. The men said to them, "Why are you looking for a living person in this place for the dead? ⁶He is not here; he has risen from the dead. Do you remember what he told you in Galilee? ⁷He said the Son of Man must be handed over to sinful people, be crucified, and rise from the dead on the third day." ⁸Then the women remembered what Jesus had said.

**23:34 Verse 34** Some early Greek copies do not have this first part of the verse. **23:43 paradise** Another word for heaven. **23:45 curtain in the Temple** A curtain divided the Most Holy Place from the other part of the Temple, the special building in Jerusalem where God commanded the Jewish people to worship him.

⁹The women left the tomb and told all these things to the eleven apostles and the other followers. ¹⁰It was Mary Magdalene, Joanna, Mary the mother of James, and some other women who told the apostles everything that had happened at the tomb. ¹¹But they did not believe the women, because it sounded like nonsense. ¹²But Peter got up and ran to the tomb. Bending down and looking in, he saw only the cloth that Jesus' body had been wrapped in. Peter went away to his home, wondering about what had happened.

## Jesus on the Road to Emmaus

¹³That same day two of Jesus' followers were going to a town named Emmaus, about seven miles from Jerusalem. ¹⁴They were talking about everything that had happened. ¹⁵While they were talking and discussing, Jesus himself came near and began walking with them, ¹⁶but they were kept from recognizing him. ¹⁷Then he said, "What are these things you are talking about while you walk?"

# "THEY WERE SAYING, 'THE LORD REALLY HAS RISEN FROM THE DEAD! HE SHOWED HIMSELF TO SIMON.' "

The two followers stopped, looking very sad. ¹⁸The one named Cleopas answered, "Are you the only visitor in Jerusalem who does not know what just happened there?"

¹⁹Jesus said to them, "What are you talking about?"

They said, "About Jesus of Nazareth. He was a prophet who said and did many powerful things before God and all the people. ²⁰Our leaders and the leading priests handed him over to be sentenced to death, and they crucified him. ²¹But we were hoping that he would free Israel. Besides this, it is now the third day since this happened. ²²And today some women among us amazed us. Early this morning they went to the tomb, ²³but they did not find his body there. They came and told us that they had seen a vision of angels who said that Jesus was alive! ²⁴So some of our group went to the tomb, too. They found it just as the women said, but they did not see Jesus."

²⁵Then Jesus said to them, "You are foolish and slow to believe everything the prophets said. ²⁶They said that the Christ must suffer these things before he enters his glory." ²⁷Then starting with what Moses and all the prophets had said about him, Jesus began to explain everything that had been written about himself in the Scriptures.

²⁸They came near the town of Emmaus, and Jesus acted as if he were going farther. ²⁹But they begged him, "Stay with us, because it is late; it is almost night." So he went in to stay with them.

³⁰When Jesus was at the table with them, he took some bread, gave thanks, divided it, and gave it to them. ³¹And then, they were allowed to recognize Jesus. But when they saw who he was, he disappeared. ³²They said to each other, "It felt like a fire burning in us when Jesus talked to us on the road and explained the Scriptures to us."

³³So the two followers got up at once and went back to Jerusalem. There they found the eleven apostles and others gathered. ³⁴They were saying, "The Lord really has risen from the dead! He showed himself to Simon."

³⁵Then the two followers told what had happened on the road and how they recognized Jesus when he divided the bread.

## Jesus Appears to His Followers

³⁶While the two followers were telling this, Jesus himself stood right in the middle of them and said, "Peace be with you."

³⁷They were fearful and terrified and thought they were seeing a ghost. ³⁸But Jesus said, "Why are you troubled? Why do you doubt what you see? ³⁹Look at my hands and my feet. It is I myself! Touch me and see, because a ghost does not have a living body as you see I have."

⁴⁰After Jesus said this, he showed them his hands and feet. ⁴¹While they still could not

## top 10
### random cds to rock out to

**10** — Satellite by P.O.D.

**9** — Jars of Clay by Jars of Clay

**8** — Momentum by tobyMac

**7** — Relient K by Relient K

**6** — The Beautiful Letdown by Switchfoot

**5** — Where Do We Go from Here by Pillar

**4** — Anthems for the Imperfect by Everyday Sunday

**3** — The Fundamental Elements of Southtown by P.O.D.

**2** — Supernatural by dc talk

**1** — Collide by Skillet

believe it because they were amazed and happy, Jesus said to them, "Do you have any food here?" 42They gave him a piece of broiled fish. 43While the followers watched, Jesus took the fish and ate it.

law of Moses, the books of the prophets, and the Psalms."

45Then Jesus opened their minds so they could understand the Scriptures. 46He said to them, "It is written that the Christ would suffer

all nations, starting at Jerusalem. 48You are witnesses of these things. 49I will send you what my Father has promised, but you must stay in Jerusalem until you have received that power from heaven."

## APPROXIMATELY HALF OF ALL NEW HIV INFECTIONS OCCUR IN PEOPLE UNDER AGE 25.

CENTERS FOR DISEASE CONTROL AND PREVENTION

### Jesus Goes Back to Heaven

50Jesus led his followers as far as Bethany, and he raised his hands and blessed them. 51While he was blessing them, he was separated from them and carried into heaven. 52They worshiped him and returned to Jerusalem very happy. 53They stayed in the Temple all the time, praising God.

44He said to them, "Remember when I was with you before? I said that everything written about me must happen—everything in the

and rise from the dead on the third day 47and that a change of hearts and lives and forgiveness of sins would be preached in his name to

# the Gospel of John isn't meant to simply be read—it needs to be explored.

From the opening chapter about Jesus coming into the world to the final assertion of the enormity of Jesus' ministry, John shows us how Jesus was completely human and completely God at the same time.

## John The Thinking-Girl's Gospel

You'll notice that John never refers to himself by name here. Instead, he uses the phrase "the follower Jesus loved" (13:23). That's a pretty bold statement. So is John being conceited? No way! He was definitely one of Jesus' closest friends along with Peter and James. Not mentioning his name is actually a reflection of John's humility, and it's also his way of honoring his close friendship with Jesus. And, FYI, Jesus had his own nickname for John. In Mark 3:17, he called John and his brother James the "Sons of Thunder."

John is considered more theological than the other three Gospels. (Theology is the study of God's characteristics and his relationship to the universe.) It's the only Gospel that offers the promise of a Helper—the Holy Spirit—to come after Jesus has ascended into heaven (16:7).

Overall, John is a pretty deep book. It's designed for thinkers and people who like symbolism, detailed teachings, and powerful readings. It's a book you can read over and over again and always find something new. Then again, every chapter of the Bible is like that!

## CHRIST COMES TO THE WORLD

**1** In the beginning there was the Word." The Word was with God, and the Word was God. ²He was with God in the beginning. ³All things were made by him, and nothing was made without him. ⁴In him there was life, and that life was the light of all people. ⁵The Light shines in the darkness, and the darkness has not overpowered it.

⁶There was a man named John" who was sent by God. ⁷He came to tell people the truth about the Light so that through him all people could hear about the Light and believe. ⁸John was not the Light, but he came to tell people the truth about the Light. ⁹The true Light that gives light to all was coming into the world!

¹⁰The Word was in the world, and the world was made by him, but the world did not know him. ¹¹He came to the world that was his own, but his own people did not accept him. ¹²But to all who did accept him and believe in him he gave the right to become children of God. ¹³They did not become his children in any human way—by any human parents or human desire. They were born of God.

¹⁴The Word became a human and lived among us. We saw his glory—the glory that belongs to the only Son of the Father—and he was full of grace and truth. ¹⁵John tells the truth about him and cries out, saying, "This is the One I told you about: 'The One who comes after me is greater than I am, because he was living before me.'"

¹⁶Because he was full of grace and truth, from him we all received one gift after another. ¹⁷The law was given through Moses, but grace and truth came through Jesus Christ. ¹⁸No one has ever seen God. But God the only Son is very close to the Father," and he has shown us what God is like.

## JOHN TELLS PEOPLE ABOUT JESUS

¹⁹Here is the truth John" told when the leaders in Jerusalem sent priests and Levites to ask him, "Who are you?"

²⁰John spoke freely and did not refuse to answer. He said, "I am not the Christ."

**[GENESIS 1–3]** Eve was a woman who had it all. She was God's original design, so she was the ultimate woman—the most beautiful, perfectly formed woman who has ever lived. She's the only woman who ever walked and talked with God in a perfect world. Can you imagine wasting all that for a piece of fruit!? Eve was simply dying for the only thing she was told she couldn't have. With one tiny bite, Eve lost paradise, for herself and for all of us. But as much as Eve's greed cost us, she's actually the ultimate example of what God's grace looks like. She totally ruined everything—she did the one thing he asked her not to do—but he still loved her unconditionally. That's what makes God, well, God.

²¹So they asked him, "Then who are you? Are you Elijah?"

He answered, "No, I am not."

"Are you the Prophet?"" they asked.

He answered, "No."

²²Then they said, "Who are you? Give us an answer to tell those who sent us. What do you say about yourself?"

²³John told them in the words of the prophet Isaiah:

"I am the voice of one
  calling out in the desert:
'Make the road straight for the Lord.'"

*Isaiah 40:3*

²⁴Some Pharisees who had been sent asked John: ²⁵"If you are not the Christ or Elijah or the Prophet, why do you baptize people?"

²⁶John answered, "I baptize with water, but there is one here with you that you don't know about. ²⁷He is the One who comes after me. I am not good enough to untie the strings of his sandals."

²⁸This all happened at Bethany on the other side of the Jordan River, where John was baptizing people.

²⁹The next day John saw Jesus coming toward him. John said, "Look, the Lamb of God," who takes away the sin of the world! ³⁰This is the One I was talking about when I said, 'A man will come after me, but he is greater than I am, because he was living before me.' ³¹Even I did not know who he was, although I came baptizing with water so that the people of Israel would know who he is."

## "IN THE BEGINNING THERE WAS THE WORD. THE WORD WAS WITH GOD, AND THE WORD WAS GOD."

³²⁻³³Then John said, "I saw the Spirit come down from heaven in the form of a dove and rest on him. Until then I did not know who the Christ was. But the God who sent me to baptize with water told me, 'You will see the Spirit come down and rest on a man; he is the One who will baptize with the Holy Spirit.' ³⁴I have

**1:1 Word** The Greek word is "logos," meaning any kind of communication; it could be translated "message." Here, it means Christ, because Christ was the way God told people about himself. **1:6 John** John the Baptist, who preached to people about Christ's coming (Matthew 3, Luke 3). **1:18 But . . . Father** This could be translated, "But the only God is very close to the Father." Also, some Greek copies say, "But the only Son is very close to the Father." **1:19 John** John the Baptist, who preached to people about Christ's coming (Matthew 3, Luke 3). **1:21 Elijah** A prophet who spoke for God. He lived hundreds of years before Christ and was expected to return before Christ (Malachi 4:5-6). **1:21 Prophet** They probably meant the prophet that God told Moses he would send (Deuteronomy 18:15-19). **1:29 Lamb of God** Name for Jesus. Jesus is like the lambs that were offered for a sacrifice to God.

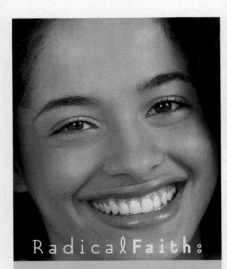

## Radical Faith:

## John 1:3-5

Have you ever gone on a long hike and enjoyed the beauty of God's creation? Maybe you've gone snorkeling and seen the mysteries and wonders of the sea. God created all the life and beauty around you and is in charge of everything that exists. He did it all—he made it and he sustains it. Consider this: The power goes out in your house and you can't see anything in the dark. What do you look for? A flashlight, of course. And what does a flashlight need to produce light? It needs batteries, right? It won't work without them. Just like that flashlight, you were created depend on one particular power source—God. You were cut out to have life and power through Jesus Christ. Just like a flashlight and batteries, only the filling of God's presence in your life will do. God is the One who has started, shaped, and maintained all things; you can know life and light through him.

seen this happen, and I tell you the truth: This man is the Son of God."

### THE FIRST FOLLOWERS OF JESUS

35The next day John[n] was there again with two of his followers. 36When he saw Jesus walking by, he said, "Look, the Lamb of God!"[n]

37The two followers heard John say this, so they followed Jesus. 38When Jesus turned and saw them following him, he asked, "What are you looking for?"

They said, "Rabbi, where are you staying?" ("Rabbi" means "Teacher.")

39He answered, "Come and see." So the two men went with Jesus and saw where he was staying and stayed there with him that day. It was about four o'clock in the afternoon.

40One of the two men who followed Jesus after they heard John speak about him was Andrew, Simon Peter's brother. 41The first thing Andrew did was to find his brother Simon and say to him, "We have found the Messiah." ("Messiah" means "Christ.")

42Then Andrew took Simon to Jesus. Jesus looked at him and said, "You are Simon son of John. You will be called Cephas." ("Cephas" means "Peter.")

43The next day Jesus decided to go to Galilee. He found Philip and said to him, "Follow me."

44Philip was from the town of Bethsaida, where Andrew and Peter lived. 45Philip found Nathanael and told him, "We have found the man that Moses wrote about in the law, and the prophets also wrote about him. He is Jesus, the son of Joseph, from Nazareth."

46But Nathanael said to Philip, "Can anything good come from Nazareth?"

Philip answered, "Come and see."

47As Jesus saw Nathanael coming toward him, he said, "Here is truly an Israelite. There is nothing false in him."

48Nathanael asked, "How do you know me?"

Jesus answered, "I saw you when you were under the fig tree, before Philip told you about me."

49Then Nathanael said to Jesus, "Teacher, you are the Son of God; you are the King of Israel."

50Jesus said to Nathanael, "Do you believe simply because I told you I saw you under the fig tree? You will see greater things than that." 51And Jesus said to them, "I tell you the truth, you will all see heaven open and 'angels of God going up and coming down'[n] on the Son of Man."

### THE WEDDING AT CANA

2 Two days later there was a wedding in the town of Cana in Galilee. Jesus' mother was there, 2and Jesus and his followers were also invited to the wedding. 3When all the wine was gone, Jesus' mother said to him, "They have no more wine."

4Jesus answered, "Dear woman, why come to me? My time has not yet come."

5His mother said to the servants, "Do whatever he tells you to do."

6In that place there were six stone water jars that the Jews used in their washing ceremony.[n] Each jar held about twenty or thirty gallons.

## beautysecret

### Acne

While acne isn't a serious threat to your health, it can affect the way you look and feel about yourself. If you're struggling with acne, avoid touching, washing, or picking at your face too much. If it's a real problem, seek professional help.

1:35 **John** John the Baptist, who preached to people about Christ's coming (Matthew 3, Luke 3). 1:36 **Lamb of God** Name for Jesus. Jesus is like the lambs that were offered for a sacrifice to God. 1:42 **Peter** The Greek name "Peter," like the Aramaic name "Cephas," means "rock." 1:51 **'angels . . . down'** These words are from Genesis 28:12. 2:6 **washing ceremony** The Jewish people washed themselves in special ways before eating, before worshiping in the Temple, and at other special times.

7Jesus said to the servants, "Fill the jars with water." So they filled the jars to the top.

8Then he said to them, "Now take some out and give it to the master of the feast."

## "I TELL YOU THE TRUTH, UNLESS ONE IS BORN AGAIN, HE CANNOT BE IN GOD'S KINGDOM."

So they took the water to the master. 9When he tasted it, the water had become wine. He did not know where the wine came from, but the servants who had brought the water knew. The master of the wedding called the bridegroom 10and said to him, "People always serve the best wine first. Later, after the guests have been drinking awhile, they serve the cheaper wine. But you have saved the best wine till now."

11So in Cana of Galilee Jesus did his first miracle. There he showed his glory, and his followers believed in him.

### JESUS IN THE TEMPLE

12After this, Jesus went to the town of Capernaum with his mother, brothers, and followers. They stayed there for just a few days. 13When it was almost time for the Jewish Passover Feast, Jesus went to Jerusalem. 14In the Temple he found people selling cattle, sheep, and doves. He saw others sitting at tables, exchanging different kinds of money. 15Jesus made a whip out of cords and forced all of them, both the sheep and cattle, to leave the Temple. He turned over the tables and scattered the money of those who were exchanging it. 16Then he said to those who were selling pigeons, "Take these things out of here! Don't make my Father's house a place for buying and selling!"

17When this happened, the followers remembered what was written in the Scriptures: "My strong love for your Temple completely controls me."[n]

18Some of his people said to Jesus, "Show us a miracle to prove you have the right to do these things."

19Jesus answered them, "Destroy this temple, and I will build it again in three days."

20They answered, "It took forty-six years to build this Temple! Do you really believe you can build it again in three days?"

21(But the temple Jesus meant was his own body. 22After Jesus was raised from the dead, his followers remembered that Jesus had said this. Then they believed the Scripture and the words Jesus had said.)

23When Jesus was in Jerusalem for the Passover Feast, many people believed in him because they saw the miracles he did. 24But Jesus did not trust himself to them because he knew them all. 25He did not need anyone to tell him about people, because he knew what was in people's minds.

### NICODEMUS COMES TO JESUS

3 There was a man named Nicodemus who was one of the Pharisees and an important Jewish leader. 2One night Nicodemus came to Jesus and said, "Teacher, we know you are a teacher sent from God, because no one can do the miracles you do unless God is with him."

3Jesus answered, "I tell you the truth, unless one is born again, he cannot be in God's kingdom."

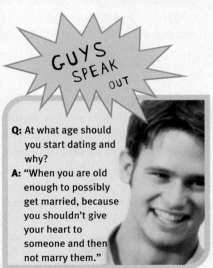

**GUYS SPEAK OUT**

Q: At what age should you start dating and why?

A: "When you are old enough to possibly get married, because you shouldn't give your heart to someone and then not marry them."

**Blab**

Q: Three of my friends recently died at 16. What's the point in going to school and working hard if your life is going to be cut short? Shouldn't I just go out and have some fun?

A: It's natural to question what's important when a friend dies. You should make the most of every day in case it's your last one, but that doesn't mean you can quit doing the work required (like going to school). You should be extra focused on what God wants you to do, how you can tell people about him, and how you can live the best in the time he has given you.

Q: My good friend died, and I just can't stop feeling sad. I feel like I am losing my faith, and nothing seems fun anymore. What do I do?

A: Grieving is natural after a loss, and it can take a while to feel normal again. You may even get angry or feel guilty. Be sad, but do not let sadness take over your life. If you feel like you can't function because you are too sad, ask your parents to let you talk to a Christian counselor.

Q: My mom has cancer, and I am scared that she might die. I don't want to tell her how I feel, because she is going through enough. What do I do?

A: The last thing your mom wants is for you, her child, to protect her. She wants to know your feelings. It can actually make her feel better. Pray together, and ask about treatment options and how you can help. Pray for her healing and for strength.

notes  2:17 "My . . . me." Quotation from Psalm 69:9.

## CHECK IT OUT

### THE GO FOUNDATION

The Go Foundation got its start from Christian bands MercyMe and Audio Adrenaline, as band members saw the need for more believers to take the gospel message worldwide. The Go Foundation connects Christians with mission-sending organizations that need people to do short-term and long-term ministry in foreign countries.

Some participants even have opportunities to do missions trips with band members. A number of mission-sending groups have partnered with the Go Foundation including the International Mission Board, G.O. Ministries Inc., Fuel International, Awe Star Ministries, iWitness Ministries, Spoken For International Youth Outreach, Mercy Ships, and International Commission.

The website offers a 10-day "Go Challenge," which includes a Bible study that leads readers through a process of discovering God's plan for the nations and His desire for everyone to be involved. It also provides application instructions and advice on how to raise support.

*Get involved by visiting* **www.thegofoundation.com.**

⁴Nicodemus said, "But if a person is already old, how can he be born again? He cannot enter his mother's body again. So how can a person be born a second time?"

⁵But Jesus answered, "I tell you the truth, unless one is born from water and the Spirit, he cannot enter God's kingdom. ⁶Human life comes from human parents, but spiritual life comes from the Spirit. ⁷Don't be surprised when I tell you, 'You must all be born again.' ⁸The wind blows where it wants to and you hear the sound of it, but you don't know where the wind comes from or where it is going. It is the same with every person who is born from the Spirit."

⁹Nicodemus asked, "How can this happen?"

¹⁰Jesus said, "You are an important teacher in Israel, and you don't understand these things? ¹¹I tell you the truth, we talk about what we know, and we tell about what we have seen, but you don't accept what we tell you. ¹²I have told you about things here on earth, and you do not believe me. So you will not believe me if I tell you about things of heaven. ¹³The only one who has ever gone up to heaven is the One who came down from heaven—the Son of Man.

¹⁴"Just as Moses lifted up the snake in the desert,ⁿ the Son of Man must also be lifted up.

¹⁵So that everyone who believes can have eternal life in him.

¹⁶"God loved the world so much that he gave his one and only Son so that whoever believes in him may not be lost, but have eternal life. ¹⁷God did not send his Son into the world to judge the world guilty, but to save the world through him. ¹⁸People who believe in God's Son are not judged guilty. Those who do not believe have already been judged guilty, because they have not believed in God's one and only Son. ¹⁹They are judged by this fact: The Light has come into the world, but they did not want light. They wanted darkness, because they were doing evil things. ²⁰All who do evil hate the light and will not come to the light, because it will show all the evil things they do. ²¹But those who follow the true way come to the light, and it shows that the things they do were done through God."

### Jesus and John the Baptist

²²After this, Jesus and his followers went into the area of Judea, where he stayed with his followers and baptized people. ²³John was also baptizing in Aenon, near Salim, because there was plenty of water there. People were going there to be baptized. ²⁴(This was before John was put into prison.)

²⁵Some of John's followers had an argument with a Jew about religious washing.ⁿ ²⁶So they came to John and said, "Teacher, remember the man who was with you on the other side of the Jordan River, the one you spoke about so much? He is baptizing, and everyone is going to him."

²⁷John answered, "A man can get only what God gives him. ²⁸You yourselves heard me say, 'I am not the Christ, but I am the one sent to prepare the way for him.' ²⁹The bride belongs only to the bridegroom. But the friend who helps the bridegroom stands by and listens to him. He is thrilled that he gets to hear the bridegroom's voice. In the same way, I am really happy. ³⁰He must become greater, and I must become less important.

### The One Who Comes from Heaven

³¹"The One who comes from above is greater than all. The one who is from the earth belongs to the earth and talks about things on the earth. But the One who comes from heaven is greater than all. ³²He tells what he has seen and heard, but no one accepts what he says. ³³Whoever accepts what he says has proven that God is true. ³⁴The One whom God sent speaks the words of God, because God gives him the Spirit fully. ³⁵The Father loves the Son and has given him power over everything.

---

**3:14 Moses . . . desert** When the Israelites were dying from snake bites, God told Moses to put a brass snake on a pole. The people who looked at the snake were healed (Numbers 21:4-9). **3:25 religious washing** The Jewish people washed themselves in special ways before eating, before worshiping in the Temple, and at other special times.

36Those who believe in the Son have eternal life, but those who do not obey the Son will never have life. God's anger stays on them."

## Jesus and a Samaritan woman

4 The Pharisees heard that Jesus was making and baptizing more followers than John, 2although Jesus himself did not baptize people, but his followers did. 3Jesus knew that the Pharisees had heard about him, so he left Judea and went back to Galilee. 4But on the way he had to go through the country of Samaria.

5In Samaria Jesus came to the town called Sychar, which is near the field Jacob gave to his son Joseph. 6Jacob's well was there. Jesus was tired from his long trip, so he sat down beside the well. It was about twelve o'clock noon. 7When a Samaritan woman came to the well to get some water, Jesus said to her, "Please give me a drink." 8(This happened while Jesus' followers were in town buying some food.)

9The woman said, "I am surprised that you ask me for a drink, since you are a Jewish man and I am a Samaritan woman." (Jewish people are not friends with Samaritans.")

10Jesus said, "If you only knew the free gift of God and who it is that is asking you for water, you would have asked him, and he would have given you living water."

11The woman said, "Sir, where will you get this living water? The well is very deep, and you have nothing to get water with. 12Are you greater than Jacob, our father, who gave us this well and drank from it himself along with his sons and flocks?"

13Jesus answered, "Everyone who drinks this water will be thirsty again, 14but whoever drinks the water I give will never be thirsty. The water I give will become a spring of water gushing up inside that person, giving eternal life."

15The woman said to him, "Sir, give me this water so I will never be thirsty again and will not have to come back here to get more water."

16Jesus told her, "Go get your husband and come back here."

17The woman answered, "I have no husband."

Jesus said to her, "You are right to say you have no husband. 18Really you have had five husbands, and the man you live with now is not your husband. You told the truth."

19The woman said, "Sir, I can see that you are a prophet. 20Our ancestors worshiped on this mountain, but you say that Jerusalem is the place where people must worship."

21Jesus said, "Believe me, woman. The time is coming when neither in Jerusalem nor on this mountain will you actually worship the Father. 22You Samaritans worship something you don't understand. We understand what we worship, because salvation comes from the Jews. 23The time is coming when the true worshipers will worship the Father in spirit and truth, and that time is here already. You see, the Father too is actively seeking such people to worship him. 24God is spirit, and those who worship him must worship in spirit and truth."

## "GOD IS SPIRIT, AND THOSE WHO WORSHIP HIM MUST WORSHIP IN SPIRIT AND TRUTH."

25The woman said, "I know that the Messiah is coming." (Messiah is the One called Christ.) "When the Messiah comes, he will explain everything to us."

26Then Jesus said, "I am he—I, the one talking to you."

27Just then his followers came back from town and were surprised to see him talking with

## Music Reviews

GROUP: BETHANY DILLON   ALBUM: BETHANY DILLON

Bethany Dillon, like Stacie Orrico, is another one of those musical teens who can practically do it all. With a debut album at 15, Bethany proves she can sing, play the guitar, and write some killer songs that engage the emotions and make you think about what's real. Her first single, "Beautiful," focuses on the desire to be beautiful to God, not just to have yourself together on the outside. Another track that describes God as "All I Need," is remarkably grown-up for someone with several years of high school to go. Bethany definitely makes you get out of yourself and into God, and that's awesome.

WHY IT ROCKS: TEEN SINGER AND SONGWRITER ADDS AN ORIGINAL, FOLKSY TOUCH TO LYRICS THAT STIR THE SOUL.

 4:9 Jewish people . . . Samaritans This can also be translated "Jewish people don't use things that Samaritans have used."

# John 4:13-14

Did you know that two-thirds of your body is made up of water? (That means if you weigh 120 pounds, then you are carrying around 80 pounds of water!) Obviously, we know that water is necessary for a ton of things—the most important being for our own survival. But no matter how much water we drink to quench our thirst, we're going to get thirsty again sometime, right?

In much of John, Jesus helped his audience get the point of his teaching by making comparisons with familiar things. Here he wanted this woman to stop looking for other ways to quench the thirst of her soul and to realize that what he was offering her was eternal. When we accept Jesus as the perfect Son of God who died for our sins, the Holy Spirit enters our lives, continually renewing us with springs of refreshing water for our soul. And that water never runs out. So next time you feel like you're in a spiritually "dry" place, remember these verses and know that God's well never runs dry.

a woman. But none of them asked, "What do you want?" or "Why are you talking with her?"

²⁸Then the woman left her water jar and went back to town. She said to the people, ²⁹"Come and see a man who told me everything I ever did. Do you think he might be the Christ?" ³⁰So the people left the town and went to see Jesus.

³¹Meanwhile, his followers were begging him, "Teacher, eat something."

³²But Jesus answered, "I have food to eat that you know nothing about."

³³So the followers asked themselves, "Did somebody already bring him food?"

³⁴Jesus said, "My food is to do what the One who sent me wants me to do and to finish his work. ³⁵You have a saying, 'Four more months till harvest.' But I tell you, open your eyes and look at the fields ready for harvest now. ³⁶Already, the one who harvests is being paid and is gathering crops for eternal life. So the one who plants and the one who harvests celebrate at the same time. ³⁷Here the saying is true, 'One person plants, and another harvests.' ³⁸I sent you to harvest a crop that you did not work on. Others did the work, and you get to finish up their work."ⁿ

³⁹Many of the Samaritans in that town believed in Jesus because of what the woman said: "He told me everything I ever did." ⁴⁰When the Samaritans came to Jesus, they begged him to stay with them, so he stayed there two more days. ⁴¹And many more believed because of the things he said.

⁴²They said to the woman, "First we believed in Jesus because of your speech, but now we believe because we heard him ourselves. We know that this man really is the Savior of the world."

## Jesus Heals an Officer's Son

⁴³Two days later, Jesus left and went to Galilee. ⁴⁴(Jesus had said before that a prophet is not respected in his own country.) ⁴⁵When Jesus arrived in Galilee, the people there welcomed him. They had seen all the things he did at the Passover Feast in Jerusalem, because they had been there, too.

⁴⁶Jesus went again to visit Cana in Galilee where he had changed the water into wine. One of the king's important officers lived in the city of Capernaum, and his son was sick. ⁴⁷When he heard that Jesus had come from Judea to Galilee, he went to Jesus and begged him to come to Capernaum and heal his son, because his son was almost dead. ⁴⁸Jesus said to him, "You people must see signs and miracles before you will believe in me."

> # "WHEN JESUS SAW THE MAN AND KNEW THAT HE HAD BEEN SICK FOR SUCH A LONG TIME, JESUS ASKED HIM, "DO YOU WANT TO BE WELL?"

⁴⁹The officer said, "Sir, come before my child dies."

⁵⁰Jesus answered, "Go. Your son will live."

The man believed what Jesus told him and went home. ⁵¹On the way the man's servants came and met him and told him, "Your son is alive."

⁵²The man asked, "What time did my son begin to get well?"

They answered, "Yesterday at one o'clock the fever left him."

⁵³The father knew that one o'clock was the exact time that Jesus had said, "Your son will live." So the man and all the people who lived in his house believed in Jesus.

⁵⁴That was the second miracle Jesus did after coming from Judea to Galilee.

## Jesus Heals a Man at a Pool

5 Later Jesus went to Jerusalem for a special feast. ²In Jerusalem there is a pool with five covered porches, which is called Bethzathaⁿ in the Hebrew language.ⁿ This pool is near the Sheep Gate. ³Many sick people were lying on the porches beside the pool. Some were blind, some were crippled, and some

**4:38 I . . . their work.** As a farmer sends workers to harvest grain, Jesus sends his followers out to bring people to God. **5:2 Bethzatha** Also called Bethsaida or Bethesda, it is a pool of water north of the Temple in Jerusalem. **5:2 Hebrew language** Hebrew or Aramaic, the languages of many people in this region in the first century.

were paralyzed." ⁵A man was lying there who had been sick for thirty-eight years. ⁶When Jesus saw the man and knew that he had been sick for such a long time, Jesus asked him, "Do you want to be well?"

⁷The sick man answered, "Sir, there is no one to help me get into the pool when the water starts moving. While I am coming to the water, someone else always gets in before me."

⁸Then Jesus said, "Stand up. Pick up your mat and walk." ⁹And immediately the man was well; he picked up his mat and began to walk.

The day this happened was a Sabbath day. ¹⁰So the Jews said to the man who had been healed, "Today is the Sabbath. It is against our law for you to carry your mat on the Sabbath day."

¹¹But he answered, "The man who made me well told me, 'Pick up your mat and walk.'"

¹²Then they asked him, "Who is the man who told you to pick up your mat and walk?"

¹³But the man who had been healed did not know who it was, because there were many people in that place, and Jesus had left.

¹⁴Later, Jesus found the man at the Temple and said to him, "See, you are well now. Stop sinning so that something worse does not happen to you."

### JESUS HAS GOD'S AUTHORITY

¹⁹But Jesus said, "I tell you the truth, the Son can do nothing alone. The Son does only what he sees the Father doing, because the Son does whatever the Father does. ²⁰The Father loves the Son and shows the Son all the things he himself does. But the Father will show the Son even greater things than this so that you can all be amazed. ²¹Just as the Father raises the dead and gives them life, so also the Son gives life to those he wants to. ²²In fact, the Father judges no one, but he has given the Son power to do all the judging ²³so that all people will honor the Son as much as they honor the Father. Anyone who does not honor the Son does not honor the Father who sent him.

²⁴"I tell you the truth, whoever hears what I say and believes in the One who sent me has eternal life. That person will not be judged guilty but has already left death and entered life. ²⁵I tell you the truth, the time is coming and is already here when the dead will hear the voice of the Son of God, and those who hear will have life. ²⁶Life comes from the Father himself, and he has allowed the Son to have life in himself as well. ²⁷And the Father has given the Son the power to judge, because he is the Son of Man. ²⁸Don't be surprised at this: A time is coming when all who are dead and in

## John 5:30

Chances are, you're living to please someone. Who is it? Someone at school? At church? At home? Yourself? God? Think about it for a moment and then take a look at Jesus' life. Who was his focus? What was his life about? If you read about Jesus for very long you can't help but notice that he was really only concerned with pleasing an audience of one—his Father in heaven. He said, "I don't try to please myself, but I try to please the One who sent me." What an honest confession! Jesus didn't live one day trying to please himself. He didn't live for his own comfort, feelings, preferences, or convenience. He didn't live to get people's attention, affirmation, or approval. Jesus was always concerned about what God was leading him to do and how he could honor God in his choices. Even in the midst of suffering, Jesus' desire for God to have his way and his will be done consumed him. What would it look like in your own life if you lived to please God the way Jesus did? If you focus on God and let him lead you, you will see him glorified in your life.

### DIDYA KNOW

**74% OF ONLINE TEENS USE INSTANT MESSAGING (IM).**

PEW INTERNET & AMERICAN LIFE PROJECT

¹⁵Then the man left and told his people that Jesus was the one who had made him well.

¹⁶Because Jesus was doing this on the Sabbath day, some evil people began to persecute him. ¹⁷But Jesus said to them, "My Father never stops working, and so I keep working, too."

¹⁸This made them try still harder to kill him. They said, "First Jesus was breaking the law about the Sabbath day. Now he says that God is his own Father, making himself equal with God!"

their graves will hear his voice. ²⁹Then they will come out of their graves. Those who did good will rise and have life forever, but those who did evil will rise to be judged guilty.

### JESUS IS GOD'S SON

³⁰"I can do nothing alone. I judge only the way I am told, so my judgment is fair. I don't try to please myself, but I try to please the One who sent me.

³¹"If only I tell people about myself, what I say is not true. ³²But there is another who tells

**5:3 Verse 3** Some Greek copies add "and they waited for the water to move." A few later copies add verse 4: "Sometimes an angel of the Lord came down to the pool and stirred up the water. After the angel did this, the first person to go into the pool was healed from any sickness he had."

about me, and I know that the things he says about me are true.

<sup>33</sup>"You have sent people to John, and he has told you the truth. <sup>34</sup>It is not that I accept such human telling; I tell you this so you can be saved. <sup>35</sup>John was like a burning and shining lamp, and you were happy to enjoy his light for a while.

<sup>36</sup>"But I have a proof about myself that is greater than that of John. The things I do, which are the things my Father gave me to do, prove that the Father sent me. <sup>37</sup>And the Father himself who sent me has given proof about me. You have never heard his voice or seen what he looks like. <sup>38</sup>His teaching does not live in you, because you don't believe in the One the Father sent. <sup>39</sup>You carefully study the Scriptures because you think they give you

eternal life. They do in fact tell about me, <sup>40</sup>but you refuse to come to me to have that life.

<sup>41</sup>"I don't need praise from people. <sup>42</sup>But I know you—I know that you don't have God's love in you. <sup>43</sup>I have come from my Father and speak for him, but you don't accept me. But when another person comes, speaking only for himself, you will accept him. <sup>44</sup>You try to get praise from each other, but you do not try to get the praise that comes from the only God. So how can you believe? <sup>45</sup>Don't think that I will stand before the Father and say you are wrong. The one who says you are wrong is Moses, the one you hoped would save you. <sup>46</sup>If you really believed Moses, you would believe me, because Moses wrote about me. <sup>47</sup>But if you don't believe what Moses wrote, how can you believe what I say?"

## MORE THAN FIVE THOUSAND FED

**6** After this, Jesus went across Lake Galilee (or, Lake Tiberias). <sup>2</sup>Many people followed him because they saw the miracles he did to heal the sick. <sup>3</sup>Jesus went up on a hill and sat down there with his followers. <sup>4</sup>It was almost the time for the Jewish Passover Feast.

<sup>5</sup>When Jesus looked up and saw a large crowd coming toward him, he said to Philip, "Where can we buy enough bread for all these people to eat?" <sup>6</sup>(Jesus asked Philip this question to test him, because Jesus already knew what he planned to do.)

<sup>7</sup>Philip answered, "We would all have to work a month to buy enough bread for each person to have only a little piece."

<sup>8</sup>Another one of his followers, Andrew, Simon Peter's brother, said, <sup>9</sup>"Here is a boy with five loaves of barley bread and two little fish, but that is not enough for so many people."

<sup>10</sup>Jesus said, "Tell the people to sit down." This was a very grassy place, and about five thousand men sat down there. <sup>11</sup>Then Jesus took the loaves of bread, thanked God for them, and gave them to the people who were sitting there. He did the same with the fish, giving as much as the people wanted.

<sup>12</sup>When they had all had enough to eat, Jesus said to his followers, "Gather the leftover pieces of fish and bread so that nothing is wasted." <sup>13</sup>So they gathered up the pieces and filled twelve baskets with the pieces left from the five barley loaves.

<sup>14</sup>When the people saw this miracle that Jesus did, they said, "He must truly be the Prophet<sup>n</sup> who is coming into the world."

<sup>15</sup>Jesus knew that the people planned to come and take him by force and make him their king, so he left and went into the hills alone.

### JESUS WALKS ON THE WATER

<sup>16</sup>That evening Jesus' followers went down to Lake Galilee. <sup>17</sup>It was dark now, and Jesus had not yet come to them. The followers got into a boat and started across the lake to Capernaum. <sup>18</sup>By now a strong wind was blowing, and the waves on the lake were getting bigger. <sup>19</sup>When they had rowed the boat about three or four miles, they saw Jesus walking on the water, coming toward the boat. The followers were afraid, <sup>20</sup>but Jesus said to them, "It is I. Do not be afraid." <sup>21</sup>Then they were glad to take him into the boat. At once the boat came to land at the place where they wanted to go.

> "WHEN THEY HAD ROWED THE BOAT ABOUT THREE OR FOUR MILES, THEY SAW JESUS WALKING ON THE WATER, COMING TOWARD THE BOAT."

### THE PEOPLE SEEK JESUS

<sup>22</sup>The next day the people who had stayed on the other side of the lake knew that Jesus had not gone in the boat with his followers but that they had left without him. And they knew that only one boat had been there. <sup>23</sup>But then some boats came from Tiberias and landed

## relationships

"And if you are nice only to your friends, you are no better than other people. Even those who don't know God are nice to their friends" (Matthew 5:47). Girls can be mean, really mean, to those who don't fit in. If you are popular, your job is to protect those who are less popular, not to torture them. When was the last time you made a new friend or let somebody new into your circle of friends? God welcomes those who come to him. If you are a God-lover, give your friendship freely.

6:14 **Prophet** They probably meant the prophet that God told Moses he would send (Deuteronomy 18:15-19).

# LEARN I+ & LIVE I+

**John 6:11**
**Learn It:** Jesus thanked God for the bread and fish he was going to give to the people.
**Live It:** Get in the habit of thanking God for your food before you eat it, even in public places.

**John 7:37**
**Learn It:** God provides the ultimate satisfaction in this life.
**Live It:** The next time you find yourself struggling with a situation, go to God first in prayer.

**John 13:5**
**Learn It:** Jesus showed his Servant attitude by washing his followers' feet.
**Live It:** Tell this part of Jesus' story to someone you love; then show your love and humility by doing something kind for the person.

near the place where the people had eaten the bread after the Lord had given thanks. [24]When the people saw that Jesus and his followers were not there now, they got into boats and went to Capernaum to find Jesus.

## JESUS, THE BREAD OF LIFE

[25]When the people found Jesus on the other side of the lake, they asked him, "Teacher, when did you come here?"

[26]Jesus answered, "I tell you the truth, you aren't looking for me because you saw me do miracles. You are looking for me because you ate the bread and were satisfied. [27]Don't work for the food that spoils. Work for the food that stays good always and gives eternal life. The Son of Man will give you this food, because on him God the Father has put his power."

[28]The people asked Jesus, "What are the things God wants us to do?"

[29]Jesus answered, "The work God wants you to do is this: Believe the One he sent."

[30]So the people asked, "What miracle will you do? If we see a miracle, we will believe you. What will you do? [31]Our fathers ate the manna in the desert. This is written in the Scriptures: 'He gave them bread from heaven to eat.' "[n]

[32]Jesus said, "I tell you the truth, it was not Moses who gave you bread from heaven; it is my Father who is giving you the true bread from heaven. [33]God's bread is the One who comes down from heaven and gives life to the world."

[34]The people said, "Sir, give us this bread always."

[35]Then Jesus said, "I am the bread that gives life. Whoever comes to me will never be hungry, and whoever believes in me will never be thirsty. [36]But as I told you before, you have seen me and still don't believe. [37]The Father gives me my people. Every one of them will come to me, and I will always accept them. [38]I came down from heaven to do what God wants me to do, not what I want to do. [39]Here is what the One who sent me wants me to do: I must not lose even one whom God gave me, but I must raise them all on the last day. [40]Those who see the Son and believe in him have eternal life, and I will raise them on the last day. This is what my Father wants."

[41]Some people began to complain about Jesus because he said, "I am the bread that comes down from heaven." [42]They said, "This is Jesus, the son of Joseph. We know his father and mother. How can he say, 'I came down from heaven'?"

[43]But Jesus answered, "Stop complaining to each other. [44]The Father is the One who sent me. No one can come to me unless the Father draws him to me, and I will raise that person up on the last day. [45]It is written in the prophets, 'They will all be taught by God.'[n] Everyone who listens to the Father and learns from him comes to me. [46]No one has seen the Father except the One who is from God; only he has seen the Father. [47]I tell you the truth, whoever believes has eternal life. [48]I am the bread that gives life. [49]Your ancestors ate the manna in the desert, but still they died. [50]Here

is the bread that comes down from heaven. Anyone who eats this bread will never die. [51]I am the living bread that came down from heaven. Anyone who eats this bread will live forever. This bread is my flesh, which I will give up so that the world may have life."

[52]Then the evil people began to argue among themselves, saying, "How can this man give us his flesh to eat?"

## "THE WORK GOD WANTS YOU TO DO IS THIS: BELIEVE THE ONE HE SENT."

[53]Jesus said, "I tell you the truth, you must eat the flesh of the Son of Man and drink his blood. Otherwise, you won't have real life in you. [54]Those who eat my flesh and drink my blood have eternal life, and I will raise them up on the last day. [55]My flesh is true food, and my blood is true drink. [56]Those who eat my flesh and drink my blood live in me, and I live in them. [57]The living Father sent me, and I live because of the Father. So whoever eats me will live because of me. [58]I am not like the bread your ancestors ate. They ate that bread and still died. I am the bread that came down from heaven, and whoever eats this bread will live forever." [59]Jesus said all these things while he was teaching in the synagogue in Capernaum.

**notes** **6:31** 'He gave . . . eat.' Quotation from Psalm 78:24. **6:45** 'They . . . God.' Quotation from Isaiah 54:13.

**Q:** My little sister has been totally hitting on my boyfriend, and it's really irritating. What can I do?

**A:** If your sister is really little, humor her. If she is a teen, take her to lunch and explain how it makes you feel when she gets too close to your guy. Ask her nicely to respect your relationship with him and to back off. If she doesn't, pray for patience.

**Q:** My whole family is a big, fat pain. My dad thinks he is funny, and he is *so* not. My kid brothers are loud and obnoxious, and my sister thinks she's the boss of the whole world. My mom refuses to let me do anything. I am so frustrated with them. How can I get past this?

**A:** You get irritated with your family the most because they are the closest people to you, and you know it is safe to feel negative emotions for them and they will still love you. (How's that for a little free analysis?) Pray that God will give you patience and help you feel love for them. Ask him to show you the good in them; he will.

**Q:** My parents want to know everywhere I am going and everybody who will be there every time I want to do something. I am a good kid. Why don't they trust me?

**A:** For them, it isn't an issue of trusting you. It's an issue of safety for you and of not trusting everybody else. You are their treasure, and they want to know that they can find you if they need you.

## THE WORDS OF ETERNAL LIFE

⁶⁰When the followers of Jesus heard this, many of them said, "This teaching is hard. Who can accept it?"

⁶¹Knowing that his followers were complaining about this, Jesus said, "Does this teaching bother you? ⁶²Then will it also bother you to see the Son of Man going back to the place where he came from? ⁶³It is the Spirit that gives life. The flesh doesn't give life. The words I told you are spirit, and they give life. ⁶⁴But some of you don't believe." (Jesus knew from the beginning who did not believe and who would turn against him.) ⁶⁵Jesus said, "That is the reason I said, 'If the Father does not bring a person to me, that one cannot come.'"

⁶⁶After Jesus said this, many of his followers left him and stopped following him.

⁶⁷Jesus asked the twelve followers, "Do you want to leave, too?"

⁶⁸Simon Peter answered him, "Lord, where would we go? You have the words that give eternal life. ⁶⁹We believe and know that you are the Holy One from God."

⁷⁰Then Jesus answered, "I chose all twelve of you, but one of you is a devil."

⁷¹Jesus was talking about Judas, the son of Simon Iscariot. Judas was one of the twelve, but later he was going to turn against Jesus.

## JESUS' BROTHERS DON'T BELIEVE

**7** After this, Jesus traveled around Galilee. He did not want to travel in Judea, because some evil people there wanted to kill him. ²It was time for the Feast of Shelters. ³So Jesus' brothers said to him, "You should leave here and go to Judea so your followers there can see the miracles you do. ⁴Anyone who wants to be well known does not hide what he does. If you are doing these things, show yourself to the world." ⁵(Even Jesus' brothers did not believe in him.)

⁶Jesus said to his brothers, "The right time for me has not yet come, but any time is right for you. ⁷The world cannot hate you, but it hates me, because I tell it the evil things it does. ⁸So you go to the feast. I will not go yet to this feast, because the right time for me has not yet come." ⁹After saying this, Jesus stayed in Galilee.

¹⁰But after Jesus' brothers had gone to the feast, Jesus went also. But he did not let people see him. ¹¹At the feast some people were looking for him and saying, "Where is that man?"

¹²Within the large crowd there, many people were whispering to each other about Jesus. Some said, "He is a good man."

Others said, "No, he fools the people." ¹³But no one was brave enough to talk about Jesus openly, because they were afraid of the older leaders.

## JESUS TEACHES AT THE FEAST

¹⁴When the feast was about half over, Jesus went to the Temple and began to teach. ¹⁵The people were amazed and said, "This man has never studied in school. How did he learn so much?"

¹⁶Jesus answered, "The things I teach are not my own, but they come from him who sent me. ¹⁷If people choose to do what God wants, they will know that my teaching comes from God and not from me. ¹⁸Those who teach their own ideas are trying to get honor for themselves. But those who try to bring honor to the one who sent him speak the truth, and there is nothing false in them. ¹⁹Moses gave you the law," but none of you obeys that law. Why are you trying to kill me?"

²⁰The people answered, "A demon has come into you. We are not trying to kill you."

²¹Jesus said to them, "I did one miracle, and you are all amazed. ²²Moses gave you the law about circumcision. (But really Moses did not give you circumcision; it came from our ancestors.) And yet you circumcise a baby on a Sabbath day. ²³If a baby can be circumcised on a Sabbath day to obey the law of Moses, why are you angry at me for healing a person's whole body on the Sabbath day? ²⁴Stop judging by the way things look, but judge by what is really right."

## IS JESUS THE CHRIST?

²⁵Then some of the people who lived in Jerusalem said, "This is the man they are try-

**7:19 law** Moses gave God's people the Law that God gave him on Mount Sinai (Exodus 34:29-32).

130

ing to kill. [26]But he is teaching where everyone can see and hear him, and no one is trying to stop him. Maybe the leaders have decided he really is the Christ. [27]But we know where this man is from. And when the real Christ comes, no one will know where he comes from."

[28]Jesus, teaching in the Temple, cried out, "Yes, you know me, and you know where I am from. But I have not come by my own authority. I was sent by the One who is true, whom you don't know. [29]But I know him, because I am from him, and he sent me."

[30]When Jesus said this, the people tried to take him. But no one was able to touch him, because it was not yet the right time. [31]But many of the people believed in Jesus. They said, "When the Christ comes, will he do more miracles than this man has done?"

## THE LEADERS TRY TO ARREST JESUS

[32]The Pharisees heard the crowd whispering these things about Jesus. So the leading priests and the Pharisees sent some Temple guards to arrest him. [33]Jesus said, "I will be with you a little while longer. Then I will go back to the One who sent me. [34]You will look for me, but you will not find me. And you cannot come where I am."

[35]Some people said to each other, "Where will this man go so we cannot find him? Will

GUYS SPEAK OUT

**Q:** What things do you worry about the most?
**A:** "I worry about my future the most."

he go to the Greek cities where our people live and teach the Greek people there? [36]What did he mean when he said, 'You will look for me, but you will not find me,' and 'You cannot come where I am'?"

## JESUS TALKS ABOUT THE SPIRIT

[37]On the last and most important day of the feast Jesus stood up and said in a loud voice, "Let anyone who is thirsty come to me and drink. [38]If anyone believes in me, rivers of living water will flow out from that person's heart, as the Scripture says." [39]Jesus was talking about the Holy Spirit. The Spirit had not yet been given, because Jesus had not yet been raised to glory. But later, those who believed in Jesus would receive the Spirit.

## THE PEOPLE ARGUE ABOUT JESUS

[40]When the people heard Jesus' words, some of them said, "This man really is the Prophet."[n]

[41]Others said, "He is the Christ."

> ## "WHEN THE PEOPLE HEARD JESUS' WORDS, SOME OF THEM SAID, 'THIS MAN REALLY IS THE PROPHET.'"

Still others said, "The Christ will not come from Galilee. [42]The Scripture says that the Christ will come from David's family and from Bethlehem, the town where David lived." [43]So the people did not agree with each other about Jesus. [44]Some of them wanted to arrest him, but no one was able to touch him.

## SOME LEADERS WON'T BELIEVE

[45]The Temple guards went back to the leading priests and the Pharisees, who asked, "Why didn't you bring Jesus?"

[46]The guards answered, "The words he says are greater than the words of any other person who has ever spoken!"

[47]The Pharisees answered, "So Jesus has fooled you also! [48]Have any of the leaders or

the Pharisees believed in him? No! [49]But these people, who know nothing about the law, are under God's curse."

[50]Nicodemus, who had gone to see Jesus before, was in that group.[n] He said, [51]"Our law does not judge a man without hearing him and knowing what he has done."

[52]They answered, "Are you from Galilee, too? Study the Scriptures, and you will learn that no prophet comes from Galilee."

---

Some early Greek manuscripts do not contain 7:53—8:11.

[[53]And everyone left and went home.

## THE WOMAN CAUGHT IN ADULTERY

**8** Jesus went to the Mount of Olives. [2]But early in the morning he went back to the Temple, and all the people came to him, and he sat and taught them. [3]The teachers of the law and the Pharisees brought a woman who had been caught in adultery. They forced her to stand before the people. [4]They said to Jesus, "Teacher, this woman was caught having sexual relations with a man who is not her husband. [5]The law of Moses commands that we stone to death every woman who does this. What do you say we should do?" [6]They were asking this to trick Jesus so that they could have some charge against him.

But Jesus bent over and started writing on the ground with his finger. [7]When they continued to ask Jesus their question, he raised up and said, "Anyone here who has never sinned can throw the first stone at her." [8]Then Jesus bent over again and wrote on the ground.

[9]Those who heard Jesus began to leave one by one, first the older men and then the others. Jesus was left there alone with the woman standing before him. [10]Jesus raised up again and asked her, "Woman, where are they? Has no one judged you guilty?"

[11]She answered, "No one, sir."

Then Jesus said, "I also don't judge you guilty. You may go now, but don't sin anymore."]

## JESUS IS THE LIGHT OF THE WORLD

[12]Later, Jesus talked to the people again, saying, "I am the light of the world. The person who follows me will never live in darkness but will have the light that gives life."

[13]The Pharisees said to Jesus, "When you talk about yourself, you are the only one to say these things are true. We cannot accept what you say."

[14]Jesus answered, "Yes, I am saying these things about myself, but they are true. I know where I came from and where I am going. But you don't know where I came from or where I am going. [15]You judge by human standards. I am not judging anyone. [16]But when I do judge, my judging is true, because I am not alone. The Father who sent me is with me. [17]Your own law says that when two witnesses say the same thing, you must accept what they say. [18]I

am one of the witnesses who speaks about myself, and the Father who sent me is the other witness."

[19]They asked, "Where is your father?"

Jesus answered, "You don't know me or my Father. If you knew me, you would know my Father, too." [20]Jesus said these things while he was teaching in the Temple, near where the money is kept. But no one arrested him, because the right time for him had not yet come.

### THE PEOPLE MISUNDERSTAND JESUS

[21]Again, Jesus said to the people, "I will leave you, and you will look for me, but you will die in your sins. You cannot come where I am going."

[22]So the Jews asked, "Will Jesus kill himself? Is that why he said, 'You cannot come where I am going'?"

[23]Jesus said, "You people are from here below, but I am from above. You belong to this world, but I don't belong to this world. [24]So I told you that you would die in your sins. Yes, you will die in your sins if you don't believe that I am he."

[25]They asked, "Then who are you?"

Jesus answered, "I am what I have told you from the beginning. [26]I have many things to say and decide about you. But I tell people only the things I have heard from the One who sent me, and he speaks the truth."

[27]The people did not understand that he was talking to them about the Father. [28]So Jesus said to them, "When you lift up the Son of Man, you will know that I am he. You will know that these things I do are not by my own authority but that I say only what the Father has taught me. [29]The One who sent me is with me. I always do what is pleasing to him, so he

has not left me alone." [30]While Jesus was saying these things, many people believed in him.

## FREEDOM FROM SIN

[31]So Jesus said to the Jews who believed in him, "If you continue to obey my teaching, you are truly my followers. [32]Then you will know the truth, and the truth will make you free."

[33]They answered, "We are Abraham's children, and we have never been anyone's slaves. So why do you say we will be free?"

[34]Jesus answered, "I tell you the truth, everyone who lives in sin is a slave to sin. [35]A slave does not stay with a family forever, but a son belongs to the family forever. [36]So if the Son makes you free, you will be truly free. [37]I know you are Abraham's children, but you want to kill me because you don't accept my teaching. [38]I am telling you what my Father has shown me, but you do what your father has told you."

[39]They answered, "Our father is Abraham."

Jesus said, "If you were really Abraham's children, you would do the things Abraham did. [40]I am a man who has told you the truth which I heard from God, but you are trying to kill me. Abraham did nothing like that. [41]So you are doing the things your own father did."

But they said, "We are not like children who never knew who their father was. God is our Father; he is the only Father we have."

## "IF YOU KNEW ME, YOU WOULD KNOW MY FATHER, TOO."

[42]Jesus said to them, "If God were really your Father, you would love me, because I came from God and now I am here. I did not come by my

DIDYA KNOW — **THREE OUT OF FIVE YOUTH WISH THEY COULD SPEND MORE TIME WITH THEIR PARENTS.** EPM COMMUNICATIONS

## beauty secret

### Blending Makeup

One of the biggest mistakes women make when applying their makeup is forgetting to blend. Use makeup brushes and sponge-tipped applicators to make sure your makeup appears natural, without a specific beginning or end—especially between your face and your neck.

own authority; God sent me. ⁴³You don't understand what I say, because you cannot accept my teaching. ⁴⁴You belong to your father the devil, and you want to do what he wants. He was a murderer from the beginning and was against the truth, because there is no truth in him. When he tells a lie, he shows what he is really like, because he is a liar and the father of lies. ⁴⁵But because I speak the truth, you don't believe me. ⁴⁶Can any of you prove that I am guilty of sin? If I am telling the truth, why don't you believe me? ⁴⁷The person who belongs to God accepts what God says. But you don't accept what God says, because you don't belong to God."

## Jesus Is Greater Than Abraham

⁴⁸They answered, "We say you are a Samaritan and have a demon in you. Are we not right?"

## "THE PERSON WHO BELONGS TO GOD ACCEPTS WHAT GOD SAYS."

⁴⁹Jesus answered, "I have no demon in me. I give honor to my Father, but you dishonor me. ⁵⁰I am not trying to get honor for myself. There is One who wants this honor for me, and he is the judge. ⁵¹I tell you the truth, whoever obeys my teaching will never die."

⁵²They said to Jesus, "Now we know that you have a demon in you! Even Abraham and the prophets died. But you say, 'Whoever obeys my teaching will never die.' ⁵³Do you think you are greater than our father Abraham, who died? And the prophets died, too. Who do you think you are?"

⁵⁴Jesus answered, "If I give honor to myself, that honor is worth nothing. The One who gives me honor is my Father, and you say he is your God. ⁵⁵You don't really know him, but I know him. If I said I did not know him, I would be a liar like you. But I do know him, and I obey what he says. ⁵⁶Your father

Abraham was very happy that he would see my day. He saw that day and was glad."

⁵⁷They said to him, "You have never seen Abraham! You are not even fifty years old."

⁵⁸Jesus answered, "I tell you the truth, before Abraham was even born, I am!" ⁵⁹When Jesus said this, the people picked up stones to throw at him. But Jesus hid himself, and then he left the Temple.

## Jesus Heals a Man Born Blind

9 As Jesus was walking along, he saw a man who had been born blind. ²His followers asked him, "Teacher, whose sin caused this man to be born blind—his own sin or his parents' sin?"

³Jesus answered, "It is not this man's sin or his parents' sin that made him be blind. This man was born blind so that God's power could be shown in him. ⁴While it is daytime, we must continue doing the work of the One who sent me. Night is coming, when no one can work. ⁵While I am in the world, I am the light of the world."

⁶After Jesus said this, he spit on the ground and made some mud with it and put the mud on the man's eyes. ⁷Then he told the man, "Go and wash in the Pool of Siloam." (Siloam means Sent.) So the man went, washed, and came back seeing.

⁸The neighbors and some people who had earlier seen this man begging said, "Isn't this the same man who used to sit and beg?"

⁹Some said, "He is the one," but others said, "No, he only looks like him."

The man himself said, "I am the man."

¹⁰They asked, "How did you get your sight?"

¹¹He answered, "The man named Jesus made some mud and put it on my eyes. Then he told me to go to Siloam and wash. So I went and washed, and then I could see."

¹²They asked him, "Where is this man?"

"I don't know," he answered.

## Pharisees Question the Healing

¹³Then the people took to the Pharisees the man who had been blind. ¹⁴The day Jesus had

## Radical Faith:

## John 9:1-3, 6-7

Tragedies, failures, heartbreaks, losses—it's usually hard to make sense of any of the bad things that happen in our lives. This man in John 9 had never seen sunlight or his mother's eyes. He had little food and money. Popular teaching of the day said that the man or his parents must have sinned since he was disabled. He was probably ignored or called a loser. But things changed when Jesus stepped into the equation. You take a broken man with profound pain and put him into the hands of the living God, and suddenly you get a glimpse of God's extreme power and goodness of heart. Jesus healed him and declared to his followers that sometimes ailments and hardships in our lives are present so that we can be less and God can be more. Would you have been able to see the beauty of God in this man's seemingly wrecked life? God will use all kinds of situations to reveal himself to you. And sometimes they will be hard to deal with. Trust that God is working in your life and that he will wonderfully and powerfully fill your life with himself.

made mud and healed his eyes was a Sabbath day. ¹⁵So now the Pharisees asked the man, "How did you get your sight?"

He answered, "He put mud on my eyes, I washed, and now I see."

¹⁶So some of the Pharisees were saying, "This man does not keep the Sabbath day, so he is not from God."

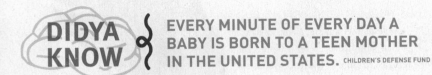

## DIDYA KNOW
**EVERY MINUTE OF EVERY DAY A BABY IS BORN TO A TEEN MOTHER IN THE UNITED STATES.** CHILDREN'S DEFENSE FUND

But others said, "A man who is a sinner can't do miracles like these." So they could not agree with each other.

¹⁷They asked the man again, "What do you say about him since it was your eyes he opened?"

The man answered, "He is a prophet."

¹⁸These leaders did not believe that he had been blind and could now see again. So they sent for the man's parents ¹⁹and asked them, "Is this your son who you say was born blind? Then how does he now see?"

²⁰His parents answered, "We know that this is our son and that he was born blind. ²¹But we don't know how he can now see. We don't know who opened his eyes. Ask him. He is old enough to speak for himself." ²²His parents said this because they were afraid of the older leaders, who had already decided that anyone who said Jesus was the Christ would be avoided. ²³That is why his parents said, "He is old enough. Ask him."

²⁴So for the second time, they called the man who had been blind. They said, "You should give God the glory by telling the truth. We know that this man is a sinner."

²⁵He answered, "I don't know if he is a sinner. One thing I do know: I was blind, and now I see."

²⁶They asked, "What did he do to you? How did he make you see again?"

²⁷He answered, "I already told you, and you didn't listen. Why do you want to hear it again? Do you want to become his followers, too?"

²⁸Then they insulted him and said, "You are his follower, but we are followers of Moses. ²⁹We know that God spoke to Moses, but we don't even know where this man comes from."

³⁰The man answered, "This is a very strange thing. You don't know where he comes from, and yet he opened my eyes. ³¹We all know that God does not listen to sinners, but he listens to anyone who worships and obeys him. ³²Nobody has ever heard of anyone giving sight to a man born blind. ³³If this man were not from God, he could do nothing."

³⁴They answered, "You were born full of sin! Are you trying to teach us?" And they threw him out.

### SPIRITUAL BLINDNESS

³⁵When Jesus heard that they had thrown him out, Jesus found him and said, "Do you believe in the Son of Man?"

³⁶He asked, "Who is the Son of Man, sir, so that I can believe in him?"

³⁷Jesus said to him, "You have seen him. The Son of Man is the one talking with you."

³⁸He said, "Lord, I believe!" Then the man worshiped Jesus.

³⁹Jesus said, "I came into this world so that the world could be judged. I came so that the blind" would see and so that those who see will become blind."

⁴⁰Some of the Pharisees who were nearby heard Jesus say this and asked, "Are you saying we are blind, too?"

⁴¹Jesus said, "If you were blind, you would not be guilty of sin. But since you keep saying you see, your guilt remains."

### THE SHEPHERD AND HIS SHEEP

**10** Jesus said, "I tell you the truth, the person who does not enter the sheepfold by the door, but climbs in some other way, is a thief and a robber. ²The one who enters by the door is the shepherd of the sheep. ³The one who guards the door opens it for him. And the sheep listen to the voice of the shepherd. He calls his own sheep by name and leads them out. ⁴When he brings all his sheep out, he goes ahead of them, and they follow him because they know his voice. ⁵But they will never follow a stranger. They will run away from him because they don't know his voice." ⁶Jesus told the people this story, but they did not understand what it meant.

> ## "JESUS SAID, 'I CAME INTO THIS WORLD SO THAT THE WORLD COULD BE JUDGED. I CAME SO THAT THE BLIND WOULD SEE AND SO THAT THOSE WHO SEE WILL BECOME BLIND.'"

### JESUS IS THE GOOD SHEPHERD

⁷So Jesus said again, "I tell you the truth, I am the door for the sheep. ⁸All the people who came before me were thieves and robbers. The sheep did not listen to them. ⁹I am the door, and the person who enters through me will be saved and will be able to come in and go out and find pasture. ¹⁰A thief comes to steal and kill and destroy, but I came to give life—life in all its fullness.

¹¹"I am the good shepherd. The good shepherd gives his life for the sheep. ¹²The worker who is paid to keep the sheep is different from the shepherd who owns them. When the worker sees a wolf coming, he runs away and leaves the sheep alone. Then the wolf attacks the sheep and scatters them. ¹³The man runs away because he is only a paid worker and does not really care about the sheep.

**9:39 blind** Jesus is talking about people who are spiritually blind, not physically blind.

14-15"I am the good shepherd. I know my sheep, as the Father knows me. And my sheep know me, as I know the Father. I give my life for the sheep. 16I have other sheep that are not in this flock, and I must bring them also. They will listen to my voice, and there will be one flock and one shepherd. 17The Father loves me because I give my life so that I can take it back again. 18No one takes it away from me; I give my own life freely. I have the right to give my life, and I have the right to take it back. This is what my Father commanded me to do."

19Again the leaders did not agree with each other because of these words of Jesus. 20Many of them said, "A demon has come into him and made him crazy. Why listen to him?"

21But others said, "A man who is crazy with a demon does not say things like this. Can a demon open the eyes of the blind?"

## Jesus is Rejected

22The time came for the Feast of Dedication at Jerusalem. It was winter, 23and Jesus was walking in the Temple in Solomon's Porch. 24Some people gathered around him and said, "How long will you make us wonder about you? If you are the Christ, tell us plainly."

25Jesus answered, "I told you already, but you did not believe. The miracles I do in my Father's name show who I am. 26But you don't believe, because you are not my sheep. 27My sheep listen to my voice; I know them, and they follow me. 28I give them eternal life, and they will never die, and no one can steal them out of my hand. 29My Father gave my sheep to me. He is greater than all, and no person can steal my sheep out of my Father's hand. 30The Father and I are one."

31Again some of the people picked up stones to kill Jesus. 32But he said to them, "I have done many good works from the Father. Which of these good works are you killing me for?"

33They answered, "We are not killing you because of any good work you did, but because you speak against God. You are only a human, but you say you are the same as God!"

34Jesus answered, "It is written in your law that God said, 'I said, you are gods.'" 35This Scripture called those people gods who received God's message, and Scripture is always true. 36So why do you say that I speak against God because I said, 'I am God's Son'? I am the one God chose and sent into the world. 37If I don't do what my Father does, then don't believe me. 38But if I do what my Father does, even though you don't believe in me, believe what I do. Then you will know and understand that the Father is in me and I am in the Father."

39They tried to take Jesus again, but he escaped from them.

40Then he went back across the Jordan River to the place where John had first baptized. Jesus stayed there, 41and many people came to him and said, "John never did a miracle, but everything John said about this man is true." 42And in that place many believed in Jesus.

## The Death of Lazarus

11 A man named Lazarus was sick. He lived in the town of Bethany, where Mary and her sister Martha lived. 2Mary was the woman who later put perfume on the Lord and wiped his feet with her hair. Mary's brother was Lazarus, the man who was now sick. 3So Mary and Martha sent someone to tell Jesus, "Lord, the one you love is sick."

4When Jesus heard this, he said, "This sickness will not end in death. It is for the glory of God, to bring glory to the Son of God." 5Jesus loved Martha and her sister and Lazarus. 6But when he heard that Lazarus was sick, he stayed where he was for two more days. 7Then Jesus said to his followers, "Let's go back to Judea."

8The followers said, "But Teacher, some people there tried to stone you to death only a short time ago. Now you want to go back there?"

## *Music Reviews*

GROUP:

SUPERCHIC[K]

ALBUM:

KARAOKE SUPERSTARS (CLASSIC HIT)

Superchic[k] was the brainchild of a guy named Max Hsu, who met two sisters at a concert and asked them if they wanted to be in a band. Max wrote and produced the songs, and this album came out before Superchic[k] had really even played live. Now Max, sisters Tricia and Melissa Brock, and a couple of other friends sing songs that have appeared on TV shows, movies, and even JC Penney commercials. Superchic[k] makes bouncy pop rock with crunchy guitars and lots of pop culture references.

**WHY IT ROCKS: SUPERCHIC[K] ADDRESSES ISSUES WE DEAL WITH DAILY, WRAPPED IN POP ROCK PACKAGES THAT ARE TONS OF FUN TO OPEN.**

**10:34 'I . . . gods.'** Quotation from Psalm 82:6.

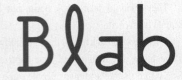

**Q:** My friend's dad is in the service, and he is fighting overseas. She is really worried about him. How can I help?

**A:** Ask her if you can pray with her regularly for her dad. Ask for a picture of him that you can put in your prayer notebook to remind you to pray. Help her write letters to him or put together a care package that you can mail. Tell her how proud you are of her dad.

**Q:** I want to be an encouragement to those fighting for our country. What can I do?

**A:** Thank men and women in military uniforms for their service whenever you see them. Call the local armed forces offices and ask them how you can obtain names of soldiers who might need letters of support or care packages. Gather donations at church or school (with permission) and mail the packages to soldiers.

**Q:** How can I support our country's leaders? I know the Bible says something about that.

**A:** It does say to live under the rule of your country's leaders. Add pictures of the president and other leaders to your prayer notebook and pray for them regularly. Ask God to give them wisdom and discernment. Visit www.presidentialprayerteam.org for other ideas.

⁹Jesus answered, "Are there not twelve hours in the day? If anyone walks in the daylight, he will not stumble, because he can see by this world's light. ¹⁰But if anyone walks at night, he stumbles because there is no light to help him see."

¹¹After Jesus said this, he added, "Our friend Lazarus has fallen asleep, but I am going there to wake him."

¹²The followers said, "But Lord, if he is only asleep, he will be all right."

¹³Jesus meant that Lazarus was dead, but his followers thought he meant Lazarus was really sleeping. ¹⁴So then Jesus said plainly, "Lazarus is dead. ¹⁵And I am glad for your sakes I was not there so that you may believe. But let's go to him now."

¹⁶Then Thomas (the one called Didymus) said to the other followers, "Let us also go so that we can die with him."

### Jesus in Bethany

¹⁷When Jesus arrived, he learned that Lazarus had already been dead and in the tomb for four days. ¹⁸Bethany was about two miles from Jerusalem. ¹⁹Many of the Jews had come there to comfort Martha and Mary about their brother.

²⁰When Martha heard that Jesus was coming, she went out to meet him, but Mary stayed home. ²¹Martha said to Jesus, "Lord, if you had been here, my brother would not have died. ²²But I know that even now God will give you anything you ask."

²³Jesus said, "Your brother will rise and live again."

²⁴Martha answered, "I know that he will rise and live again in the resurrection" on the last day."

²⁵Jesus said to her, "I am the resurrection and the life. Those who believe in me will have life even if they die. ²⁶And everyone who lives and believes in me will never die. Martha, do you believe this?"

²⁷Martha answered, "Yes, Lord. I believe that you are the Christ, the Son of God, the One coming to the world."

### Jesus Cries

²⁸After Martha said this, she went back and talked to her sister Mary alone. Martha said, "The Teacher is here and he is asking for you." ²⁹When Mary heard this, she got up quickly and went to Jesus. ³⁰Jesus had not yet come into the town but was still at the place where Martha had met him. ³¹The Jews were with Mary in the house, comforting her. When they saw her stand and leave quickly, they followed her, thinking she was going to the tomb to cry there.

³²But Mary went to the place where Jesus was. When she saw him, she fell at his feet and said, "Lord, if you had been here, my brother would not have died."

## "THEN JESUS SAID TO HER, 'DIDN'T I TELL YOU THAT IF YOU BELIEVED YOU WOULD SEE THE GLORY OF GOD?' "

³³When Jesus saw Mary crying and the Jews who came with her also crying, he was upset and was deeply troubled. ³⁴He asked, "Where did you bury him?"

"Come and see, Lord," they said.

³⁵Jesus cried.

³⁶So the Jews said, "See how much he loved him."

³⁷But some of them said, "If Jesus opened the eyes of the blind man, why couldn't he keep Lazarus from dying?"

### Jesus Raises Lazarus

³⁸Again feeling very upset, Jesus came to the tomb. It was a cave with a large stone covering the entrance. ³⁹Jesus said, "Move the stone away."

Martha, the sister of the dead man, said, "But, Lord, it has been four days since he died. There will be a bad smell."

⁴⁰Then Jesus said to her, "Didn't I tell you that if you believed you would see the glory of God?"

 **notes**    11:24 **resurrection** Being raised from the dead to live again.

136

[41]So they moved the stone away from the entrance. Then Jesus looked up and said, "Father, I thank you that you heard me. [42]I know that you always hear me, but I said these things because of the people here around me. I want them to believe that you sent me." [43]After Jesus said this, he cried out in a loud voice, "Lazarus, come out!" [44]The dead man came out, his hands and feet wrapped with pieces of cloth, and a cloth around his face.

Jesus said to them, "Take the cloth off of him and let him go."

### THE PLAN TO KILL JESUS

[45]Many of the people, who had come to visit Mary and saw what Jesus did, believed in him. [46]But some of them went to the Pharisees and told them what Jesus had done. [47]Then the leading priests and Pharisees called a meeting of the council. They asked, "What should we do? This man is doing many miracles. [48]If we let him continue doing these things, everyone will believe in him. Then the Romans will come and take away our Temple and our nation."

[49]One of the men there was Caiaphas, the high priest that year. He said, "You people know nothing! [50]You don't realize that it is better for one man to die for the people than for the whole nation to be destroyed."

[51]Caiaphas did not think of this himself. As high priest that year, he was really prophesying that Jesus would die for their nation [52]and for God's scattered children to bring them all together and make them one.

[53]That day they started planning to kill Jesus. [54]So Jesus no longer traveled openly among the people. He left there and went to a place near the desert, to a town called Ephraim and stayed there with his followers.

[55]It was almost time for the Passover Feast. Many from the country went up to Jerusalem before the Passover to do the special things to make themselves pure. [56]The people looked for Jesus and stood in the Temple asking each other, "Is he coming to the Feast? What do you think?" [57]But the leading priests and the Pharisees had given orders that if anyone

BIBLE BIOS

## Hagar

[GENESIS 16] As Sarah's maidservant, Hagar was pretty much obligated to do whatever Sarah wanted. When Sarah got impatient waiting for God to fulfill his promise to give her a child, she insisted that Hagar sleep with her husband Abraham so she might have a baby for them. When Hagar did what she was told, sure enough, she got pregnant. Then what did Sarah do? She became jealous and treated Hagar even worse. Rather than going to God for help, Hagar ran away. When she finally stopped, she found that God was waiting to answer and keep her life from spinning out of control. Hagar's problems were big, but God was there with a solution. She just had to ask.

knew where Jesus was, he must tell them. Then they could arrest him.

> "MANY FROM THE COUNTRY WENT UP TO JERUSALEM BEFORE THE PASSOVER TO DO THE SPECIAL THINGS TO MAKE THEMSELVES PURE."

### JESUS WITH FRIENDS IN BETHANY

12 Six days before the Passover Feast, Jesus went to Bethany, where Lazarus lived. (Lazarus is the man Jesus raised from the dead.) [2]There they had a dinner for Jesus. Martha served the food, and Lazarus was one of the people eating with Jesus. [3]Mary brought in a pint of very expensive perfume made from pure nard. She poured the perfume on Jesus' feet, and then she wiped his feet with her hair. And the sweet smell from the perfume filled the whole house.

[4]Judas Iscariot, one of Jesus' followers who would later turn against him, was there. Judas said, [5]"This perfume was worth three hundred coins." Why wasn't it sold and the money given to the poor?" [6]But Judas did not really care about the poor; he said this because he was a thief. He was the one who kept the money box, and he often stole from it.

[7]Jesus answered, "Leave her alone. It was right for her to save this perfume for today, the day for me to be prepared for burial. [8]You will always have the poor with you, but you will not always have me."

### THE PLOT AGAINST LAZARUS

[9]A large crowd of people heard that Jesus was in Bethany. So they went there to see not only Jesus but Lazarus, whom Jesus raised from the dead. [10]So the leading priests made plans to kill Lazarus, too. [11]Because of Lazarus many of the Jews were leaving them and believing in Jesus.

**12:5 coins** One coin, a denarius, was the average pay for one day's work.

137

## Radical Faith:

# John 12:25-26

Often, we tend to give ourselves over to whatever matters most to us in life. Jesus says that those who love their lives will actually lose them and those who hate their lives will actually live. At first glance, this statement seems like a riddle. What does he mean by hating your life? Basically Jesus is talking about putting God's agenda above your own—with an end result of having a life that is deeply devoted to God. If you live only to build up your own life by striving for achievements, cool stuff, popularity, a comfortable lifestyle, or personal pleasure, you will end up empty and unsatisfied. You'll have nothing in the end. But if you live aiming to build up God's kingdom and giving everything you can to him, you'll know true purpose, joy, and life. God honors such a life. Give control of your life to Christ. Don't live consumed with yourself. Be concerned with following Jesus' teaching and staying in his presence. You'll either spend your life living for yourself or for him. What are you doing right now?

## JESUS ENTERS JERUSALEM

¹²The next day a great crowd who had come to Jerusalem for the Passover Feast heard that Jesus was coming there. ¹³So they took branches of palm trees and went out to meet Jesus, shouting,

"Praise" God!
God bless the One who comes in the name of the Lord!
God bless the King of Israel!"

*Psalm 118:25-26*

¹⁴Jesus found a colt and sat on it. This was as the Scripture says,

¹⁵"Don't be afraid, people of Jerusalem!
Your king is coming,
sitting on the colt of a donkey."

*Zechariah 9:9*

¹⁶The followers of Jesus did not understand this at first. But after Jesus was raised to glory, they remembered that this had been written about him and that they had done these things to him.

## PEOPLE TELL ABOUT JESUS

¹⁷There had been many people with Jesus when he raised Lazarus from the dead and told him to come out of the tomb. Now they were telling others about what Jesus did. ¹⁸Many people went out to meet Jesus, because they had heard about this miracle. ¹⁹So the Pharisees said to each other, "You can see that nothing is going right for us. Look! The whole world is following him."

## JESUS TALKS ABOUT HIS DEATH

²⁰There were some Greek people, too, who came to Jerusalem to worship at the Passover Feast. ²¹They went to Philip, who was from Bethsaida in Galilee, and said, "Sir, we would like to see Jesus." ²²Philip told Andrew, and then Andrew and Philip told Jesus.

²³Jesus said to them, "The time has come for the Son of Man to receive his glory. ²⁴I tell you the truth, a grain of wheat must fall to the ground and die to make many seeds. But if it never dies, it remains only a single seed. ²⁵Those who love their lives will lose them, but those who hate their lives in this world will keep true life forever. ²⁶Whoever serves me must follow me. Then my servant will be with me everywhere I am. My Father will honor anyone who serves me.

²⁷"Now I am very troubled. Should I say, 'Father, save me from this time'? No, I came to this time so I could suffer. ²⁸Father, bring glory to your name!"

Then a voice came from heaven, "I have brought glory to it, and I will do it again." ²⁹The crowd standing there, who heard the voice, said it was thunder.

But others said, "An angel has spoken to him."

³⁰Jesus said, "That voice was for your sake, not mine. ³¹Now is the time for the world to be judged; now the ruler of this world will be thrown down. ³²If I am lifted up from the earth, I will draw all people toward me." ³³Jesus said this to show how he would die.

³⁴The crowd said, "We have heard from the law that the Christ will live forever. So why do you say, 'The Son of Man must be lifted up'? Who is this 'Son of Man'?"

³⁵Then Jesus said, "The light will be with you for a little longer, so walk while you have the light. Then the darkness will not catch you. If you walk in the darkness, you will not know where you are going. ³⁶Believe in the light while you still have it so that you will become children of light." When Jesus had said this, he left and hid himself from them.

## SOME PEOPLE WON'T BELIEVE IN JESUS

³⁷Though Jesus had done many miracles in front of the people, they still did not believe in him. ³⁸This was to bring about what Isaiah the prophet had said:

"Lord, who believed what we told them?
Who saw the Lord's power in this?"

*Isaiah 53:1*

³⁹This is why the people could not believe: Isaiah also had said,

⁴⁰"He has blinded their eyes,
and he has closed their minds.
Otherwise they would see with their eyes

12:13 **Praise** Literally, "Hosanna," a Hebrew word used at first in praying to God for help, but at this time it was probably a shout of joy used in praising God or his Messiah.

and understand in their minds
and come back to me and be healed."

*Isaiah 6:10*

⁴¹Isaiah said this because he saw Jesus' glory and spoke about him.

⁴²But many believed in Jesus, even many of the leaders. But because of the Pharisees, they did not say they believed in him for fear they would be put out of the synagogue. ⁴³They loved praise from people more than praise from God.

⁴⁴Then Jesus cried out, "Whoever believes in me is really believing in the One who sent me. ⁴⁵Whoever sees me sees the One who sent me. ⁴⁶I have come as light into the world so that whoever believes in me would not stay in darkness.

⁴⁷"Anyone who hears my words and does not obey them, I do not judge, because I did not come to judge the world, but to save the world. ⁴⁸There is a judge for those who refuse to believe in me and do not accept my words. The word I have taught will be their judge on the last day. ⁴⁹The things I taught were not from myself. The Father who sent me told me what to say and what to teach. ⁵⁰And I know that eternal life comes from what the Father commands. So whatever I say is what the Father told me to say."

## Bible Basics

God refers to himself by many names throughout the Bible so that we can get to know him and get closer to him. We can begin to understand his personality and attributes by the names he has in Scripture. Among the many are Wonderful Counselor, Powerful God, Father Who Lives Forever, I Am Who I Am, Prince of Peace, Lord of lords, King of kings, Immanuel (which means "God is with us"), the Alpha and Omega (the beginning and the end), and the Great Shepherd. A quick look at this list shows us that God has existed since before time began. He will live forever, and he treats us as his much-loved children. He looks after us as a shepherd would a precious flock, listens and gives wise advice, calms us, brings peace in our lives, and has supreme authority. Wow!

### JESUS WASHES HIS FOLLOWERS' FEET

**13** It was almost time for the Passover Feast. Jesus knew that it was time for him to leave this world and go back to the Father. He had always loved those who were his own in the world, and he loved them all the way to the end.

²Jesus and his followers were at the evening meal. The devil had already persuaded Judas Iscariot, the son of Simon, to turn against Jesus. ³Jesus knew that the Father had given him power over everything and that he had come from God and was going back to God. ⁴So during the meal Jesus stood up and took off his outer clothing. Taking a towel, he wrapped it around his waist. ⁵Then he poured water into a bowl and began to wash the followers' feet, drying them with the towel that was wrapped around him.

⁶Jesus came to Simon Peter, who said to him, "Lord, are you going to wash my feet?"

## ⊙➡ CHECK IT OUT

### RONALD MCDONALD CHARITIES

The Ronald McDonald Charities have been helping families with seriously ill children since 1974. The Ronald McDonald Houses provides a homelike atmosphere where families of hospitalized children can stay and eat meals for free or for a small fee in order to be close to the hospital and their children. The houses have family areas, playrooms, a community kitchen, and other advantages to help families stay connected.

Other programs include the Ronald McDonald Care Mobiles, which since 2000 have provided immunizations, medical, and dental care to underserved children; Ronald McDonald Family Rooms, comfortable rooms within hospitals where families can stay close to children undergoing treatment; and the RMHC scholarship programs for deserving African-American, Asian, and Hispanic-American students.

Ronald McDonald Charities need volunteers to help care for the houses, including cooking, cleaning, answering phones, and checking families in and out of the properties.

*Get involved by visiting **www.rmhc.com**.*

7Jesus answered, "You don't understand now what I am doing, but you will understand later."

8Peter said, "No, you will never wash my feet."

Jesus answered, "If I don't wash your feet, you are not one of my people."

9Simon Peter answered, "Lord, then wash not only my feet, but wash my hands and my head, too!"

10Jesus said, "After a person has had a bath, his whole body is clean. He needs only to wash his feet. And you men are clean, but not all of you." 11Jesus knew who would turn against him, and that is why he said, "Not all of you are clean."

12When he had finished washing their feet, he put on his clothes and sat down again. He asked, "Do you understand what I have just done for you? 13You call me 'Teacher' and 'Lord,' and you are right, because that is what I am. 14If I, your Lord and Teacher, have washed your feet, you also should wash each other's feet. 15I did this as an example so that you should do as I have done for you. 16I tell you the truth, a servant is not greater than his master. A messenger is not greater than the one who sent him. 17If you know these things, you will be happy if you do them.

18"I am not talking about all of you. I know those I have chosen. But this is to bring about what the Scripture said: 'The man who ate at my table has turned against me.'" 19I am telling you this now before it happens so that when it happens, you will believe that I am he. 20I tell you the truth, whoever accepts anyone I send also accepts me. And whoever accepts me also accepts the One who sent me."

## JESUS TALKS ABOUT HIS DEATH

21After Jesus said this, he was very troubled. He said openly, "I tell you the truth, one of you will turn against me."

22The followers all looked at each other, because they did not know whom Jesus was talking about. 23One of the followers sitting" next to Jesus was the follower Jesus loved. 24Simon Peter motioned to him to ask Jesus whom he was talking about.

25That follower leaned closer to Jesus and asked, "Lord, who is it?"

26Jesus answered, "I will dip this bread into the dish. The man I give it to is the man who will turn against me." So Jesus took a piece of bread, dipped it, and gave it to Judas Iscariot, the son of Simon. 27As soon as Judas took the bread, Satan entered him. Jesus said to him, "The thing that you will do—do it quickly." 28No one at the table understood why Jesus said this to Judas. 29Since he was the one who kept the money box, some of the followers thought Jesus was telling him to buy what was needed for the feast or to give something to the poor.

30Judas took the bread Jesus gave him and immediately went out. It was night.

31When Judas was gone, Jesus said, "Now the Son of Man receives his glory, and God receives glory through him. 32If God receives glory through him, then God will give glory to the Son through himself. And God will give him glory quickly."

## "I GIVE YOU A NEW COMMAND: LOVE EACH OTHER. YOU MUST LOVE EACH OTHER AS I HAVE LOVED YOU."

33Jesus said, "My children, I will be with you only a little longer. You will look for me, and what I told the Jews, I tell you now: Where I am going you cannot come.

34"I give you a new command: Love each other. You must love each other as I have loved you. 35All people will know that you are my followers if you love each other."

## PETER WILL SAY HE DOESN'T KNOW JESUS

36Simon Peter asked Jesus, "Lord, where are you going?"

Jesus answered, "Where I am going you cannot follow now, but you will follow later."

37Peter asked, "Lord, why can't I follow you now? I am ready to die for you!"

38Jesus answered, "Are you ready to die for me? I tell you the truth, before the rooster crows, you will say three times that you don't know me."

## JESUS COMFORTS HIS FOLLOWERS

14 Jesus said, "Don't let your hearts be troubled. Trust in God, and trust in me. 2There are many rooms in my Father's house; I would not tell you this if it were not true. I am going there to prepare a place for you. 3After I go and prepare a place for you, I will come back and take you to be with me so that you may be where I am. 4You know the way to the place where I am going."

# relationships

"Dear friends, you are like foreigners and strangers in this world. I beg you to avoid the evil things your bodies want to do that fight against your soul" (1 Peter 2:11). If you have never been popular, don't try to change yourself to move up the social ladder. If you love God and show it, chances are people may think you are different. Hang in there—God will see you through. Be friendly, and ask God to help you not take it personally. He will bring you real friends who will love and accept you for you.

**notes** 13:18 'The man . . . me.' Quotation from Psalm 41:9. 13:23 sitting Literally, "lying." The people of that time ate lying down and leaning on one arm.

**140**

[5]Thomas said to Jesus, "Lord, we don't know where you are going. So how can we know the way?"

[6]Jesus answered, "I am the way, and the truth, and the life. The only way to the Father is through me. [7]If you really knew me, you would know my Father, too. But now you do know him, and you have seen him."

[8]Philip said to him, "Lord, show us the Father. That is all we need."

[9]Jesus answered, "I have been with you a long time now. Do you still not know me, Philip? Whoever has seen me has seen the Father. So why do you say, 'Show us the Father'? [10]Don't you believe that I am in the Father and the Father is in me? The words I say to you don't come from me, but the Father lives in me and does his own work. [11]Believe me when I say that I am in the Father and the Father is in me. Or believe because of the miracles I have done. [12]I tell you the truth, whoever believes in me will do the same things that I do. Those who believe will do even greater things than these, because I am going to the Father. [13]And if you ask for anything in my name, I will do it for you so that the Father's glory will be shown through the Son. [14]If you ask me for anything in my name, I will do it.

## THE PROMISE OF THE HOLY SPIRIT

[15]"If you love me, you will obey my commands. [16]I will ask the Father, and he will give you another Helper" to be with you forever— [17]the Spirit of truth. The world cannot accept him, because it does not see him or know him. But you know him, because he lives with you and he will be in you.

[18]"I will not leave you all alone like orphans; I will come back to you. [19]In a little while the world will not see me anymore, but you will see me. Because I live, you will live, too. [20]On that day you will know that I am in my Father, and that you are in me and I am in you. [21]Those who know my commands and obey them are the ones who love me, and my Father will love those who love me. I will love them and will show myself to them."

[22]Then Judas (not Judas Iscariot) said, "But, Lord, why do you plan to show yourself to us and not to the rest of the world?"

[23]Jesus answered, "If people love me, they will obey my teaching. My Father will love them, and we will come to them and make our home with them. [24]Those who do not love me do not obey my teaching. This teaching that you hear is not really mine; it is from my Father, who sent me.

[25]"I have told you all these things while I am with you. [26]But the Helper will teach you everything and will cause you to remember all that I told you. This Helper is the Holy Spirit whom the Father will send in my name.

[27]"I leave you peace; my peace I give you. I do not give it to you as the world does. So don't let your hearts be troubled or afraid. [28]You heard me say to you, 'I am going, but I am coming back to you.' If you loved me, you should be happy that I am going back to the Father, because he is greater than I am. [29]I have told you this now, before it happens, so that when it happens, you will believe. [30]I will not talk with you much longer, because the ruler of this world is coming. He has no power over me, [31]but the world must know that I love the Father, so I do exactly what the Father told me to do.

"Come now, let us go.

## JESUS IS LIKE A VINE

**15** "I am the true vine; my Father is the gardener. [2]He cuts off every branch of

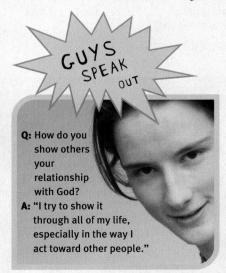

## John 14:27

What does *peace* mean to you? Do you feel peaceful if you're in a nice, quiet place or listening to some relaxing music? Or maybe you consider a cease-fire between you and your brother for more than one afternoon peaceful. Finishing a big project at school may also give you peace of mind that you did a good job. Some people declutter their homes to create a peaceful atmosphere. Others go on tropical vacations so they can relax and discover inner peace. (Hawaii, anyone?)

But even though most of these things are beneficial to you and can help you rest and relax, they never seem to last long enough, do they? Vacations end. You have another big test next week. Your brother trashes your room. Houses get messy and chaotic. And we start to worry and get anxious all over again. The peace that Jesus offers us is far more lasting than anything we can create ourselves. He offers us eternal peace—so we can know that no matter how chaotic things get and how out of control our lives can seem sometimes, we have been offered eternal life and the knowledge that God is in control. Not even the best travel agent in the world can guarantee that.

notes    **14:16 Helper** "Counselor" or "Comforter." Jesus is talking about the Holy Spirit.

# Quiz

# are you too BODY-conscious?

**FOR EACH STATEMENT, CIRCLE THE NUMBER ON THE SCALE THAT BEST DESCRIBES HOW YOU FEEL.**

WHEN I LOOK IN THE MIRROR, I'M GENERALLY PLEASED WITH WHAT I SEE.

NEVER 1 2 3 4 5 6 7 8 9 10 ALWAYS

I DON'T LIKE TO LOOK AT PICTURES OF MYSELF.

HATE IT 1 2 3 4 5 6 7 8 9 10 DON'T MIND IT

I TEND TO JUDGE OTHER WOMEN BY THE WAY THEY LOOK.

ABSOLUTELY ME 1 2 3 4 5 6 7 8 9 10 NOT ME

I LIKE TO TRY NEW STYLES AND TO EXPERIMENT WITH CLOTHES.

NEVER 1 2 3 4 5 6 7 8 9 10 ALL OF THE TIME

EATING OUT WITH OTHER PEOPLE IS ABSOLUTELY NO FUN FOR ME.

I AGREE 1 2 3 4 5 6 7 8 9 10 I DISAGREE

I CAN NAME ONE PART OF MY BODY THAT I REALLY LIKE.

NOPE, NOT ONE 1 2 3 4 5 6 7 8 9 10 I HAVE LOTS

I FEEL THAT I SHOULD LOOK LIKE THE MODELS AND ACTRESSES I SEE ON TV AND IN MAGAZINES.

ABSOLUTELY 1 2 3 4 5 6 7 8 9 10 I DON'T THINK ABOUT IT

EVERY CALORIE THAT GOES INTO MY MOUTH IS COUNTED.

EVERY ONE 1 2 3 4 5 6 7 8 9 10 NOT ONE

WHEN I PASS A MIRROR, I HAVE TO STOP AND SEE HOW I LOOK.

EVERY TIME 1 2 3 4 5 6 7 8 9 10 NEVER

I HAVE SKIPPED OUT ON GOING TO A PARTY OR A GET-TOGETHER BECAUSE I FELT FAT AND/OR UNATTRACTIVE.

OFTEN 1 2 3 4 5 6 7 8 9 10 NOT ONCE

## ADD UP YOUR SCORE:

**IF YOU SCORED BETWEEN 10 AND 39, YOU ARE OBSESSED:**
It's no news to you that our culture praises the perfection of the body. But listen, it's NOT the most important thing in life, contrary to how you may feel! Read Psalm 139 and reflect on how God created every little thing about you—yes, even the parts of your body you don't like! He knows you inside and out and loves everything about you that makes you who you are. If you continue to concentrate on having the perfect body, you will only be miserable and unhappy. Share with a good friend or a parent how much you struggle with this and ask them to pray for you. You don't have to be a prisoner to your own body!

**IF YOU SCORED BETWEEN 40 AND 59, YOU ARE AVERAGE:**
You are average in that you are concerned with your body and how you look, but you don't let it totally control your life. Remember that God is much more interested in the condition of your heart than your body and that how you look is not the most important thing about you, regardless of what the world says. It's hard to deal with sometimes, but pray that God will shift your focus from the outside to the inside and allow him to work in you.

**IF YOU SCORED 60 +, YOU ARE NOT CONCERNED:**
Kudos! You have somehow managed to avoid the obsession our culture has with weight and body image. Encourage your friends who tend to struggle with these issues, being sensitive to their struggle and praying for them. Continue to maintain a healthy lifestyle, and good health will no doubt follow.

mine that does not produce fruit. And he trims and cleans every branch that produces fruit so that it will produce even more fruit. ³You are already clean because of the words I have spoken to you. ⁴Remain in me, and I will remain in you. A branch cannot produce fruit alone but must remain in the vine. In the same way, you cannot produce fruit alone but must remain in me.

⁵"I am the vine, and you are the branches. If any remain in me and I remain in them, they produce much fruit. But without me they can do nothing. ⁶If any do not remain in me, they are like a branch that is thrown away and then dies. People pick up dead branches, throw them into the fire, and burn them. ⁷If you remain in me and follow my teachings, you can ask anything you want, and it will be given to you. ⁸You should produce much fruit and show that you are my followers, which brings glory to my Father. ⁹I loved you as the Father loved me. Now remain in my love. ¹⁰I have obeyed my Father's commands, and I remain in his love. In the same way, if you obey my commands, you will remain in my love. ¹¹I have told you these things so that you can have the same joy I have and so that your joy will be the fullest possible joy.

¹²"This is my command: Love each other as I have loved you. ¹³The greatest love a person can show is to die for his friends. ¹⁴You are my friends if you do what I command you. ¹⁵I no longer call you servants, because a servant does not know what his master is doing. But I call you friends, because I have made known to you everything I heard from my Father. ¹⁶You did not choose me; I chose you. And I gave you this work: to go and produce fruit, fruit that will last. Then the Father will give you anything you ask for in my name. ¹⁷This is my command: Love each other.

### JESUS WARNS HIS FOLLOWERS

¹⁸"If the world hates you, remember that it hated me first. ¹⁹If you belonged to the world, it would love you as it loves its own. But I have chosen you out of the world, so you don't belong to it. That is why the world hates you.

²⁰Remember what I told you: A servant is not greater than his master. If people did wrong to me, they will do wrong to you, too. And if they obeyed my teaching, they will obey yours, too. ²¹They will do all this to you on account of me, because they do not know the One who sent me. ²²If I had not come and spoken to them, they would not be guilty of sin, but now they have no excuse for their sin. ²³Whoever hates me also hates my Father. ²⁴I did works among them that no one else has ever done. If I had not done these works, they would not be guilty of sin. But now they have seen what I have done, and yet they have hated both me and my Father. ²⁵But this happened so that what is written in their law would be true: 'They hated me for no reason.'ⁿ

²⁶"I will send you the Helperⁿ from the Father; he is the Spirit of truth who comes from the Father. When he comes, he will tell about me, ²⁷and you also must tell people about me, because you have been with me from the beginning.

**16** "I have told you these things to keep you from giving up. ²People will put you out of their synagogues. Yes, the time is coming when those who kill you will think they are offering service to God. ³They will do this because they have not known the Father and they have not known me. ⁴I have told you these things now so that when the time comes you will remember that I warned you.

### THE WORK OF THE HOLY SPIRIT

"I did not tell you these things at the beginning, because I was with you then. ⁵Now I am going back to the One who sent me. But none of you asks me, 'Where are you going?' ⁶Your hearts are filled with sadness because I have told you these things. ⁷But I tell you the truth, it is better for you that I go away. When I go away, I will send the Helperⁿ to you. If I do not go away, the Helper will not come. ⁸When the Helper comes, he will prove to the people of the world the truth about sin, about being right with God, and about judgment. ⁹He will prove to them that sin is not believing in me. ¹⁰He will prove to them that being right with

## John 15:5, 8-10

Where do you belong? Do you ever feel like you don't quite fit, no matter where you turn? Guess what? You belong with God. The truth is that if you've given yourself to God, you are completely united with him. He's made it so that you and he fit together. You're a part of him. In this passage, Jesus says you're a branch on his vine—you belong in a position connected to him. When you believe in God's grace and salvation through Jesus, you become an extension of him; and disconnected from him, you will suffer. However, connected and united with God, you will become more like him and others will see him in you. But you've got to stay totally connected to God to keep things that way. Every day, God invites you to become closer to him. So go to him and be renewed, reconnected, and redirected. Let him remind you about his values, his priorities, and the way he wants you to treat others. Remain in and receive his love—by spending time with him in the Word and obeying him. Live the way God calls you to live by staying where you really fit—close by his side.

**15:25** *'They . . . reason.'* These words could be from Psalm 35:19 or Psalm 69:4.　**15:26; 16:7** **Helper** "Counselor" or "Comforter." Jesus is talking about the Holy Spirit.

God comes from my going to the Father and not being seen anymore. ¹¹And the Helper will prove to them that judgment happened when the ruler of this world was judged.

¹²"I have many more things to say to you, but they are too much for you now. ¹³But when the Spirit of truth comes, he will lead you into all truth. He will not speak his own words, but he will speak only what he hears, and he will tell you what is to come. ¹⁴The Spirit of truth will bring glory to me, because he will take what I have to say and tell it to you. ¹⁵All that the Father has is mine. That is why I said that the Spirit will take what I have to say and tell it to you.

## "I TOLD YOU THESE THINGS SO THAT YOU CAN HAVE PEACE IN ME. IN THIS WORLD YOU WILL HAVE TROUBLE, BUT BE BRAVE!"

### SADNESS WILL BECOME HAPPINESS

¹⁶"After a little while you will not see me, and then after a little while you will see me again."

¹⁷Some of the followers said to each other, "What does Jesus mean when he says, 'After a little while you will not see me, and then after a little while you will see me again'? And what does he mean when he says, 'Because I am going to the Father'?" ¹⁸They also asked, "What does he mean by 'a little while'? We don't understand what he is saying."

¹⁹Jesus saw that the followers wanted to ask him about this, so he said to them, "Are you asking each other what I meant when I said, 'After a little while you will not see me, and then after a little while you will see me again'? ²⁰I tell you the truth, you will cry and be sad, but the world will be happy. You will be sad, but your sadness will become joy. ²¹When a woman gives birth to a baby, she has pain, because her time has come. But when her baby is born, she forgets the pain, because she is so happy that a child has been born into the world. ²²It is the same with you. Now you are sad, but I will see you again and you will be happy, and no one will take away your joy. ²³In that day you will not ask me for anything. I tell you the truth, my Father will give you anything you ask for in my name. ²⁴Until now you have not asked for anything in my name. Ask and you will receive, so that your joy will be the fullest possible joy.

### VICTORY OVER THE WORLD

²⁵"I have told you these things, using stories that hide the meaning. But the time will come when I will not use stories like that to tell you things; I will speak to you in plain words about the Father. ²⁶In that day you will ask the Father for things in my name. I mean, I will not need to ask the Father for you. ²⁷The Father himself loves you. He loves you because you loved me and believed that I came from God. ²⁸I came from the Father into the world. Now I am leaving the world and going back to the Father."

²⁹Then the followers of Jesus said, "You are speaking clearly to us now and are not using stories that are hard to understand. ³⁰We can see now that you know all things. You can answer a person's question even before it is asked. This makes us believe you came from God."

³¹Jesus answered, "So now you believe? ³²Listen to me; a time is coming when you will be scattered, each to his own home. That time is now here. You will leave me alone, but I am never really alone, because the Father is with me.

³³"I told you these things so that you can have peace in me. In this world you will have trouble, but be brave! I have defeated the world."

### JESUS PRAYS FOR HIS FOLLOWERS

**17** After Jesus said these things, he looked toward heaven and prayed,

## Promises!

# John 15:16

You make a lot of choices every day. Some of them are small and some of them have bigger consequences: *What should I wear today? Should I study after school or hang out with my friends? Do I want to watch TV or surf the web for a while? How far should I go with my boyfriend?* In the thousand decisions that make up our lives every day, one big decision we have to make is whether or not to follow God. For most of us, it's a daily struggle.

In this verse, Jesus says that we do not choose him but he chooses us. Why does he say this? Because we are sinful by nature and want to have our own way all the time, and more often than not, we tend to choose our own selfishness over being close to God. God knows this about us. He knows we struggle. So he is saying that he chooses us—the God of the whole universe picks you to be a part of his family!

You are not some meaningless blip on the map of history and humanity. God chose you from the beginning to be one of his own and to use you in great ways.

**top 10**

**random ways to share faith with friends**

**10** Invite friends to a Christian concert or festival.

**9** Be true to your beliefs, not wishy-washy.

**8** Know your stuff so you are believable.

**7** Show that you have joy and peace; others will want it.

**6** Simply share how God has made a difference in your life.

**5** Pray for your friends by name every day.

**4** Sign your emails with your "signature" Bible verse.

**3** Be a godly example.

**2** Invite friends to your youth group.

**1** Read *Revolve* during lunch.

"Father, the time has come. Give glory to your Son so that the Son can give glory to you. [2]You gave the Son power over all people so that the Son could give eternal life to all those you gave him. [3]And this is eternal life: that people know you, the only true God, and that they know Jesus Christ, the One you sent. [4]Having finished the work you gave me to do, I brought you glory on earth. [5]And now, Father, give me glory with you; give me the glory I had with you before the world was made.

[6]"I showed what you are like to those you gave me from the world. They belonged to you, and you gave them to me, and they have obeyed your teaching. [7]Now they know that everything you gave me comes from you. [8]I gave them the teachings you gave me, and they accepted them. They knew that I truly came from you, and they believed that you sent me. [9]I am praying for them. I am not praying for people in the world but for those you gave me, because they are yours. [10]All I have is yours, and all you have is mine. And my glory is shown through them. [11]I am coming to you; I will not stay in the world any longer. But they are still in the world. Holy Father, keep them safe by the power of your name, the name you gave me, so that they will be one, just as you and I are one. [12]While I was with them, I kept them safe by the power of your name, the name you gave me. I protected them, and only one of them, the one worthy of destruction, was lost so that the Scripture would come true.

[13]"I am coming to you now. But I pray these things while I am still in the world so that these followers can have all of my joy in them. [14]I have given them your teaching. And the world has hated them, because they don't belong to the world, just as I don't belong to the world. [15]I am not asking you to take them out of the world but to keep them safe from the Evil One. [16]They don't belong to the world, just as I don't belong to the world. [17]Make them ready for your service through your truth; your teaching is truth. [18]I have sent them into the world, just as you sent me into the world. [19]For their sake, I am making myself ready to serve so that they can be ready for their service of the truth.

[20]"I pray for these followers, but I am also praying for all those who will believe in me because of their teaching. [21]Father, I pray that they can be one. As you are in me and I am in you, I pray that they can also be one in us. Then the world will believe that you sent me. [22]I have given these people the glory that you gave me so that they can be one, just as you and I are one. [23]I will be in them and you will be in me so that they will be completely one. Then the world will know that you sent me and that you loved them just as much as you loved me.

[24]"Father, I want these people that you gave me to be with me where I am. I want them to see my glory, which you gave me because you loved me before the world was made. [25]Father,

**beauty secret**

## Outside Appearance

What's the first thing you notice about someone? Their looks? Clothes? Style? It's easy to judge people by their appearances. First Samuel 16:7 reminds us, "People look at the outside of a person, but the LORD looks at the heart." Take God's perspective the next time you meet someone.

# Music Reviews

**GROUP:** STACIE ORRICO

**ALBUM:** STACIE ORRICO

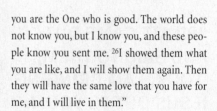

If you like modern R&B mixed with pop (think Beyoncé and J.Lo), and you haven't heard of Stacie Orrico, then grab this one and pop it in the player. Stacie Orrico signed with ForeFront Records when she was just 14, and this self-titled release from the teenage singer-songwriter is her first for a major mainstream label (Virgin Records). Stacie wrote or cowrote lots of the songs on this album, including the pop hit about crushin' on a bad boy "Stuck," the MTV fave "(there's gotta be) More to Life," and the ballad about trust "Strong Enough."

**WHY IT ROCKS: STACIE IS ONE MODERN TEEN POP STAR WHO YOU'LL LOVE.**

you are the One who is good. The world does not know you, but I know you, and these people know you sent me. 26I showed them what you are like, and I will show them again. Then they will have the same love that you have for me, and I will live in them."

## Jesus is Arrested

**18** When Jesus finished praying, he went with his followers across the Kidron Valley. On the other side there was a garden, and Jesus and his followers went into it.

2Judas knew where this place was, because Jesus met there often with his followers. Judas was the one who turned against Jesus. 3So Judas came there with a group of soldiers and some guards from the leading priests and the Pharisees. They were carrying torches, lanterns, and weapons.

4Knowing everything that would happen to him, Jesus went out and asked, "Who is it you are looking for?"

5They answered, "Jesus from Nazareth."

"I am he," Jesus said. (Judas, the one who turned against Jesus, was standing there with them.) 6When Jesus said, "I am he," they moved back and fell to the ground.

7Jesus asked them again, "Who is it you are looking for?"

They said, "Jesus of Nazareth."

8"I told you that I am he," Jesus said. "So if you are looking for me, let the others go." 9This happened so that the words Jesus said before would come true: "I have not lost any of the ones you gave me."

10Simon Peter, who had a sword, pulled it out and struck the servant of the high priest, cutting off his right ear. (The servant's name was Malchus.) 11Jesus said to Peter, "Put your sword back. Shouldn't I drink the cup" the Father gave me?"

**DIDYA KNOW** AROUND 96% OF TEENS LISTEN TO THE RADIO EACH WEEK. HORIZON MEDIA RESEARCH

## Jesus is Brought Before Annas

12Then the soldiers with their commander and the guards arrested Jesus. They tied him 13and led him first to Annas, the father-in-law of Caiaphas, the high priest that year. 14Caiaphas was the one who told the Jews that it would be better if one man died for all the people.

## Peter Says He Doesn't Know Jesus

15Simon Peter and another one of Jesus' followers went along after Jesus. This follower knew the high priest, so he went with Jesus into the high priest's courtyard. 16But Peter waited outside near the door. The follower who knew the high priest came back outside, spoke to the girl at the door, and brought Peter inside. 17The girl at the door said to Peter, "Aren't you also one of that man's followers?"

Peter answered, "No, I am not!"

18It was cold, so the servants and guards had built a fire and were standing around it, warming themselves. Peter also was standing with them, warming himself.

## The High Priest Questions Jesus

19The high priest asked Jesus questions about his followers and his teaching. 20Jesus answered, "I have spoken openly to everyone. I have always taught in synagogues and in the Temple, where all the Jews come together. I never said anything in secret. 21So why do you question me? Ask the people who heard my teaching. They know what I said."

 **notes** **18:11 cup** Jesus is talking about the painful things that will happen to him. Accepting these things will be very hard, like drinking a cup of something bitter.

## Blab

**Q:** My best friend and my boyfriend are each jealous of the time I spend with the other, and it is wearing me out. What do I do?

**A:** Reassure them both that they are not losing you just because the other one is in your life. Make sure you still spend time with your best friend, and don't drop her because you're so wrapped up in your crush. Let each know that the other is important to you, and ask them to put aside their differences for you.

**Q:** My BFF is sneaking out with a much older guy. Her parents have no clue. Should I tell somebody?

**A:** Any time the word "sneaking" is involved, the parents should be told. If she has to hide her actions, even your friend knows she is not doing the right thing. An older man could be physically dangerous to your friend. If you love her, hold her accountable. And let somebody know.

**Q:** A close friend of my family sexually molested me. He says no one will believe me if I tell, and he might be right. I am afraid my parents will just get mad. Should I tell them?

**A:** It is always wrong for an adult to force himself or herself sexually in any way on a minor. It is against the law in most cases, even if the minor consents. If you do not tell your parents, their friend may molest you again or do the same to other girls. He needs help, and you need freedom from guilt. Pray hard; then take the plunge and tell.

---

22When Jesus said this, one of the guards standing there hit him. The guard said, "Is that the way you answer the high priest?"

23Jesus answered him, "If I said something wrong, then show what it was. But if what I said is true, why do you hit me?"

24Then Annas sent Jesus, who was still tied, to Caiaphas the high priest.

### PETER SAYS AGAIN HE DOESN'T KNOW JESUS

25As Simon Peter was standing and warming himself, they said to him, "Aren't you one of that man's followers?"

Peter said it was not true; he said, "No, I am not."

26One of the servants of the high priest was there. This servant was a relative of the man whose ear Peter had cut off. The servant said, "Didn't I see you with him in the garden?"

27Again Peter said it wasn't true. At once a rooster crowed.

### JESUS IS BROUGHT BEFORE PILATE

28Early in the morning they led Jesus from Caiaphas's house to the Roman governor's palace. They would not go inside the palace, because they did not want to make themselves unclean;[n] they wanted to eat the Passover meal. 29So Pilate went outside to them and asked, "What charges do you bring against this man?"

30They answered, "If he were not a criminal, we wouldn't have brought him to you."

31Pilate said to them, "Take him yourselves and judge him by your own law."

"But we are not allowed to put anyone to death," the Jews answered. 32(This happened so that what Jesus said about how he would die would come true.)

33Then Pilate went back inside the palace and called Jesus to him and asked, "Are you the king of the Jews?"

34Jesus said, "Is that your own question, or did others tell you about me?"

35Pilate answered, "I am not one of you. It was your own people and their leading priests who handed you over to me. What have you done wrong?"

36Jesus answered, "My kingdom does not belong to this world. If it belonged to this world, my servants would fight so that I would not be given over to the Jews. But my kingdom is from another place."

37Pilate said, "So you are a king!"

Jesus answered, "You are the one saying I am a king. This is why I was born and came into the world: to tell people the truth. And everyone who belongs to the truth listens to me."

38Pilate said, "What is truth?" After he said this, he went out to the crowd again and said to them, "I find nothing against this man. 39But it is your custom that I free one prisoner to you at Passover time. Do you want me to free the 'king of the Jews'?"

> "PILATE CAME OUT AND SAID TO THEM, 'LOOK, I AM BRINGING JESUS OUT TO YOU. I WANT YOU TO KNOW THAT I FIND NOTHING AGAINST HIM.'"

40They shouted back, "No, not him! Let Barabbas go free!" (Barabbas was a robber.)

19 Then Pilate ordered that Jesus be taken away and whipped. 2The soldiers made a crown from some thorny branches and put it on Jesus' head and put a purple robe around him. 3Then they came to him many times and said, "Hail, King of the Jews!" and hit him in the face.

4Again Pilate came out and said to them, "Look, I am bringing Jesus out to you. I want you to know that I find nothing against him." 5So Jesus came out, wearing the crown of thorns and the purple robe. Pilate said to them, "Here is the man!"

6When the leading priests and the guards saw Jesus, they shouted, "Crucify him! Crucify him!"

---

notes **18:28 unclean** Going into the Roman palace would make them unfit to eat the Passover Feast, according to their Law.

# MaY

**1**

**2** Mother's Day is the second Sunday in May. Do something special that will surprise mom.

**3**

**4**

**5** Write a note of thanks to your parents. Post it on their bathroom mirror.

**6** Take time to paint your nails.

**7**

**8** Give your favorite teachers notes of appreciation.

**9**

**10** Pray for a person of influence: Pray for Bono and his efforts to battle AIDS through www.data.org. It's his birthday.

**11** Read Philippians 4. Tell a friend about what you learn.

**12**

**13**

**14** Choose to have a good attitude today, no matter what happens.

**15**

**16** Make a list of all the blessings in your life.

**17** Spend time talking with a neighbor.

**18**

**19**

**20** Do something your stepparent asks of you without complaint.

**21** Make and mail cards to some of your family members, including aunts and uncles.

**22**

**23**

**24** Celebrate family by setting up a night where you can all be together.

**25**

**26** Clip out the Bible memory cards in the back of this Bible. Memorize a verse.

**27**

**28** Take an afternoon nap. Rest is good for you.

**29**

**30**

**31**

Memorial Day is celebrated the last Monday in May. Work with your church to set up a time to honor soldiers who've died for our country.

# LEARN I✞ & LIVE I✞

**John 14:23**
**Learn It:** If people love Jesus, they will obey his teaching.
**Live It:** Read the four Gospels; compare and contrast their accounts of Jesus' life, death, and resurrection.

**John 19:30**
**Learn It:** Jesus bowed his head and died.
**Live It:** Watch the *Jesus* film or *The Passion of the Christ* (as long as your parents approve) with friends and marvel at Christ's sacrifice for you.

**John 20:14**
**Learn It:** Mary Magdalene saw the resurrected Jesus.
**Live It:** Step into Mary's shoes, and journal about what it must have been like to meet Jesus alive again.

But Pilate answered, "Crucify him yourselves, because I find nothing against him."

⁷The leaders answered, "We have a law that says he should die, because he said he is the Son of God."

⁸When Pilate heard this, he was even more afraid. ⁹He went back inside the palace and asked Jesus, "Where do you come from?" But Jesus did not answer him. ¹⁰Pilate said, "You refuse to speak to me? Don't you know I have power to set you free and power to have you crucified?"

¹¹Jesus answered, "The only power you have over me is the power given to you by God. The man who turned me in to you is guilty of a greater sin."

¹²After this, Pilate tried to let Jesus go. But some in the crowd cried out, "Anyone who makes himself king is against Caesar. If you let this man go, you are no friend of Caesar."

¹³When Pilate heard what they were saying, he brought Jesus out and sat down on the judge's seat at the place called The Stone Pavement. (In the Hebrew language" the name is Gabbatha.) ¹⁴It was about noon on Preparation Day of Passover week. Pilate said to the crowd, "Here is your king!"

¹⁵They shouted, "Take him away! Take him away! Crucify him!"

Pilate asked them, "Do you want me to crucify your king?"

The leading priests answered, "The only king we have is Caesar."

¹⁶So Pilate handed Jesus over to them to be crucified.

## JESUS IS CRUCIFIED

The soldiers took charge of Jesus. ¹⁷Carrying his own cross, Jesus went out to a place called The Place of the Skull, which in the Hebrew language" is called Golgotha. ¹⁸There they crucified Jesus. They also crucified two other men, one on each side, with Jesus in the middle. ¹⁹Pilate wrote a sign and put it on the cross. It read: JESUS OF NAZARETH, THE KING OF THE JEWS. ²⁰The sign was written in Hebrew, in Latin, and in Greek. Many of the people read the sign, because the place where Jesus was crucified was near the city. ²¹The leading priests said to Pilate, "Don't write, 'The King of the Jews.' But write, 'This man said, "I am the King of the Jews." ' "

²²Pilate answered, "What I have written, I have written."

²³After the soldiers crucified Jesus, they took his clothes and divided them into four parts, with each soldier getting one part. They also took his long shirt, which was all one piece of cloth, woven from top to bottom. ²⁴So the soldiers said to each other, "We should not tear this into parts. Let's throw lots to see who will get it." This happened so that this Scripture would come true:

"They divided my clothes among them,
    and they threw lots for my clothing."

*Psalm 22:18*

So the soldiers did this.

²⁵Standing near his cross were Jesus' mother, his mother's sister, Mary the wife of Clopas, and Mary Magdalene. ²⁶When Jesus saw his mother and the follower he loved standing nearby, he said to his mother, "Dear woman, here is your son." ²⁷Then he said to the follower, "Here is your mother." From that time on, the follower took her to live in his home.

## JESUS DIES

²⁸After this, Jesus knew that everything had been done. So that the Scripture would come true, he said, "I am thirsty."" ²⁹There was a jar full of vinegar there, so the soldiers soaked a sponge in it, put the sponge on a branch of a hyssop plant, and lifted it to Jesus' mouth. ³⁰When Jesus tasted the vinegar, he said, "It is finished." Then he bowed his head and died.

³¹This day was Preparation Day, and the next day was a special Sabbath day. Since the religious leaders did not want the bodies to stay on the cross on the Sabbath day, they

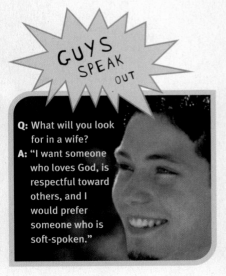

**GUYS SPEAK OUT**

**Q:** What will you look for in a wife?
**A:** "I want someone who loves God, is respectful toward others, and I would prefer someone who is soft-spoken."

**19:13** Hebrew language Hebrew or Aramaic, the languages of many people in this region in the first century. **19:17** Hebrew language Hebrew or Aramaic, the languages of many people in this region in the first century. **19:28** "I am thirsty." Read Psalms 22:15; 69:21.

asked Pilate to order that the legs of the men be broken" and the bodies be taken away. ³²So the soldiers came and broke the legs of the first man on the cross beside Jesus. Then they broke the legs of the man on the other cross beside Jesus. ³³But when the soldiers came to Jesus and saw that he was already dead, they did not break his legs. ³⁴But one of the soldiers stuck his spear into Jesus' side, and at once blood and water came out. ³⁵(The one who saw this happen is the one who told us this, and whatever he says is true. And he knows that he tells the truth, and he tells it so that you might believe.) ³⁶These things happened to make the Scripture come true: "Not one of his bones will be broken."" ³⁷And another Scripture says, "They will look at the one they stabbed.""

## "THEY HAVE TAKEN AWAY MY LORD, AND I DON'T KNOW WHERE THEY HAVE PUT HIM."

### JESUS IS BURIED

³⁸Later, Joseph from Arimathea asked Pilate if he could take the body of Jesus. (Joseph was a secret follower of Jesus, because he was afraid of some of the leaders.) Pilate gave his permission, so Joseph came and took Jesus' body away. ³⁹Nicodemus, who earlier had come to Jesus at night, went with Joseph. He brought about seventy-five pounds of myrrh and aloes. ⁴⁰These two men took Jesus' body and wrapped it with the spices in pieces of linen cloth, which is how they bury the dead. ⁴¹In the place where Jesus was crucified, there was a garden. In the garden was a new tomb that had never been used before. ⁴²The men laid Jesus in that tomb because it was nearby, and they were preparing to start their Sabbath day.

### JESUS' TOMB IS EMPTY

**20** Early on the first day of the week, Mary Magdalene went to the tomb while it was still dark. When she saw that the large stone had been moved away from the tomb, ²she ran to Simon Peter and the follower whom Jesus loved. Mary said, "They have taken the Lord out of the tomb, and we don't know where they have put him."

³So Peter and the other follower started for the tomb. ⁴They were both running, but the other follower ran faster than Peter and reached the tomb first. ⁵He bent down and looked in and saw the strips of linen cloth lying there, but he did not go in. ⁶Then following him, Simon Peter arrived and went into the tomb and saw the strips of linen lying there. ⁷He also saw the cloth that had been around Jesus' head, which was folded up and laid in a different place from the strips of linen. ⁸Then the other follower, who had reached the tomb first, also went in. He saw and believed. ⁹(They did not yet understand from the Scriptures that Jesus must rise from the dead.)

### JESUS APPEARS TO MARY MAGDALENE

¹⁰Then the followers went back home. ¹¹But Mary stood outside the tomb, crying. As she was crying, she bent down and looked inside the tomb. ¹²She saw two angels dressed in white, sitting where Jesus' body had been, one at the head and one at the feet.

¹³They asked her, "Woman, why are you crying?"

She answered, "They have taken away my Lord, and I don't know where they have put him." ¹⁴When Mary said this, she turned around and saw Jesus standing there, but she did not know it was Jesus.

¹⁵Jesus asked her, "Woman, why are you crying? Whom are you looking for?"

Thinking he was the gardener, she said to him, "Did you take him away, sir? Tell me where you put him, and I will get him."

¹⁶Jesus said to her, "Mary."

Mary turned toward Jesus and said in Hebrew," "Rabboni." (This means Teacher.)

¹⁷Jesus said to her, "Don't hold on to me, because I have not yet gone up to the Father. But go to my brothers and tell them, 'I am

### Radical Faith:

# John 20:21

Have you ever wanted to be a part of the in crowd? Well, everyone who is part of God's kingdom is invited to be in on doing something really big. We're talking about connecting with the greatest power source in the world here! God is doing mind-blowing things all over the globe as he's moving forward with his kingdom. The great news is that he's asking you to join him in advancing his kingdom. Jesus is sending you as his representative. His instructions are pretty clear. He is simply asking you to do what he did— reach out to others, embrace the hurting, bring healing to them, and share the Good News with everyone. Jesus sought out hurting people in order to bring them to the life and love of God. He made it clear that what's essential is to love other people and care for them. God wants you to spend your energy helping others know and honor him. In John 17:4, Jesus prays to God, "Having finished the work you gave me to do, I brought you glory on earth." Make it your goal to make that same statement true of your life.

**19:31 broken** The breaking of their bones would make them die sooner. **19:36 "Not one . . . broken."** Quotation from Psalm 34:20. The idea is from Exodus 12:46; Numbers 9:12. **19:37 "They . . . stabbed."** Quotation from Zechariah 12:10. **20:16 Hebrew language** Hebrew or Aramaic, the languages of many people in this region in the first century.

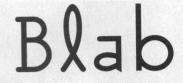

**Q:** I want to go to church, but my parents don't. I don't drive yet. Any suggestions?

**A:** Ask your parents if they would mind driving you, or call the church and see if they have a bus that can pick you up. If they don't, ask them to recommend someone in your area who would not mind giving you a ride. If you can't make it to church, there are lots of good sermons on the radio, television, and on the Internet. See if your pastor puts his sermons online.

**Q:** All my friends know what they want to be when they go to college, but I don't have a clue. Is something wrong with me?

**A:** Not at all. God reveals his plans for each person's life when he is ready. Keep seeking him, work hard, and hone your special talents and abilities. Continue to help others, and ask God to give you a passion for something and clear direction to discover it.

**Q:** My friends want to be lawyers and accountants. I haven't admitted it, but secretly, I just want to get married and be a mom someday. Is that okay?

**A:** Certainly! In fact, it's one of the highest callings for a woman, despite what all those who champion women's rights say. You still need to develop your talents and work hard in school, but take time to learn homemaking skills like cooking and cleaning along the way. If you are unsure if homemaking is enough, read the description of a great wife and mom in Proverbs 31.

going back to my Father and your Father, to my God and your God.' "

18Mary Magdalene went and said to the followers, "I saw the Lord!" And she told them what Jesus had said to her.

### Jesus appears to his followers

19When it was evening on the first day of the week, the followers were together. The doors were locked, because they were afraid of the older leaders. Then Jesus came and stood right in the middle of them and said, "Peace be with you." 20After he said this, he showed them his hands and his side. The followers were thrilled when they saw the Lord.

21Then Jesus said again, "Peace be with you. As the Father sent me, I now send you." 22After he said this, he breathed on them and said, "Receive the Holy Spirit. 23If you forgive anyone his sins, they are forgiven. If you don't forgive them, they are not forgiven."

### Jesus appears to Thomas

24Thomas (called Didymus), who was one of the twelve, was not with them when Jesus came. 25The other followers kept telling Thomas, "We saw the Lord."

But Thomas said, "I will not believe it until I see the nail marks in his hands and put my finger where the nails were and put my hand into his side."

26A week later the followers were in the house again, and Thomas was with them. The doors were locked, but Jesus came in and stood right in the middle of them. He said, "Peace be with you." 27Then he said to Thomas, "Put your finger here, and look at my hands. Put your hand here in my side. Stop being an unbeliever and believe."

28Thomas said to him, "My Lord and my God!"

29Then Jesus told him, "You believe because you see me. Those who believe without seeing me will be truly happy."

### Why John wrote this book

30Jesus did many other miracles in the presence of his followers that are not written in this book. 31But these are written so that you may believe that Jesus is the Christ, the Son of God. Then, by believing, you may have life through his name.

### Jesus appears to seven followers

21 Later, Jesus showed himself to his followers again—this time at Lake Galilee.ⁿ This is how he showed himself: 2Some of the followers were together: Simon Peter, Thomas (called Didymus), Nathanael from Cana in Galilee, the two sons of Zebedee, and two other followers. 3Simon Peter said, "I am going out to fish."

The others said, "We will go with you." So they went out and got into the boat. They fished that night but caught nothing.

4Early the next morning Jesus stood on the shore, but the followers did not know it was Jesus. 5Then he said to them, "Friends, did you catch any fish?"

They answered, "No."

> **"YOU BELIEVE BECAUSE YOU SEE ME. THOSE WHO BELIEVE WITHOUT SEEING ME WILL BE TRULY HAPPY."**

6He said, "Throw your net on the right side of the boat, and you will find some." So they did, and they caught so many fish they could not pull the net back into the boat.

7The follower whom Jesus loved said to Peter, "It is the Lord!" When Peter heard him say this, he wrapped his coat around himself. (Peter had taken his clothes off.) Then he jumped into the water. 8The other followers went to shore in the boat, dragging the net full of fish. They were not very far from shore, only about a hundred yards. 9When the followers stepped out of the boat and onto the shore, they saw a fire of hot coals. There were fish on the fire, and there was bread.

<sup>10</sup>Then Jesus said, "Bring some of the fish you just caught."

<sup>11</sup>Simon Peter went into the boat and pulled the net to the shore. It was full of big fish, one hundred fifty-three in all, but even though there were so many, the net did not tear. <sup>12</sup>Jesus said to them, "Come and eat." None of the followers dared ask him, "Who are you?" because they knew it was the Lord. <sup>13</sup>Jesus came and took the bread and gave it to them, along with the fish.

<sup>14</sup>This was now the third time Jesus showed himself to his followers after he was raised from the dead.

## Jesus Talks to Peter

<sup>15</sup>When they finished eating, Jesus said to Simon Peter, "Simon son of John do you love me more than these?"

He answered, "Yes, Lord, you know that I love you."

Jesus said, "Feed my lambs."

<sup>16</sup>Again Jesus said, "Simon son of John do you love me?"

He answered, "Yes, Lord, you know that I love you."

Jesus said, "Take care of my sheep."

<sup>17</sup>A third time he said, "Simon son of John do you love me?"

Peter was hurt because Jesus asked him the third time, "Do you love me?" Peter said, "Lord, you know everything; you know that I love you!"

He said to him, "Feed my sheep. <sup>18</sup>I tell you the truth, when you were younger, you tied your own belt and went where you wanted. But when you are old, you will put out your hands and someone else will tie you and take you where you don't want to go." <sup>19</sup>(Jesus said this to show how Peter would die to give glory to God.) Then Jesus said to Peter, "Follow me!"

<sup>20</sup>Peter turned and saw that the follower Jesus loved was walking behind them. (This was the follower who had leaned against Jesus at the supper and had said, "Lord, who will turn against you?") <sup>21</sup>When Peter saw him behind them, he asked Jesus, "Lord, what about him?"

<sup>22</sup>Jesus answered, "If I want him to live until I come back, that is not your business. You follow me."

<sup>23</sup>So a story spread among the followers that this one would not die. But Jesus did not say he would not die. He only said, "If I want him to live until I come back, that is not your business."

<sup>24</sup>That follower is the one who is telling these things and who has now written them down. We know that what he says is true.

<sup>25</sup>There are many other things Jesus did. If every one of them were written down, I suppose the whole world would not be big enough for all the books that would be written.

## BIBLE BIOS

### Hannah

[1 SAMUEL 1] Hannah had a problem that many women today struggle with: She desperately wanted to have a baby, but couldn't get pregnant. But instead of focusing on the other gifts God had given her, what she *didn't* have became the focus of her life. Hannah prayed for God to bless her with a son and promised to give the child back to him if he would give her one. She wanted a son who would serve the Lord all his days. In the end, God performed a miracle and gave Hannah a son, Samuel. And when the time was right, Hannah kept her promise. She and her husband took Samuel to the house of the Lord at Shiloh to stay with the priest, Eli. This time, she *literally* gave her heart's desire to the Lord.

# Y ou've read Luke's vivid account

of Jesus' birth. You've learned what Jesus taught in Matthew and what he did in Mark. John told you about the Helper coming. So, now what?

## Acts  What the Holy Spirit Did Through Regular People

Acts, written by Luke, is a sort of sequel to the Gospels. It begins with Jesus being taken up into heaven. But before he goes, he promises his followers that the Holy Spirit will empower them to be witnesses of all they have seen and experienced. They probably didn't have any idea what they were in for!

Scholars consider Acts to be the first book of church history. For the first time, believers are trying to follow in Jesus' footsteps without him present in the flesh. We see the successes—and setbacks—of this baby church in its first three decades.

We also meet Paul—also called Saul, but definitely a different Saul than the king from the Old Testament. A close friend of Luke's, Paul was one of the most influential men in the Bible, and he's the author of several New Testament letters.

Acts, or "The Acts of the Apostles," might be better titled "The Acts of the Holy Spirit Through Common Men." It's the power of the Holy Spirit flowing through followers of Jesus, allowing them to perform miracles in his name, spreading to both Jews and Gentiles, and, finally, sparking the beginnings the Christian movement that's still alive today.

## LUKE WRITES ANOTHER BOOK

1 To Theophilus.

The first book I wrote was about everything Jesus began to do and teach ²until the day he was taken up into heaven. Before this, with the help of the Holy Spirit, Jesus told the apostles he had chosen what they should do. ³After his death, he showed himself to them and proved in many ways that he was alive. The apostles saw Jesus during the forty days after he was raised from the dead, and he spoke to them about the kingdom of God. ⁴Once when he was eating with them, he told them not to leave Jerusalem. He said, "Wait here to receive the promise from the Father which I told you about. ⁵John baptized people with water, but in a few days you will be baptized with the Holy Spirit."

## JESUS IS TAKEN UP INTO HEAVEN

⁶When the apostles were all together, they asked Jesus, "Lord, are you now going to give the kingdom back to Israel?"

⁷Jesus said to them, "The Father is the only One who has the authority to decide dates and times. These things are not for you to know. ⁸But when the Holy Spirit comes to you, you will receive power. You will be my witnesses—in Jerusalem, in all of Judea, in Samaria, and in every part of the world."

⁹After he said this, as they were watching, he was lifted up, and a cloud hid him from their sight. ¹⁰As he was going, they were looking into the sky. Suddenly, two men wearing white clothes stood beside them. ¹¹They said, "Men of Galilee, why are you standing here looking into the sky? Jesus, whom you saw taken up from you into heaven, will come back in the same way you saw him go."

## A NEW APOSTLE IS CHOSEN

¹²Then they went back to Jerusalem from the Mount of Olives. (This mountain is about half a mile from Jerusalem.) ¹³When they entered the city, they went to the upstairs room where they were staying. Peter, John, James, Andrew, Philip, Thomas, Bartholomew, Matthew, James son of Alphaeus, Simon (known as the Zealot), and Judas son of James were there. ¹⁴They all continued praying together with some women, including Mary the mother of Jesus, and Jesus' brothers.

¹⁵During this time there was a meeting of the believers (about one hundred twenty of them). Peter stood up and said, ¹⁶⁻¹⁷"Brothers and sisters," in the Scriptures the Holy Spirit said through David something that must happen involving Judas. He was one of our own group and served together with us. He led those who arrested Jesus." ¹⁸(Judas bought a field with the money he got for his evil act. But he fell to his death, his body burst open, and all his intestines poured out. ¹⁹Everyone in Jerusalem learned about this so they named this place Akeldama. In their language Akeldama means "Field of Blood.") ²⁰"In the Book of Psalms," Peter said, "this is written:

'May his place be empty;

leave no one to live in it.' *Psalm 69:25*

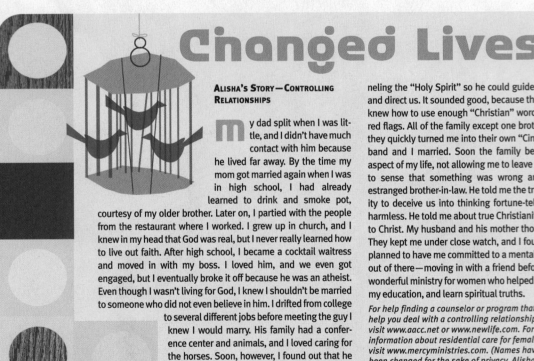

# Changed Lives

### ALISHA'S STORY—CONTROLLING RELATIONSHIPS

My dad split when I was little, and I didn't have much contact with him because he lived far away. By the time my mom got married again when I was in high school, I had already learned to drink and smoke pot, courtesy of my older brother. Later on, I partied with the people from the restaurant where I worked. I grew up in church, and I knew in my head that God was real, but I never really learned how to live out faith. After high school, I became a cocktail waitress and moved in with my boss. I loved him, and we even got engaged, but I eventually broke it off because he was an atheist. Even though I wasn't living for God, I knew I shouldn't be married to someone who did not even believe in him. I drifted from college to several different jobs before meeting the guy I knew I would marry. His family had a conference center and animals, and I loved caring for the horses. Soon, however, I found out that he and his family were spiritually different. They took me to psychics and told me we were chan-

neling the "Holy Spirit" so he could guide and direct us. It sounded good, because they knew how to use enough "Christian" words not to throw up any red flags. All of the family except one brother was involved, and they quickly turned me into their own "Cinderella" after my husband and I married. Soon the family began controlling every aspect of my life, not allowing me to leave their property. I began to sense that something was wrong and later ran into the estranged brother-in-law. He told me the truth about Satan's ability to deceive us into thinking fortune-tellers and psychics are harmless. He told me about true Christianity, and I gave my heart to Christ. My husband and his mother thought I had gone crazy. They kept me under close watch, and I found out that the family planned to have me committed to a mental hospital. I quickly got out of there—moving in with a friend before being taken in by a wonderful ministry for women who helped me get on my feet, get my education, and learn spiritual truths.

*For help finding a counselor or program that can help you deal with a controlling relationship visit www.aacc.net or www.newlife.com. For information about residential care for females, visit www.mercyministries.com. (Names have been changed for the sake of privacy. Alisha tells her story after going through biblically based counseling with Mercy Ministries.)*

 **1:16-17 Brothers and sisters** Although the Greek text says "Brothers" here and throughout this book, the words of the speakers were meant for the entire church, including men and women.

156

And it is also written:

'Let another man replace him as leader.'

*Psalm 109:8*

²¹⁻²²"So now a man must become a witness with us of Jesus' being raised from the dead. He must be one of the men who were part of our group during all the time the Lord Jesus was among us—from the time John was baptizing people until the day Jesus was taken up from us to heaven."

²³They put the names of two men before the group. One was Joseph Barsabbas, who was also called Justus. The other was Matthias. ²⁴⁻²⁵The apostles prayed, "Lord, you know the thoughts of everyone. Show us which one of these two you have chosen to do this work. Show us who should be an apostle in place of Judas, who turned away and went where he belongs." ²⁶Then they used lots to choose between them, and the lots showed that Matthias was the one. So he became an apostle with the other eleven.

## THE COMING OF THE HOLY SPIRIT

2 When the day of Pentecost came, they were all together in one place. ²Suddenly a noise like a strong, blowing wind came from heaven and filled the whole house where they were sitting. ³They saw something like flames of fire that were separated and stood over each person there. ⁴They were all filled with the Holy Spirit, and they began to speak different languages" by the power the Holy Spirit was giving them.

⁵There were some religious Jews staying in Jerusalem who were from every country in the world. ⁶When they heard this noise, a crowd came together. They were all surprised, because each one heard them speaking in his own language. ⁷They were completely amazed at this. They said, "Look! Aren't all these people that we hear speaking from Galilee? ⁸Then how is it possible that we each hear them in our own languages? We are from different places: ⁹Parthia, Media, Elam, Mesopotamia, Judea, Cappadocia, Pontus, Asia, ¹⁰Phrygia, Pamphylia, Egypt, the areas of Libya near Cyrene, Rome ¹¹(both Jews and those who had become Jews), Crete, and Arabia. But we hear them telling in our own languages about the great things God has done!" ¹²They were all amazed and confused, asking each other, "What does this mean?"

¹³But others were making fun of them, saying, "They have had too much wine."

## PETER SPEAKS TO THE PEOPLE

¹⁴But Peter stood up with the eleven apostles, and in a loud voice he spoke to the crowd: "My fellow Jews, and all of you who are in Jerusalem, listen to me. Pay attention to what I have to say. ¹⁵These people are not drunk, as you think; it is only nine o'clock in the morning! ¹⁶But Joel the prophet wrote about what is happening here today:

¹⁷'God says: In the last days
   I will pour out my Spirit on all kinds of
     people.
Your sons and daughters will prophesy.
   Your young men will see visions,
   and your old men will dream dreams.
¹⁸At that time I will pour out my Spirit
   also on my male slaves and female slaves,
   and they will prophesy.
¹⁹I will show miracles
   in the sky and on the earth:
   blood, fire, and thick smoke.
²⁰The sun will become dark,
   the moon red as blood,
   before the overwhelming and glorious
     day of the Lord will come.
²¹Then anyone who calls on the Lord will be
   saved.'

*Joel 2:28-32*

²²"People of Israel, listen to these words: Jesus from Nazareth was a very special man. God clearly showed this to you by the miracles, wonders, and signs he did through Jesus. You all know this, because it happened right here among you. ²³Jesus was given to you, and with the help of those who don't know the law, you put him to death by nailing him to a cross. But this was God's plan which he had made long ago; he knew all this would happen. ²⁴God raised Jesus from the dead and set him free from the pain of death, because death could not hold him. ²⁵For David said this about him:

## RadicalFaith:

# Acts 1:6-7

Any good author knows his characters inside and out. He or she sees the whole story and knows exactly how everything should play out. Do you know that there is an imaginative, exciting, wise, and trustworthy Author of your life? When you've got big questions you want answered, sometimes it's hard to be patient until you get answers. But God can give all you need to stay strong and steady in the middle of your journey. There are lots of things you can know for sure. Deuteronomy 32:4 says, "He is like a rock. What he does is perfect and he is always fair. He is a faithful God who does no wrong, who is right and fair." When you're upset and confused, find a place where you can sit quietly for a few minutes. Think about God's character and spend time praying and reading about what he shows you clearly in his Word. Only God knows the details of his plan for your life, but you can know that he's faithful. He's constantly working in you. Sometimes it's not so much about you understanding everything that happens, but is more about understanding who he is. Put your trust in him. And you'll find that getting closer to God is even better than having had the answers all along.

 **2:4 languages** This can also be translated "tongues."

# CHECK IT OUT

## LOCKS OF LOVE

Locks of Love is a nonprofit organization that provides hairpieces to financially disadvantaged young people under the age of 18 who are suffering from long-term, medically related hair loss. The organization uses donated human hair to create extremely realistic prosthetics (sometimes called wigs) to help restore kids' self-esteem and confidence.

Locks of Love collects donated hair and sends it to prosthetic companies to be made into high-quality prosthetics. Donations are used to pay for the hairpieces, and Locks of Love fund-raisers are held all over the United States. Volunteers are needed to organize these events, and donations are needed to pay for prosthetics to be made. A volunteer kit is available for download on the organization's website, as well as a Locks of Love banner that can be added to your website. You can also learn about how to donate your own hair—all you need are ten or more inches to cut off.

*Get involved by visiting www.locksoflove.org.*

'I keep the Lord before me always.

Because he is close by my side,

I will not be hurt.

²⁶So I am glad, and I rejoice.

Even my body has hope,

²⁷because you will not leave me in the grave.

You will not let your Holy One rot.

²⁸You will teach me how to live a holy life.

Being with you will fill me with joy.'

*Psalm 16:8-11*

²⁹"Brothers and sisters, I can tell you truly that David, our ancestor, died and was buried. His grave is still here with us today. ³⁰He was a prophet and knew God had promised him that he would make a person from David's family a king just as he was." ³¹Knowing this before it happened, David talked about the Christ rising from the dead. He said:

'He was not left in the grave.

His body did not rot.'

³²So Jesus is the One whom God raised from the dead. And we are all witnesses to this. ³³Jesus was lifted up to heaven and is now at God's right side. The Father has given the Holy Spirit to Jesus as he promised. So Jesus has poured out that Spirit, and this is what you now see and hear. ³⁴David was not the one who was lifted up to heaven, but he said:

'The Lord said to my Lord,

"Sit by me at my right side,

³⁵until I put your enemies under your

control."ⁿ *Psalm 110:1*

³⁶"So, all the people of Israel should know this truly: God has made Jesus —the man you nailed to the cross—both Lord and Christ."

³⁷When the people heard this, they felt guilty and asked Peter and the other apostles, "What shall we do?"

³⁸Peter said to them, "Change your hearts and lives and be baptized, each one of you, in the name of Jesus Christ for the forgiveness of your sins. And you will receive the gift of the Holy Spirit. ³⁹This promise is for you, for your children, and for all who are far away. It is for everyone the Lord our God calls to himself."

⁴⁰Peter warned them with many other words. He begged them, "Save yourselves from the evil of today's people!" ⁴¹Then those people

# LEARN I+ & LIVE I+

### Acts 2:4
**Learn It:** The followers of Jesus were filled with the Holy Spirit.
**Live It:** Study teachings on the Holy Spirit, and ask God to reveal what he does in your life today.

### Acts 2:42
**Learn It:** Jesus' followers spent their time learning, sharing, eating, and praying together.
**Live It:** Get together with friends regularly to learn, share, eat, and pray.

### Acts 4:12
**Learn It:** Jesus is the only One who can save people.
**Live It:** Learn about other religions, but do not be deceived into thinking that all religions lead to the same God.

**2:30 God . . . was** See 2 Samuel 7:13; Psalm 132:11." **2:35 until . . . control** Literally, "until I make your enemies a footstool for your feet."

# Music Reviews

| GROUP: | ALBUM: |
| --- | --- |
| TODD AGNEW | GRACE LIKE RAIN |

Gravelly voiced worship leader Todd Agnew paints a magnificent picture of God in "This Fragile Breath (The Thunder Song)" that stays with the listener long after the last note fades away. Todd then expands the vision with "Grace Like Rain," a remake of the classic hymn, with his own lyrics and gripping melody attached. Todd's deep, throaty vocals and melding of blues, gospel, and rock make him, along with Jeremy Camp, one of the modern rock leaders of the pack.

**WHY IT ROCKS: TODD'S RICH VOICE WITH LOTS OF GUITAR MAKES FOR PRAISE THAT ROCKS THE PEWS.**

who accepted what Peter said were baptized. About three thousand people were added to the number of believers that day. ⁴²They spent their time learning the apostles' teaching, sharing, breaking bread," and praying together.

## THE BELIEVERS SHARE

⁴³The apostles were doing many miracles and signs, and everyone felt great respect for God. ⁴⁴All the believers were together and shared everything. ⁴⁵They would sell their land and the things they owned and then divide the money and give it to anyone who needed it. ⁴⁶The believers met together in the Temple every day. They ate together in their homes, happy to share their food with joyful hearts. ⁴⁷They praised God and were liked by all the people. Every day the Lord added those who were being saved to the group of believers.

## PETER HEALS A CRIPPLED MAN

**3** One day Peter and John went to the Temple at three o'clock, the time set each day for the afternoon prayer service. ²There, at the Temple gate called Beautiful Gate, was a man who had been crippled all his life. Every day he was carried to this gate to beg for money from the people going into the Temple. ³The man saw Peter and John going into the Temple and asked them for money. ⁴Peter and John looked straight at him and said, "Look at us!" ⁵The man looked at them, thinking they were going to give him some money. ⁶But Peter said, "I don't have any silver or gold, but I do have something else I can give you. By the power of Jesus Christ from Nazareth, stand up and walk!" ⁷Then Peter took the man's right hand and lifted him up. Immediately the man's feet and ankles became strong. ⁸He jumped up, stood on his feet, and began to walk. He went into the Temple with them, walking and jumping and praising God. ⁹⁻¹⁰All the people recognized him as the crippled man who always sat by the Beautiful Gate begging for money. Now they saw this same man walking and praising God, and they were amazed. They wondered how this could happen.

# "BY THE POWER OF JESUS CHRIST FROM NAZARETH, STAND UP AND WALK!"

## PETER SPEAKS TO THE PEOPLE

¹¹While the man was holding on to Peter and John, all the people were amazed and ran to them at Solomon's Porch. ¹²When Peter saw this, he said to them, "People of Israel, why are you surprised? You are looking at us as if it were our own power or goodness that made this man walk. ¹³The God of Abraham, Isaac, and Jacob, the God of our ancestors, gave glory to Jesus, his servant. But you handed him over to be killed. Pilate decided to let him go free, but you told Pilate you did not want Jesus. ¹⁴You did not want the One who is holy and good but asked Pilate to give you a murderer" instead. ¹⁵And so you killed the One who gives life, but God raised him from the dead. We are witnesses to this. ¹⁶It was faith in Jesus that made this crippled man well. You can see this man, and you know him. He was made completely well because of trust in Jesus, and you all saw it happen!

¹⁷"Brothers and sisters, I know you did those things to Jesus because neither you nor your leaders understood what you were doing. ¹⁸God said through the prophets that his Christ would suffer and die. And now God has made these things come true in this way. ¹⁹So you must change your hearts and lives! Come back to God, and he will forgive your sins. Then the Lord will send the time of rest. ²⁰And he will send Jesus, the One he chose to be the Christ. ²¹But Jesus must stay in heaven until the time comes when all things will be made right again. God told about this time long ago when he spoke through his holy prophets.

 **2:42 breaking bread** This may mean a meal as in verse 46, or the Lord's Supper, the special meal Jesus told his followers to eat to remember him (Luke 22:14-20). **3:14 murderer** Barabbas, the man the crowd asked Pilate to set free instead of Jesus (Luke 23:18).

**Q:** I want to thank my parents for always being there. What are three things I could do to show them?

**A:** You could wash your dad's car, offer to babysit younger siblings so your parents can go out on a date, or make dinner for them and do the dishes afterward. Look for ways to spend time with them and let them in on what's happening in your life.

**Q:** How can I prove to my parents that I am ready to have my own car?

**A:** You can best prove you are ready to be trusted with a car when you are trustworthy in every area. Work hard at school, have a good attitude at home, and develop their trust by always being where you say you will be and arriving home on time. Oh yeah, and show them that you drive safely and responsibly, too.

**Q:** My parents want to know everything about me, but I want to keep a lot of things to myself. Don't I have a right to privacy?

**A:** You do have a right to privacy, but what do you have to hide? You should not shut out the people who love you most. Your parents realize that you are changing into a young adult and want to get to know the new you. They are interested in who you are as a person; they are not just being nosy. Let them into your life. You'll be amazed at how happy you'll make them.

22Moses said, 'The Lord your God will give you a prophet like me, who is one of your own people. You must listen to everything he tells you. 23Anyone who does not listen to that prophet will die, cut off from God's people.'" 24Samuel, and all the other prophets who spoke for God after Samuel, told about this time now. 25You are descendants of the prophets. You have received the agreement God made with your ancestors. He said to your father Abraham, 'Through your descendants all the nations on the earth will be blessed.'" 26God has raised up his servant Jesus and sent him to you first to bless you by turning each of you away from doing evil."

## PETER AND JOHN AT THE COUNCIL

4 While Peter and John were speaking to the people, priests, the captain of the soldiers that guarded the Temple, and Sadducees came up to them. 2They were upset because the two apostles were teaching the people and were preaching that people will rise from the dead through the power of Jesus. 3The older leaders grabbed Peter and John and put them in jail. Since it was already night, they kept them in jail until the next day. 4But many of those who had heard Peter and John preach believed the things they said. There were now about five thousand in the group of believers.

5The next day the rulers, the older leaders, and the teachers of the law met in Jerusalem. 6Annas the high priest, Caiaphas, John, and Alexander were there, as well as everyone from the high priest's family. 7They made Peter and John stand before them and then asked them, "By what power or authority did you do this?"

8Then Peter, filled with the Holy Spirit, said to them, "Rulers of the people and you older leaders, 9are you questioning us about a good thing that was done to a crippled man? Are you asking us who made him well? 10We want all of you and all the people to know that this man was made well by the power of Jesus Christ from Nazareth. You crucified him, but God raised him from the dead. This man was crippled, but he is now well and able to stand here before you because of the power of Jesus. 11Jesus is

'the stone" that you builders rejected,
which has become the cornerstone.'

*Psalm 118:22*

12Jesus is the only One who can save people. His name is the only power in the world that has been given to save people. We must be saved through him."

13The leaders saw that Peter and John were not afraid to speak, and they understood that these men had no special training or education. So they were amazed. Then they realized that Peter and John had been with Jesus. 14Because they saw the healed man standing there beside the two apostles, they could say nothing against them. 15After the leaders ordered them to leave the meeting, they began to talk to each other. 16They said, "What shall we do with these men? Everyone in Jerusalem knows they have done a great miracle, and we cannot say it is not true.

### Blushing Shadows

Some makeup artists suggest using blush on your eyes as a time-saver. But the rosy colors of blushes can make your eyes look red and unhealthy. Instead, invest in an eye shadow shade of pink. It's worth the extra money.

 notes  3:22-23 'The Lord . . . people.' Quotation from Deuteronomy 18:15, 19.  3:25 'Through . . . blessed.' Quotation from Genesis 22:18; 26:4.  4:11 stone A symbol meaning Jesus.

160

[17]But to keep it from spreading among the people, we must warn them not to talk to people anymore using that name."

[18]So they called Peter and John in again and told them not to speak or to teach at all in the name of Jesus. [19]But Peter and John answered them, "You decide what God would want. Should we obey you or God? [20]We cannot keep quiet. We must speak about what we have seen and heard." [21]The leaders warned the apostles again and let them go free. They could not find a way to punish them, because all the people were praising God for what had been done. [22]The man who received the miracle of healing was more than forty years old.

## THE BELIEVERS PRAY

[23]After Peter and John left the meeting of leaders, they went to their own group and told them everything the leading priests and the older leaders had said to them. [24]When the believers heard this, they prayed to God together, "Lord, you are the One who made the sky, the earth, the sea, and everything in them. [25]By the Holy Spirit, through our father David your servant, you said:

'Why are the nations so angry?
    Why are the people making useless plans?
[26]The kings of the earth prepare to fight,
    and their leaders make plans together against the Lord
    and his Christ.'                    *Psalm 2:1-2*

[27]These things really happened when Herod, Pontius Pilate, and some of the people all came together against Jesus here in Jerusalem. Jesus is your holy servant, the One you made to be the Christ. [28]These people made your plan happen because of your power and your will. [29]And now, Lord, listen to their threats. Lord, help us, your servants, to speak your word without fear. [30]Help us to be brave by showing us your power to heal. Give proofs and make miracles happen by the power of Jesus, your holy servant."

[31]After they had prayed, the place where they were meeting was shaken. They were all filled with the Holy Spirit, and they spoke God's word without fear.

## THE BELIEVERS SHARE

[32]The group of believers were united in their hearts and spirit. All those in the group acted as though their private property belonged to everyone in the group. In fact, they shared everything. [33]With great power the apostles were telling people that the Lord Jesus was truly raised from the dead. And God blessed all the believers very much. [34]No one in the group needed anything. From time to time those who owned fields or houses sold them, brought the money, [35]and gave it to the apostles. Then the money was given to anyone who needed it.

[36]One of the believers was named Joseph, a Levite born in Cyprus. The apostles called him Barnabas (which means "one who encourages"). [37]Joseph owned a field, sold it, brought the money, and gave it to the apostles.

## ANANIAS AND SAPPHIRA DIE

5 But a man named Ananias and his wife Sapphira sold some land. [2]He kept back part of the money for himself; his wife knew about this and agreed to it. But he brought the rest of the money and gave it to the apostles.

[3]Peter said, "Ananias, why did you let Satan rule your thoughts to lie to the Holy Spirit and to keep for yourself part of the money you received for the land? [4]Before you sold the land, it belonged to you. And even after you sold it, you could have used the money any way you wanted. Why did you think of doing this? You lied to God, not to us!" [5-6]When Ananias heard this, he fell down and died. Some young men came in, wrapped up his body, carried it out, and buried it. And everyone who heard about this was filled with fear.

[7]About three hours later his wife came in, but she did not know what had happened. [8]Peter said to her, "Tell me, was the money you got for your field this much?"

Sapphira answered, "Yes, that was the price."

[9]Peter said to her, "Why did you and your husband agree to test the Spirit of the Lord? Look! The men who buried your husband are at the door, and they will carry you out." [10]At that moment Sapphira fell down by his feet and died. When the young men came in and saw that she was dead, they carried her out and buried her beside her husband. [11]The whole church and all the others who heard about these things were filled with fear.

---

# Bible Basics

The **Passover** is a special occasion still celebrated by those of the Jewish faith to commemorate the time before Christ when God protected the firstborn sons of the Israelites from death. God sent Moses to tell the king (the pharaoh) of Egypt, who was keeping the Israelites in slavery, to let them go. When the king refused, God sent terrible plagues to the Egyptians. Still, the king would not let the Israelites leave. God told Moses that during the night he would pass over each house in Egypt and kill all the firstborn males—human and animal. The only exceptions would be those in the houses that were marked with blood from a special sacrifice the Lord instructed the Israelites to make. If the Israelites' doorframes were properly marked with the blood, the Lord "passed over" their homes and saved their sons. However, all the Egyptian firstborn sons died and the king then allowed the Israelites to leave.

## THE APOSTLES HEAL MANY

[12]The apostles did many signs and miracles among the people. And they would all meet together on Solomon's Porch. [13]None of the others dared to join them, but all the people respected them. [14]More and more men and women believed in the Lord and were added to the group of believers. [15]The people placed their sick on beds and mats in the streets, hoping that when Peter passed by at least his shadow might fall on them. [16]Crowds came from all the towns around Jerusalem, bringing their sick and those who were bothered by evil spirits, and all of them were healed.

## LEADERS TRY TO STOP THE APOSTLES

[17]The high priest and all his friends (a group called the Sadducees) became very jealous. [18]They took the apostles and put them in jail. [19]But during the night, an angel of the Lord opened the doors of the jail and led the apostles outside. The angel said, [20]"Go stand in the Temple and tell the people everything about this new life." [21]When the apostles heard this, they obeyed and went into the Temple early in the morning and continued teaching.

## "THE ANGEL SAID, 'GO STAND IN THE TEMPLE AND TELL THE PEOPLE EVERYTHING ABOUT THIS NEW LIFE.'"

When the high priest and his friends arrived, they called a meeting of the leaders and all the important older men. They sent some men to the jail to bring the apostles to them. [22]But, upon arriving, the officers could not find the apostles. So they went back and reported to the leaders. [23]They said, "The jail was closed and locked, and the guards were standing at the doors. But when we opened the doors, the jail was empty!" [24]Hearing this, the captain of the Temple guards and the leading priests were confused and wondered what was happening.

[25]Then someone came and told them, "Listen! The men you put in jail are standing in the Temple teaching the people." [26]Then the captain and his men went out and brought the apostles back. But the soldiers did not use force, because they were afraid the people would stone them to death.

[27]The soldiers brought the apostles to the meeting and made them stand before the leaders. The high priest questioned them, [28]saying, "We gave you strict orders not to continue teaching in that name. But look, you have filled Jerusalem with your teaching and are trying to make us responsible for this man's death."

[29]Peter and the other apostles answered, "We must obey God, not human authority! [30]You killed Jesus by hanging him on a cross. But God, the God of our ancestors, raised Jesus up from the dead! [31]Jesus is the One whom God raised to be on his right side, as Leader and Savior. Through him, all people could change their hearts and lives and have their sins forgiven. [32]We saw all these things happen. The Holy Spirit, whom God has given to all who obey him, also proves these things are true."

[33]When the leaders heard this, they became angry and wanted to kill them. [34]But a Pharisee named Gamaliel stood up in the meeting. He was a teacher of the law, and all the people respected him. He ordered the apostles to leave the meeting for a little while. [35]Then he said, "People of Israel, be careful what you are planning to do to these men. [36]Remember when Theudas appeared? He said he was a great man, and about four hundred men joined him. But he was killed, and all his followers were scattered; they were able to do nothing. [37]Later, a man named Judas came from Galilee at the time of the registration." He also led a group of followers and was killed, and all his followers were scattered. [38]And so now I tell you: Stay away from these men, and leave them alone. If their plan comes from human authority, it will fail. [39]But if it is from God, you will not be able to stop them. You might even be fighting against God himself!"

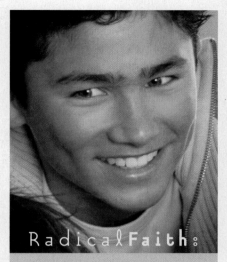

RadicalFaith:

## Acts 5:40-42

The followers were living out their worst nightmare. The people hated and made fun of them, they were busted by the authorities, and got beaten to a bloody pulp. Could things have been worse? What could they do after all that? Start sobbing and yell out, "God, how could you let this happen?" Not these guys. Peter and the other followers are a great example of how to handle pain and rejection. They were obeying Jesus' direction to preach the good news, and things got really ugly fast. But they kept obeying. Oddly enough, they actually found immense joy in the suffering. You can have a lot of hope and strength when you're suffering for God. Jesus even warned them of this persecution before his death: "I told you these things so that you can have peace in me. In this world you will have trouble, but be brave! I have defeated the world" (John 16:33). Jesus certainly knew rejection and persecution, but he also knew that God's power was greater. Sharing in Christ's sufferings now means you'll share in his joy when he returns and every knee bows before him. So if you're going through a tough time because of your faith, remember that God is faithful—he has not forgotten you!

**notes** 5:37 **registration** Census. A counting of all the people and the things they own.

The leaders agreed with what Gamaliel said. [40]They called the apostles in, beat them, and told them not to speak in the name of Jesus again. Then they let them go free. [41]The apostles left the meeting full of joy because they were given the honor of suffering disgrace for Jesus. [42]Every day in the Temple and in people's homes they continued teaching the people and telling the Good News—that Jesus is the Christ.

## seven leaders are chosen

**6** The number of followers was growing. But during this same time, the Greek-speaking followers had an argument with the other followers. The Greek-speaking widows were not getting their share of the food that was given out every day. [2]The twelve apostles called the whole group of followers together and said, "It is not right for us to stop our work of teaching God's word in order to serve tables. [3]So, brothers and sisters, choose seven of your own men who are good, full of the Spirit and full of wisdom. We will put them in charge of this work. [4]Then we can continue to pray and to teach the word of God."

[5]The whole group liked the idea, so they chose these seven men: Stephen (a man with great faith and full of the Holy Spirit), Philip,[n] Procorus, Nicanor, Timon, Parmenas, and Nicolas (a man from Antioch who had become a follower of the Jewish religion). [6]Then they put these men before the apostles, who prayed and laid their hands[n] on them.

[7]The word of God was continuing to spread. The group of followers in Jerusalem increased, and a great number of the Jewish priests believed and obeyed.

## stephen is accused

[8]Stephen was richly blessed by God who gave him the power to do great miracles and signs among the people. [9]But some people were against him. They belonged to the synagogue of Free Men[n] (as it was called), which included people from Cyrene, Alexandria, Cilicia, and Asia. They all came and argued with Stephen.

[10]But the Spirit was helping him to speak with wisdom, and his words were so strong that they could not argue with him. [11]So they secretly urged some men to say, "We heard Stephen speak against Moses and against God."

[12]This upset the people, the older leaders, and the teachers of the law. They came and grabbed Stephen and brought him to a meeting of the leaders. [13]They brought in some people to tell lies about Stephen, saying, "This man is always speaking against this holy place and the law of Moses. [14]We heard him say that Jesus from Nazareth will destroy this place and that Jesus will change the customs Moses gave us." [15]All the people in the meeting were watching Stephen closely and saw that his face looked like the face of an angel.

## stephen's speech

**7** The high priest said to Stephen, "Are these things true?"

[2]Stephen answered, "Brothers and fathers, listen to me. Our glorious God appeared to Abraham, our ancestor, in Mesopotamia before he lived in Haran. [3]God said to Abraham, 'Leave your country and your relatives, and go to the land I will show you.'[n] [4]So Abraham left the country of Chaldea and went to live in Haran. After Abraham's father died, God sent him to this place where you now live. [5]God did not give Abraham any of this land, not even a foot of it. But God promised that he would give this land to him and his descendants, even before Abraham had a child. [6]This is what God said to him: 'Your descendants will be strangers in a land they don't own. The people there will make them slaves and will mistreat them for four hundred years. [7]But I will punish the nation where they are slaves. Then your descendants will leave that land and will worship me in this place.'[n] [8]God made an agreement with Abraham, the sign of which was circumcision. And so when Abraham had his son Isaac, Abraham circumcised him when he was eight days old. Isaac also circumcised his son Jacob, and Jacob did the same for his sons, the twelve ancestors[n] of our people.

[9]"Jacob's sons became jealous of Joseph and sold him to be a slave in Egypt. But God was with him [10]and saved him from all his troubles. The king of Egypt liked Joseph and respected him because of the wisdom God gave him. The king made him governor of Egypt and put him in charge of all the people in his palace.

[11]"Then all the land of Egypt and Canaan became so dry that nothing would grow, and the people suffered very much. Jacob's sons, our ancestors, could not find anything to eat. [12]But when Jacob heard there was grain in Egypt, he sent his sons there. This was their first trip to Egypt. [13]When they went there a second time, Joseph told his brothers who he was, and the king learned about Joseph's family. [14]Then Joseph sent messengers to invite Jacob, his father, to come to Egypt along with

GUYS SPEAK OUT

Q: How do you have fun with your family?
A: "We play a lot of board games. That's fun."

**notes** **6:5 Philip** Not the apostle named Philip. **6:6 laid their hands** The laying on of hands had many purposes, including the giving of a blessing, power, or authority. **6:9 Free Men** Jewish people who had been slaves or whose fathers had been slaves, but were now free. **7:3 'Leave . . . you.'** Quotation from Genesis 12:1. **7:6-7 'Your descendants . . . place.'** Quotation from Genesis 15:13-14 and Exodus 3:12. **7:8 twelve ancestors** Important ancestors of the people of Israel; the leaders of the twelve tribes of Israel.

all his relatives (seventy-five persons altogether). ¹⁵So Jacob went down to Egypt, where he and his sons died. ¹⁶Later their bodies were moved to Shechem and put in a grave there. (It was the same grave Abraham had bought for a sum of money from the sons of Hamor in Shechem.)

¹⁷"The promise God made to Abraham was soon to come true, and the number of people in Egypt grew large. ¹⁸Then a new king, who did not know who Joseph was, began to rule Egypt. ¹⁹This king tricked our people and was cruel to our ancestors, forcing them to leave their babies outside to die. ²⁰At this time Moses was born, and he was very beautiful. For three months Moses was cared for in his father's house. ²¹When they put Moses outside, the king's daughter adopted him and raised him as if he were her own son. ²²The Egyptians taught Moses everything they knew, and he was a powerful man in what he said and did.

²³"When Moses was about forty years old, he thought it would be good to visit his own people, the people of Israel. ²⁴Moses saw an Egyptian mistreating one of his people, so he defended the Israelite and punished the Egyptian by killing him. ²⁵Moses thought his own people would understand that God was using him to save them, but they did not. ²⁶The next day when Moses saw two men of Israel fighting, he tried to make peace between them. He said, 'Men, you are brothers. Why are you hurting each other?' ²⁷The man who was hurting the other pushed Moses away and said, 'Who made you our ruler and judge? ²⁸Are you going to kill me as you killed the Egyptian yesterday?'" ²⁹When Moses heard him say this, he left Egypt and went to live in the land of Midian where he was a stranger. While Moses lived in Midian, he had two sons.

³⁰"Forty years later an angel appeared to Moses in the flames of a burning bush as he was in the desert near Mount Sinai. ³¹When Moses saw this, he was amazed and went near to look closer. Moses heard the Lord's voice say, ³²'I am the God of your ancestors, the God of Abraham, Isaac, and Jacob.'" Moses began to shake with fear and was afraid to look. ³³The Lord said to him, 'Take off your sandals, because you are standing on holy ground. ³⁴I have seen the troubles my people have suffered in Egypt. I have heard their cries and have come down to save them. And now, Moses, I am sending you back to Egypt.'"

³⁵"This Moses was the same man the two men of Israel rejected, saying, 'Who made you a ruler and judge?'" Moses is the same man God sent to be a ruler and savior, with the help of the angel that Moses saw in the burning bush. ³⁶So Moses led the people out of Egypt. He worked miracles and signs in Egypt, at the Red Sea, and then in the desert for forty years. ³⁷This is the same Moses that said to the people of Israel, 'God will give you a prophet like me, who is one of your own people.'" ³⁸This is the Moses who was with the gathering of the Israelites in the desert. He was with the angel that spoke to him at Mount Sinai, and he was with our ancestors. He received commands from God that give life, and he gave those commands to us.

³⁹"But our ancestors did not want to obey Moses. They rejected him and wanted to go back to Egypt. ⁴⁰They said to Aaron, 'Make us gods who will lead us. Moses led us out of Egypt, but we don't know what has happened to him.' ⁴¹So the people made an idol that looked like a calf. Then they brought sacrifices to it and were proud of what they had made with their own hands. ⁴²But God turned against them and did not try to stop them from worshiping the sun, moon, and stars. This is what is written in the book of the prophets: God says,

'People of Israel, you did not bring me
    sacrifices and offerings
    while you traveled in the desert for forty
    years.
⁴³You have carried with you
    the tent to worship Molech
    and the idols of the star god Rephan that
    you made to worship.
So I will send you away beyond Babylon.'

*Amos 5:25-27*

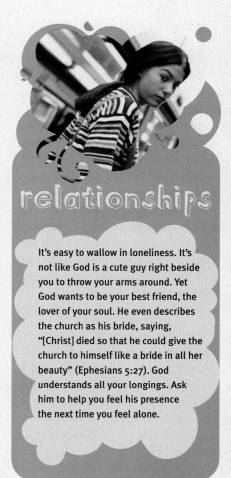

# relationships

It's easy to wallow in loneliness. It's not like God is a cute guy right beside you to throw your arms around. Yet God wants to be your best friend, the lover of your soul. He even describes the church as his bride, saying, "[Christ] died so that he could give the church to himself like a bride in all her beauty" (Ephesians 5:27). God understands all your longings. Ask him to help you feel his presence the next time you feel alone.

⁴⁴"The Holy Tent where God spoke to our ancestors was with them in the desert. God told Moses how to make this Tent, and he made it like the plan God showed him. ⁴⁵Later, Joshua led our ancestors to capture the lands of the other nations. Our people went in, and God forced the other people out. When our people went into this new land, they took with them this same Tent they had received from their ancestors. They kept it until the time of David, ⁴⁶who pleased God and asked God to let him build a house for him, the God of Jacob. ⁴⁷But Solomon was the one who built the Temple.

⁴⁸"But the Most High does not live in houses that people build with their hands. As the prophet says:
⁴⁹'Heaven is my throne,
    and the earth is my footstool.

**notes**  **7:27-28 'Who . . . yesterday?'** Quotation from Exodus 2:14.  **7:32 'I am . . . Jacob.'** Quotation from Exodus 3:6.  **7:33-34 'Take . . . Egypt.'** Quotation from Exodus 3:5-10.  **7:35 'Who . . . judge?'** Quotation from Exodus 2:14.  **7:37 'God . . . people.'** Quotation from Deuteronomy 18:15.  **7:40 'Make . . . him.'** Quotation from Exodus 32:1.

165

So do you think you can build a house for
me? says the Lord.

Do I need a place to rest?

50Remember, my hand made all these
things!' " *Isaiah 66:1-2*

51Stephen continued speaking: "You stubborn people! You have not given your hearts to God, nor will you listen to him! You are always against what the Holy Spirit is trying to tell you, just as your ancestors were. 52Your ancestors tried to hurt every prophet who ever lived. Those prophets said long ago that the One who is good would come, but your ancestors killed them. And now you have turned against and killed the One who is good. 53You received the law of Moses, which God gave you through his angels, but you haven't obeyed it."

### STEPHEN IS KILLED

54When the leaders heard this, they became furious. They were so mad they were grinding their teeth at Stephen. 55But Stephen was full of the Holy Spirit. He looked up to heaven and saw the glory of God and Jesus standing at God's right side. 56He said, "Look! I see heaven open and the Son of Man standing at God's right side."

57Then they shouted loudly and covered their ears and all ran at Stephen. 58They took him out of the city and began to throw stones at him to kill him. And those who told lies against Stephen left their coats with a young man named Saul. 59While they were throwing stones, Stephen prayed, "Lord Jesus, receive my spirit." 60He fell on his knees and cried in a loud voice, "Lord, do not hold this sin against them." After Stephen said this, he died.

**8** Saul agreed that the killing of Stephen was good.

### TROUBLES FOR THE BELIEVERS

On that day the church of Jerusalem began to be persecuted, and all the believers, except the apostles, were scattered throughout Judea and Samaria.

2And some religious people buried Stephen and cried loudly for him. 3Saul was also trying to destroy the church, going from house to house, dragging out men and women and putting them in jail. 4And wherever they were scattered, they told people the Good News.

### PHILIP PREACHES IN SAMARIA

5Philip went to the city of Samaria and preached about the Christ. 6When the people there heard Philip and saw the miracles he was doing, they all listened carefully to what he said. 7Many of these people had evil spirits in them, but Philip made the evil spirits leave. The spirits made a loud noise when they came out. Philip also healed many weak and crippled people there. 8So the people in that city were very happy.

9But there was a man named Simon in that city. Before Philip came there, Simon had practiced magic and amazed all the people of Samaria. He bragged and called himself a great man. 10All the people—the least important and the most important—paid attention to Simon, saying, "This man has the power of God, called 'the Great Power'!" 11Simon had amazed them with his magic so long that the people became his followers. 12But when Philip told them the Good News about the kingdom of God and the power of Jesus Christ, men and women believed Philip and were baptized. 13Simon himself believed, and after he was baptized, he stayed very close to Philip. When he saw the miracles and the powerful things Philip did, Simon was amazed.

14When the apostles who were still in Jerusalem heard that the people of Samaria had accepted the word of God, they sent Peter and John to them. 15When Peter and John arrived, they prayed that the Samaritan believers might receive the Holy Spirit. 16These people had been baptized in the name of the Lord Jesus, but the Holy Spirit had not yet come upon any of them. 17Then, when the two apostles began laying their hands on the people, they received the Holy Spirit.

18Simon saw that the Spirit was given to people when the apostles laid their hands on them. So he offered the apostles money, 19saying, "Give me also this power so that anyone on whom I lay my hands will receive the Holy Spirit."

20Peter said to him, "You and your money should both be destroyed, because you thought you could buy God's gift with money. 21You cannot share with us in this work since your heart is not right before God. 22Change your heart! Turn away from this evil thing you

## LEARN I+ & LIVE I+

**Acts 8:4**
**Learn It:** Wherever the followers of Jesus were scattered, they shared their faith.
**Live It:** Wherever you go, from the grocery store to the classroom, ask God for opportunities to share your faith.

**Acts 14:28**
**Learn It:** Paul and Barnabas stayed in Antioch with believers for a long time.
**Live It:** The next time you are at Bible study or church, enjoy your time with other believers. Do not be in a hurry to leave.

**Romans 1:8**
**Learn It:** Paul thanked God for the Christians in Rome who were spreading the Good News.
**Live It:** Make a list of the people who have helped you get to know God. Write letters thanking them.

# *Music Reviews*

| GROUP: | ALBUM: |
|---|---|
| JEREMY CAMP | STAY |

Jeremy Camp's story grabbed fans' hearts almost before his music gained their attention. As a young twentysomething, Jeremy became widowed. *Stay* captures his struggles with faith through that heartbreaking loss in lyrics that will grip your heart. Songs like "I Still Believe" and "Walk By Faith" outline his determination not to let his heartache destroy his belief in God. Jeremy's music can be compared to Creed and Dave Matthews, yet it has originality, too. This one is a must-have for modern rock and modern worship fans alike.

**WHY IT ROCKS: JEREMY IS PROOF THAT BAD THINGS CAN HAPPEN TO GOOD PEOPLE, BUT HE SHOWS THAT IT'S POSSIBLE TO SEE THROUGH THE BAD AND REALIZE THAT GOD IS STILL THERE.**

have done, and pray to the Lord. Maybe he will forgive you for thinking this. <sup>23</sup>I see that you are full of bitter jealousy and ruled by sin."

<sup>24</sup>Simon answered, "Both of you pray for me to the Lord so the things you have said will not happen to me."

<sup>25</sup>After Peter and John told the people what they had seen Jesus do and after they had spoken the message of the Lord, they went back to Jerusalem. On the way, they went through many Samaritan towns and preached the Good News to the people.

## PHILIP TEACHES AN ETHIOPIAN

<sup>26</sup>An angel of the Lord said to Philip, "Get ready and go south to the road that leads down to Gaza from Jerusalem—the desert road." <sup>27</sup>So Philip got ready and went. On the road he saw a man from Ethiopia, a eunuch. He was an important officer in the service of Candace, the queen of the Ethiopians; he was responsible for taking care of all her money. He had gone to Jerusalem to worship. <sup>28</sup>Now, as he was on his way home, he was sitting in his chariot reading from the Book of Isaiah, the prophet. <sup>29</sup>The Spirit said to Philip, "Go to that chariot and stay near it."

<sup>30</sup>So when Philip ran toward the chariot, he heard the man reading from Isaiah the prophet. Philip asked, "Do you understand what you are reading?"

<sup>31</sup>He answered, "How can I understand unless someone explains it to me?" Then he invited Philip to climb in and sit with him. <sup>32</sup>The portion of Scripture he was reading was this:

"He was like a sheep being led to be killed.

He was quiet, as a lamb is quiet while its wool is being cut;

he never opened his mouth.

<sup>33</sup>    He was shamed and was treated unfairly.

He died without children to continue his family.

His life on earth has ended." *Isaiah 53:7-8*

<sup>34</sup>The officer said to Philip, "Please tell me, who is the prophet talking about —himself or someone else?" <sup>35</sup>Philip began to speak, and starting with this same Scripture, he told the man the Good News about Jesus.

<sup>36</sup>While they were traveling down the road, they came to some water. The officer said, "Look, here is water. What is stopping me from being baptized?" <sup>37n</sup> <sup>38</sup>Then the officer commanded the chariot to stop. Both Philip and the officer went down into the water, and Philip baptized him. <sup>39</sup>When they came up out of the water, the Spirit of the Lord took Philip away; the officer never saw him again. And the officer continued on his way home, full of joy. <sup>40</sup>But Philip appeared in a city called Azotus

and preached the Good News in all the towns on the way from Azotus to Caesarea.

## SAUL IS CONVERTED

**9** In Jerusalem Saul was still threatening the followers of the Lord by saying he would kill them. So he went to the high priest <sup>2</sup>and asked him to write letters to the synagogues in the city of Damascus. Then if Saul found any followers of Christ's Way, men or women, he would arrest them and bring them back to Jerusalem.

<sup>3</sup>So Saul headed toward Damascus. As he came near the city, a bright light from heaven suddenly flashed around him. <sup>4</sup>Saul fell to the ground and heard a voice saying to him, "Saul, Saul! Why are you persecuting me?"

<sup>5</sup>Saul said, "Who are you, Lord?"

## "I AM JESUS, WHOM YOU ARE PERSECUTING."

The voice answered, "I am Jesus, whom you are persecuting. <sup>6</sup>Get up now and go into the city. Someone there will tell you what you must do."

<sup>7</sup>The people traveling with Saul stood there but said nothing. They heard the voice, but

**8:37 Verse 37** Some late copies of Acts add verse 37: "Philip answered, 'If you believe with all your heart, you can.' The officer said, 'I believe that Jesus Christ is the Son of God.'"

**167**

## Blab

**Q:** I have been going to church all my life, and I love Jesus. But I want to go deeper. How can I get to the next level in my faith?

**A:** Just keep asking God, and he will give you what you desire. The Bible promises that if you seek him, you will find him. Ask your youth leader or pastor to recommend some good books or Bible study tools that can help you learn more, be faithful in your quiet times, and wait expectantly for God to show up.

**Q:** I know the Bible says Jesus is coming back someday to take believers to heaven. Is it wrong for me to want more time on earth first?

**A:** God created this earth for people to enjoy, and he understands that you want to be here for a while. He knows that you cannot understand how great heaven is and that you want the opportunity to experience things like being an adult, getting married, and having a career and kids. Pray that he will give you an enthusiasm for his return, while also living to the fullest here on earth.

**Q:** Do I need to memorize Bible verses?

**A:** Yes, you should. The Bible is our instruction manual, our defense, and our armor against temptation. You may not always have one handy to flip open when you need it. If you know key verses on topics like anger, prayer, fear, temptation, and love, you are able to remember them right away and apply them when you need them.

they saw no one. ⁸Saul got up from the ground and opened his eyes, but he could not see. So those with Saul took his hand and led him into Damascus. ⁹For three days Saul could not see and did not eat or drink.

¹⁰There was a follower of Jesus in Damascus named Ananias. The Lord spoke to Ananias in a vision, "Ananias!"

Ananias answered, "Here I am, Lord."

¹¹The Lord said to him, "Get up and go to Straight Street. Find the house of Judas," and ask for a man named Saul from the city of Tarsus. He is there now, praying. ¹²Saul has seen a vision in which a man named Ananias comes to him and lays his hands on him. Then he is able to see again."

¹³But Ananias answered, "Lord, many people have told me about this man and the terrible things he did to your holy people in Jerusalem. ¹⁴Now he has come here to Damascus, and the leading priests have given him the power to arrest everyone who worships you."

¹⁵But the Lord said to Ananias, "Go! I have chosen Saul for an important work. He must tell about me to those who are not Jews, to kings, and to the people of Israel. ¹⁶I will show him how much he must suffer for my name."

¹⁷So Ananias went to the house of Judas. He laid his hands on Saul and said, "Brother Saul, the Lord Jesus sent me. He is the one you saw on the road on your way here. He sent me so that you can see again and be filled with the Holy Spirit." ¹⁸Immediately, something that looked like fish scales fell from Saul's eyes, and he was able to see again! Then Saul got up and was baptized. ¹⁹After he ate some food, his strength returned.

### Saul Preaches in Damascus

Saul stayed with the followers of Jesus in Damascus for a few days. ²⁰Soon he began to preach about Jesus in the synagogues, saying, "Jesus is the Son of God."

²¹All the people who heard him were amazed. They said, "This is the man who was in Jerusalem trying to destroy those who trust in this name! He came here to arrest the fol-

lowers of Jesus and take them back to the leading priests."

²²But Saul grew more powerful. His proofs that Jesus is the Christ were so strong that his own people in Damascus could not argue with him.

²³After many days, they made plans to kill Saul. ²⁴They were watching the city gates day and night, but Saul learned about their plan. ²⁵One night some followers of Saul helped him leave the city by lowering him in a basket through an opening in the city wall.

### Saul Preaches in Jerusalem

²⁶When Saul went to Jerusalem, he tried to join the group of followers, but they were all afraid of him. They did not believe he was really a follower. ²⁷But Barnabas accepted Saul and took him to the apostles. Barnabas explained to them that Saul had seen the Lord on the road and the Lord had spoken to Saul. Then he told them how boldly Saul had preached in the name of Jesus in Damascus.

²⁸And so Saul stayed with the followers, going everywhere in Jerusalem, preaching boldly in the name of the Lord. ²⁹He would often talk and argue with the Jewish people who spoke Greek, but they were trying to kill him. ³⁰When the followers learned about this, they took Saul to Caesarea and from there sent him to Tarsus.

³¹The church everywhere in Judea, Galilee, and Samaria had a time of peace and became stronger. Respecting the Lord by the way they lived, and being encouraged by the Holy Spirit, the group of believers continued to grow.

### Peter Heals Aeneas

³²As Peter was traveling through all the area, he visited God's people who lived in Lydda. ³³There he met a man named Aeneas, who was paralyzed and had not been able to leave his bed for the past eight years. ³⁴Peter said to him, "Aeneas, Jesus Christ heals you. Stand up and make your bed." Aeneas stood up immediately. ³⁵All the people living in Lydda and on the Plain of Sharon saw him and turned to the Lord.

notes    **9:11 Judas** This is not either of the apostles named Judas.

## Peter Heals Tabitha

³⁶In the city of Joppa there was a follower named Tabitha (whose Greek name was Dorcas). She was always doing good deeds and kind acts. ³⁷While Peter was in Lydda, Tabitha became sick and died. Her body was washed and put in a room upstairs. ³⁸Since Lydda is near Joppa and the followers in Joppa heard that Peter was in Lydda, they sent two messengers to Peter. They begged him, "Hurry, please come to us!" ³⁹So Peter got ready and went with them. When he arrived, they took him to the upstairs room where all the widows stood around Peter, crying. They showed him the shirts and coats Tabitha had made when she was still alive. ⁴⁰Peter sent everyone out of the room and kneeled and prayed. Then he turned to the body and said, "Tabitha, stand up." She opened her eyes, and when she saw Peter, she sat up. ⁴¹He gave her his hand and helped her up. Then he called the saints and the widows into the room and showed them that Tabitha was alive. ⁴²People everywhere in Joppa learned about this, and many believed in the Lord. ⁴³Peter stayed in Joppa for many days with a man named Simon who was a tanner.

## Peter Teaches Cornelius

**10** At Caesarea there was a man named Cornelius, an officer in the Italian group of the Roman army. ²Cornelius was a religious man. He and all the other people who lived in his house worshiped the true God. He gave much of his money to the poor and prayed to God often. ³One afternoon about three o'clock, Cornelius clearly saw a vision. An angel of God came to him and said, "Cornelius!"

⁴Cornelius stared at the angel. He became afraid and said, "What do you want, Lord?"

The angel said, "God has heard your prayers. He has seen that you give to the poor, and he remembers you. ⁵Send some men now to Joppa to bring back a man named Simon who is also called Peter. ⁶He is staying with a man, also named Simon, who is a tanner and has a house beside the sea." ⁷When the angel who spoke to Cornelius left, Cornelius called two of his ser-vants and a soldier, a religious man who worked for him. ⁸Cornelius explained everything to them and sent them to Joppa.

⁹About noon the next day as they came near Joppa, Peter was going up to the roof* to pray. ¹⁰He was hungry and wanted to eat, but while the food was being prepared, he had a vision. ¹¹He saw heaven opened and something coming down that looked like a big sheet being lowered to earth by its four corners. ¹²In it were all kinds of animals, reptiles, and birds. ¹³Then a voice said to Peter, "Get up, Peter; kill and eat."

¹⁴But Peter said, "No, Lord! I have never eaten food that is unholy or unclean."

¹⁵But the voice said to him again, "God has made these things clean so don't call them 'unholy'!" ¹⁶This happened three times, and at once the sheet was taken back to heaven.

¹⁷While Peter was wondering what this vision meant, the men Cornelius sent had found Simon's house and were standing at the gate. ¹⁸They asked, "Is Simon Peter staying here?"

¹⁹While Peter was still thinking about the vision, the Spirit said to him, "Listen, three men are looking for you. ²⁰Get up and go downstairs. Go with them without doubting, because I have sent them to you."

²¹So Peter went down to the men and said, "I am the one you are looking for. Why did you come here?"

²²They said, "A holy angel spoke to Cornelius, an army officer and a good man; he worships God. All the people respect him. The angel told Cornelius to ask you to come to his house so that he can hear what you have to say." ²³So Peter asked the men to come in and spend the night.

**DIDYA KNOW**

**ALMOST TWO-THIRDS OF CHILDREN'S BEDROOMS HAVE A TV.**

KNOWLEDGE NETWORKS/SRI

**notes** 10:9 **roof** In Bible times houses were built with flat roofs. The roof was used for drying things such as flax and fruit. And it was used as an extra room, as a place for worship, and as a cool place to sleep in the summer.

## Radical Faith:

## Acts 10:42-43

If you were given the undercover heads-up that a deadly tornado was about to hit, you'd be telling your neighbors, right? If a terrible epidemic hit and you found the antidote needed for survival, you'd chase people down to give them the cure, wouldn't you? If you were homeless and hungry and you found a place with a ton of food, you'd surely point others in need in the right direction. Finding forgiveness for sins through Jesus means being saved from destruction, suffering, and death. You have to tell people about it! You can't just sit on this too-good-to-be-true information. You can't let others continue in the direction of devastation when they can be snatched up into safety. It isn't undercover info; get the word out! Many people don't know that their sins mean certain spiritual death (Romans 6:23) and that everyone who believes in Jesus will be forgiven of their sins. There is a way to have eternal life. Peter spent his days telling people about Jesus, wherever he was. And many were saved because of Peter. Be like Peter, and let people know that God's made a way for them, too.

The next day Peter got ready and went with them, and some of the followers from Joppa joined him. ²⁴On the following day they came to Caesarea. Cornelius was waiting for them and had called together his relatives and close friends. ²⁵When Peter entered, Cornelius met him, fell at his feet, and worshiped him. ²⁶But Peter helped him up, saying, "Stand up. I too am only a human." ²⁷As he talked with Cornelius, Peter went inside where he saw many people gathered. ²⁸He said, "You people understand that it is against our law for Jewish people to associate with or visit anyone who is not Jewish. But God has shown me that I should not call any person 'unholy' or 'unclean.' ²⁹That is why I did not argue when I was asked to come here. Now, please tell me why you sent for me."

³⁰Cornelius said, "Four days ago, I was praying in my house at this same time—three o'clock in the afternoon. Suddenly, there was a man standing before me wearing shining clothes. ³¹He said, 'Cornelius, God has heard your prayer and has seen that you give to the poor and remembers you. ³²So send some men to Joppa and ask Simon Peter to come. Peter is staying in the house of a man, also named Simon, who is a tanner and has a house beside the sea.' ³³So I sent for you immediately, and it was very good of you to come. Now we are all here before God to hear everything the Lord has commanded you to tell us."

³⁴Peter began to speak: "I really understand now that to God every person is the same. ³⁵In every country God accepts anyone who worships him and does what is right. ³⁶You know the message that God has sent to the people of Israel is the Good News that peace has come through Jesus Christ. Jesus is the Lord of all people! ³⁷You know what has happened all over Judea, beginning in Galilee after John" preached to the people about baptism. ³⁸You know about Jesus from Nazareth, that God gave him the Holy Spirit and power. You know how Jesus went everywhere doing good and healing those who were ruled by the devil, because God was with him. ³⁹We saw what

Jesus did in Judea and in Jerusalem, but the Jews in Jerusalem killed him by hanging him on a cross. ⁴⁰Yet, on the third day, God raised Jesus to life and caused him to be seen, ⁴¹not by all the people, but only by the witnesses God had already chosen. And we are those witnesses who ate and drank with him after he was raised from the dead. ⁴²He told us to preach to the people and to tell them that he is the one whom God chose to be the judge of the living and the dead. ⁴³All the prophets say it is true that all who believe in Jesus will be forgiven of their sins through Jesus' name."

⁴⁴While Peter was still saying this, the Holy Spirit came down on all those who were listening. ⁴⁵The Jewish believers who came with Peter were amazed that the gift of the Holy Spirit had been given even to the nations. ⁴⁶These believers heard them speaking in different languages" and praising God. Then Peter said, ⁴⁷"Can anyone keep these people from being baptized with water? They have received the Holy Spirit just as we did!" ⁴⁸So Peter ordered that they be baptized in the name of Jesus Christ. Then they asked Peter to stay with them for a few days.

### PETER RETURNS TO JERUSALEM

11 The apostles and the believers in Judea heard that some who were not Jewish had accepted God's teaching too. ²But when Peter came to Jerusalem, some people argued with him. ³They said, "You went into the homes of people who are not circumcised and ate with them!"

⁴So Peter explained the whole story to them. ⁵He said, "I was in the city of Joppa, and while I was praying, I had a vision. I saw something that looked like a big sheet being lowered from heaven by its four corners. It came very close to me. ⁶I looked inside it and saw animals, wild beasts, reptiles, and birds. ⁷I heard a voice say to me, 'Get up, Peter. Kill and eat.' ⁸But I said, 'No, Lord! I have never eaten anything that is unholy or unclean.' ⁹But the voice from heaven spoke again, 'God has made these things clean, so don't call them unholy.' ¹⁰This happened three times. Then the whole thing

notes  **10:37 John** John the Baptist, who preached to people about Christ's coming (Luke 3).   **10:46 languages** This can also be translated "tongues."

was taken back to heaven. [11]Right then three men who were sent to me from Caesarea came to the house where I was staying. [12]The Spirit told me to go with them without doubting. These six believers here also went with me, and we entered the house of Cornelius. [13]He told us about the angel he saw standing in his house. The angel said to him, 'Send some men to Joppa and invite Simon Peter to come. [14]By the words he will say to you, you and all your family will be saved.' [15]When I began my speech, the Holy Spirit came on them just as he came on us at the beginning. [16]Then I remembered the words of the Lord. He said, 'John baptized with water, but you will be baptized with the Holy Spirit.' [17]Since God gave them the same gift he gave us who believed in the Lord Jesus Christ, how could I stop the work of God?"

[18]When the believers heard this, they stopped arguing. They praised God and said, "So God is allowing even other nations to turn to him and live."

## THE GOOD NEWS COMES TO ANTIOCH

[19]Many of the believers were scattered when they were persecuted after Stephen was killed. Some of them went as far as Phoenicia, Cyprus, and Antioch telling the message to others, but only to Jews. [20]Some of these believers were people from Cyprus and Cyrene. When they came to Antioch, they spoke also to Greeks, telling them the Good News about the Lord Jesus. [21]The Lord was helping the believers, and a large group of people believed and turned to the Lord.

[22]The church in Jerusalem heard about all of this, so they sent Barnabas to Antioch. [23-24]Barnabas was a good man, full of the Holy Spirit and full of faith. When he reached Antioch and saw how God had blessed the people, he was glad. He encouraged all the believers in Antioch always to obey the Lord with all their hearts, and many people became followers of the Lord.

[25]Then Barnabas went to the city of Tarsus to look for Saul, [26]and when he found Saul, he brought him to Antioch. For a whole year Saul and Barnabas met with the church and taught many people there. In Antioch the followers were called Christians for the first time.

[27]About that time some prophets came from Jerusalem to Antioch. [28]One of them, named Agabus, stood up and spoke with the help of the Holy Spirit. He said, "A very hard time is coming to the whole world. There will be no food to eat." (This happened when Claudius ruled.) [29]The believers all decided to help the followers who lived in Judea, as much as each one could. [30]They gathered the money and gave it to Barnabas and Saul, who brought it to the elders in Judea.

## HEROD AGRIPPA HURTS THE CHURCH

**12** During that same time King Herod began to mistreat some who

---

---

## Blab

**Q:** I'm not sure what qualities I should look for in the guy I want to marry—except for good looks and a hot body. Where should I start?

**A:** Good looks don't hurt, but they aren't going to last. Go for a good heart and a firm commitment to Christ. Your guy needs to love God more than he loves you. That's the only way he can understand how to love you the right way. He should be gentle and cherish you. He should also be an emotionally healthy person, so that you are not a crutch he needs to feel good about himself.

**Q:** I like a guy at school, and he likes me, but he isn't very popular. If my friends see me with him, they're definitely going to give me a hard time. Is it okay to ask him not to pay attention to me at school?

**A:** No way! It is so not okay to treat people differently in different situations. How would that make you feel? Ask God to work in your heart to help you care about others more than you care about the way they see you. Your guy deserves better.

**Q:** My boyfriend and I just had sex for the first time. Now I feel really guilty. I don't want to do it again, but he does. What can I do?

**A:** Ask Jesus to forgive you, and make sure you get tested for sexually transmitted diseases (unless you absolutely know for sure that he was a virgin, too) and pregnancy. From now on, don't be alone with your boyfriend—ever—anywhere you might be tempted. Tell him what you did was wrong and that you will not do it again.

# top 10

## random ways to keep your own standards

**10** Date guys who act like Christians and don't just say they are.

**9** Forget procrastinating. Do your work early and with excellence.

**8** Know before you date how far you'll go physically. Don't cross your own line.

**7** Stay away from strangers online.

**6** Put filters on your Internet.

**5** Ask God to help you capture wrong thoughts before they take root.

**4** Don't spend time alone in houses, cars, or (especially) bedrooms with boyfriends.

**3** Choose friends who respect your values.

**2** Decide ahead of time what is okay in movies and stick to it.

**1** Consider what you watch on TV.

belonged to the church. [2]He ordered James, the brother of John, to be killed by the sword. [3]Herod saw that some of the people liked this, so he decided to arrest Peter, too. (This happened during the time of the Feast of Unleavened Bread.)

[4]After Herod arrested Peter, he put him in jail and handed him over to be guarded by sixteen soldiers. Herod planned to bring Peter before the people for trial after the Passover Feast. [5]So Peter was kept in jail, but the church prayed earnestly to God for him.

## PETER LEAVES THE JAIL

[6]The night before Herod was to bring him to trial, Peter was sleeping between two soldiers, bound with two chains. Other soldiers were guarding the door of the jail. [7]Suddenly, an angel of the Lord stood there, and a light shined in the cell. The angel struck Peter on the side and woke him up. "Hurry! Get up!" the angel said. And the chains fell off Peter's hands. [8]Then the angel told him, "Get dressed and put on your sandals." And Peter did. Then the angel said, "Put on your coat and follow me." [9]So Peter followed him out, but he did not know if what the angel was doing was real; he thought he might be seeing a vision. [10]They went past the first and second guards and came to the iron gate that separated them from the city. The gate opened by itself for them, and they went through it. When they had walked down one street, the angel suddenly left him.

[11]Then Peter realized what had happened. He thought, "Now I know that the Lord really sent his angel to me. He rescued me from Herod and from all the things the people thought would happen."

[12]When he considered this, he went to the home of Mary, the mother of John Mark. Many people were gathered there, praying. [13]Peter knocked on the outside door, and a servant girl named Rhoda came to answer it. [14]When she recognized Peter's voice, she was so happy she forgot to open the door. Instead, she ran inside and told the group, "Peter is at the door!"

[15]They said to her, "You are crazy!" But she kept on saying it was true, so they said, "It must be Peter's angel."

[16]Peter continued to knock, and when they opened the door, they saw him and were amazed. [17]Peter made a sign with his hand to tell them to be quiet. He explained how the Lord led him out of the jail, and he said, "Tell James and the other believers what happened." Then he left to go to another place.

[18]The next day the soldiers were very upset and wondered what had happened to Peter. [19]Herod looked everywhere for him but could not find him. So he questioned the guards and ordered that they be killed.

## THE DEATH OF HEROD AGRIPPA

Later Herod moved from Judea and went to the city of Caesarea, where he stayed. [20]Herod was very angry with the people of Tyre and Sidon, but the people of those cities all came in a group to him. After convincing Blastus, the king's personal servant, to be on their side, they asked Herod for peace, because their country got its food from his country.

[21]On a chosen day Herod put on his royal robes, sat on his throne, and made a speech to the people. [22]They shouted, "This is the voice of a god, not a human!" [23]Because Herod did not give the glory to God, an angel of the Lord immediately caused him to become sick, and he was eaten by worms and died.

[24]God's message continued to spread and reach people.

[25]After Barnabas and Saul finished their task in Jerusalem, they returned to Antioch, taking John Mark with them.

## BARNABAS AND SAUL ARE CHOSEN

**13** In the church at Antioch there were these prophets and teachers: Barnabas, Simeon (also called Niger), Lucius (from the city of Cyrene), Manaen (who had grown up with Herod, the ruler), and Saul. [2]They were all worshiping the Lord and giving up eating for a certain time." During this time the Holy Spirit said to them, "Set apart for me Barnabas

**13:2 giving up . . . time** This is called "fasting." The people would give up eating for a special time of prayer and worship to God. It was also done sometimes to show sadness and disappointment.

172

and Saul to do a special work for which I have chosen them."

[3]So after they gave up eating and prayed, they laid their hands on[n] Barnabas and Saul and sent them out.

## Barnabas and Saul in Cyprus

[4]Barnabas and Saul, sent out by the Holy Spirit, went to the city of Seleucia. From there they sailed to the island of Cyprus. [5]When they came to Salamis, they preached the Good News of God in the synagogues. John Mark was with them to help.

[6]They went across the whole island to Paphos where they met a magician named Bar-Jesus. He was a false prophet [7]who always stayed close to Sergius Paulus, the governor and a smart man. He asked Barnabas and Saul to come to him, because he wanted to hear the message of God. [8]But Elymas, the magician, was against them. (Elymas is the name for Bar-Jesus in the Greek language.) He tried to stop the governor from believing in Jesus. [9]But Saul, who was also called Paul, was filled with the Holy Spirit. He looked straight at Elymas [10]and said, "You son of the devil! You are an enemy of everything that is right! You are full of evil tricks and lies, always trying to change the Lord's truths into lies. [11]Now the Lord will touch you, and you will be blind. For a time you will not be able to see anything—not even the light from the sun."

Then everything became dark for Elymas, and he walked around, trying to find someone to lead him by the hand. [12]When the governor saw this, he believed because he was amazed at the teaching about the Lord.

## Paul and Barnabas Leave Cyprus

[13]Paul and those with him sailed from Paphos and came to Perga, in Pamphylia. There John Mark left them to return to Jerusalem. [14]They continued their trip from Perga and went to Antioch, a city in Pisidia. On the Sabbath day they went into the synagogue and sat down. [15]After the law of Moses and the writings of the prophets were read, the leaders of the synagogue sent a message to Paul and Barnabas: "Brothers, if you have any message that will encourage the people, please speak."

[16]Paul stood up, raised his hand, and said, "You Israelites and you who worship God, please listen! [17]The God of the Israelites chose our ancestors. He made the people great during the time they lived in Egypt, and he brought them out of that country with great power. [18]And he was patient with them for forty years in the desert. [19]God destroyed seven nations in the land of Canaan and gave the land to his people. [20]All this happened in about four hundred fifty years.

"After this, God gave them judges until the time of Samuel the prophet. [21]Then the people asked for a king, so God gave them Saul son of Kish. Saul was from the tribe of Benjamin and was king for forty years. [22]After God took him away, God made David their king. God said about him: 'I have found in David son of Jesse the kind of man I want. He will do all I want him to do.' [23]So God has brought Jesus, one of David's descendants, to Israel to be its Savior, as he promised. [24]Before Jesus came, John[n] preached to all the people of Israel about a baptism of changed hearts and lives. [25]When he was finishing his work, he said, 'Who do you think I am? I am not the Christ. He is coming later, and I am not worthy to untie his sandals.'

[26]"Brothers, sons of the family of Abraham, and others who worship God, listen! The news about this salvation has been sent to us. [27]Those who live in Jerusalem and their leaders did not realize that Jesus was the Savior. They did not understand the words that the prophets wrote, which are read every Sabbath day. But they made them come true when they said Jesus was guilty. [28]They could not find any real reason for Jesus to be put to death, but they asked Pilate to have him killed. [29]When they had done to him all that the Scriptures had said, they took him down from the cross and laid him in a tomb. [30]But God raised him up from the dead! [31]After this, for many days, those who had gone with Jesus from Galilee to Jerusalem saw him. They are now his witnesses

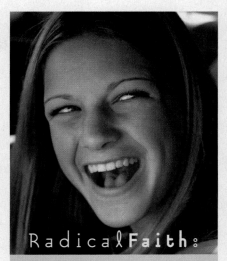

## Radical Faith:

# Acts 12:5-7

Is prayer the first place you go when you are in trouble, or is it your last resort? When Peter's friends found out he was in prison, they didn't strategize a plan to break him out. Nope, they went to their knees. Did you know that when a believing person prays that great things can happen? Praying is the *most* you can do in any situation, not the least. Think about who you're talking to for a moment. This is the God who poured down bread from heaven to feed his people, who parted the sea so his people could escape the Egyptians, and who broke Peter's prison chains. This is the God who told Jeremiah that nothing was impossible for him (Jeremiah 32:27). This is the God with endless wisdom and ultimate authority, and you're able to call on him at any given moment. You're in a position to connect with God and to ask him for wisdom and guidance in your life. Turn to him for everything, and don't limit your prayers to the ordinary. Remember, he's a God who does the unthinkable. There are no limitations on how he might bring glory to himself as he works in you, leads you, and walks through everything with you.

**13:3 laid their hands on** The laying on of hands had many purposes, including the giving of a blessing, power, or authority. **13:24 John** John the Baptist, who preached to people about Christ's coming (Luke 3).

173

to the people. ³²We tell you the Good News about the promise God made to our ancestors. ³³God has made this promise come true for us, his children, by raising Jesus from the dead. We read about this also in Psalm 2:

'You are my Son.

Today I have become your Father.'

*Psalm 2:7*

³⁴God raised Jesus from the dead, and he will never go back to the grave and become dust. So God said:

'I will give you the holy and sure blessings that I promised to David.'    *Isaiah 55:3*

³⁵But in another place God says:

'You will not let your Holy One rot.'

*Psalm 16:10*

³⁶David did God's will during his lifetime. Then he died and was buried beside his ancestors, and his body did rot in the grave. ³⁷But the One God raised from the dead did not rot in the grave. ³⁸⁻³⁹Brothers, understand what we are telling you: You can have forgiveness of your sins through Jesus. The law of Moses could not free you from your sins. But through Jesus everyone who believes is free from all sins. ⁴⁰Be careful! Don't let what the prophets said happen to you:

⁴¹'Listen, you people who doubt!

You can wonder, and then die.

I will do something in your lifetime

that you won't believe even when you are told about it!' "    *Habakkuk 1:5*

⁴²While Paul and Barnabas were leaving the synagogue, the people asked them to tell them more about these things on the next Sabbath. ⁴³When the meeting was over, many people with those who had changed to worship God followed Paul and Barnabas from that place. Paul and Barnabas were persuading them to continue trusting in God's grace.

⁴⁴On the next Sabbath day, almost everyone in the city came to hear the word of the Lord. ⁴⁵Seeing the crowd, the Jewish people became very jealous and said insulting things and argued against what Paul said. ⁴⁶But Paul and Barnabas spoke very boldly, saying, "We must speak the message of God to you first. But you refuse to listen. You are judging yourselves not worthy of having eternal life! So we will now go to the people of other nations. ⁴⁷This is what the Lord told us to do, saying:

'I have made you a light for the nations;

you will show people all over the world the way to be saved.' "    *Isaiah 49:6*

⁴⁸When those who were not Jewish heard Paul say this, they were happy and gave honor to the message of the Lord. And the people who were chosen to have life forever believed the message.

⁴⁹So the message of the Lord was spreading through the whole country. ⁵⁰But the Jewish people stirred up some of the important religious women and the leaders of the city. They started trouble against Paul and Barnabas and forced them out of their area. ⁵¹So Paul and Barnabas shook the dust off their feet[n] and went to Iconium. ⁵²But the followers were filled with joy and the Holy Spirit.

## PAUL AND BARNABAS IN ICONIUM

**14** In Iconium, Paul and Barnabas went as usual to the synagogue. They spoke so well that a great many Jews and Greeks believed. ²But some people who did not believe excited the others and turned them against the believers. ³Paul and Barnabas stayed in Iconium a long time and spoke bravely for the Lord. He showed that their message about his grace was true by giving them the power to work miracles and signs. ⁴But the city was divided. Some of the people agreed with the Jews, and others believed the apostles.

⁵Some who were not Jews, some Jews, and some of their rulers wanted to mistreat Paul and Barnabas and to stone them to death. ⁶When Paul and Barnabas learned about this, they ran away to Lystra and Derbe, cities in Lycaonia, and to the areas around those cities. ⁷They announced the Good News there, too.

## PAUL IN LYSTRA AND DERBE

⁸In Lystra there sat a man who had been born crippled; he had never walked. ⁹As this man was listening to Paul speak, Paul looked

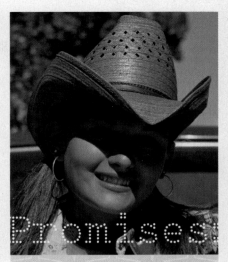

# Acts 13:38-39

Do you ever feel like your life is dictated by a never-ending list of rules? Curfews and chores are set by your parents. Your principal tells you what time you must be at school and when you can leave. Teachers give you homework to do every night. The government tells you how fast you can drive. Your soccer coach makes you run twenty laps every day. Ugh!

The teenage years can sometimes make you feel that you don't have a lot of control over your life. It can leave you feeling frustrated or even rebellious. Why can't you just live your life the way you want? Well, to state the annoyingly obvious: Rules can be good for you. They can protect you and keep you focused. (Probably what your parents have told you all along, huh?) But rules aren't everything, especially when it comes to your relationship with God. No matter how well you keep the rules, they won't save you. What great freedom we have in knowing that salvation comes from belief in God alone and not by how well we follow the rules!

No exceptions.

**13:51 shook . . . feet** A warning. It showed that they had rejected these people.

175

## Promises!

### Acts 13:47

The modern Olympic custom of carrying a torch from Athens to the site of the games is a very cool thing. Each time the Olympic games are held, one single flame travels all around the world—passing from nation to nation—until it makes a full trip around the globe and arrives at the opening ceremonies of the games. This singular flame represents all of the hopes and dreams of the athletes and is a symbol of unity among the nations. The flame is never extinguished, but is passed from torch to torch as it makes its international journey. Each person chosen to carry the torch for a short leg of its trip is honored to be a part of such an extraordinary event.

Actually, if you think about it, you are a lot like that Olympic flame. You have a light inside you that cannot be extinguished if you are a child of God. You are a light that stands out in the darkness of the world and that light is God's love and salvation. What a privilege!

straight at him and saw that he believed God could heal him. [10]So he cried out, "Stand up on your feet!" The man jumped up and began walking around. [11]When the crowds saw what Paul did, they shouted in the Lycaonian language, "The gods have become like humans and have come down to us!" [12]Then the people began to call Barnabas "Zeus"[n] and Paul "Hermes,"[n] because he was the main speaker. [13]The priest in the temple of Zeus, which was near the city, brought some bulls and flowers to the city gates. He and the people wanted to offer a sacrifice to Paul and Barnabas. [14]But when the apostles, Barnabas and Paul, heard about it, they tore their clothes. They ran in among the people, shouting, [15]"Friends, why are you doing these things? We are only human beings like you. We are bringing you the Good News and are telling you to turn away from these worthless things and turn to the living God. He is the One who made the sky, the earth, the sea, and everything in them. [16]In the past, God let all the nations do what they wanted. [17]Yet he proved he is real by showing kindness, by giving you rain from heaven and crops at the right times, by giving you food and filling your hearts with joy." [18]Even with these words, they were barely able to keep the crowd from offering sacrifices to them.

[19]Then some evil people came from Antioch and Iconium and persuaded the people to turn against Paul. So they threw stones at him and dragged him out of town, thinking they had killed him. [20]But the followers gathered around him, and he got up and went back into the town. The next day he and Barnabas left and went to the city of Derbe.

### THE RETURN TO ANTIOCH IN SYRIA

[21]Paul and Barnabas told the Good News in Derbe, and many became followers. Paul and Barnabas returned to Lystra, Iconium, and Antioch, [22]making the followers of Jesus stronger and helping them stay in the faith. They said, "We must suffer many things to enter God's kingdom." [23]They chose elders for each church, by praying and giving up eating for a certain time.[n] These elders had trusted

the Lord, so Paul and Barnabas put them in the Lord's care.

[24]Then they went through Pisidia and came to Pamphylia. [25]When they had preached the message in Perga, they went down to Attalia. [26]And from there they sailed away to Antioch where the believers had put them into God's care and had sent them out to do this work. Now they had finished.

[27]When they arrived in Antioch, Paul and Barnabas gathered the church together. They told the church all about what God had done with them and how God had made it possible for those who were not Jewish to believe. [28]And they stayed there a long time with the followers.

### THE MEETING AT JERUSALEM

15 Then some people came to Antioch from Judea and began teaching the non-Jewish believers: "You cannot be saved if you are not circumcised as Moses taught us." [2]Paul and Barnabas were against this teaching and argued with them about it. So the church decided to send Paul, Barnabas, and some others to Jerusalem where they could talk more about this with the apostles and elders.

[3]The church helped them leave on the trip, and they went through the countries of Phoenicia and Samaria, telling all about how the other nations had turned to God. This made all the believers very happy. [4]When they

**GUYS SPEAK OUT**

**Q:** How do you know God is real?
**A:** "He shows himself to me every day, when I look at creation."

**14:12 "Zeus"** The Greeks believed in many false gods, of whom Zeus was most important.  **14:12 "Hermes"** The Greeks believed he was a messenger for the other gods.  **14:23 giving . . . time** This is called "fasting." The people would give up eating for a special time of prayer and worship to God. It was also done sometimes to show sadness and disappointment.

**176**

# CHECK IT OUT

## WORLD VISION

World Vision has been working to make an impact around the world since 1950, with various programs that cover a wide range of needs for those around the world including addressing the AIDS crisis in Africa, giving children soccer balls, and sending school supply kits to underprivileged areas. World Vision works with churches and community leaders in foreign countries to help care for children and families in need, to teach them life skills (including abstinence and fidelity) and how to be the hands and feet of Christ.

Volunteers can give donations or sponsor a child for $30 a month. You can also take part in a 30-hour "famine" to bring attention to the devastating effects of poverty around the world and to raise funds. The SchoolTools program encourages anyone who wants to help to fill gallon-size plastic zipper bags with pencils, pens, notebooks, crayons, erasers, and rulers and package them with a personalized greeting card. These can then be shipped to World Vision to be distributed to children in need.

*Get involved by visiting www.worldvision.org.*

arrived in Jerusalem, they were welcomed by the apostles, the elders, and the church. Paul, Barnabas, and the others told about everything God had done with them. 5But some of the believers who belonged to the Pharisee group came forward and said, "The non-Jewish believers must be circumcised. They must be told to obey the law of Moses."

6The apostles and the elders gathered to consider this problem. 7After a long debate, Peter stood up and said to them, "Brothers, you know that in the early days God chose me from among you to preach the Good News to the nations. They heard the Good News from me, and they believed. 8God, who knows the thoughts of everyone, accepted them. He showed this to us by giving them the Holy Spirit, just as he did to us. 9To God, those people are not different from us. When they believed, he made their hearts pure. 10So now why are you testing God by putting a heavy load around the necks of the non-Jewish believers? It is a load that neither we nor our ancestors were able to carry. 11But we believe that we and they too will be saved by the grace of the Lord Jesus."

12Then the whole group became quiet. They listened to Paul and Barnabas tell about all the miracles and signs that God did through them among the people. 13After they finished speaking, James said, "Brothers, listen to me. 14Simon has told us how God showed his love for those people. For the first time he is accepting from among them a people to be his own. 15The words of the prophets agree with this too:

# Music Reviews

| GROUP: | ALBUM: |
|---|---|
| RELIENT K | RELIENT K (CLASSIC HIT) |

Relient K burst onto the scene in 2000 with this self-titled debut that combines fun and frenzy with a dose of faith. "My Girlfriend," a story about shock rocker Marilyn Manson's music turning a friend away from God, even caused a stir on MTV. Singer and primary songwriter Matt Thiessen constantly mixes pop culture references with pop-punk music in a mixture that sets toes tapping and fans singing along. Check out "Wake Up Call" and the hilarious tracks "Hello McFly" and "Charles in Charge."

**WHY IT ROCKS: RELIENT K CAPTURES THE COOL OF BLINK-182 WHILE STILL FANNING THE FLAMES OF FAITH.**

¹⁶'After these things I will return.
The kingdom of David is like a fallen
tent.
But I will rebuild its ruins,
and I will set it up.
¹⁷Then those people who are left alive may
ask the Lord for help,
and the other nations that belong to me,
says the Lord,
who will make it happen.
¹⁸And these things have been known for a
long time.'                    *Amos 9:11-12*

¹⁹"So I think we should not bother the other people who are turning to God. ²⁰Instead, we should write a letter to them telling them these things: Stay away from food that has been offered to idols (which makes it unclean), any kind of sexual sin, eating animals that have been strangled, and blood. ²¹They should do

## relationships

"All people will know that you are my followers if you love each other" (John 13:35). Guys are often described as players, but what about girls? Do you really care about your current crush or does he just look good on your arm? Real love doesn't play with others' affections, and those who love God are instructed to love others more than they love themselves. If you are just using your guy and don't know if you really care for him, gently break it off and wait for the one God has in mind for you.

these things, because for a long time in every city the law of Moses has been taught. And it is still read in the synagogue every Sabbath day."

### LETTER TO NON-JEWISH BELIEVERS

²²The apostles, the elders, and the whole church decided to send some of their men with Paul and Barnabas to Antioch. They chose Judas Barsabbas and Silas, who were respected by the believers. ²³They sent the following letter with them:

From the apostles and elders, your brothers.
To all the non-Jewish believers in Antioch, Syria, and Cilicia:
Greetings!
²⁴We have heard that some of our group have come to you and said things that trouble and upset you. But we did not tell them to do this. ²⁵We have all agreed to choose some messengers and send them to you with our dear friends Barnabas and Paul—²⁶people who have given their lives to serve our Lord Jesus Christ. ²⁷So we are sending Judas and Silas, who will tell you the same things. ²⁸It has pleased the Holy Spirit that you should not have a heavy load to carry, and we agree. You need to do only these things: ²⁹Stay away from any food that has been offered to idols, eating any animals that have been strangled, and blood, and any kind of sexual sin. If you stay away from these things, you will do well.
Good-bye.

³⁰So they left Jerusalem and went to Antioch where they gathered the church and gave them the letter. ³¹When they read it, they were very happy because of the encouraging message. ³²Judas and Silas, who were also prophets, said many things to encourage the believers and make them stronger. ³³After

some time Judas and Silas were sent off in peace by the believers, and they went back to those who had sent them. ³⁴ⁿ

³⁵But Paul and Barnabas stayed in Antioch and, along with many others, preached the Good News and taught the people the message of the Lord.

### DIDYA KNOW

ONE IN TEN HIGH SCHOOL SENIORS REPORTS USING AN ILLEGAL DRUG OTHER THAN MARIJUANA IN THE PAST MONTH. CHILD TRENDS DATABANK

### PAUL AND BARNABAS SEPARATE

³⁶After some time, Paul said to Barnabas, "We should go back to all those towns where we preached the message of the Lord. Let's visit the believers and see how they are doing."
³⁷Barnabas wanted to take John Mark with them, ³⁸but he had left them at Pamphylia; he did not continue with them in the work. So Paul did not think it was a good idea to take him. ³⁹Paul and Barnabas had such a serious argument about this that they separated and went different ways. Barnabas took Mark and sailed to Cyprus, ⁴⁰but Paul chose Silas and left. The believers in Antioch put Paul into the Lord's care, ⁴¹and he went through Syria and Cilicia, giving strength to the churches.

### TIMOTHY GOES WITH PAUL

**16** Paul came to Derbe and Lystra, where a follower named Timothy lived. Timothy's mother was Jewish and a believer, but his father was a Greek.
²The believers in Lystra and Iconium respected Timothy and said good things about him. ³Paul wanted Timothy to travel with him, but all the people living in that area knew that Timothy's father was Greek. So Paul circumcised Timothy to please his mother's people. ⁴Paul and those with him traveled from town to town and gave the decisions made by the apostles and elders in Jerusalem for the people to obey. ⁵So the churches became stronger in the faith and grew larger every day.

**15:34 Verse 34** Some Greek copies add verse 34: ". . . but Silas decided to remain there."

## PAUL IS CALLED OUT OF ASIA

⁶Paul and those with him went through the areas of Phrygia and Galatia since the Holy Spirit did not let them preach the Good News in the country of Asia. ⁷When they came near the country of Mysia, they tried to go into Bithynia, but the Spirit of Jesus did not let them. ⁸So they passed by Mysia and went to Troas. ⁹That night Paul saw in a vision a man from Macedonia. The man stood and begged, "Come over to Macedonia and help us." ¹⁰After Paul had seen the vision, we immediately prepared to leave for Macedonia, understanding that God had called us to tell the Good News to those people.

## LYDIA BECOMES A CHRISTIAN

¹¹We left Troas and sailed straight to the island of Samothrace. The next day we sailed to Neapolis." ¹²Then we went by land to Philippi, a Roman colony" and the leading city in that part of Macedonia. We stayed there for several days.

¹³On the Sabbath day we went outside the city gate to the river where we thought we would find a special place for prayer. Some women had gathered there, so we sat down and talked with them. ¹⁴One of the listeners was a woman named Lydia from the city of Thyatira whose job was selling purple cloth. She worshiped God, and he opened her mind to pay attention to what Paul was saying. ¹⁵She and all the people in her house were baptized. Then she invited us to her home, saying, "If you think I am truly a believer in the Lord, then come stay in my house." And she persuaded us to stay with her.

## PAUL AND SILAS IN JAIL

¹⁶Once, while we were going to the place for prayer, a servant girl met us. She had a special spirit" in her, and she earned a lot of money for her owners by telling fortunes. ¹⁷This girl followed Paul and us, shouting, "These men are servants of the Most High God. They are telling you how you can be saved."

¹⁸She kept this up for many days. This bothered Paul, so he turned and said to the spirit, "By the power of Jesus Christ, I command you to come out of her!" Immediately, the spirit came out.

¹⁹When the owners of the servant girl saw this, they knew that now they could not use her to make money. So they grabbed Paul and Silas and dragged them before the city rulers in the marketplace. ²⁰They brought Paul and Silas to the Roman rulers and said, "These men are Jews and are making trouble in our city. ²¹They are teaching things that are not right for us as Romans to do."

## "BELIEVE IN THE LORD JESUS AND YOU WILL BE SAVED."

²²The crowd joined the attack against them. The Roman officers tore the clothes of Paul and Silas and had them beaten with rods. ²³Then Paul and Silas were thrown into jail, and the jailer was ordered to guard them carefully. ²⁴When he heard this order, he put them far inside the jail and pinned their feet down between large blocks of wood.

²⁵About midnight Paul and Silas were praying and singing songs to God as the other prisoners listened. ²⁶Suddenly, there was a strong earthquake that shook the foundation of the jail. Then all the doors of the jail broke open, and all the prisoners were freed from their chains. ²⁷The jailer woke up and saw that the jail doors were open. Thinking that the prisoners had already escaped, he got his sword and was about to kill himself." ²⁸But Paul shouted, "Don't hurt yourself! We are all here."

²⁹The jailer told someone to bring a light. Then he ran inside and, shaking with fear, fell down before Paul and Silas. ³⁰He brought them outside and said, "Men, what must I do to be saved?"

³¹They said to him, "Believe in the Lord Jesus and you will be saved—you and all the people in your house." ³²So Paul and Silas told the message of the Lord to the jailer and all the people in his house. ³³At that hour of the night the jailer took Paul and Silas and washed their wounds. Then he and all his people were baptized immediately. ³⁴After this the jailer took Paul and Silas home and gave them food. He and his family were very happy because they now believed in God.

³⁵The next morning, the Roman officers sent the police to tell the jailer, "Let these men go free."

---

# Bible Basics

**The Ten Commandments** are more than just rules being fought over in courts today. They were actually laws on how to live life, written with God's own finger on tablets of clay and handed to Moses to be shared with the people of Israel. The Ten Commandments teach how to behave toward God and toward each other and are still rules to follow today. The first four commandments speak to the way we should act toward God, such as not taking his name in vain and not having any other gods but him. The last six remind us how we should treat each other, telling us not to kill each other, to honor our parents, not to commit adultery (tell that to the writers of the soaps on TV, right?), and not to be jealous of each other's stuff.

---

**16:11 Neapolis** City in Macedonia. It was the first city Paul visited on the continent of Europe.   **16:12 Roman colony** A town begun by Romans with Roman laws, customs, and privileges.   **16:16 spirit** This was a spirit from the devil, which caused her to say she had special knowledge.   **16:27 kill himself** He thought the leaders would kill him for letting the prisoners escape.

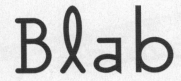

³⁶The jailer said to Paul, "The officers have sent an order to let you go free. You can leave now. Go in peace."

³⁷But Paul said to the police, "They beat us in public without a trial, even though we are Roman citizens." And they threw us in jail. Now they want to make us go away quietly! No! Let them come themselves and bring us out."

³⁸The police told the Roman officers what Paul said. When the officers heard that Paul and Silas were Roman citizens, they were afraid. ³⁹So they came and told Paul and Silas they were sorry and took them out of jail and asked them to leave the city. ⁴⁰So when they came out of the jail, they went to Lydia's house where they saw some of the believers and encouraged them. Then they left.

## Paul and Silas in Thessalonica

**17** Paul and Silas traveled through Amphipolis and Apollonia and came to Thessalonica where there was a synagogue. ²Paul went into the synagogue as he always did, and on each Sabbath day for three weeks, he talked with his fellow Jews about the Scriptures. ³He explained and proved that the Christ must die and then rise from the dead. He said, "This Jesus I am telling you about is the Christ." ⁴Some of them were convinced and joined Paul and Silas, along with many of the Greeks who worshiped God and many of the important women.

⁵But some others became jealous. So they got some evil men from the marketplace, formed a mob, and started a riot. They ran to Jason's house, looking for Paul and Silas, wanting to bring them out to the people. ⁶But when they did not find them, they dragged Jason and some other believers to the leaders of the city. The people were yelling, "These people have made trouble everywhere in the world, and now they have come here too! ⁷Jason is keeping them in his house. All of them do things against the laws of Caesar, saying there is another king, called Jesus."

⁸When the people and the leaders of the city heard these things, they became very upset. ⁹They made Jason and the others put up a sum of money. Then they let the believers go free.

## Paul and Silas Go to Berea

¹⁰That same night the believers sent Paul and Silas to Berea where they went to the synagogue. ¹¹These people were more willing to listen than the people in Thessalonica. The Bereans were eager to hear what Paul and Silas said and studied the Scriptures every day to find out if these things were true. ¹²So, many of them believed, as well as many important Greek women and men. ¹³But the people in Thessalonica learned that Paul was preaching the word of God in Berea, too. So they came there, upsetting the people and making trouble. ¹⁴The believers quickly sent Paul away to the coast, but Silas and Timothy stayed in Berea. ¹⁵The people leading Paul went with him to Athens. Then they carried a message from Paul back to Silas and Timothy for them to come to him as soon as they could.

## Paul Preaches in Athens

¹⁶While Paul was waiting for Silas and Timothy in Athens, he was troubled because he saw that the city was full of idols. ¹⁷In the synagogue, he talked with the Jews and the Greeks who worshiped God. He also talked every day with people in the marketplace.

¹⁸Some of the Epicurean and Stoic philosophers" argued with him, saying, "This man doesn't know what he is talking about. What is he trying to say?" Others said, "He seems to be telling us about some other gods," because Paul was telling them about Jesus and his rising from the dead. ¹⁹They got Paul and took him to a meeting of the Areopagus," where they said, "Please explain to us this new idea you have been teaching. ²⁰The things you are saying are new to us, and we want to know what this teaching means." ²¹(All the people of Athens and those from other countries who lived there always used their time to talk about the newest ideas.)

²²Then Paul stood before the meeting of the Areopagus and said, "People of Athens, I can

# June

**1** Play a board game with your brother or sister.

**2**

**3**

**4** Pray for a person of influence. It's Angelina Jolie's birthday.

**5**

**6** National Yo-Yo Day. You know what to do.

**7**

**8** Eat an extra serving of vegetables today.

**9** Spend an evening with your family without the TV.

**10** Get up early and take in the sunrise. Thank God for his creation.

**11** Be thinking about what you can do for your dad. Father's Day is the third Sunday in June.

**12**

**13** This is National Juggling Day. Give it a try.

**14** Write a letter to someone you care about.

**15**

**16**

**17** Think of someone who was mean to you. Do something nice for him or her.

**18** Put together a time capsule. Bury it. Dig it up in five years.

**19**

**20** Water the plants in the house.

**21** Read the Book of Ephesians today. Pick a verse and memorize it.

**22** The donut was invented on this day in 1847. Go ahead and have a glazed one.

**23**

**24** IM someone you haven't talked to in a while. Rekindle an old friendship.

**25**

**26** Sit outside for an hour and enjoy God's creation.

**27** Tell your mom three things you love about her today.

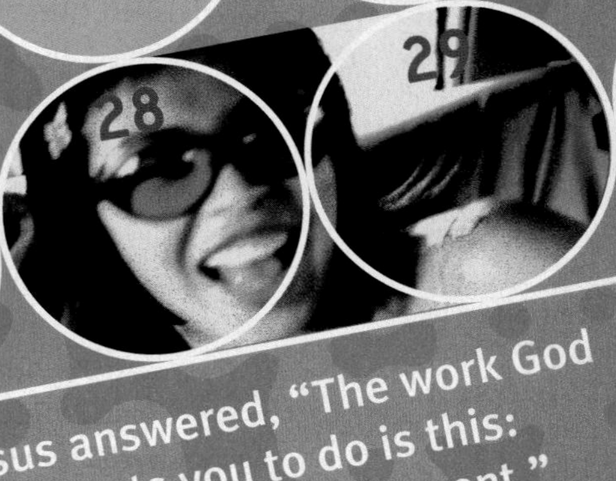

**28**

**29**

**30** Sing some praise songs this morning.

Jesus answered, "The work God wants you to do is this: Believe the One he sent." —John 6:29

## Acts 17:24-28

Every day you walk around, breathing in and out and experiencing life. But do you acknowledge and worship God in the midst of all of it? The people Paul met in Athens sure didn't seem to notice God. Instead, they worshiped anything that caught their attention. Paul stepped onto the scene to find people giving their energy and their love to things with surface appeal but no substance. They didn't even know what they were worshiping— there was nothing really *to* know. Paul told these people they were way off. He told them about one that was truly worthy of worship—the God whose genius is all over this world and the design of humanity and whose power keeps everything together. He is the One you see in the beauty of colors, forms, and textures around you. He's in the sweet moments with people you adore and in the thrills of the exciting parts of life. He creates the joy, depth, loveliness, and meaning in life. You live because of the one true God—the God of beauty, power, and wonder. Delight in knowing him, worshiping him, and experiencing him in your life.

see you are very religious in all things. 23As I was going through your city, I saw the objects you worship. I found an altar that had these words written on it: TO A GOD WHO IS NOT KNOWN. You worship a god that you don't know, and this is the God I am telling you about! 24The God who made the whole world and everything in it is the Lord of the land and the sky. He does not live in temples built by human hands. 25This God is the One who gives life, breath, and everything else to people. He does not need any help from them; he has everything he needs. 26God began by making one person, and from him came all the different people who live everywhere in the world. God decided exactly when and where they must live. 27God wanted them to look for him and perhaps search all around for him and find him, though he is not far from any of us: 28'We live in him. We walk in him. We are in him.' Some of your own poets have said: 'For we are his children.' 29Since we are God's children, you must not think that God is like something that people imagine or make from gold, silver, or rock. 30In the past, people did not understand God, and he ignored this. But now, God tells all people in the world to change their hearts and lives. 31God has set a day that he will judge all the world with fairness, by the man he chose long ago. And God has proved this to everyone by raising that man from the dead!"

32When the people heard about Jesus being raised from the dead, some of them laughed. But others said, "We will hear more about this from you later." 33So Paul went away from them. 34But some of the people believed Paul and joined him. Among those who believed was Dionysius, a member of the Areopagus, a woman named Damaris, and some others.

### PAUL IN CORINTH

**18** Later Paul left Athens and went to Corinth. 2Here he met a Jew named Aquila who had been born in the country of Pontus. But Aquila and his wife, Priscilla, had recently moved to Corinth from Italy, because Claudius" commanded that all Jews must leave Rome. Paul went to visit Aquila and Priscilla. 3Because they were tentmakers, just as he was, he stayed with them and worked with them. 4Every Sabbath day he talked with the Jews and Greeks in the synagogue, trying to persuade them to believe in Jesus.

5Silas and Timothy came from Macedonia and joined Paul in Corinth. After this, Paul spent all his time telling people the Good News, showing them that Jesus is the Christ. 6But they would not accept Paul's teaching and said some evil things. So he shook off the dust from his clothes" and said to them, "If you are not saved, it will be your own fault! I have done all I can do! After this, I will go only to other nations." 7Paul left the synagogue and moved into the home of Titius Justus, next to the synagogue. This man worshiped God. 8Crispus was the leader of that synagogue, and he and all the people living in his house believed in the Lord. Many others in Corinth also listened to Paul and believed and were baptized.

> ## "THE GOD WHO MADE THE WHOLE WORLD AND EVERYTHING IN IT IS THE LORD OF THE LAND AND THE SKY."

9During the night, the Lord told Paul in a vision: "Don't be afraid. Continue talking to people and don't be quiet. 10I am with you, and no one will hurt you because many of my people are in this city." 11Paul stayed there for a year and a half, teaching God's word to the people.

### PAUL IS BROUGHT BEFORE GALLIO

12When Gallio was the governor of the country of Southern Greece, some people came together against Paul and took him to the court. 13They said, "This man is teaching people to worship God in a way that is against our law."

14Paul was about to say something, but Gallio spoke, saying, "I would listen to you if

notes

**18:2 Claudius** The emperor (ruler) of Rome, A.D. 41-54.  **18:6 shook . . . clothes** This was a warning to show that Paul was finished talking to the people in that city.

**182**

you were complaining about a crime or some wrong. [15]But the things you are saying are only questions about words and names—arguments about your own law. So you must solve this problem yourselves. I don't want to be a judge of these things." [16]And Gallio made them leave the court.

## "WHEN THE PEOPLE HEARD ABOUT JESUS BEING RAISED FROM THE DEAD, SOME OF THEM LAUGHED."

[17]Then they all grabbed Sosthenes, the leader of the synagogue, and beat him there before the court. But this did not bother Gallio.

### Paul Returns to Antioch

[18]Paul stayed with the believers for many more days. Then he left and sailed for Syria, with Priscilla and Aquila. At Cenchrea Paul cut off his hair,[n] because he had made a promise to God. [19]Then they went to Ephesus, where Paul left Priscilla and Aquila. While Paul was there, he went into the synagogue and talked with the people. [20]When they asked him to stay with them longer, he refused. [21]But as he left, he said, "I will come back to you again if God wants me to." And so he sailed away from Ephesus.

[22]When Paul landed at Caesarea, he went and gave greetings to the church in Jerusalem. After that, Paul went to Antioch. [23]He stayed there for a while and then left and went through the regions of Galatia and Phrygia. He traveled from town to town in these regions, giving strength to all the followers.

### Apollos in Ephesus and Corinth

[24]A Jew named Apollos came to Ephesus. He was born in the city of Alexandria and was a good speaker who knew the Scriptures well. [25]He had been taught about the way of the Lord and was always very excited when he spoke and taught the truth about Jesus. But the only baptism Apollos knew about was the baptism that John[n] taught. [26]Apollos began to speak very boldly in the synagogue, and when Priscilla and Aquila heard him, they took him to their home and helped him better understand the way of God. [27]Now Apollos wanted to go to the country of Southern Greece. So the believers helped him and wrote a letter to the followers there, asking them to accept him. These followers had believed in Jesus because of God's grace, and when Apollos arrived, he helped them very much. [28]He argued very strongly with the Jews before all the people, clearly proving with the Scriptures that Jesus is the Christ.

### Paul in Ephesus

19 While Apollos was in Corinth, Paul was visiting some places on the way to Ephesus. There he found some followers [2]and asked them, "Did you receive the Holy Spirit when you believed?"

They said, "We have never even heard of a Holy Spirit."

[3]So he asked, "What kind of baptism did you have?"

They said, "It was the baptism that John taught."

## "WHEN THEY HEARD THIS, THEY WERE BAPTIZED IN THE NAME OF THE LORD JESUS."

[4]Paul said, "John's baptism was a baptism of changed hearts and lives. He told people to believe in the one who would come after him, and that one is Jesus."

[5]When they heard this, they were baptized in the name of the Lord Jesus. [6]Then Paul laid his hands on them,[n] and the Holy Spirit came upon them. They began speaking different languages[n] and prophesying. [7]There were about twelve people in this group.

[8]Paul went into the synagogue and spoke out boldly for three months. He talked with the people and persuaded them to accept the things he said about the kingdom of God. [9]But some of them became stubborn. They refused to believe and said evil things about the Way of Jesus before all the people. So Paul left them, and taking the followers with him, he went to the school of a man named Tyrannus. There Paul talked with people every day [10]for two years. Because of his work, every Jew and Greek in the country of Asia heard the word of the Lord.

### The Sons of Sceva

[11]God used Paul to do some very special miracles. [12]Some people took handkerchiefs and clothes that Paul had used and put them on the sick. When they did this, the sick were healed and evil spirits left them.

## beauty secret

### Warm Colors

Thinking about warming up the rich tones in your hair? If you're a brunette, then enrich your color with a cappuccino- or light coffee-colored dye. If you're a redhead, try a cherry color that will add dimension. If you're a blonde, try a hint of sunlight to accentuate your hair color.

**notes** **18:18 cut . . . hair** Jews did this to show that the time of a special promise to God was finished. **18:25 John** John the Baptist, who preached to people about Christ's coming (Luke 3). **19:6 laid his hands on them** The laying on of hands had many purposes, including the giving of a blessing, power, or authority. **19:6 languages** This can also be translated "tongues."

# Quiz

# WHAT'S YOUR money ID?

**1. YOU GET AN AFTER-SCHOOL JOB BECAUSE:**

A. You like having a little extra spending money.
B. You're saving for that great ski trip everyone's going on at the end of the year.
C. You need to start investing. How else will you be a millionaire by the time you're 30?

**2. YOU'VE DECIDED TO CHOOSE A PROFESSION BASED ENTIRELY ON HOW MUCH MONEY YOU'LL MAKE.**

A. True.
B. False.

**3. WHICH OF THE FOLLOWING PEOPLE OF INFLUENCE DO YOU MOST ADMIRE?**

A. Mother Teresa.
B. Jennifer Aniston.
C. Oprah Winfrey.

**4. DO YOU POUT OR COMPLAIN TO YOUR PARENTS BECAUSE YOU DON'T HAVE THE BEST AND NEWEST CLOTHES, SHOES, CAR, ETC.?**

A. Often.
B. Not really.
C. Sometimes.

**5. YOU TEND TO JUDGE PEOPLE MAINLY BY:**

A. How they treat others.
B. Their personality and their friends.
C. What they're wearing and what they're driving.

**6. DO YOU EVER THINK THAT YOUR LIFE WOULD BE MUCH EASIER IF YOU HAD MORE MONEY?**

A. No.
B. Yes.

---

**SCORING:** 1. A=1, B=3, C=5    2. A=5, B=0    3. A=1, B=3, C=5    4. A=5, B=1, C=3    5. A=1, B=3, C=5    6. A=0, B=5

---

**A SCORE OF 18 + = BETTY BLING**

Okay, it may be time to rethink your priorities. Consider this: When you die, can you take your money and all your stuff with you? No! Most people believe that money is the key to everything. Don't believe the lie! You'll just end up frustrated and disappointed.

**A SCORE OF 11-17 = MONEY MAVEN**

You're not totally obsessed with money, but you probably do think about it a good bit. That's okay—it's normal. Just make sure you keep it in perspective. Life is about more than the bling.

**A SCORE OF 4-10 = DIMESTORE DIVA**

You know what's truly important in life and have a good hold on money's place in your life. And you're probably a great bargain shopper to boot!

13But some people also were traveling around and making evil spirits go out of people. They tried to use the name of the Lord Jesus to force the evil spirits out. They would say, "By the same Jesus that Paul talks about, I order you to come out!" 14Seven sons of Sceva, a leading priest, were doing this.

15But one time an evil spirit said to them, "I know Jesus, and I know about Paul, but who are you?"

16Then the man who had the evil spirit jumped on them. Because he was so much stronger than all of them, they ran away from the house naked and hurt. 17All the people in Ephesus—Jews and Greeks—learned about this and were filled with fear and gave great honor to the Lord Jesus. 18Many of the believers began to confess openly and tell all the evil things they had done. 19Some of them who had used magic brought their magic books and burned them before everyone. Those books were worth about fifty thousand silver coins."

20So in a powerful way the word of the Lord kept spreading and growing.

21After these things, Paul decided to go to Jerusalem, planning to go through the countries of Macedonia and Southern Greece and then on to Jerusalem. He said, "After I have been to Jerusalem, I must also visit Rome." 22Paul sent Timothy and Erastus, two of his helpers, ahead to Macedonia, but he himself stayed in Asia for a while.

## TROUBLE IN EPHESUS

23And during that time, there was some serious trouble in Ephesus about the Way of Jesus. 24A man named Demetrius, who worked with silver, made little silver models that looked like the temple of the goddess Artemis." Those who did this work made much money. 25Demetrius had a meeting with them and some others who did the same kind of work. He told them, "Men, you know that we make a lot of money from our business. 26But look at what this man Paul is doing. He has convinced and turned away many people in Ephesus and in almost all of Asia! He says the gods made by human hands are not real. 27There is a danger that our business will lose its good name, but there is also another danger: People will begin to think that the temple of the great goddess Artemis is not important. Her greatness will be destroyed, and Artemis is the goddess that everyone in Asia and the whole world worships."

28When the others heard this, they became very angry and shouted, "Artemis, the goddess of Ephesus, is great!" 29The whole city became confused. The people grabbed Gaius and Aristarchus, who were from Macedonia and were traveling with Paul, and ran to the theater. 30Paul wanted to go in and talk to the crowd, but the followers did not let him. 31Also, some leaders of Asia who were friends of Paul sent him a message, begging him not to go into the theater. 32Some people were shouting one thing, and some were shouting another. The meeting was completely confused; most of them did not know why they had come together. 33They put a man named Alexander in front of the people, and some of them told him what to do. Alexander waved his hand so he could explain things to the people. 34But when they saw that Alexander was a Jew, they all shouted the same thing for two hours: "Great is Artemis of Ephesus!"

35Then the city clerk made the crowd be quiet. He said, "People of Ephesus, everyone knows that Ephesus is the city that keeps the temple of the great goddess Artemis and her holy stone" that fell from heaven. 36Since no one can say this is not true, you should be quiet. Stop and think before you do anything. 37You brought these men here, but they have not said anything evil against our goddess or stolen anything from her temple. 38If Demetrius and those who work with him have a charge against anyone they should go to the courts and judges where they can argue with each other. 39If there is something else you want to talk about, it can be decided at the regular town meeting of the people. 40I say this because some people might see this trouble today and say that we are rioting. We could not explain this, because there is no real reason for this meeting." 41After the city clerk said these things, he told the people to go home.

## PAUL IN MACEDONIA AND GREECE

20 When the trouble stopped, Paul sent for the followers to come to him. After he encouraged them and then told them good-bye, he left and went to the country of Macedonia. 2He said many things to strengthen the followers in the different places on his way through Macedonia. Then he went to Greece, 3where he stayed for three months. He was ready to sail for Syria, but some evil people were planning something against him. So Paul decided to go back through Macedonia

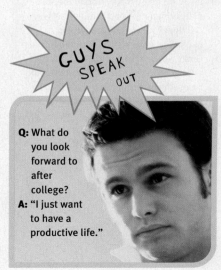

**notes** **19:19 fifty thousand silver coins** Probably drachmas. One coin was enough to pay a worker for one day's labor. **19:24 Artemis** A Greek goddess that the people of Asia Minor worshiped. **19:35 holy stone** Probably a meteorite or stone that the people thought looked like Artemis.

# Radical Faith:

# Acts 20:24

Some people live to be well liked, have the perfect look, own the best stuff, have the most fun, or make a name for themselves. Other people live with no big goals or dreams, but just kind of live each day with no specific purpose in mind. What fills your mind and your heart? How do you live each day? Paul lived fully, deeply, and intensely. He knew he lived for a purpose and he made every day count. He did nothing for the sake of personal success or impressing people. He was driven and compelled by God's agenda to bring people to life through Jesus. Paul saw his life counting for nothing if it couldn't be used by God in the work of his kingdom. Read through Acts—see how Paul would do anything to make God more well known and to see God's will carried out. If Paul's time, energy, abilities—his whole life—could be used, what could God do with your life? Ask yourself: What am I living for? Make God the goal of all you do. He'll use you in ways you could never imagine.

to Syria. ⁴The men who went with him were Sopater son of Pyrrhus, from the city of Berea; Aristarchus and Secundus, from the city of Thessalonica; Gaius, from Derbe; Timothy; and Tychicus and Trophimus, two men from the country of Asia. ⁵These men went on ahead and waited for us at Troas. ⁶We sailed from Philippi after the Feast of Unleavened Bread. Five days later we met them in Troas, where we stayed for seven days.

## PAUL'S LAST VISIT TO TROAS

⁷On the first day of the week,ⁿ we all met together to break bread,ⁿ and Paul spoke to the group. Because he was planning to leave the next day, he kept on talking until midnight. ⁸We were all together in a room upstairs, and there were many lamps in the room. ⁹A young man named Eutychus was sitting in the window. As Paul continued talking, Eutychus was falling into a deep sleep. Finally, he went sound asleep and fell to the ground from the third floor. When they picked him up, he was dead. ¹⁰Paul went down to Eutychus, knelt down, and put his arms around him. He said, "Don't worry. He is alive now." ¹¹Then Paul went upstairs again, broke bread, and ate. He spoke to them a long time, until it was early morning, and then he left. ¹²They took the young man home alive and were greatly comforted.

## THE TRIP FROM TROAS TO MILETUS

¹³We went on ahead of Paul and sailed for the city of Assos, where he wanted to join us on the ship. Paul planned it this way because he wanted to go to Assos by land. ¹⁴When he met us there, we took him aboard and went to Mitylene. ¹⁵We sailed from Mitylene and the next day came to a place near Kios. The following day we sailed to Samos, and the next day we reached Miletus. ¹⁶Paul had already decided not to stop at Ephesus, because he did not want to stay too long in the country of Asia. He was hurrying to be in Jerusalem on the day of Pentecost, if that were possible.

## THE ELDERS FROM EPHESUS

¹⁷Now from Miletus Paul sent to Ephesus and called for the elders of the church. ¹⁸When they came to him, he said, "You know about my life from the first day I came to Asia. You know the way I lived all the time I was with you. ¹⁹The evil people made plans against me, which troubled me very much. But you know I always served the Lord unselfishly, and I often cried. ²⁰You know I preached to you and did not hold back anything that would help you. You know that I taught you in public and in your homes. ²¹I warned both Jews and Greeks to change their lives and turn to God and believe in our Lord Jesus. ²²But now I must obey the Holy Spirit and go to Jerusalem. I don't know what will happen to me there. ²³I know only that in every city the Holy Spirit tells me that troubles and even jail wait for me. ²⁴I don't care about my own life. The most important thing is that I complete my mission, the work that the Lord Jesus gave me—to tell people the Good News about God's grace.

²⁵"And now, I know that none of you among whom I was preaching the kingdom of God will ever see me again. ²⁶So today I tell you that if any of you should be lost, I am not responsible, ²⁷because I have told you everything God wants you to know. ²⁸Be careful for yourselves and for all the people the Holy Spirit has given to you to care for. You must be like shepherds to the church of God,ⁿ which he bought with the death of his own son. ²⁹I know that after I leave, some people will come like wild wolves and try to destroy the flock. ³⁰Also, some from your own group will rise up and twist the truth and will lead away followers after them. ³¹So be careful! Always remember that for three years, day and night, I never stopped warning each of you, and I often cried over you.

³²"Now I am putting you in the care of God and the message about his grace. It is able to give you strength, and it will give you the blessings God has for all his holy people. ³³When I was with you, I never wanted anyone's money or fine clothes. ³⁴You know I always worked to take care of my own needs

20:7 **first day of the week** Sunday, which for Jews began at sunset on our Saturday. But if in this part of Asia a different system of time was used, then the meeting was on our Sunday night. 20:7 **break bread** Probably the Lord's Supper, the special meal that Jesus told his followers to eat to remember him (Luke 22:14-20). 20:28 **of God** Some Greek copies say, "of the Lord."

and the needs of those who were with me. 35I showed you in all things that you should work as I did and help the weak. I taught you to remember the words Jesus said: 'It is more blessed to give than to receive.' "

36When Paul had said this, he knelt down with all of them and prayed. 37-38And they all cried because Paul had said they would never see him again. They put their arms around him and kissed him. Then they went with him to the ship.

## Paul Goes to Jerusalem

21 After we all said good-bye to them, we sailed straight to the island of Cos. The next day we reached Rhodes, and from there we went to Patara. 2There we found a ship going to Phoenicia, so we went aboard and sailed away. 3We sailed near the island of Cyprus, seeing it to the north, but we sailed on to Syria. We stopped at Tyre because the ship needed to unload its cargo there. 4We found some followers in Tyre and stayed with them for seven days. Through the Holy Spirit they warned Paul not to go to Jerusalem. 5When we finished our visit, we left and continued our trip. All the followers, even the women and children, came outside the city with us. After we all knelt on the beach and prayed, 6we said good-bye and got on the ship, and the followers went back home.

7We continued our trip from Tyre and arrived at Ptolemais, where we greeted the believers and stayed with them for a day. 8The next day we left Ptolemais and went to the city of Caesarea. There we went into the home of Philip the preacher, one of the seven helpers," and stayed with him. 9He had four unmarried daughters who had the gift of prophesying. 10After we had been there for some time, a prophet named Agabus arrived from Judea. 11He came to us and borrowed Paul's belt and used it to tie his own hands and feet. He said, "The Holy Spirit says, 'This is how evil people in Jerusalem will tie up the man who wears this belt. Then they will give him to the older leaders.' "

12When we all heard this, we and the people there begged Paul not to go to Jerusalem. 13But

# Leah

[GENESIS 29 AND 30] Leah was in an awkward position. Her manipulative father tricked Jacob, her sister Rachel's true love, into marrying her instead. So there she was—married to a guy who was in love with someone else whom he also married. And when Leah began to have many children while Rachel had trouble getting pregnant, it drove a wedge between the two sisters that would never quite go away. It was a painful time for Leah, who cried out to God for relief. And while God didn't change Jacob's heart, he did give Leah seven children of her own, who surrounded her with the love of family. He rewarded her with a son, Judah, who began the lineage of David, through which Jesus would be born.

he said, "Why are you crying and making me so sad? I am not only ready to be tied up in Jerusalem, I am ready to die for the Lord Jesus!"

14We could not persuade him to stay away from Jerusalem. So we stopped begging him and said, "We pray that what the Lord wants will be done."

15After this, we got ready and started on our way to Jerusalem. 16Some of the followers from Caesarea went with us and took us to the home of Mnason, where we would stay. He was from Cyprus and was one of the first followers.

## Paul Visits James

17In Jerusalem the believers were glad to see us. 18The next day Paul went with us to visit James, and all the elders were there. 19Paul greeted them and told them everything God had done among the other nations through him. 20When they heard this, they praised God. Then they said to Paul, "Brother, you can see that many thousands of our people have become believers. And they think it is very important to obey the law of Moses. 21They

have heard about your teaching, that you tell our people who live among the nations to leave the law of Moses. They have heard that you tell them not to circumcise their children and not to obey customs. 22What should we do? They will learn that you have come. 23So we will tell you what to do: Four of our men have made a promise to God. 24Take these men with you and share in their cleansing ceremony." Pay their expenses so they can shave their heads." Then it will prove to everyone that what they have heard about you is not true and that you follow the law of Moses in your own life. 25We have already sent a letter to the non-Jewish believers. The letter said: 'Do not eat food that has been offered to idols, or blood, or animals that have been strangled. Do not take part in sexual sin.' "

26The next day Paul took the four men and shared in the cleansing ceremony with them. Then he went to the Temple and announced the time when the days of the cleansing ceremony would be finished. On the last day an offering would be given for each of the men.

27When the seven days were almost over,

notes 21:8 helpers The seven men chosen for a special work described in Acts 6:1-6. Sometimes they are called "deacons." 21:24 cleansing ceremony The special things Jews did to end the Nazirite promise. 21:24 shave their heads Jews did this to show that their promise was finished.

# Blab

**Q:** I really can't stand my brother, no matter how hard I try. He's always bursting into my room without knocking, taking my stuff, and teasing me on purpose. What can I do?

**A:** Ask God to help you be the peacemaker. Write down ten good things about your brother. Look at the list when he makes you mad. Tell your brother in a calm voice what things specifically upset you. Sometimes siblings just want to see if they can get a rise out of you. Don't give him one, and he'll tire of teasing.

**Q:** My little sister wants to go everywhere with me and my friends. I don't want to hurt her feelings, but I am 16 and she is only 14. I don't want her always tagging along. What can I do?

**A:** Plan some times when she can come along, or when the two of you can do things together. Take her out for a mocha and explain how you feel. She may pout at first, but make a deal about how often she can come out with you, so she knows you aren't dropping her completely.

**Q:** My parents always buy me nice presents, but secretly I am usually disappointed in what they pick. Am I really selfish?

**A:** No. God probably gave you a romantic personality, where your expectations are always high, and reality often disappoints. You may not be able to help your initial reaction, but you can still be thankful for the gift and the thought that went into it. Before the next gift occasion, tell your parents some specific things you'd like to have, or ask for gift cards so you can pick out your own things.

some of his people from Asia saw Paul at the Temple. They caused all the people to be upset and grabbed Paul. [28]They shouted, "People of Israel, help us! This is the man who goes everywhere teaching against the law of Moses, against our people, and against this Temple. Now he has brought some Greeks into the Temple and has made this holy place unclean!" [29](They said this because they had seen Trophimus, a man from Ephesus, with Paul in Jerusalem. They thought that Paul had brought him into the Temple.)

[30]All the people in Jerusalem became upset. Together they ran, took Paul, and dragged him out of the Temple. The Temple doors were closed immediately. [31]While they were trying to kill Paul, the commander of the Roman army in Jerusalem learned that there was trouble in the whole city. [32]Immediately he took some officers and soldiers and ran to the place where the crowd was gathered. When the people saw them, they stopped beating Paul. [33]The commander went to Paul and arrested him. He told his soldiers to tie Paul with two chains. Then he asked who he was and what he had done wrong. [34]Some in the crowd were yelling one thing, and some were yelling another. Because of all this confusion and shouting, the commander could not learn what had happened. So he ordered the soldiers to take Paul to the army building. [35]When Paul came to the steps, the soldiers had to carry him because the people were ready to hurt him. [36]The whole mob was following them, shouting, "Kill him!"

[37]As the soldiers were about to take Paul into the army building, he spoke to the commander, "May I say something to you?"

The commander said, "Do you speak Greek? [38]I thought you were the Egyptian who started some trouble against the government not long ago and led four thousand killers out to the desert."

[39]Paul said, "No, I am a Jew from Tarsus in the country of Cilicia. I am a citizen of that important city. Please, let me speak to the people."

[40]The commander gave permission, so Paul stood on the steps and waved his hand to quiet the people. When there was silence, he spoke to them in the Hebrew language.

## "ALL THE PEOPLE IN JERUSALEM BECAME UPSET."

### Paul Speaks to the People

**22** Paul said, "Friends, fellow Jews, listen to my defense to you." [2]When they heard him speaking the Hebrew language," they became very quiet. Paul said, [3]"I am a Jew, born in Tarsus in the country of Cilicia, but I grew up in this city. I was a student of Gamaliel," who carefully taught me everything about the law of our ancestors. I was very serious about serving God, just as are all of you here today. [4]I persecuted the people who followed the Way of Jesus, and some of them were even killed. I arrested men and women and put them in jail. [5]The high priest and the whole council of older leaders can tell you this is true. They gave me letters to the brothers in Damascus. So I was going there to arrest these people and bring them back to Jerusalem to be punished.

[6]"About noon when I came near Damascus, a bright light from heaven suddenly flashed all around me. [7]I fell to the ground and heard a voice saying, 'Saul, Saul, why are you persecuting me?' [8]I asked, 'Who are you, Lord?' The voice said, 'I am Jesus from Nazareth whom you are persecuting.' [9]Those who were with me did not hear the voice, but they saw the light. [10]I said, 'What shall I do, Lord?' The Lord answered, 'Get up and go to Damascus. There you will be told about all the things I have planned for you to do.' [11]I could not see, because the bright light had made me blind. So my companions led me into Damascus.

[12]"There a man named Ananias came to me. He was a religious man; he obeyed the law of Moses, and all the Jews who lived there respected him. [13]He stood by me and said, 'Brother Saul, see again!' Immediately I was

**22:2 Hebrew language** Or Aramaic, the languages of many people in this region in the first century. **22:3 Gamaliel** A very important teacher of the Pharisees, a Jewish religious group (Acts 5:34).

able to see him. ¹⁴He said, 'The God of our ancestors chose you long ago to know his plan, to see the Righteous One, and to hear words from him. ¹⁵You will be his witness to all people, telling them about what you have seen and heard. ¹⁶Now, why wait any longer? Get up, be

**FIVE OUT OF TEN AMERICAN TEENS OWN SOME KIND OF WIRELESS DEVICE.** MEDIAPOST COMMUNICATIONS

baptized, and wash your sins away, trusting in him to save you.'

¹⁷"Later, when I returned to Jerusalem, I was praying in the Temple, and I saw a vision. ¹⁸I saw the Lord saying to me, 'Hurry! Leave Jerusalem now! The people here will not accept the truth about me.' ¹⁹But I said, 'Lord, they know that in every synagogue I put the believers in jail and beat them. ²⁰They also know I was there when Stephen, your witness, was killed. I stood there agreeing and holding the coats of those who were killing him!' ²¹But the Lord said to me, 'Leave now. I will send you far away to the other nations.' "

²²The crowd listened to Paul until he said this. Then they began shouting, "Kill him! Get him out of the world! He should not be allowed to live!" ²³They shouted, threw off their coats,ⁿ and threw dust into the air.ⁿ

²⁴Then the commander ordered the soldiers to take Paul into the army building and beat him. He wanted to make Paul tell why the people were shouting against him like this. ²⁵But as the soldiers were tying him up, preparing to beat him, Paul said to an officer nearby, "Do you have the right to beat a Roman citizenⁿ who has not been proven guilty?"

²⁶When the officer heard this, he went to the commander and reported it. The officer said, "Do you know what you are doing? This man is a Roman citizen."

²⁷The commander came to Paul and said, "Tell me, are you really a Roman citizen?"

He answered, "Yes."

²⁸The commander said, "I paid a lot of money to become a Roman citizen."

But Paul said, "I was born a citizen."

²⁹The men who were preparing to question Paul moved away from him immediately. The commander was frightened because he had already tied Paul, and Paul was a Roman citizen.

## Paul Speaks to Leaders

³⁰The next day the commander decided to learn why the Jews were accusing Paul. So he ordered the leading priests and the council to meet. The commander took Paul's chains off. Then he brought Paul out and stood him before their meeting.

**23** Paul looked at the council and said, "Brothers, I have lived my life without guilt feelings before God up to this day." ²Ananias,ⁿ the high priest, heard this and told the men who were standing near Paul to hit him on the mouth. ³Paul said to Ananias, "God will hit you, too! You are like a wall that has been painted white. You sit there and judge me, using the law of Moses, but you are telling them to hit me, and that is against the law."

⁴The men standing near Paul said to him, "You cannot insult God's high priest like that!"

⁵Paul said, "Brothers, I did not know this man was the high priest. It is written in the Scriptures, 'You must not curse a leader of your people.' "ⁿ

⁶Some of the men in the meeting were Sadducees, and others were Pharisees. Knowing this, Paul shouted to them, "My brothers, I am a Pharisee, and my father was a Pharisee. I am on trial here because I believe that people will rise from the dead."

⁷When Paul said this, there was an argument between the Pharisees and the Sadducees, and the group was divided. ⁸(The Sadducees do not believe in angels or spirits or that people will rise from the dead. But the Pharisees believe in them all.) ⁹So there was a great uproar. Some of the teachers of the law,

**Promises**

## Acts 22:3-16

Do you ever think that maybe God's gift of grace is too good to be true? C'mon, God is really going to forgive *anyone* of *any* sin? What about murderers? Liars? Thieves? There are some pretty bad things going on out there that people do every day. All you have to do is listen to your local nightly news to find out that everything isn't so great in your community and in our world.

Consider Saul. A smart and highly educated guy, Saul was respected in the Jewish community, but he really wasn't such a nice guy. He helped to track down Christians and to expose them for their faith; he even stuck around to watch while some of them were killed for their beliefs. Not someone who would be in God's favor, right? One of amazing things about God is that he loves for us to be redeemed from the awful things we can sometimes do. God caught Saul one day and changed his life forever. His name became Paul and his unwavering devotion to God after that day would make him one of the greatest leaders in the early church. Don't sell God or yourself short—he can do amazing things with anyone!

**notes** **22:23 threw off their coats** This showed that the people were very angry with Paul. **22:23 threw dust into the air** This showed even greater anger. **22:25 Roman citizen** Roman law said that Roman citizens must not be beaten before they had a trial. **23:2 Ananias** This is not the same man named Ananias in Acts 22:12. **23:5 'You . . . people.'** Quotation from Exodus 22:28.

189

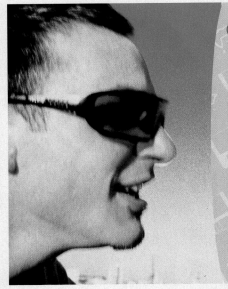

who were Pharisees, stood up and argued, "We find nothing wrong with this man. Maybe an angel or a spirit did speak to him."

¹⁰The argument was beginning to turn into such a fight that the commander was afraid some evil people would tear Paul to pieces. So he told the soldiers to go down and take Paul away and put him in the army building.

¹¹The next night the Lord came and stood by Paul. He said, "Be brave! You have told people in Jerusalem about me. You must do the same in Rome."

¹²In the morning some evil people made a plan to kill Paul, and they took an oath not to eat or drink anything until they had killed him. ¹³There were more than forty men who made this plan. ¹⁴They went to the leading priests and the older leaders and said, "We have taken an oath not to eat or drink until we have killed Paul. ¹⁵So this is what we want you to do: Send a message to the commander to bring Paul out to you as though you want to ask him more questions. We will be waiting to kill him while he is on the way here."

¹⁶But Paul's nephew heard about this plan and went to the army building and told Paul. ¹⁷Then Paul called one of the officers and said, "Take this young man to the commander. He has a message for him."

¹⁸So the officer brought Paul's nephew to the commander and said, "The prisoner, Paul, asked me to bring this young man to you. He wants to tell you something."

¹⁹The commander took the young man's hand and led him to a place where they could be alone. He asked, "What do you want to tell me?"

²⁰The young man said, "The Jews have decided to ask you to bring Paul down to their council meeting tomorrow. They want you to think they are going to ask him more questions. ²¹But don't believe them! More than forty men are hiding and waiting to kill Paul. They have all taken an oath not to eat or drink until they have killed him. Now they are waiting for you to agree."

²²The commander sent the young man away, ordering him, "Don't tell anyone that you have told me about their plan."

### Paul Is Sent to Caesarea

²³Then the commander called two officers and said, "I need some men to go to Caesarea. Get two hundred soldiers, seventy horsemen, and two hundred men with spears ready to leave at nine o'clock tonight. ²⁴Get some horses for Paul to ride so he can be taken to Governor Felix safely." ²⁵And he wrote a letter that said:

²⁶From Claudius Lysias.

To the Most Excellent Governor Felix: Greetings.

²⁷Some of the Jews had taken this man and planned to kill him. But I learned that he is a Roman citizen, so I went with my soldiers and saved him. ²⁸I wanted to know why they were accusing him, so I brought him before their council meeting. ²⁹I learned that these people said Paul did some things that were wrong by their own laws, but no charge was worthy of jail or death. ³⁰When I was told that some of them were planning to kill Paul, I sent him to you at once. I also told them to tell you what they have against him.

³¹So the soldiers did what they were told and took Paul and brought him to the city of Antipatris that night. ³²The next day the horsemen went with Paul to Caesarea, but the other soldiers went back to the army building in Jerusalem. ³³When the horsemen came to Caesarea and gave the letter to the governor, they turned Paul over to him. ³⁴The governor read the letter and asked Paul, "What area are you from?" When he learned that Paul was from Cilicia, ³⁵he said, "I will hear your case when those who are against you come here, too." Then the governor gave orders for Paul to be kept under guard in Herod's palace.

## PAUL IS ACCUSED

**24** Five days later Ananias, the high priest, went to the city of Caesarea with some of the older leaders and a lawyer named Tertullus. They had come to make

## DIDYA KNOW

**TWO IN FIVE TEENS ADMIT TO FEELING PERSONALLY PRESSURED ABOUT SEX AND RELATIONSHIPS.**

KAISER FAMILY FOUNDATION AND *SEVENTEEN*

charges against Paul before the governor. ²Paul was called into the meeting, and Tertullus began to accuse him, saying, "Most Excellent Felix! Our people enjoy much peace because of you, and many wrong things in our country are being made right through your wise help. ³We accept these things always and in every place, and we are thankful for them. ⁴But not wanting to take any more of your time, I beg you to be kind and listen to our few words. ⁵We have found this man to be a troublemaker, stirring up his people everywhere in the world. He is a leader of the Nazarene group. ⁶Also, he was trying to make the Temple unclean, but we stopped him." ⁸By asking him questions yourself, you can decide if all these things are true." ⁹The others agreed and said that all of this was true.

¹⁰When the governor made a sign for Paul to speak, Paul said, "Governor Felix, I know you have been a judge over this nation for a long time. So I am happy to defend myself before you. ¹¹You can learn for yourself that I went to worship in Jerusalem only twelve days ago. ¹²Those who are accusing me did not find me arguing with anyone in the Temple or stirring up the people in the synagogues or in the city. ¹³They cannot prove the things they are saying against me now. ¹⁴But I will tell you this: I worship the God of our ancestors as a follower of the Way of Jesus. The others say that the Way of Jesus is not the right way. But I believe everything that is taught in the law of Moses and that is written in the books of the Prophets. ¹⁵I have the same hope in God that they have—the hope that all people, good and bad, will surely be raised from the dead. ¹⁶This

is why I always try to do what I believe is right before God and people.

¹⁷"After being away from Jerusalem for several years, I went back to bring money to my people and to offer sacrifices. ¹⁸I was doing this when they found me in the Temple. I had finished the cleansing ceremony and had not made any trouble; no people were gathering around me. ¹⁹But there were some people from the country of Asia who should be here, standing before you. If I have really done anything wrong, they are the ones who should accuse me. ²⁰Or ask these people here if they found any wrong in me when I stood before the council in Jerusalem. ²¹But I did shout one thing when I stood before them: 'You are judging me today because I believe that people will rise from the dead!' "

²²Felix already understood much about the Way of Jesus. He stopped the trial and said, "When commander Lysias comes here, I will decide your case." ²³Felix told the officer to keep Paul guarded but to give him some freedom and to let his friends bring what he needed.

## PAUL SPEAKS TO FELIX AND HIS WIFE

²⁴After some days Felix came with his wife, Drusilla, who was Jewish, and asked for Paul to be brought to him. He listened to Paul talk about believing in Christ Jesus. ²⁵But Felix became afraid when Paul spoke about living right, self-control, and the time when God will judge the world. He said, "Go away now. When I have more time, I will call for you." ²⁶At the same time Felix hoped that Paul would give him some money, so he often sent for Paul and talked with him.

²⁷But after two years, Felix was replaced by Porcius Festus as governor. But Felix had left Paul in prison to please the Jews.

## PAUL ASKS TO SEE CAESAR

**25** Three days after Festus became governor, he went from Caesarea to Jerusalem. ²There the leading priests and the important leaders made charges against Paul before Festus. ³They asked Festus to do them a favor. They wanted him to send Paul back to Jerusalem, because they had a plan to kill him on the way. ⁴But Festus answered that Paul would be kept in Caesarea and that he himself was returning there soon. ⁵He said, "Some of your leaders should go with me. They can accuse the man there in Caesarea, if he has really done something wrong."

⁶Festus stayed in Jerusalem another eight or ten days and then went back to Caesarea. The next day he told the soldiers to bring Paul before him. Festus was seated on the judge's seat ⁷when Paul came into the room. The

## relationships

Different people feel love in different ways. Some get a head rush when they receive gifts. Some like compliments; others want to just spend time with you. Follow Jesus' command in John 13:34, which states: "Love each other. You must love each other as I have loved you." Learn the love languages of your family, friends, and your guy. Practice speaking love to them in the ways they will understand best.

people who had come from Jerusalem stood around him, making serious charges against him, which they could not prove. [8]This is what Paul said to defend himself: "I have done nothing wrong against the law, against the Temple, or against Caesar."

[9]But Festus wanted to please the people. So he asked Paul, "Do you want to go to Jerusalem for me to judge you there on these charges?"

[10]Paul said, "I am standing at Caesar's judgment seat now, where I should be judged. I have done nothing wrong to them; you know this is true. [11]If I have done something wrong and the law says I must die, I do not ask to be saved from death. But if these charges are not true, then no one can give me to them. I want Caesar to hear my case!"

[12]Festus talked about this with his advisers. Then he said, "You have asked to see Caesar, so you will go to Caesar!"

## Paul Before King Agrippa

[13]A few days later King Agrippa and Bernice came to Caesarea to visit Festus. [14]They stayed there for some time, and Festus told the king about Paul's case. Festus said, "There is a man that Felix left in prison. [15]When I went to Jerusalem, the leading priests and the older leaders there made charges against him, asking me to sentence him to death. [16]But I answered, 'When a man is accused of a crime, Romans do not hand him over until he has been allowed to face his accusers and defend himself against their charges.' [17]So when these people came here to Caesarea for the trial, I did not waste time. The next day I sat on the judge's seat and commanded that the man be brought in. [18]They stood up and accused him, but not of any serious crime as I thought they would. [19]The things they said were about their own religion and about a man named Jesus who died. But Paul said that he is still alive. [20]Not knowing how to find out about these questions, I asked Paul, 'Do you want to go to Jerusalem and be judged there?' [21]But he asked to be kept in Caesarea. He wants a decision from the emperor." So I ordered that he be held until I could send him to Caesar."

[22]Agrippa said to Festus, "I would also like to hear this man myself."

Festus said, "Tomorrow you will hear him."

[23]The next day Agrippa and Bernice appeared with great show, acting like very important people. They went into the judgment room with the army leaders and the important men of Caesarea. Then Festus ordered the soldiers to bring Paul in. [24]Festus said, "King Agrippa and all who are gathered here with us, you see this man. All the people, here and in Jerusalem, have complained to me about him, shouting that he should not live any longer. [25]When I judged him, I found no reason to order his death. But since he asked to be judged by Caesar, I decided to send him. [26]But I have nothing definite to write the emperor about him. So I have brought him before all of you—especially you, King Agrippa. I hope you can question him and give me something to write. [27]I think it is foolish to send a prisoner to Caesar without telling what charges are against him."

## Paul Defends Himself

26 Agrippa said to Paul, "You may now speak to defend yourself."

Then Paul raised his hand and began to speak. [2]He said, "King Agrippa, I am very happy to stand before you and will answer all the charges the evil people make against me. [3]You know so much about all the customs and the things they argue about, so please listen to me patiently.

[4]"All my people know about my whole life, how I lived from the beginning in my own country and later in Jerusalem. [5]They have known me for a long time. If they want to, they can tell you that I was a good Pharisee. And the

# Music Reviews

GROUP: **PILLAR**

ALBUM: **WHERE DO WE GO FROM HERE**

The title of this third album spotlights this hard rock band's record label journey from Christian label Flicker to mainstream major label MCA and back to Flicker again. Still, Pillar has crossover success with *Where Do We Go From Here,* as rock fans love the blistering single "Bring Me Down." Frontman Rob Beckley continues to write positive lyrics with biblical allusions, although they are not overtly Christian. Pillar has been compared to the Foo Fighters and even Incubus with its intense brand of aggressive rock.

WHY IT ROCKS: ROB BECKLEY AND THE BAND MAKE POSITIVE MUSIC FROM A BIBLICAL WORLDVIEW THAT ROCKS HARD.

notes

25:21 **emperor** The ruler of the Roman Empire, which was almost all the known world.

Pharisees obey the laws of my tradition more carefully than any other group. ⁶Now I am on trial because I hope for the promise that God made to our ancestors. ⁷This is the promise that the twelve tribes of our people hope to receive as they serve God day and night. My king, they have accused me because I hope for this same promise! ⁸Why do any of you people think it is impossible for God to raise people from the dead?

⁹"I, too, thought I ought to do many things against Jesus from Nazareth. ¹⁰And that is what I did in Jerusalem. The leading priests gave me the power to put many of God's people in jail, and when they were being killed, I agreed it was a good thing. ¹¹In every synagogue, I often punished them and tried to make them speak against Jesus. I was so angry against them I even went to other cities to find them and punish them.

¹²"One time the leading priests gave me permission and the power to go to Damascus. ¹³On the way there, at noon, I saw a light from heaven. It was brighter than the sun and flashed all around me and those who were traveling with me. ¹⁴We all fell to the ground. Then I heard a voice speaking to me in the Hebrew language," saying, 'Saul, Saul, why are you persecuting me? You are only hurting yourself by fighting me.' ¹⁵I said, 'Who are you, Lord?' The Lord said, 'I am Jesus, the one you are persecuting. ¹⁶Stand up! I have chosen you to be my servant and my witness—you will tell people the things that you have seen and the things that I will show you. This is why I have come to you today. ¹⁷I will keep you safe from your own people and also from the others. I am sending you to them ¹⁸to open their eyes so that they may turn away from darkness to the light, away from the power of Satan and to God. Then their sins can be forgiven, and they can have a place with those people who have been made holy by believing in me.'

¹⁹"King Agrippa, after I had this vision from heaven, I obeyed it. ²⁰I began telling people that they should change their hearts and lives and turn to God and do things to show they really had changed. I told this first to those in Damascus, then in Jerusalem, and in every part of Judea, and also to the other people. ²¹This is why the Jews took me and were trying to kill me in the Temple. ²²But God has helped me, and so I stand here today, telling all people, small and great, what I have seen. But I am saying only what Moses and the prophets said would happen— ²³that the Christ would die, and as the first to rise from the dead, he would bring light to all people."

## PAUL TRIES TO PERSUADE AGRIPPA

²⁴While Paul was saying these things to defend himself, Festus said loudly, "Paul, you are out of your mind! Too much study has driven you crazy!"

²⁵Paul said, "Most excellent Festus, I am not crazy. My words are true and sensible. ²⁶King Agrippa knows about these things, and I can speak freely to him. I know he has heard about all of these things, because they did not happen off in a corner. ²⁷King Agrippa, do you believe what the prophets wrote? I know you believe."

²⁸King Agrippa said to Paul, "Do you think you can persuade me to become a Christian in such a short time?"

²⁹Paul said, "Whether it is a short or a long time, I pray to God that not only you but every person listening to me today would be saved and be like me—except for these chains I have."

³⁰Then King Agrippa, Governor Festus, Bernice, and all the people sitting with them stood up ³¹and left the room. Talking to each other, they said, "There is no reason why this man should die or be put in jail." ³²And Agrippa said to Festus, "We could let this man go free, but he has asked Caesar to hear his case."

## PAUL SAILS FOR ROME

**27** It was decided that we would sail for Italy. An officer named Julius, who served in the emperor's" army, guarded Paul and some other prisoners. ²We got on a

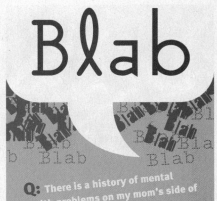

**Q:** There is a history of mental health problems on my mom's side of the family for at least three generations. How can I be sure I won't be crazy?

**A:** The Bible says that Christians can take a stand against things that run in families for generations and stand on his Word to break the cycle. If you suspect that you might suffer from a chemical imbalance, find a Christian therapist and discuss your concerns.

**Q:** I am afraid of nearly everything—airplanes, snakes, mice, elevators, certain foods, and most people. It is getting hard to even go outside. What can I do?

**A:** There are many Bible verses that instruct us not to be afraid. Find some of them and write them on cards that you place around your room, on the bathroom mirror, and in your locker. Ask friends or family members to pray over you that God will remove your fears, and pray yourself. Finally, conquer your fears by actually doing the things that frighten you.

**Q:** Some days I just want to sleep all day and never get up. Is that normal?

**A:** It's normal if you stay up late all the time, but not if you are just trying to block out the world. Sleeping too much when you aren't really physically tired can be a sign of depression or illness. Tell your parents how you feel, and see a doctor if you can't seem to get moving.

**26:14 Hebrew language** Hebrew or Aramaic, the languages of many people in this region in the first century.    **27:1 emperor** The ruler of the Roman Empire, which was almost all the known world.

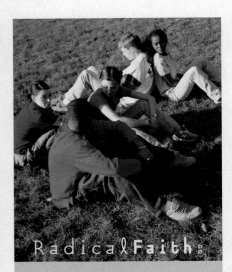

## RadicalFaith

# Acts 26:16-18

For a while, Paul lived to deny Christ and make life hard for Christians. But Jesus stepped into Paul's life and transformed him into an entirely new person. Paul saw Jesus as Lord, and the truth went straight to his heart. Paul developed new desires, new drives, new dreams, and a whole new direction for his life. Paul received this job description: Tell everyone about God's love and how he sent Jesus as a redemption for their sins. And you know what? This same job description applies to you, as well. God opens people's eyes to see things they can't on their own, and he wants to use you in the process of helping others come to him. Not everyone will embrace what you have to say, but don't get discouraged. Learn a lesson from Paul's life—anyone can go from denying Christ to living for him. Pray for this to happen in the lives of people you know. God can do it! And take on the same job Jesus gave Paul. Be a part of what God is doing in the world!

ship that was from the city of Adramyttium and was about to sail to different ports in the country of Asia. Aristarchus, a man from the city of Thessalonica in Macedonia, went with us. ³The next day we came to Sidon. Julius was very good to Paul and gave him freedom to go visit his friends, who took care of his needs. ⁴We left Sidon and sailed close to the island of Cyprus, because the wind was blowing against us. ⁵We went across the sea by Cilicia and Pamphylia and landed at the city of Myra, in Lycia. ⁶There the officer found a ship from Alexandria that was going to Italy, so he put us on it.

⁷We sailed slowly for many days. We had a hard time reaching Cnidus because the wind was blowing against us, and we could not go any farther. So we sailed by the south side of the island of Crete near Salmone. ⁸Sailing past it was hard. Then we came to a place called Fair Havens, near the city of Lasea.

⁹We had lost much time, and it was now dangerous to sail, because it was already after the Day of Cleansing." So Paul warned them, ¹⁰"Men, I can see there will be a lot of trouble on this trip. The ship, the cargo, and even our lives may be lost." ¹¹But the captain and the owner of the ship did not agree with Paul, and the officer believed what the captain and owner of the ship said. ¹²Since that harbor was not a good place for the ship to stay for the winter, most of the men decided that the ship should leave. They hoped we could go to Phoenix and stay there for the winter. Phoenix, a city on the island of Crete, had a harbor which faced southwest and northwest.

## THE STORM

¹³When a good wind began to blow from the south, the men on the ship thought, "This is the wind we wanted, and now we have it." So they pulled up the anchor, and we sailed very close to the island of Crete. ¹⁴But then a very strong wind named the "northeaster" came from the island. ¹⁵The ship was caught in it and could not sail against it. So we stopped trying and let the wind carry us. ¹⁶When we went below a small island named Cauda, we

were barely able to bring in the lifeboat. ¹⁷After the men took the lifeboat in, they tied ropes around the ship to hold it together. The men were afraid that the ship would hit the sandbanks of Syrtis," so they lowered the sail and let the wind carry the ship. ¹⁸The next day the storm was blowing us so hard that the men threw out some of the cargo. ¹⁹A day later with their own hands they threw out the ship's equipment. ²⁰When we could not see the sun or the stars for many days, and the storm was very bad, we lost all hope of being saved.

²¹After the men had gone without food for a long time, Paul stood up before them and said, "Men, you should have listened to me. You should not have sailed from Crete. Then you would not have all this trouble and loss. ²²But now I tell you to cheer up because none of you will die. Only the ship will be lost. ²³Last night an angel came to me from the God I belong to and worship. ²⁴The angel said, 'Paul, do not be afraid. You must stand before Caesar. And God has promised you that he will save the lives of everyone sailing with you.' ²⁵So men, have courage. I trust in God that everything will happen as his angel told me. ²⁶But we will crash on an island."

²⁷On the fourteenth night we were still being carried around in the Adriatic Sea." About midnight the sailors thought we were close to land, ²⁸so they lowered a rope with a weight on

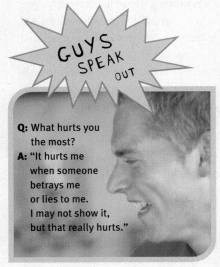

GUYS SPEAK OUT

**Q:** What hurts you the most?
**A:** "It hurts me when someone betrays me or lies to me. I may not show it, but that really hurts."

**27:9  Day of Cleansing** An important Jewish holy day in the fall of the year. This was the time of year that bad storms arose on the sea.   **27:17  Syrtis** Shallow area in the sea near the Libyan coast.
**27:27  Adriatic Sea** The sea between Greece and Italy, including the central Mediterranean.

the end of it into the water. They found that the water was one hundred twenty feet deep. They went a little farther and lowered the rope again. It was ninety feet deep. 29The sailors were afraid that we would hit the rocks, so they threw four anchors into the water and prayed for daylight to come. 30Some of the sailors wanted to leave the ship, and they lowered the lifeboat, pretending they were throwing more anchors from the front of the ship. 31But Paul told the officer and the other soldiers, "If these men do not stay in the ship, your lives cannot be saved." 32So the soldiers cut the ropes and let the lifeboat fall into the water.

33Just before dawn Paul began persuading all the people to eat something. He said, "For the past fourteen days you have been waiting and watching and not eating. 34Now I beg you to eat something. You need it to stay alive. None of you will lose even one hair off your heads." 35After he said this, Paul took some bread and thanked God for it before all of them. He broke off a piece and began eating. 36They all felt better and started eating, too. 37There were two hundred seventy-six people on the ship. 38When they had eaten all they wanted, they began making the ship lighter by throwing the grain into the sea.

## "WHEN DAYLIGHT CAME, THE SAILORS SAW LAND."

### THE SHIP IS DESTROYED

39When daylight came, the sailors saw land. They did not know what land it was, but they saw a bay with a beach and wanted to sail the ship to the beach if they could. 40So they cut the ropes to the anchors and left the anchors in the sea. At the same time, they untied the ropes that were holding the rudders. Then they raised the front sail into the wind and sailed toward the beach. 41But the ship hit a sandbank. The front of the ship stuck there and could not move, but the back of the ship began to break up from the big waves.

42The soldiers decided to kill the prisoners so none of them could swim away and escape. 43But Julius, the officer, wanted to let Paul live and did not allow the soldiers to kill the prisoners. Instead he ordered everyone who could swim to jump into the water first and swim to land. 44The rest were to follow using wooden boards or pieces of the ship. And this is how all the people made it safely to land.

### PAUL ON THE ISLAND OF MALTA

28 When we were safe on land, we learned that the island was called Malta. 2The people who lived there were very good to us. Because it was raining and very cold, they made a fire and welcomed all of us. 3Paul gathered a pile of sticks and was putting them on the fire when a poisonous snake came out because of the heat and bit him on the hand. 4The people living on the island saw the snake hanging from Paul's hand and said to each other, "This man must be a murderer! He did not die in the sea, but Justice" does not want him to live." 5But Paul shook the snake off into the fire and was not hurt. 6The people thought that Paul would swell up or fall down dead. They waited and watched him for a long time, but nothing bad happened to him. So they changed their minds and said, "He is a god!"

7There were some fields around there owned by Publius, an important man on the island. He welcomed us into his home and was very good to us for three days. 8Publius' father was sick with a fever and dysentery." Paul went to him, prayed, and put his hands on the man and healed him. 9After this, all the other sick people on the island came to Paul, and he healed them, too. 10-11The people on the island gave us many honors. When we were ready to leave, three months later, they gave us the things we needed.

### PAUL GOES TO ROME

We got on a ship from Alexandria that had stayed on the island during the winter. On the front of the ship was the sign of the twin gods." 12We stopped at Syracuse for three days.

13From there we sailed to Rhegium. The next day a wind began to blow from the south, and a day later we came to Puteoli. 14We found some believers there who asked us to stay with them for a week. Finally, we came to Rome. 15The believers in Rome heard that we were there and came out as far as the Market of Appius" and the Three Inns" to meet us. When Paul saw them, he was encouraged and thanked God.

### PAUL IN ROME

16When we arrived at Rome, Paul was allowed to live alone, with the soldier who guarded him.

17Three days later Paul sent for the leaders there. When they came together, he said, "Brothers, I have done nothing against our people or the customs of our ancestors. But I was arrested in Jerusalem and given to the Romans.

## beautysecret

### Refresh Day-Old Hair

Did you just wake up from sleeping on yesterday's great hairstyle? Instead of washing and blowing out your hair again, freshen it up by using three or four large Velcro rollers on the hair around your face. Add a touch of hair spray, and you're ready to go.

**28:4 Justice** The people thought there was a god named Justice who would punish bad people. **28:8 dysentery** A sickness like diarrhea. **28:10-11 twin gods** Statues of Castor and Pollux, gods in old Greek tales. **28:15 Market of Appius** A town about twenty-seven miles from Rome. **28:15 Three Inns** A town about thirty miles from Rome.

[18]After they asked me many questions, they could find no reason why I should be killed. They wanted to let me go free, [19]but the evil people there argued against that. So I had to ask to come to Rome to have my trial before Caesar. But I have no charge to bring against my own people. [20]That is why I wanted to see you and talk with you. I am bound with this chain because I believe in the hope of Israel."

## "I WANT YOU TO KNOW THAT GOD HAS ALSO SENT HIS SALVATION TO ALL NATIONS, AND THEY WILL LISTEN!"

[21]They answered Paul, "We have received no letters from Judea about you. None of our Jewish brothers who have come from there brought news or told us anything bad about you. [22]But we want to hear your ideas, because we know that people everywhere are speaking against this religious group."

[23]Paul and the people chose a day for a meeting and on that day many more of the Jews met with Paul at the place he was staying. He spoke to them all day long. Using the law of Moses and the prophets' writings, he explained the kingdom of God, and he tried to persuade them to believe these things about Jesus. [24]Some believed what Paul said, but others did not. [25]So they argued and began leaving after Paul said one more thing to them: "The Holy Spirit spoke the truth to your ancestors through Isaiah the prophet, saying,

[26]'Go to this people and say:

You will listen and listen, but you will not understand.

You will look and look, but you will not learn,

[27]because these people have become stubborn.

They don't hear with their ears,

and they have closed their eyes.

Otherwise, they might really understand what they see with their eyes

and hear with their ears.

They might really understand in their minds

and come back to me and be healed.'

*Isaiah 6:9-10*

[28]"I want you to know that God has also sent his salvation to all nations, and they will listen!" [29]n

[30]Paul stayed two full years in his own rented house and welcomed all people who came to visit him. [31]He boldly preached about the kingdom of God and taught about the Lord Jesus Christ, and no one tried to stop him.

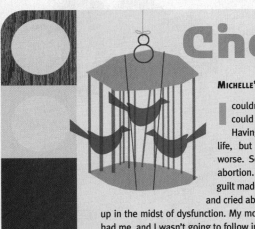

# Changed Lives

### MICHELLE'S STORY—CHOOSING LIFE

I couldn't believe my ears. How could I be pregnant with twins? Having a baby would ruin my life, but having two would be worse. So I decided to have an abortion. Immediately, waves of guilt made me sick, and I lay there and cried about what I'd done. I grew up in the midst of dysfunction. My mom was a teen when she had me, and I wasn't going to follow in her footsteps. My mom had to work so hard that, at six years old, I was already taking care of my four-year-old brother and one-year-old sister. My mom eventually got married, but my stepfather and I did not get along. He treated my mom badly, and I lost respect for him and for her. I struggled in school, and my mom lost interest in us kids when she became depressed. She would lock us out of the house all day so she could lie around and watch television. I thought I was dumb, fat, and ugly. In high school when boys began to want to date me, I liked the attention but wanted to be a good girl. Then a boy raped me, and I just gave up. I struggled with poor self-image and rejection but managed to get to college. Then I got pregnant with the twins. I told myself it was no big deal, but the abortion deeply affected me. I dropped out of school and ended up moving in with a new guy I didn't even really like, just to escape my family's house. That guy tortured and threatened me for years. Then I gave my life over to God, and my family helped me escape. They gave me a bus ticket, and I stayed in a homeless shelter. I was too sick to work, and I discovered I was pregnant again. This time, I knew I would have the baby and give it up for adoption. I found a women's ministry that took me in, and there I finally faced my past and began to heal. I had the baby and gave it to a Christian family. I was able to go back to school and continue to work for the ministry who helped me. I want to tell people who feel desperate that abortion is not the answer. It's just one mistake on top of another.

*For more information about choosing life, visit www.optionline.org or www.prolife.com. For information about residential care for females, visit mercyministries.com. (Names have been changed for the sake of privacy. Michelle tells her story after going through biblically based counseling with Mercy Ministries.)*

**28:29 Verse 29** Some late Greek copies add verse 29: "After Paul said this, the Jews left. They were arguing very much with each other."

# *i*f you're looking for one of the best

chapters in the Bible to clearly state what Jesus did for you on the cross, try reading Romans 5. Not only does it describe the unique sacrifice Jesus Christ made, but it also explains why his death was necessary for us to have eternal life. Verse 6 gets right to the point: "When we were unable to help ourselves, at the moment of our need, Christ died for us."

# Romans christian faith 101

Cliffs Notes on Romans would go something like this: We have all sinned (3:23), and we need to be made right with God by his grace—or free, unearned favor (3:24)—through faith—or complete trust—in the blood of Jesus' death (3:25). It's not about what we *do*, but rather about what Jesus already *did* on the cross.

And that's what this letter from Paul to the Roman Christians is really about—the basics of the Christian faith. Of course, reading and understanding Romans can be anything *but* basic. Paul deals with some pretty abstract concepts (grace, faith, righteousness, sin, spiritual gifts), but if you can hang in there with him, he has an extremely relevant message for believers today.

But don't take our word for it. Read on.

1 From Paul, a servant of Christ Jesus. God called me to be an apostle and chose me to tell the Good News.

²God promised this Good News long ago through his prophets, as it is written in the Holy Scriptures. ³⁻⁴The Good News is about God's Son, Jesus Christ our Lord. As a man, he was born from the family of David. But through the Spirit of holiness he was appointed to be God's Son with great power by rising from the dead. ⁵Through Christ, God gave me the special work of an apostle, which was to lead people of all nations to believe and obey. I do this work for him. ⁶And you who are in Rome are also called to belong to Jesus Christ.

⁷To all of you in Rome whom God loves and has called to be his holy people:

Grace and peace to you from God our Father and the Lord Jesus Christ.

## A PRAYER OF THANKS

⁸First I want to say that I thank my God through Jesus Christ for all of you, because people everywhere in the world are talking about your faith. ⁹God, whom I serve with my whole heart by telling the Good News about his Son, knows that I always mention you ¹⁰every time I pray. I pray that I will be allowed to come to you, and this will happen if God wants it. ¹¹I want very much to see you, to give you some spiritual gift to make you strong. ¹²I mean that I want us to help each other with the faith we have. Your faith will help me, and my faith will help you. ¹³Brothers and sisters," I want you to know that I planned many times to come to you, but this has not been possible. I wanted to come so that I could help you grow spiritually as I have helped the other non-Jewish people.

¹⁴I have a duty to all people—Greeks and those who are not Greeks, the wise and the foolish. ¹⁵That is why I want so much to preach the Good News to you in Rome.

¹⁶I am proud of the Good News, because it is the power God uses to save everyone who believes—to save the Jews first, and also to

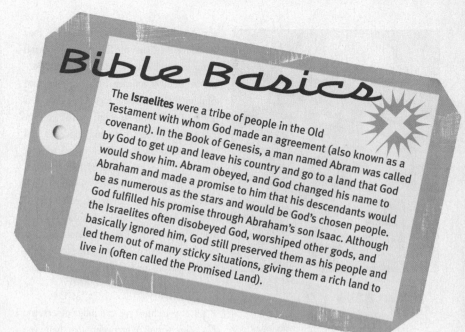

**Bible Basics**

The **Israelites** were a tribe of people in the Old Testament with whom God made an agreement (also known as a covenant). In the Book of Genesis, a man named Abram was called by God to get up and leave his country and go to a land that God would show him. Abram obeyed, and God changed his name to Abraham and made a promise to him that his descendants would be as numerous as the stars and would be God's chosen people. God fulfilled his promise through Abraham's son Isaac. Although the Israelites often disobeyed God, worshiped other gods, and basically ignored him, God still preserved them as his people and led them out of many sticky situations, giving them a rich land to live in (often called the Promised Land).

save those who are not Jews. ¹⁷The Good News shows how God makes people right with himself—that it begins and ends with faith. As the Scripture says, "But those who are right with God will live by trusting in him."ⁿ

> ## "GOD PROMISED THIS GOOD NEWS LONG AGO THROUGH HIS PROPHETS, AS IT IS WRITTEN IN THE HOLY SCRIPTURES."

## ALL PEOPLE HAVE DONE WRONG

¹⁸God's anger is shown from heaven against all the evil and wrong things people do. By their own evil lives they hide the truth. ¹⁹God shows his anger because some knowledge of him has been made clear to them. Yes, God has shown himself to them. ²⁰There are things about him that people cannot see—his eternal power and all the things that make him God. But since the beginning of the world those things have been easy to understand by what God has made. So people have no excuse for

the bad things they do. ²¹They knew God, but they did not give glory to God or thank him. Their thinking became useless. Their foolish minds were filled with darkness. ²²They said they were wise, but they became fools. ²³They traded the glory of God who lives forever for the worship of idols made to look like earthly people, birds, animals, and snakes.

²⁴Because they did these things, God left them and let them go their sinful way, wanting only to do evil. As a result, they became full of sexual sin, using their bodies wrongly with each other. ²⁵They traded the truth of God for a lie. They worshiped and served what had been created instead of the God who created those things, who should be praised forever. Amen.

²⁶Because people did those things, God left them and let them do the shameful things they wanted to do. Women stopped having natural sex and started having sex with other women. ²⁷In the same way, men stopped having natural sex and began wanting each other. Men did shameful things with other men, and in their bodies they received the punishment for those wrongs.

²⁸People did not think it was important to have a true knowledge of God. So God left them and allowed them to have their own

**1:13 Brothers and sisters** Although the Greek text says "Brothers" here and throughout this book, Paul's words were meant for the entire church, including men and women. **1:17 "But those . . . him."** Quotation from Habakkuk 2:4.

199

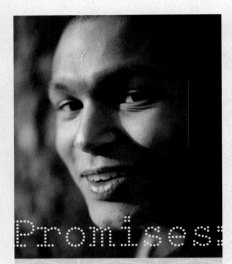

# Romans 1:2

Have you ever wondered why Jesus and others in the New Testament refer often to old scriptures or prophecies? Or maybe you've noticed that in this version of the Bible, there are references to Old Testament scriptures throughout. It's no mistake that these scriptures are noted.

The Jews of Jesus' day understood a few things very well—namely, the old scriptures and prophecies. They studied hard and knew what prophets of old predicted about God's work in their people and how he would send them a Messiah. Jesus, therefore, often used the exact wording of these scriptures so that the Jews would know he was knowledgeable about the things of God. He also wanted them to understand that he was the fulfillment of the scriptures that they had been waiting for—that he was the Messiah. Prophets throughout the years had predicted exact details of the Messiah's birth, life, and death; and Jesus' life fulfilled every one of those prophecies. Many Jews, however, still didn't want to believe because Jesus wasn't quite what they were expecting.

Jesus isn't easy to define or sum up in a few sentences. But we can confidently know that he was God's perfect Son, our Messiah and Savior.

worthless thinking and to do things they should not do. ²⁹They are filled with every kind of sin, evil, selfishness, and hatred. They are full of jealousy, murder, fighting, lying, and thinking the worst about each other. They gossip ³⁰and say evil things about each other. They hate God. They are rude and conceited and brag about themselves. They invent ways of doing evil. They do not obey their parents. ³¹They are foolish, they do not keep their promises, and they show no kindness or mercy to others. ³²They know God's law says that those who live like this should die. But they themselves not only continue to do these evil things, they applaud others who do them.

## YOU PEOPLE ALSO ARE SINFUL

2 If you think you can judge others, you are wrong. When you judge them, you are really judging yourself guilty, because you do the same things they do. ²God judges those who do wrong things, and we know that his judging is right. ³You judge those who do wrong, but you do wrong yourselves. Do you think you will be able to escape the judgment of God? ⁴He has been very kind and patient, waiting for you to change, but you think nothing of his kindness. Perhaps you do not understand that God is kind to you so you will change your hearts and lives. ⁵But you are stubborn and refuse to change, so you are making your own punishment even greater on the day he shows his anger. On that day everyone will see God's right judgments. ⁶God will reward or punish every person for what that person has done. ⁷Some people, by always continuing to do good, live for God's glory, for honor, and for life that has no end. God will give them life forever. ⁸But other people are selfish. They refuse to follow truth and, instead, follow evil. God will give them his punishment and anger. ⁹He will give trouble and suffering to everyone who does evil—to the Jews first and also to those who are not Jews. ¹⁰But he will give glory, honor, and peace to everyone who does good—to the Jews first and also to those who are not Jews. ¹¹For God judges all people in the same way.

¹²People who do not have the law and who are sinners will be lost, although they do not have the law. And, in the same way, those who have the law and are sinners will be judged by the law. ¹³Hearing the law does not make people right with God. It is those who obey the law who will be right with him. ¹⁴(Those who are not Jews do not have the law, but when they freely do what the law commands, they are the law for themselves. This is true even though they do not have the law. ¹⁵They show that in their hearts they know what is right and wrong, just as the law commands. And they show this by their consciences. Sometimes their thoughts tell them they did wrong, and sometimes their thoughts tell them they did right.) ¹⁶All these things will happen on the day when God, through Christ Jesus, will judge people's secret thoughts. The Good News that I preach says this.

## THE JEWS AND THE LAW

¹⁷What about you? You call yourself a Jew. You trust in the law of Moses and brag that you are close to God. ¹⁸You know what he wants you to do and what is important, because you have learned the law. ¹⁹You think you are a guide for the blind and a light for those who are in darkness. ²⁰You think you can show foolish people what is right and teach those who know nothing. You have the law; so you think you know everything and have all truth. ²¹You teach others, so why don't you teach yourself? You tell others not to steal, but you steal. ²²You say that others must not take part in adultery, but you are guilty of that sin. You hate idols, but you steal from temples. ²³You brag about having God's law, but you bring shame to God by breaking his law, ²⁴just as the Scriptures say: "Those who are not Jews speak against God's name because of you."ⁿ

²⁵If you follow the law, your circumcision has meaning. But if you break the law, it is as if you were never circumcised. ²⁶People who are not Jews are not circumcised, but if they do what the law says, it is as if they were circumcised. ²⁷You Jews have the written law and circumcision, but you break the law. So those who are not

2:24 "Those . . . you." Quotation from Isaiah 52:5; Ezekiel 36:20.

200

circumcised in their bodies, but still obey the law, will show that you are guilty. [28]They can do this because a person is not a true Jew if he is only a Jew in his physical body; true circumcision is not only on the outside of the body. [29]A person is a Jew only if he is a Jew inside; true circumcision is done in the heart by the Spirit, not by the written law. Such a person gets praise from God rather than from people.

**3** So, do Jews have anything that other people do not have? Is there anything special about being circumcised? [2]Yes, of course, there is in every way. The most important thing is this: God trusted the Jews with his teachings. [3]If some Jews were not faithful to him, will that stop God from doing what he promised? [4]No! God will continue to be true even when every person is false. As the Scriptures say:

"So you will be shown to be right when you speak,

and you will win your case." *Psalm 51:4*

[5]When we do wrong, that shows more clearly that God is right. So can we say that God is wrong to punish us? (I am talking as people might talk.) [6]No! If God could not punish us, he could not judge the world.

[7]A person might say, "When I lie, it really gives him glory, because my lie shows God's truth. So why am I judged a sinner?" [8]It would be the same to say, "We should do evil so that good will come." Some people find fault with us and say we teach this, but they are wrong and deserve the punishment they will receive.

## ALL PEOPLE ARE GUILTY

[9]So are we Jews better than others? No! We have already said that Jews and those who are not Jews are all guilty of sin. [10]As the Scriptures say:

"There is no one who always does what is right,

not even one.

[11]There is no one who understands.

There is no one who looks to God for help.

[12]All have turned away.

Together, everyone has become useless.

## Mary

**[MATTHEW 1 AND 2]** Before the angel's visit, everything was going Mary's way. She was engaged to a great man and wedding plans were in the works. But the angel Gabriel's news hit hard, like a hurricane ripping her world apart. A baby? Now? Mary could have said, "Isn't there someone else?" or "Can't this whole thing just wait until after my wedding?" But she didn't. Terrified at the thought, Mary still believed Gabriel when he told her she was to be the mother of Jesus. All her life, she'd heard about the coming Messiah. She knew there was no higher calling than to give birth to the Son of God. And as Mary put God's will ahead of her own, the world was changed forever.

There is no one who does anything good;

there is not even one." *Psalm 14:1-3*

[13]"Their throats are like open graves;

they use their tongues for telling lies."

*Psalm 5:9*

"Their words are like snake poison."

*Psalm 140:3*

[14] "Their mouths are full of cursing and hate." *Psalm 10:7*

[15]"They are always ready to kill people.

[16] Everywhere they go they cause ruin and misery.

[17]They don't know how to live in peace."

*Isaiah 59:7-8*

[18] "They have no fear of God." *Psalm 36:1*

[19]We know that the law's commands are for those who have the law. This stops all excuses and brings the whole world under God's judgment, [20]because no one can be made right with God by following the law. The law only shows us our sin.

## HOW GOD MAKES PEOPLE RIGHT

[21]But God has a way to make people right with him without the law, and he has now shown us that way which the law and the prophets told us about. [22]God makes people right with himself through their faith in Jesus Christ. This is true for all who believe in Christ, because all people are the same: [23]All have sinned and are not good enough for God's glory, [24]and all need to be made right with God by his grace, which is a free gift. They need to be made free from sin through Jesus Christ. [25]God gave him as a way to forgive sin through faith in the blood of Jesus' death. This showed that God always does what is right and fair, as in the past when he was patient and did not punish people for their sins. [26]And God gave Jesus to show today that he does what is right. God did this so he could judge rightly and so he could make right any person who has faith in Jesus.

[27]So do we have a reason to brag about ourselves? No! And why not? It is the way of faith that stops all bragging, not the way of trying to obey the law. [28]A person is made right with God through faith, not through obeying the law. [29]Is God only the God of the Jews? Is he not also the God of those who are not Jews? [30]Of course he is,

# Blab

**Q:** My cousin's boyfriend kissed me last week. Should I tell my cousin? What should I do?

**A:** Her boyfriend treated you and your cousin with disrespect when he put the moves on you. Tell your cousin, but do it gently. Be prepared for her to be mad at you. Tell her you are sorry (even if it wasn't your fault) and that she deserves to be treated better. If she stays with him anyway, make sure you are never alone with him.

**Q:** I like my best friend's boyfriend. I just can't help it. I feel terrible, and she'd kill me if she knew. What do I do?

**A:** Capture those thoughts every time they come into your head and repeat the verse, "Love your neighbor as you love yourself." If you love your best friend, you would never betray her. Ask God to remove your desire for her boyfriend, and keep yourself from spending time alone with him or time dreaming about him. Get up and get busy with something else.

**Q:** My boyfriend wants to give me a promise ring, but my parents say I can't accept it. Why can't they see that we are really in love?

**A:** They want you to have all that life has to offer you while you are young, like freedom to travel, college, and the pursuit of your dreams. They know from having more life experience that sometimes those who marry early or put a relationship ahead of the other things often lose the chance to do those things. Honor your parents, and wait. If it's true love, the right time will come.

because there is only one God. He will make Jews right with him by their faith, and he will also make those who are not Jews right with him through their faith. [31]So do we destroy the law by following the way of faith? No! Faith causes us to be what the law truly wants.

## THE EXAMPLE OF ABRAHAM

4 So what can we say that Abraham,[n] the father of our people, learned about faith? [2]If Abraham was made right by the things he did, he had a reason to brag. But this is not God's view, [3]because the Scripture says, "Abraham believed God, and God accepted Abraham's faith, and that faith made him right with God."[n]

[4]When people work, their pay is not given as a gift, but as something earned. [5]But people cannot do any work that will make them right with God. So they must trust in him, who makes even evil people right in his sight. Then God accepts their faith, and that makes them right with him. [6]David said the same thing. He said that people are truly blessed when God, without paying attention to good deeds, makes people right with himself.

[7]"Happy are they
    whose sins are forgiven,
    whose wrongs are pardoned.
[8]Happy is the person
    whom the Lord does not consider
    guilty."          *Psalm 32:1-2*

[9]Is this blessing only for those who are circumcised or also for those who are not circumcised? We have already said that God accepted Abraham's faith and that faith made him right with God. [10]So how did this happen? Did God accept Abraham before or after he was circumcised? It was before his circumcision. [11]Abraham was circumcised to show that he was right with God through faith before he was circumcised. So Abraham is the father of all those who believe but are not circumcised; he is the father of all believers who are accepted as being right with God. [12]And Abraham is also the father of those who have been circumcised and who live following the

faith that our father Abraham had before he was circumcised.

## GOD KEEPS HIS PROMISE

[13]Abraham[n] and his descendants received the promise that they would get the whole world. He did not receive that promise through the law, but through being right with God by his faith. [14]If people could receive what God promised by following the law, then faith is worthless. And God's promise to Abraham is worthless, [15]because the law can only bring God's anger. But if there is no law, there is nothing to disobey.

> ## "ABRAHAM AND HIS DESCENDANTS RECEIVED THE PROMISE THAT THEY WOULD GET THE WHOLE WORLD."

[16]So people receive God's promise by having faith. This happens so the promise can be a free gift. Then all of Abraham's children can have that promise. It is not only for those who live under the law of Moses but for anyone who

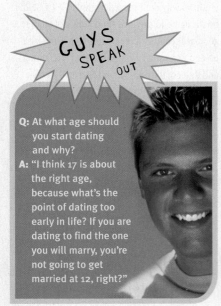

**GUYS SPEAK OUT**

**Q:** At what age should you start dating and why?
**A:** "I think 17 is about the right age, because what's the point of dating too early in life? If you are dating to find the one you will marry, you're not going to get married at 12, right?"

**notes**          **4:1 Abraham** Most respected ancestor of the Jews. Every Jew hoped to see Abraham.          **4:3 "Abraham . . . God."** Quotation from Genesis 15:6.          **4:13 Abraham** Most respected ancestor of the Jews. Every Jew hoped to see Abraham.

202

## LEARN I+ & LIVE I+

### Romans 1:14
**Learn It:** Paul said he had a duty to share the story of Jesus with all people.
**Live It:** Be willing to talk about God to anyone he puts in your path, not just to those you pick.

### Romans 2:13
**Learn It:** It isn't enough to hear the law; you must obey it.
**Live It:** Get into the habit of reading through the Bible carefully and regularly so you will know what God wants you to do and how to do it.

### Romans 3:24
**Learn It:** Everyone needs God's free gift of grace.
**Live It:** Place a slip of paper with the words "God's grace" on it in a small box. Set it out as a reminder that God's gift of redemption is free to you and to everyone who accepts it.

lives with faith like that of Abraham, who is the father of us all. [17]As it is written in the Scriptures: "I am making you a father of many nations."[n] This is true before God, the God Abraham believed, the God who gives life to the dead and who creates something out of nothing.

[18]There was no hope that Abraham would have children. But Abraham believed God and continued hoping, and so he became the father of many nations. As God told him, "Your descendants also will be too many to count."[n] [19]Abraham was almost a hundred years old, much past the age for having children, and Sarah could not have children. Abraham thought about all this, but his faith in God did not become weak. [20]He never doubted that God would keep his promise, and he never stopped believing. He grew stronger in his faith and gave praise to God. [21]Abraham felt sure that God was able to do what he had promised. [22]So, "God accepted Abraham's faith, and that faith made him right with God."[n] [23]Those words ("God accepted Abraham's faith") were written not only for Abraham [24]but also for us. God will accept us also because we believe in the One who raised Jesus our Lord from the dead. [25]Jesus was given to die for our sins, and he was raised from the dead to make us right with God.

## RIGHT WITH GOD

**5** Since we have been made right with God by our faith, we have peace with God. This happened through our Lord Jesus Christ, [2]who has brought us into that blessing of God's grace that we now enjoy. And we are happy because of the hope we have of sharing God's glory. [3]We also have joy with our troubles, because we know that these troubles produce patience. [4]And patience produces character, and character produces hope. [5]And this hope will never disappoint us, because God has poured out his love to fill our hearts. He gave us his love through the Holy Spirit, whom God has given to us.

[6]When we were unable to help ourselves, at the moment of our need, Christ died for us, although we were living against God. [7]Very few people will die to save the life of someone else. Although perhaps for a good person someone might possibly die. [8]But God shows his great love for us in this way: Christ died for us while we were still sinners.

[9]So through Christ we will surely be saved from God's anger, because we have been made right with God by the blood of Christ's death. [10]While we were God's enemies, he made friends with us through the death of his Son. Surely, now that we are his friends, he will save us through his Son's life. [11]And not only that, but now we are also very happy in God

through our Lord Jesus Christ. Through him we are now God's friends again.

## ADAM AND CHRIST COMPARED

[12]Sin came into the world because of what one man did, and with sin came death. This is why everyone must die—because everyone sinned. [13]Sin was in the world before the law of Moses, but sin is not counted against us as breaking a command when there is no law. [14]But from the time of Adam to the time of Moses, everyone had to die, even those who

## DIDYA KNOW

**SEVEN IN TEN TEENS SAY THEY HAVE ACCIDENTALLY BEEN EXPOSED TO PORNOGRAPHY ON THE INTERNET.** KAISER FAMILY FOUNDATION

had not sinned by breaking a command, as Adam had.

Adam was like the One who was coming in the future. [15]But God's free gift is not like Adam's sin. Many people died because of the sin of that one man. But the grace from God was much greater; many people received God's gift of life by the grace of the one man, Jesus Christ. [16]After Adam sinned once, he was judged guilty. But the gift of God is different. God's free gift came after many sins, and it makes people right with God. [17]One man sinned, and so death ruled all people because of that one man. But now those people who accept God's full grace and the great gift of being made right with him will surely have

 **notes** 4:17 "I . . . nations." Quotation from Genesis 17:5. 4:18 "Your . . . count." Quotation from Genesis 15:5. 4:22 "God . . . God." Quotation from Genesis 15:6.

203

## top 10

### random acts of kindness

**10** Pray regularly for your friends.

**9** Help someone with his or her homework.

**8** Fulfill a needy family's Christmas list.

**7** Volunteer at your church.

**6** Baby-sit for free for a single mom or struggling family.

**5** Give a restaurant or grocery gift certificate to someone who's hungry.

**4** Buy a special gift for your pastor or his family.

**3** Give money or volunteer your time at a local Christian radio station.

**2** Send a "thank you" email to your senator or the president.

**1** Write notes of encouragement to parents, pastors, and friends.

true life and rule through the one man, Jesus Christ.

18So as one sin of Adam brought the punishment of death to all people, one good act that Christ did makes all people right with God. And that brings true life for all. 19One man disobeyed God, and many became sinners. In the same way, one man obeyed God, and many will be made right. 20The law came to make sin worse. But when sin grew worse, God's grace increased. 21Sin once used death to rule us, but God gave people more of his grace so that grace could rule by making people right with him. And this brings life forever through Jesus Christ our Lord.

### DEAD TO SIN BUT ALIVE IN CHRIST

6 So do you think we should continue sinning so that God will give us even more grace? 2No! We died to our old sinful lives, so how can we continue living with sin? 3Did you forget that all of us became part of Christ when we were baptized? We shared his death in our baptism. 4When we were baptized, we were buried with Christ and shared his death. So, just as Christ was raised from the dead by the wonderful power of the Father, we also can live a new life.

5Christ died, and we have been joined with him by dying too. So we will also be joined with him by rising from the dead as he did. 6We know that our old life died with Christ on the cross so that our sinful selves would have no power over us and we would not be slaves to sin. 7Anyone who has died is made free from sin's control.

8If we died with Christ, we know we will also live with him. 9Christ was raised from the dead, and we know that he cannot die again. Death has no power over him now. 10Yes, when Christ died, he died to defeat the power of sin one time—enough for all time. He now has a new life, and his new life is with God. 11In the same way, you should see yourselves as being dead to the power of sin and alive with God through Christ Jesus.

12So, do not let sin control your life here on earth so that you do what your sinful self wants to do. 13Do not offer the parts of your body to serve sin, as things to be used in doing evil. Instead, offer yourselves to God as people who have died and now live. Offer the parts of your body to God to be used in doing good. 14Sin will not be your master, because you are not under law but under God's grace.

### BE SLAVES OF RIGHTEOUSNESS

15So what should we do? Should we sin because we are under grace and not under law? No! 16Surely you know that when you give yourselves like slaves to obey someone, then you are really slaves of that person. The person you obey is your master. You can follow sin, which brings spiritual death, or you can obey God, which makes you right with him. 17In the past you were slaves to sin—sin controlled you. But thank God, you fully obeyed the things that you were taught. 18You were made free from sin, and now you are slaves to good-

## beauty secret

### Freckle Facts

Freckles are natural spots on the skin where pigment is increased. Produced by cells that make melanin (the stuff that gives skin its color), freckles get darker when the amount of melanin in your skin increases. You can minimize your freckles by wearing sunscreen.

ness. [19]I use this example because this is hard for you to understand. In the past you offered the parts of your body to be slaves to sin and evil; you lived only for evil. In the same way now you must give yourselves to be slaves of goodness. Then you will live only for God.

## "GOD GIVES US A FREE GIFT—LIFE FOREVER IN CHRIST JESUS OUR LORD."

[20]In the past you were slaves to sin, and goodness did not control you. [21]You did evil things, and now you are ashamed of them. Those things only bring death. [22]But now you are free from sin and have become slaves of God. This brings you a life that is only for God, and this gives you life forever. [23]When people sin, they earn what sin pays—death. But God gives us a free gift—life forever in Christ Jesus our Lord.

### an example from marriage

**7** Brothers and sisters, all of you understand the law of Moses. So surely you know that the law rules over people only while they are alive. [2]For example, a woman must stay married to her husband as long as he is alive. But if her husband dies, she is free from the law of marriage. [3]But if she marries another man while her husband is still alive, the law says she is guilty of adultery. But if her husband dies, she is free from the law of marriage. Then if she marries another man, she is not guilty of adultery.

[4]In the same way, my brothers and sisters, your old selves died, and you became free from the law through the body of Christ. This happened so that you might belong to someone else—the One who was raised from the dead—and so that we might be used in service to God. [5]In the past, we were ruled by our sinful selves. The law made us want to do sinful things that controlled our bodies, so the things we did were bringing us death. [6]In the past, the law held us like prisoners, but our old selves died, and we were made free from the law. So now we serve God in a new way with the Spirit, and not in the old way with written rules.

### OUR FIGHT against sin

[7]You might think I am saying that sin and the law are the same thing. That is not true. But the law was the only way I could learn what sin meant. I would never have known what it means to want to take something belonging to someone else if the law had not said, "You must not want to take your neighbor's things."[n] [8]And sin found a way to use that command and cause me to want all kinds of things I should not want. But without the law, sin has no power. [9]I was alive before I knew the law. But when the law's command came to me, then sin began to live, [10]and I died. The command was meant to bring life, but for me it brought death. [11]Sin found a way to fool me by using the command to make me die.

[12]So the law is holy, and the command is holy and right and good. [13]Does this mean that something that is good brought death to me? No! Sin used something that is good to bring death to me. This happened so that I could see what sin is really like; the command was used to show that sin is very evil.

### THE war WITHIN US

[14]We know that the law is spiritual, but I am not spiritual since sin rules me as if I were its slave. [15]I do not understand the things I do. I do not do what I want to do, and I do the things I hate. [16]And if I do not want to do the hated things I do, that means I agree that the law is good. [17]But I am not really the one who is doing these hated things; it is sin living in me that does them. [18]Yes, I know that nothing good lives in me—I mean nothing good lives in the part of me that is earthly and sinful. I want to do the things that are good, but I do not do them. [19]I do not do the good things I want to do, but I do the bad things I do not want to do. [20]So if I do things I do not want to do, then I am not the one doing them. It is sin living in me that does those things.

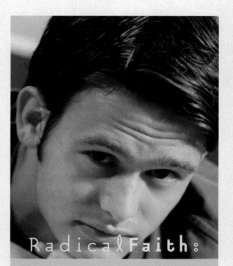

### Radical Faith:

## Romans 3:22-26

Sometimes we think that being a nice and good person is all that's important. But did you know that even the best people are impure and sinful deep down? And, if there is any sin in you at all, you are not good enough for God's glory. Like it or not, we as human beings are, by nature, sinful. It all goes back to Adam and Eve. We were born with selfish tendencies and a mind that wants to do what we want to do. That's why we need to be "born again" (check out 1 Peter 1:23). God is completely pure and perfect, so we need to be made right with God. This can only happen when we are freed from our sinful natures and have a new kind of nature put in us. And that happens when you receive God's grace and believe in Jesus Christ his Son. Jesus replaces your sinfulness with his righteousness through the sacrifice of his life. You're just fooling yourself if you think you haven't sinned or don't need a savior (1 John 1:8, 10). "All have sinned and are not good enough for God's glory" (Romans 3:23). You'll get nowhere trying to become good through anything else or anyone other than Jesus. God said it; you can believe it.

**notes** 7:7 **"You . . . things."** Quotation from Exodus 20:17.

# CHECK IT OUT

## STUDENT GLOBAL AIDS CAMPAIGN

The Student Global AIDS Campaign is a national, student-based organization dedicated to ending the global AIDS pandemic by pressuring politicians, civil society, and corporations to address and help end this crisis. The 75 chapters on high school, college, and university campuses around the United States work together to plan nationwide advocacy campaigns to fight for funding, access to AIDS medicines, debt cancellation, and other issues that are crucial in ending the AIDS pandemic.

Global statistics show 42 million people are infected with HIV/AIDS around the world, with an additional 15,000 becoming infected every day, and 8,200 people dying every day. Student Global AIDS Campaign chapters participate in national campaigns, as well as develop their own projects, such as educating students about the global AIDS crisis and their role in fighting it by holding teach-ins, film screenings, and lectures. Members also lobby, write letters, and make phone calls to the president and members of Congress about AIDS. They also hold rallies and press events to gain public attention.

*Get involved by visiting www.fightglobalaids.org.*

²¹So I have learned this rule: When I want to do good, evil is there with me. ²²In my mind, I am happy with God's law. ²³But I see another law working in my body, which makes war against the law that my mind accepts. That other law working in my body is the law of sin, and it makes me its prisoner. ²⁴What a miserable man I am! Who will save me from this body that brings me death? ²⁵I thank God for saving me through Jesus Christ our Lord!

So in my mind I am a slave to God's law, but in my sinful self I am a slave to the law of sin.

## BE RULED BY THE SPIRIT

**8** So now, those who are in Christ Jesus are not judged guilty. ²Through Christ Jesus the law of the Spirit that brings life made me free from the law that brings sin and death. ³The law was without power, because the law was made weak by our sinful selves. But God did what the law could not do. He sent his own Son to earth with the same human life that others use for sin. By sending his Son to be an offering for sin, God used a human life to destroy sin. ⁴He did this so that we could be the kind of people the law correctly wants us to be. Now we do not live following our sinful selves, but we live following the Spirit.

⁵Those who live following their sinful selves think only about things that their sinful selves want. But those who live following the Spirit are thinking about the things the Spirit wants them to do. ⁶If people's thinking is controlled by the sinful self, there is death. But if their thinking is controlled by the Spirit, there is life and peace. ⁷When people's thinking is controlled by the sinful self, they are against God, because they refuse to obey God's law and really are not even able to obey God's law. ⁸Those people who are ruled by their sinful selves cannot please God.

**DIDYA KNOW** ALMOST ONE IN FIVE HIGH SCHOOL GUYS SAY THEY'VE DRIVEN AFTER DRINKING. CHILD TRENDS DATABANK

## "THOSE WHO LIVE FOLLOWING THEIR SINFUL SELVES THINK ONLY ABOUT THINGS THAT THEIR SINFUL SELVES WANT."

⁹But you are not ruled by your sinful selves. You are ruled by the Spirit, if that Spirit of God really lives in you. But the person who does not have the Spirit of Christ does not belong to Christ. ¹⁰Your body will always be dead because of sin. But if Christ is in you, then the Spirit gives you life, because Christ made you right with God. ¹¹God raised Jesus from the dead, and if God's Spirit is living in you, he will also give life to your bodies that die. God is the One who raised Christ from the dead, and he will give life through his Spirit that lives in you.

¹²So, my brothers and sisters, we must not be ruled by our sinful selves or live the way our sinful selves want. ¹³If you use your lives to do the wrong things your sinful selves want, you will die spiritually. But if you use the Spirit's help to stop doing the wrong things you do with your body, you will have true life.

¹⁴The true children of God are those who let God's Spirit lead them. ¹⁵The Spirit we received does not make us slaves again to fear; it makes

## Promises!

# Romans 6:6

Do you have any bad habits? C'mon, fess up. Do you bite your fingernails? Smack your gum? Talk with your mouth open while you're eating? Always late for school? Gossip too much? Or maybe you have habits that are harder to break, like smoking or using language you shouldn't use? Maybe you have tried and tried to break your nasty habits, but they don't go away easily.

We humans are creatures of habit—not to mention that we are really prone to sinful behavior. But, just like you can work to break a bad habit, you can also break sin's control on your life. When you accept Jesus as Savior, sin doesn't have a hold on you anymore. That was your old life—you new life in Christ frees you of that.

So does this mean that you will never sin again? No. But it does mean that you don't have to define yourself by your sin anymore. When you do struggle with sin, you can pray and ask God to forgive you and to help you overcome it. The old has gone and the new has come!

us children of God. With that Spirit we cry out, "Father."[n] [16]And the Spirit himself joins with our spirits to say we are God's children. [17]If we are God's children, we will receive blessings from God together with Christ. But we must suffer as Christ suffered so that we will have glory as Christ has glory.

### OUR FUTURE GLORY

[18]The sufferings we have now are nothing compared to the great glory that will be shown to us. [19]Everything God made is waiting with excitement for God to show his children's glory completely. [20]Everything God made was changed to become useless, not by its own wish but because God wanted it and because all along there was this hope: [21]that everything God made would be set free from ruin to have the freedom and glory that belong to God's children.

[22]We know that everything God made has been waiting until now in pain, like a woman ready to give birth. [23]Not only the world, but we also have been waiting with pain inside us. We have the Spirit as the first part of God's promise. So we are waiting for God to finish making us his own children, which means our bodies will be made free. [24]We were saved, and we have this hope. If we see what we are waiting for, that is not really hope. People do not hope for something they already have. [25]But we are hoping for something we do not have yet, and we are waiting for it patiently.

[26]Also, the Spirit helps us with our weakness. We do not know how to pray as we should. But the Spirit himself speaks to God for us, even begs God for us with deep feelings that words cannot explain. [27]God can see what is in people's hearts. And he knows what is in the mind of the Spirit, because the Spirit speaks to God for his people in the way God wants.

[28]We know that in everything God works for the good of those who love him. They are the people he called, because that was his plan. [29]God knew them before he made the world, and he decided that they would be like his Son so that Jesus would be the firstborn[n] of many

brothers. [30]God planned for them to be like his Son; and those he planned to be like his Son, he also called; and those he called, he also made right with him; and those he made right, he also glorified.

### GOD'S LOVE IN CHRIST JESUS

[31]So what should we say about this? If God is with us, no one can defeat us. [32]He did not spare his own Son but gave him for us all. So with Jesus, God will surely give us all things. [33]Who can accuse the people God has chosen? No one, because God is the One who makes them right. [34]Who can say God's people are guilty? No one, because Christ Jesus died, but he was also raised from the dead, and now he is on God's right side, begging God for us. [35]Can anything separate us from the love Christ has for us? Can troubles or problems or

## relationships

"Whoever does not care for his own relatives, especially his own family members, has turned against the faith and is worse than someone who does not believe in God" (1 Timothy 5:8). Ouch! That can be a tough verse. Got a grandpa that drives you nuts? A mom who gets on your nerves? A little brother who can be a big pain? In order to love God effectively, you've got to love them all anyway. Just keep trying every day, and ask God to help you see the good in them.

notes    **8:15 "Father"** Literally, "Abba, Father." Jewish children called their fathers "Abba."    **8:29 firstborn** Here this probably means that Christ was the first in God's family to share God's glory.

208

sufferings or hunger or nakedness or danger or violent death? <sup>36</sup>As it is written in the Scriptures:

"For you we are in danger of death all the time.
People think we are worth no more than sheep to be killed." *Psalm 44:22*

<sup>37</sup>But in all these things we have full victory through God who showed his love for us. <sup>38</sup>Yes, I am sure that neither death, nor life, nor angels, nor ruling spirits, nothing now, nothing in the future, no powers, <sup>39</sup>nothing above us, nothing below us, nor anything else in the whole world will ever be able to separate us from the love of God that is in Christ Jesus our Lord.

## "SO GOD SHOWS MERCY WHERE HE WANTS TO SHOW MERCY, AND HE MAKES STUBBORN THE PEOPLE HE WANTS TO MAKE STUBBORN."

### GOD AND THE JEWISH PEOPLE

9 I am in Christ, and I am telling you the truth; I do not lie. My conscience is ruled by the Holy Spirit, and it tells me I am not lying. <sup>2</sup>I have great sorrow and always feel much sadness. <sup>3</sup>I wish I could help my Jewish brothers and sisters, my people. I would even wish that I were cursed and cut off from Christ if that would help them. <sup>4</sup>They are the people of Israel, God's chosen children. They have seen the glory of God, and they have the agreements that God made between himself and his people. God gave them the law of Moses and the right way of worship and his promises. <sup>5</sup>They are the descendants of our great ancestors, and they are the earthly family into which Christ was born, who is God over all. Praise him forever!<sup>n</sup> Amen.

<sup>6</sup>It is not that God failed to keep his promise to them. But only some of the people of Israel are truly God's people,<sup>n</sup> <sup>7</sup>and only some of Abraham's<sup>n</sup> descendants are true children of Abraham. But God said to Abraham: "The descendants I promised you will be from Isaac."<sup>n</sup> <sup>8</sup>This means that not all of Abraham's descendants are God's true children. Abraham's true children are those who become God's children because of the promise God made to Abraham. <sup>9</sup>God's promise to Abraham was this: "At the right time I will return, and Sarah will have a son."<sup>n</sup> <sup>10</sup>And that is not all. Rebekah's sons had the same father, our father Isaac. <sup>11-12</sup>But before the two boys were born, God told Rebekah, "The older will serve the younger."<sup>n</sup> This was before the boys had done anything good or bad. God said this so that the one chosen would be chosen because of God's own plan. He was chosen because he was the one God wanted to call, not because of anything he did. <sup>13</sup>As the Scripture says, "I loved Jacob, but I hated Esau."<sup>n</sup>

<sup>14</sup>So what should we say about this? Is God unfair? In no way. <sup>15</sup>God said to Moses, "I will show kindness to anyone to whom I want to show kindness, and I will show mercy to anyone to whom I want to show mercy."<sup>n</sup> <sup>16</sup>So God will choose the one to whom he decides to show mercy; his choice does not depend on what people want or try to do. <sup>17</sup>The Scripture says to the king of Egypt: "I made you king for this reason: to show my power in you so that my name will be talked about in all the earth."<sup>n</sup> <sup>18</sup>So God shows mercy where he wants to show mercy, and he makes stubborn the people he wants to make stubborn.

<sup>19</sup>So one of you will ask me: "Then why does God blame us for our sins? Who can fight his will?" <sup>20</sup>You are only human, and human beings have no right to question God. An object should not ask the person who made it, "Why did you make me like this?" <sup>21</sup>The potter can make anything he wants to make. He can use the same clay to make one thing for special use and another thing for daily use.

<sup>22</sup>It is the same way with God. He wanted to

## RadicalFaith:

# Romans 6:22-23

When you understand how awful your sins are, you're in a position to see more clearly the character, genius, and heart of God. The truth is, you deserve his wrath. We all do. Sin brings harsh judgment, punishment, and painful consequences. Sin brings death. On the cross, Christ took the consequences of your sin—death and eternal separation from God—and paid the price to free you from those consequences. This gift from God results in forgiveness and a life that's controlled by his goodness, not by your sin. Jesus died for every sin you struggle with—so you don't have to be slave to it. You've been given "a life that is only for God, and this gives you life forever." Now and always, there's a way for you to be with him. Think about what that says about God. He loves you so much that he's willing to do whatever it takes to make a way for you to be in his presence. Christ's sacrifice covers the sin that keeps us from God. Spend your life receiving the gift of God's presence, believing he loves you, and responding to his grace in obedience.

# LEARN I+ & LIVE I+

**Romans 5:8**
**Learn It:** Christ died for us while we were still sinners.
**Live It:** When you share the Good News of Christ with others, be sure to emphasize God's great love.

**Romans 6:1-2**
**Learn It:** Should we sin so that God can give us more grace? No!
**Live It:** Take a shower and put on clean clothes to remind yourself that you are clean and covered by grace. Try not to get dirty today—inside or out.

**Romans 6:13**
**Learn It:** Do not let your body do sinful things; offer your body to God to do good things.
**Live It:** Get rid of any CDs or DVDs that you wouldn't want Christ to catch you hearing or watching.

show his anger and to let people see his power. But he patiently stayed with those people he was angry with—people who were made ready to be destroyed. ²³He waited with patience so that he could make known his rich glory to the people who receive his mercy. He has prepared these people to have his glory, ²⁴and we are those people whom God called. He called us not from the Jews only but also from those who are not Jews. ²⁵As the Scripture says in Hosea:

"I will say, 'You are my people'
to those I had called 'not my people.'
And I will show my love
to those people I did not love."

*Hosea 2:1, 23*

²⁶"They were called,
'You are not my people,'

but later they will be called
'children of the living God.'" *Hosea 1:10*

²⁷And Isaiah cries out about Israel:
"The people of Israel are many,
like the grains of sand by the sea.
But only a few of them will be saved,
²⁸ because the Lord will quickly and
completely punish the
people on the earth." *Isaiah 10:22-23*

²⁹It is as Isaiah said:
"The Lord All-Powerful
allowed a few of our descendants to live.
Otherwise we would have been completely destroyed
like the cities of Sodom and
Gomorrah."ⁿ *Isaiah 1:9*

³⁰So what does all this mean? Those who

are not Jews were not trying to make themselves right with God, but they were made right with God because of their faith. ³¹The people of Israel tried to follow a law to make themselves right with God. But they did not succeed, ³²because they tried to make themselves right by the things they did instead of trusting in God to make them right. They stumbled over the stone that causes people to stumble. ³³As it is written in the Scripture:

"I will put in Jerusalem a stone that causes
people to stumble,
a rock that makes them fall.
Anyone who trusts in him will never be
disappointed." *Isaiah 8:14; 28:16*

**10** Brothers and sisters, the thing I want most is for all the Jews to be saved.

# Music Reviews

**GROUP:** SIXPENCE NONE THE RICHER

**ALBUM:** THE BEST OF

Pop band Sixpence None the Richer has officially disbanded (as singer Leigh Nash enjoys being a first-time mom), but their music lives on. So while the group is no more, fans can relive their favorite musical moments with *The Best of Sixpence None the Richer*. The project has eighteen songs featuring Leigh's ethereal vocals on such crossover hits as "There She Goes" and "Kiss Me" (in two versions), plus three new songs.

WHY IT ROCKS: IT'S THE LAST CHANCE TO HEAR NEW TUNES FROM THIS OUTSTANDING CROSSOVER POP GROUP WHILE ENJOYING PAST HITS.

**notes** **9:29 Sodom and Gomorrah** Two cities that God destroyed because the people were so evil.

That is my prayer to God. ²I can say this about them: They really try to follow God, but they do not know the right way. ³Because they did not know the way that God makes people right with him, they tried to make themselves right in their own way. So they did not accept God's way of making people right. ⁴Christ ended the law so that everyone who believes in him may be right with God.

⁵Moses writes about being made right by following the law. He says, "A person who obeys these things will live because of them."ⁿ ⁶But this is what the Scripture says about being made right through faith: "Don't say to yourself, 'Who will go up into heaven?' " (That means, "Who will go up to heaven and bring Christ down to earth?") ⁷"And do not say, 'Who will go down into the world below?' " (That means, "Who will go down and bring Christ up

from the dead?") ⁸This is what the Scripture says: "The word is near you; it is in your mouth and in your heart."ⁿ That is the teaching of faith that we are telling. ⁹If you use your mouth to say, "Jesus is Lord," and if you believe in your heart that God raised Jesus from the dead, you will be saved. ¹⁰We believe with our hearts, and so we are made right with God. And we use our mouths to say that we believe, and so we are saved. ¹¹As the Scripture says, "Anyone who trusts in him will never be disappointed."ⁿ ¹²That Scripture says "anyone" because there is no difference between those who are Jews and those who are not. The same Lord is the Lord of all and gives many blessings to all who trust in him, ¹³as the Scripture says, "Anyone who calls on the Lord will be saved."ⁿ

¹⁴But before people can ask the Lord for help, they must believe in him; and before they can believe in him, they must hear about him; and for them to hear about the Lord, someone must tell them; ¹⁵and before someone can go and tell them, that person must be sent. It is written, "How beautiful is the person who comes to bring good news."ⁿ ¹⁶But not all the Jews accepted the good news. Isaiah said, "Lord, who believed what we told them?"ⁿ ¹⁷So faith comes from hearing the Good News, and people hear the Good News when someone tells them about Christ.

¹⁸But I ask: Didn't people hear the Good News? Yes, they heard—as the Scripture says:

"Their message went out through all the
    world;
their words go everywhere on earth."

*Psalm 19:4*

¹⁹Again I ask: Didn't the people of Israel understand? Yes, they did understand. First, Moses says:

"I will use those who are not a nation to
    make you jealous.
I will use a nation that does not
    understand to make you angry."

*Deuteronomy 32:21*

²⁰Then Isaiah is bold enough to say:

"I was found by those who were not asking
    me for help.

## beautysecret

### Nail Care

If you paint your nails on a regular basis, try not to use nail polish remover more than once a week. It dries out your nails, which cause them to crack and split more often. A thick, clear top coat will help reduce any chipping or cracking of your nails.

# Blab

**Q:** I'm afraid to admit I am a Christian at school, because I don't think I know enough to defend my faith. How can I get more comfortable standing up for what I believe?

**A:** Find books on apologetics (books that help you explain and defend your faith). See if your church or another local church offers classes on the basics of faith, and sign up. Finally, keep studying your Bible and ask God for wisdom and courage. He'll give you the right words.

**Q:** I like to read my horoscope, but a friend told me it's wrong for Christians to do that. Is it really wrong?

**A:** It is wrong, because you are putting your faith in something other than God. Horoscopes, which seem harmless, are actually a tool used by Satan to manipulate people by giving them false ideas of their future. Astrologers, psychics, and fortune-tellers are condemned in the Bible, because they represent what can happen when people start trying to do God's job.

**Q:** I act one way with my youth group and really feel close to God there, but then I get to school and cuss and gossip with my friends and sort of forget what I believe. How can I change?

**A:** Remember that God will work in you continually if you pray, spend time with him, and read his Word. When you mess up, confess to God and ask him to forgive you and help you not to do it again. Check out what the Bible says about people who keep sinning. That should help you want to change your ways.

**notes**    **10:5** "A person . . . them." Quotation from Leviticus 18:5.    **10:6-8** Verses 6-8 Quotations from Deuteronomy 9:4; 30:12-14; Psalm 107:26.    **10:11** "Anyone . . . disappointed." Quotation from Isaiah 28:16.    **10:13** "Anyone . . . saved." Quotation from Joel 2:32.    **10:15** "How . . . news." Quotation from Isaiah 52:7.    **10:16** "Lord, . . . them?" Quotation from Isaiah 53:1.

**211**

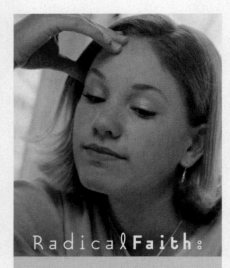

Radical Faith:

# Romans 8:31-34

Do you maybe ever think that God could never *really* accept you? Do you think the idea that he would save you is too good to be true? Well it *is* really good—a better gift than anything else in the world—but it's tough to grasp sometimes. Check out 2 Corinthians 5:17. Nothing can make you anything less than what God has made you in Christ—a wonderful new creation he treasures. In Christ you have real forgiveness, big strength, and deep love. No power, situation, or person can keep you from it (Romans 8:35-39). Believe God. The salvation he offers is based on how good he is, not how good you are. His authority in your life makes you what you are and leads you through every step. Nothing can ever interfere with his power to work good things in and through your life.

I made myself known to people who
were not looking for me."         *Isaiah 65:1*
²¹But about Israel God says,
"All day long I stood ready to accept
people who disobey and are stubborn."
*Isaiah 65:2*

## GOD SHOWS MERCY TO ALL PEOPLE

11 So I ask: Did God throw out his people? No! I myself am an Israelite from the family of Abraham, from the tribe of Benjamin. ²God chose the Israelites to be his people before they were born, and he has not thrown his people out. Surely you know what the Scripture says about Elijah, how he prayed to God against the people of Israel. ³"Lord," he said, "they have killed your prophets, and they have destroyed your altars. I am the only prophet left, and now they are trying to kill me, too."ⁿ ⁴But what answer did God give

 **77% OF YOUTH SAY IT'S IMPORTANT TO BUY THE RIGHT BRANDS.** BKG YOUTH

Elijah? He said, "But I have left seven thousand people in Israel who have never bowed down before Baal."ⁿ ⁵It is the same now. There are a few people that God has chosen by his grace. ⁶And if he chose them by grace, it is not for the things they have done. If they could be made God's people by what they did, God's gift of grace would not really be a gift.

⁷So this is what has happened: Although the Israelites tried to be right with God, they did not succeed, but the ones God chose did become right with him. The others were made stubborn and refused to listen to God. ⁸As it is written in the Scriptures:
"God gave the people a dull mind so they
could not understand."        *Isaiah 29:10*
"He closed their eyes so they could not see
and their ears so they could not hear.
This continues until today."
*Deuteronomy 29:4*

⁹And David says:
"Let their own feasts trap them and cause
their ruin;
let their feasts cause them to stumble
and be paid back.
¹⁰Let their eyes be closed so they cannot see
and their backs be forever weak from
troubles."        *Psalm 69:22-23*

¹¹So I ask: When the Jews fell, did that fall destroy them? No! But their mistake brought salvation to those who are not Jews, in order to make the Jews jealous. ¹²The Jews' mistake brought rich blessings for the world, and the Jews' loss brought rich blessings for the non-Jewish people. So surely the world will receive much richer blessings when enough Jews become the kind of people God wants.

¹³Now I am speaking to you who are not Jews. I am an apostle to those who are not Jews, and since I have that work, I will make

the most of it. ¹⁴I hope I can make my own people jealous and, in that way, help some of them to be saved. ¹⁵When God turned away from the Jews, he became friends with other people in the world. So when God accepts the Jews, surely that will bring them life after death.

¹⁶If the first piece of bread is offered to God, then the whole loaf is made holy. If the roots of a tree are holy, then the tree's branches are holy too.

¹⁷It is as if some of the branches from an olive tree have been broken off. You non-Jewish people are like the branch of a wild olive tree that has been joined to that first tree. You now share the strength and life of the first tree, the Jews. ¹⁸So do not brag about those branches that were broken off. If you brag, remember that you do not support the root, but the root supports you. ¹⁹You will say, "Branches were

 **11:3 "They . . . too."** Quotation from 1 Kings 19:10, 14.   **11:4 "But . . . Baal."** Quotation from 1 Kings 19:18.

broken off so that I could be joined to their tree." ²⁰That is true. But those branches were broken off because they did not believe, and you continue to be part of the tree only because you believe. Do not be proud, but be afraid. ²¹If God did not let the natural branches of that tree stay, then he will not let you stay if you don't believe.

²²So you see that God is kind and also very strict. He punishes those who stop following him. But God is kind to you, if you continue following in his kindness. If you do not, you will be cut off from the tree. ²³And if the Jews will believe in God again, he will accept them back. God is able to put them back where they were. ²⁴It is not natural for a wild branch to be part of a good tree. And you who are not Jews are like a branch cut from a wild olive tree and joined to a good olive tree. But since those Jews are like a branch that grew from the good tree, surely they can be joined to their own tree again.

²⁵I want you to understand this secret, brothers and sisters, so you will understand that you do not know everything: Part of Israel has been made stubborn, but that will change when many who are not Jews have come to God. ²⁶And that is how all Israel will be saved. It is written in the Scriptures:

"The Savior will come from Jerusalem;
he will take away all evil from the family of Jacob."

²⁷And I will make this agreement with those people

when I take away their sins."

*Isaiah 59:20-21; 27:9*

²⁸The Jews refuse to accept the Good News, so they are God's enemies. This has happened to help you who are not Jews. But the Jews are still God's chosen people, and he loves them very much because of the promises he made to their ancestors. ²⁹God never changes his mind about the people he calls and the things he gives them. ³⁰At one time you refused to obey God. But now you have received mercy, because those people refused to obey. ³¹And now the Jews refuse to obey, because God showed mercy to you. But this happened so

## BIBLE BIOS

## Mary and Martha

[LUKE 10] This is the story of two sisters, Mary and Martha, who were total polar opposites. Mary was a laidback achiever; Martha was a competent over-achiever. So it was little wonder that the two had trouble getting along, especially when their good friend Jesus was coming for a visit. Both Mary and Martha had the gift of hospitality. While Martha dashed frantically about the kitchen, cooking and taking care of the details, Mary was all about enjoying the company, captivated by all Jesus had to say. Needless to say, Martha was ticked. But Jesus gently pointed out that Martha's priorities were out of order. Most of us, if we admit it, might get a bit miffed that the overachiever didn't get the best rap, but Jesus wanted us to know that our deeds and our works can never take the place of simply being in God's presence.

 **11:26 Jacob** Father of the twelve family groups of Israel, the people God chose to be his people.

# July

**1** Watch the sunset with a friend.

**2**

**3**

**4** It's the Fourth of July: Celebrate our nation's birthday. Enjoy picnics and fireworks!

**5**

**6** Rent a comedy and spend time laughing with your family.

**7** Don't forget to make time to spend with God today.

**8**

**9** Pray for a person of influence: It's Tom Hanks's birthday.

**10** Pray for a person of influence: It's Jessica Simpson's birthday.

**11**

**12** Try lifting some weights to get in shape.

**13** Pray for a person of influence: Harrison Ford is having a birthday today.

**14**

**15**

**16** Do something nice for your brother or sister without letting him or her know!

**17**

**18** Go for a long walk. Enjoy God's creation.

**19** Read Acts 1 and 2. Tell a friend what you learn.

**20** Have a water balloon fight. Remember to play fair and have fun.

**21**

**22** Give yourself a facial. It's important to take care of your skin.

**23** Make time to clean out your email folders.

**24**

**25**

**26** Think about what you'd say if someone asked you why Jesus is the only way to heaven.

**27** Surprise your parents by cleaning your room.

**28** Write a letter to God. Fill it with your prayers.

**29**

**30** Pray for a person of influence: It's Arnold Schwarzenegger's birthday.

**31** Ask your parents to share stories from their childhood.

Surprise your parent(s) by remembering their holiday—National Parents' Day is the fourth Sunday of July.

# LEARN I+ & LIVE I+

**Romans 11:22**
**Learn It:** God is kind, but he also wants to bring those who are disobeying him back into line.
**Live It:** When things go wrong, ask God if he is trying to correct any sin in your life. Listen for his answer.

**Romans 12:5**
**Learn It:** Christians must all work together, and God says we belong to each other.
**Live It:** Thank at least one church member for the job he or she does in your Christian family.

**Romans 12:8**
**Learn It:** You should use the gifts God has given you.
**Live It:** Take a spiritual gifts assessment and learn what your God-given gifts are. Use them for him.

that they also can receive mercy from him. 32God has given all people over to their stubborn ways so that he can show mercy to all.

## PRAISE TO GOD

33Yes, God's riches are very great, and his wisdom and knowledge have no end! No one can explain the things God decides or understand his ways. 34As the Scripture says,

"Who has known the mind of the Lord, or who has been able to give him advice?" *Isaiah 40:13*

35"No one has ever given God anything that he must pay back." *Job 41:11*

36Yes, God made all things, and everything continues through him and for him. To him be the glory forever! Amen.

## GIVE YOUR LIVES TO GOD

12 So brothers and sisters, since God has shown us great mercy, I beg you to offer your lives as a living sacrifice to him. Your offering must be only for God and pleasing to him, which is the spiritual way for you to worship. 2Do not change yourselves to be like the people of this world, but be changed within by a new way of thinking. Then you will be able to decide what God wants for you; you will know what is good and pleasing to him and what is perfect. 3Because God has given me a special gift, I have something to say to everyone among you. Do not think you are better than you are. You must decide what you really are by the amount of faith God has given you. 4Each one of us has a body with many parts, and these parts all have different uses. 5In the same way, we are many, but in Christ we are all one body. Each one is a part of that body, and each part belongs to all the other parts. 6We all have different gifts, each of which came because of the grace God gave us. The person who has the gift of prophecy should use that gift in agreement with the faith. 7Anyone who has the gift of serving should serve. Anyone who has the gift of teaching should teach. 8Whoever has the gift of encouraging others should encourage. Whoever has the gift of giving to others should give freely. Anyone who has the gift of being a leader should try hard when he leads. Whoever has the gift of showing mercy to others should do so with joy.

9Your love must be real. Hate what is evil,

## ⊙► CHECK IT OUT

### GIRL SCOUTS OF THE U.S.A.

Girl Scouts isn't an old-fashioned organization where girls dress up in vests and beanies and add badges to their sashes. Studio 2B is a Girls Scouts program and national network for girls ages 11 to 17 that wants to help them "Become, Belong, Believe, and Build" by getting together with other girls in their community and developing skills and talents to build better communities.

The Studio 2B program also helps girls reach their dreamed-of destinations through travel with Outward Bound programs and Sea World/Busch Gardens Adventure Camps, plus wilderness camps, ropes courses, scuba diving trips, dog sledding expeditions, and other extreme adventures.

At home, Studio 2B members can stop by the website to chat, take quizzes, participate in national polls, post their own stories and poems, and find out more about teens around the world.

*Get involved by visiting* **www.studio2b.org.**

and hold on to what is good. [10]Love each other like brothers and sisters. Give each other more honor than you want for yourselves. [11]Do not be lazy but work hard, serving the Lord with all your heart. [12]Be joyful because you have hope. Be patient when trouble comes, and pray at all times. [13]Share with God's people who need help. Bring strangers in need into your homes.

## "WISH GOOD FOR THOSE WHO HARM YOU; WISH THEM WELL AND DO NOT CURSE THEM."

[14]Wish good for those who harm you; wish them well and do not curse them. [15]Be happy with those who are happy, and be sad with those who are sad. [16]Live in peace with each other. Do not be proud, but make friends with those who seem unimportant. Do not think how smart you are.

[17]If someone does wrong to you, do not pay him back by doing wrong to him. Try to do what everyone thinks is right. [18]Do your best to live in peace with everyone. [19]My friends, do not try to punish others when they wrong you, but wait for God to punish them with his anger. It is written: "I will punish those who do

wrong; I will repay them,"[n] says the Lord. [20]But you should do this:

"If your enemy is hungry, feed him;
    if he is thirsty, give him a drink.
Doing this will be like pouring burning
    coals on his head."    *Proverbs 25:21-22*

[21]Do not let evil defeat you, but defeat evil by doing good.

### CHRISTIANS SHOULD OBEY THE LAW

**13** All of you must yield to the government rulers. No one rules unless God has given him the power to rule, and no one rules now without that power from God. [2]So those who are against the government are really against what God has commanded. And they will bring punishment on themselves. [3]Those who do right do not have to fear the rulers; only those who do wrong fear them. Do you want to be unafraid of the rulers? Then do what is right, and they will praise you. [4]The ruler is God's servant to help you. But if you do wrong, then be afraid. He has the power to punish; he is God's servant to punish those who do wrong. [5]So you must yield to the government, not only because you might be punished, but because you know it is right.

[6]This is also why you pay taxes. Rulers are working for God and give their time to their work. [7]Pay everyone, then, what you owe. If you owe any kind of tax, pay it. Show respect and honor to them all.

### LOVING OTHERS

[8]Do not owe people anything, except always owe love to each other, because the person who loves others has obeyed all the law. [9]The law says, "You must not be guilty of adultery. You must not murder anyone. You must not steal. You must not want to take your neighbor's things."[n] All these commands and all others are really only one rule: "Love your neighbor as you love yourself."[n] [10]Love never hurts a neighbor, so loving is obeying all the law.

[11]Do this because we live in an important time. It is now time for you to wake up from your sleep, because our salvation is nearer now

RadicalFaith:

## Romans 12:1-2

What do worship and sacrifice mean to you? You worship God not because an adult makes you or because it's the right thing to be seen doing. You do it because God has given you abundant life. He totally embraces you as a flawed, hopeless, and rejected mistake-maker. And he offers his presence, beauty, and purity to fix places in you that are empty, dark, broken, damaged, and desperate. This is mercy. In your shock and outrageous gratitude, you want to do anything God says. By offering a sacrifice to God, you are showing that you have an attitude and a willingness to do whatever it takes to obey him. Being a walking sacrifice means daily shedding your desires and going after God's desires. Spend time with him so you can understand what he's like and what he wants for your life. God wants you to look and think like him—and not like the world—because that's the best possible way to live. He'll reshape everything inside you so that you become more like him, but you have to let him in and give him the control.

### GUYS SPEAK OUT

**Q:** What do you worry about the most?
**A:** "I worry the most about what other people think about me, and also about what I am going to do with my life."

notes    **12:19** "I . . . them" Quotation from Deuteronomy 32:35.    **13:9** "You . . . things." Quotation from Exodus 20:13-15, 17.    **13:9** "Love . . . yourself." Quotation from Leviticus 19:18.

217

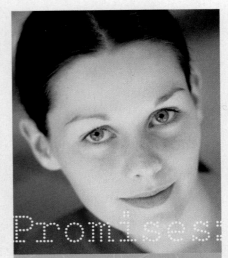

## Romans 12:3-8

Take a good look at your hands. Have you ever stopped to think about what all they do for you? What about your feet? You would be able to do a lot less without hands and feet, wouldn't you? Your teeth chew your food. Your heart keeps blood flowing. Your nose allows you to breathe. Your spine helps you stand tall. All the parts of your body do amazing things, and each part's function is crucial to the rest of the body. Take one part away and the whole body suffers.

The same concept applies to the body of Christ (a.k.a. the church). You may think that because you can't speak in front of people or sing that you don't have much to contribute to the body. But that is absolutely not true! God has given you a special gift that is unique and one that fulfills a great purpose in the body. Maybe you love children and can teach toddlers about Christ's love. Or you may be good at greeting new people and can make them feel welcome when they come to youth group. Stop and ask yourself what you're really passionate about. Pray about how you can use your specific gifts to serve and just do it! The body needs you!

than when we first believed. 12The "night"[n] is almost finished, and the "day"[n] is almost here. So we should stop doing things that belong to darkness and take up the weapons used for fighting in the light. 13Let us live in a right way, like people who belong to the day. We should not have wild parties or get drunk. There should be no sexual sins of any kind, no fighting or jealousy. 14But clothe yourselves with the Lord Jesus Christ and forget about satisfying your sinful self.

## DO NOT CRITICIZE OTHER PEOPLE

14 Accept into your group someone who is weak in faith, and do not argue about opinions. 2One person believes it is right to eat all kinds of food.[n] But another, who is weak, believes it is right to eat only vegetables. 3The one who knows that it is right to eat any kind of food must not reject the one who eats only vegetables. And the person who eats only vegetables must not think that the one who eats all foods is wrong, because God has accepted that person. 4You cannot judge another person's servant. The master decides if the servant is doing well or not. And the Lord's servant will do well because the Lord helps him do well.

5Some think that one day is more important than another, and others think that every day is the same. Let all be sure in their own mind. 6Those who think one day is more important than other days are doing that for the Lord. And those who eat all kinds of food are doing that for the Lord, and they give thanks to God. Others who refuse to eat some foods do that for the Lord, and they give thanks to God. 7We do not live or die for ourselves. 8If we live, we are living for the Lord, and if we die, we are dying for the Lord. So living or dying, we belong to the Lord.

9The reason Christ died and rose from the dead to live again was so he would be Lord over both the dead and the living. 10So why do you judge your brothers or sisters in Christ? And why do you think you are better than they are? We will all stand before God to be judged, 11because it is written in the Scriptures:

"'As surely as I live,' says the Lord,
'Everyone will bow before me;
everyone will say that I am God.'"

*Isaiah 45:23*

12So each of us will have to answer to God.

## DO NOT CAUSE OTHERS TO SIN

13For that reason we should stop judging each other. We must make up our minds not to do anything that will make another Christian sin. 14I am in the Lord Jesus, and I know that there is no food that is wrong to eat. But if a person believes something is wrong, that thing is wrong for him. 15If you hurt your brother's or sister's faith because of something you eat, you are not really following the way of love. Do not destroy someone's faith by eating food he thinks is wrong, because Christ died for him. 16Do not allow what you think is good to become what others say is evil. 17In the kingdom of God, eating and drinking are not important. The important things are living right with God, peace, and joy in the Holy Spirit. 18Anyone who serves Christ by living this way is pleasing God and will be accepted by other people.

19So let us try to do what makes peace and helps one another. 20Do not let the eating of food destroy the work of God. All foods are all right to eat, but it is wrong to eat food that causes someone else to sin. 21It is better not to eat meat or drink wine or do anything that will cause your brother or sister to sin.

22Your beliefs about these things should be kept secret between you and God. People are happy if they can do what they think is right

**13:12 "night"** This is used as a symbol of the sinful world we live in. This world will soon end.  **13:12 "day"** This is used as a symbol of the good time that is coming, when we will be with God.  **14:2 all . . . food** The Jewish law said there were some foods Jews should not eat. When Jews became Christians, some of them did not understand they could now eat all foods.

without feeling guilty. ²³But those who eat something without being sure it is right are wrong because they did not believe it was right. Anything that is done without believing it is right is a sin.

**15** We who are strong in faith should help the weak with their weaknesses, and not please only ourselves. ²Let each of us please our neighbors for their good, to help them be stronger in faith. ³Even Christ did not live to please himself. It was as the Scriptures said: "When people insult you, it hurts me."ⁿ ⁴Everything that was written in the past was written to teach us. The Scriptures give us patience and encouragement so that we can have hope. ⁵Patience and encouragement come from God. And I pray that God will help you all agree with each other the way Christ Jesus wants. ⁶Then you will all be joined together, and you will give glory to God the Father of our Lord Jesus Christ. ⁷Christ accepted you, so you should accept each other, which will bring glory to God. ⁸I tell you that Christ became a servant of the Jews to show that God's promises to the Jewish ancestors are true. ⁹And he also did this so that those who are not Jews could give glory to God for the mercy he gives to them. It is written in the Scriptures:

"So I will praise you among the non-Jewish people.

I will sing praises to your name."

*Psalm 18:49*

¹⁰The Scripture also says,

"Be happy, you who are not Jews, together with his people." *Deuteronomy 32:43*

¹¹Again the Scripture says,

"All you who are not Jews, praise the Lord.

All you people, sing praises to him."

*Psalm 117:1*

¹²And Isaiah says,

"A new king will come from the family of Jesse.ⁿ

He will come to rule over the non-Jewish people,

and they will have hope because of him."

*Isaiah 11:10*

## Bible Basics

What is **sin**? Well, literally it is "a word, thought, or act against the law of God." Sin sounds like it would be obviously bad, but it can actually be a lot of fun—at first. The problem with sin is that it is only fun until the consequences of your actions come back to haunt you big time. Sin separates you from being close to God and from being able to hear his voice. It is anything that you do that God has said not to do, but it is also anything you don't do that you know God wants you to do. What sin can do is masquerade as a good time, while actually destroying your life. So not cool! Just a few sins worth mentioning: gossiping, lying, and disobeying authority. The awesome thing is that God will forgive us for our sins—every time—if we ask him to.

¹³I pray that the God who gives hope will fill you with much joy and peace while you trust in him. Then your hope will overflow by the power of the Holy Spirit.

> **"A NEW KING WILL COME FROM THE FAMILY OF JESSE. HE WILL COME TO RULE OVER THE NON-JEWISH PEOPLE, AND THEY WILL HAVE HOPE BECAUSE OF HIM."**

### PAUL TALKS ABOUT HIS WORK

¹⁴My brothers and sisters, I am sure that you are full of goodness. I know that you have all the knowledge you need and that you are able to teach each other. ¹⁵But I have written to you very openly about some things I wanted you to remember. I did this because God gave me this special gift: ¹⁶to be a minister of Christ Jesus to those who are not Jews. I served God by teaching his Good News, so that the non-Jewish people could be an offering that God would accept—an offering made holy by the Holy Spirit.

¹⁷So I am proud of what I have done for God in Christ Jesus. ¹⁸I will not talk about anything except what Christ has done through me in leading those who are not Jews to obey God. They have obeyed God because of what I have said and done, ¹⁹because of the power of miracles and the great things they saw, and because of the power of the Holy Spirit. I preached the Good News from Jerusalem all the way around to Illyricum, and so I have finished that part of my work. ²⁰I always want to preach the Good News in places where people have never heard of Christ, because I do not want to build on the work someone else has already started. ²¹But it is written in the Scriptures:

"Those who were not told about him will see,

and those who have not heard about him will understand." *Isaiah 52:15*

### PAUL'S PLAN TO VISIT ROME

²²This is the reason I was stopped many times from coming to you. ²³Now I have finished my work here. Since for many years I have wanted to come to you, ²⁴I hope to visit you on my way to Spain. After I enjoy being

**notes** 15:3 "When . . . me." Quotation from Psalm 69:9. 15:12 **Jesse** Jesse was the father of David, king of Israel. Jesus was from their family.

219

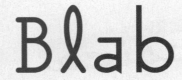

**Q:** I feel like I am a different person around different people. Sometimes I'm a prep. Other times I feel punk. Am I just a fake?

**A:** You are at an age where you are discovering your identity and developing your talents and skills. It is natural to want to "try on" different styles, but try not to adopt different attitudes. Be loving and kind, and ask God to help you find the perfect fit for you.

**Q:** My breasts have grown really big over the last year, and they are embarrassing. Is there anything I can do?

**A:** Go to a lingerie store where the professional ladies there can help you choose bras that fit correctly and help you feel comfortable. It might be embarrassing, but the right bras can help a lot. Ask God to help you accept your body's changes and to show you how beautiful he thinks you are. If they are so large that they cause your back to hurt, ask your mom about discussing their size with a doctor.

**Q:** I never used to have hair "down there," and I hate it. It's ugly, and it bothers me. Is it all right to shave?

**A:** Talk to your mom about it, and be careful if you decide to take off some of the hair around your bikini line. You can develop severe razor burn that is itchy and uncomfortable (and far worse than a little hair) or you may cut yourself. Pray that God will help you feel comfortable with the way your body is changing. He will.

with you for a while, I hope you can help me on my trip. ²⁵Now I am going to Jerusalem to help God's people. ²⁶The believers in Macedonia and Southern Greece were happy to give their money to help the poor among God's people at Jerusalem. ²⁷They were happy to do this, and really they owe it to them. These who are not Jews have shared in the Jews' spiritual blessings, so they should use their material possessions to help the Jews. ²⁸After I am sure the poor in Jerusalem get the money that has been given for them, I will leave for Spain and stop and visit you. ²⁹I know that when I come to you I will bring Christ's full blessing.

³⁰Brothers and sisters, I beg you to help me in my work by praying to God for me. Do this because of our Lord Jesus and the love that the Holy Spirit gives us. ³¹Pray that I will be saved from the nonbelievers in Judea and that this help I bring to Jerusalem will please God's people there. ³²Then, if God wants me to, I will come to you with joy, and together you and I will have a time of rest. ³³The God who gives peace be with you all. Amen.

## GREETINGS TO THE CHRISTIANS

**16** I recommend to you our sister Phoebe, who is a helper" in the church in Cenchrea. ²I ask you to accept her in the Lord in the way God's people should. Help her with anything she needs, because she has helped me and many other people also.

³Give my greetings to Priscilla and Aquila, who work together with me in Christ Jesus ⁴and who risked their own lives to save my life. I am thankful to them, and all the non-Jewish churches are thankful as well. ⁵Also, greet for me the church that meets at their house.

Greetings to my dear friend Epenetus, who was the first person in the country of Asia to follow Christ. ⁶Greetings to Mary, who worked very hard for you. ⁷Greetings to Andronicus and Junia, my relatives, who were in prison with me. They are very important apostles. They were believers in Christ before I was. ⁸Greetings to Ampliatus, my dear friend in the Lord. ⁹Greetings to Urbanus, a worker

together with me for Christ. And greetings to my dear friend Stachys. ¹⁰Greetings to Apelles, who was tested and proved that he truly loves Christ. Greetings to all those who are in the family of Aristobulus. ¹¹Greetings to Herodion, my fellow citizen. Greetings to all those in the family of Narcissus who belong to the Lord. ¹²Greetings to Tryphena and Tryphosa, women who work very hard for the Lord. Greetings to my dear friend Persis, who also has worked very hard for the Lord. ¹³Greetings to Rufus, who is a special person in the Lord, and to his mother, who has been like a mother to me also. ¹⁴Greetings to Asyncritus, Phlegon, Hermes, Patrobas, Hermas, and all the brothers who are with them. ¹⁵Greetings to Philologus and Julia, Nereus and his sister, and Olympas, and to all God's people with them. ¹⁶Greet each other with a holy kiss. All of Christ's churches send greetings to you.

¹⁷Brothers and sisters, I ask you to look out for those who cause people to be against each other and who upset other people's faith. They are against the true teaching you learned, so stay away from them. ¹⁸Such people are not serving our Lord Christ but are only doing what pleases themselves. They use fancy talk and fine words to fool the minds of those who do not know about evil. ¹⁹All the believers have

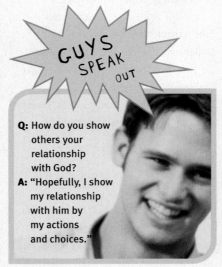

GUYS SPEAK OUT

**Q:** How do you show others your relationship with God?
**A:** "Hopefully, I show my relationship with him by my actions and choices."

**16:1 helper** Literally, "deaconess." This might mean the same as one of the special women helpers in 1 Timothy 3:11.

# LEARN I+ & LIVE I+

**Romans 13:2**
**Learn It:** Christians should respect their government.
**Live It:** Pray for the president, Congress, and the Supreme Court each day.

**Romans 14:13**
**Learn It:** You shouldn't do something that might make someone else sin.
**Live It:** If you are with someone who is tempted to eat too much, stay away from buffets. If your friend is tempted to take a drink at a party, talk your friend out of going to the party.

**Romans 15:1**
**Learn It:** The strong in faith should help the weak.
**Live It:** Start a Bible study and invite some new believers. Mentor them in the faith.

heard that you obey, so I am very happy because of you. But I want you to be wise in what is good and innocent in what is evil.

[20]The God who brings peace will soon defeat Satan and give you power over him.

The grace of our Lord Jesus be with you.

[21]Timothy, a worker together with me, sends greetings, as well as Lucius, Jason, and Sosipater, my relatives.

[22]I am Tertius, and I am writing this letter from Paul. I send greetings to you in the Lord.

[23]Gaius is letting me and the whole church here use his home. He also sends greetings to you, as do Erastus, the city treasurer, and our brother Quartus. [24n]

[25]Glory to God who can make you strong in faith by the Good News that I tell people and by the message about Jesus Christ. The message about Christ is the secret that was hidden for long ages past but is now made known. [26]It has been made clear through the writings of the prophets. And by the command of the eternal God it is made known to all nations that they might believe and obey.

[27]To the only wise God be glory forever through Jesus Christ! Amen.

**16:24 Verse 24** Some Greek copies add verse 24: "The grace of our Lord Jesus Christ be with all of you. Amen."

# *t*his letter from Paul to the believers

in Corinth was in response to a cry for help from church leaders there. It seems that even though Paul had stayed in Corinth for nearly two years, teaching believers there about key Christian beliefs, it only took them about

# 1 Corinthians
## Loving Correction for Immature Believers

the same amount of time to forget all they had learned and go back to their sinful ways. This troubled church was dealing with divisiveness among its members in the form of frivolous lawsuits, sexual immorality, corrupt leaders, idol worship, and drunkenness, to name a few. But their main sin was that they were unwilling to set themselves apart from the unbelievers around them.

So Paul, with all the patience he can muster, lovingly corrects this immature group of believers. Using the human body as his model, he describes how each member of the church should be working together in unity. And in chapter 13, he gives one of the most quoted passages in the Bible (especially at weddings) that tells how everything we say and do should be motivated by love. It's something that Paul just doesn't talk about, but something he tries to live through his actions and his letters.

223

# Blab

**Q:** I discovered that if I touch myself "down there," it feels really good. I want to know—is masturbating okay? I don't fantasize, and it keeps me from wanting to go too far with my boyfriend.

**A:** The Bible doesn't speak directly about masturbating, but it says a lot about keeping your thoughts and actions pure. Sex was designed for two people—a man and a woman—within the bounds of marriage. Pleasuring yourself doesn't fulfill that design and can lead you down the dangerous road of fantasizing, pornography, or wanting to try the real thing before marriage.

**Q:** My guy's parents are going to be gone this weekend, and he wants me to spend the night. He says we won't go all the way; he just wants to be with me and cuddle together. I don't want to let him down, and I really want to be with him. What do I do?

**A:** Stay home where you belong. Spending the night with him is playing with fire sexually and robbing your future husband of being the first guy you spend the night with. It would also involve lying to your parents and deceiving his, which is an all-around bad deal. Tell him "no."

**Q:** I am 16, and I have slept with five guys. I am a Christian, but every time a guy wants to have sex, it feels so good to be liked and wanted that I just do it. How can I stop?

**A:** Do not put yourself in any situation where you are alone with any guy. Go out with girlfriends or in groups. Ask God to forgive you and help you remain sexually pure from now on. Read the Bible verses that deal with sexual sin, and beg God for self-control.

1 From Paul. God called me to be an apostle of Christ Jesus because that is what God wanted. Also from Sosthenes, our brother in Christ.

²To the church of God in Corinth, to you who have been made holy in Christ Jesus. You were called to be God's holy people with all people everywhere who pray in the name of the Lord Jesus Christ—their Lord and ours:

³Grace and peace to you from God our Father and the Lord Jesus Christ.

## PAUL GIVES THANKS TO GOD

⁴I always thank my God for you because of the grace God has given you in Christ Jesus. ⁵I thank God because in Christ you have been made rich in every way, in all your speaking and in all your knowledge. ⁶Just as our witness about Christ has been guaranteed to you, ⁷so you have every gift from God while you wait for our Lord Jesus Christ to come again. ⁸Jesus will keep you strong until the end so that there will be no wrong in you on the day our Lord Jesus Christ comes again. ⁹God, who has called you to share everything with his Son, Jesus Christ our Lord, is faithful.

## PROBLEMS IN THE CHURCH

¹⁰I beg you, brothers and sisters,ⁿ by the name of our Lord Jesus Christ that all of you agree with each other and not be split into groups. I beg that you be completely joined together by having the same kind of thinking and the same purpose. ¹¹My brothers and sisters, some people from Chloe's family have told me quite plainly that there are quarrels among you. ¹²This is what I mean: One of you says, "I follow Paul"; another says, "I follow Apollos"; another says, "I follow Peter"; and another says, "I follow Christ." ¹³Christ has been divided up into different groups! Did Paul die on the cross for you? No! Were you baptized in the name of Paul? No! ¹⁴I thank God I did not baptize any of you except Crispus and Gaius ¹⁵so that now no one can say you were baptized in my name. ¹⁶(I also baptized the family of Stephanas, but I do not remember that I

baptized anyone else.) ¹⁷Christ did not send me to baptize people but to preach the Good News. And he sent me to preach the Good News without using words of human wisdom so that the crossⁿ of Christ would not lose its power.

# "GOD HAS MADE THE WISDOM OF THE WORLD FOOLISH."

## CHRIST IS GOD'S POWER AND WISDOM

¹⁸The teaching about the cross is foolishness to those who are being lost, but to us who

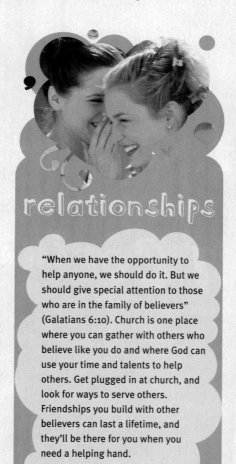

## relationships

"When we have the opportunity to help anyone, we should do it. But we should give special attention to those who are in the family of believers" (Galatians 6:10). Church is one place where you can gather with others who believe like you do and where God can use your time and talents to help others. Get plugged in at church, and look for ways to serve others. Friendships you build with other believers can last a lifetime, and they'll be there for you when you need a helping hand.

**notes** **1:10 brothers and sisters** Although the Greek text says "brothers" here and throughout this book, Paul's words were meant for the entire church, including men and women. **1:17 cross** Paul uses the cross as a picture of the Good News, the story of Christ's death and rising from the dead for people's sins. The cross, or Christ's death, was God's way to save people.

are being saved it is the power of God. ¹⁹It is written in the Scriptures:

"I will cause the wise men to lose their
    wisdom;
  I will make the wise men unable to
    understand."                      *Isaiah 29:14*

²⁰Where is the wise person? Where is the educated person? Where is the skilled talker of this world? God has made the wisdom of the world foolish. ²¹In the wisdom of God the world did not know God through its own wisdom. So God chose to use the message that sounds foolish to save those who believe. ²²The Jews ask for miracles, and the Greeks want wisdom. ²³But we preach a crucified Christ. This is a big problem to the Jews, and it is foolishness to those who are not Jews. ²⁴But Christ is the power of God and the wisdom of God to those people God has called—Jews and Greeks. ²⁵Even the foolishness of God is wiser than human wisdom, and the weakness of God is stronger than human strength.

²⁶Brothers and sisters, look at what you were when God called you. Not many of you were wise in the way the world judges wisdom. Not many of you had great influence. Not many of you came from important families. ²⁷But God chose the foolish things of the world to shame the wise, and he chose the weak things of the world to shame the strong. ²⁸He chose what the world thinks is unimportant and what the world looks down on and thinks is nothing in order to destroy what the world thinks is important. ²⁹God did this so that no one can brag in his presence. ³⁰Because of God you are in Christ Jesus, who has become for us wisdom from God. In Christ we are put right with God, and have been made holy, and have been set free from sin. ³¹So, as the Scripture says, "If someone wants to brag, he should brag only about the Lord."*ⁿ*

## THE MESSAGE OF CHRIST'S DEATH

**2** Dear brothers and sisters, when I came to you, I did not come preaching God's secret with fancy words or a show of human wisdom. ²I decided that while I was with you I would forget about everything except Jesus Christ and his death on the cross. ³So when I came to you, I was weak and fearful and trembling. ⁴My teaching and preaching were not with words of human wisdom that persuade people but with proof of the power that the Spirit gives. ⁵This was so that your faith would be in God's power and not in human wisdom.

### GOD'S WISDOM

⁶However, I speak a wisdom to those who are mature. But this wisdom is not from this world or from the rulers of this world, who are losing their power. ⁷I speak God's secret wisdom, which he has kept hidden. Before the world began, God planned this wisdom for our glory. ⁸None of the rulers of this world understood it. If they had, they would not have crucified the Lord of glory. ⁹But as it is written in the Scriptures:

"No one has ever seen this,
  and no one has ever heard about it.
No one has ever imagined
    what God has prepared for those
      who love him."            *Isaiah 64:4*

¹⁰But God has shown us these things through the Spirit.

## "NO ONE HAS EVER IMAGINED WHAT GOD HAS PREPARED FOR THOSE WHO LOVE HIM."

The Spirit searches out all things, even the deep secrets of God. ¹¹Who knows the thoughts that another person has? Only a person's spirit that lives within him knows his thoughts. It is the same with God. No one knows the thoughts of God except the Spirit of God. ¹²Now we did not receive the spirit of the world, but we received the Spirit that is from God so that we can know all that God has given us. ¹³And we speak about these things, not with words taught us by human wisdom but with words taught us by the Spirit. And so we explain spiritual truths to spiritual people. ¹⁴A person who

## Promises!

# 1 Corinthians 2:9

What is the most beautiful place in the world that you can think of? Maybe you're thinking of a spectacular tropical beach with crystal blue water and palm trees. Or maybe the first thing that comes to mind is a majestic, snow-covered mountain range under a clear blue sky. You could be thinking of a beautiful countryside with rolling green hills and ponds and lakes. Isn't God's creation amazing? There are so many unique, exquisite places on earth that put us in awe of God's creativity.

If he has given us such amazing places on earth, what must heaven be like? It's fun to imagine what God has in store for us there. He promises that it will be an amazing place for those who accept his salvation. Perhaps it will be like a beautiful resort area. Or it could be the craziest, most topsy-turvy, sky-painted-orange kind of place like nothing we have ever before experienced on earth.

Either way, once we get to heaven we will be amazed and able to stand in the presence of the God of the universe. It will be breathtaking!

**notes** 1:31 "If . . . Lord." Quotation from Jeremiah 9:24.

# Radical Faith:

## 1 Corinthians 2:12-14

Does it surprise you when you realize how different you are from nonbelievers around you? Following God sets you on a way different track from that of the majority. They can't get it, so don't even expect them to. You have the Spirit of God in you, not the spirit of the world, so your perspective, value system, and information source are totally different from those of nonbelievers. It's like you've been given earphones to listen to God's voice, while other people don't have the hookup. They're just kind of wandering and searching. They've got no vertical communication going on. What they live by is the distorted and deadening view of the spirit of the world. So they may not respond to things with insight from God like you will. When they rip on you or become weird and distant because you're making choices that glorify God, don't be surprised. Let it be, and continue in your way with God. Pray for them, and pray that God would bring into your life people who know him and can encourage you in your journey. If you're feeling alone, be patient. Stay strong. God is faithful.

does not have the Spirit does not accept the truths that come from the Spirit of God. That person thinks they are foolish and cannot understand them, because they can only be judged to be true by the Spirit. [15]The spiritual person is able to judge all things, but no one can judge him. The Scripture says:

[16]"Who has known the mind of the Lord?
    Who has been able to teach him?"

*Isaiah 40:13*

But we have the mind of Christ.

## FOLLOWING PEOPLE IS WRONG

3 Brothers and sisters, in the past I could not talk to you as I talk to spiritual people. I had to talk to you as I would to people without the Spirit—babies in Christ. [2]The teaching I gave you was like milk, not solid food, because you were not able to take solid food. And even now you are not ready. [3]You are still not spiritual, because there is jealousy and quarreling among you, and this shows that you are not spiritual. You are acting like people of the world. [4]One of you says, "I belong to Paul," and another says, "I belong to Apollos." When you say things like this, you are acting like people of the world.

[5]Is Apollos important? No! Is Paul important? No! We are only servants of God who helped you believe. Each one of us did the work God gave us to do. [6]I planted the seed, and Apollos watered it. But God is the One who made it grow. [7]So the one who plants is not important, and the one who waters is not important. Only God, who makes things grow, is important. [8]The one who plants and the one who waters have the same purpose, and each will be rewarded for his own work. [9]We are God's workers, working together; you are like God's farm, God's house.

[10]Using the gift God gave me, I laid the foundation of that house like an expert builder. Others are building on that foundation, but all people should be careful how they build on it. [11]The foundation that has already been laid is Jesus Christ, and no one can lay down any other foundation. [12]But if people

build on that foundation, using gold, silver, jewels, wood, grass, or straw, [13]their work will be clearly seen, because the Day of Judgment[n] will make it visible. That Day will appear with fire, and the fire will test everyone's work to show what sort of work it was. [14]If the building that has been put on the foundation still stands, the builder will get a reward. [15]But if the building is burned up, the builder will suffer loss. The builder will be saved, but it will be as one who escaped from a fire.

# "DON'T YOU KNOW THAT YOU ARE GOD'S TEMPLE AND THAT GOD'S SPIRIT LIVES IN YOU?"

[16]Don't you know that you are God's temple and that God's Spirit lives in you? [17]If anyone destroys God's temple, God will destroy that person, because God's temple is holy and you are that temple.

[18]Do not fool yourselves. If you think you are wise in this world, you should become a fool so that you can become truly wise, [19]because the wisdom of this world is foolishness with God. It is written in the Scriptures, "He catches those who are wise in their own clever traps."[n] [20]It is also written in the Scriptures, "The Lord knows what wise people think. He knows their thoughts are just a puff of wind."[n] [21]So you should not brag about human leaders. All things belong to you: [22]Paul, Apollos, and Peter; the world, life, death, the present, and the future—all these belong to you. [23]And you belong to Christ, and Christ belongs to God.

## APOSTLES ARE SERVANTS OF CHRIST

4 People should think of us as servants of Christ, the ones God has trusted with his secrets. [2]Now in this way those who are trusted with something valuable must show they are worthy of that trust. [3]As for myself, I

**3:13 Day of Judgment** The day Christ will come to judge all people and take his people home to live with him. **3:19 "He . . . traps."** Quotation from Job 5:13. **3:20 "The Lord . . . wind."** Quotation from Psalm 94:11.

226

# Music Reviews

| GROUP: | ALBUM: |
|---|---|
| DC TALK | JESUS FREAK [CLASSIC HIT] |

Toby McKeehan (tobyMac), Michael Tait (Tait), and Kevin Max (KMax) changed the course of contemporary Christian music when they gained a Dove Award (Christian music's equivalent of the Grammy®) for Artist of the Year and best Rock Recorded Song for this disc in 1996. *Jesus Freak* mixed elements of grunge, metal, pop, and rap into a blend of modern music that still stands the test of time. Other hits include the trio's heavenly harmonies on the slow songs "Colored People" and "Between You and Me."

WHY IT ROCKS: TOBYMAC'S ENERGETIC RAPS MATCHED WITH LUSCIOUS VOCALS FROM KMAX AND TAIT MAKE FOR A MELTING POT OF GREAT MUSIC.

do not care if I am judged by you or by any human court. I do not even judge myself. ⁴I know of no wrong I have done, but this does not make me right before the Lord. The Lord is the One who judges me. ⁵So do not judge before the right time; wait until the Lord comes. He will bring to light things that are now hidden in darkness, and will make known the secret purposes of people's hearts. Then God will praise each one of them.

⁶Brothers and sisters, I have used Apollos and myself as examples so you could learn through us the meaning of the saying, "Follow only what is written in the Scriptures." Then you will not be more proud of one person than another. ⁷Who says you are better than others? What do you have that was not given to you? And if it was given to you, why do you brag as if you did not receive it as a gift?

⁸You think you already have everything you need. You think you are rich. You think you have become kings without us. I wish you really were kings so we could be kings together with you. ⁹But it seems to me that God has put us apostles in last place, like those sentenced to die. We are like a show for the whole world to see—angels and people. ¹⁰We are fools for Christ's sake, but you are very wise in Christ. We are weak, but you are strong. You receive honor, but we are shamed. ¹¹Even to this very hour we do not have enough to eat or drink or to wear. We are often beaten, and we have no homes in which to live. ¹²We work hard with our own hands for our food. When people curse us, we bless them. When they hurt us, we put up with it. ¹³When they tell evil lies about us, we speak nice words about them. Even today, we are treated as though we were the garbage of the world—the filth of the earth.

# LEARN IT & LIVE IT

### 1 Corinthians 1:27-28
**Learn It:** God uses the least important to do the most important work.
**Live It:** Believe that God can use you in a mighty way, even if you feel young, weak, or unpopular. He will!

### 1 Corinthians 3:2
**Learn It:** Paul said the Corinthians were still acting like baby Christians and needed to mature.
**Live It:** Determine to grow in your faith by starting a daily quiet time of prayer and Bible study.

### 1 Corinthians 4:5
**Learn It:** Do not judge people. God will bring hidden things to light and reveal secrets. Then he will praise them.
**Live It:** Be careful not to misjudge someone's motives because of what you see on the surface. Trust that they are doing the right thing, and remember that God will take care of it if they are not.

# Quiz

# WHAT'S YOUR STUDY STYLE?

**1. YOUR YOUTH GROUP WANTS TO START A NEW BIBLE STUDY. THERE ARE SEVERAL WAYS TO DO THE STUDY AND YOU PREFER TO:**

A. Watch the video sessions.
B. Use the discussion questions.
C. Utilize the workbook.
D. Read the book and answer the study questions.

**2. YOU AND THREE FRIENDS ARE RESPONSIBLE FOR A GROUP PROJECT AT SCHOOL. YOU VOLUNTEER TO BE IN CHARGE OF THE:**

A. Visual aids.
B. Presentation.
C. Research.
D. Outline.

**3. THERE'S A BIG TEST COMING UP. TO PREPARE, YOU:**

A. Make flashcards from the information.
B. Attend group study sessions offered by the teacher.
C. Reread your notes several times.
D. Find a friend and go over the material out loud.

**4. YOU AND A FRIEND HAVE A GOAL TO MEMORIZE THREE BIBLE VERSES THIS MONTH. HOW DO YOU DO IT?**

A. Make a game out of it and recite the verses back and forth to each other.
B. Recite the verses to yourself every night three times.
C. Write the verses on note cards and put them on your bathroom mirror.
D. Make up songs with the verses to help you remember them.

**5. YOUR TEACHER ASSIGNS YOU A BOOK REPORT AND ALLOWS YOU TO CHOOSE THE FORMAT IN WHICH TO PRESENT IT. YOU CHOOSE TO GIVE YOUR REPORT IN THE FORM OF:**

A. A paper.
B. A verbal presentation to the class.
C. A skit.
D. An art project.

**SCORING:**   1. A=3, B=4, C=2, D=1   2. A=3, B=4, C=1, D=2   3. A=2, B=3, C=1, D=4   4. A=3, B=1, C=2, D=4   5. A=1, B=3, C=4, D=2

**IF YOU SCORED 15-20, YOUR STUDY STYLE IS INTERACTIVE:**
You work best when you are actively doing something to help you learn. We're not likely to see you in a library any time soon.

**IF YOU SCORED 9-14, YOUR STUDY STYLE IS MIX-IT-UP:**
You are comfortable working alone or in groups, depending on the nature of the project at hand. Sometimes you like to study alone, and other times you like to do something verbal or visual to improve your skills.

**IF YOU SCORED 5-8, YOUR STUDY STYLE IS LONER:**
Preferring to work alone, group projects probably make you crazy. You are at your best working alone and hitting the books in the library or in a quiet coffee shop.

[14]I am not trying to make you feel ashamed. I am writing this to give you a warning as my own dear children. [15]For though you may have ten thousand teachers in Christ, you do not

**YOUTH WHO START DRINKING BEFORE AGE 15 ARE FOUR TIMES MORE LIKELY TO DEVELOP ALCOHOLISM AT SOME POINT IN THEIR LIVES.**

NATIONAL INSTITUTE ON ALCOHOL ABUSE AND ALCOHOLISM

have many fathers. Through the Good News I became your father in Christ Jesus, [16]so I beg you, please follow my example. [17]That is why I am sending to you Timothy, my son in the Lord. I love Timothy, and he is faithful. He will help you remember my way of life in Christ Jesus, just as I teach it in all the churches everywhere.

**"SOME OF YOU HAVE BECOME PROUD, THINKING THAT I WILL NOT COME TO YOU AGAIN. BUT I WILL COME TO YOU VERY SOON IF THE LORD WISHES."**

[18]Some of you have become proud, thinking that I will not come to you again. [19]But I will come to you very soon if the Lord wishes. Then I will know what the proud ones do, not what they say, [20]because the kingdom of God is present not in talk but in power. [21]Which do you want: that I come to you with punishment or with love and gentleness?

### WICKEDNESS IN THE CHURCH

5 It is actually being said that there is sexual sin among you. And it is a kind that does not happen even among people who do not know God. A man there has his father's wife. [2]And you are proud! You should have been filled with sadness so that the man who did this should be put out of your group. [3]I am not there with you in person, but I am with you in spirit. And I have already judged the man who did that sin as if I were really there. [4]When you meet together in the name of our Lord Jesus, and I meet with you in spirit with the power of our Lord Jesus, [5]then hand this man over to Satan. So his sinful self[n] will be destroyed, and his spirit will be saved on the day of the Lord.

[6]Your bragging is not good. You know the saying, "Just a little yeast makes the whole batch of dough rise." [7]Take out all the old yeast so that you will be a new batch of dough without yeast, which you really are. For Christ, our Passover lamb, has been sacrificed. [8]So let us celebrate this feast, but not with the bread that has the old yeast—the yeast of sin and wickedness. Let us celebrate this feast with the bread that has no yeast—the bread of goodness and truth.

[9]I wrote you in my earlier letter not to associate with those who sin sexually. [10]But I did not mean you should not associate with those of this world who sin sexually, or with the greedy, or robbers, or those who worship idols. To get away from them you would have to leave this world. [11]I am writing to tell you that you must not associate with those who call themselves believers in Christ but who sin sexually, or are greedy, or worship idols, or abuse others with words, or get drunk, or cheat people. Do not even eat with people like that.

[12-13]It is not my business to judge those who are not part of the church. God will judge them. But you must judge the people who are part of the church. The Scripture says, "You must get rid of the evil person among you."[n]

# top10
## great fiction reads for fun

**10** True Colors series by Melody Carlson

**9** Sierra Jensen Series by Robin Jones Gunn

**8** *This Present Darkness* and *Piercing the Darkness* by Frank Peretti

**7** Degrees of Guilt series by Melody Carlson, Sigmund Brouwer, and Dandi Daley Mackall

**6** The Veritas Project series by Frank Peretti

**5** Newpointe 911 series by Terri Blackstock

**4** *The Princess* by Lori Wick

**3** Love Comes Softly Series by Janette Oke

**2** Diary of a Teenage Girl series by Melody Carlson

**1** The Christy Miller Series by Robin Jones Gunn

**5:5 sinful self** Literally, "flesh." This could also mean his body. **5:12-13 "You . . . you."** Quotation from Deuteronomy 17:7; 19:19; 22:21, 24; 24:7.

## JUDGING PROBLEMS AMONG CHRISTIANS

6 When you have something against another Christian, how can you bring yourself to go before judges who are not right with God? Why do you not let God's people decide who is right? ²Surely you know that God's people will judge the world. So if you are to judge the world, are you not able to judge small cases as well? ³You know that in the future we will judge angels, so surely we can judge the ordinary things of this life. ⁴If you have ordinary cases that must be judged, are you going to appoint people as judges who mean nothing to the church? ⁵I say this to shame you. Surely there is someone among you wise enough to judge a complaint between believers. ⁶But now one believer goes to court against another believer—and you do this in front of unbelievers!

## beauty secret

### Lovely Lips

Have you ever accidentally bought the wrong color of lipstick? No worries. Just try mixing it with different shades of lipstick. You just might discover a new, unique color that works for you. Remember that it's not just what you put on your lips that makes you beautiful. It's also what comes out of them.

⁷The fact that you have lawsuits against each other shows that you are already defeated. Why not let yourselves be wronged? Why not let yourselves be cheated? ⁸But you yourselves do wrong and cheat, and you do this to other believers!

⁹⁻¹⁰Surely you know that the people who do wrong will not inherit God's kingdom. Do not be fooled. Those who sin sexually, worship idols, take part in adultery, those who are male prostitutes, or men who have sexual relations with other men, those who steal, are greedy, get drunk, lie about others, or rob—these people will not inherit God's kingdom. ¹¹In the past, some of you were like that, but you were washed clean. You were made holy, and you were made right with God in the name of the Lord Jesus Christ and in the Spirit of our God.

## USE YOUR BODIES FOR GOD'S GLORY

¹²"I am allowed to do all things," but all things are not good for me to do. "I am allowed to do all things," but I will not let anything make me its slave. ¹³"Food is for the stomach, and the stomach for food," but God will destroy them both. The body is not for sexual sin but for the Lord, and the Lord is for the body. ¹⁴By his power God has raised the Lord from the dead and will also raise us from the dead. ¹⁵Surely you know that your bodies are parts of Christ himself. So I must never take the parts of Christ and join them to a prostitute! ¹⁶It is written in the Scriptures, "The two will become one body."ⁿ So you should know that anyone who joins with a prostitute becomes one body with the prostitute. ¹⁷But the one who joins with the Lord is one spirit with the Lord.

¹⁸So run away from sexual sin. Every other sin people do is outside their bodies, but those who sin sexually sin against their own bodies. ¹⁹You should know that your body is a temple for the Holy Spirit who is in you. You have received the Holy Spirit from God. So you do not belong to yourselves, ²⁰because you were bought by God for a price. So honor God with your bodies.

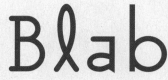

**Q:** A friend of mine came over, and now my necklace is missing. I think she took it. What do I do?

**A:** First of all, it is never right to accuse someone of doing something unless you actually saw them do it. Tear your room apart before jumping to any conclusions, because chances are it just fell behind the dresser or under the bed. If you see her with the necklace on, take an adult with you to gently confront her. Whether you get the necklace back or not, you need to forgive her.

**Q:** I am going to sing in the school talent night, and I really want to win first place. Is that wrong?

**A:** It is not wrong to feel good about the talents God has blessed you with, but it is wrong to feel superior to others or brag about them, because that does not show love for others above yourself. Do your very best and hope for the best, but ask God to help you be happy for whoever takes the top spot. If it is you, give God the glory.

**Q:** I am afraid that terrorists will bomb us. How can I fight this fear?

**A:** Pray. Remember how much God loves you, and read 1 John 4:18 that says "perfect love drives out fear." Even if the worst-case scenario did happen, God would be with you to see you through. In the meantime, ask him to help you keep your speculation of what might happen under control.

**notes** 6:16 "The two . . . body." Quotation from Genesis 2:24.

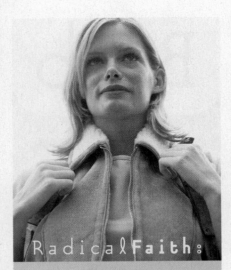

Radical Faith:

## 1 Corinthians 7:34-35

Chances are you haven't walked down the aisle just yet. But you can probably hardly wait for that lucky guy to be by your side, right? Being in a relationship is really exciting to think about, but maybe it's not in your life right now. Here's a newsflash: That's OK. You don't start living when your future husband walks into your life. You've got a lot of life to live right now! You've got all you need, and God's got a lot in mind for you today. You are his creation, his daughter, his servant, and his bride. . . explore all the ways you can relate to him. Let God have your heart in every sense. Do you know there are special ways that you reflect him by just being who you are? God can use your abilities and passions in great ways. Your body, your mind, and your spirit belong to God. Grow in him, show his love to others, and strive to know him more. Get grounded in who you are in him. Whenever you do end up walking down the aisle, there will be someone loving, worshiping, and knowing God right alongside you. But God will still be the main event. So live like it now.

## About Marriage

7 Now I will discuss the things you wrote me about. It is good for a man not to have sexual relations with a woman. 2But because sexual sin is a danger, each man should have his own wife, and each woman should have her own husband. 3The husband should give his wife all that he owes her as his wife. And the wife should give her husband all that she owes him as her husband. 4The wife does not have full rights over her own body; her husband shares them. And the husband does not have full rights over his own body; his wife shares them. 5Do not refuse to give your bodies to each other, unless you both agree to stay away from sexual relations for a time so you can give your time to prayer. Then come together again so Satan cannot tempt you because of a lack of self-control. 6I say this to give you permission to stay away from sexual relations for a time. It is not a command to do so. 7I wish that everyone were like me, but each person has his own gift from God. One has one gift, another has another gift.

8Now for those who are not married and for the widows I say this: It is good for them to stay unmarried as I am. 9But if they cannot control themselves, they should marry. It is better to marry than to burn with sexual desire.

10Now I give this command for the married people. (The command is not from me; it is from the Lord.) A wife should not leave her husband. 11But if she does leave, she must not marry again, or she should make up with her husband. Also the husband should not divorce his wife.

12For all the others I say this (I am saying this, not the Lord): If a Christian man has a wife who is not a believer, and she is happy to live with him, he must not divorce her. 13And if a Christian woman has a husband who is not a believer, and he is happy to live with her, she must not divorce him. 14The husband who is not a believer is made holy through his believing wife. And the wife who is not a believer is made holy through her believing husband. If this were not true, your children would not be clean, but now your children are holy.

15But if those who are not believers decide to leave, let them leave. When this happens, the Christian man or woman is free. But God called us to live in peace. 16Wife, you don't know; maybe you will save your husband. And husband, you don't know; maybe you will save your wife.

## "YOU ALL WERE BOUGHT AT A GREAT PRICE, SO DO NOT BECOME SLAVES OF PEOPLE."

## Live as God Called You

17But in any case each one of you should continue to live the way God has given you to live—the way you were when God called you. This is a rule I make in all the churches. 18If a man was already circumcised when he was called, he should not undo his circumcision. If a man was without circumcision when he was called, he should not be circumcised. 19It is not important if a man is circumcised or not. The important thing is obeying God's commands. 20Each one of you should stay the way you were when God called you. 21If you were a slave when God called you, do not let that bother you. But if you can be free, then make good use of your freedom. 22Those who were slaves when the Lord called them are free persons who belong to the Lord. In the same way, those who were free when they were called are now Christ's slaves. 23You all were bought at a great price, so do not become slaves of people. 24Brothers and sisters, each of you should stay as you were when you were called, and stay there with God.

## Questions About Getting Married

25Now I write about people who are not married. I have no command from the Lord about this; I give my opinion. But I can be trusted, because the Lord has shown me mercy. ²⁶The present time is a time of trouble, so I think it is good for you to stay the way you are. ²⁷If you have a wife, do not try to become free from her. If you are not married, do not try to find a wife. ²⁸But if you decide to marry, you have not sinned. And if a girl who has never married decides to marry, she has not sinned. But those who marry will have trouble in this life, and I want you to be free from trouble.

²⁹Brothers and sisters, this is what I mean: We do not have much time left. So starting now, those who have wives should live as if they had no wives. ³⁰Those who are crying should live as if they were not crying. Those who are happy should live as if they were not happy. Those who buy things should live as if they own nothing. ³¹Those who use the things of the world should live as if they were not using them, because this world in its present form will soon be gone.

³²I want you to be free from worry. A man who is not married is busy with the Lord's work, trying to please the Lord. ³³But a man who is married is busy with things of the world, trying to please his wife. ³⁴He must think about two things—pleasing his wife and pleasing the Lord. A woman who is not married or a girl who has never married is busy with the Lord's work. She wants to be holy in body and spirit. But a married woman is busy with things of the world, as to how she can please her husband. ³⁵I am saying this to help you, not to limit you. But I want you to live in the right way, to give yourselves fully to the Lord without concern for other things.

## BIBLE BIOS

### Michal

**[1 Samuel 18 and 19]** All Michal wanted was to love and be loved. David was such a handsome guy, and she'd had a crush on him for a long time. So when Michal's father, Saul, offered her to David as a wife, she thought she was headed straight for the life she'd only dreamed of. But her dad was only using Michal as a way to get rid of David by making him fight the Philistines before taking her hand in marriage; a battle Saul never expected David to win. But David's life was spared, and Saul allowed David to marry her.

But that wasn't the end of the story. Michal then found herself caught between her father and David in a terrible feud, and she saved David's life by helping him to escape.

³⁶If a man thinks he is not doing the right thing with the girl he is engaged to, if she is almost past the best age to marry and he feels he should marry her, he should do what he wants. They should get married. It is no sin. ³⁷But if a man is sure in his mind that there is no need for marriage, and has his own desires under control, and has decided not to marry the one to whom he is engaged, he is doing the right thing. ³⁸So the man who marries his girl does right, but the man who does not marry will do better.

³⁹A woman must stay with her husband as long as he lives. But if her husband dies, she is free to marry any man she wants, but she must marry in the Lord. ⁴⁰The woman is happier if she does not marry again. This is my opinion, but I believe I also have God's Spirit.

# LEARN I+ & LIVE I+

### 1 Corinthians 6:12
**Learn It:** You are allowed to do a lot of things, but not everything is good for you.
**Live It:** When you have a variety of choices, always go with the best one.

### 1 Corinthians 6:20
**Learn It:** Your body was bought by God for the price of Christ's blood. Honor God with it.
**Live It:** Write down three things you can do to keep from dishonoring God with your body.

### 1 Corinthians 7:32
**Learn It:** If you are not married, be busy with the Lord's work, pleasing the Lord.
**Live It:** Instead of worrying about being alone, use your gifts and talents and put them to work wherever God calls you to go.

# CHECK IT OUT

## MARCH OF DIMES

Since 1938, the March of Dimes has worked as a national voluntary health agency to save millions of babies from death and disability by preventing birth defects and infant mortality. The March of Dimes funds research programs, education, and advocacy to save babies. In 2003, the organization launched a five-year campaign to address the increasing rate of premature birth.

For the past 50 years, the March of Dimes has recruited young volunteers for leadership roles. Today, the Team Youth program involves nearly one million students and advisers working toward a common goal—giving every baby a healthy start. *American Idol* winner Kelly Clarkson currently serves as Team Youth Celebrity Ambassador, and teens can help with her by joining Chain Reaction for high school students or the Collegiate Council for college students. Volunteers help educate and raise funds through a variety of fun opportunities.

*Get involved by visiting* **www.marchofdimes.com.**

## ABOUT FOOD OFFERED TO IDOLS

8 Now I will write about meat that is sacrificed to idols. We know that "we all have knowledge." Knowledge puffs you up with pride, but love builds up. ²If you think you know something, you do not yet know anything as you should. ³But if any person loves God, that person is known by God.

⁴So this is what I say about eating meat sacrificed to idols: We know that an idol is really nothing in the world, and we know there is only one God. ⁵Even though there are things called gods, in heaven or on earth (and there are many "gods" and "lords"), ⁶for us there is only one God—our Father. All things came from him, and we live for him. And there is only one Lord—Jesus Christ. All things were made through him, and we also were made through him.

**DIDYA KNOW** ONLY 2% OF TEENS PLAY VIDEO GAMES WITH THEIR PARENTS.

KAISER FAMILY FOUNDATION

⁷But not all people know this. Some people are still so used to idols that when they eat meat, they still think of it as being sacrificed to an idol. Because their conscience is weak, when they eat it, they feel guilty. ⁸But food will not bring us closer to God. Refusing to eat does not make us less pleasing to God, and eating does not make us better in God's sight.

## "BUT BE CAREFUL THAT YOUR FREEDOM DOES NOT CAUSE THOSE WHO ARE WEAK IN FAITH TO FALL INTO SIN."

⁹But be careful that your freedom does not cause those who are weak in faith to fall into sin. ¹⁰You have "knowledge," so you eat in an idol's temple." But someone who is weak in faith might see you eating there and be encouraged to eat meat sacrificed to idols while thinking it is wrong to do so. ¹¹This weak believer for whom Christ died is ruined because of your "knowledge." ¹²When you sin against your brothers and sisters in Christ like this and cause them to do what they feel is wrong, you are also sinning against Christ. ¹³So if the food I eat causes them to fall into sin, I will never eat meat again so that I will not cause any of them to sin.

## PAUL IS LIKE THE OTHER APOSTLES

9 I am a free man. I am an apostle. I have seen Jesus our Lord. You people are all an example of my work in the Lord. ²If others do not accept me as an apostle, surely you do, because you are proof that I am an apostle in the Lord.

³This is the answer I give people who want to judge me: ⁴Do we not have the right to eat and drink? ⁵Do we not have the right to bring a believing wife with us when we travel as do the other apostles and the Lord's brothers and Peter? ⁶Are Barnabas and I the only ones who must work to earn our living? ⁷No soldier ever serves in the army and pays his own salary. No one ever plants a vineyard without eating some of the grapes. No person takes care of a flock without drinking some of the milk.

⁸I do not say this by human authority; God's law also says the same thing. ⁹It is written in the law of Moses: "When an ox is working in the grain, do not cover its mouth to keep it from eating."" When God said this, was he thinking only about oxen? No. ¹⁰He was really talking about us.

notes **8:10 idol's temple** Building where a god is worshiped. **9:9 "When an ox . . . eating."** Quotation from Deuteronomy 25:4.

Yes, that Scripture was written for us, because it goes on to say: "The one who plows and the one who works in the grain should hope to get some of the grain for their work." [11]Since we planted spiritual seed among you, is it too much if we should harvest from you some things for this life? [12]If others have the right to get something from you, surely we have this right, too. But we do not use it. No, we put up with everything ourselves so that we will not keep anyone from believing the Good News of Christ. [13]Surely you know that those who work at the Temple get their food from the Temple, and those who serve at the altar get part of what is offered at the altar. [14]In the same way, the Lord has commanded that those who tell the Good News should get their living from this work.

[15]But I have not used any of these rights. And I am not writing this now to get anything from you. I would rather die than to have my reason for bragging taken away. [16]Telling the Good News does not give me any reason for bragging. Telling the Good News is my duty—something I must do. And how terrible it will be for me if I do not tell the Good News. [17]If I preach because it is my own choice, I have a

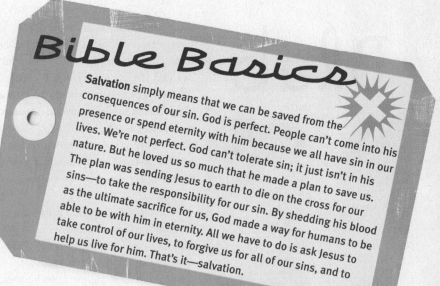

**Bible Basics**

**Salvation** simply means that we can be saved from the consequences of our sin. God is perfect. People can't come into his presence or spend eternity with him because we all have sin in our lives. We're not perfect. God can't tolerate sin; it just isn't in his nature. But he loved us so much that he made a plan to save us. The plan was sending Jesus to earth to die on the cross for our sins—to take the responsibility for our sin. By shedding his blood as the ultimate sacrifice for us, God made a way for humans to be able to be with him in eternity. All we have to do is ask Jesus to take control of our lives, to forgive us for all of our sins, and to help us live for him. That's it—salvation.

reward. But if I preach and it is not my choice to do so, I am only doing the duty that was given to me. [18]So what reward do I get? This is my reward: that when I tell the Good News I can offer it freely. I do not use my full rights in my work of preaching the Good News.

[19]I am free and belong to no one. But I make myself a slave to all people to win as many as I can. [20]To the Jews I became like a Jew to win the Jews. I myself am not ruled by the law. But to those who are ruled by the law I became like a person who is ruled by the law. I did this to win those who are ruled by the law. [21]To those who are without the law I became like a person who is without the law. I did this to win those people who are without the law. (But really, I am not without God's law—I am ruled by Christ's law.) [22]To those who are weak, I became weak so I could win the weak. I have become all things to all people so I could save some of them in any way possible. [23]I do all this because of the Good News and so I can share in its blessings.

[24]You know that in a race all the runners run, but only one gets the prize. So run to win! [25]All those who compete in the games use self-control so they can win a crown. That crown is an earthly thing that lasts only a short time, but our crown will never be destroyed. [26]So I

do not run without a goal. I fight like a boxer who is hitting something—not just the air. [27]I treat my body hard and make it my slave so that I myself will not be disqualified after I have preached to others.

> ## "I AM FREE AND BELONG TO NO ONE. BUT I MAKE MYSELF A SLAVE TO ALL PEOPLE TO WIN AS MANY AS I CAN."

### WARNINGS FROM ISRAEL'S PAST

**10** Brothers and sisters, I want you to know what happened to our ancestors who followed Moses. They were all under the cloud and all went through the sea. [2]They were all baptized as followers of Moses in the cloud and in the sea. [3]They all ate the same spiritual food, [4]and all drank the same spiritual drink. They drank from that spiritual rock that followed them, and that rock was Christ. [5]But God was not pleased with most of them, so they died in the desert.

[6]And these things happened as examples for us, to stop us from wanting evil things as

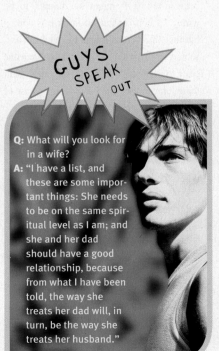

**GUYS SPEAK OUT**

Q: What will you look for in a wife?
A: "I have a list, and these are some important things: She needs to be on the same spiritual level as I am; and she and her dad should have a good relationship, because from what I have been told, the way she treats her dad will, in turn, be the way she treats her husband."

235

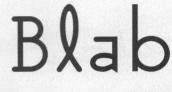

**Q:** You always hear about guys having problems with porn and wanting sex, but I do, too. Sometimes I can't help looking at pictures or reading erotic stories on the Internet. Then I play with myself and feel gross. What can I do?

**A:** Only get on the Internet in a room full of people. Don't have it in your bedroom or get online when no one is home. Get rid of any magazines or videos you have, and don't get more. Pray that God will keep your thoughts and actions pure, and tell him you are sorry.

**Q:** My parents have seen my boyfriend and me hug and kiss. Now they think we're going "too far." But we're really not. How can we get them to trust us?

**A:** If you are already hugging and kissing, that means that you can only go further—and your parents know that. Remember, they were teens, too, and they have more experience than you do. Try to keep in mind that your parents are really on your side, and reassure them by being open about your relationship. Also, cut down on the PDA (public displays of affection) and the private displays, too.

**Q:** I find it much easier to get along with guys than girls. Is it okay that all my best friends are guys?

**A:** Lots of girls find friendships with guys easier, because they come with less emotional baggage than relationships with girls. Keep a balance, though, of guys and girls in your life. And make sure you are not fooling yourself into thinking you just want to be friends with a guy when you really want more.

those people did. 7Do not worship idols, as some of them did. Just as it is written in the Scriptures: "They sat down to eat and drink, and then they got up and sinned sexually."" 8We must not take part in sexual sins, as some of them did. In one day twenty-three thousand of them died because of their sins. 9We must not test Christ as some of them did; they were killed by snakes. 10Do not complain as some of them did; they were killed by the angel that destroys.

11The things that happened to those people are examples. They were written down to teach us, because we live in a time when all these things of the past have reached their goal. 12If you think you are strong, you should be careful not to fall. 13The only temptation that has come to you is that which everyone has. But you can trust God, who will not permit you to be tempted more than you can stand. But when you are tempted, he will also give you a way to escape so that you will be able to stand it.

14So, my dear friends, run away from the worship of idols. 15I am speaking to you as to intelligent people; judge for yourselves what I say. 16We give thanks for the cup of blessing," which is a sharing in the blood of Christ. And the bread that we break is a sharing in the body of Christ. 17Because there is one loaf of bread, we who are many are one body, because we all share that one loaf.

18Think about the Israelites: Do not those who eat the sacrifices share in the altar? 19I do not mean that the food sacrificed to an idol is important. I do not mean that an idol is anything at all. 20But I say that what is sacrificed to idols is offered to demons, not to God. And I do not want you to share anything with demons. 21You cannot drink the cup of the Lord and the cup of demons also. You cannot share in the Lord's table and the table of demons. 22Are we trying to make the Lord jealous? We are not stronger than he is, are we?

## HOW TO USE CHRISTIAN FREEDOM

23"We are allowed to do all things," but all things are not good for us to do. "We are allowed to do all things," but not all things help others grow stronger. 24Do not look out only for yourselves. Look out for the good of others also.

# "IF YOU EAT OR DRINK, OR IF YOU DO ANYTHING, DO IT ALL FOR THE GLORY OF GOD."

25Eat any meat that is sold in the meat market. Do not ask questions to see if it is meat you think is wrong to eat. 26You may eat it, "because the earth belongs to the Lord, and everything in it."″

27Those who are not believers may invite you to eat with them. If you want to go, eat anything that is put before you. Do not ask questions to see if you think it might be wrong to eat. 28But if anyone says to you, "That food was offered to idols," do not eat it. Do not eat it because of that person who told you and because eating it might be thought to be wrong. 29I don't mean you think it is wrong, but the other person might. But why, you ask, should my freedom be judged by someone else's conscience? 30If I eat the meal with thankfulness, why am I criticized because of something for which I thank God?

31The answer is, if you eat or drink, or if you do anything, do it all for the glory of God. 32Never do anything that might hurt others— Jews, Greeks, or God's church— 33just as I, also, try to please everybody in every way. I am not trying to do what is good for me but what is good for most people so they can be saved.

11 Follow my example, as I follow the example of Christ.

## BEING UNDER AUTHORITY

2I praise you because you remember me in everything, and you follow closely the teachings just as I gave them to you. 3But I want you to understand this: The head of every man is

 10:7 "They . . . sexually." Quotation from Exodus 32:6. 10:16 cup of blessing The cup of the fruit of the vine that Christians thank God for and drink at the Lord's Supper. 10:26 "because . . . it" Quotation from Psalms 24:1; 50:12; 89:11.

236

Christ, the head of a woman is the man," and the head of Christ is God. ⁴Every man who prays or prophesies with his head covered brings shame to his head. ⁵But every woman who prays or prophesies with her head uncovered brings shame to her head. She is the same as a woman who has her head shaved. ⁶If a woman does not cover her head, she should have her hair cut off. But since it is shameful for a woman to cut off her hair or to shave her head, she should cover her head. ⁷But a man should not cover his head, because he is the likeness and glory of God. But woman is man's glory. ⁸Man did not come from woman, but woman came from man. ⁹And man was not made for woman, but woman was made for man. ¹⁰So that is why a woman should have a symbol of authority on her head, because of the angels.

¹¹But in the Lord women are not independent of men, and men are not independent of women. ¹²This is true because woman came from man, but also man is born from woman. But everything comes from God. ¹³Decide this for yourselves: Is it right for a woman to pray to God with her head uncovered? ¹⁴Even nature itself teaches you that wearing long hair is shameful for a man. ¹⁵But long hair is a woman's glory. Long hair is given to her as a covering. ¹⁶Some people may still want to argue about this, but I would add that neither we nor the churches of God have any other practice.

## THE LORD'S SUPPER

¹⁷In the things I tell you now I do not praise you, because when you come together you do more harm than good. ¹⁸First, I hear that when you meet together as a church you are divided, and I believe some of this. ¹⁹(It is necessary to have differences among you so that it may be clear which of you really have God's approval.) ²⁰When you come together, you are not really eating the Lord's Supper." ²¹This is because when you eat, each person eats without waiting for the others. Some people do not get enough to eat, while others have too much to drink. ²²You can eat and drink in your own homes! You seem to think God's church is not important, and you embarrass those who are poor. What should I tell you? Should I praise you? I do not praise you for doing this.

²³The teaching I gave you is the same teaching I received from the Lord: On the night when the Lord Jesus was handed over to be killed, he took bread ²⁴and gave thanks for it. Then he broke the bread and said, "This is my body; it is for you. Do this to remember me." ²⁵In the same way, after they ate, Jesus took the cup. He said, "This cup is the new agreement that is sealed with the blood of my death. When you drink this, do it to remember me." ²⁶Every time you eat this bread and drink this cup you are telling others about the Lord's death until he comes.

## relationships

"The way you give to others is the way God will give to you, but God will give you even more" (Mark 4:24). Are you a giver or a taker? Your parents buy you school clothes, give you spending money, and help you get the things you need. What have you given them recently? Practice giving them not only small gifts, but also aim for good grades, put on lots of smiles, hand out hugs, and show your appreciation. A good attitude goes a long way and won't go unrewarded.

## RadicalFaith

## 1 Corinthians 10:13

Everyone has weaknesses. And all of us have something we like to do even though we know we shouldn't. Are there things in your life that trigger you to sin or to compromise your beliefs? When you're in a spot where you're tempted to sin, God promises that there's always a way out. Sometimes that means leaving the situation. Sometimes it means simply saying "no." And sometimes it means making choices that won't make you popular. But if you think and pray hard enough, you will always discover an exit strategy. The fact is, God won't let any temptation come your way that he won't help you overcome—you're not alone here. And God won't allow more than you're able to bear come your way—you've got his power at hand and his provision at work. Remember that Jesus is able to understand your weaknesses, because he also experienced temptation (though he didn't sin) while he was on earth (Hebrews 4:15). He knows what it's like, and you can go to him anytime and ask for help. He will "give you a way to escape so that you will be able to stand it."

 **notes** **11:3 the man** This could also mean "her husband." **11:20 Lord's Supper** The meal Jesus told his followers to eat to remember him (Luke 22:14-20).

# LEARN I+ & LIVE I+

**1 Corinthians 10:7**
**Learn It:** Do not worship idols.
**Live It:** Anything you consider a priority above God, that you think about more, spend more time on, love more, is an idol in your life. Be careful not to elevate your crush—or yourself—above God.

**1 Corinthians 11:11**
**Learn It:** Men and women in the Lord are not independent of each other.
**Live It:** Avoid joining the popular trend of "male-bashing." Boys are not stinky, mean, or stupid. God created men and women to need each other.

**1 Corinthians 12:26**
**Learn It:** If one part of the body of Christ (the church) suffers, everyone suffers.
**Live It:** Minister to someone who is hurting today by giving them a gift, a smile, or an offer to pray with them.

<sup>27</sup>So a person who eats the bread or drinks the cup of the Lord in a way that is not worthy of it will be guilty of sinning against the body and the blood of the Lord. <sup>28</sup>Look into your own hearts before you eat the bread and drink the cup, <sup>29</sup>because all who eat the bread and drink the cup without recognizing the body eat and drink judgment against themselves. <sup>30</sup>That is why many in your group are sick and weak, and many have died. <sup>31</sup>But if we judged ourselves in the right way, God would not judge us. <sup>32</sup>But when the Lord judges us, he punishes us so that we will not be destroyed along with the world.

<sup>33</sup>So my brothers and sisters, when you come together to eat, wait for each other. <sup>34</sup>Anyone who is too hungry should eat at home so that in meeting together you will not bring God's judgment on yourselves. I will tell you what to do about the other things when I come.

## GIFTS FROM THE HOLY SPIRIT

12 Now, brothers and sisters, I want you to understand about spiritual gifts. <sup>2</sup>You know the way you lived before you were believers. You let yourselves be influenced and led away to worship idols—things that could

# Changed Lives

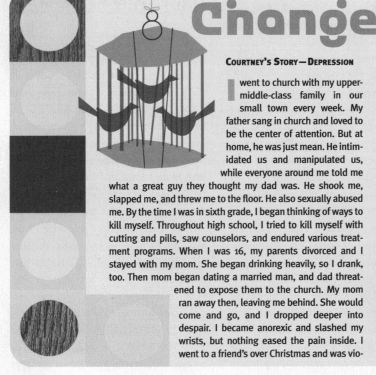

### COURTNEY'S STORY—DEPRESSION

I went to church with my upper-middle-class family in our small town every week. My father sang in church and loved to be the center of attention. But at home, he was just mean. He intimidated us and manipulated us, while everyone around me told me what a great guy they thought my dad was. He shook me, slapped me, and threw me to the floor. He also sexually abused me. By the time I was in sixth grade, I began thinking of ways to kill myself. Throughout high school, I tried to kill myself with cutting and pills, saw counselors, and endured various treatment programs. When I was 16, my parents divorced and I stayed with my mom. She began drinking heavily, so I drank, too. Then mom began dating a married man, and dad threatened to expose them to the church. My mom ran away then, leaving me behind. She would come and go, and I dropped deeper into despair. I became anorexic and slashed my wrists, but nothing eased the pain inside. I went to a friend's over Christmas and was vio-lently raped by a man staying at their house. My father told me it was my fault; the authorities told me they would not press charges. My parents punished me for being raped. The summer after I graduated from high school, I went to a Christian camp where I heard about a program for girls with problems like mine. At first, I didn't like the program. I was confronted and expected to play by the rules, and I didn't like it. I ran away. I started college, but my eating disorder and depression became so severe that I was hospitalized several times. The school asked me to leave. With nowhere to go, I tried to kill myself again. I woke up in intensive care and realized God wasn't going to let me take my life. I went back to the Christian program. This time, I was ready to listen and to heal. It took hard work and discipline, but today I have forgiven my father and healed a lot emotionally. Now I can share my testimony with other girls who are struggling.

*To find help in overcoming depression and other mental health issues, visit www.aacc.net, www.newlife.com, or www.christianprograms-forteens.com. For information about residential care for females, visit mercyministries.com. (Names have been changed for the sake of privacy. Courtney tells her story after going through biblically based counseling with Mercy Ministries.)*

# beauty secret

## Facial Scrub

For a homemade facial scrub, combine two tablespoons of cornmeal and water into a thick paste. Gently rub onto your face as if you were using soap. Rinse off the paste with a soft cloth and enjoy softer skin.

not speak. ³So I want you to understand that no one who is speaking with the help of God's Spirit says, "Jesus be cursed." And no one can say, "Jesus is Lord," without the help of the Holy Spirit.

⁴There are different kinds of gifts, but they are all from the same Spirit. ⁵There are different ways to serve but the same Lord to serve. ⁶And there are different ways that God works through people but the same God. God works in all of us in everything we do. ⁷Something from the Spirit can be seen in each person, for the common good. ⁸The Spirit gives one person the ability to speak with wisdom, and the same Spirit gives another the ability to speak with knowledge. ⁹The same Spirit gives faith to one person. And, to another, that one Spirit gives gifts of healing. ¹⁰The Spirit gives to another person the power to do miracles, to another the ability to prophesy. And he gives to another the ability to know the difference between good

and evil spirits. The Spirit gives one person the ability to speak in different kinds of languages" and to another the ability to interpret those languages. ¹¹One Spirit, the same Spirit, does all these things, and the Spirit decides what to give each person.

## THE BODY OF CHRIST WORKS TOGETHER

¹²A person's body is only one thing, but it has many parts. Though there are many parts to a body, all those parts make only one body. Christ is like that also. ¹³Some of us are Jews, and some are Greeks. Some of us are slaves, and some are free. But we were all baptized into one body through one Spirit. And we were all made to share in the one Spirit.

¹⁴The human body has many parts. ¹⁵The foot might say, "Because I am not a hand, I am not part of the body." But saying this would not stop the foot from being a part of the body. ¹⁶The ear might say, "Because I am not an eye, I am not part of the body." But saying this would not stop the ear from being a part of the body. ¹⁷If the whole body were an eye, it would not be able to hear. If the whole body were an ear, it would not be able to smell. ¹⁸⁻¹⁹If each part of the body were the same part, there would be no body. But truly God put all the parts, each one of them, in the body as he wanted them. ²⁰So then there are many parts, but only one body.

²¹The eye cannot say to the hand, "I don't need you!" And the head cannot say to the foot, "I don't need you!" ²²No! Those parts of the body that seem to be the weaker are really necessary. ²³And the parts of the body we think are less deserving are the parts to which we give the most honor. We give special respect to the parts we want to hide. ²⁴The more respectable parts of our body need no special care. But God put the body together and gave more honor to the parts that need it ²⁵so our body would not be divided. God wanted the different parts to care the same for each other. ²⁶If one part of the body suffers, all the other parts suffer with it. Or if one part of our body is honored, all the other parts share its honor.

²⁷Together you are the body of Christ, and each one of you is a part of that body. ²⁸In the church God has given a place first to apostles, second to prophets, and third to teachers. Then God has given a place to those who do miracles, those who have gifts of healing, those who can help others, those who are able to govern, and those who can speak in different languages." ²⁹Not all are apostles. Not all are prophets. Not all are teachers. Not all do miracles. ³⁰Not all have gifts of healing. Not all speak in different languages. Not all interpret those languages. ³¹But you should truly want to have the greater gifts.

## "I MAY GIVE AWAY EVERYTHING I HAVE, AND I MAY EVEN GIVE MY BODY AS AN OFFERING TO BE BURNED. BUT I GAIN NOTHING IF I DO NOT HAVE LOVE."

### LOVE IS THE GREATEST GIFT

And now I will show you the best way of all.

**13** I may speak in different languages" of people or even angels. But if I do not have love, I am only a noisy bell or a crashing cymbal. ²I may have the gift of prophecy. I may understand all the secret things of God and have all knowledge, and I may have faith so great I can move mountains. But even with all these things, if I do not have love, then I am nothing. ³I may give away everything I have, and I may even give my body as an offering to be burned." But I gain nothing if I do not have love.

⁴Love is patient and kind. Love is not jealous, it does not brag, and it is not proud. ⁵Love is not rude, is not selfish, and does not get upset with others. Love does not count up wrongs that have been done. ⁶Love is not happy

**notes** 12:10, 28; 13:1 **languages** This can also be translated "tongues." 13:3 **Verse 3** Other Greek copies read: "hand over my body in order that I may brag."

with evil but is happy with the truth. ⁷Love patiently accepts all things. It always trusts, always hopes, and always remains strong.

⁸Love never ends. There are gifts of prophecy, but they will be ended. There are gifts of speaking in different languages, but those gifts will stop. There is the gift of knowledge, but it will come to an end. ⁹The reason is that our knowledge and our ability to prophesy are not perfect. ¹⁰But when perfection comes, the things that are not perfect will end. ¹¹When I was a child, I talked like a child, I thought like a child, I reasoned like a child. When I became a man, I stopped those childish ways. ¹²It is the same with us. Now we see a dim reflection, as if we were looking into a mirror, but then we shall see clearly. Now I know only a part, but then I will know fully, as God has known me. ¹³So these three things continue forever: faith, hope, and love. And the greatest of these is love.

## DESIRE SPIRITUAL GIFTS

**14** You should seek after love, and you should truly want to have the spiritual gifts, especially the gift of prophecy. ²I will explain why. Those who have the gift of speaking in different languages" are not speaking to people; they are speaking to God. No one understands them; they are speaking secret things through the Spirit. ³But those who

prophesy are speaking to people to give them strength, encouragement, and comfort. ⁴The ones who speak in different languages are helping only themselves, but those who prophesy are helping the whole church. ⁵I wish all of you had the gift of speaking in different kinds of languages, but more, I wish you would prophesy. Those who prophesy are greater than those who can only speak in different languages—unless someone is there who can explain what is said so that the whole church can be helped.

⁶Brothers and sisters, will it help you if I come to you speaking in different languages? No! It will help you only if I bring you a new truth or some new knowledge, or prophecy, or teaching. ⁷It is the same as with lifeless things that make sounds—like a flute or a harp. If they do not make clear musical notes, you will not know what is being played. ⁸And in a war, if the trumpet does not give a clear sound, who will prepare for battle? ⁹It is the same with you. Unless you speak clearly with your tongue, no one can understand what you are saying. You will be talking into the air! ¹⁰It may be true that there are all kinds of sounds in the world, and none is without meaning. ¹¹But unless I understand the meaning of what someone says to me, I will be a foreigner to him, and he will be a foreigner to me. ¹²It is the same with you. Since you want spiritual gifts very much, seek most of all to have the gifts that help the church grow stronger.

¹³The one who has the gift of speaking in a different language should pray for the gift to interpret what is spoken. ¹⁴If I pray in a different language, my spirit is praying, but my mind does nothing. ¹⁵So what should I do? I will pray with my spirit, but I will also pray with my mind. I will sing with my spirit, but I will also sing with my mind. ¹⁶If you praise God with your spirit, those persons there without understanding cannot say amen" to your prayer of thanks, because they do not know what you are saying. ¹⁷You may be thanking God in a good way, but the other person is not helped.

¹⁸I thank God that I speak in different kinds of languages more than all of you. ¹⁹But in the

## Promises

# 1 Corinthians 13:4-8

What's your favorite romantic movie? You know, the one you watch over and over again and still get misty every time you see it? Maybe you still wait breathlessly until the critical moment when Cupid begins to work his magic and, finally, the couple comes together and admits how much they love each other. Then you smile and sit back, wondering when the fairy tale will happen to you and when you will hear an "I love you" from someone special. Think you're sappy or weird? Don't—there are lots of other women right there with you.

We use the word *love* so freely every day. You *love* your favorite pair of jeans. You *love* your dog or kitty cat. Your friend *loves* your new pair of shoes. You have a crush that you are so *in love* with. But in this passage we see that love means so much more than an occasional infatuation. In fact, 1 John 4:8 says "God is love." Replace "love" in this passage with "God" and see all of the amazing qualities that describe God. Wow! If God can love you so freely, maybe you can try to love someone this 1 Corinthians 13 way today.

### GUYS SPEAK OUT

**Q:** How far is "too far" when you are dating?
**A:** "This is just my opinion, but I don't even want to kiss before being married."

 **14:2 languages** This can also be translated "tongues." **14:16 amen** To say amen means to agree with the things that were said.

241

# Blab

**Q:** My parents and I seem to fight all the time. How can I make our relationship better?

**A:** Sit down with your parents, and have an honest conversation about the things you are having the most conflict over. Take notes, and make a list of your frustrations and theirs. See if you can compromise on issues that come up repeatedly, like curfew or cleaning your room. Tell them you want to have a good relationship with them, and pray together. Then just keep trying.

**Q:** I live with my mom, and I am having a hard time wanting to visit my dad. I love him, but his place is a bachelor pad. It's dirty, and he has a roommate. How can I honor my dad and not get weirded out staying with him?

**A:** Try to remember how much he loves you and wants to see you. Then ask him if you can help him get the place cleaned up. When you are out to dinner or somewhere neutral, share your feelings with him and brainstorm together changes you can make to feel more comfortable over there.

**Q:** My parents do not have any money, and I am afraid I won't be able to go to college. What can I do to get ready without burdening my parents too much?

**A:** Isaiah 65:24 says God will supply your needs before you even ask, and Matthew 7:7 says to ask and God will give to you. You can trust him to help you afford college. In the meantime, do your part by getting good grades, participating in extracurricular activities, and making yourself a great scholarship candidate.

church meetings I would rather speak five words I understand in order to teach others than thousands of words in a different language.

²⁰Brothers and sisters, do not think like children. In evil things be like babies, but in your thinking you should be like adults. ²¹It is written in the Scriptures:

"With people who use strange words and foreign languages
I will speak to these people.
But even then they will not listen to me,"

*Isaiah 28:11-12*

says the Lord.

²²So the gift of speaking in different kinds of languages is a proof for those who do not believe, not for those who do believe. And prophecy is for people who believe, not for those who do not believe. ²³Suppose the whole church meets together and everyone speaks in different languages. If some people come in who do not understand or do not believe, they will say you are crazy. ²⁴But suppose everyone is prophesying and some people come in who do not believe or do not understand. If everyone is prophesying, their sin will be shown to them, and they will be judged by all that they hear. ²⁵The secret things in their hearts will be made known. So they will bow down and worship God saying, "Truly, God is with you."

## MEETINGS SHOULD HELP THE CHURCH

²⁶So, brothers and sisters, what should you do? When you meet together, one person has a song, and another has a teaching. Another has a new truth from God. Another speaks in a different language,ⁿ and another person interprets that language. The purpose of all these things should be to help the church grow strong. ²⁷When you meet together, if anyone speaks in a different language, it should be only two, or not more than three, who speak. They should speak one after the other, and someone else should interpret. ²⁸But if there is no interpreter, then those who speak in a different language should be quiet in the church

meeting. They should speak only to themselves and to God.

²⁹Only two or three prophets should speak, and the others should judge what they say. ³⁰If a message from God comes to another person who is sitting, the first speaker should stop. ³¹You can all prophesy one after the other. In this way all the people can be taught and encouraged. ³²The spirits of prophets are under the control of the prophets themselves. ³³God is not a God of confusion but a God of peace.

As is true in all the churches of God's people, ³⁴women should keep quiet in the church meetings. They are not allowed to speak, but they must yield to this rule as the law says. ³⁵If they want to learn something, they should ask their own husbands at home. It is shameful for a woman to speak in the church meeting. ³⁶Did God's teaching come from you? Or are you the only ones to whom it has come?

³⁷Those who think they are prophets or spiritual persons should understand that what I am writing to you is the Lord's command. ³⁸Those who ignore this will be ignored by God.

³⁹So my brothers and sisters, you should truly want to prophesy. But do not stop people from using the gift of speaking in different kinds of languages. ⁴⁰But let everything be done in a right and orderly way.

## "NOW, BROTHERS AND SISTERS, I WANT YOU TO REMEMBER THE GOOD NEWS I BROUGHT TO YOU."

### THE GOOD NEWS ABOUT CHRIST

**15** Now, brothers and sisters, I want you to remember the Good News I brought to you. You received this Good News and continue strong in it. ²And you are being saved by it if you continue believing what I told you. If you do not, then you believed for nothing.

**notes** **14:26 language** This can also be translated "tongue."

# Music Reviews

| GROUP: | ALBUM: |
|---|---|
| AUDIO ADRENALINE | WORLDWIDE |

Audio Adrenaline fans who loved the band's 2001 album *Lift,* with hits "Ocean Floor" and "Beautiful," or the 1999 disc *Underdog,* with singles "Get Down" and "Good Life," will be gratified to know that their boys are back and still going strong on *Worldwide*. The theme for *Worldwide* is all about going out and telling others about Jesus, urging everyone to get involved through songs like "Dirty," "Go and Be," and the challenging "Church Punks."

**WHY IT ROCKS: AUDIO A ROCKS WHILE GETTING YOU OUT OF YOURSELF AND FOCUSED ON OTHERS WHO NEED TO HEAR ABOUT HIM.**

³I passed on to you what I received, of which this was most important: that Christ died for our sins, as the Scriptures say; ⁴that he was buried and was raised to life on the third day as the Scriptures say; ⁵and that he was seen by Peter and then by the twelve apostles. ⁶After that, Jesus was seen by more than five hundred of the believers at the same time. Most of them are still living today, but some have died. ⁷Then he was seen by James and later by all the apostles. ⁸Last of all he was seen by me—as by a person not born at the normal time. ⁹All the other apostles are greater than I am. I am not even good enough to be called an apostle, because I persecuted the church of God. ¹⁰But God's grace has made me what I am, and his grace to me was not wasted. I worked harder than all the other apostles. (But it was not I really; it was God's grace that was with me.) ¹¹So if I preached to you or the other apostles preached to you, we all preach the same thing, and this is what you believed.

## WE WILL BE RAISED FROM THE DEAD

¹²Now since we preached that Christ was raised from the dead, why do some of you say that people will not be raised from the dead? ¹³If no one is ever raised from the dead, then Christ has not been raised. ¹⁴And if Christ has

not been raised, then our preaching is worth nothing, and your faith is worth nothing. ¹⁵And also, we are guilty of lying about God, because we testified of him that he raised Christ from the dead. But if people are not raised from the dead, then God never raised Christ. ¹⁶If the dead are not raised, Christ has not been raised either. ¹⁷And if Christ has not been raised, then your faith has nothing to it; you are still guilty of your sins. ¹⁸And those in Christ who have already died are lost. ¹⁹If our

**NONAGGRESSIVE TEENS WHO PLAY A LOT OF VIOLENT VIDEO GAMES ARE TEN TIMES MORE LIKELY TO BE INVOLVED IN FIGHTS THAN OTHER NONAGGRESSIVE TEENS WHO DON'T PLAY VIOLENT GAMES.** RESEARCHER PAUL LYNCH

hope in Christ is for this life only, we should be pitied more than anyone else in the world.

²⁰But Christ has truly been raised from the dead—the first one and proof that those who sleep in death will also be raised. ²¹Death has come because of what one man did, but the rising from death also comes because of one man. ²²In Adam all of us die. In the same way, in Christ all of us will be made alive again. ²³But everyone will be raised to life in the right order. Christ was first to be raised. When

Christ comes again, those who belong to him will be raised to life, ²⁴and then the end will come. At that time Christ will destroy all rulers, authorities, and powers, and he will hand over the kingdom to God the Father. ²⁵Christ must rule until he puts all enemies under his control. ²⁶The last enemy to be destroyed will be death. ²⁷The Scripture says that God put all things under his control." When it says "all things" are under him, it is clear this does not include God himself. God is

the One who put everything under his control. ²⁸After everything has been put under the Son, then he will put himself under God, who had put all things under him. Then God will be the complete ruler over everything.

²⁹If the dead are never raised, what will people do who are being baptized for the dead? If the dead are not raised at all, why are people being baptized for them?

³⁰And what about us? Why do we put ourselves in danger every hour? ³¹I die every day.

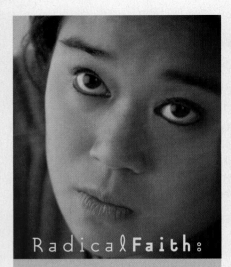

## RadicalFaith:

# 1 Corinthians 15:54-57

If you've been anywhere near death, you know the devastation it brings. God never intended for us to have to experience death and separation from each other; death is a result of sin coming into the world. He aches over the pain that his people experience because of death, and he walks through every step of suffering and grief with us. He has compassion on our pain and fear regarding death and replaces that fear with hope. Because death is not the end of the story. When God raised Jesus from the dead, he conquered the power of death for good. Christ did not stay dead, and neither will you if you are in him. There is more life to come. In fact, our earthly lives are just the beginning. You can relax, knowing that God is bigger than death and that he has turned it into a way to show his power and glory to the entire world. He's had clear victory over it. He's made it a gateway into his rest. You can be sure today that the healing, joy, goodness, peace, and perfection that will be in heaven will far surpass any present human pain and dread of death.

That is true, brothers and sisters, just as it is true that I brag about you in Christ Jesus our Lord. [32]If I fought wild animals in Ephesus only with human hopes, I have gained nothing. If the dead are not raised, "Let us eat and drink, because tomorrow we will die."[n]

[33]Do not be fooled: "Bad friends will ruin good habits." [34]Come back to your right way of thinking and stop sinning. Some of you do not know God—I say this to shame you.

## WHAT KIND OF BODY WILL WE HAVE?

[35]But someone may ask, "How are the dead raised? What kind of body will they have?" [36]Foolish person! When you sow a seed, it must die in the ground before it can live and grow. [37]And when you sow it, it does not have the same "body" it will have later. What you sow is only a bare seed, maybe wheat or something else. [38]But God gives it a body that he has planned for it, and God gives each kind of seed its own body. [39]All things made of flesh are not the same: People have one kind of flesh, animals have another, birds have another, and fish have another. [40]Also there are heavenly bodies and earthly bodies. But the beauty of the heavenly bodies is one kind, and the beauty of the earthly bodies is another. [41]The sun has one kind of beauty, the moon has another beauty, and the stars have another. And each star is different in its beauty.

[42]It is the same with the dead who are raised to life. The body that is "planted" will ruin and decay, but it is raised to a life that cannot be destroyed. [43]When the body is "planted," it is without honor, but it is raised in glory. When the body is "planted," it is weak, but when it is raised, it is powerful. [44]The body that is "planted" is a physical body. When it is raised, it is a spiritual body.

There is a physical body, and there is also a spiritual body. [45]It is written in the Scriptures: "The first man, Adam, became a living person."[n] But the last Adam became a spirit that gives life. [46]The spiritual did not come first, but the physical and then the spiritual. [47]The first man came from the dust of the earth. The second man came from heaven. [48]People who belong to the earth are like the first man of earth. But those people who belong to heaven are like the man of heaven. [49]Just as we were made like the man of earth, so we will also be made like the man of heaven.

[50]I tell you this, brothers and sisters: Flesh and blood cannot have a part in the kingdom of God. Something that will ruin cannot have a part in something that never ruins. [51]But look! I tell you this secret: We will not all sleep in death, but we will all be changed. [52]It will take only a second—as quickly as an eye blinks—when the last trumpet sounds. The trumpet will sound, and those who have died will be raised to live forever, and we will all be changed. [53]This body that can be destroyed must clothe itself with something that can never be destroyed. And this body that dies must clothe itself with something that can never die. [54]So this body that can be destroyed will clothe itself with that which can never be destroyed, and this body that dies will clothe itself with that which can never die. When this happens, this Scripture will be made true:

"Death is destroyed forever in victory."

*Isaiah 25:8*

[55]"Death, where is your victory?

Death, where is your pain?" *Hosea 13:14*

[56]Death's power to hurt is sin, and the power of sin is the law. [57]But we thank God! He gives us the victory through our Lord Jesus Christ.

[58]So my dear brothers and sisters, stand strong. Do not let anything change you. Always give yourselves fully to the work of the Lord, because you know that your work in the Lord is never wasted.

## THE GIFT FOR OTHER BELIEVERS

**16** Now I will write about the collection of money for God's people. Do the same thing I told the Galatian churches to do: [2]On the first day of every week, each one of you should put aside money as you have been blessed. Save it up so you will not have to collect money after I come. [3]When I arrive, I will send whomever you approve to take your gift

---

**15:32** "Let us . . . die." Quotation from Isaiah 22:13; 56:12. **15:45** "The first . . . person." Quotation from Genesis 2:7.

244

# August

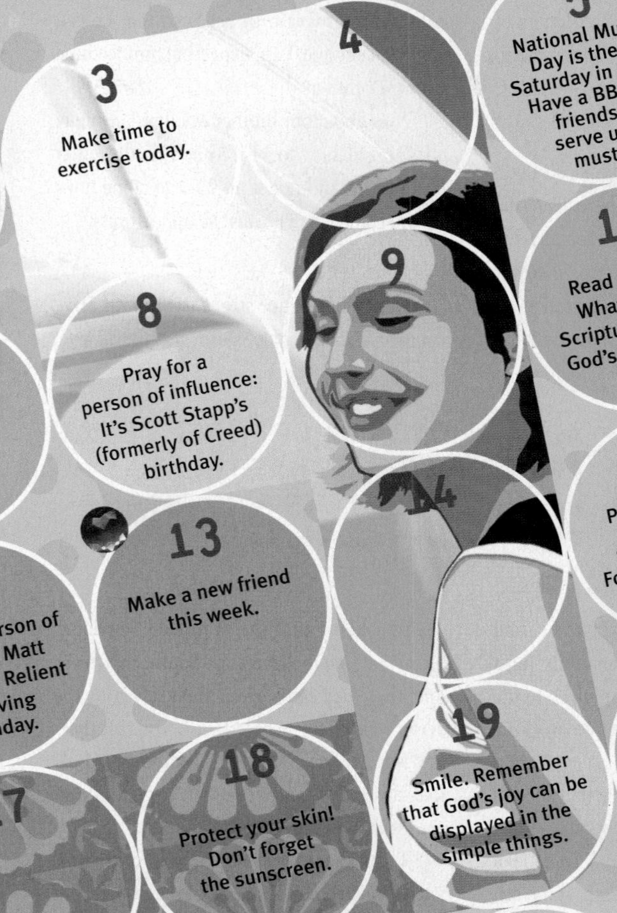

**1**

**2** Take care of your feet. Give yourself a pedicure.

**3** Make time to exercise today.

**4**

**5** National Mustard Day is the first Saturday in August. Have a BBQ with friends and serve up the mustard.

**6** National Fresh Breath Day. Don't forget to brush and use mouthwash.

**7**

**8** Pray for a person of influence: It's Scott Stapp's (formerly of Creed) birthday.

**9**

**10** Read Isaiah 43. What does the Scripture say about God's love for you?

**11**

**12** Pray for a person of influence: Matt Thiessen of Relient K is having a birthday.

**13** Make a new friend this week.

**14**

**15** Pray for a person of influence: Switchfoot's Tim Foreman is celebrating a birthday.

**16** Pray for a person of influence: It's Madonna's birthday.

**17**

**18** Protect your skin! Don't forget the sunscreen.

**19** Smile. Remember that God's joy can be displayed in the simple things.

**20**

**21**

**22** Share your faith with someone you've been praying for.

**23**

**24** Go on a date night with your dad. Enjoy spending time with him.

**25** Pray for a person of influence: Sean Connery is having a birthday.

**26**

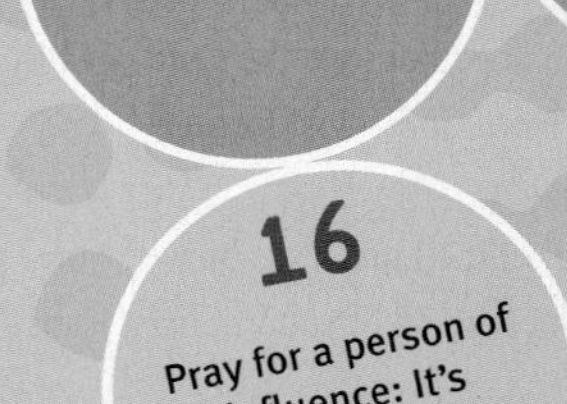

**27** Bake cookies with one of your sisters or brothers.

**28** Surprise your step-parent by cleaning the cars.

**29**

**30** Go through your clothes and donate the ones you're not wearing.

**31** Pick up the phone and call your grandparents to tell them how much you love them.

God gives us a free gift— life forever in Christ Jesus our Lord. —Romans 6:23

to Jerusalem. I will send them with letters of introduction, ⁴and if it seems good for me to go also, they will go along with me.

## PAUL'S PLANS

⁵I plan to go through Macedonia, so I will come to you after I go through there. ⁶Perhaps I will stay with you for a time or even all winter. Then you can help me on my trip, wherever I go. ⁷I do not want to see you now just in passing. I hope to stay a longer time with you if the Lord allows it. ⁸But I will stay at Ephesus until Pentecost, ⁹because a good opportunity for a great and growing work has been given to me now. And there are many people working against me.

¹⁰If Timothy comes to you, see to it that he has nothing to fear with you, because he is working for the Lord just as I am. ¹¹So none of you should treat Timothy as unimportant, but help him on his trip in peace so that he can come back to me. I am expecting him to come with the brothers.

¹²Now about our brother Apollos: I strongly encouraged him to visit you with the other brothers. He did not at all want to come now; he will come when he has the opportunity.

## PAUL ENDS HIS LETTER

¹³Be alert. Continue strong in the faith. Have courage, and be strong. ¹⁴Do everything in love.

¹⁵You know that the family of Stephanas were the first believers in Southern Greece and that they have given themselves to the service of God's people. I ask you, brothers and sisters, ¹⁶to follow the leading of people like these and anyone else who works and serves with them.

¹⁷I am happy that Stephanas, Fortunatus, and Achaicus have come. You are not here, but they have filled your place. ¹⁸They have refreshed my spirit and yours. You should recognize the value of people like these.

> **"BE ALERT. CONTINUE STRONG IN THE FAITH. HAVE COURAGE, AND BE STRONG. DO EVERYTHING IN LOVE."**

¹⁹The churches in the country of Asia send greetings to you. Aquila and Priscilla greet you in the Lord, as does the church that meets in their house. ²⁰All the brothers and sisters here send greetings. Give each other a holy kiss when you meet.

²¹I, Paul, am writing this greeting with my own hand.

²²If anyone does not love the Lord, let him be separated from God—lost forever!

Come, O Lord!

²³The grace of the Lord Jesus be with you. ²⁴My love be with all of you in Christ Jesus.

## DIDYA KNOW

**ALMOST TWO OUT OF THREE TEENS ARE CONCERNED THAT THEIR INTERNET USE CUTS INTO FAMILY TIME.** PEW INTERNET & AMERICAN LIFE PROJECT

# i t's a wonder that Paul didn't give up

on the Corinthians. Here they are, once again in chaos. Paul had already visited them once, trying to undo the work of false teachers who had influenced believers there. But instead of being welcomed with open arms, his character and motives were attacked by the same people he had loved, trained, and encouraged in the faith.

# 2 Corinthians
## Paul Patiently Instructs the Believers at Corinth . . . Again

Paul could have defended himself aggressively, condemning those who had turned their backs on him. Instead, he wrote this heartfelt letter, full of mercy and forgiveness. Does he tackle the issues head-on? Absolutely. But by sharing some of his personal joys and struggles, Paul is able to defend his credibility and continue delivering the message of God's love and provision for us.

One of the most powerful passages deals with what Paul describes as "a painful physical problem" (12:7). The literal translation is "a thorn in the flesh." We don't know exactly what type of ailment Paul was dealing with, but we know that he asked the Lord three times to remove the problem. God's response was surprising: "My grace is enough for you. When you are weak, my power is made perfect in you." So the next time you feel less-than-strong, think of how God responded to Paul and know that God has got your back.

From Paul, an apostle of Christ Jesus. I am an apostle because that is what God wanted. Also from Timothy our brother in Christ.

To the church of God in Corinth, and to all of God's people everywhere in Southern Greece:

²Grace and peace to you from God our Father and the Lord Jesus Christ.

### PAUL GIVES THANKS TO GOD

³Praise be to the God and Father of our Lord Jesus Christ. God is the Father who is full of mercy and all comfort. ⁴He comforts us every time we have trouble, so when others have trouble, we can comfort them with the same comfort God gives us. ⁵We share in the many sufferings of Christ. In the same way, much comfort comes to us through Christ. ⁶If we have troubles, it is for your comfort and salvation, and if we have comfort, you also have comfort. This helps you to accept patiently the same sufferings we have. ⁷Our hope for you is strong, knowing that you share in our sufferings and also in the comfort we receive.

## "GOD IS THE FATHER WHO IS FULL OF MERCY AND ALL COMFORT."

⁸Brothers and sisters,ⁿ we want you to know about the trouble we suffered in Asia. We had great burdens there that were beyond our own strength. We even gave up hope of living. ⁹Truly, in our own hearts we believed we would die. But this happened so we would not trust in ourselves but in God, who raises people from the dead. ¹⁰God saved us from these great dangers of death, and he will continue to save us. We have put our hope in him, and he will save us again. ¹¹And you can help us with your prayers. Then many people will give thanks for us—that God blessed us because of their many prayers.

### THE CHANGE IN PAUL'S PLANS

¹²This is what we are proud of, and I can say it with a clear conscience: In everything we have done in the world, and especially with you, we have had an honest and sincere heart from God. We did this by God's grace, not by the kind of wisdom the world has. ¹³⁻¹⁴We write to you only what you can read and understand. And I hope that as you have understood some things about us, you may come to know everything about us. Then you can be proud of us, as we will be proud of you on the day our Lord Jesus Christ comes again.

¹⁵I was so sure of all this that I made plans to visit you first so you could be blessed twice. ¹⁶I planned to visit you on my way to Macedonia and again on my way back. I wanted to get help from you for my trip to Judea. ¹⁷Do you think that I made these plans without really meaning it? Or maybe you think I make plans as the world does, so that I say yes, yes and at the same time no, no.

¹⁸But if you can believe God, you can believe that what we tell you is never both yes and no. ¹⁹The Son of God, Jesus Christ, that Silas and Timothy and I preached to you, was not yes and no. In Christ it has always been yes. ²⁰The yes to all of God's promises is in Christ, and through Christ we say yes to the glory of God. ²¹Remember, God is the One who makes you and us strong in Christ. God made us his chosen people. ²²He put his mark on us to show that we are his, and he put his Spirit in our hearts to be a guarantee for all he has promised.

²³I tell you this, and I ask God to be my witness that this is true: The reason I did not come back to Corinth was to keep you from being punished or hurt. ²⁴We are not trying to control your faith. You are strong in faith. But we are workers with you for your own joy.

So I decided that my next visit to you would not be another one to make you sad. ²If I make you sad, who will make me glad? Only you can make me glad—particularly the person whom I made sad. ³I wrote you a letter for this reason: that when I came to

### RadicalFaith:

## 2 Corinthians 1:8-10

Do you have days when you have to face things you don't think you can handle? Everyone does. But what do you turn to in the hard times? What do you put your hope in? In 2 Corinthians, the apostle Paul said he could only rely on God to get him through the hard things in his life. He suffered so much pain and hardship in Asia that he found himself thinking there was no way he'd ever survive. Some time or another you may find yourself in situations like Paul, facing burdens and trials, whether they are physical or emotional. And through Paul's example of his unwavering faith in God, we can know that God will be just as powerful and protecting in our lives. We often forget his power and run to other things that we think may save us. But no relationship, no drug, no achievement, no image, and no reckless behavior will bring you what you really want. Nothing in the world and nothing in your own power can bring the strength and peace that you need. Those things only come from God. In whatever you will face today, go into it relying on God's power and his Word.

**notes** 1:8 **Brothers and sisters** Although the Greek text says "Brothers" here and throughout this book, Paul's words were meant for the entire church, including men and women.

you I would not be made sad by the people who should make me happy. I felt sure of all of you, that you would share my joy. ⁴When I wrote to you before, I was very troubled and unhappy in my heart, and I wrote with many tears. I did not write to make you sad, but to let you know how much I love you.

### FORGIVE THE SINNER

⁵Someone there among you has caused sadness, not to me, but to all of you. I mean he caused sadness to all in some way. (I do not want to make it sound worse than it really is.) ⁶The punishment that most of you gave him is enough for him. ⁷But now you should forgive him and comfort him to keep him from having too much sadness and giving up completely. ⁸So I beg you to show that you love him. ⁹I wrote you to test you and to see if you obey in everything. ¹⁰If you forgive someone, I also forgive him. And what I have forgiven—if I had anything to forgive—I forgave it for you, as if Christ were with me. ¹¹I did this so that Satan would not win anything from us, because we know very well what Satan's plans are.

### PAUL'S CONCERN IN TROAS

¹²When I came to Troas to preach the Good News of Christ, the Lord gave me a good opportunity there. ¹³But I had no peace, because I did not find my brother Titus. So I said good-bye to them at Troas and went to Macedonia.

### VICTORY THROUGH CHRIST

¹⁴But thanks be to God, who always leads us in victory through Christ. God uses us to spread his knowledge everywhere like a sweet-smelling perfume. ¹⁵Our offering to God is this: We are the sweet smell of Christ among those who are being saved and among those who are being lost. ¹⁶To those who are lost, we are the smell of death that brings death, but to those who are being saved, we are the smell of life

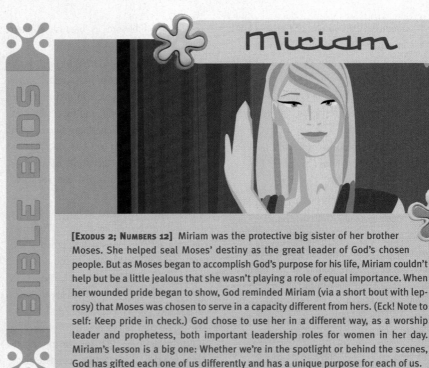

**BIBLE BIOS**

# Miriam

**[EXODUS 2; NUMBERS 12]** Miriam was the protective big sister of her brother Moses. She helped seal Moses' destiny as the great leader of God's chosen people. But as Moses began to accomplish God's purpose for his life, Miriam couldn't help but be a little jealous that she wasn't playing a role of equal importance. When her wounded pride began to show, God reminded Miriam (via a short bout with leprosy) that Moses was chosen to serve in a capacity different from hers. (Eck! Note to self: Keep pride in check.) God chose to use her in a different way, as a worship leader and prophetess, both important leadership roles for women in her day. Miriam's lesson is a big one: Whether we're in the spotlight or behind the scenes, God has gifted each one of us differently and has a unique purpose for each of us.

# ● ➡ CHECK IT OUT

## CHRISTIAN COWBOYS

The Fellowship of Christian Cowboys (FCC), which includes cowgirls, operates "to present to cowboys and all whom they influence, the challenge and adventure of receiving Jesus Christ as Savior and Lord; and to disciple them in their commitment to serve Jesus in their relationships and in the fellowship of the church." The organization hopes to spread the gospel to every rodeo arena and ranchland in the nation.

To reach out, the Fellowship of Christian Cowboys sponsors church services at youth, college, and adult rodeos, horse shows, and roping events. There are local chapters around the country that meet for Bible study, fellowship, and to organize the Cowboy Church services at events. FCC sponsors Rodeo Bible Camps for young people interested in improving their horsemanship and rodeo skills and provides ministry materials for distribution at Cowboy Church, booths, and other livestock related events.

To help, you can send a donation to the national organization and you'll receive a Cowboy Bible, decal, and newsletter subscription; or you can contact a local chapter to join.

*Get involved by visiting* **www.christiancowboys.com**.

that brings life. So who is able to do this work? [17]We do not sell the word of God for a profit as many other people do. But in Christ we speak the truth before God, as messengers of God.

### servants of the new agreement

3 Are we starting to brag about ourselves again? Do we need letters of introduction to you or from you, like some other people? [2]You yourselves are our letter, written on our hearts, known and read by everyone. [3]You show that you are a letter from Christ sent through us. This letter is not written with ink but with the Spirit of the living God. It is not written on stone tablets[n] but on human hearts.

## "THE WRITTEN LAW BRINGS DEATH, BUT THE SPIRIT GIVES LIFE."

[4]We can say this, because through Christ we feel certain before God. [5]We are not saying that we can do this work ourselves. It is God who makes us able to do all that we do. [6]He made us able to be servants of a new agreement from himself to his people. This new agreement is not a written law, but it is of the Spirit. The written law brings death, but the Spirit gives life.

[7]The law that brought death was written in words on stone. It came with God's glory, which

### Bible Basics

**Heaven** is described in the Bible as the place God lives and reigns. It is also the place where humans who believe in him and have asked for his forgiveness will spend eternity. Other details the Bible gives us about heaven include that it has streets made of gold and twelve gates, each made of a single pearl. It is where Jesus sits on the throne at the right hand of God. The Bible also mentions that there will be a great wedding feast, with Jesus as the bridegroom and all of the Christians as his beautiful bride. Heaven will be a place where there will be no more tears, death, sin, or sorrow.

made Moses' face so bright that the Israelites could not continue to look at it. But that glory later disappeared. [8]So surely the new way that brings the Spirit has even more glory. [9]If the law that judged people guilty of sin had glory, surely the new way that makes people right with God has much greater glory. [10]That old law had glory, but it really loses its glory when it is compared to the much greater glory of this new way. [11]If that law which disappeared came with glory, then this new way which continues forever has much greater glory.

[12]We have this hope, so we are very bold. [13]We are not like Moses, who put a covering over his face so the Israelites would not see it.

The glory was disappearing, and Moses did not want them to see it end. [14]But their minds were closed, and even today that same covering hides the meaning when they read the old agreement. That covering is taken away only through Christ. [15]Even today, when they read the law of Moses, there is a covering over their minds. [16]But when a person changes and follows the Lord, that covering is taken away. [17]The Lord is the Spirit, and where the Spirit of the Lord is, there is freedom. [18]Our faces, then, are not covered. We all show the Lord's glory, and we are being changed to be like him. This change in us brings ever greater glory, which comes from the Lord, who is the Spirit.

## LEARN I✞ & LIVE I✞

**1 Corinthians 13:11**
**Learn It:** As children, we acted in childish ways. As mature Christians, we should act mature.
**Live It:** List five ways you have grown in your faith since accepting Christ as your Savior.

**2 Corinthians 3:17**
**Learn It:** Where the spirit of the Lord is, there is freedom.
**Live It:** Act like you have freedom in the Lord. Be enthusiastic and joy-filled. Be passionate about what he has done for you.

**2 Corinthians 4:9**
**Learn It:** Sometimes we are persecuted for Christ, but he does not leave us.
**Live It:** Pray for Christians who live in places where Christianity is illegal.

**3:3 stone tablets** Meaning the Law of Moses that was written on stone tablets (Exodus 24:12; 25:16).

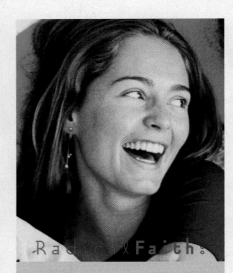

## 2 Corinthians 4:16-18

What do you tend to think about the most—things you can see or things you can't see? When hard times come, it's often really easy just to focus on those hard things in our lives—whether they involve physical ailments, tough circumstances, or emotional pain. But whatever you're going through right now, you can know that it's not going to last forever. There will be an end to it. And this time of pain is so small compared to the hope we have that we will one day be with God forever. All that will last is what God says and what God does. When you're struggling, know that God has put the all-surpassing power of his presence in you and makes you able to withstand anything imaginable. Hope can reign in you every day. Through him, you can be complete and heal from all your pain. You can rest and delight in his presence. What will last for eternity is living with the One who is holy, almighty, and lovely—the wonderful God who draws you close and will always be in control. Ask him to help you spend every day on earth with an eternal perspective, having a clear idea from him of what will last and what won't. Ask him to help you see what is worth your time and your focus.

## PREACHING THE GOOD NEWS

4 God, with his mercy, gave us this work to do, so we don't give up. [2]But we have turned away from secret and shameful ways. We use no trickery, and we do not change the teaching of God. We teach the truth plainly, showing everyone who we are. Then they can know in their hearts what kind of people we are in God's sight. [3]If the Good News that we preach is hidden, it is hidden only to those who are lost. [4]The devil who rules this world has blinded the minds of those who do not believe. They cannot see the light of the Good News— the Good News about the glory of Christ, who is exactly like God. [5]We do not preach about ourselves, but we preach that Jesus Christ is Lord and that we are your servants for Jesus. [6]God once said, "Let the light shine out of the darkness!" This is the same God who made his light shine in our hearts by letting us know the glory of God that is in the face of Christ.

## SPIRITUAL TREASURE IN CLAY JARS

[7]We have this treasure from God, but we are like clay jars that hold the treasure. This shows that the great power is from God, not from us. [8]We have troubles all around us, but we are not defeated. We do not know what to do, but we do not give up the hope of living. [9]We are persecuted, but God does not leave us. We are hurt sometimes, but we are not destroyed. [10]We carry the death of Jesus in our own bodies so that the life of Jesus can also be seen in our bodies. [11]We are alive, but for Jesus we are always in danger of death so that the life of Jesus can be seen in our bodies that die. [12]So death is working in us, but life is working in you.

[13]It is written in the Scriptures, "I believed, so I spoke."[n] Our faith is like this, too. We believe, and so we speak. [14]God raised the Lord Jesus from the dead, and we know that God will also raise us with Jesus. God will bring us together with you, and we will stand before him. [15]All these things are for you. And so the grace of God that is being given to more and more people will bring increasing thanks to God for his glory.

## LIVING BY FAITH

[16]So we do not give up. Our physical body is becoming older and weaker, but our spirit inside us is made new every day. [17]We have small troubles for a while now, but they are helping us gain an eternal glory that is much greater than the troubles. [18]We set our eyes not on what we see but on what we cannot see. What we see will last only a short time, but what we cannot see will last forever.

> **"WE KNOW THAT OUR BODY—THE TENT WE LIVE IN HERE ON EARTH—WILL BE DESTROYED. BUT WHEN THAT HAPPENS, GOD WILL HAVE A HOUSE FOR US."**

5 We know that our body—the tent we live in here on earth—will be destroyed. But when that happens, God will have a house for us. It will not be a house made by human hands; instead, it will be a home in heaven that will last forever. [2]But now we groan in this tent. We want God to give us our heavenly home, [3]because it will clothe us so we will not be naked. [4]While we live in this body, we have burdens, and we groan. We do not want to be naked, but we want to be clothed with our heavenly home. Then this body that dies will be fully covered with life. [5]This is what God made us for, and he has given us the Spirit to be a guarantee for this new life.

[6]So we always have courage. We know that while we live in this body, we are away from the Lord. [7]We live by what we believe, not by what we can see. [8]So I say that we have courage. We really want to be away from this body and be at home with the Lord. [9]Our only goal is to please God whether we live here or there, [10]because we must all stand before Christ to be judged.

 **notes** 4:13 "I . . . spoke." Quotation from Psalm 116:10.

252

Each of us will receive what we should get—good or bad—for the things we did in the earthly body.

### BECOMING FRIENDS WITH GOD

11Since we know what it means to fear the Lord, we try to help people accept the truth about us. God knows what we really are, and I hope that in your hearts you know, too. 12We are not trying to prove ourselves to you again, but we are telling you about ourselves so you will be proud of us. Then you will have an answer for those who are proud about things that can be seen rather than what is in the heart. 13If we are out of our minds, it is for God. If we have our right minds, it is for you. 14The love of Christ controls us, because we know that One died for all, so all have died. 15Christ died for all so that those who live would not continue to live for themselves. He died for

them and was raised from the dead so that they would live for him.

16From this time on we do not think of anyone as the world does. In the past we thought of Christ as the world thinks, but we no longer think of him in that way. 17If anyone belongs to Christ, there is a new creation. The old things have gone; everything is made new! 18All this is from God. Through Christ, God made peace between us and himself, and God gave us the work of telling everyone about the peace we can have with him. 19God was in Christ, making peace between the world and himself. In Christ, God did not hold the world guilty of its sins. And he gave us this message of peace. 20So we have been sent to speak for Christ. It is as if God is calling to you through us. We speak for Christ when we beg you to be at peace with God. 21Christ had no sin, but God made him become sin so that in Christ we could become right with God.

6 We are workers together with God, so we beg you: Do not let the grace that you received from God be for nothing. 2God says,

"At the right time I heard your prayers.
On the day of salvation I helped you."

*Isaiah 49:8*

I tell you that the "right time" is now, and the "day of salvation" is now.

3We do not want anyone to find fault with our work, so nothing we do will be a problem for anyone. 4But in every way we show we are servants of God: in accepting many hard things, in troubles, in difficulties, and in great problems. 5We are beaten and thrown into prison. We meet those who become upset with us and start riots. We work hard, and sometimes we get no sleep or food. 6We show we are servants of God by our pure lives, our understanding, patience, and kindness, by the Holy Spirit, by true love, 7by speaking the truth, and by God's power. We use our right living to defend ourselves against everything. 8Some people honor us, but others blame us. Some people say evil things about us, but others say good things. Some people say we are liars, but

## beautysecret

### Hangnails

Hangnails are the small pieces of dead skin next to your fingernails. They are the result of chronic dry skin, overexposure to water, or a lack of vitamins in your diet. Rather than tear or bite hangnails, trim them carefully. Use moisturizing lotions and eat more vegetables and fruit.

Promises!

## 2 Corinthians 4:17-18

Got a problem? What comes to your mind when you think about that problem? Do you figure out the best way to fix it quickly so that you can get on with your life, or do you step back and wait it out as long as possible? If you're like most of us, you probably just want to find a solution right away.

No one has to remind you that life can be hard. Chances are, you are faced with something that stresses you out almost every day. You failed a test. Your friends suddenly decide they don't want to hang out with you anymore. You feel totally overwhelmed by your after-school activities and can't juggle your responsibilities anymore. Frustrating and hurtful things happen all the time. And everyday life has a way of keeping our minds very occupied and focused on the here and now.

But God promises us so much more than we can see here on earth. He wants us to realize that we don't have to be tied down to our everyday troubles. We can set our eyes and our focus on God and what he has in store for us—things that are eternal.

# Blab

**Q:** Everyone else at school is getting so excited about college. I just feel worried about it. What's wrong with me?

**A:** Nothing. Some people like to try new things; some do not. College is a great chance to mature and discover some of God's purposes for you, but it is normal to be concerned about all the upcoming changes. Pray for peace about your college decision. If you feel you are not ready to go away, look into schools in your own area.

**Q:** I hate high school. It seems so boring and stupid. Why can't I just get my G.E.D. or drop out and start working now?

**A:** If you are old enough, technically you can. However, it may not be the best choice for your future. Typically, high school diplomas are more accepted for scholarships, grants, and college admission than a G.E.D. And dropping out to work almost guarantees you years of low-paying jobs ahead. God asks us to do our best in everything we do. You need to finish high school; ask him for the grace to do it with excellence and a good attitude.

**Q:** I didn't make cheerleading, and I am really bummed. How come I am never quite good enough?

**A:** You are God's absolutely perfect design for you; and when frustrating things happen, you need to trust that he has a reason for it. Maybe you didn't make cheerleading because God knows you are going to be the lead in the school play. Or maybe he wants you to spend the time helping others instead. Ask him to comfort you and show you what you should do next.

we speak the truth. [9]We are not known, but we are well known. We seem to be dying, but we continue to live. We are punished, but we are not killed. [10]We have much sadness, but we are always rejoicing. We are poor, but we are making many people rich in faith. We have nothing, but really we have everything.

[11]We have spoken freely to you in Corinth and have opened our hearts to you. [12]Our feelings of love for you have not stopped, but you have stopped your feelings of love for us. [13]I speak to you as if you were my children. Do to us as we have done—open your hearts to us.

## warning about non-christians

[14]You are not the same as those who do not believe. So do not join yourselves to them. Good and bad do not belong together. Light and darkness cannot share together. [15]How can Christ and Belial, the devil, have any agreement? What can a believer have together with a nonbeliever? [16]The temple of God cannot have any agreement with idols, and we are the temple of the living God. As God said: "I will live with them and walk with them. And I will be their God, and they will be my people."

[17]"Leave those people,
and be separate, says the Lord.
Touch nothing that is unclean,
and I will accept you."

*Isaiah 52:11; Ezekiel 20:34, 41*

[18]"I will be your father,
and you will be my sons and daughters,
says the Lord Almighty." *2 Samuel 7:14*

7 Dear friends, we have these promises from God, so we should make ourselves pure—free from anything that makes body or soul unclean. We should try to become holy in the way we live, because we respect God.

## paul's joy

[2]Open your hearts to us. We have not done wrong to anyone, we have not ruined the faith of anyone, and we have not cheated anyone. [3]I do not say this to blame you. I told you before that we love you so much we would live or die with you. [4]I feel very sure of you and am very

proud of you. You give me much comfort, and in all of our troubles I have great joy.

[5]When we came into Macedonia, we had no rest. We found trouble all around us. We had fighting on the outside and fear on the inside. [6]But God, who comforts those who are troubled, comforted us when Titus came. [7]We were comforted, not only by his coming but also by the comfort you gave him. Titus told us about your wish to see me and that you are very sorry for what you did. He also told me about your great care for me, and when I heard this, I was much happier.

[8]Even if my letter made you sad, I am not sorry I wrote it. At first I was sorry, because it made you sad, but you were sad only for a short time. [9]Now I am happy, not because you were made sad, but because your sorrow made you change your lives. You became sad in the way God wanted you to, so you were not hurt by us in any way. [10]The kind of sorrow God wants makes people change their hearts and lives. This leads to salvation, and you cannot be sorry for that. But the kind of sorrow the world has brings death. [11]See what this sorrow—the sorrow God wanted you to have—has done to you: It has made you very serious. It made you want to prove you were not wrong.

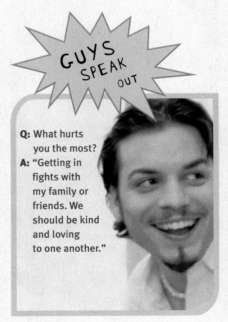

**GUYS SPEAK OUT**

**Q:** What hurts you the most?
**A:** "Getting in fights with my family or friends. We should be kind and loving to one another."

 notes 6:16 "I . . . people." Quotation from Leviticus 26:11-12; Jeremiah 32:38; Ezekiel 37:27.

254

It made you angry and afraid. It made you want to see me. It made you care. It made you want the right thing to be done. You proved you were innocent in the problem. [12]I wrote that letter, not because of the one who did the wrong or because of the person who was hurt. I wrote the letter so you could see, before God, the great care you have for us. [13]That is why we were comforted.

**DIDYA KNOW**

**HALF OF ALL TEENS SAY THEY ARE CONCERNED THEY MIGHT GO FURTHER SEXUALLY THAN THEY HAD PLANNED TO BECAUSE THEY WERE DRINKING OR USING DRUGS.** KAISER FAMILY FOUNDATION AND MTV

Not only were we very comforted, we were even happier to see that Titus was so happy. All of you made him feel much better. [14]I bragged to Titus about you, and you showed that I was right. Everything we said to you was true, and you have proved that what we bragged about to Titus is true. [15]And his love for you is stronger when he remembers that you all ready to obey. You welcomed him with respect and fear. [16]I am very happy that I can trust you fully.

## CHRISTIAN GIVING

8 And now, brothers and sisters, we want you to know about the grace God gave the churches in Macedonia. [2]They have been tested by great troubles, and they are very poor. But they gave much because of their great joy. [3]I can tell you that they gave as much as they were able and even more than they could afford. No one told them to do it. [4]But they begged and pleaded with us to let them share in this service for God's people. [5]And they gave in a way we did not expect: They first gave themselves to the Lord and to us. This is what God wants. [6]So we asked Titus to help you finish this special work of grace since he is the one who started it. [7]You are rich in everything—in faith, in speaking, in knowledge, in truly wanting to help, and in the love you learned from us. In the same way, be strong also in the grace of giving.

[8]I am not commanding you to give. But I want to see if your love is true by comparing you with others that really want to help. [9]You know the grace of our Lord Jesus Christ. You know that Christ was rich, but for you he became poor so that by his becoming poor you might become rich.

[10]This is what I think you should do: Last year you were the first to want to give, and you were the first who gave. [11]So now finish the work you started. Then your "doing" will be equal to your "wanting to do." Give from what you have. [12]If you want to give, your gift will be accepted. It will be judged by what you have, not by what you do not have. [13]We do not want you to have troubles while other people are at ease, but we want everything to be equal. [14]At this time you have plenty. What you have can help others who are in need. Then later, when they have plenty, they can help you when you are in need, and all will be equal. [15]As it is written in the Scriptures, "The person who gathered more did not have too much, nor did the person who gathered less have too little."

## TITUS AND HIS COMPANIONS HELP

[16]I thank God because he gave Titus the same love for you that I have. [17]Titus accepted what we asked him to do. He wanted very much to go to you, and this was his own idea. [18]We are sending with him the brother who is praised by all the churches because of his service in preaching the Good News. [19]Also, this brother was chosen by the churches to go with us when we deliver this gift of money. We are doing this service to bring glory to the Lord and to show that we really want to help. [20]We are being careful so that no one will criticize us for the way we are handling this large gift. [21]We are trying hard to do what the

**top 10**

**random ways to connect with your family**

**10** Pray out loud for each other.

**9** Share the "highs" and "lows" of your day.

**8** Watch a video and eat popcorn.

**7** Throw a ball together.

**6** Go for a walk.

**5** Take a road trip.

**4** Visit a theme park.

**3** Read a book out loud together.

**2** Play a board game.

**1** Cook dinner for everyone.

notes **8:15** "The person . . . little." Quotation from Exodus 16:18.

# Music Reviews

| GROUP: | ALBUM: |
|---|---|
| JARS OF CLAY | JARS OF CLAY (CLASSIC HIT) |

It's hard to believe that this Jars of Clay debut is now more than ten years old, but it contains great string-backed pop tunes that still get radio play today. Who could forget the crossover single "Flood" or the chanting monks who start the song "Liquid"? Nearly every song on this disc, from "Love Song for a Savior" to the beautiful "Worlds Apart," became a radio single then and definitely deserves a listen today. If you've never checked it out, don't wait any longer.

**WHY IT ROCKS: JARS OF CLAY BROKE NEW MUSICAL GROUND WITH THIS OUTSTANDING DEBUT THAT STILL HOLDS UP TEN YEARS LATER.**

Lord accepts as right and also what people think is right.

<sup>22</sup>Also, we are sending with them our brother, who is always ready to help. He has proved this to us in many ways, and he wants to help even more now, because he has much faith in you.

## "WE ARE TRYING HARD TO DO WHAT THE LORD ACCEPTS AS RIGHT AND ALSO WHAT PEOPLE THINK IS RIGHT."

<sup>23</sup>Now about Titus—he is my partner who is working with me to help you. And about the other brothers—they are sent from the churches, and they bring glory to Christ. <sup>24</sup>So show these men the proof of your love and the reason we are proud of you. Then all the churches can see it.

### Help for Fellow Christians

**9** I really do not need to write you about this help for God's people. <sup>2</sup>I know you want to help. I have been bragging about this to the people in Macedonia, telling them that you in Southern Greece have been ready to give since last year. And your desire to give has made most of them ready to give also. <sup>3</sup>But I

am sending the brothers to you so that our bragging about you in this will not be empty words. I want you to be ready, as I said you would be. <sup>4</sup>If any of the people from Macedonia come with me and find that you are not ready, we will be ashamed that we were so sure of you. (And you will be ashamed, too!) <sup>5</sup>So I thought I should ask these brothers to go to you before we do. They will finish getting in order the generous gift you promised so it will be ready when we come. And it will be a generous gift—not one that you did not want to give.

<sup>6</sup>Remember this: The person who plants a little will have a small harvest, but the person who plants a lot will have a big harvest. <sup>7</sup>Each

# LEARN I+ & LIVE I+

**2 Corinthians 6:3**
**Learn It:** We do not want to do anything that will cause anyone to doubt our work.
**Live It:** Whatever job you have to do today—from a massive school project to making your bed—do it to the very best of your abilities.

**2 Corinthians 6:14**
**Learn It:** Do not join yourself to unbelievers.
**Live It:** Love nonbelievers, but do not put them in the role of best friends or boyfriends. You may think you can bend over the fence and pull someone up, but most likely you will fall over.

**2 Corinthians 8:12**
**Learn It:** Your gift will be judged by what you have, not by what you don't have.
**Live It:** Give with a motive of pleasing God, not worrying about whether you can give as much as someone else.

## Radical Faith:

## 2 Corinthians 9:8

Would you say that you're a generous person? Do you give what's in your hands or within your reach to help someone else who needs it? Maybe sometimes you'd like to give, but you're worried about having what you need for yourself or you just don't want to let your things go. God calls you to be generous in every way and to care for others. All the things he's given you, both physical and spiritual resources, are intended to be used for his eternal and very important purposes. And when you give all you possibly can to others, you will begin to notice how God abundantly provides you. When you're generous—and not just with your money, but also with your time and talents—you will find that God will actually give you more than you need to help you do a ton of good works for his glory. Offer what you've got. He'll keep providing you with physical resources (Matthew 6:25-26) and unlimited spiritual resources (Ephesians 1:3). Ask God to help you see what spiritual gifts he's given you, and then use them. You've got a whole lot to give!

one should give as you have decided in your heart to give. You should not be sad when you give, and you should not give because you feel forced to give. God loves the person who gives happily. [8]And God can give you more blessings than you need. Then you will always have plenty of everything—enough to give to every good work. [9]It is written in the Scriptures:

"He gives freely to the poor.

The things he does are right and will
continue forever." *Psalm 112:9*

[10]God is the One who gives seed to the farmer and bread for food. He will give you all the seed you need and make it grow so there will be a great harvest from your goodness. [11]He will make you rich in every way so that you can always give freely. And your giving through us will cause many to give thanks to God. [12]This service you do not only helps the needs of God's people, it also brings many more thanks to God. [13]It is a proof of your faith. Many people will praise God because you obey the Good News of Christ—the gospel you say you believe—and because you freely share with them and with all others. [14]And when they pray, they will wish they could be with you because of the great grace that God has given you. [15]Thanks be to God for his gift that is too wonderful for words.

### PAUL DEFENDS HIS MINISTRY

10 I, Paul, am begging you with the gentleness and the kindness of Christ. Some people say that I am easy on you when I am with you and bold when I am away. [2]They think we live in a worldly way, and I plan to be very bold with them when I come. I beg you that when I come I will not need to use that same boldness with you. [3]We do live in the world, but we do not fight in the same way the world fights. [4]We fight with weapons that are different from those the world uses. Our weapons have power from God that can destroy the enemy's strong places. We destroy people's arguments [5]and every proud thing that raises itself against the knowledge of God. We capture every thought and make it give up and obey

Christ. [6]We are ready to punish anyone there who does not obey, but first we want you to obey fully.

[7]You must look at the facts before you. If you feel sure that you belong to Christ, you must remember that we belong to Christ just as you do. [8]It is true that we brag freely about the authority the Lord gave us. But this authority is to build you up, not to tear you down. So I will not be ashamed. [9]I do not want you to think I am trying to scare you with my letters. [10]Some people say, "Paul's letters are powerful and sound important, but when he is with us, he is weak. And his speaking is nothing." [11]They should know this: We are not there with you now, so we say these things in letters. But when we are there with you, we will show the same authority that we show in our letters.

## relationships

"In every way be an example of doing good deeds" (Titus 2:7). You show others what kind of relationship you have with God by the things you do. If you act one way at church and another way at school, people will notice. Non-Christians often call Christians "hypocrites" because so many believers talk about God, but don't act the way he wants them to. Do the right thing simply because it's the right thing, whether anyone else is doing it or not.

¹²We do not dare to compare ourselves with those who think they are very important. They use themselves to measure themselves, and they judge themselves by what they themselves are. This shows that they know nothing. ¹³But we will not brag about things outside the work that was given us to do. We will limit our bragging to the work that God gave us, and this includes our work with you. ¹⁴We are not bragging too much, as we would be if we had not already come to you. But we have come to you with the Good News of Christ. ¹⁵We limit our bragging to the work that is ours, not what others have done. We hope that as your faith continues to grow, you will help our work to grow much larger. ¹⁶We want to tell the Good News in the areas beyond your city. We do not want to brag about work that has already been done in another person's area. ¹⁷But, "If someone wants to brag, he should brag only about the Lord."ⁿ ¹⁸It is not those who say they are good who are accepted but those who the Lord thinks are good.

## "HE GIVES FREELY TO THE POOR. THE THINGS HE DOES ARE RIGHT AND WILL CONTINUE FOREVER."

### Paul and the False Apostles

11 I wish you would be patient with me even when I am a little foolish, but you are already doing that. ²I am jealous over you with a jealousy that comes from God. I promised to give you to Christ, as your only husband. I want to give you as his pure bride. ³But I am afraid that your minds will be led away from your true and pure following of Christ just as Eve was tricked by the snake with his evil ways. ⁴You are very patient with anyone who comes to you and preaches a different Jesus from the one we preached. You are very willing to accept a spirit or gospel that is different from the Spirit and Good News you received from us.

⁵I do not think that those "great apostles" are any better than I am. ⁶I may not be a trained speaker, but I do have knowledge. We have shown this to you clearly in every way.

⁷I preached God's Good News to you without pay. I made myself unimportant to make you important. Do you think that was wrong? ⁸I accepted pay from other churches, taking their money so I could serve you. ⁹If I needed something when I was with you, I did not trouble any of you. The brothers who came from Macedonia gave me all that I needed. I did not allow myself to depend on you in any way, and I will never depend on you. ¹⁰No one in Southern Greece will stop me from bragging about that. I say this with the truth of Christ in me. ¹¹And why do I not depend on you? Do you think it is because I do not love you? God knows that I love you.

¹²And I will continue doing what I am doing now, because I want to stop those people from having a reason to brag. They would like to say that the work they brag about is the same as ours. ¹³Such men are not true apostles but are workers who lie. They change themselves to look like apostles of Christ. ¹⁴This does not surprise us. Even Satan changes himself to look like an angel of light.ⁿ ¹⁵So it does not surprise us if Satan's servants also make themselves look like servants who work for what is right. But in the end they will be punished for what they do.

### Paul Tells About His Sufferings

¹⁶I tell you again: No one should think I am a fool. But if you think so, accept me as you would accept a fool. Then I can brag a little, too. ¹⁷When I brag because I feel sure of myself, I am not talking as the Lord would talk but as a fool. ¹⁸Many people are bragging about their lives in the world. So I will brag too. ¹⁹You are wise, so you will gladly be patient with fools! ²⁰You are even patient with those who order you around, or use you, or trick you, or think they are better than you, or hit you in the face. ²¹It is shameful to me to say

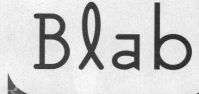

**Blab**

**Q:** I just found out that I have a sexually transmitted disease that I will have for the rest of my life. I am so ashamed! Will anyone ever love me now?

**A:** Sex outside of marriage has devastating consequences. If you have asked God to forgive you and are not having sex now, leave the future in his hands. He can bring into your life someone who will love you no matter what you have done in the past and no matter what you may face with this disease.

**Q:** I got a little drunk at a party last weekend and drove home. I had promised my parents I would never get behind the wheel if I had had any alcohol. I got home okay, and I don't want to be grounded. Do I have to tell them?

**A:** Yes, part of the process of redemption is confessing your sin. You disobeyed. Your parents will be disappointed and mad, but take the punishment and learn your lesson. Tell them it won't happen again, and then prove it when they allow you to drive again.

**Q:** My parents let me drive the car around our property before I had a license. They also allow me to drink some of their wine. If they say it's okay to break the law, is it?

**A:** It really isn't. The Scriptures make it clear that we are to obey the laws of our land—unless the laws break God's laws. Thank them for the offer to drive and to taste wine, but tell them you want to wait until it is legal.

**10:17** "If . . . Lord." Quotation from Jeremiah 9:24. **11:14 angel of light** Messenger from God. The devil fools people so that they think he is from God.

259

# LEARN I+ & LIVE I+

**2 Corinthians 9:7**
**Learn It:** You should give to God when you feel good about it. He wants you to give happily.
**Live It:** Give $20, a bag of groceries, or a gift certificate to someone who needs it.

**2 Corinthians 10:4-5**
**Learn It:** You can take sinful thoughts captive.
**Live It:** The next time you find yourself thinking something inappropriate, stop yourself. Offer up a prayer to God or sing a song of praise.

**2 Corinthians 11:4**
**Learn It:** Accepting false teachings about Christ is a mistake.
**Live It:** Study the Bible as much as you can so that you are not fooled by things that sound good or close to the truth but that are not the truth.

this, but we were too "weak" to do those things to you!

But if anyone else is brave enough to brag, then I also will be brave and brag. (I am talking as a fool.) ²²Are they Hebrews?" So am I. Are they Israelites? So am I. Are they from Abra-ham's family? So am I. ²³Are they serving Christ? I am serving him more. (I am crazy to talk like this.) I have worked much harder than they. I have been in prison more often. I have been hurt more in beatings. I have been near death many times. ²⁴Five times the Jews have given me their punishment of thirty-nine lashes with a whip. ²⁵Three different times I was beaten with rods. One time I was almost stoned to death. Three times I was in ships that wrecked, and one of those times I spent a night and a day in the sea. ²⁶I have gone on many travels and have been in danger from rivers, thieves, my own people, the Jews, and those who are not Jews. I have been in danger in cities, in places where no one lives, and on the sea. And I have been in danger with false Christians. ²⁷I have done hard and tiring work, and many times I did not sleep. I have been hungry and thirsty, and many times I have been without food. I have been cold and without clothes. ²⁸Besides all this, there is on me every day the load of my concern for all the churches. ²⁹I feel weak every time someone is weak, and I feel upset every time someone is led into sin.

³⁰If I must brag, I will brag about the things that show I am weak. ³¹God knows I am not lying. He is the God and Father of the Lord Jesus Christ, and he is to be praised forever. ³²When I was in Damascus, the governor under King Aretas wanted to arrest me, so he put guards around the city. ³³But my friends lowered me in a basket through a hole in the city wall. So I escaped from the governor.

## beauty secret

### Warts

Warts are excess skin growths caused by viruses in the papillomavirus (HPV) family—which has more than sixty members. Common warts grow on the back of your hands, arms, face, and elbows; and plantar warts grow on the soles of your feet. See a doctor to remove any warts rather than trying do-it-yourself methods.

## A SPECIAL BLESSING IN PAUL'S LIFE

**12** I must continue to brag. It will do no good, but I will talk now about visions and revelations" from the Lord. ²I know a man in Christ who was taken up to the third heaven fourteen years ago. I do not know whether the man was in his body or out of his body, but God knows. ³⁻⁴And I know that this man was taken up to paradise." I don't know if he was in his body or away from his body, but God knows. He heard things he is not able to explain, things that no human is allowed to tell. ⁵I will brag about a man like that, but I will not brag about myself, except about my weaknesses. ⁶But if I wanted to brag about myself, I would not be a fool, because I would be telling the truth. But I will not brag about myself. I do not want people to think more of me than what they see me do or hear me say.

## "MY GRACE IS ENOUGH FOR YOU. WHEN YOU ARE WEAK, MY POWER IS MADE PERFECT IN YOU."

⁷So that I would not become too proud of the wonderful things that were shown to me, a painful physical problem" was given to me. This problem was a messenger from Satan,

**11:22 Hebrews** A name for the Jews that some Jews were very proud of. **12:1 revelations** Revelation is making known a truth that was hidden. **12:3-4 paradise** Another word for heaven. **12:7 painful physical problem** Literally, "thorn in the flesh."

260

sent to beat me and keep me from being too proud. [8]I begged the Lord three times to take this problem away from me. [9]But he said to me, "My grace is enough for you. When you are weak, my power is made perfect in you." So I am very happy to brag about my weaknesses. Then Christ's power can live in me. [10]For this reason I am happy when I have weaknesses, insults, hard times, sufferings, and all kinds of troubles for Christ. Because when I am weak, then I am truly strong.

## DIDYA KNOW

**UNACCOMPANIED YOUTHS AGES 13 TO 16 ARE ABLE TO BUY M-RATED VIDEO GAMES 85% OF THE TIME.**

FEDERAL TRADE COMMISSION

### PAUL'S LOVE FOR THE CHRISTIANS

[11]I have been talking like a fool, but you made me do it. You are the ones who should say good things about me. I am worth nothing, but those "great apostles" are not worth any more than I am! [12]When I was with you, I patiently did the things that prove I am an apostle—signs, wonders, and miracles. [13]So you received everything that the other churches have

### GUYS SPEAK OUT

**Q:** What do you like to do on dates?
**A:** "I like to do whatever she wants to do. (And that's probably the best thing, right?)"

received. Only one thing was different: I was not a burden to you. Forgive me for this!

[14]I am now ready to visit you the third time, and I will not be a burden to you. I want nothing from you, except you. Children should not have to save up to give to their parents. Parents should save to give to their children. [15]So I am happy to give everything I have for you, even myself. If I love you more, will you love me less?

[16]It is clear I was not a burden to you, but you think I was tricky and lied to catch you. [17]Did I cheat you by using any of the messengers I sent to you? No, you know I did not. [18]I asked Titus to go to you, and I sent our brother with him. Titus did not cheat you, did he? No, you know that Titus and I did the same thing and with the same spirit.

[19]Do you think we have been defending ourselves to you all this time? We have been speaking in Christ and before God. You are our dear friends, and everything we do is to make you stronger. [20]I am afraid that when I come, you will not be what I want you to be, and I will not be what you want me to be. I am afraid that among you there may be arguing, jealousy, anger, selfish fighting, evil talk, gossip, pride, and confusion. [21]I am afraid that when I come to you again, my God will make me ashamed before you. I may be saddened by many of those who have sinned because they have not changed their hearts or turned from their sexual sins and the shameful things they have done.

### FINAL WARNINGS AND GREETINGS

**13** I will come to you for the third time. "Every case must be proved by two or three witnesses."[n] [2]When I was with you the

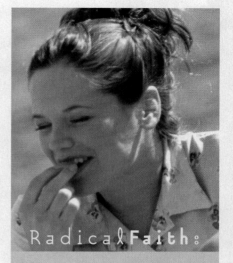

### Radical Faith:

## 2 Corinthians 12:7-10

Limitations, struggles, and failures can easily get you down. So it's so cool to know that God created you just the way you are for a reason, and he wants you to know that he fills in all the gaps in your abilities. And that allows his power to shine through you! It's even more exciting than somehow having it all together on your own. That's why Paul said he was actually OK with all the things he couldn't do. He was even OK with adversity and physical pain. He didn't like it, but he could accept it because he knew he could find God in it. When Paul found himself weak and struggling quite a bit, he stayed cool about it. Those tough times helped him understand and depend on God's strength and grace. He learned that it was only when he operated with God's power, not his own, that worthwhile things happened. And God got a lot of glory and recognition through Paul's life. God made Paul solid and effective. So don't get down on yourself about what you can't do or what holds you back. Rather, embrace what God can do. Remember that in every tough situation, God has something to teach you.

notes
**13:1 "Every . . . witnesses."** Quotation from Deuteronomy 19:15.

quiz

# IS HE a PLaYeR?

SO YOU'VE GOT A GUY AND YOU THINK HE'S THE BEST THING SINCE THE IPOD. TAKE A LOOK AT THE QUESTIONS BELOW TO SEE IF THEY DESCRIBE HIM.

**1. IS HE SUPER-SWEET TO YOU WHEN YOU'RE HANGING OUT OR CHATTING ON THE PHONE BUT IGNORES YOU IN FRONT OF HIS FRIENDS?**

A. Yes.
B. No.

**2. DOES HE HAVE A REPUTATION FOR HAVING A DIFFERENT DATE TO EVERY SCHOOL DANCE?**

A. Yes.
B. No.

**3. DOES HE OFTEN PROMISE TO CALL YOU BUT DOESN'T?**

A. Yes.
B. No.

**4. HE COMES TO YOUR PARTY BUT ENDS UP TALKING TO THE NEW GIRL IN CLASS ALL NIGHT.**

A. True.
B. False.

**5. HAVE YOU TWO BEEN "DATING" FOR SEVERAL MONTHS BUT HE HAS YET TO CALL YOU HIS GIRLFRIEND OR EVEN BRING UP THE SUBJECT?**

A. No.
B. Yes.

**6. YOU'VE BEEN HANGING OUT AND YOU'RE CONVINCED HE REALLY LIKES YOU, BUT THEN HE WON'T CALL OR SEE YOU FOR A COUPLE OF WEEKS.**

A. True.
B. False.

**7. YOU'VE SEEN HIM OUT WITH ANOTHER GIRL, BUT HE INSISTS THEY'RE JUST FRIENDS.**

A. False.
B. True.

**8. NO ONE REALLY KNOWS ABOUT YOUR RELATIONSHIP. HE LIKES THAT IT'S YOUR "LITTLE SECRET."**

A. True.
B. False.

**9. HAS HE BROKEN A FEW DATES WITH YOU AT THE LAST MINUTE?**

A. Yes.
B. No.

**10. HE PUSHES YOU TO GO FARTHER PHYSICALLY THAN YOU'RE WILLING TO GO.**

A. False.
B. True.

**IF YOU ANSWERED YES/TRUE TO FOUR OR MORE QUESTIONS, YOU PROBABLY HAVE A PLAYER ON YOUR HANDS!**

You may be asking, "So what is a player and what's the big deal anyway?" A player is a someone who is "playing" with your heart. Whether it's entirely intentional or not, he's a tease. And although he seems to be pretty into you, he's not looking for any kind of commitment. You should be concerned because the reality is that you are probably going to get hurt. You may be investing a lot in this relationship but you won't get much in return. He's not worth it. Protect your heart and get rid of this guy!

second time, I gave a warning to those who had sinned. Now I am away from you, and I give a warning to all the others. When I come to you again, I will not be easy with them. [3]You want proof that Christ is speaking through me. My proof is that he is not weak among you, but he is powerful. [4]It is true that he was weak when he was killed on the cross, but he lives now by God's power. It is true that we are weak in Christ, but for you we will be alive in Christ by God's power.

[5]Look closely at yourselves. Test yourselves to see if you are living in the faith. You know that Jesus Christ is in you—unless you fail the test. [6]But I hope you will see that we ourselves have not failed the test. [7]We pray to God that you will not do anything wrong. It is not important to see that we have passed the test, but it is important that you do what is right, even if it seems we have failed. [8]We cannot do anything against the truth, but only for the truth. [9]We are happy to be weak, if you are strong, and we pray that you will become complete. [10]I am writing this while I am away from you so that when I come I will not have to be harsh in my use of authority. The Lord gave me this authority to build you up, not to tear you down.

## BIBLE BIOS

# Naomi

[**BOOK OF RUTH**] Naomi had to be the mother of all mothers-in-law, because both of her daughters-in-law adored her! Despite her own troubles (she had left home with her husband and sons to escape famine), Naomi treated her sons' wives, Ruth and Orpah, as her very own daughters. She didn't care that they were of a different nationality and religious tradition. Later, when tragedy struck and left all three women widowed, Naomi encouraged the girls to return to their own fathers' homes so they could eventually remarry. Orpah returned home, but Ruth chose to stay with Naomi in a foreign land, instead of starting a new life of her own. Naomi showed Ruth and Orpah, as much as is humanly possible, what God's unconditional love is like. And God blessed her with a new family through Ruth.

[11]Now, brothers and sisters, I say good-bye. Try to be complete. Do what I have asked you to do. Agree with each other, and live in peace. Then the God of love and peace will be with you.

[12]Greet each other with a holy kiss. [13]All of God's holy people send greetings to you.

[14]The grace of the Lord Jesus Christ, the love of God, and the fellowship of the Holy Spirit be with you all.

**S**ome people look at the Christian faith in terms of what we should and shouldn't do as Christians: Christians are supposed to read their Bible. ... Christians aren't supposed to lie. ... Christians are supposed to pray. ... Christians aren't supposed to cheat. ... You get the point.

# Galatians
### freedom in christ

That's exactly what the believers in Galatia were struggling with. Certain teachers were undermining the belief that Jesus' death on the cross was what makes people right with God. (Remember Romans 3?) Instead, they were convincing the Galatians that they must adhere to every morsel of the Old Testament Jewish law to earn favor with God. They were preaching a legalistic religion that depended on what each person did—not on what Jesus had already done.

Paul's message in Galatians is this: If our faith is just a list of dos and don'ts, we're missing the point. Jesus gave us freedom from the old laws when he defeated death through his resurrection. "We have freedom now, because Christ made us free. So stand strong. Do not change and go back into the slavery of the law" (5:1). It's a freedom that should be embraced rather than abused, though. "Do not use your freedom as an excuse to do what pleases your sinful self. Serve each other with love" (5:13).

1 From Paul, an apostle. I was not chosen to be an apostle by human beings, nor was I sent from human beings. I was made an apostle through Jesus Christ and God the Father who raised Jesus from the dead. [2]This letter is also from all those of God's family[n] who are with me.

To the churches in Galatia:[n]

[3]Grace and peace to you from God our Father and the Lord Jesus Christ. [4]Jesus gave himself for our sins to free us from this evil world we live in, as God the Father planned. [5]The glory belongs to God forever and ever. Amen.

## THE ONLY GOOD NEWS

[6]God, by his grace through Christ, called you to become his people. So I am amazed that you are turning away so quickly and believing something different than the Good News. [7]Really, there is no other Good News. But some people are confusing you; they want to change the Good News of Christ. [8]We preached to you the Good News. So if we ourselves, or even an angel from heaven, should preach to you something different, we should be judged guilty! [9]I said this before, and now I say it again: You have already accepted the Good News. If anyone is preaching something different to you, he should be judged guilty!

[10]Do you think I am trying to make people accept me? No, God is the One I am trying to please. Am I trying to please people? If I still wanted to please people, I would not be a servant of Christ.

## PAUL'S AUTHORITY IS FROM GOD

[11]Brothers and sisters,[n] I want you to know that the Good News I preached to you was not made up by human beings. [12]I did not get it from humans, nor did anyone teach it to me, but Jesus Christ showed it to me.

[13]You have heard about my past life in the Jewish religion. I attacked the church of God and tried to destroy it. [14]I was becoming a leader in the Jewish religion, doing better than most other Jews of my age. I tried harder than anyone else to follow the teachings handed down by our ancestors.

[15]But God had special plans for me and set me apart for his work even before I was born. He called me through his grace [16]and showed his son to me so that I might tell the Good News about him to those who are not Jewish. When God called me, I did not get advice or help from any person. [17]I did not go to Jerusalem to see those who were apostles before I was. But, without waiting, I went away to Arabia and later went back to Damascus.

[18]After three years I went to Jerusalem to meet Peter and stayed with him for fifteen days. [19]I met no other apostles, except James, the brother of the Lord. [20]God knows that these things I write are not lies. [21]Later, I went to the areas of Syria and Cilicia.

[22]In Judea the churches in Christ had never met me. [23]They had only heard it said, "This man who was attacking us is now preaching the same faith that he once tried to destroy." [24]And these believers praised God because of me.

## OTHER APOSTLES ACCEPTED PAUL

2 After fourteen years I went to Jerusalem again, this time with Barnabas. I also took Titus with me. [2]I went because God showed me I should go. I met with the believers there, and in private I told their leaders the Good News that I preach to the non-Jewish people. I did not want my past work and the work I am now doing to be wasted. [3]Titus was with me, but he was not forced to be circumcised, even though he was a Greek. [4]We talked about this problem because some false believers had come into our group secretly. They came in like spies to overturn the freedom we have in Christ Jesus. They wanted to make us slaves. [5]But we did not give in to those false believers for a minute. We wanted the truth of the Good News to continue for you.

[6]Those leaders who seemed to be important did not change the Good News that I preach. (It doesn't matter to me if they were "important" or not. To God everyone is the

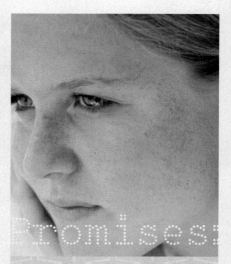

## Galatians 1:11-12

Rumors are funny creatures. One little piece of truth is thrown out there and suddenly it gets out of control. For example, consider this statement: Kara thinks Josh is nice and pretty cute. Then one person tells another, who tells another, who tells another . . . you get the point. Pretty soon, the simple statement has grown into the rumor that Kara and Josh have been secretly dating for months! Ugh. Poor Kara.

Human beings are good at coming up with crazy stories. Check out any video store or library and you will see all kinds of tales that may be great for entertainment, but don't contain much truth or reality. Fortunately, the story of Jesus' death and resurrection is not a random story created from someone's imagination. We can trust that what we read in the Bible is the actual word of God and what it contains is right and true. Who could ever imagine that God could love us as much as he does and therefore give Jesus as a sacrifice for us? That's a story that is beyond even the greatest writer.

 **notes** 1:2 those . . . family The Greek text says "brothers." 1:2 Galatia Probably the same country where Paul preached and began churches on his first missionary trip. Read the Book of Acts, chapters 13 and 14. 1:11 Brothers and sisters Although the Greek text says "Brothers" here and throughout this book, Paul's words were meant for the entire church, including men and women.

## CHECK IT OUT

### YOUTH WITH A MISSION (YWAM)/KING'S KIDS INTERNATIONAL

When 20-year-old college student Loren Cunningham saw a vision during his prayer time of waves of young people spreading all over the world, he never dreamed the vision would become reality. In 1960, Cunningham started Youth With a Mission, a missions organization dedicated to helping send young Christians around the world to spread the good news of Jesus.

By the year 2000, YWAM had more than 11,000 staff from over 130 countries. For young adults, it offers 11- to 12-week Discipleship Training Schools (DTS) to prepare messengers of the gospel, helping students to know God in depth. The goal is to form Christian character and establish biblical relationships while developing a daily walk with God. The DTS classes are typically followed by a 12-week outreach.

To get a preview of YWAM, teens can join King's Kids International, where ages 8 to 18 participate in short-term missions and mission camps around the world during summers and other school breaks. King's Kids do hands-on service, form worship teams, reach unchurched young people, and receive discipleship and training.

*Get involved by visiting www.ywam.org or www.kkint.net.*

---

same.) ⁷But these leaders saw that I had been given the work of telling the Good News to those who are not Jewish, just as Peter had the work of telling the Jews. ⁸God gave Peter the power to work as an apostle for the Jewish people. But he also gave me the power to work as an apostle for those who are not Jews. ⁹James, Peter, and John, who seemed to be the leaders, understood that God had given me this special grace, so they accepted Barnabas and me. They agreed that they would go to the Jewish people and that we should go to those who are not Jewish. ¹⁰The only thing they asked us was to remember to help the poor—something I really wanted to do.

### PAUL SHOWS THAT PETER WAS WRONG

¹¹When Peter came to Antioch, I challenged him to his face, because he was wrong. ¹²Peter ate with the non-Jewish people until some Jewish people sent from James came to Antioch. When they arrived, Peter stopped eating with those who weren't Jewish, and he separated himself from them. He was afraid of the Jews. ¹³So Peter was a hypocrite, as were the other Jewish believers who joined with him. Even Barnabas was influenced by what these Jewish believers did. ¹⁴When I saw they were not following the truth of the Good News, I spoke to Peter in front of them all. I said, "Peter, you are a Jew, but you are not living like a Jew. You are living like those who are not Jewish. So why do you now try to force those who are not Jewish to live like Jews?"

¹⁵We were not born as non-Jewish "sinners," but as Jews. ¹⁶Yet we know that a person is made right with God not by following the law, but by trusting in Jesus Christ. So we, too, have put our faith in Christ Jesus, that we might be

---

## LEARN I+ & LIVE I+

**2 Corinthians 12:9-10**
**Learn It:** When we are weak, Christ's power in us is even more apparent.
**Live It:** Think of the toughest thing you are going through, and ask a friend to help you lean on Christ through it.

**Galatians 2:10**
**Learn It:** Remember the poor.
**Live It:** Find a way to help the poor in your community. Volunteer at a shelter, donate nice clothes that you don't need, or fulfill a family's Christmas wishes.

**Galatians 4:7**
**Learn It:** You are not a slave; you are God's child, and he will bless you.
**Live It:** Tell Satan to get lost the next time he tries to make you feel bad about yourself, and don't lug around a big burden of guilt.

made right with God because we trusted in Christ. It is not because we followed the law, because no one can be made right with God by following the law.

## "DOES GOD GIVE YOU THE SPIRIT AND WORK MIRACLES AMONG YOU BECAUSE YOU FOLLOW THE LAW? NO, HE DOES THESE THINGS BECAUSE YOU HEARD THE GOOD NEWS AND BELIEVED IT."

[17]We Jews came to Christ, trying to be made right with God, and it became clear that we are sinners, too. Does this mean that Christ encourages sin? No! [18]But I would really be wrong to begin teaching again those things that I gave up. [19]It was the law that put me to death, and I died to the law so that I can now live for God. [20]I was put to death on the cross with Christ, and I do not live anymore—it is Christ who lives in me. I still live in my body, but I live by faith in the Son of God who loved me and gave himself to save me. [21]By saying these things I am not going against God's grace. Just the opposite, if the law could make us right with God, then Christ's death would be useless.

### BLESSING COMES THROUGH FAITH

**3** You people in Galatia were told very clearly about the death of Jesus Christ on the cross. But you were foolish; you let someone trick you. [2]Tell me this one thing: How did you receive the Holy Spirit? Did you receive the Spirit by following the law? No, you received the Spirit because you heard the Good News and believed it. [3]You began your life in Christ by the Spirit. Now are you trying to make it complete by your own power? That is foolish. [4]Were all your experiences wasted? I hope not! [5]Does God give you the Spirit and work miracles among you because you follow the law? No, he does these things because you heard the Good News and believed it.

[6]The Scriptures say the same thing about Abraham: "Abraham believed God, and God accepted Abraham's faith, and that faith made him right with God."[n] [7]So you should know that the true children of Abraham are those who have faith. [8]The Scriptures, telling what would happen in the future, said that God would make the non-Jewish people right through their faith. This Good News was told to Abraham beforehand, as the Scripture says: "All nations will be blessed through you."[n] [9]So all who believe as Abraham believed are blessed just as Abraham was. [10]But those who depend on following the law to make them right are under a curse, because the Scriptures say, "Anyone will be cursed who does not always obey what is written in the Book of the Law."[n] [11]Now it is clear that no one can be made right with God by the law, because the Scriptures say, "Those who are right with God will live by trusting in him."[n] [12]The law is not based on faith. It says, "A person who obeys these things will live because of them."[n] [13]Christ took away the curse the law put on us. He changed places with us and put himself under that curse. It is written in the Scriptures, "Anyone whose body is displayed on a tree[n] is cursed." [14]Christ did this so that God's blessing promised to Abraham might come through Jesus Christ to those who are not Jews. Jesus died so that by our believing we could receive the Spirit that God promised.

### THE LAW AND THE PROMISE

[15]Brothers and sisters, let us think in human terms: Even an agreement made between two persons is firm. After that agreement is accepted by both people, no one can stop it or add anything to it. [16]God made promises both to Abraham and to his descendant. God did not say, "and to your descendants." That would mean many people. But God said, "and to your descendant." That

Radical Faith:

## Galatians 2:19-21

Paul finally realized something really important: He'd never be acceptable, right, or good if he spent his life just trying really hard to be that way on his own. He had to quit trying to do things on his own—living for rules alone—and depend on the grace that Christ's death and resurrection brings. But how does that really work? Putting your faith in Jesus makes you totally united with him—you share in what he's experienced. He died so you can have new life. It was your sin that was paid for on the cross, and now God sees you as perfect because your sin died in Jesus' death. Then he rose from the grave to give you grace that is greater than sin and death and every mistake you've made. No need for rules or performances. You can't rely on your own power to be OK; you're made right only by grace and being united with Jesus' death and life. And since his life is now in you, you can talk to him every day. You go where he goes. Your life lived with Christ is all about him, and it's lived out by faith. He loves you, has saved you, and has called you to a life full of purpose.

**notes**    **3:6 "Abraham . . . God."** Quotation from Genesis 15:6.   **3:8 "All . . . you."** Quotation from Genesis 12:3 and 18:18.   **3:10 "Anyone . . . Law."** Quotation from Deuteronomy 27:26.   **3:11 "Those . . . him."** Quotation from Habakkuk 2:4.   **3:12 "A person . . . them."** Quotation from Leviticus 18:5.   **3:13 displayed on a tree** Deuteronomy 21:22-23 says that when a person was killed for doing wrong, the body was hung on a tree to show shame. Paul means that the cross of Jesus was like that.

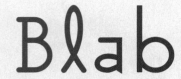

**Q:** I think R-ratings are so stupid. They are not really any worse than PG-13, and I'll be 17 next month. If the theater doesn't ask how old I am, can't I go to the R-rated movie I want to see?

**A:** Nope. You gotta obey the rules, because doing right is always the right thing to do. Besides, R-ratings mean the movie has a lot of sex, violence, or bad language. Before you see it, ask yourself if you would be comfortable watching it if Jesus was in the seat next to you.

**Q:** I learned from my friends how to throw up right after I eat. It's really easy if you do it right away, and I don't want to gain weight. Is this wrong?

**A:** Making yourself throw up is actually an eating disorder called bulimia, and it can seriously affect your health. Eventually, it can even kill you. Ask God to help you have self-control in your eating, and do not obsess about your weight. If you can't stop, you need to get help.

**Q:** Is there really a point to studying history? I am going to be an accountant. What do I need history for?

**A:** History for a Christian should be very exciting, because it shows God's hand at work throughout the ages. It also helps you see where others went wrong, so you can avoid their mistakes. History is one of the subjects needed to become a well-rounded adult (and it really helps you when you play along with *Jeopardy!*). Try to see it from God's perspective. It's not just history; it's his-story.

means only one person; that person is Christ. 17This is what I mean: God had an agreement with Abraham and promised to keep it. The law, which came four hundred thirty years later, cannot change that agreement and so destroy God's promise to Abraham. 18If the law could give us Abraham's blessing, then the promise would not be necessary. But that is not possible, because God freely gave his blessings to Abraham through the promise he had made.

19So what was the law for? It was given to show that the wrong things people do are against God's will. And it continued until the special descendant, who had been promised, came. The law was given through angels who used Moses for a mediator" to give the law to people. 20But a mediator is not needed when there is only one side, and God is only one.

## THE PURPOSE OF THE LAW OF MOSES

21Does this mean that the law is against God's promises? Never! That would be true only if the law could make us right. But God did not give a law that can bring life. 22Instead, the Scriptures showed that the whole world is bound by sin. This was so the promise would be given through faith to people who believe in Jesus Christ.

23Before this faith came, we were all held prisoners by the law. We had no freedom until God showed us the way of faith that was coming. 24In other words, the law was our guardian leading us to Christ so that we could be made right with God through faith. 25Now the way of faith has come, and we no longer live under a guardian.

26-27You were all baptized into Christ, and so you were all clothed with Christ. This means that you are all children of God through faith in Christ Jesus. 28In Christ, there is no difference between Jew and Greek, slave and free person, male and female. You are all the same in Christ Jesus. 29You belong to Christ, so you are Abraham's descendants. You will inherit all of God's blessings because of the promise God made to Abraham.

4 I want to tell you this: While those who will inherit their fathers' property are still children, they are no different from slaves. It does not matter that the children own everything. 2While they are children, they must obey those who are chosen to care for them. But when the children reach the age set by their fathers, they are free. 3It is the same for us. We were once like children, slaves to the useless rules of this world. 4But when the right time came, God sent his Son who was born of a woman and lived under the law. 5God did this so he could buy freedom for those who were under the law and so we could become his children.

6Since you are God's children, God sent the Spirit of his Son into your hearts, and the Spirit cries out, "Father."" 7So now you are not a slave; you are God's child, and God will give you the blessing he promised, because you are his child.

### PAUL'S LOVE FOR THE CHRISTIANS

8In the past you did not know God. You were slaves to gods that were not real. 9But now you know the true God. Really, it is God who knows you. So why do you turn back to those weak and useless rules you followed before? Do you want to be slaves to those things again? 10You still follow teachings about special days,

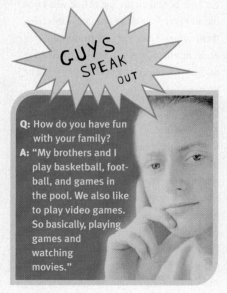

**GUYS SPEAK OUT**

**Q:** How do you have fun with your family?
**A:** "My brothers and I play basketball, football, and games in the pool. We also like to play video games. So basically, playing games and watching movies."

 **notes**     **3:19 mediator** A person who helps one person talk to or give something to another person.     **4:6 "Father"** Literally, "Abba, Father." Jewish children called their fathers "Abba."

268

months, seasons, and years. ¹¹I am afraid for you, that my work for you has been wasted.

## "WE HAD NO FREEDOM UNTIL GOD SHOWED US THE WAY OF FAITH THAT WAS COMING."

¹²Brothers and sisters, I became like you, so I beg you to become like me. You were very good to me before. ¹³You remember that it was because of an illness that I came to you the first time, preaching the Good News. ¹⁴Though

## relationships

"He will make peace between parents and their children" (Luke 1:17). Did you know that your parents are on your side? It may not seem like it when they say "no" to the party on Friday night, but they really are looking out for you. You want independence; they give you boundaries. It's natural that you will push against each other, but remember that they are on your team. They created you and love you more than anyone. Ask God to make peace between you and your parents the next time you're on opposite sides. He promises he will.

my sickness was a trouble for you, you did not hate me or make me leave. But you welcomed me as an angel from God, as if I were Jesus Christ himself! ¹⁵You were very happy then, but where is that joy now? I am ready to testify that you would have taken out your eyes and given them to me if that were possible. ¹⁶Now am I your enemy because I tell you the truth?

¹⁷Those people" are working hard to persuade you, but this is not good for you. They want to persuade you to turn against us and follow only them. ¹⁸It is good for people to show interest in you, but only if their purpose is good. This is always true, not just when I am with you. ¹⁹My little children, again I feel the pain of childbirth for you until you truly become like Christ. ²⁰I wish I could be with you now and could change the way I am talking to you, because I do not know what to think about you.

### The example of Hagar and Sarah

²¹Some of you still want to be under the law. Tell me, do you know what the law says? ²²The Scriptures say that Abraham had two sons. The mother of one son was a slave woman, and the mother of the other son was a free woman. ²³Abraham's son from the slave woman was born in the normal human way. But the son from the free woman was born because of the promise God made to Abraham.

²⁴This story teaches something else: The two women are like the two agreements between God and his people. One agreement is the law that God made on Mount Sinai," and the people who are under this agreement are like slaves. The mother named Hagar is like that agreement. ²⁵She is like Mount Sinai in Arabia and is a picture of the earthly Jewish city of Jerusalem. This city and its people, the Jews, are slaves to the law. ²⁶But the heavenly Jerusalem, which is above, is like the free woman. She is our mother. ²⁷It is written in the Scriptures:

"Be happy, Jerusalem.
You are like a woman who never gave birth to children.

## Galatians 3:29

Have you ever made a promise to someone that you knew you couldn't keep? Has someone you trusted ever broken a promise to you? What exactly does a promise mean? A promise is a commitment from one person to another, given in good faith that each person will hold up his or her end of the bargain. So if someone makes a promise to you and breaks it, how do you feel? Your trust in that person is probably broken, and you feel let down.

Thousands of years ago, God made some promises to Abraham. Although Abraham (Abram at the time; see Genesis 15) had no children and was very old, God promised that his descendants would be as numerous as the stars in the sky. Abraham believed and obeyed God, and God kept his promise. Even today, Abraham is considered a forefather of many, many nations. God kept his promise to Abraham, as well as to many other believers told about in the Bible. He doesn't break his promises to us either, and we can trust that he will never let us down.

 **4:17 Those people** They are the false teachers who were bothering the believers in Galatia (Galatians 1:7). **4:24 Mount Sinai** Mountain in Arabia where God gave his Law to Moses (Exodus 19 and 20).

## Music Reviews

**GROUP:** MERCYME

**ALBUM:** UNDONE

MercyMe rocketed to success with "I Can Only Imagine," a single that topped charts on several musical formats in mainstream and Christian radio. Their album, *Undone,* also caught crossover attention with the first single "Here With Me." It's a great song of worship, and the whole album is full of rich lyrics and great tunes. If "Imagine" got you thinking about the hereafter, the heavenly follow-up "Homesick" will keep you longing for it.

**WHY IT ROCKS: MERCYME IS A GREAT BAND GETTING THE WORD OUT INTO THE WORLD WITH POWERFUL PRAISE AND WORSHIP THAT USHERS YOU INTO GOD'S PRESENCE.**

Start singing and shout for joy.
 You never felt the pain of giving birth,
but you will have more children
 than the woman who has a husband."

*Isaiah 54:1*

28My brothers and sisters, you are God's children because of his promise, as Isaac was then. 29The son who was born in the normal way treated the other son badly. It is the same today. 30But what does the Scripture say? "Throw out the slave woman and her son. The son of the slave woman should not inherit anything. The son of the free woman should receive it all." 31So, my brothers and sisters, we are not children of the slave woman, but of the free woman.

### KEEP YOUR FREEDOM

5 We have freedom now, because Christ made us free. So stand strong. Do not change and go back into the slavery of the law. 2Listen, I Paul tell you that if you go back to the law by being circumcised, Christ does you no good. 3Again, I warn every man: If you allow yourselves to be circumcised, you must follow all the law. 4If you try to be made right with God through the law, your life with Christ is over—you have left God's grace. 5But we have the true hope that comes from being made right with God, and by the Spirit we wait eagerly for this hope. 6When we are in Christ Jesus, it is not important if we are circumcised or not. The important thing is faith—the kind of faith that works through love.

7You were running a good race. Who stopped you from following the true way? 8This change did not come from the One who chose you. 9Be careful! "Just a little yeast makes the whole batch of dough rise." 10But I trust in the Lord that you will not believe those different ideas. Whoever is confusing you with such ideas will be punished.

## LEARN I+ & LIVE I+

**Galatians 5:15**
**Learn It:** If Christians hurt each other and tear each other apart, they will destroy each other.
**Live It:** When you are tempted to say things that are hurtful, remember that your tongue can do a ton of damage.

**Galatians 6:9**
**Learn It:** Don't become tired of doing the right thing. God will reward you.
**Live It:** The next time being good just feels boring, rejuvenate yourself by doing a random act of kindness anonymously or getting together with friends who can keep you going.

**Ephesians 1:7**
**Learn It:** We have forgiveness of sins because of the blood Christ shed through his death on the cross.
**Live It:** Pray for a friend who does not know Christ.

notes

4:30 "Throw . . . all." Quotation from Genesis 21:10.

## RadicalFaith:

# Galatians
## 5:24-25

Before God came onto the scene in your life, you probably just followed whatever whim or idea came to you. But God has shown us that there is a better way to live. And that is to live a life totally surrendered to him. But it's not easy. Even when you want to obey, you will still deal with the temptation to do what you know isn't right. When Jesus was crucified, he willingly allowed his life to be taken. He did this so that God's will could be carried out. And just like Jesus allowed his life to be under God's control, you can do the same with your life. You can allow your sinful impulses be taken over by God. Paul says, "Those who belong to Christ Jesus have crucified their own sinful selves." He says they have "given up" on the wrong stuff they did before God took over their lives. Ask God to help you understand how to get closer to him and how to surrender all areas of your life to him. With God alive in you, you have the ability to follow the impulses of his Spirit instead of the impulses of your own sinful nature.

[11]My brothers and sisters, I do not teach that a man must be circumcised. If I teach circumcision, why am I still being attacked? If I still taught circumcision, my preaching about the cross would not be a problem. [12]I wish the people who are bothering you would castrate[n] themselves!

[13]My brothers and sisters, God called you to be free, but do not use your freedom as an excuse to do what pleases your sinful self. Serve each other with love. [14]The whole law is made complete in this one command: "Love your neighbor as you love yourself."[n] [15]If you go on hurting each other and tearing each other apart, be careful, or you will completely destroy each other.

### THE SPIRIT AND HUMAN NATURE

[16]So I tell you: Live by following the Spirit. Then you will not do what your sinful selves want. [17]Our sinful selves want what is against the Spirit, and the Spirit wants what is against our sinful selves. The two are against each other, so you cannot do just what you please. [18]But if the Spirit is leading you, you are not under the law.

[19]The wrong things the sinful self does are clear: being sexually unfaithful, not being pure, taking part in sexual sins, [20]worshiping gods, doing witchcraft, hating, making trouble, being jealous, being angry, being selfish, making people angry with each other, causing divisions among people, [21]feeling envy, being drunk, having wild and wasteful parties, and doing other things like these. I warn you now as I warned you before: Those who do these things will not inherit God's kingdom. [22]But the Spirit produces the fruit of love, joy, peace, patience, kindness, goodness, faithfulness, [23]gentleness, self-control. There is no law that says these things are wrong. [24]Those who belong to Christ Jesus have crucified their own sinful selves. They have given up their old selfish feelings and the evil things they wanted to do. [25]We get our new life from the Spirit, so we should follow the Spirit. [26]We must not be proud or make trouble with each other or be jealous of each other.

**Q:** My brother has been using drugs, fighting with my parents, and generally wreaking havoc in our family. I am so mad at him, yet I love him and want to help him. What can I do?

**A:** Your brother has to decide for himself to quit using drugs, but you can share with him (when he is sober and not angry) how it makes you feel. Pray for him a lot, every time you think of him, and support your parents through this difficult time. Educate yourself about addictions and determine not to follow in your brother's footsteps.

**Q:** My parents aren't Christians, and they party a lot. I don't want to get them in trouble, but it freaks me out that they are breaking the law. And it makes me mad. What can I do?

**A:** If your parents are breaking the law and getting high, it puts you in danger. Take an adult with you, and confront them when they are sober. Tell them you love them but will be forced to report them if they don't stop using. You don't want them to go to jail, but you could be saving their lives—and yours. Pray for them most of all, and be a good witness to them.

**Q:** How can I tell my friends about Christ without turning them off?

**A:** Use actions, not words. Be kind, loving, generous, slow to anger, forgiving, faithful, joyful, and peaceful in tough situations. Those consistent qualities will make others want to know how you can be so nice and stay so calm. Then you can tell them.

 **5:12 castrate** To cut off part of the male sex organ. Paul uses this word because it is similar to "circumcision." Paul wanted to show that he is very upset with the false teachers. **5:14 "Love . . . yourself."** Quotation from Leviticus 19:18.

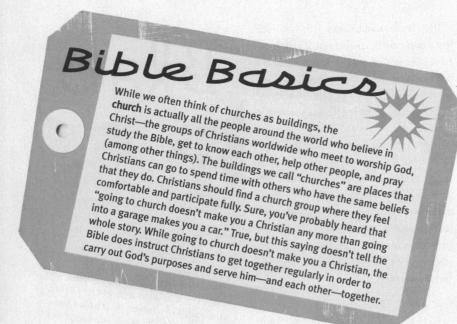

## Bible Basics

While we often think of churches as buildings, the **church** is actually all the people around the world who believe in Christ—the groups of Christians worldwide who meet to worship God, study the Bible, get to know each other, help other people, and pray (among other things). The buildings we call "churches" are places that Christians can go to spend time with others who have the same beliefs that they do. Christians should find a church group where they feel comfortable and participate fully. Sure, you've probably heard that "going to church doesn't make you a Christian any more than going into a garage makes you a car." True, but this saying doesn't tell the whole story. While going to church doesn't make you a Christian, the Bible does instruct Christians to get together regularly in order to carry out God's purposes and serve him—and each other—together.

### HELP EACH OTHER

6 Brothers and sisters, if someone in your group does something wrong, you who are spiritual should go to that person and gently help make him right again. But be careful, because you might be tempted to sin, too. ²By helping each other with your troubles, you truly obey the law of Christ. ³If anyone thinks he is important when he really is not, he is only fooling himself. ⁴Each person should judge his own actions and not compare himself with others. Then he can be proud for what he himself has done. ⁵Each person must be responsible for himself.

⁶Anyone who is learning the teaching of God should share all the good things he has with his teacher.

### LIFE IS LIKE PLANTING A FIELD

⁷Do not be fooled: You cannot cheat God. People harvest only what they plant. ⁸If they plant to satisfy their sinful selves, their sinful selves will bring them ruin. But if they plant to please the Spirit, they will receive eternal life from the Spirit. ⁹We must not become tired of doing good. We will receive our harvest of eternal life at the right time if we do not give up. ¹⁰When we have the opportunity to help anyone, we should do it. But we should give special attention to those who are in the family of believers.

### PAUL ENDS HIS LETTER

¹¹See what large letters I use to write this myself. ¹²Some people are trying to force you to be circumcised so the Jews will accept them. They are afraid they will be attacked if they follow only the cross of Christ." ¹³Those who are circumcised do not obey the law themselves, but they want you to be circumcised so they can brag about what they forced you to do. ¹⁴I hope I will never brag about things like that. The cross of our Lord Jesus Christ is my only reason for bragging. Through the cross of Jesus my world was crucified, and I died to the world. ¹⁵It is not important if a man is circumcised or uncircumcised. The important thing is being the new people God has made. ¹⁶Peace and mercy to those who follow this rule—and to all of God's people.

¹⁷So do not give me any more trouble. I have scars on my body that show" I belong to Christ Jesus.

¹⁸My brothers and sisters, the grace of our Lord Jesus Christ be with your spirit. Amen.

**notes**  **6:12 cross of Christ** Paul uses the cross as a picture of the Good News, the story of Christ's death and rising from the dead to pay for our sins. The cross, or Christ's death, was God's way to save us.  **6:17 that show** Many times Paul was beaten and whipped by people who were against him because he was teaching about Christ. The scars were from these beatings.

# *i*n one sentence, the theme of Ephesians

is this: "You are joined together with peace through the Spirit, so make every effort to continue together in this way" (4:3). Paul uses this letter to encourage the believers at Ephesus to get along with each other. Some scholars believe this letter was meant to be circulated among several churches in Asia Minor— a sort of chain letter, but without the "curse" if you break the chain. That theory makes sense, since Paul's message here is universal to all believers.

# Ephesians
## Unity in the Body of Christ

The first three chapters of Ephesians deal mostly with theology and doctrine (teaching on the belief system of the Christian faith), while the last three chapters are practical in nature, showing us specific ways we can live together in peace as Christians.

The end of chapter 5 has some great insight into how husbands and wives should relate to each other. And pay close attention to the beginning of chapter 6—this passage deals with relationships between children and their parents. (Don't worry. The responsibility is not all on the kids' shoulders; parents, too, are accountable for their actions.) Finally, Paul uses a great metaphor about putting on the full armor of God before entering into battle against the devil.

## Promises:

## Ephesians 1:19

Think God is powerful? You bet he is. Genesis 1 tells us that God created the whole universe by simply speaking it into existence. Now that's power. In fact, God's awesome power is constantly displayed throughout Scripture. He caused a Great Flood (Genesis 6-8) to destroy the earth. He ripped the Temple curtain in half when Jesus died (Matthew 27). He parted the Red Sea so the Israelites could escape the king of Egypt (Exodus 14). Jesus performed many great miracles while on earth, including raising the dead (the Gospels). And there are countless other examples.

God's power is real and it is great. He continues to show us his power today by answering prayers and changing lives. When we as believers come to him, believing that he has the power to make things happen, he never lets us down. He always listens to us and hears our prayers. God alone has the power to save us from our sins and make us whole again when we're broken. We can believe in his great power to work in our lives each day.

1 From Paul, an apostle of Christ Jesus. I am an apostle because that is what God wanted.

To God's holy people living in Ephesus, believers in Christ Jesus:

²Grace and peace to you from God our Father and the Lord Jesus Christ.

**"IN CHRIST WE WERE CHOSEN TO BE GOD'S PEOPLE, BECAUSE FROM THE VERY BEGINNING GOD HAD DECIDED THIS IN KEEPING WITH HIS PLAN."**

### SPIRITUAL BLESSINGS IN CHRIST

³Praise be to the God and Father of our Lord Jesus Christ. In Christ, God has given us every spiritual blessing in the heavenly world. ⁴That is, in Christ, he chose us before the world was made so that we would be his holy people—people without blame before him. ⁵Because of his love, God had already decided to make us his own children through Jesus Christ. That was what he wanted and what pleased him, ⁶and it brings praise to God because of his wonderful grace. God gave that grace to us freely, in Christ, the One he loves. ⁷In Christ we are set free by the blood of his death, and so we have forgiveness of sins. How rich is God's grace, ⁸which he has given to us so fully and freely. God, with full wisdom and understanding, ⁹let us know his secret purpose. This was what God wanted, and he planned to do it through Christ. ¹⁰His goal was to carry out his plan, when the right time came, that all things in heaven and on earth would be joined together in Christ as the head.

¹¹In Christ we were chosen to be God's people, because from the very beginning God had decided this in keeping with his plan. And he

## Radical Faith:

## Ephesians 2:10

In every sense, God has made you what you are. You're a great catch, an amazing treasure, and a delightful and fascinating expression of God's beauty. You are adored and enjoyed by your Creator. Whenever you don't feel accepted by people on earth, don't let their actions define you. People can't truly see you as God can, and only he has authority to define who you are. God tells you that he formed you the way you are with much care and he is always at work in you (Psalm 139). He works to make you more like him and more beautiful in your heart, in your mind, and in your spirit. He sings over you with joy. Meanwhile, you've got to be who you are, whether people like it or not. Be the authentic you. You've got nothing to prove and nothing to lose by being totally real. God receives you entirely. He sees you as his precious work of art. He just loves you and wants you close to him. Believe the message from God's powerful and eternal Word—that he adores you—over the message of your own circumstances, which is ever-changing and temporary.

# LEARN I+ & LIVE I+

**Ephesians 1:13**
**Learn It:** When you believed in Christ, God put his stamp of ownership on you by giving you the Holy Spirit.
**Live It:** Did you know that you are a designer brand? You were bought with Christ's blood, and that's a priceless brand name.

**Ephesians 2:10**
**Learn It:** God has a special purpose for you that he planned long ago.
**Live It:** Ask God for direction every day before you decide how to spend the time he has given you.

**Ephesians 3:20**
**Learn It:** With God's power in us, we can do more than we ever imagined.
**Live It:** Pray first for wisdom; then list five spiritual goals you have.

is the One who makes everything agree with what he decides and wants. [12]We are the first people who hoped in Christ, and we were chosen so that we would bring praise to God's glory. [13]So it is with you. When you heard the true teaching—the Good News about your salvation—you believed in Christ. And in Christ, God put his special mark of ownership on you by giving you the Holy Spirit that he had promised. [14]That Holy Spirit is the guarantee that we will receive what God promised for his people until God gives full freedom to those who are his—to bring praise to God's glory.

## PAUL'S PRAYER

[15]That is why since I heard about your faith in the Lord Jesus and your love for all God's people, [16]I have not stopped giving thanks to God for you. I always remember you in my prayers, [17]asking the God of our Lord Jesus Christ, the glorious Father, to give you a spirit of wisdom and revelation so that you will know him better. [18]I pray also that you will have greater understanding in your heart so you will know the hope to which he has called us and that you will know how rich and glorious are the blessings God has promised his holy people. [19]And you will know that God's power is very great for us who believe. That power is the same as the great strength [20]God used to raise Christ from the dead and put him at his right side in the heavenly world. [21]God

has put Christ over all rulers, authorities, powers, and kings, not only in this world but also in the next. [22]God put everything under his power and made him the head over everything for the church, [23]which is Christ's body. The church is filled with Christ, and Christ fills everything in every way.

## WE NOW HAVE LIFE

2 In the past you were spiritually dead because of your sins and the things you did against God. [2]Yes, in the past you lived the way the world lives, following the ruler of the evil powers that are above the earth. That same spirit is now working in those who refuse to obey God. [3]In the past all of us lived like them, trying to please our sinful selves and doing all the things our bodies and minds wanted. We should have suffered God's anger because of the way we were. We were the same as all other people.

[4]But God's mercy is great, and he loved us very much. [5]Though we were spiritually dead because of the things we did against God, he gave us new life with Christ. You have been saved by God's grace. [6]And he raised us up with Christ and gave us a seat with him in the heavens. He did this for those in Christ Jesus [7]so that for all future time he could show the very great riches of his grace by being kind to us in Christ Jesus. [8]I mean that you have been saved by grace through believing. You did not save yourselves; it was a gift from God. [9]It was

not the result of your own efforts, so you cannot brag about it. [10]God has made us what we are. In Christ Jesus, God made us to do good works, which God planned in advance for us to live our lives doing.

## beauty secret

### H₂O

Water is good for your skin, energy, and overall health. You can't live more than a few days without water—it's essential for survival. Maybe that's one reason that Jesus offered the woman at the well "living water" (John 4:10-15). He is the only One who can satisfy our soul's deepest desires.

# September

**1**

**2** Labor Day is the first Monday of September. Take a day off and enjoy rest.

**3**

**4** Pray for a person of influence: It's Beyoncé Knowles's birthday.

**5** Introduce yourself to one of the new students at school. Kindness goes a long way.

**6**

**7** Grandparents' Day is the first Sunday after Labor Day. Send them a homemade gift.

**8** Pray for a person of influence: It's Pink's birthday.

**9** Pray for a person of influence: Adam Sandler is having a birthday today.

**10**

**11** Pray for those who lost loved ones during the WTC bombings. Pray for God's protection on our country.

**12**

**13** Spend some time visiting a lonely elderly person today.

**14**

**15** lucky

**16** Water the plants in the yard for your parents.

**17**

**18** Make a fun little gift for your mom.

**19** Read John 14–17. Make a list of three new things you learned about Jesus.

**20**

**21** On July 23, 1904, Charles E. Menches invented the ice cream cone. Take a friend out for ice cream.

**22**

**23**

**24**

**25** Pray for a person of influence: It's Will Smith's birthday.

**26** Talk to your family about sponsoring a child through www.compassion.com.

**27** Pray for a person of influence: Avril Lavigne is having a birthday.

**28** Pray for a person of influence: It's Hilary Duff's birthday.

**29**

**30** Read the Book of Galatians today. Record what you learned in your journal.

Do not let evil defeat you, but defeat evil by doing good.
—Romans 12:21

## ONE IN CHRIST

[11] You were not born Jewish. You are the people the Jews call "uncircumcised."[n] Those who call you "uncircumcised" call themselves "circumcised." (Their circumcision is only something they themselves do on their bodies.) [12] Remember that in the past you were without Christ. You were not citizens of Israel, and you had no part in the agreements[n] with the promise that God made to his people. You had no hope, and you did not know God. [13] But now in Christ Jesus, you who were far away from God are brought near through the blood of Christ's death. [14] Christ himself is our peace. He made both Jewish people and those who are not Jews one people. They were separated as if there were a wall between them, but Christ broke down that wall of hate by giving his own body. [15] The Jewish law had many commands and rules, but Christ ended that law. His purpose was to make the two groups of people become one new people in him and in this way make peace. [16] It was also Christ's purpose to end the hatred between the two groups, to make them into one body, and to bring them back to God. Christ did all this with his death on the cross. [17] Christ came and preached peace to you who were far away from God, and to those who were near to God. [18] Yes, it is through Christ we all have the right to come to the Father in one Spirit.

[19] Now you who are not Jewish are not foreigners or strangers any longer, but are citizens together with God's holy people. You belong to God's family. [20] You are like a building that was built on the foundation of the apostles and prophets. Christ Jesus himself is the most important stone[n] in that building, [21] and that whole building is joined together in Christ. He makes it grow and become a holy temple in the Lord. [22] And in Christ you, too, are being built together with the Jews into a place where God lives through the Spirit.

## PAUL'S WORK IN TELLING THE GOOD NEWS

3 So I, Paul, am a prisoner of Christ Jesus for you who are not Jews. [2] Surely you have heard that God gave me this work

## Peninnah

[1 SAMUEL 1] Peninnah (we'll call her Penny) was married to Elkanah (let's call him Elk, for short). Elk also had another wife (Hannah), whom he loved; and all three of them had to live together under the same roof. Penny and Hannah had to share Elk's affections, but Hannah clearly had his heart. When the time came for Elk to divvy up the fruits of his labor, he always gave Hannah twice as much as Penny. Just like Leah's situation with Jacob and Rachel, Penny was the fertile one. She was a great mom to all the little Elks, but even that didn't make her husband love her more. It was a bitter pill to swallow, and swallow it she did. Instead of asking for God's help or comfort, she became obsessed with making Hannah's life miserable. She even made fun of her for not being able to get pregnant, which was cruelty beyond compare. Bitterness turned this second fiddle into a mean woman who couldn't enjoy any of the blessings she'd been given.

# LEARN I+ & LIVE I+

### Ephesians 4:2
**Learn It:** Always be gentle, humble, and patient. Accept each other.
**Live It:** Practice saying only nice things to people for a whole day. Stretch it into a week. See how long you can keep it up until you have made a positive change.

### Ephesians 4:16
**Learn It:** Christians depend on Christ, but they also must work together to grow and to love the world.
**Live It:** Spend time with God to determine how he wants to use you to benefit his church.

### Ephesians 4:19
**Learn It:** Unbelievers do not feel ashamed over their sin, and they do evil.
**Live It:** Keep your conscience sharp by listening to it regularly. Do not ignore the little voice that tries to warn you when you are about to do wrong.

**notes** **2:11 uncircumcised** People not having the mark of circumcision as the Jews had. **2:12 agreements** The agreements that God gave to his people in the Old Testament. **2:20 most important stone** Literally, "cornerstone." The first and most important stone in a building.

# CHECK IT OUT

## FELLOWSHIP OF CHRISTIAN ATHLETES

For more than 50 years, the Fellowship of Christian Athletes (FCA) has been challenging coaches and athletes on the professional, college, high school, junior high, and youth levels to use athletics to impact the world for Jesus Christ. FCA is the largest interdenominational, school-based, Christian sports organization in America. FCA aims to serve local communities by equipping, empowering, and encouraging people to make a difference for Christ.

On junior high, high school, and college campuses, FCA clubs are called "Huddles." If you are a current or former member of recognized school athletic teams or carry an interest in athletics, you are qualified to join a Huddle or can request information on starting one.

Some Huddles meet on campus; some meet in homes. They meet weekly or twice a month. All aim to encourage, serve their local communities, learn more about Jesus, and affect others' lives for him. For example, the Lawton (Oklahoma) High FCA Huddle recently sent care packages and letters to U.S. troops fighting in Iraq.

*Get involved by visiting www.fca.org.*

through his grace to help you. ³He let me know his secret by showing it to me. I have already written a little about this. ⁴If you read what I wrote then, you can see that I truly understand the secret about the Christ. ⁵People who lived in other times were not told that secret. But now, through the Spirit, God has shown that secret to his holy apostles and prophets. ⁶This is that secret: that through the Good News those who are not Jews will share with the Jews in God's blessing. They belong to the same body, and they share together in the promise that God made in Christ Jesus.

⁷By God's special gift of grace given to me through his power, I became a servant to tell that Good News. ⁸I am the least important of all God's people, but God gave me this gift—to tell those who are not Jews the Good News about the riches of Christ, which are too great to understand fully. ⁹And God gave me the work of telling all people about the plan for his secret, which has been hidden in him since the beginning of time. He is the One who created everything. ¹⁰His purpose was that through the church all the rulers and powers in the heavenly world will now know God's wisdom, which has so many forms. ¹¹This agrees with the purpose God had since the beginning of time, and he carried out his plan through Christ Jesus our Lord. ¹²In Christ we can come before God with freedom and without fear. We can do this through faith in Christ. ¹³So I ask you not to become discouraged because of the sufferings I am having for you. My sufferings are for your glory.

### THE LOVE OF CHRIST

¹⁴So I bow in prayer before the Father ¹⁵from whom every family in heaven and on earth gets its true name. ¹⁶I ask the Father in his great glory to give you the power to be strong inwardly through his Spirit. ¹⁷I pray

# LEARN I+ & LIVE I+

**Ephesians 5:4**
**Learn It:** Do not speak foolishly or tell evil jokes.
**Live It:** Are the jokes you tell really funny or are they rude and risqué? Don't read or pass along dirty emails, hurtful jokes, or other things that would be offensive to God.

**Ephesians 5:18**
**Learn It:** Do not get drunk; it will ruin you.
**Live It:** Whenever the Bible mentions drunkenness, it warns not to go there. Period. End of story.

**Ephesians 5:28**
**Learn It:** Husbands should love their wives as they love themselves.
**Live It:** Look for selfless giving as a trait you want in the man who might one day be your husband.

that Christ will live in your hearts by faith and that your life will be strong in love and be built on love. 18And I pray that you and all God's holy people will have the power to understand the greatness of Christ's love—how wide and how long and how high and how deep that love is. 19Christ's love is greater than anyone can ever know, but I pray that you will be able to know that love. Then you can be filled with the fullness of God.

20With God's power working in us, God can do much, much more than anything we can ask or imagine. 21To him be glory in the church and in Christ Jesus for all time, forever and ever. Amen.

> ## "WITH GOD'S POWER WORKING IN US, GOD CAN DO MUCH, MUCH MORE THAN ANYTHING WE CAN ASK OR IMAGINE."

### THE UNITY OF THE BODY

4 I am in prison because I belong to the Lord. God chose you to be his people, so I urge you now to live the life to which God called you. 2Always be humble, gentle, and

**GUYS SPEAK OUT**

**Q:** How do you know God is real?
**A:** "By studying science. Just looking at the things of this world will tell you there is a creator."

patient, accepting each other in love. 3You are joined together with peace through the Spirit, so make every effort to continue together in this way. 4There is one body and one Spirit, and God called you to have one hope. 5There is one Lord, one faith, and one baptism. 6There is one God and Father of everything. He rules everything and is everywhere and is in everything.

7Christ gave each one of us the special gift of grace, showing how generous he is. 8That is why it says in the Scriptures,

"When he went up to the heights,
   he led a parade of captives,
   and he gave gifts to people." *Psalm 68:18*

9When it says, "He went up," what does it mean? It means that he first came down to the earth. 10So Jesus came down, and he is the same One who went up above all the heaven. Christ did that to fill everything with his presence. 11And Christ gave gifts to people—he made some to be apostles, some to be prophets, some to go and tell the Good News, and some to have the work of caring for and teaching God's people. 12Christ gave those gifts to prepare God's holy people for the work of serving, to make the body of Christ stronger. 13This work must continue until we are all joined together in the same faith and in the same knowledge of the Son of God. We must become like a mature person, growing until we become like Christ and have his perfection.

14Then we will no longer be babies. We will not be tossed about like a ship that the waves carry one way and then another. We will not be influenced by every new teaching we hear from people who are trying to fool us. They make plans and try any kind of trick to fool people into following the wrong path. 15No! Speaking the truth with love, we will grow up in every way into Christ, who is the head. 16The whole body depends on Christ, and all the parts of the body are joined and held together. Each part does its own work to make the whole body grow and be strong with love.

### THE WAY YOU SHOULD LIVE

17In the Lord's name, I tell you this. Do not continue living like those who do not believe.

**Promises:**

## Ephesians 5:8

It's easy to tell the difference between light and darkness, right? That's a no-brainer. In the light, everything is exactly what it appears to be. Nothing is hidden. But in the darkness, things become unknown and sometimes scary. Remember when you were a little kid and when you woke up in the middle of the night, the lamp in the corner of your room suddenly seemed to have transformed into a scary, awful monster? Darkness has a way of distorting the truth and suddenly changing our perspective.

Paul liked to use illustrations of light and darkness to help us understand the change that Christ makes in our lives. Apart from him, our sinful nature produces darkness in our souls. We are covered in darkness because of our selfish desires and worldly perspective. But, when Christ enters our lives, we are filled with all of his light and his good qualities. He exposes truth (or light) into our lives to take away the darkness and the creatures of fear and doubt that lurk in the shadows. He brings it all to light so we can see his love.

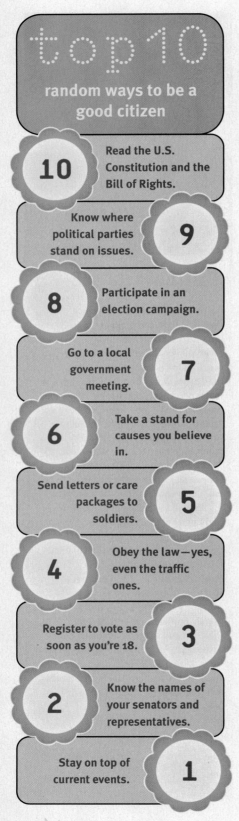

**top10**

random ways to be a good citizen

**10** Read the U.S. Constitution and the Bill of Rights.

**9** Know where political parties stand on issues.

**8** Participate in an election campaign.

**7** Go to a local government meeting.

**6** Take a stand for causes you believe in.

**5** Send letters or care packages to soldiers.

**4** Obey the law—yes, even the traffic ones.

**3** Register to vote as soon as you're 18.

**2** Know the names of your senators and representatives.

**1** Stay on top of current events.

Their thoughts are worth nothing. [18]They do not understand, and they know nothing, because they refuse to listen. So they cannot have the life that God gives. [19]They have lost all feeling of shame, and they use their lives for doing evil. They continually want to do all kinds of evil. [20]But what you learned in Christ was not like this. [21]I know that you heard about him, and you are in him, so you were taught the truth that is in Jesus. [22]You were taught to leave your old self—to stop living the evil way you lived before. That old self becomes worse, because people are fooled by the evil things they want to do. [23]But you were taught to be made new in your hearts, [24]to become a new person. That new person is made to be like God—made to be truly good and holy.

[25]So you must stop telling lies. Tell each other the truth, because we all belong to each other in the same body." [26]When you are angry, do not sin, and be sure to stop being angry before the end of the day. [27]Do not give the devil a way to defeat you. [28]Those who are stealing must stop stealing and start working. They should earn an honest living for themselves. Then they will have something to share with those who are poor.

[29]When you talk, do not say harmful things, but say what people need—words that will help others become stronger. Then what you say will do good to those who listen to you. [30]And do not make the Holy Spirit sad. The Spirit is God's proof that you belong to him. God gave you the Spirit to show that God will make you free when the final day comes. [31]Do not be bitter or angry or mad. Never shout angrily or say things to hurt others. Never do anything evil. [32]Be kind and loving to each other, and forgive each other just as God forgave you in Christ.

## LIVING IN THE LIGHT

5 You are God's children whom he loves, so try to be like him. [2]Live a life of love just as Christ loved us and gave himself for us as a sweet-smelling offering and sacrifice to God.

[3]But there must be no sexual sin among you, or any kind of evil or greed. Those things are not right for God's holy people. [4]Also, there must be no evil talk among you, and you must not speak foolishly or tell evil jokes. These things are not right for you. Instead, you should be giving thanks to God. [5]You can be sure of this: No one will have a place in the kingdom of Christ and of God who sins sexually, or does evil things, or is greedy. Anyone who is greedy is serving a false god.

## "WAKE UP, SLEEPER! RISE FROM DEATH, AND CHRIST WILL SHINE ON YOU."

[6]Do not let anyone fool you by telling you things that are not true, because these things will bring God's anger on those who do not obey him. [7]So have nothing to do with them. [8]In the past you were full of darkness, but now you are full of light in the Lord. So live like children who belong to the light. [9]Light brings every kind of goodness, right living, and truth. [10]Try to learn what pleases the Lord. [11]Have nothing to do with the things done in darkness, which are not worth anything. But show that they are wrong. [12]It is shameful even to talk about what those people do in secret. [13]But the light makes all things easy to see, [14]and everything that is made easy to see can become light. This is why it is said:

"Wake up, sleeper!
  Rise from death,
  and Christ will shine on you."

[15]So be very careful how you live. Do not live like those who are not wise, but live wisely. [16]Use every chance you have for doing good, because these are evil times. [17]So do not be foolish but learn what the Lord wants you to do. [18]Do not be drunk with wine, which will ruin you, but be filled with the Spirit. [19]Speak to each other with psalms, hymns, and spiritual songs, singing and making music in your

**notes**   4:25 Tell . . . body. Quotation from Zechariah 8:16.

280

hearts to the Lord. 20Always give thanks to God the Father for everything, in the name of our Lord Jesus Christ.

## wives and husbands

21Yield to obey each other because you respect Christ.

22Wives, yield to your husbands, as you do to the Lord, 23because the husband is the head of the wife, as Christ is the head of the church. And he is the Savior of the body, which is the church. 24As the church yields to Christ, so you wives should yield to your husbands in everything.

25Husbands, love your wives as Christ loved the church and gave himself for it 26to make it belong to God. Christ used the word to make the church clean by washing it with water. 27He died so that he could give the church to himself like a bride in all her beauty. He died so that the church could be pure and without fault, with no evil or sin or any other wrong thing in it. 28In the same way, husbands should love their wives as they love their own bodies. The man who loves his wife loves himself. 29No one ever hates his own body, but feeds and takes care of it. And that is what Christ does for the church, 30because we are parts of his body. 31The Scripture says, "So a man will leave his father and mother and be united with his wife, and the two will become one body."ⁿ 32That secret is very important—I am talking about Christ and the church. 33But each one of you must love his wife as he loves himself, and a wife must respect her husband.

## children and parents

6 Children, obey your parents as the Lord wants, because this is the right thing to do. 2The command says, "Honor your father and mother."ⁿ This is the first command

that has a promise with it— 3"Then everything will be well with you, and you will have a long life on the earth."ⁿ

4Fathers, do not make your children angry, but raise them with the training and teaching of the Lord.

## slaves and masters

5Slaves, obey your masters here on earth with fear and respect and from a sincere heart, just as you obey Christ. 6You must do this not only while they are watching you, to please them. With all your heart you must do what God wants as people who are obeying Christ.

7Do your work with enthusiasm. Work as if you were serving the Lord, not as if you were serving only men and women. 8Remember that the Lord will give a reward to everyone, slave or free, for doing good.

9Masters, in the same way, be good to your slaves. Do not threaten them. Remember that the One who is your Master and their Master is in heaven, and he treats everyone alike.

## wear the full armor of god

10Finally, be strong in the Lord and in his great power. 11Put on the full armor of God so that you can fight against the devil's evil tricks. 12Our fight is not against people on earth but against the rulers and authorities and the powers of this world's darkness, against the spiritual powers of evil in the heavenly world. 13That is why you need to put on God's full armor. Then on the day of evil you will be able to stand strong. And when you have finished the whole fight, you will still be standing. 14So stand strong, with the belt of truth tied around your waist and the protection of right living on your chest. 15On your feet wear the Good News of peace to help you stand strong. 16And also use the shield of faith

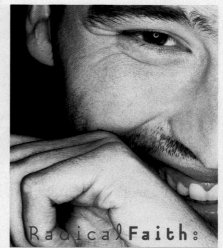

Radical Faith:

## Ephesians 6:10-13

One thing you can always count on is that Satan will try to convince you to stray from God and steer toward destruction. You can't defend yourself with the stuff you're made of—this is about fighting forces in the spiritual realm—so you're going to have to fight with the stuff God's made of. Paul doesn't just say, "Be strong"; he says, "Be strong in the Lord and in *his* great power"(emphasis added). He doesn't suggest just giving it your best. That simply won't cut it. You have access to the supernatural power of God that can knock down every evil and deceptive attack that comes your way. God is bigger than anything you'll face. Notice there's no dangling question mark about what will happen if you follow Paul's words here. He says you *will* be able to stand firm. He says when the fight comes to an end, you'll still be going strong because you were fighting with God's armor and power. So cling to God in every way, ask for his Spirit to control you, and live devoted to him. Study and memorize Scripture, and stay dependent in prayer. Put all your faith in his ability and truth and walk with him so that you can be victorious.

**notes** 5:31 "So . . . body." Quotation from Genesis 2:24. 6:2 "Honor . . . mother." Quotation from Exodus 20:12; Deuteronomy 5:16. 6:3 "Then . . . earth." Quotation from Exodus 20:12; Deuteronomy 5:16.

281

# LEARN I✝ & LIVE I✝

**Ephesians 6:1**
**Learn It:** Obey your parents because it is the right thing to do.
**Live It:** Do whatever your mom asks you to do today with a smile. You'll be surprised at how happy it makes her.

**Ephesians 6:11**
**Learn It:** Fight off the devil by wearing the armor of God.
**Live It:** Read Ephesians 6:11-18 and memorize the pieces of armor God has given to help you defend yourself against attacks on your faith.

**Ephesians 6:19**
**Learn It:** Pray for those in church leadership who share the Good News.
**Live It:** Add your pastor to your prayer list. Thank God for the way he is using your pastor to reach and teach you and others the Good News.

with which you can stop all the burning arrows of the Evil One. [17]Accept God's salvation as your helmet, and take the sword of the Spirit, which is the word of God. [18]Pray in the Spirit at all times with all kinds of prayers, asking for everything you need. To do this you must always be ready and never give up. Always pray for all God's people.

[19]Also pray for me that when I speak, God will give me words so that I can tell the secret of the Good News without fear. [20]I have been sent to preach this Good News, and I am doing that now, here in prison. Pray that when I preach the Good News I will speak without fear, as I should.

## FINAL GREETINGS

[21]I am sending to you Tychicus, our brother whom we love and a faithful servant of the Lord's work. He will tell you everything that is happening with me. Then you will know how I am and what I am doing. [22]I am sending him to you for this reason—so that you will know how we are, and he can encourage you.

[23]Peace and love with faith to you from God the Father and the Lord Jesus Christ. [24]Grace to all of you who love our Lord Jesus Christ with love that never ends.

**i** magine this: Paul is in prison. He is locked up, probably not eating very well, and almost certainly physically uncomfortable. He's exhausted—in body and in spirit. No one would fault him for rolling over in defeat. But Paul does something rather unexpected. He writes a thank-you note.

# Philippians
### A Letter of Joy and Thanks

Yep, a thank-you note. Hearing of his imprisonment and discomfort, the Philippians had sent Paul a gift. In the midst of his unfortunate circumstances, Paul takes the time to remember his manners. Beyond just thanking the believers at Philippi, Paul uses this letter to express his immense joy, despite his circumstances.

Paul has learned a great lesson—how to be content in Christ. It's a tough lesson, but one he wants everyone to share in. He wants the Philippians to experience the same contagious joy that he feels. He wants them to live beyond circumstance and embrace the happiness that money can't buy.

Surely, if Paul can be happy in prison, you can be happy in Algebra class. Or Social Studies. Or Biology. (You get the point.)

# Blab

**Q:** Does it really matter what kind of music I listen to? I like the beat more than the words.

**A:** The words matter, because they are getting locked into your memory for the rest of your life. You may think you only listen to the music, but c'mon, you can remember all the words to all the songs you knew as a little kid, right? Music sticks with you, and it does affect you. Choose music with words that are positive, not profane. Better yet, find music in the style you like that glorifies God. There's great Christian rock, rap, industrial, folk, techno, punk, you name it. Check it out.

**Q:** I wouldn't mind listening to Christian music; but when I turn to the Christian station, I don't know any of the songs and I love to sing along. What can I do?

**A:** Instead of flipping past it, find a good contemporary Christian or Christian rock station on the radio or Internet and make that all you play for the next two weeks straight. After two weeks of listening daily, you'll know all the songs in rotation. Then the new habit will be easy to keep.

**Q:** I still sleep with my favorite stuffed animal from when I was little. Am I a complete dork?

**A:** Not at all. There is nothing wrong with having sentimental attachment to a few things, as long as they don't become a crutch that you have to have. If that becomes the case, ask God to replace that object of your affections with himself. He is your comfort, not an old teddy bear.

1 From Paul and Timothy, servants of Christ Jesus.

To all of God's holy people in Christ Jesus who live in Philippi, including your elders and deacons:

²Grace and peace to you from God our Father and the Lord Jesus Christ.

## Paul's Prayer

³I thank my God every time I remember you, ⁴always praying with joy for all of you. ⁵I thank God for the help you gave me while I preached the Good News—help you gave from the first day you believed until now. ⁶God began doing a good work in you, and I am sure he will continue it until it is finished when Jesus Christ comes again.

⁷And I know that I am right to think like this about all of you, because I have you in my heart. All of you share in God's grace with me while I am in prison and while I am defending and proving the truth of the Good News. ⁸God knows that I want to see you very much, because I love all of you with the love of Christ Jesus.

⁹This is my prayer for you: that your love will grow more and more; that you will have knowledge and understanding with your love; ¹⁰that you will see the difference between good and bad and will choose the good; that you will be pure and without wrong for the coming of Christ; ¹¹that you will do many good things with the help of Christ to bring glory and praise to God.

## Paul's Troubles Help the Work

¹²I want you brothers and sisters" to know that what has happened to me has helped to spread the Good News. ¹³All the palace guards and everyone else knows that I am in prison because I am a believer in Christ. ¹⁴Because I am in prison, most of the believers have become more bold in Christ and are not afraid to speak the word of God.

¹⁵It is true that some preach about Christ because they are jealous and ambitious, but others preach about Christ because they want to help. ¹⁶They preach because they have love, and they know that God gave me the work of defending the Good News. ¹⁷But the others preach about Christ for selfish and wrong reasons, wanting to make trouble for me in prison.

## "WHEN YOU DO THINGS, DO NOT LET SELFISHNESS OR PRIDE BE YOUR GUIDE."

¹⁸But it doesn't matter. The important thing is that in every way, whether for right or wrong reasons, they are preaching about Christ. So I am happy, and I will continue to be happy. ¹⁹Because you are praying for me and the Spirit of Jesus Christ is helping me, I know this trouble will bring my freedom. ²⁰I expect and hope that I will not fail Christ in anything but that I will have the courage now, as always, to show the greatness of Christ in my life here on earth, whether I live or die. ²¹To me the only important thing about living is Christ, and dying would be profit for me. ²²If I continue living in my body, I will be able to work for the Lord. I do not know what to choose—living or dying. ²³It is hard to choose between the two. I want to leave this life and be with Christ, which is much better, ²⁴but you need me here in my body. ²⁵Since I am sure of this, I know I will stay with you to help you grow and have joy in your faith. ²⁶You will be very happy in Christ Jesus when I am with you again.

²⁷Only one thing concerns me: Be sure that you live in a way that brings honor to the Good News of Christ. Then whether I come and visit you or am away from you, I will hear that you are standing strong with one purpose, that you work together as one for the faith of the Good News, ²⁸and that you are not afraid of those who are against you. All of this is proof that your enemies will be destroyed but that you will be saved by God. ²⁹God gave you the honor not only of believing in Christ but also of suf-

---

**notes** 1:12 **brothers and sisters** Although the Greek text says "brothers" here and throughout this book, Paul's words were meant for the entire church, including men and women.

fering for him, both of which bring glory to Christ. ³⁰When I was with you, you saw the struggles I had, and you hear about the struggles I am having now. You yourselves are having the same kind of struggles.

2 Does your life in Christ give you strength? Does his love comfort you? Do we share together in the spirit? Do you have mercy and kindness? ²If so, make me very happy by having the same thoughts, sharing the same love, and having one mind and purpose. ³When you do things, do not let selfishness or pride be your guide. Instead, be humble and give more honor to others than to yourselves. ⁴Do not be interested only in your own life, but be interested in the lives of others.

## BE UNSELFISH LIKE CHRIST

⁵In your lives you must think and act like Christ Jesus.

## beautysecret

### Broken Lipstick?

**Have you ever had the end of your lipstick break off? It can be pretty frustrating. Instead of throwing the whole tube away, place the two broken ends together gently. Put the cap on the lipstick and place it in the freezer for 10 to 20 minutes. Your lipstick should be ready to go again.**

⁶Christ himself was like God in everything.
But he did not think that being equal with God was something to be used for his own benefit.
⁷But he gave up his place with God and made himself nothing.
He was born to be a man and became like a servant.
⁸And when he was living as a man, he humbled himself and was fully obedient to God,
even when that caused his death— death on a cross.
⁹So God raised him to the highest place.
God made his name greater than every other name
¹⁰so that every knee will bow to the name of Jesus—
everyone in heaven, on earth, and under the earth.
¹¹And everyone will confess that Jesus Christ is Lord
and bring glory to God the Father.

## BE THE PEOPLE GOD WANTS YOU TO BE

¹²My dear friends, you have always obeyed God when I was with you. It is even more important that you obey now while I am away from you. Keep on working to complete your salvation with fear and trembling, ¹³because God is working in you to help you want to do and be able to do what pleases him.

¹⁴Do everything without complaining or arguing. ¹⁵Then you will be innocent and without any wrong. You will be God's children without fault. But you are living with crooked and mean people all around you, among whom you shine like stars in the dark world. ¹⁶You offer the teaching that gives life. So when Christ comes again, I can be happy because my work was not wasted. I ran the race and won.

¹⁷Your faith makes you offer your lives as a sacrifice in serving God. If I have to offer my own blood with your sacrifice, I will be happy and full of joy with all of you. ¹⁸You also should be happy and full of joy with me.

## Promises

## Philippians 2:13

Ever feel like you just can't do anything right? Maybe everything in your spiritual life seems to be going great and you feel like you are doing a decent job of pleasing and obeying God, when—boom! You mess up and feel like you're back to square one. Mission failed.

Listen, God knows very well that you are not perfect—and that you can never be perfect, for that matter. The only perfect human being was Jesus Christ. No saint, priest, or preacher has even come close. "Okay," you may say, "then what's the point? Why even try?" Well, because it is noted throughout Scripture that God wants us to obey him—he demands it, even. He appreciates and honors the "baby steps" that we take in trying to be obedient to him; and, as this verse says, he even helps us along the way. When you fall, he will pick you up again, dust you off, and set you on your way again.

He continues to work in you and through you—one "baby step" at a time.

# Music Reviews

**GROUP:** SKILLET

**ALBUM:** ALIEN YOUTH (CLASSIC HIT)

Skillet may become the next big thing in electronic/industrial rock as far as mainstream music is concerned, but Christian music fans have known about the band's heavy hooks for years. On *Alien Youth,* gravelly voiced frontman John Cooper, his wife Korey, and other band members sing about "worldwide Jesus domination" on the title song and keep the hits coming with power ballads "You Are My Hope" and "One Real Thing." Skillet grinds guitars, adds the staccato beats of rapid-fire drumming, and sets it off with keyboards that create the band's unique brand of rock 'n' roll.

**WHY IT ROCKS: SKILLET ROCKS HARD.**

## TIMOTHY AND EPAPHRODITUS

¹⁹I hope in the Lord Jesus to send Timothy to you soon. I will be happy to learn how you are. ²⁰I have no one else like Timothy, who truly cares for you. ²¹Other people are interested only in their own lives, not in the work of Jesus Christ. ²²You know the kind of person Timothy is. You know he has served with me in telling the Good News, as a son serves his father. ²³I plan to send him to you quickly when I know what will happen to me. ²⁴I am sure that the Lord will help me to come to you soon.

²⁵Epaphroditus, my brother in Christ, works and serves with me in the army of Christ. When I needed help, you sent him to me. I think now that I must send him back to you, ²⁶because he wants very much to see all of you. He is worried because you heard that he was sick. ²⁷Yes, he was sick, and nearly died, but God had mercy on him and me too so that I would not have more sadness. ²⁸I want very much to send him to you so that when you see him you can be happy, and I can stop worrying about you. ²⁹Welcome him in the Lord with much joy. Give honor to people like him, ³⁰because he almost died for the work of Christ. He risked his life to give me the help you could not give in your service to me.

## THE IMPORTANCE OF CHRIST

**3** My brothers and sisters, be full of joy in the Lord. It is no trouble for me to write the same things to you again, and it will help you to be more ready. ²Watch out for those who do evil, who are like dogs, who demand to cut" the body. ³We are the ones who are truly circumcised. We worship God through his Spirit, and our pride is in Christ Jesus. We do not put trust in ourselves or anything we can do, ⁴although I might be able to put trust in myself. If anyone thinks he has a reason to trust in himself, he should know that I have greater reason for trusting in myself. ⁵I was circumcised eight days after my birth. I am from the people of Israel and the tribe of Benjamin. I am a Hebrew, and my parents were Hebrews. I had a strict view of the law, which is why I became a Pharisee. ⁶I was so

# LEARN I✝ & LIVE I✝

**Philippians 1:10**
**Learn It:** It's important to be able to see the difference between right and wrong.
**Live It:** Make a list of all the choices you have to make this week, and ask God if they are right or wrong.

**Philippians 2:4**
**Learn It:** Be interested in others' lives, not just your own.
**Live It:** Notice how many times you talk about yourself today. Try counting how many times you say "I" and "me."

**Philippians 2:12**
**Learn It:** Learn to obey even when no one is watching.
**Live It:** God knows your motives; he sees your actions. Try to do the right thing for the right reasons.

**3:2 cut** The word in Greek is like the word "circumcise," but it means "to cut completely off."

enthusiastic I tried to hurt the church. No one could find fault with the way I obeyed the law of Moses. [7]Those things were important to me, but now I think they are worth nothing because of Christ. [8]Not only those things, but I think that all things are worth nothing compared with the greatness of knowing Christ Jesus my Lord. Because of him, I have lost all those things, and now I know they are worthless trash. This allows me to have Christ [9]and to belong to him. Now I am right with God, not because I followed the law, but because I believed in Christ. God uses my faith to make me right with him. [10]I want to know Christ and the power that raised him from the dead. I want to share in his sufferings and become like him in his death. [11]Then I have hope that I myself will be raised from the dead.

## CONTINUING TOWARD OUR GOAL

[12]I do not mean that I am already as God wants me to be. I have not yet reached that goal, but I continue trying to reach it and to make it mine. Christ wants me to do that, which is the reason he made me his. [13]Brothers and sisters, I know that I have not yet reached that goal, but there is one thing I always do. Forgetting the past and straining toward what is ahead, [14]I keep trying to reach the goal and get the prize for which God called me through Christ to the life above.

# Bible Basics

**Evangelism** may sound like a big, scary deal, but it's not. It's a lot like talking about yourself. Instead of just sharing with someone about your day, your family, or your friends, evangelism is sharing with other people about the friendship you have with Christ. It is building relationships with others and explaining to them what a difference Christ has made in your life. Since getting to know him, has he helped you through hard times, made you feel better inside, or given you a feeling of peace that you are doing the right thing? Sure he has, and those are the kinds of things that other people want, too. They're hungry to hear that somebody loves them and thinks they are special, that they matter and their life has a purpose. When you share about Christ, whether in a personal conversation with a close friend or on a stage in front of thousands, that's evangelism.

# Changed Lives

### VICKI'S STORY—CHRISTIAN ADOPTION

My boyfriend and I made some mistakes and soon found out we were pregnant with twins. We were not ready to be parents, but we knew we wanted our babies to live. We decided to give them up for adoption and wanted to place them with a Christian family involved in ministry. I also wanted them to be placed in a family where one of the spouses was either a twin or had a twin in their family. Little did I know how God would work things out. I never thought I would get pregnant. My mother had died of cancer just a year before, and I was still reeling from her death. My boyfriend and I made bad choices and had sex when we knew we shouldn't, forcing us to deal with consequences that would be painful for the rest of our lives. My boyfriend's family and mine agreed that we should pursue adoption, but it wasn't an easy decision. We chose a Christian organization that could help place our babies. At first, the director did not know if she could meet all of our criteria for birthparents. She said our list was too specific.

But one day, when she was preparing to speak at a youth conference, the director said God kept putting us in her thoughts. She finally gave up trying to prepare her speech and began waiting for God to share what he wanted to tell her. He gave her the names of a couple in high-profile ministry who had never had children, but she had no idea if they wanted to adopt or if there were twins in their family. But God knew. The husband was a twin, and he and his wife were excited about the prospect of adopting. In fact, a man at their church had recently told them that he felt they would be parents soon, possibly with twins. The confirmation on both sides let us know that God's hand was already working in our babies' lives. Letting my daughters go was the hardest thing I have ever done. But today, I have graduated from Bible school and am working full time. And I have been blessed to help turn a wonderful couple into a family.

*For more information on Christian adoption, contact www.bethany.org. You can also check out www.perigee.net/~cas/ or call them at (800) 453-1011. For information about residential care for females, visit mercyministries.com. (Names have been changed for the sake of privacy. Vicki tells her story after going through biblically based counseling with Mercy Ministries.)*

# Radical Faith:

## Philippians 4:6-7

Is it really possible to not worry at all? Seems a little far-fetched, huh? But God tells you not to worry, so there must be a way to avoid it. For every command God gives, he provides you with the ability to carry it out with the help of the Holy Spirit. When you worry, you're underestimating God's goodness, power, and wisdom. So honoring him is not what you're most concerned about. If you believe that there is nothing God can't handle, then act like it. Paul says to replace your worry with prayer and that God will give you peace in his presence. God doesn't say, "Don't care about anything." He says, "Come running to me with everything. Trust me to work in your heart and in your situation. Believe that only I can handle it perfectly. Stay close to me, fully trust me, and I'll keep you in my peace." With God's help you can keep your heart from restlessness and keep your mind from fear and worry. You can only do that by continually being reminded of God's truth, being thankful, and being open with him. So stay put in his Word, and keep up the conversation.

15All of us who are spiritually mature should think this way, too. And if there are things you do not agree with, God will make them clear to you. 16But we should continue following the truth we already have.

17Brothers and sisters, all of you should try to follow my example and to copy those who live the way we showed you. 18Many people live like enemies of the cross of Christ. I have often told you about them, and it makes me cry to tell you about them now. 19In the end, they will be destroyed. They do whatever their bodies want, they are proud of their shameful acts, and they think only about earthly things. 20But our homeland is in heaven, and we are waiting for our Savior, the Lord Jesus Christ, to come from heaven. 21By his power to rule all things, he will change our simple bodies and make them like his own glorious body.

## WHAT THE CHRISTIANS ARE TO DO

4 My dear brothers and sisters, I love you and want to see you. You bring me joy and make me proud of you, so stand strong in the Lord as I have told you.

2I ask Euodia and Syntyche to agree in the Lord. 3And I ask you, my faithful friend, to help these women. They served with me in telling the Good News, together with Clement and others who worked with me, whose names are written in the book of life.*n*

understand it, will keep your hearts and minds in Christ Jesus.

## "BROTHERS AND SISTERS, THINK ABOUT THE THINGS THAT ARE GOOD AND WORTHY OF PRAISE."

8Brothers and sisters, think about the things that are good and worthy of praise. Think about the things that are true and honorable and right and pure and beautiful and respected. 9Do what you learned and received from me, what I told you, and what you saw me do. And the God who gives peace will be with you.

## PAUL THANKS THE CHRISTIANS

10I am very happy in the Lord that you have shown your care for me again. You continued to care about me, but there was no way for you to show it. 11I am not telling you this because I need anything. I have learned to be satisfied with the things I have and with everything that happens. 12I know how to live when I am poor, and I know how to live when I have plenty. I have learned the secret of being happy at any time in everything that happens, when I have enough to eat and when I go hungry,

**WHAT TEENS CONSIDER TO BE THE MOST PRESTIGIOUS JOBS: 1) DOCTOR (55%), 2) MEMBER OF CONGRESS (41%), 3) MILITARY OFFICER (40%), 4) FIREMAN (38%), 5) SCIENTIST (36%), 6) ACTOR (36%), 7) POLICE OFFICER (32%), 8) ATHLETE (31%), 9) LAWYER (29%), 10) ENTERTAINER (29%).** WWW.HARRISINTERACTIVE.COM

4Be full of joy in the Lord always. I will say again, be full of joy.

5Let everyone see that you are gentle and kind. The Lord is coming soon. 6Do not worry about anything, but pray and ask God for everything you need, always giving thanks. 7And God's peace, which is so great we cannot

when I have more than I need and when I do not have enough. 13I can do all things through Christ, because he gives me strength.

14But it was good that you helped me when I needed it. 15You Philippians remember when I first preached the Good News there. When I left Macedonia, you were the only church that gave

 **notes** 4:3 **book of life** God's book that has the names of all God's chosen people (Revelation 3:5; 21:27).

**Philippians 2:14**
**Learn It:** Do everything without complaining or arguing.
**Live It:** Here's a tall order: do not complain about anything today. Concentrate on giving compliments, and give in gracefully before arguments even start.

**Philippians 3:17**
**Learn It:** Copy the lives of those who live the right way.
**Live It:** Choose a couple of spiritual mentors who are further along in the faith, and copy their good spiritual habits.

**Philippians 4:4**
**Learn It:** Always be full of the joy in the Lord.
**Live It:** Have you checked your attitude lately? Dress up in something fun, dance around the room, and exude joy today.

me help. [16]Several times you sent me things I needed when I was in Thessalonica. [17]Really, it is not that I want to receive gifts from you, but I want you to have the good that comes from giving. [18]And now I have everything, and more. I have all I need, because Epaphroditus brought your gift to me. It is like a sweet-smelling sacrifice offered to God, who accepts that sacrifice and is pleased with it. [19]My God will use his wonderful riches in Christ Jesus to give you everything you need. [20]Glory to our God and Father forever and ever! Amen.

[21]Greet each of God's people in Christ. Those who are with me send greetings to you. [22]All of God's people greet you, particularly those from the palace of Caesar.

[23]The grace of the Lord Jesus Christ be with you all.

# tolerance. It's a major buzz word

in today's society. The mantra of "live and let live" pervades our culture, warning us not to make waves, not to step on anyone else's toes. In a tolerant world, truth is relative. There are many ways to God. Perhaps there are even many gods. And shouldn't we be tolerant of other religions? Don't they each have some truth to them?

# Colossians
### Back to a Pure Christian Faith

Tolerance is a great idea in most circumstances. We definitely need to be tolerant of differing personalities, races, income levels, and cultures. But when we become too tolerant of other belief systems, Christianity can become polluted by false religions.

That's exactly what was happening in Colossae. Believers there were treating their faith like an all-you-can-eat buffet, taking a little of this and a little of that. Meanwhile, the most basic, critical teachings of the Christian faith were being watered down and reduced to mere suggestions. Paul steps in, denouncing this philosophy as heresy—a teaching that goes against a particular religion—in this case, against Christianity. Then he reminds the Colossians of the truth of the Good News. And that's something we all need to be reminded of from time to time.

Radical Faith:

## Colossians 1:10-13

How do you live a life that honors God? What does that look like? God will definitely help you to understand how to live a life pleasing to him if you ask for his help. Pray that you'll stay filled with his presence, and do your best to learn and to submit to his Word. If you do that, you'll see God work. You'll produce fruit—your character will change, and people will see God in you. You'll understand more about how God works, what he's done in the past, and what he has planned for your future. Knowing more of him will direct you in how to live. He will give you his strength so that you can be steady and patient when things seem long and hard. You're no longer trapped in darkness and hopelessness; God has permitted you to take part in his love, rest, freedom, life, and glory. He's "made you able to have a share in all that he has prepared for his people" (Colossians 1:12). What a wonderful God. You can spend your life giving thanks to him and offering him a heart that wants to please him. Keep looking to him, and he'll lead in you in a life that honors and reflects him.

1 From Paul, an apostle of Christ Jesus. I am an apostle because that is what God wanted. Also from Timothy, our brother.

²To the holy and faithful brothers and sisters" in Christ that live in Colossae:

Grace and peace to you from God our Father.

³In our prayers for you we always thank God, the Father of our Lord Jesus Christ, ⁴because we have heard about the faith you have in Christ Jesus and the love you have for all of God's people. ⁵You have this faith and love because of your hope, and what you hope for is kept safe for you in heaven. You learned about this hope when you heard the message about the truth, the Good News ⁶that was told to you. Everywhere in the world that Good News is bringing blessings and is growing. This has happened with you, too, since you heard the Good News and understood the truth about the grace of God. ⁷You learned about God's grace from Epaphras, whom we love. He works together with us and is a faithful servant of Christ for us. ⁸He also told us about the love you have from the Holy Spirit.

⁹Because of this, since the day we heard about you, we have continued praying for you, asking God that you will know fully what he wants. We pray that you will also have great wisdom and understanding in spiritual things ¹⁰so that you will live the kind of life that honors and pleases the Lord in every way. You will produce fruit in every good work and grow in the knowledge of God. ¹¹God will strengthen you with his own great power so that you will not give up when troubles come, but you will be patient. ¹²And you will joyfully give thanks to the Father who has made you able to have a share in all that he has prepared for his people in the kingdom of light. ¹³God has freed us from the power of darkness, and he brought us into the kingdom of his dear Son. ¹⁴The Son paid for our sins, and in him we have forgiveness.

### THE IMPORTANCE OF CHRIST

¹⁵No one can see God, but Jesus Christ is exactly like him. He ranks higher than everything that has been made. ¹⁶Through his

Promises:

## Colossians 1:14

Reality TV is one of the hottest things going today. In various (and usually weird) ways, each show explores issues that we as humans face every day such as temptation, greed, fear, romance, friendship—and even redemption. In one popular makeover show called "What Not to Wear," two fashion stylists swoop in and rescue one fashion victim from their unsightly appearance. The stylists take the person's offending wardrobe and get rid of it, coaching the victim on what they should buy before giving them $5,000 to spend on a new wardrobe. The goal of the stylists is to redeem the person from their fashion faux pas and give them a shining new appearance.

Sound familiar? Once, we were apart from God and no amount of law-keeping or cleaning ourselves up could make us right with him. So Jesus came and paid for our sins, allowing us an opportunity to get rid of the old and bring in the new. Because of what Jesus did, we can pray directly to God, asking forgiveness for sins and accepting his grace.

Now that's a makeover to get excited about!

notes    **1:2 brothers and sisters** Although the Greek text says "brothers" here and throughout this book, Paul's words were meant for the entire church, including men and women.

# LEARN I+ & LIVE I+

**Philippians 4:11**
**Learn It:** Be satisfied with what you have, and be happy no matter what happens.
**Live It:** Read in Philippians every day for a week, and put Paul's words into practice.

**Philippians 4:13**
**Learn It:** Christ gives me strength to do anything.
**Live It:** Figure out one grim task that you have been putting off, whether it is cleaning out your closet or facing someone you haven't spoken to in years, and ask Christ to help you do it.

**Colossians 1:9-10**
**Learn It:** It's important to know how God wants his people to live.
**Live It:** Over the next thirty days, pray that God will give you wisdom in all your decisions and choices.

power all things were made—things in heaven and on earth, things seen and unseen, all powers, authorities, lords, and rulers. All things were made through Christ and for Christ. ¹⁷He was there before anything was made, and all things continue because of him. ¹⁸He is the head of the body, which is the church. Everything comes from him. He is the first one who was raised from the dead. So in all things Jesus has first place. ¹⁹God was pleased for all of himself to live in Christ. ²⁰And through Christ, God has brought all things back to himself again—things on earth and things in heaven. God made peace through the blood of Christ's death on the cross.

²¹At one time you were separated from God. You were his enemies in your minds, and the evil things you did were against God. ²²But now God has made you his friends again. He did this through Christ's death in the body so that he might bring you into God's presence as people who are holy, with no wrong, and with nothing of which God can judge you guilty. ²³This will happen if you continue strong and sure in your faith. You must not be moved away from the hope brought to you by the Good News that you heard. That same Good News has been told to everyone in the world, and I, Paul, help in preaching that Good News.

## PAUL'S WORK FOR THE CHURCH

²⁴I am happy in my sufferings for you. There are things that Christ must still suffer through his body, the church. I am accepting, in my body, my part of these things that must be suffered. ²⁵I became a servant of the church because God gave me a special work to do that helps you, and that work is to tell fully the message of God. ²⁶This message is the secret that was hidden from everyone since the beginning of time, but now it is made known to God's holy people. ²⁷God decided to let his people know this rich and glorious secret which he has for all people. This secret is Christ himself, who is in you. He is our only hope for glory. ²⁸So we continue to preach Christ to each person, using all wisdom to warn and to teach everyone, in order to bring each one into God's presence as a mature person in Christ. ²⁹To do this, I work and struggle, using Christ's great strength that works so powerfully in me.

2 I want you to know how hard I work for you, those in Laodicea, and others who have never seen me. ²I want them to be strengthened and joined together with love so that they may be rich in their understanding. This leads to their knowing fully God's secret, that is, Christ himself. ³In him all the treasures of wisdom and knowledge are safely kept.

⁴I say this so that no one can fool you by arguments that seem good, but are false. ⁵Though I am absent from you in my body, my heart is with you, and I am happy to see your good lives and your strong faith in Christ.

## CONTINUE TO LIVE IN CHRIST

⁶As you received Christ Jesus the Lord, so continue to live in him. ⁷Keep your roots deep in him and have your lives built on him. Be strong in the faith, just as you were taught, and always be thankful.

⁸Be sure that no one leads you away with

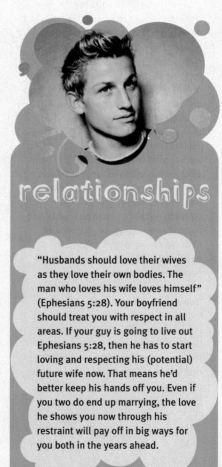

## relationships

"Husbands should love their wives as they love their own bodies. The man who loves his wife loves himself" (Ephesians 5:28). Your boyfriend should treat you with respect in all areas. If your guy is going to live out Ephesians 5:28, then he has to start loving and respecting his (potential) future wife now. That means he'd better keep his hands off you. Even if you two do end up marrying, the love he shows you now through his restraint will pay off in big ways for you both in the years ahead.

false and empty teaching that is only human, which comes from the ruling spirits of this world, and not from Christ. ⁹All of God lives in Christ fully (even when Christ was on earth), ¹⁰and you have a full and true life in Christ, who is ruler over all rulers and powers.

¹¹Also in Christ you had a different kind of circumcision, a circumcision not done by hands. It was through Christ's circumcision, that is, his death, that you were made free from the power of your sinful self. ¹²When you were baptized, you were buried with Christ, and you were raised up with him through your faith in God's power that was shown when he raised Christ from the dead. ¹³When you were spiritually dead because of your sins and because you were not free from the power of your sinful self, God made you alive with Christ, and he forgave all our sins. ¹⁴He canceled the debt, which listed all the rules we failed to follow. He took away that record with its rules and nailed it to the cross. ¹⁵God stripped the spiritual rulers and powers of their authority. With the cross, he won the victory and showed the world that they were powerless.

## DON'T FOLLOW PEOPLE'S RULES

¹⁶So do not let anyone make rules for you about eating and drinking or about a religious feast, a New Moon Festival, or a Sabbath day.

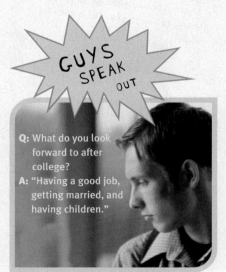

# BIBLE BIOS

# Rachel

[GENESIS 29–33; 35] Jacob loved Rachel so much that he agreed to work for her father for seven years in order to marry her. But when the wedding day came around, Rachel's sister, Leah, was the bride wearing the veil, so poor Jacob had to work for seven more years to marry his true love. But even then, Rachel would always have to share Jacob with her sister. And not only that, Leah was a baby-making factory, giving Jacob many children, while Rachel continually had trouble getting pregnant. Frustrated, Rachel became jealous. Somehow, she forgot about the fourteen years he had worked to win her hand. She just couldn't accept the fact that she did not have to earn Jacob's love. Sound familiar? Some of us, like Rachel, spend a lifetime trying to win God's love and approval, a treasure we already possess. But the truth is, we cannot earn what he's already given.

¹⁷These things were like a shadow of what was to come. But what is true and real has come and is found in Christ. ¹⁸Do not let anyone disqualify you by making you humiliate yourself and worship angels. Such people enter into visions, which fill them with foolish pride because of their human way of thinking. ¹⁹They do not hold tightly to Christ, the head. It is from him that all the parts of the body are cared for and held together. So it grows in the way God wants it to grow.

²⁰Since you died with Christ and were made free from the ruling spirits of the world, why do you act as if you still belong to this world by following rules like these: ²¹"Don't eat this," "Don't taste that," "Don't even touch that thing"? ²²These rules refer to earthly things that are gone as soon as they are used. They are only man-made commands and teachings. ²³They seem to be wise, but they are only part of a man-made religion. They make people pretend not to be proud and make them punish their bodies, but they do not really control the evil desires of the sinful self.

## YOUR NEW LIFE IN CHRIST

3 Since you were raised from the dead with Christ, aim at what is in heaven, where Christ is sitting at the right hand of God. ²Think only about the things in heaven, not the things on earth. ³Your old sinful self has died, and your new life is kept with Christ in God. ⁴Christ is our life, and when he comes again, you will share in his glory.

## "GOD STRIPPED THE SPIRITUAL RULERS AND POWERS OF THEIR AUTHORITY."

⁵So put all evil things out of your life: sexual sinning, doing evil, letting evil thoughts control you, wanting things that are evil, and greed. This is really serving a false god. ⁶These things make God angry.ⁿ ⁷In your past, evil life you also did these things.

⁸But now also put these things out of your

3:6 These . . . angry Some Greek copies add: "against the people who do not obey God."

life: anger, bad temper, doing or saying things to hurt others, and using evil words when you talk. 9Do not lie to each other. You have left your old sinful life and the things you did before. 10You have begun to live the new life, in which you are being made new and are becoming like the One who made you. This new life brings you the true knowledge of God. 11In the new life there is no difference between Greeks and Jews, those who are circumcised and those who are not circumcised, or people who are foreigners, or Scythians." There is no difference between slaves and free people. But Christ is in all believers, and Christ is all that is important.

## "EVERYTHING YOU DO OR SAY SHOULD BE DONE TO OBEY JESUS YOUR LORD."

12God has chosen you and made you his holy people. He loves you. So always do these things: Show mercy to others, be kind, humble, gentle, and patient. 13Get along with each other, and forgive each other. If someone does wrong to you, forgive that person because the Lord forgave you. 14Do all these things; but most important, love each other. Love is what holds you all together in perfect unity. 15Let the peace that Christ gives control your thinking, because you were all called together in one body" to have peace. Always be thankful. 16Let the teaching of Christ live in you richly. Use all wisdom to teach and instruct each other by singing psalms, hymns, and spiritual songs with thankfulness in your hearts to God. 17Everything you do or say should be done to obey Jesus your Lord. And in all you do, give thanks to God the Father through Jesus.

### YOUR New LIFE WITH OTHER PEOPLE

18Wives, yield to the authority of your husbands, because this is the right thing to do in the Lord.

### Radical Faith:

## Colossians 3:1-2

As a believer, Christ has given you a new life that is eternal. While you're still here on earth, your thoughts and actions should be more like heaven (which is eternal and full of brilliant life and beauty) than the world (which is temporary, empty, and wasting away). Don't live like people of the world: "They do whatever their bodies want, they are proud of their shameful acts, and they think only of earthly things" (Philippians 3:19). That kind of life is exactly what Christ saved you from! Don't fall back into it. Instead we should be living with our eyes on heaven. When Jesus returns, you will want to look more like him than the world. You are God's and who he's making you to be won't always fit in with the rest of the world. But you won't be here forever. You're made to belong with God in his home in heaven and that's where you're headed. Set your mind on things that are eternal. Keep your life free of things that don't honor God. Ask him to help you learn how to change. Live with your eyes on God and your mind on heaven. It's so much better than anything of the world.

# Blab

**Q:** Is it okay to go braless?

**A:** If your breasts are very small and the material of your shirt is thick enough that it is not noticeable, maybe. For everyone else, no way. First of all, not giving your breasts support will eventually contribute to their sagging. Second, your breasts are very attractive to guys. Frankly, they love 'em and would like to get their hands on them. Without a bra, your nipples are much more noticeable and a distraction and temptation for men.

**Q:** I pledged not to have sexual intercourse until I get married, but having oral sex is okay, right?

**A:** Nope, but nice try. Sexual sin is sexual sin. With oral sex, you still run the risk of getting a sexually transmitted disease, not to mention low self-esteem and feeling used. Your body belongs to you and God until you marry the right guy. Same goes for his.

**Q:** I want to wear a ring to remind me to remain pure. Does it have to be a certain kind?

**A:** Several Christian companies design purity rings. A ring may be given to you after you take a pledge at church or by your parents. If you want to participate in a pledge, ask your youth pastor about it. Or ask your parents to draw one up with you.

notes: **3:11 Scythians** The Scythians were known as very wild and cruel people.  **3:15 body** The spiritual body of Christ, meaning the church or his people.

# LEARN I+ & LIVE I+

**Colossians 1:18**
**Learn It:** In everything, Jesus has first place.
**Live It:** Make a first place blue ribbon that says, "Jesus has 1st place," and hang it in your locker or in your room as a reminder of who comes first.

**Colossians 2:7**
**Learn It:** Keep your roots deep in Christ, be strong in the faith, and be thankful.
**Live It:** Ask God to help your roots in him grow deep.

**Colossians 3:8**
**Learn It:** Get rid of your bad temper, hurting others, and saying wicked things.
**Live It:** Are you quick to get angry and let people have it? Make a list of people you need to apologize to because of your temper, and then tell them you're sorry.

¹⁹Husbands, love your wives and be gentle with them.

²⁰Children, obey your parents in all things, because this pleases the Lord.

²¹Fathers, do not nag your children. If you are too hard to please, they may want to stop trying.

²²Slaves, obey your masters in all things. Do not obey just when they are watching you, to gain their favor, but serve them honestly, because you respect the Lord. ²³In all the work you are doing, work the best you can. Work as if you were doing it for the Lord, not for people. ²⁴Remember that you will receive your reward from the Lord, which he promised to his people. You are serving the Lord Christ. ²⁵But remember that anyone who does wrong will be punished for that wrong, and the Lord treats everyone the same.

4 Masters, give what is good and fair to your slaves. Remember that you have a Master in heaven.

## WHAT THE CHRISTIANS ARE TO DO

²Continue praying, keeping alert, and always thanking God. ³Also pray for us that God will give us an opportunity to tell people his message. Pray that we can preach the secret that God has made known about Christ. This is why I am in prison. ⁴Pray that I can speak in a way that will make it clear, as I should.

⁵Be wise in the way you act with people who are not believers, making the most of every opportunity. ⁶When you talk, you should always be kind and pleasant so you will be able to answer everyone in the way you should.

## NEWS ABOUT THE PEOPLE WITH PAUL

⁷Tychicus is my dear brother in Christ and a faithful minister and servant with me in the Lord. He will tell you all the things that are happening to me. ⁸This is why I am sending

# Music Reviews

**GROUP:** CASTING CROWNS  **ALBUM:** CASTING CROWNS

Casting Crowns is an Atlanta-based band of youth leaders whose main goal is to help youth pastors around the country engage teens in enthusiastic worship and study. Part of that vision included making music, and the music rocketed them to the top of the Christian radio charts with their first single "If We Are the Body," which challenges Christians to show that we love God by loving people. Other eye-openers include "What If His People Prayed" and the beautiful "Who Am I?"

**WHY IT ROCKS:** LEAD SINGER MARK HALL REMINDS US THROUGH BEAUTIFUL TUNES TO LOVE OTHERS LIKE CHRIST WOULD.

him: so you may know how we are and he may encourage you. 9I send him with Onesimus, a faithful and dear brother in Christ, and one of your group. They will tell you all that has happened here.

10Aristarchus, a prisoner with me, and Mark, the cousin of Barnabas, greet you. (I have already told you what to do about Mark. If he comes, welcome him.) 11Jesus, who is called Justus, also greets you. These are the only Jewish believers who work with me for the kingdom of God, and they have been a comfort to me.

12Epaphras, a servant of Jesus Christ, from your group, also greets you. He always prays for you that you will grow to be spiritually mature and have everything God wants for you. 13I know he has worked hard for you and the people in Laodicea and in Hierapolis. 14Demas and our dear friend Luke, the doctor, greet you.

15Greet the brothers in Laodicea. And greet Nympha and the church that meets in her house. 16After this letter is read to you, be sure it is also read to the church in Laodicea. And you read the letter that I wrote to Laodicea. 17Tell Archippus, "Be sure to finish the work the Lord gave you."

18I, Paul, greet you and write this with my own hand. Remember me in prison. Grace be with you.

**t**hessalonica was the
largest city in Macedonia

and was an ideal mission field for Paul and Silas. It was a hub of
political and commercial activity, and there were plenty of sinners who
needed to know about Jesus. Unfortunately, Paul and Silas were so good
at preaching the Good News and converting sinners that a group of angry Jews
had them thrown out of the city.

# 1 Thessalonians

## Paul Finishes a Message Cut Short

Thessalonica was the largest city in Macedonia and was an ideal mission field
for Paul and Silas. It was a hub of political and commercial activity, and there were
plenty of sinners who needed to know about Jesus. Unfortunately, Paul and Silas
were so good at preaching the Good News and converting sinners that a group of
angry Jews had them thrown out of the city.

Since his time in Thessalonica was cut short, Paul sent this letter via Timothy to
the believers there, both to encourage them and to complete his message that had
been interrupted. Paul addresses some of the false accusations made against him,
and he comforts the persecuted flock of believers. He reminds them to keep
living lives that please God.

Paul's message concentrates on Christ's return to the earth to gather
believers. He notes that it's OK to be concerned about the return of Jesus, but
not to be so caught up in waiting that one loses sight of what's important
today. For Thessalonians and all believers who still haven't found their
place in this world, Paul challenges them to live honorable
lives, work hard, and earn the respect of others.

297

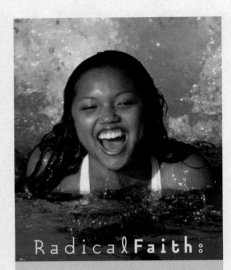

## RadicalFaith:

# 1 Thessalonians 1:9

What do you think about a lot? Did you ever realize that what you think or care about the most is actually what you are worshiping? It could be anything—a person, an idea, or a goal. God calls anything other than himself that takes first place in your heart an idol. And God made your heart to be filled perfectly only with him; he hates it when you try to put petty substitutes in his place. The Thessalonians were all about giving their time, attention, and devotion to anything other than God, but then they made a huge switch and turned to God. People around them were shocked at the transformation. The Thessalonians found out that everything else wasn't worthwhile. They discovered that God really does satisfy the longing soul—that he fills the hungry heart with goodness. They encountered something supernatural, something that went way past all the physical and temporary things around them. If you're looking for significance, purpose, deep joy, and connection, let the living God take over your life in a new way. When you make him the object of your affection, focus, and commitment, you'll discover a whole new life. You will find the most delight in knowing, worshiping, and walking with him.

1 From Paul, Silas, and Timothy.

To the church in Thessalonica, the church in God the Father and the Lord Jesus Christ:

Grace and peace to you.

## THE FAITH OF THE THESSALONIANS

[2]We always thank God for all of you and mention you when we pray. [3]We continually recall before God our Father the things you have done because of your faith and the work you have done because of your love. And we thank him that you continue to be strong because of your hope in our Lord Jesus Christ.

[4]Brothers and sisters," God loves you, and we know he has chosen you, [5]because the Good News we brought to you came not only with words, but with power, with the Holy Spirit, and with sure knowledge that it is true. Also you know how we lived when we were with you in order to help you. [6]And you became like us and like the Lord. You suffered much, but still you accepted the teaching with the joy that comes from the Holy Spirit. [7]So you became an example to all the believers in Macedonia and Southern Greece. [8]And the Lord's teaching spread from you not only into Macedonia and Southern Greece, but now your faith in God has become known everywhere. So we do not need to say anything about it. [9]People everywhere are telling about the way you accepted us when we were there with you. They tell how you stopped worshiping idols and began serving the living and true God. [10]And you wait for God's Son, whom God raised from the dead, to come from heaven. He is Jesus, who saves us from God's angry judgment that is sure to come.

## PAUL'S WORK IN THESSALONICA

2 Brothers and sisters, you know our visit to you was not a failure. [2]Before we came to you, we suffered in Philippi. People there insulted us, as you know, and many people were against us. But our God helped us to be brave and to tell you his Good News. [3]Our appeal does not come from lies or wrong reasons, nor were we trying to trick you. [4]But we speak the Good News because God tested us and trusted us to do it. When we speak, we are not trying to please people, but God, who tests our hearts. [5]You know that we never tried to influence you by saying nice things about you. We were not trying to get your money; we had no selfishness to hide from you. God knows that this is true. [6]We were not looking for human praise, from you or anyone else, [7]even though as apostles of Christ we could have used our authority over you.

But we were very gentle with you, like a mother caring for her little children. [8]Because we loved you, we were happy to share not only God's Good News with you, but even our own lives. You had become so dear to us! [9]Brothers and sisters, I know you remember our hard work and difficulties. We worked night and day so we would not burden any of you while we preached God's Good News to you.

## "AND IT REALLY IS GOD'S MESSAGE WHICH WORKS IN YOU WHO BELIEVE."

[10]When we were with you, we lived in a holy and honest way, without fault. You know this is true, and so does God. [11]You know that we

**DIDYA KNOW**

## MORE THAN HALF OF TEENS LIVE IN HOMES WHERE THE TV IS USUALLY ON DURING MEALTIMES.

**KAISER FAMILY FOUNDATION**

**notes**   1:4 **Brothers and sisters** Although the Greek text says "Brothers" here and throughout this book, Paul's words were meant for the entire church, including men and women.

298

# LEARN I+ & LIVE I+

**Colossians 3:18**
**Learn It:** The Lord wants the wife to let the husband have authority.
**Live It:** How politically correct is your thinking? Ask Christian women who have been married for years what giving their husband authority looks like.

**Colossians 4:5**
**Learn It:** Be wise in the way you act around unbelievers, and make the most of every chance to share your faith.
**Live It:** Find three friends who need to hear the Good News, and ask God to give you just the right way to approach them.

**1 Thessalonians 1:4**
**Learn It:** God loves you, and he chose you.
**Live It:** Think about how it feels to be picked to be the lead character in a play or to be the one everyone wants on their team. God picked you to be on his team. Thank him for that today!

treated each of you as a father treats his own children. ¹²We encouraged you, we urged you, and we insisted that you live good lives for God, who calls you to his glorious kingdom.

¹³Also, we always thank God because when you heard his message from us, you accepted it as the word of God, not the words of humans. And it really is God's message which works in you who believe. ¹⁴Brothers and sisters, your experiences have been like those of God's churches in Christ that are in Judea." You suffered from the people of your own country, as they suffered from the Jews, ¹⁵who killed both the Lord Jesus and the prophets and forced us to leave that country. They do not please God

and are against all people. ¹⁶They try to stop us from teaching those who are not Jews so they may be saved. By doing this, they are increasing their sins to the limit. The anger of God has come to them at last.

## PAUL WANTS TO VISIT THEM AGAIN

¹⁷Brothers and sisters, though we were separated from you for a short time, our thoughts were still with you. We wanted very much to see you and tried hard to do so. ¹⁸We wanted to come to you. I, Paul, tried to come more than once, but Satan stopped us. ¹⁹You are our hope, our joy, and the crown we will take pride in

when our Lord Jesus Christ comes. ²⁰Truly you are our glory and our joy.

3 When we could not wait any longer, we decided it was best to stay in Athens alone ²and send Timothy to you. Timothy, our brother, works with us for God and helps us tell people the Good News about Christ. We sent him to strengthen and encourage you in your faith ³so none of you would be upset by these troubles. You yourselves know that we must face these troubles. ⁴Even when we were with you, we told you we all would have to suffer, and you know it has happened. ⁵Because of this, when I could wait no longer, I sent Timothy to you so I could learn about your faith. I was

## ◉➜ CHECK IT OUT

### MERCY SHIPS

Since 1978, Mercy Ships has performed more than 2 million services and impacted over 5.5 million people through free medical care and surgical operations. Doctors and surgeons who volunteer their time have performed more than 18,000 operations such as cataract removal, straightening of crossed eyes, and facial reconstruction. Medical teams and volunteers have treated more than 300,000 people in village medical clinics, performed 110,000 dental treatments, and educated more than 5,500 local health care and professional workers, who have in turn trained tens to hundreds of thousands in primary health care.

Mercy Ships have provided more than $21 million in medical equipment, hospital supplies, and medicines, and completed close to 350 construction and agriculture projects that include building schools, clinics, orphanages, and water wells.

Short-term volunteers can participate from two weeks to a full year on a Mercy Ship, and the ships also need donations of money and supplies when in port.

*Get involved by visiting* **www.mercyships.org**.

**notes**    **2:14 Judea** The Jewish land where Jesus lived and taught and where the church first began.

# Quiz

# HOW CONFIDENT ARE YOU?

**1. SOME OF YOUR FRIENDS MENTION THAT YOU SHOULD RUN FOR STUDENT COUNCIL. THE THOUGHT OF DOING THIS IS:**

A.   Slightly intriguing.
B.   Absolutely terrifying.
C.   Exciting.
D.   Interesting.

**2. YOU CREATE A FUNKY SELF-PORTRAIT IN ART CLASS. WHAT DO YOU DO WITH IT?**

A.   Hang it in your room at home.
B.   Ask the art teacher to display it on her wall of student art.
C.   Allow your mom to hang it in the family room.

D.   Shove it into the back of your locker as soon as the paint dries.

**3. YOU'RE WALKING DOWN THE HALL AND NOTICE SOMEONE YOU BARELY RECOGNIZE WAVING IN YOUR DIRECTION. YOU:**

A.   Assume they're waving at you and run over to say hello.
B.   Smile and walk their way.
C.   Ignore them—there's no way they're waving at you.
D.   Turn around to see who's behind you.

**4. YOUR ENGLISH TEACHER LOVES CLASS PARTICIPATION. YOU'RE DISCUSSING *HAMLET* AND YOU CAN TELL SHE'S ABOUT**

TO CALL ON YOU. YOU READ UP, SO YOU KNOW THE ANSWER. YOU FEEL:

A.   Ready and eager to answer.
B.   A little nervous.
C.   Indifferent.
D.   Very anxious.

**5. WHEN IT COMES TO MEETING NEW PEOPLE, YOU ARE:**

A.   Friendly.
B.   Enthusiastic.
C.   A little shy.
D.   Totally self-conscious.

---

**SCORING:** 1. A=4, B=5, C=2, D=3   2. A=4, B=2, C=3, D=5   3. A=2, B=4, C=5, D=3   4. A=2, B=4, C=3, D=5   5. A=3, B=2, C=4, D=5

---

**A SCORE OF 20-25 = SHRINKING VIOLET:**

You have very little confidence in yourself or your abilities. You have more to offer than you may realize, so don't be afraid to acknowledge your good qualities and talents more often. Surround yourself with positive people and try to take a few new chances.

**A SCORE OF 15-19 = BALANCED GAL:**

You are confident and friendly, without being cocky or making others feel insecure. You are comfortable with yourself and confident in your abilities—great qualities to have! Be on the lookout for others who are less confident and encourage them.

**A SCORE OF 10-14 = SUPER CONFIDENT:**

Confidence is a great thing—and, boy, do you have it in abundance! Be sure to encourage others with your enthusiasm while being careful not to make others feel inferior. You like to run the show, but step back every once in a while and let someone else make the plans.

# Blab

**Q:** My parents think I should "try out" guys before I get married. They think I should have sex and live with somebody before I decide whether I want them for life. How can I show them that's the wrong approach?

**A:** Live out your purity and faith in front of them. There are also studies you can find that show that couples who live together before marriage are even more likely to divorce than those who don't. Ask God to help you show them his plan in Scripture. If they still don't believe, let it go; but uphold God's standards in your life.

**Q:** My parents drink wine with dinner. Is that wrong?

**A:** The Bible does not forbid the drinking of alcohol but speaks very clearly against getting drunk.

**Q:** My parents are atheists and do not want me to worship God. I am a Christian and want to grow in my faith. What do I do?

**A:** When people want you to deny your faith, you have to honor God above them. Living with parents who are atheists is somewhat like living in a country where people are persecuted for being Christian. They go underground to worship and study, but they still worship and study. Pray for your parents, and ask God to soften their hearts toward him.

afraid the devil had tempted you, and then our hard work would have been wasted.

⁶But Timothy now has come back to us from you and has brought us good news about your faith and love. He told us that you always remember us in a good way and that you want to see us just as much as we want to see you. ⁷So, brothers and sisters, while we have much trouble and suffering, we are encouraged about you because of your faith. ⁸Our life is really full if you stand strong in the Lord. ⁹We have so much joy before our God because of you. We cannot thank him enough for all the joy we feel. ¹⁰Night and day we continue praying with all our heart that we can see you again and give you all the things you need to make your faith strong.

## "MAY THE LORD MAKE YOUR LOVE GROW MORE AND MULTIPLY FOR EACH OTHER AND FOR ALL PEOPLE."

¹¹Now may our God and Father himself and our Lord Jesus prepare the way for us to come to you. ¹²May the Lord make your love grow more and multiply for each other and for all people so that you will love others as we love you. ¹³May your hearts be made strong so that you will be holy and without fault before our God and Father when our Lord Jesus comes with all his holy ones.

### a Life that pleases God

4 Brothers and sisters, we taught you how to live in a way that will please God, and you are living that way. Now we ask and encourage you in the Lord Jesus to live that way even more. ²You know what we told you to do by the authority of the Lord Jesus. ³God wants you to be holy and to stay away from sexual sins. ⁴He wants each of you to learn to control your own body*ⁿ* in a way that is holy and honorable. ⁵Don't use your body for sexual sin like the people who do not know God.

## 1 Thessalonians 4:16-18

One of the greatest sources of hope Christians have is knowing that one day Jesus will return to earth and we will go to be with him for eternity. It is often hard to look around at the world today and have a lot of hope. Wars and cultural violence ravage nations. Starvation and disease kill millions of innocent children every year. Greed abounds. Chaos seems to be everywhere.

But one day, all the chaos and pain in the world will end. Jesus will return and be the ruler of all the earth. And those who know him and have accepted him will finally be in the presence of the lover of their souls. Not only can we look forward to peace once again reigning on earth, but we will also be able to be with the Lord forever. We will finally be face-to-face with him and will able to praise and honor him. But we shouldn't live our lives just sitting around waiting for Jesus to return—that's not what he commands us to do. While we're here on earth, we need to spend our time caring for others and loving them as Christ would, so that they may come to know him as well.

**notes**    **4:4 learn . . . body** This might also mean "learn to live with your own wife."

## 1 Thessalonians 5:5-10

Walking into a completely dark room isn't very smart, is it? You'll probably trip and fall over something you can't see. Before Christ saved you, you were spiritually in the dark, tripping and falling over your sin. Do you still find yourself still stumbling around even though Christ has saved you? As a child of God, you are freed from the darkness of your sin, but Satan wants you to stay in that darkness. He aims to make sin appealing, but that is deceiving. Choose to live a life pleasing to God. Don't put yourself in a situation where you know you'll be tempted to do stuff that won't honor God or things that would make you ashamed of in his presence. It may feel like God won't notice, but he sees everything. Instead, choose self-control. Just because you convince yourself you can get away with it, it doesn't mean you should do it. Capture every thought that comes to you mind and take it to Jesus. Make even your thoughts obey Christ, and then do whatever he leads (2 Corinthians 10:5). You have love, strength, faith, and hope of salvation from God to help keep you in the light. So live like it!

[6]Also, do not wrong or cheat another Christian in this way. The Lord will punish people who do those things as we have already told you and warned you. [7]God called us to be holy and does not want us to live in sin. [8]So the person who refuses to obey this teaching is disobeying God, not simply a human teaching. And God is the One who gives us his Holy Spirit.

[9]We do not need to write you about having love for your Christian family, because God has already taught you to love each other. [10]And truly you do love the Christians in all of Macedonia. Brothers and sisters, now we encourage you to love them even more. [11]Do all you can to live a peaceful life. Take care of your own business, and do your own work as we have already told you. [12]If you do, then people who are not believers will respect you, and you will not have to depend on others for what you need.

## "ENCOURAGE THE PEOPLE WHO ARE AFRAID. HELP THOSE WHO ARE WEAK. BE PATIENT WITH EVERYONE."

### THE LORD'S COMING

[13]Brothers and sisters, we want you to know about those Christians who have died so you will not be sad, as others who have no hope. [14]We believe that Jesus died and that he rose again. So, because of him, God will raise with Jesus those who have died. [15]What we tell you now is the Lord's own message. We who are living when the Lord comes again will not go before those who have already died. [16]The Lord himself will come down from heaven with a loud command, with the voice of the archangel,[n] and with the trumpet call of God. And those who have died believing in Christ will rise first. [17]After that, we who are still alive will be gathered up with them in the clouds to meet the Lord in the air. And we will be with the Lord forever. [18]So encourage each other with these words.

## beautysecret

### Light

Different types of light affect the way your makeup looks. If you're putting on makeup in the morning, stand by a window for natural light. In the evening, try to use white lights (rather than yellow, incandescent bulbs). Just remember that the most important light in your life is Christ shining through you.

### BE READY FOR THE LORD'S COMING

5 Now, brothers and sisters, we do not need to write you about times and dates. [2]You know very well that the day the Lord comes again will be a surprise, like a thief that comes in the night. [3]While people are saying, "We have peace and we are safe," they will be destroyed quickly. It is like pains that come quickly to a woman having a baby. Those people will not escape. [4]But you, brothers and sisters, are not living in darkness, and so that day will not surprise you like a thief. [5]You are all people who belong to the light and to the day. We do not belong to the night or to darkness. [6]So we should not be like other people who are sleeping, but we should be alert and have self-control. [7]Those who sleep, sleep at night. Those who get drunk, get drunk at night. [8]But we belong to the day, so we should control our-

notes     4:16 archangel The leader among God's angels or messengers.

selves. We should wear faith and love to protect us, and the hope of salvation should be our helmet. [9]God did not choose us to suffer his anger but to have salvation through our Lord Jesus Christ. [10]Jesus died for us so that we can live together with him, whether we are alive or dead when he comes. [11]So encourage each other and give each other strength, just as you are doing now.

## Final Instructions and Greetings

[12]Now, brothers and sisters, we ask you to appreciate those who work hard among you, who lead you in the Lord and teach you. [13]Respect them with a very special love because of the work they do.

Live in peace with each other. [14]We ask you, brothers and sisters, to warn those who do not work. Encourage the people who are afraid. Help those who are weak. Be patient with everyone. [15]Be sure that no one pays back wrong for wrong, but always try to do what is good for each other and for all people.

[16]Always be joyful. [17]Pray continually, [18]and give thanks whatever happens. That is what God wants for you in Christ Jesus.

[19]Do not hold back the work of the Holy Spirit. [20]Do not treat prophecy as if it were unimportant. [21]But test everything. Keep what is good, [22]and stay away from everything that is evil.

[23]Now may God himself, the God of peace, make you pure, belonging only to him. May your whole self—spirit, soul, and body—be kept safe and without fault when our Lord Jesus Christ comes. [24]You can trust the One who calls you to do that for you.

[25]Brothers and sisters, pray for us.

[26]Give each other a holy kiss when you meet. [27]I tell you by the authority of the Lord to read this letter to all the believers.

[28]The grace of our Lord Jesus Christ be with you.

## Bible Basics

In the biblical stories of the life of Jesus (found in the Bible books Matthew, Mark, Luke, and John), Jesus had dinner with his followers shortly before he was arrested and then crucified. Matthew, Mark, and Luke record that, at dinner, he took a cup (filled with fruit of the vine, or wine) and passed it around the table, instructing his followers to drink it. Then he broke bread and passed the pieces around, repeating the ritual and telling them to eat the bread. Christ was trying to let his followers know that he was headed for death, but only temporarily. He wanted them to remember the sacrifice he was about to make, that his body (the bread) was going to be broken and his blood (the fruit of the vine, or wine) shed for their sins—and ours. Today, churches still serve bread (or crackers or wafers) and the fruit of the vine (wine or grape juice) in remembrance of and reverence for what Christ did for us. This observance is known as **communion**.

# LEARN I+ & LIVE I+

**1 Thessalonians 1:6**
**Learn It:** True Christians may suffer for their faith, but they still joyfully accept the teaching of the Holy Spirit.
**Live It:** Do not let hard times in your life pull you away from God.

**1 Thessalonians 4:4**
**Learn It:** God wants you to exercise control over your body in way that honors him and is holy.
**Live It:** With a friend create a pledge of ten specific ways you will stay out of tricky situations that might lead to sexual sin. Sign it together.

**1 Thessalonians 4:11**
**Learn It:** Take care of your own business, do your own work, and do all you can to live peacefully.
**Live It:** Ask God to help you not gossip for one week. Make a chart and check off the days.

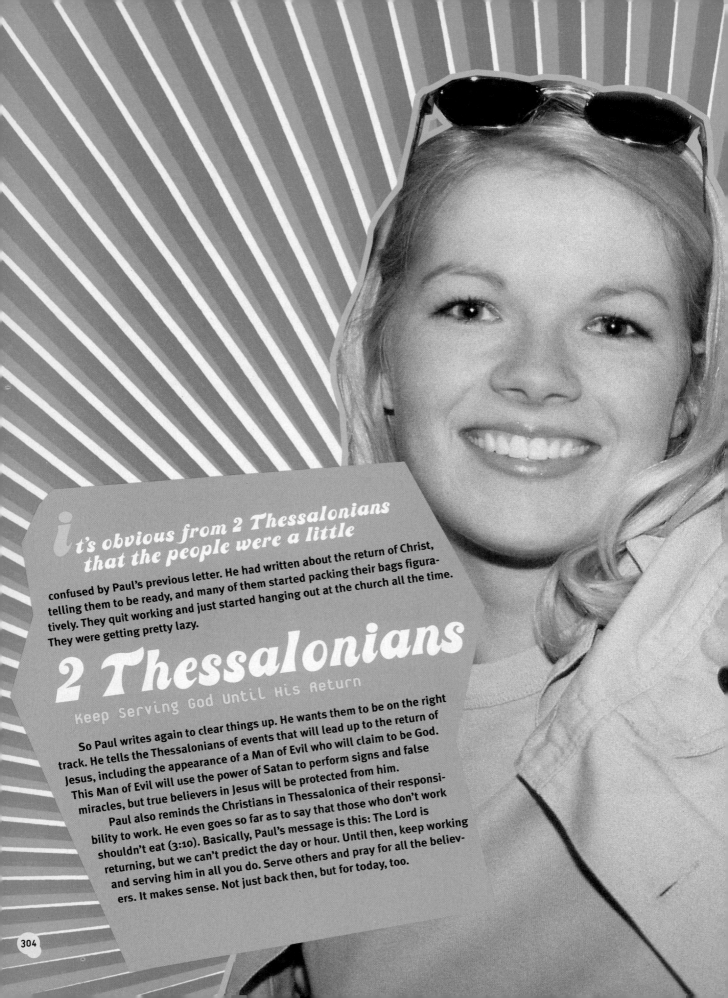

**i**t's obvious from 2 Thessalonians that the people were a little confused by Paul's previous letter. He had written about the return of Christ, telling them to be ready, and many of them started packing their bags figuratively. They quit working and just started hanging out at the church all the time. They were getting pretty lazy.

# 2 Thessalonians
### Keep Serving God Until His Return

So Paul writes again to clear things up. He wants them to be on the right track. He tells the Thessalonians of events that will lead up to the return of Jesus, including the appearance of a Man of Evil who will claim to be God. This Man of Evil will use the power of Satan to perform signs and false miracles, but true believers in Jesus will be protected from him.

Paul also reminds the Christians in Thessalonica of their responsibility to work. He even goes so far as to say that those who don't work shouldn't eat (3:10). Basically, Paul's message is this: The Lord is returning, but we can't predict the day or hour. Until then, keep working and serving him in all you do. Serve others and pray for all the believers. It makes sense. Not just back then, but for today, too.

1 From Paul, Silas, and Timothy.

To the church in Thessalonica in God our Father and the Lord Jesus Christ:

²Grace and peace to you from God the Father and the Lord Jesus Christ.

## PAUL TALKS ABOUT GOD'S JUDGMENT

³We must always thank God for you, brothers and sisters." This is only right, because your faith is growing more and more, and the love that every one of you has for each other is increasing. ⁴So we brag about you to the other churches of God. We tell them about the way you continue to be strong and have faith even though you are being treated badly and are suffering many troubles.

⁵This is proof that God is right in his judgment. He wants you to be counted worthy of his kingdom for which you are suffering. ⁶God will do what is right. He will give trouble to those who trouble you. ⁷And he will give rest to you who are troubled and to us also when the Lord Jesus appears with burning fire from heaven with his powerful angels. ⁸Then he will punish those who do not know God and who do not obey the Good News about our Lord Jesus Christ. ⁹Those people will be punished with a destruction that continues forever. They will be kept away from the Lord and from his great power. ¹⁰This will happen on the day when the Lord Jesus comes to receive glory because of his holy people. And all the people

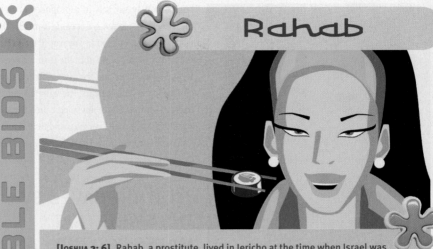

## BIBLE BIOS

# Rahab

[JOSHUA 2; 6] Rahab, a prostitute, lived in Jericho at the time when Israel was at war with her city. Two Israelite spies ended up at her home during the conflict, but rather than turn them in, she helped protect them. She made a powerful choice to honor their God and actually ended up saving their lives. It was a courageous act, and she has been honored with her name being among the few women listed in the family tree of Jesus. Yep—she's there in the genealogy. In Hebrews 11, she is also recognized as one of the great people of faith in the Bible. Rahab's story reminds us that no one is beyond redemption—and anyone can be used by God.

who have believed will be amazed at Jesus. You will be in that group, because you believed what we told you.

¹¹That is why we always pray for you, asking our God to help you live the kind of life he called you to live. We pray that with his power God will help you do the good things you want and perform the works that come from your faith. ¹²We pray all this so that the name of our Lord Jesus Christ will have glory in you, and you will have

glory in him. That glory comes from the grace of our God and the Lord Jesus Christ.

## EVIL THINGS WILL HAPPEN

2 Brothers and sisters, we have something to say about the coming of our Lord Jesus Christ and the time when we will meet together with him. ²Do not become easily upset in your thinking or afraid if you hear that the day of the Lord has already come.

# LEARN I+ & LIVE I+

**1 Thessalonians 5:17**
**Learn It:** Pray continually.
**Live It:** Do what it says. Talk to God before school or work, in the car, while you are working, during lunch, before bed, and any other time you can. Make him your best friend.

**2 Thessalonians 1:11**
**Learn It:** Paul, Silas, and Timothy prayed for their friends and let them know it.
**Live It:** Do you remember to pray for your friends regularly? Create a prayer notebook with their pictures in it, and list prayer needs.

**2 Thessalonians 3:11**
**Learn It:** Refusing to work and meddling in others' lives are no-nos.
**Live It:** Ask yourself honestly if you are a hard worker. Aim for excellence in everything that you do.

notes    **1:3 brothers and sisters** Although the Greek text says "brothers" here and throughout this book, Paul's words were meant for the entire church, including men and women.

## Promises:

# 2 Thessalonians 3:3

Felt attacked lately? Beaten down? Relentlessly tempted and discouraged? Satan loves to get us down and to make us feel weak. We're easy targets because it's easy for us to get discouraged and feel like we can't do anything to defeat the sin in our lives.

But guess what? God has complete control. Satan has no power over God and has little control over you as a Christian under the ultimate control of God. So does this mean that Satan won't tempt you or try to keep you from living the abundant life God wants you to live? The answer is a definite "no." Satan knows that he can't have you, but he will try hard to steal your joy and your effectiveness in reaching others for Christ.

When you get down and feel attacked by Satan, pray to God for wisdom and strength. He has the power to answer.

Someone may say this in a prophecy or in a message or in a letter as if it came from us. ³Do not let anyone fool you in any way. That day of the Lord will not come until the turning away" from God happens and the Man of Evil, who is on his way to hell, appears. ⁴He will be against and put himself above anything called God or anything that people worship. And that Man of Evil will even go into God's Temple and sit there and say that he is God.

# "YOU ARE SAVED BY THE SPIRIT THAT MAKES YOU HOLY AND BY YOUR FAITH IN THE TRUTH."

⁵I told you when I was with you that all this would happen. Do you not remember? ⁶And now you know what is stopping that Man of Evil so he will appear at the right time. ⁷The secret power of evil is already working in the world, but there is one who is stopping that power. And he will continue to stop it until he is taken out of the way. ⁸Then that Man of Evil will appear, and the Lord Jesus will kill him with the breath that comes from his mouth and will destroy him with the glory of his coming. ⁹The Man of Evil will come by the power of Satan. He will have great power, and he will do many different false miracles, signs, and wonders. ¹⁰He will use every kind of evil to trick those who are lost. They will die, because they refused to love the truth. (If they loved the truth, they would be saved.) ¹¹For this reason God sends them something powerful that leads them away from the truth so they will believe a lie. ¹²So all those will be judged guilty who did not believe the truth, but enjoyed doing evil.

## YOU ARE CHOSEN FOR SALVATION

¹³Brothers and sisters, whom the Lord loves, God chose you from the beginning to be saved. So we must always thank God for you. You are saved by the Spirit that makes you holy and by your faith in the truth. ¹⁴God used the Good News that we preached to call you to be saved so you can share in the glory of our Lord Jesus Christ. ¹⁵So, brothers and sisters, stand strong and continue to believe the teachings we gave you in our speaking and in our letter.

¹⁶⁻¹⁷May our Lord Jesus Christ himself and God our Father encourage you and strengthen you in every good thing you do and say. God loved us, and through his grace he gave us a good hope and encouragement that continues forever.

## PRAY FOR US

3 And now, brothers and sisters, pray for us that the Lord's teaching will continue to spread quickly and that people will give honor to that teaching, just as happened with you. ²And pray that we will be protected from

## relationships

"Children, obey your parents as the Lord wants, because this is the right thing to do" (Ephesians 6:1). That's a tough one when you feel like telling them to just leave you alone. You might think you can get out of obeying if you keep reading to verse 4, which says that fathers shouldn't make their children angry. Not so much. Your dad might make you mad, but you're still on the hook. The verse doesn't say obey *unless* your dad makes you mad. It just says to obey. What dad does with verse 4 is his issue with God, not yours.

# October

**1** October is Pastor Appreciation Month. Buy a gift for your pastor youth leader.

**2**

**3** Pray for a person of influence: Ashlee Simpson is having a birthday.

**4** Pray for a person of influence: It's Alicia Silverstone's birthday.

**5**

**6**

**7** Try reading the Bible every night before you go to bed.

**8**

**9** Collect fall leaves and use them to make your own artwork.

**10** Take your dog for a long walk. If you don't have a dog, then take a friend.

**11**

**12** Treat your parents to breakfast in bed.

**13**

**14** Give your teacher a thank-you note just because.

**15** Pray for a person of influence: Jaci Velasquez is having a birthday.

**16** Text message (or tell) your dad three things you love about him today.

**17** Memorize Hebrews 11:1 today. Write the verse on a card. Place it by your mirror.

**18**

**19**

**20** Read Psalm 100. Tell a friend what you learned.

**21**

**22** Pray for a person of influence: Jon Foreman of Switchfoot is having a birthday.

**23** Think about what you'd say if someone asked you why you believe in God.

**24**

**25** Go to church with a friend this weekend. Check out a different denomination.

**26** Pray for a person of influence: It's Hillary Clinton's birthday.

**27**

**28** Open a dictionary and look for three words you don't know. Memorize their spellings and meanings.

**29** Plan for a restful Sabbath this week. A day off is good for the mind, body, and soul.

**30**

**31** Halloween

Switch to Standard Time on the last Sunday of October—turn your clocks back one hour.

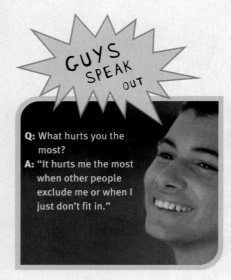

stubborn and evil people, because not all people believe.

³But the Lord is faithful and will give you strength and will protect you from the Evil One. ⁴The Lord makes us feel sure that you are doing and will continue to do the things we told you. ⁵May the Lord lead your hearts into God's love and Christ's patience.

## THE DUTY TO WORK

⁶Brothers and sisters, by the authority of our Lord Jesus Christ we command you to stay away from any believer who refuses to work and does not follow the teaching we gave you. ⁷You yourselves know that you should live as we live. We were not lazy when we were with you. ⁸And when we ate another person's food, we always paid for it. We worked very hard night and day so we would not be an expense to any of you. ⁹We had the right to ask you to help us, but we worked to take care of ourselves so we would be an example for you to follow. ¹⁰When we were with you, we gave you this rule: "Anyone who refuses to work should not eat."

¹¹We hear that some people in your group refuse to work. They do nothing but busy themselves in other people's lives. ¹²We command those people and beg them in the Lord Jesus Christ to work quietly and earn their own food. ¹³But you, brothers and sisters, never become tired of doing good.

¹⁴If some people do not obey what we tell you in this letter, then take note of them. Have nothing to do with them so they will feel ashamed. ¹⁵But do not treat them as enemies. Warn them as fellow believers.

## FINAL WORDS

¹⁶Now may the Lord of peace give you peace at all times and in every way. The Lord be with all of you.

¹⁷I, Paul, end this letter now in my own handwriting. All my letters have this to show they are from me. This is the way I write.

¹⁸The grace of our Lord Jesus Christ be with you all.

**DIDYA KNOW**

**TEENS RANK VOLUNTEERING, THE ENVIRONMENT, AND EATING HEALTHY AS THE TOP THREE ACTIVITIES THEY CONSIDER "COOL."**
TEENAGE MARKETING AND LIFESTYLE STUDY

# d o you have a mentor? Do you have

someone you mentor? Paul was a mentor and friend to a young guy named Timothy. They had traveled together, and Paul even called Timothy "a true child to me" in the opening of this letter. In their special relationship, Timothy could learn from Paul and grow in his spiritual life.

# 1 Timothy

## Gentle Instruction from a Mentor to His Protégé

After a few years of serving as Paul's assistant, Timothy was finally ready to pastor a church alone. He faced the challenges that any new minister encounters, and Timothy still had a lot to learn. Like any loving father about to hand over the car keys for the first time, Paul gave Timothy step-by-step instruction on getting the juvenile church out of the garage and safely on the road to real growth.

Much of the letter concentrates on the formation of church structure— who is qualified to be an elder, what it takes to be a deacon, who should speak and when they should do it, etc. But it also has a lot to say about getting along with each other. This letter also warns the young church to avoid false teaching and to concentrate solely on the truth. Most of all, 1 Timothy serves as an encouragement for a young minister on his own for the first time.

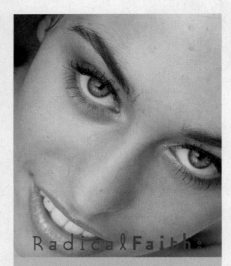

Radical Faith

## 1 Timothy 1:15-16

Do your past mistakes haunt you? Do you feel like you've messed up so many times that you can't possibly be fixed? Even though Paul was an important leader of the church, he referred to himself as the worst of sinners—he hadn't always been close to God. In fact, he had spent much of his life doing a lot of things wrong. But all that changed when he encountered God; and he came to live a life of love, devotion, and service to God. Looking back, Paul said that God used all his mistakes for good because through his life God showed the world his goodness and patience. But Paul never saw himself as a perfect Christian or leader. He saw himself as a person who needed and received mercy from God. He knew that he had to depend on God's grace for everything that he was. It's hard to face your flaws—it can be painful and dark to look at them—but it is never hopeless because the sins you've committed are not beyond God's goodness and forgiveness. His love is great, and his acceptance of you isn't based on your efforts. Your failures don't have the last say if you're with Jesus. He is the great healer and mercy-giver.

1 From Paul, an apostle of Christ Jesus, by the command of God our Savior and Christ Jesus our hope.

2To Timothy, a true child to me because you believe:

Grace, mercy, and peace from God the Father and Christ Jesus our Lord.

### warning against false teaching

3I asked you to stay longer in Ephesus when I went into Macedonia so you could command some people there to stop teaching false things. 4Tell them not to spend their time on stories that are not true and on long lists of names in family histories. These things only bring arguments; they do not help God's work, which is done in faith. 5The purpose of this command is for people to have love, a love that comes from a pure heart and a good conscience and a true faith. 6Some people have missed these things and turned to useless talk. 7They want to be teachers of the law, but they do not understand either what they are talking about or what they are sure about.

## "WE KNOW THAT THE LAW IS GOOD IF SOMEONE USES IT LAWFULLY."

8But we know that the law is good if someone uses it lawfully. 9We also know that the law is not made for good people but for those who are against the law and for those who refuse to follow it. It is for people who are against God and are sinful, who are not holy and have no religion, who kill their fathers and mothers, who murder, 10who take part in sexual sins, who have sexual relations with people of the same sex, who sell slaves, who tell lies, who speak falsely, and who do anything against the true teaching of God. 11That teaching is part of the Good News of the blessed God that he gave me to tell.

Promises

## 1 Timothy 1:16

Can a person ever do something so bad that he or she is excluded from God's grace? Are all people and their sins really equal in the presence of God? What about murderers? Rapists? Thieves? Even terrorists?

In our legal and moral system today, we judge people in varying degrees based on the severity of their crime. Prison sentences can be light (community service) or heavy (life in prison) depending on exactly what the person has done. We are used to this type of justice, so it's hard for us to imagine that God views all of our sins in the same way—he hates them. And whether you lied to your mom this morning or stole a car from a parking lot this afternoon, your sin equally separates you from God and he offers the same grace and forgiveness to cover either sin.

God is just and he is holy. Let's leave the judgment of others up to him and be thankful that his grace is big enough to cover any sin.

# LEARN I+ & LIVE I+

**1 Timothy 1:9-10**
**Learn It:** The law is not made for those who do the right thing already, but for those who would break the law.
**Live It:** Laws, especially God's laws, are there for your physical, emotional, and spiritual protection. Obey them.

**1 Timothy 1:15**
**Learn It:** Paul admitted that he was a sinner, but Christ saved him.
**Live It:** Recall some of the things you have done wrong—not to wallow in the past—but to recognize just how much Christ has done for you.

**1 Timothy 2:2**
**Learn It:** Pray for rulers and those in authority.
**Live It:** Add teachers, police officers, parents, and those in authority over you to your prayer notebook. This week spend fifteen minutes each day praying for them.

## THANKS FOR GOD'S MERCY

12I thank Christ Jesus our Lord, who gave me strength, because he trusted me and gave me this work of serving him. 13In the past I spoke against Christ and persecuted him and did all kinds of things to hurt him. But God showed me mercy, because I did not know what I was doing. I did not believe. 14But the grace of our Lord was fully given to me, and with that grace came the faith and love that are in Christ Jesus.

15What I say is true, and you should fully accept it: Christ Jesus came into the world to save sinners, of whom I am the worst. 16But I was given mercy so that in me, the worst of all sinners, Christ Jesus could show that he has patience without limit. His patience with me made me an example for those who would believe in him and have life forever. 17To the King that rules forever, who will never die, who cannot be seen, the only God, be honor and glory forever and ever. Amen.

18Timothy, my child, I am giving you a command that agrees with the prophecies that were given about you in the past. I tell you this so you can follow them and fight the good fight. 19Continue to have faith and do what you know is right. Some people have rejected this, and their faith has been shipwrecked. 20Hymenaeus and Alexander have done that, and I have given them to Satan so they will learn not to speak against God.

## SOME RULES FOR MEN AND WOMEN

2 First, I tell you to pray for all people, asking God for what they need and being thankful to him. 2Pray for rulers and for all who have authority so that we can have quiet and peaceful lives full of worship and respect for God. 3This is good, and it pleases God our Savior, 4who wants all people to be saved and to know the truth. 5There is one God and one way human beings can reach God. That way is through Christ Jesus, who is

# ⊙➤ CHECK IT OUT

## PROJECT ANGEL TREE

Not many ministries can say that they were started by a former bank robber, but Project Angel Tree has an unusual history. Angel Tree founder Mary Kay Beard was once on the FBI's Most Wanted List, but turned her life back over to Jesus while behind bars. She decided that when she got out of prison that she wanted to make a difference for him.

Beard decided the best way to reach the hearts of prisoners was to help them give to their children. She had spent a number of Christmas holidays in prison watching moms wrap up anything they could for their children. It was heartbreaking. So Beard decided to develop the Angel Tree project, which allows volunteers to buy gifts for the child of an inmate to be given to the child from their incarcerated parent.

Through local churches, volunteers can buy specific presents for children at Christmastime, deliver gifts, teach Bible studies, or be a counselor at an Angel Tree camp. You can add the Angel Tree ministry to your prayer list, donate money and gift baskets, or even hold clothing drives.

*Get involved by visiting www.angeltree.org.*

## top 10

### random ways to make an impact on your world

**10** Make others wonder what you have that they don't.

**9** Speak up when others don't.

**8** Fight for the underdog.

**7** Do your very best.

**6** Aim high.

**5** Uphold your moral standards in front of others.

**4** Share your faith boldly when others ask.

**3** Tell the truth—always.

**2** Show others you respect authority.

**1** Study hard.

himself human. 6He gave himself as a payment to free all people. He is proof that came at the right time. 7That is why I was chosen to tell the Good News and to be an apostle. (I am telling the truth; I am not lying.) I was chosen to teach those who are not Jews to believe and to know the truth.

8So, I want the men everywhere to pray, lifting up their hands in a holy manner, without anger and arguments.

9Also, women should wear proper clothes that show respect and self-control, not using braided hair or gold or pearls or expensive clothes. 10Instead, they should do good deeds, which is right for women who say they worship God.

11Let a woman learn by listening quietly and being ready to cooperate in everything. 12But I do not allow a woman to teach or to have authority over a man, but to listen quietly, 13because Adam was formed first and then Eve. 14And Adam was not tricked, but the woman was tricked and became a sinner. 15But she will be saved through having children if they continue in faith, love, and holiness, with self-control.

### ELDERS IN THE CHURCH

3 What I say is true: Anyone wanting to become an elder desires a good work. 2An elder must not give people a reason to criticize him, and he must have only one wife. He must be self-controlled, wise, respected by others, ready to welcome guests, and able to teach. 3He must not drink too much wine or like to fight, but rather be gentle and peaceable, not loving money. 4He must be a good family leader, having children who cooperate with full respect. 5(If someone does not know how to lead the family, how can that person take care of God's church?) 6But an elder must not be a new believer, or he might be too proud of himself and be judged guilty just as the devil was. 7An elder must also have the respect of people who are not in the church so he will not be criticized by others and caught in the devil's trap.

### DEACONS IN THE CHURCH

8In the same way, deacons must be respected by others, not saying things they do not mean. They must not drink too much wine or try to get rich by cheating others. 9With a clear conscience they must follow the secret of the faith that God made known to us. 10Test them first. Then let them serve as deacons if you find nothing wrong in them. 11In the same way, women" must be respected by others. They must not speak evil of others. They must be self-controlled and trustworthy in everything. 12Deacons must have only one wife and be good leaders of their children and their own families. 13Those who serve well as deacons are making an honorable place for themselves, and they will be very bold in their faith in Christ Jesus.

### THE SECRET OF OUR LIFE

14Although I hope I can come to you soon, I am writing these things to you now. 15Then,

## beautysecret

### Longer Eyelashes

Do you have short or light-colored eyelashes? If so, you can make them appear longer by applying brown mascara to your eyelashes. After a few minutes, add black mascara at the very tips. It will create the illusion that your lashes are longer.

---

notes **3:11 women** This might mean the wives of the deacons, or it might mean women who serve in the same way as deacons.

## RadicalFaith:

# 1 Timothy 4:12-13

Do you like to stick out in a crowd, or do you try to blend in? In this passage, it's pretty clear that God has a big role for you in this world. God wants you to be like him in the middle of the crowd. That means the stuff you do will probably be different from the stuff everyone else is doing. But who cares—God wants to show himself through you! People may not value or recognize godliness in you, but don't hold back. Step up to the position God's given you. If no one around you is living for God, don't be afraid to be the brave one. Let it be seen that he's alive in you through your words, actions, love, and strength of character. It ought to be said of you: "Look at the God that shines out of that girl." It won't always be easy, and others won't always get it; but God will be beaming with joy over your obedience. If you live to please him and you want your walk with him to change the world around you, toss out any fears lurking in you. Take off in the direction of him. You won't regret it.

even if I am delayed, you will know how to live in the family of God. That family is the church of the living God, the support and foundation of the truth. [16]Without doubt, the secret of our life of worship is great:

He was shown to us in a human body,
    proved right in spirit,
and seen by angels.
    He was preached to those who are not
        Jews,
believed in by the world,
    and taken up in glory.

### a warning about false teachers

4 Now the Holy Spirit clearly says that in the later times some people will stop believing the faith. They will follow spirits that lie and teachings of demons. [2]Such teachings come from the false words of liars whose consciences are destroyed as if by a hot iron. [3]They forbid people to marry and tell them not to eat certain foods which God created to be eaten with thanks by people who believe and know the truth. [4]Everything God made is good, and nothing should be refused if it is accepted with thanks, [5]because it is made holy by what God has said and by prayer.

## "HE WAS PREACHED TO THOSE WHO ARE NOT JEWS, BELIEVED IN BY THE WORLD, AND TAKEN UP IN GLORY."

### be a good servant of christ

[6]By telling these things to the brothers and sisters,[n] you will be a good servant of Christ Jesus. You will be made strong by the words of the faith and the good teaching which you have been following. [7]But do not follow foolish stories that disagree with God's truth, but train yourself to serve God. [8]Training your body helps you in some ways, but serving God helps

## Promises:

# 1 Timothy 4:12

You're never too young to make a difference in the world. Granted, you may not be able to vote (or even drive yet, for that matter), but think of all the amazing things that teenagers just like you do every day. They stand up for their faith. They give of their time and their money to help those who really need it. They even win Olympic medals and act as ambassadors for our country. They sell millions of records. They fight for the underdog. In the Bible, teenagers are a big part of many major events. Mary gave birth to Jesus, and David was chosen to lead his entire nation when they were both only teenagers.

Think that just because you're young you can't make a difference? Absolutely not! God loves you, values your gifts and abilities, cherishes you, and pretty much just thinks you're awesome. You have a lot to give to the world today. Chances are, you are full of passion and great ideas that can change things for the better. Use your energy and your gifts now. Your school, your community, and your friends need you. Don't wait!

**4:6 brothers and sisters** Although the Greek text says "brothers" here and throughout this book, Paul's words refer to the entire church, including men and women.

you in every way by bringing you blessings in this life and in the future life, too. ⁹What I say is true, and you should fully accept it. ¹⁰This is why we work and struggle: We hope in the living God who is the Savior of all people, especially of those who believe.

⁷Tell the believers to do these things so that no one can criticize them. ⁸Whoever does not care for his own relatives, especially his own family members, has turned against the faith and is worse than someone who does not believe in God.

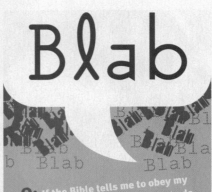

## Blab

**Q:** If the Bible tells me to obey my parents, but my parents tell me to do something God says not to do, whom do I obey?

**A:** God comes first, even ahead of your parents. You don't have to be in their face about it; but you should never directly disobey God's Word for anyone, even your mom and dad. Pray for them and for strength for yourself. Surround yourself with believers who can support you.

**Q:** I have no friends, and at school everybody acts like they hate me. What do I do?

**A:** Ask God to help you be a friend to others. Get involved in activities by joining a club or starting a Bible study. Even if you are shy, you can hold your head up, make eye contact, and smile. If kids are really hostile or are torturing you and they won't stop, ask your parents if you can change schools or possibly be home schooled. If you have to stay in the same school and they won't stop, ask a teacher or administrator to help you.

**Q:** How can I be sure that God really loves me?

**A:** Read his Word. He loved you so much that he sacrificed the most precious thing to him—his Son—to die for you. Throughout its pages, the Bible talks about how much God loves. Whenever a verse talks about God's love, insert your name and feel how much he loves *you*.

¹¹Command and teach these things. ¹²Do not let anyone treat you as if you are unimportant because you are young. Instead, be an example to the believers with your words, your actions, your love, your faith, and your pure life. ¹³Until I come, continue to read the Scriptures to the people, strengthen them, and teach them. ¹⁴Use the gift you have, which was given to you through prophecy when the group of elders laid their hands on[n] you. ¹⁵Continue to do those things; give your life to doing them so your progress may be seen by everyone. ¹⁶Be careful in your life and in your teaching. If you continue to live and teach rightly, you will save both yourself and those who listen to you.

## RULES FOR LIVING WITH OTHERS

**5** Do not speak angrily to an older man, but plead with him as if he were your father. Treat younger men like brothers, ²older women like mothers, and younger women like sisters. Always treat them in a pure way.

³Take care of widows who are truly widows. ⁴But if a widow has children or grandchildren, let them first learn to do their duty to their own family and to repay their parents or grandparents. That pleases God. ⁵The true widow, who is all alone, puts her hope in God and continues to pray night and day for God's help. ⁶But the widow who uses her life to please herself is really dead while she is alive.

⁹To be on the list of widows, a woman must be at least sixty years old. She must have been faithful to her husband. ¹⁰She must be known for her good works—works such as raising her children, welcoming strangers, washing the feet of God's people, helping those in trouble, and giving her life to do all kinds of good deeds.

¹¹But do not put younger widows on that list. After they give themselves to Christ, they are pulled away from him by their physical needs, and then they want to marry again. ¹²They will be judged for not doing what they first promised to do. ¹³Besides that, they learn to waste their time, going from house to house.

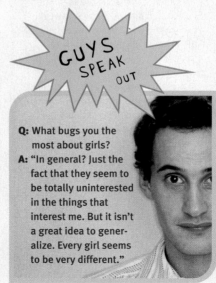

**GUYS SPEAK OUT**

**Q:** What bugs you the most about girls?
**A:** "In general? Just the fact that they seem to be totally uninterested in the things that interest me. But it isn't a great idea to generalize. Every girl seems to be very different."

 **notes** 4:14 **laid their hands on** The laying on of hands had many purposes, including the giving of a blessing, power, or authority.

314

# Music Reviews

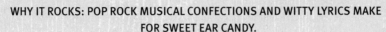

**GROUP:** NEWSBOYS

**ALBUM:** TAKE ME TO YOUR LEADER (CLASSIC HIT)

If you're a fan of Newsboys' worship music like current faves "Amazing Love" and "He Reigns," then you'll really appreciate digging into the band's archives and coming up with the 1996 album *Take Me to Your Leader.* Packed with clever phrases, puns, and plays-on-words, this disc is one of the best ever. Check out the pop rock title hit, the rockin' "God Is Not a Secret," the hilarious circus tale "Reality," the upbeat anthem "Breakfast," plus the poignant reminder that we need to forgive on "Let It Go."

**WHY IT ROCKS: POP ROCK MUSICAL CONFECTIONS AND WITTY LYRICS MAKE FOR SWEET EAR CANDY.**

And they not only waste their time but also begin to gossip and busy themselves with other people's lives, saying things they should not say. ¹⁴So I want the younger widows to marry, have children, and manage their homes. Then no enemy will have any reason to criticize them. ¹⁵But some have already turned away to follow Satan.

¹⁶If any woman who is a believer has widows in her family, she should care for them herself. The church should not have to care for them. Then it will be able to take care of those who are truly widows.

¹⁷The elders who lead the church well should receive double honor, especially those who work hard by speaking and teaching, ¹⁸because the Scripture says: "When an ox is working in the grain, do not cover its mouth to keep it from eating,"ⁿ and "A worker should be given his pay."ⁿ

¹⁹Do not listen to someone who accuses an elder, without two or three witnesses. ²⁰Tell those who continue sinning that they are wrong. Do this in front of the whole church so that the others will have a warning.

²¹Before God and Christ Jesus and the chosen angels, I command you to do these things without showing favor of any kind to anyone.

²²Think carefully before you lay your hands onⁿ anyone, and don't share in the sins of others. Keep yourself pure.

²³Stop drinking only water, but drink a little wine to help your stomach and your frequent sicknesses.

²⁴The sins of some people are easy to see even before they are judged, but the sins of others are seen only later. ²⁵So also good deeds are easy to see, but even those that are not easily seen cannot stay hidden.

**6** All who are slaves under a yoke should show full respect to their masters so no one will speak against God's name and our

# LEARN I+ & LIVE I+

**1 Timothy 2:11**
**Learn It:** Learn by listening quietly and being cooperative.
**Live It:** God knows girls like to talk, and he needs to remind us to use our ears more than our mouths. Try to go a whole day without speaking. Make a list of what you learn.

**1 Timothy 4:4**
**Learn It:** The things God made are good.
**Live It:** Make an alphabetical list from *A* to *Z* of the good things God made for you. (Zebras, anyone?)

**1 Timothy 4:12**
**Learn It:** Do not let anyone treat you like you are not important because you are young. Instead be a good example.
**Live It:** Start a charity organization, witness to people at your school, or lead a Bible study. You are never too young to serve God.

5:18 **"When . . . eating,"** Quotation from Deuteronomy 25:4. 5:18 **"A worker . . . pay."** Quotation from Luke 10:7. 5:22 **lay your hands on** The laying on of hands had many purposes, including the giving of a blessing, power, or authority.

### RadicalFaith:

# 1 Timothy 6:7-10

Think about all the stuff that you have in your closet, on your shelves, and in the corners of your room. Your room is probably packed with all kinds of stuff—most of which you probably don't use. And chances are, if given the money, you'd buy even more stuff to put in there. It's really easy to think that having lots of stuff and being the envy of all your friends will actually make you more than you are. But God lets you in on a secret in this passage about the real situation with money: Whatever you get into your hands here on earth will eventually disappear. And none of it will add a thing to who you really are in the end. From his perspective, God says that none of it even matters and getting caught up in money and stuff can even bring about a lot of mistakes and pain. Don't be fooled. Believe it or not, your satisfaction will not come from having certain material things. If you've got food when you're hungry and clothes on your body, then you're totally set and have much more than most of the world. What's really worth gaining isn't sold in any store. Ask God to help you discover what's really important in life.

teaching. [2]The slaves whose masters are believers should not show their masters any less respect because they are believers. They should serve their masters even better, because they are helping believers they love.

You must teach and preach these things.

### FALSE TEACHING AND TRUE RICHES

[3]Anyone who has a different teaching does not agree with the true teaching of our Lord Jesus Christ and the teaching that shows the true way to serve God. [4]This person is full of pride and understands nothing, but is sick with a love for arguing and fighting about words. This brings jealousy, fighting, speaking against others, evil mistrust, [5]and constant quarrels from those who have evil minds and have lost the truth. They think that serving God is a way to get rich.

[6]Serving God does make us very rich, if we are satisfied with what we have. [7]We brought nothing into the world, so we can take nothing out. [8]But, if we have food and clothes, we will be satisfied with that. [9]Those who want to become rich bring temptation to themselves and are caught in a trap. They want many foolish and harmful things that ruin and destroy people. [10]The love of money causes all kinds of evil. Some people have left the faith, because they wanted to get more money, but they have caused themselves much sorrow.

## "THEY THINK THAT SERVING GOD IS A WAY TO GET RICH."

### SOME THINGS TO REMEMBER

[11]But you, man of God, run away from all those things. Instead, live in the right way, serve God, have faith, love, patience, and gentleness. [12]Fight the good fight of faith, grabbing hold of the life that continues forever. You were called to have that life when you confessed the good confession before many witnesses. [13]In the sight of God, who gives life to everything, and of Christ Jesus, I give you a

**Q:** I am pregnant, and I just want to die. I don't know what to do. Help!

**A:** God will be with you through this, and he still loves you. You need to tell the baby's father, and you need to tell your parents. If you can't face them alone, take a sibling or friend. Tell them you are sorry, and ask for their support. Choose life, and do not consider abortion. Find a crisis pregnancy center in your area. They can counsel you and help you get ready for your baby, whether you decide to keep it or give it up for adoption.

**Q:** Sometimes in my dreams, I have sex with somebody, something I have never done in real life. Are my dreams making me sin?

**A:** It's not unusual for you to have sexual dreams in your teens. When you pray, ask God to be in control of not only your daily activities but of your whole mind, as well. Ask him to keep sexual dreams from occurring. If they happen again, ask him to help you not to dwell on them, and get on with your day.

**Q:** I had to stay after school for help in math, and my teacher kept leaning across my desk and brushing against my breasts. I am hoping it was an accident, but it happened several times. What do you think?

**A:** Once is an accident; a bunch of times is not. Teachers can't mess with students, period. Tell your parents, and ask them to go with you to tell an administrator. Ask to change math classes, and pray that God will help you forgive your teacher.

# LEARN I+ & LIVE I+

**1 Timothy 5:8**
**Learn It:** You must care for your relatives and family members.
**Live It:** If you have a beef with a parent, sibling, stepparent, cousin, or other relative, get it straightened out.

**1 Timothy 6:7**
**Learn It:** We were born with nothing, and we will take nothing with us when we die.
**Live It:** Make sure your list of things to achieve is not all about getting stuff you want.

**2 Timothy 1:5**
**Learn It:** Timothy did the right thing by serving God, just like his ancestors did.
**Live It:** Investigate your spiritual family tree. Find out what family members in your past lived by faith.

command. Christ Jesus made the good confession when he stood before Pontius Pilate. ¹⁴Do what you were commanded to do without wrong or blame until our Lord Jesus Christ comes again. ¹⁵God will make that happen at the right time. He is the blessed and only Ruler, the King of all kings and the Lord of all lords. ¹⁶He is the only One who never dies. He lives in light so bright no one can go near it. No one has ever seen God, or can see him. May honor and power belong to God forever. Amen.

¹⁷Command those who are rich with things of this world not to be proud. Tell them to hope in God, not in their uncertain riches. God richly gives us everything to enjoy. ¹⁸Tell the rich people to do good, to be rich in doing good deeds, to be generous and ready to share. ¹⁹By doing that, they will be saving a treasure for themselves as a strong foundation for the future. Then they will be able to have the life that is true life.

²⁰Timothy, guard what God has trusted to you. Stay away from foolish, useless talk and from the arguments of what is falsely called "knowledge." ²¹By saying they have that "knowledge," some have missed the true faith.

Grace be with you.

**Paul is again in a Roman prison,** and this time the conditions are harsh. He's in a cold, dark cell in chains, with no hope of being released. He is virtually alone, with only Luke for company. Knowing the end of his life is near, Paul writes this second letter to Timothy as he awaits his own execution.

# 2 Timothy

## Paul's Passing of the Torch to Timothy

Sounds depressing, doesn't it? But rather than ruminating over his coming fate, Paul is heeding this urgency by reminding Timothy of all that they have both learned. Knowing he will be passing a torch of responsibility for other believers on to Timothy, Paul wants to make sure Timothy is steadfast in the faith and prepared to continue spreading the Good News. He also wants Timothy and the church to be prepared when hard times come their way.

It's interesting that most of Paul's statements in this letter are imperative. (In case you don't remember that from your grammar lessons, an imperative means the sentence is in the form of a command—"Do your best." or "Remember this!" or "Preach the Good News.") Paul knows his time is short, so he gets right to the point of telling Timothy what needs to be done.

1 From Paul, an apostle of Christ Jesus by the will of God. God sent me to tell about the promise of life that is in Christ Jesus.

²To Timothy, a dear child to me:

Grace, mercy, and peace to you from God the Father and Christ Jesus our Lord.

## ENCOURAGEMENT FOR TIMOTHY

³I thank God as I always mention you in my prayers, day and night. I serve him, doing what I know is right as my ancestors did. ⁴Remembering that you cried for me, I want very much to see you so I can be filled with joy. ⁵I remember your true faith. That faith first lived in your grandmother Lois and in your mother Eunice, and I know you now have that same faith. ⁶This is why I remind you to keep using the gift God gave you when I laid my hands on" you. Now let it grow, as a small flame grows into a fire. ⁷God did not give us a spirit that makes us afraid but a spirit of power and love and self-control.

⁸So do not be ashamed to tell people about our Lord Jesus, and do not be ashamed of me, in prison for the Lord. But suffer with me for the Good News. God, who gives us the strength to do that, ⁹saved us and made us his holy people. That was not because of anything we did ourselves but because of God's purpose and grace. That grace was given to us through Christ Jesus before time began, ¹⁰but it is now shown to us by the coming of our Savior Christ Jesus. He destroyed death, and through the Good News he showed us the way to have life that cannot be destroyed. ¹¹I was chosen to tell that Good News and to be an apostle and a teacher. ¹²I am suffering now because I tell the Good News, but I am not ashamed, because I know Jesus, the One in whom I have believed. And I am sure he is able to protect what he has trusted me with until that day." ¹³Follow the pattern of true teachings that you heard from me in faith and love, which are in Christ Jesus. ¹⁴Protect the truth that you were given; protect it with the help of the Holy Spirit who lives in us.

¹⁵You know that everyone in the country of Asia has left me, even Phygelus and Hermogenes. ¹⁶May the Lord show mercy to the family of Onesiphorus, who has often helped me and was not ashamed that I was in prison. ¹⁷When he came to Rome, he looked eagerly for me until he found me. ¹⁸May the Lord allow him to find mercy from the Lord on that day. You know how many ways he helped me in Ephesus.

## A LOYAL SOLDIER OF CHRIST JESUS

2 You then, Timothy, my child, be strong in the grace we have in Christ Jesus. ²You should teach people whom you can trust the things you and many others have heard me say. Then they will be able to teach others. ³Share in the troubles we have like a good soldier of Christ Jesus. ⁴A soldier wants to please the enlisting officer, so no one serving in the

## relationships

"Promise not to awaken or excite my feelings of love until it is ready" (Song of Solomon 8:4). It's fun to have guys fall for you, but are you really ready for a relationship? Love requires time and commitment. That means you may be tempted to dump friends, jobs, and schoolwork when you shouldn't. Real love waits not only to have sex, but also to fall in love in the first place. Ask God to help you stay off the dating merry-go-round until you are ready to love the one he has for you.

## Promises

### 2 Timothy 1:7

Genetics are a big part of what makes you who you are. Whether you like it or not, you have inherited a lot of traits from your parents. Maybe those are good traits—such as musical abilities, great hair, athleticism, or a nice smile. And maybe you've inherited a few things you're not crazy about either, such as a big feet or a short temper.

As children of God, we inherit some pretty amazing traits of his. Some of them we have to work toward (like patience and self-control) and some may come a little easier (like kindness). So when we are faced with hard times and are tempted to be afraid, to doubt, and to act selfishly, we can know that those reactions are not from God. We can instead claim the wonderful gifts he has given us and overcome our circumstances. Celebrate today the amazing gifts that God gives to us: the ability to love, kindness, peacefulness, joy, strength, courage, empathy, and self-control. What others can you think of?

 **1:6 laid my hands on** The laying on of hands had many purposes, including the giving of a blessing, power, or authority. **1:12 day** The day Christ will come to judge all people and take his people to live with him.

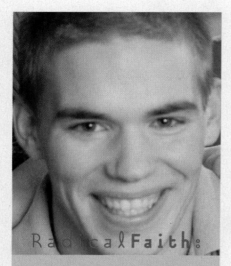

army wastes time with everyday matters. [5]Also an athlete who takes part in a contest must obey all the rules in order to win. [6]The farmer who works hard should be the first person to get some of the food that was grown. [7]Think about what I am saying, because the Lord will give you the ability to understand everything.

## "THE LORD WILL GIVE YOU THE ABILITY TO UNDERSTAND EVERYTHING."

[8]Remember Jesus Christ, who was raised from the dead, who is from the family of David. This is the Good News I preach, [9]and I am suffering because of it to the point of being bound with chains like a criminal. But God's teaching is not in chains. [10]So I patiently accept all these troubles so that those whom God has chosen can have the salvation that is in Christ Jesus. With that salvation comes glory that never ends.

[11]This teaching is true:

If we died with him, we will also live with him.

[12]If we accept suffering, we will also rule with him.

If we refuse to accept him, he will refuse to accept us.

[13]If we are not faithful, he will still be faithful,

because he cannot be false to himself.

### a worker pleasing to God

[14]Continue teaching these things, warning people in God's presence not to argue about words. It does not help anyone, and it ruins those who listen. [15]Make every effort to give yourself to God as the kind of person he will accept. Be a worker who is not ashamed and who uses the true teaching in the right way. [16]Stay away from foolish, useless talk, because that will lead people further away from God. [17]Their evil teaching will spread like a sickness inside the body. Hymenaeus and Philetus are

like that. [18]They have left the true teaching, saying that the rising from the dead has already taken place, and so they are destroying the faith of some people. [19]But God's strong foundation continues to stand. These words are written on the seal: "The Lord knows those who belong to him,"" and "Everyone who wants to belong to the Lord must stop doing wrong."

[20]In a large house there are not only things made of gold and silver, but also things made of wood and clay. Some things are used for special purposes, and others are made for ordinary jobs. [21]All who make themselves clean from evil will be used for special purposes. They will be made holy, useful to the Master, ready to do any good work.

## beautysecret

### Jewelry

What's your favorite piece of jewelry? Why do you like it so much? Did you know the Bible compares wisdom and good sense to a piece of jewelry? It says, "My child, hold on to wisdom and good sense. Don't let them out of your sight. They will give you life and beauty like a necklace around your neck" (Proverbs 3:21-22).

## RadicalFaith:

## 2 Timothy 2:21-22

Have you ever tried to use a device that didn't work because it wasn't quite clean? Take a vacuum, for instance. If the bag inside the vacuum has a ton of gunk in it, the vacuum won't work. All the stuff in the dirty bag gets in the way of the vacuum being useful. Our lives can be the same way. God wants to make you his instrument—doing his good works is something he created you for (Ephesians 2:10). So you've got to clean out all the things in your life that get in the way and clear your life of things that don't reflect God. Maybe you need to clean out your bad attitude, disobedience, or a nasty habit. But even though we all have major messes in our lives, God can still work through us as long as our hearts long to honor him. He uses broken, dirty, and flawed things for his glory because his love doesn't depend on our never making messes or mistakes. When you decide you want to be used by God, make room for him to use your life to its fullest capacity for his glory.

notes 2:19 "The Lord . . . him" Quotation from Numbers 16:5.

320

# *Music Reviews*

**GROUP:** JENNIFER KNAPP

**ALBUM:** THE COLLECTION

With bluesy riffs and a sound reminiscent of Melissa Etheridge and Alanis Morrisette, Jennifer Knapp created a body of music in just three albums that contained a wealth of hits before taking a few years off to wait for the Lord's direction. While fans have been holding their breaths to see if Jennifer will return to the stage and recording studio, Gotee released a two-disc set that contains hits, demos, previously unreleased songs, and duets with other artists.

**WHY IT ROCKS: JENNIFER KNAPP IS A ONE-OF-A-KIND ARTIST WHOSE POIGNANT LYRICS AND EMOTIVE VOCALS GRAB YOU AND WON'T LET GO.**

## "TRY HARD TO LIVE RIGHT AND TO HAVE FAITH, LOVE, AND PEACE."

22But run away from the evil young people like to do. Try hard to live right and to have faith, love, and peace, together with those who trust in the Lord from pure hearts. 23Stay away from foolish and stupid arguments, because you know they grow into quarrels. 24And a servant of the Lord must not quarrel but must be kind to everyone, a good teacher, and patient. 25The Lord's servant must gently teach those who disagree. Then maybe God will let them change their minds so they can accept the truth. 26And they may wake up and escape from the trap of the devil, who catches them to do what he wants.

### The Last Days

3 Remember this! In the last days there will be many troubles, 2because people will love themselves, love money, brag, and be proud. They will say evil things against others and will not obey their parents or be thankful or be the kind of people God wants. 3They will not love others, will refuse to forgive, will gossip, and will not control themselves. They will be cruel, will hate what is good, 4will turn against their friends, and will do foolish things without thinking. They will be conceited, will love pleasure instead of God, 5and will act as if they serve God but will not have his power. Stay away from those people. 6Some of them go into homes and get control of silly women who are full of sin and are led by many evil desires. 7These women are always learning new teachings, but they are never able to understand the truth fully. 8Just as Jannes and Jambres were against Moses, these people are against the truth. Their thinking has been ruined, and they have failed in trying to follow the faith. 9But they will not be successful in

# LEARN I+ & LIVE I+

**2 Timothy 1:12**
**Learn It:** You will suffer for sharing the Good News, but do not be ashamed.
**Live It:** At some point in your life, you will suffer for being a Christian—either emotionally or physically. Pray that God will help you remain true to him when you hurt.

**2 Timothy 2:13**
**Learn It:** Even when we are unfaithful, God is faithful, because it is his nature.
**Live It:** Make a list of the ways God has shown himself faithful to you.

**2 Timothy 2:23**
**Learn It:** Don't get into foolish arguments, which lead to quarrels.
**Live It:** Ask God to forgive you if you have a tendency to argue with others. Pray that he will help you accept that you may not always be right.

what they do, because as with Jannes and Jambres, everyone will see that they are foolish.

## OBEY THE TEACHINGS

10But you have followed what I teach, the way I live, my goal, faith, patience, and love. You know I never give up. 11You know how I have been hurt and have suffered, as in Antioch, Iconium, and Lystra. I have suffered, but the Lord saved me from all those troubles. 12Everyone who wants to live as God desires, in Christ Jesus, will be hurt. 13But people who are evil and cheat others will go from bad to worse. They will fool others, but they will also be fooling themselves.

14But you should continue following the teachings you learned. You know they are true, because you trust those who taught you. 15Since you were a child you have known the Holy Scriptures which are able to make you wise. And that wisdom leads to salvation through faith in Christ Jesus. 16All Scripture is given by God and is useful for teaching, for showing people what is wrong in their lives, for correcting faults, and for teaching how to live right. 17Using the Scriptures, the person who serves God will be capable, having all that is needed to do every good work.

**DIDYA KNOW**

TODAY'S MOVIES CONTAIN SIGNIFICANTLY MORE VIOLENCE, SEX, AND PROFANITY ON AVERAGE THAN MOVIES OF THE SAME RATING A DECADE AGO. WWW.HSPS.HARVARD.EDU

4 I give you a command in the presence of God and Christ Jesus, the One who will judge the living and the dead, and by his coming and his kingdom: 2Preach the Good News. Be ready at all times, and tell people what they need to do. Tell them when they are wrong. Encourage them with great patience and careful teaching, 3because the time will come when people will not listen to the true teaching but will find many more teachers who please them by saying the things they want to hear. 4They will stop listening to the truth and will begin to follow false stories. 5But you should control yourself at all times, accept troubles, do the work of telling the Good News, and complete all the duties of a servant of God.

6My life is being given as an offering to God, and the time has come for me to leave this life. 7I have fought the good fight, I have finished the race, I have kept the faith. 8Now, a crown is being held for me—a crown for being

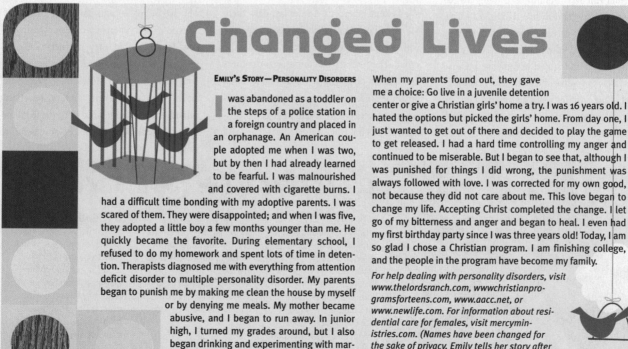

# Changed Lives

### EMILY'S STORY—PERSONALITY DISORDERS

I was abandoned as a toddler on the steps of a police station in a foreign country and placed in an orphanage. An American couple adopted me when I was two, but by then I had already learned to be fearful. I was malnourished and covered with cigarette burns. I had a difficult time bonding with my adoptive parents. I was scared of them. They were disappointed; and when I was five, they adopted a little boy a few months younger than me. He quickly became the favorite. During elementary school, I refused to do my homework and spent lots of time in detention. Therapists diagnosed me with everything from attention deficit disorder to multiple personality disorder. My parents began to punish me by making me clean the house by myself or by denying me meals. My mother became abusive, and I began to run away. In junior high, I turned my grades around, but I also began drinking and experimenting with marijuana. I got a job at a veterinary hospital and began sniffing the tranquilizers to get high.

When my parents found out, they gave me a choice: Go live in a juvenile detention center or give a Christian girls' home a try. I was 16 years old. I hated the options but picked the girls' home. From day one, I just wanted to get out of there and decided to play the game to get released. I had a hard time controlling my anger and continued to be miserable. But I began to see that, although I was punished for things I did wrong, the punishment was always followed with love. I was corrected for my own good, not because they did not care about me. This love began to change my life. Accepting Christ completed the change. I let go of my bitterness and anger and began to heal. I even had my first birthday party since I was three years old! Today, I am so glad I chose a Christian program. I am finishing college, and the people in the program have become my family.

*For help dealing with personality disorders, visit www.thelordsranch.com, wwwchristianprogramsforteens.com, www.aacc.net, or www.newlife.com. For information about residential care for females, visit mercyministries.com. (Names have been changed for the sake of privacy. Emily tells her story after going through biblically based counseling with Mercy Ministries.)*

right with God. The Lord, the judge who judges rightly, will give the crown to me on that day"—not only to me but to all those who have waited with love for him to come again.

## PERSONAL WORDS

9Do your best to come to me as soon as you can, 10because Demas, who loved this world, left me and went to Thessalonica. Crescens went to Galatia, and Titus went to Dalmatia. 11Luke is the only one still with me. Get Mark and bring him with you when you come, because he can help me in my work here. 12I sent Tychicus to Ephesus. 13When I was in Troas, I left my coat there with Carpus. So when you come, bring it to me, along with my books, particularly the ones written on parchment." 14Alexander the metalworker did many harmful things against me. The Lord will punish him for what he did. 15You also should be careful that he does not hurt you, because he fought strongly against our teaching.

16The first time I defended myself, no one helped me; everyone left me. May they be forgiven. 17But the Lord stayed with me and gave me strength so I could fully tell the Good News to all those who are not Jews. So I was saved from the lion's mouth. 18The Lord will save me when anyone tries to hurt me, and he will bring me safely to his heavenly kingdom. Glory forever and ever be the Lord's. Amen.

## "THE LORD STAYED WITH ME AND GAVE ME STRENGTH SO I COULD FULLY TELL THE GOOD NEWS."

## FINAL GREETINGS

19Greet Priscilla and Aquila and the family of Onesiphorus. 20Erastus stayed in Corinth, and I left Trophimus sick in Miletus. 21Try as hard as you can to come to me before winter.

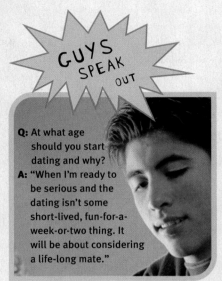

**GUYS SPEAK OUT**

**Q:** At what age should you start dating and why?
**A:** "When I'm ready to be serious and the dating isn't some short-lived, fun-for-a-week-or-two thing. It will be about considering a life-long mate."

Eubulus sends greetings to you. Also Pudens, Linus, Claudia, and all the brothers and sisters in Christ greet you.

22The Lord be with your spirit. Grace be with you.

# Paul and Titus had ministered together

on the Island of Crete for a considerable period of time. With their ministry underway and an established church there, Paul left Titus to continue to strengthen the work they had begun in Crete.

## Titus More Truth to Live By

Crete wasn't exactly an easy mission field. Paul quotes a local prophet who said this about his own people: "Cretans are always liars, evil animals, and lazy people who do nothing but eat" (1:12). Those aren't exactly kind words, but Paul doesn't disagree. He warns Titus to firmly preach against those doing wrong. He offers specific guidance on how Titus's church should be managed in Crete. Titus needed some solid direction and Paul delivered.

Some of the information in the Book of Titus may sound suspiciously like stuff Paul has mentioned in previous letters, but that's to be expected. Paul was responsible for starting many of the New Testament churches. He was also a mentor to Timothy. Paul wrote a lot of letters to a lot of different people. It's inevitable that he would repeat himself at times. But the great news is that what he repeats is solid truth, pure and simple; and Paul is emphatic about getting the message across.

1 From Paul, a servant of God and an apostle of Jesus Christ. I was sent to help the faith of God's chosen people and to help them know the truth that shows people how to serve God. ²That faith and that knowledge come from the hope for life forever, which God promised to us before time began. And God cannot lie. ³At the right time God let the world know about that life through preaching. He trusted me with that work, and I preached by the command of God our Savior.

⁴To Titus, my true child in the faith we share:

Grace and peace from God the Father and Christ Jesus our Savior.

## TITUS' WORK IN CRETE

⁵I left you in Crete so you could finish doing the things that still needed to be done and so you could appoint elders in every town, as I directed you. ⁶An elder must not be guilty of doing wrong, must have only one wife, and must have believing children. They must not be known as children who are wild and do not cooperate. ⁷As God's manager, an elder must not be guilty of doing wrong, being selfish, or becoming angry quickly. He must not drink too much wine, like to fight, or try to get rich by cheating others. ⁸An elder must be ready to welcome guests, love what is good, be wise, live right, and be holy and self-controlled. ⁹By holding on to the trustworthy word just as we teach it, an elder can help people by using true teaching, and he can show those who are against the true teaching that they are wrong.

¹⁰There are many people who refuse to cooperate, who talk about worthless things and lead others into the wrong way—mainly those who say all who are not Jews must be circumcised. ¹¹These people must be stopped, because they are upsetting whole families by teaching things they should not teach, which they do to get rich by cheating people. ¹²Even one of their own prophets said, "Cretans are always liars, evil animals, and lazy people who do nothing but eat." ¹³The words that prophet said are true. So firmly tell those people they are wrong so they may become strong in the faith, ¹⁴not

## Bible Basics

**Prayer** simply means talking to God. You can do it in the morning or at night, on your knees or while driving in your car (just remember to keep your eyes open!). You don't have to use any special words or phrases. If you need help getting started, Jesus did teach people how to pray with words that many Christians still speak in church services today—a prayer we call the "Lord's Prayer" (see Matthew 6:9-13). In this prayer, Jesus first blessed God and praised him, then asked that God's will be done on earth—just like it is in heaven. Jesus then asked God for material things like food and asked for forgiveness of sins. Finally, he prayed for protection against temptation and to be saved from evil. Many people end their prayers with the word *Amen*, which means "May it be."

# ⊙➤ CHECK IT OUT

## VOLUNTEERMATCH

VolunteerMatch is an organization that exists solely to match kids, teens, seniors, groups, and adult volunteers with local organizations that need their help. VolunteerMatch has a mission to help everyone find a great place to volunteer and offers a variety of online services to support a community of nonprofit, volunteer, and business leaders committed to getting involved.

To see what's available in your area, simply go to the site and enter your zip code. A list of volunteer opportunities within a geographical radius of your choosing (five miles and up) will pop up. Easy-to-identify symbols let you know if the opportunity is right for your age or group. A quick search of Hernando County, Florida, recently pulled up opportunities ranging from helping the Florida Fish & Wildlife Conservation Commission monitor trails in a local wildlife area to hosting a foreign exchange student.

*Get involved by visiting www.volunteermatch.org.*

RadicalFaith:

# Titus 2:11-14

Let's say you're given a small role in a play and after a few weeks of rehearsal, you get cast as another character. This role is larger and different from your other one, but better. You don't know what you did to deserve it, but you're excited anyway. Being with Jesus is like being handed a whole new role in life. What he shows you and calls you to is totally different from the world around you and what you're used to—but better. Jesus paid the price to set you free from evil and to give you a new life. But that doesn't mean you'll never struggle with sin again. Is it okay to sin sometimes and have just a taste of the world's ways because you know you'll have forgiveness for those sins? Paul asked that question, too—check it out in Romans 6:1-2. He concluded that since Jesus has saved you from that stuff, there's no reason why you should return to it. You've been handed something new that's better than anything sin could offer. You have every reason to turn away from the ways of the world and turn to God. Let God's gift of grace, eternal life, and a permanent relationship with him motivate you to daily obedience.

accepting Jewish false stories and the commands of people who reject the truth. ¹⁵To those who are pure, all things are pure, but to those who are full of sin and do not believe, nothing is pure. Both their minds and their consciences have been ruined. ¹⁶They say they know God, but their actions show they do not accept him. They are hateful people, they refuse to obey, and they are useless for doing anything good.

## FOLLOWING THE TRUE TEACHING

2 But you must tell everyone what to do to follow the true teaching. ²Teach older men to be self-controlled, serious, wise, strong in faith, in love, and in patience.

³In the same way, teach older women to be holy in their behavior, not speaking against others or enslaved to too much wine, but teaching what is good. ⁴Then they can teach the young women to love their husbands, to love their children, ⁵to be wise and pure, to be good workers at home, to be kind, and to yield to their husbands. Then no one will be able to criticize the teaching God gave us.

## "IN EVERY WAY BE AN EXAMPLE OF DOING GOOD DEEDS."

⁶In the same way, encourage young men to be wise. ⁷In every way be an example of doing good deeds. When you teach, do it with honesty and seriousness. ⁸Speak the truth so that you cannot be criticized. Then those who are against you will be ashamed because there is nothing bad to say about us.

⁹Slaves should yield to their own masters at all times, trying to please them and not arguing with them. ¹⁰They should not steal from them but should show their masters they can be fully trusted so that in everything they do they will make the teaching of God our Savior attractive.

¹¹That is the way we should live, because God's grace that can save everyone has come.

Blab

**Q:** My brother is autistic and sometimes I am embarrassed to be out with him in public because he acts so weird. Am I a terrible person?

**A:** You are not terrible. It is normal to want to fit in and not be conspicuous as a teen. However, ask God to help you see your brother the way he sees him, as his special creation. Go out of your way to love your brother the best you can. If people want to know why he acts the way he does, do not be embarrassed. You have a chance to help educate them.

**Q:** My mom hits me really hard. Once, she even broke my arm. She is always sorry afterwards, and I have never told anyone. What should I do?

**A:** If your mom is physically abusing you, she needs help and so do you. Even if you have never spoken up before, do it now. Tell your mom she must get counseling, or you will report the abuse. Call a child abuse hotline, or tell a trusted adult at church or school. Pray for your mom, but do not allow her to hurt you anymore.

**Q:** I really want my dad to quit smoking. How can I help him?

**A:** Pray and keep praying. Your dad has to want to quit, and smoking is an extremely difficult addiction to kick. If you nag him about it, you'll just make him mad—and possibly more stubborn.

<sup>12</sup>It teaches us not to live against God nor to do the evil things the world wants to do. Instead, that grace teaches us to live now in a wise and right way and in a way that shows we serve God. <sup>13</sup>We should live like that while we wait for our great hope and the coming of the glory of our great God and Savior Jesus Christ. <sup>14</sup>He gave himself for us so he might pay the price to free us from all evil and to make us pure people who belong only to him—people who are always wanting to do good deeds.

<sup>15</sup>Say these things and encourage the people and tell them what is wrong in their lives, with all authority. Do not let anyone treat you as if you were unimportant.

## THE RIGHT WAY TO LIVE

3 Remind the believers to yield to the authority of rulers and government leaders, to obey them, to be ready to do good, <sup>2</sup>to speak no evil about anyone, to live in peace, and to be gentle and polite to all people.

<sup>3</sup>In the past we also were foolish. We did not obey, we were wrong, and we were slaves to many things our bodies wanted and enjoyed. We spent our lives doing evil and being jealous. People hated us, and we hated each other. <sup>4</sup>But when the kindness and love of God our Savior was shown, <sup>5</sup>he saved us because of his

mercy. It was not because of good deeds we did to be right with him. He saved us through the washing that made us new people through the Holy Spirit. <sup>6</sup>God poured out richly upon us that Holy Spirit through Jesus Christ our

Savior. <sup>7</sup>Being made right with God by his grace, we could have the hope of receiving the life that never ends.

<sup>8</sup>This teaching is true, and I want you to be sure the people understand these things. Then those who believe in God will be careful to use

their lives for doing good. These things are good and will help everyone.

<sup>9</sup>But stay away from those who have foolish arguments and talk about useless family histories and argue and quarrel about the law.

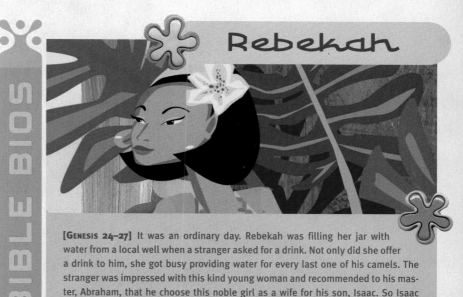

**Rebekah**

[GENESIS 24–27] It was an ordinary day. Rebekah was filling her jar with water from a local well when a stranger asked for a drink. Not only did she offer a drink to him, she got busy providing water for every last one of his camels. The stranger was impressed with this kind young woman and recommended to his master, Abraham, that he choose this noble girl as a wife for his son, Isaac. So Isaac became her husband, and Rebekah eventually had twin sons. God had told them that one son would serve the other; but instead of enjoying and nurturing both her boys and letting God take care of the details, Rebekah took matters into her own hands and gave all her affection to one son, Jacob. The result was a big family mess. One of the big lessons from Rebekah's life is to trust God to be faithful to his word.

Those things are worth nothing and will not help anyone. <sup>10</sup>After a first and second warning, avoid someone who causes arguments. <sup>11</sup>You can know that such people are evil and sinful; their own sins prove them wrong.

## SOME THINGS TO REMEMBER

<sup>12</sup>When I send Artemas or Tychicus to you, make every effort to come to me at Nicopolis, because I have decided to stay there this winter. <sup>13</sup>Do all you can to help Zenas the lawyer and Apollos on their journey so that they have everything they need. <sup>14</sup>Our people must learn to use their lives for doing good deeds to provide what is necessary so that their lives will not be useless.

<sup>15</sup>All who are with me greet you. Greet those who love us in the faith.

Grace be with you all.

**DIDYA KNOW**

THE MOST POPULAR SLEEPOVER ACTIVITY FOR GIRLS AGES 8-14 IS TRUTH OR DARE GAMES (33%), FOLLOWED BY DOING NAILS (25%), AND WATCHING TV (25%). WWW.WIZARDS.COM

**P**hilemon, the recipient of this letter was a prominent member of the church at Colossae who had become a Christian under Paul's ministry. Onesimus, a slave belonging to Philemon, was not a believer in Christ. For reasons we aren't told, Onesimus stole some money from his master and then ran away to Rome. Again, we aren't told exactly how, but Onesimus somehow met Paul in Rome and became a Christian.

# Philemon
## An Appeal for Mercy and Forgiveness

Paul grew to love this runaway slave as a dear friend and wanted Onesimus to remain in Rome with him. But Paul also knew that by stealing and fleeing from Philemon, Onesimus had not only broken Roman law but he had also broken God's laws for right living.

(An aside: Paul doesn't tackle the bigger picture of the rightness or wrongness of slavery here. It's a complicated issue, because slavery in biblical times was quite different from slavery in modern history. Slave labor was used for many of the occupations of the day—teaching, playing music, accounting, etc.—and slaves could purchase their freedom for a price. Most were treated decently, and many became friends with their masters and even a part of the family.)

OK, back to our story. Knowing that Onesimus must face his master, Paul arms him with this letter, urging Philemon to treat Onesimus graciously and to show forgiveness, welcoming him as a brother in Christ rather than as simply a slave.

¹From Paul, a prisoner of Christ Jesus, and from Timothy, our brother.

To Philemon, our dear friend and worker with us; ²to Apphia, our sister; to Archippus, a worker with us; and to the church that meets in your home:

³Grace and peace to you from God our Father and the Lord Jesus Christ.

## PHILEMON'S LOVE AND FAITH

⁴I always thank my God when I mention you in my prayers, ⁵because I hear about the love you have for all God's holy people and the faith you have in the Lord Jesus. ⁶I pray that the faith you share may make you understand every blessing we have in Christ. ⁷I have great joy and comfort, my brother, because the love

might help me while I am in prison for the Good News. ¹⁴But I did not want to do anything without asking you first so that any good you do for me will be because you want to do it, not because I forced you. ¹⁵Maybe Onesimus was separated from you for a short time so you could have him back forever— ¹⁶no longer as a slave, but better than a slave, as a loved brother. I love him very much, but you will love him even more, both as a person and as a believer in the Lord.

¹⁷So if you consider me your partner, welcome Onesimus as you would welcome me. ¹⁸If he has done anything wrong to you or if he owes you anything, charge that to me. ¹⁹I, Paul, am writing this with my own hand. I will pay it back, and I will say nothing about what you owe me for your own life. ²⁰So, my brother, I

**NEARLY ONE IN TEN HIGH SCHOOL STUDENTS EXPERIENCED PHYSICAL VIOLENCE BY A BOYFRIEND OR GIRLFRIEND IN THE PAST YEAR.**

WWW.CHILDTRENDSDATABANK.ORG

you have shown to God's people has refreshed them.

## ACCEPT ONESIMUS AS A BROTHER

⁸So, in Christ, I could be bold and order you to do what is right. ⁹But because I love you, I am pleading with you instead. I, Paul, an old man now and also a prisoner for Christ Jesus, ¹⁰am pleading with you for my child Onesimus, who became my child while I was in prison. ¹¹In the past he was useless to you, but now he has become useful for both you and me.

¹²I am sending him back to you, and with him I am sending my own heart. ¹³I wanted to keep him with me so that in your place he

ask that you do this for me in the Lord: Refresh my heart in Christ. ²¹I write this letter, knowing that you will do what I ask you and even more.

²²One more thing—prepare a room for me in which to stay, because I hope God will answer your prayers and I will be able to come to you.

## FINAL GREETINGS

²³Epaphras, a prisoner with me for Christ Jesus, sends greetings to you. ²⁴And also Mark, Aristarchus, Demas, and Luke, workers together with me, send greetings.

²⁵The grace of our Lord Jesus Christ be with your spirit.

top 10

**random ways to put other people first**

**10** Listen instead of talk.

**9** Give someone a shoulder rub.

**8** Say you're sorry when you mess up.

**7** Give up your seat.

**6** Share your stuff.

**5** Give more than you keep.

**4** Help carry someone's bags.

**3** Volunteer for the jobs no one else wants.

**2** Open doors for people.

**1** Let other drivers in, even the pushy ones.

## We don't know who wrote the Book

of Hebrews; and while scholars have speculated about this for centuries, that knowledge isn't necessary for us to appreciate the book's message. Since so much emphasis is placed on the Old Testament priesthood and on sacrifices, and because the Old Testament is quoted throughout, most scholars believe the book was written to a community of Hebrews. (Makes sense, considering the name, eh?) Some of them were likely believers in Jesus as the Messiah, but it's also likely that some were not.

# Hebrews
### A New High Priest and a New Agreement

Here we have a mystery author, writing to a group of what may or may not have been Hebrews, who may or may not have been Christians. What could possibly be relevant to us today?

First of all, Hebrews contains one of the best and clearest explanations of faith (11:1), as well as great biblical examples of men and women who exercised great faith—many of whom are still sources of inspiration today. But the main theme of Hebrews is that we have a new high priest in Jesus Christ and a new agreement (or a new covenant) because of his perfect sacrifice. This new agreement cancelled out the need for animal sacrifices and gave all believers full access to God.

## GOD SPOKE THROUGH HIS SON

**1** In the past God spoke to our ancestors through the prophets many times and in many different ways. ²But now in these last days God has spoken to us through his Son. God has chosen his Son to own all things, and through him he made the world. ³The Son reflects the glory of God and shows exactly what God is like. He holds everything together with his powerful word. When the Son made people clean from their sins, he sat down at the right side of God, the Great One in heaven. ⁴The Son became much greater than the angels, and God gave him a name that is much greater than theirs.

⁵This is because God never said to any of the angels,

"You are my Son.
　Today I have become your Father."

*Psalm 2:7*

Nor did God say of any angel,

"I will be his Father,
　and he will be my Son." *2 Samuel 7:14*

⁶And when God brings his firstborn Son into the world, he says,

"Let all God's angels worship him."ⁿ

*Psalm 97:7*

⁷This is what God said about the angels:

"God makes his angels become like winds.
　He makes his servants become like
　　flames of fire." *Psalm 104:4*

⁸But God said this about his Son:

"God, your throne will last forever and ever.

You will rule your kingdom with
　fairness.
⁹You love right and hate evil,
　so God has chosen you from among
　　your friends;
　he has set you apart with much joy."

*Psalm 45:6-7*

¹⁰God also says,

"Lord, in the beginning you made the
　earth,
　and your hands made the skies.

## "GOD HAS CHOSEN HIS SON TO OWN ALL THINGS, AND THROUGH HIM HE MADE THE WORLD."

¹¹They will be destroyed, but you will
　remain.
　They will all wear out like clothes.
¹²You will fold them like a coat.
　And, like clothes, you will change them.
But you never change,
　and your life will never end."

*Psalm 102:25-27*

¹³And God never said this to an angel:

"Sit by me at my right side
until I put your enemies under your
　control."ⁿ *Psalm 110:1*

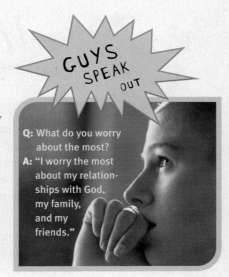

¹⁴All the angels are spirits who serve God and are sent to help those who will receive salvation.

## OUR SALVATION IS GREAT

**2** So we must be more careful to follow what we were taught. Then we will not stray away from the truth. ²The teaching God spoke through angels was shown to be true, and anyone who did not follow it or obey it received the punishment that was earned. ³So surely we also will be punished if we ignore this great salvation. The Lord himself first told about this salvation, and it was proven true to us by those who heard him. ⁴God also proved it by using wonders, great signs, many kinds of

# LEARN I+ & LIVE I+

**Titus 3:3**
**Learn It:** Do not be a slave to what your body wants.
**Live It:** Control your body, instead of letting it control you. Drink enough water. Eat healthy meals regularly. Stop biting your nails. Ask God to help you break one bad habit over the next thirty days.

**Philemon 20**
**Learn It:** Paul asked Philemon to refresh his heart in Christ.
**Live It:** Do what you can to encourage and bring joy to your Christian friends.

**Hebrews 1:3**
**Learn It:** Jesus reflected the glory of God.
**Live It:** Read through the Bible, and list all the names of God that you can find. Study a list of his attributes.

**notes** **1:6 "Let . . . him."** These words are found in Deuteronomy 32:43 in the Septuagint, the Greek version of the Old Testament, and in a Hebrew copy among the Dead Sea Scrolls. **1:13 until . . . control** Literally, "until I make your enemies a footstool for your feet."

# Music Reviews

**GROUP:** REBECCA ST. JAMES

**ALBUM:** WAIT FOR ME

Australian native Rebecca St. James came to the United States with her family when she signed a record deal before she could even drive. For the last ten years, Rebecca has rocked Christian fans with searing music and her message of staying true to God, true to yourself, and true to your body by remaining sexually pure before marriage. After a decade of music, it's time for fans to get all their favorites in one place, and *Wait for Me* captures Rebecca's past hits and more recent favorites.

**WHY IT ROCKS: REBECCA'S INTEGRITY AND COMMITMENT TO LIVE WHAT SHE BELIEVES SHINES THROUGH HER MUSIC.**

miracles, and by giving people gifts through the Holy Spirit, just as he wanted.

## CHRIST BECAME LIKE HUMANS

⁵God did not choose angels to be the rulers of the new world that was coming, which is what we have been talking about. ⁶It is written in the Scriptures,

"Why are people important to you?
Why do you take care of human beings?
⁷You made them a little lower than the angels
and crowned them with glory and honor.
⁸You put all things under their control."

*Psalm 8:4-6*

When God put everything under their control, there was nothing left that they did not rule. Still, we do not yet see them ruling over everything. ⁹But we see Jesus, who for a short time was made lower than the angels. And now he is wearing a crown of glory and honor because he suffered and died. And by God's grace, he died for everyone.

¹⁰God is the One who made all things, and all things are for his glory. He wanted to have many children share his glory, so he made the One who leads people to salvation perfect through suffering. ¹¹Jesus, who makes people holy, and those who are made holy are from the same family.

So he is not ashamed to call them his brothers and sisters." ¹²He says,

"Then, I will tell my fellow Israelites about you;
I will praise you in the public meeting."

*Psalm 22:22*

¹³He also says,

"I will trust in God." *Isaiah 8:17*

And he also says,

"I am here, and with me are the children God has given me." *Isaiah 8:18*

¹⁴Since these children are people with physical bodies, Jesus himself became like them. He did this so that, by dying, he could destroy the one who has the power of death—the devil— ¹⁵and free those who were like slaves all their lives because of their fear of death. ¹⁶Clearly, it is not angels that Jesus helps, but the people who are from Abraham." ¹⁷For this reason Jesus had to be made like his brothers in every way so he could be their merciful and faithful high priest in service to God. Then Jesus could bring forgiveness for their sins. ¹⁸And now he can help those who are tempted, because he himself suffered and was tempted.

## JESUS IS GREATER THAN MOSES

**3** So all of you holy brothers and sisters, who were called by God, think about Jesus, who was sent to us and is the high priest of our faith. ²Jesus was faithful to God as

Moses was in God's family. ³Jesus has more honor than Moses, just as the builder of a house has more honor than the house itself. ⁴Every house is built by someone, but the builder of everything is God himself. ⁵Moses was faithful in God's family as a servant, and he told what God would say in the future. ⁶But Christ is faithful as a Son over God's house. And we are God's house if we keep on being very sure about our great hope.

## WE MUST CONTINUE TO FOLLOW GOD

⁷So it is as the Holy Spirit says:

"Today listen to what he says.
⁸Do not be stubborn as in the past
when you turned against God,
when you tested God in the desert.
⁹There your ancestors tried me and tested me
and saw the things I did for forty years.
¹⁰I was angry with them.
I said, 'They are not loyal to me
and have not understood my ways.'
¹¹I was angry and made a promise,
'They will never enter my rest.'"

*Psalm 95:7-11*

¹²So brothers and sisters, be careful that none of you has an evil, unbelieving heart that will turn you away from the living God. ¹³But

**2:11 brothers and sisters** Although the Greek text says "brothers" here and throughout this book, the writer's words were meant for the entire church, including men and women. **2:16 Abraham** Most respected ancestor of the Jews. Every Jew hoped to see Abraham. **3:11 rest** A place of rest God promised to give his people.

encourage each other every day while it is "today."[n] Help each other so none of you will become hardened because sin has tricked you. [14]We all share in Christ if we keep till the end the sure faith we had in the beginning. [15]This is what the Scripture says:

"Today listen to what he says.

Do not be stubborn as in the past
when you turned against God."

*Psalm 95:7-8*

[16]Who heard God's voice and was against him? It was all those people Moses led out of Egypt. [17]And with whom was God angry for forty years? He was angry with those who sinned, who died in the desert. [18]And to whom was God talking when he promised that they would never enter his rest? He was talking to those who did not obey him. [19]So we see they were not allowed to enter and have God's rest, because they did not believe.

# beautysecret

## Overkill

**Have you ever seen someone who tried a new style but went over-the-top? To avoid a gaudy, excessive look, stand in front of the mirror and turn around quickly. Does something stand out and distract from your outfit? If so, consider removing it or asking a friend whether you should leave it at home.**

4 Now, since God has left us the promise that we may enter his rest, let us be very careful so none of you will fail to enter. [2]The Good News was preached to us just as it was to them. But the teaching they heard did not help them, because they heard it but did not accept it with faith. [3]We who have believed are able to enter and have God's rest. As God has said,

"I was angry and made a promise,
'They will never enter my rest.' "

*Psalm 95:11*

But God's work was finished from the time he made the world. [4]In the Scriptures he talked about the seventh day of the week: "And on the seventh day God rested from all his works."[n] [5]And again in the Scripture God said, "They will never enter my rest."

[6]It is still true that some people will enter God's rest, but those who first heard the way to be saved did not enter, because they did not obey. [7]So God planned another day, called "today." He spoke about that day through David a long time later in the same Scripture used before:

"Today listen to what he says.

Do not be stubborn." *Psalm 95:7-8*

[8]We know that Joshua[n] did not lead the people into that rest, because God spoke later about another day. [9]This shows that the rest[n] for God's people is still coming. [10]Anyone who enters God's rest will rest from his work as God did. [11]Let us try as hard as we can to enter God's rest so that no one will fail by following the example of those who refused to obey.

[12]God's word is alive and working and is sharper than a double-edged sword. It cuts all the way into us, where the soul and the spirit are joined, to the center of our joints and bones. And it judges the thoughts and feelings in our hearts. [13]Nothing in all the world can be hidden from God. Everything is clear and lies open before him, and to him we must explain the way we have lived.

### JESUS IS OUR HIGH PRIEST

[14]Since we have a great high priest, Jesus the Son of God, who has gone into heaven, let us hold on to the faith we have. [15]For our high

Radical Faith

# Hebrews 4:14-16

If you've got the right connections, you can get into places that other people can't. Getting to go backstage or landing a sweet job can happen just because of whom you know. Knowing Jesus is a little bit like that. Jesus has gone to heaven and sits next to God the Father. He is in a special position that is filled with authority and power. There are so many reasons to be secure and stay firm in your faith in Christ, and plenty of them are explained well in the Book of Hebrews. Jesus is the perfect high priest who takes over your weaknesses and makes you right with God (see Hebrews 7). Through him you can come to God in sincere prayer. He has the power to accomplish what is right in your heart, in your life, and in your world; and he's inviting you to come closer. Have a lifestyle of prayer. God communicates the importance of that quite a bit, instructing you to devote yourself to prayer (Colossians 4:2), to pray continually and relentlessly (Ephesians 6:18), and to stay alert and self-controlled so you can keep praying (Mark 14:38). Live in the privilege Jesus has given you, and pursue close communication with God every day.

notes
**3:13 "today"** This word is taken from verse 7. It means that it is important to do these things now. **4:4 "And . . . works."** Quotation from Genesis 2:2. **4:8 Joshua** After Moses died, Joshua became leader of the Jewish people and led them into the land that God promised to give them. **4:9 rest** Literally, "sabbath rest," meaning a sharing in the rest that God began after he created the world.

333

## Promises:

# Hebrews 4:15-16

Sometimes it's easy to feel like no one understands you. You are a highly unique person with all kinds of dreams and desires that only you can truly understand. Sure, others can give it a shot, but they may never completely understand everything that goes on inside your head. So when you're upset or want someone to sympathize with you, it's often hard for some else to really "get you" and understand how you're feeling.

How reassuring and comforting to know that God knows and completely understands every nook and cranny of who you are. And he knows this not only because he created you and is connected to you spiritually, but because he (Jesus) came to earth in human form and essentially lived in your shoes. He understands frustration, anger, fear, love, and doubt because he was human and experienced our human emotions. And even though he was perfect and without sin, he really does understand you. We worship and believe in a God who doesn't continually look down on us and shake his head in disappointment when we mess up. He understands that life can be hard and he wants you to talk to him about it. Go on; he understands.

priest is able to understand our weaknesses. When he lived on earth, he was tempted in every way that we are, but he did not sin. 16Let us, then, feel very sure that we can come before God's throne where there is grace. There we can receive mercy and grace to help us when we need it.

5 Every high priest is chosen from among other people. He is given the work of going before God for them to offer gifts and sacrifices for sins. 2Since he himself is weak, he is able to be gentle with those who do not understand and who are doing wrong things. 3Because he is weak, the high priest must offer sacrifices for his own sins and also for the sins of the people.

4To be a high priest is an honor, but no one chooses himself for this work. He must be called by God as Aaron" was. 5So also Christ did not choose himself to have the honor of being a high priest, but God chose him. God said to him,
"You are my Son.
Today I have become your Father."

*Psalm 2:7*

6And in another Scripture God says,
"You are a priest forever,
a priest like Melchizedek."" *Psalm 110:4*

7While Jesus lived on earth, he prayed to God and asked God for help. He prayed with loud cries and tears to the One who could save him from death, and his prayer was heard because he trusted God. 8Even though Jesus was the Son of God, he learned obedience by what he suffered. 9And because his obedience was perfect, he was able to give eternal salvation to all who obey him. 10In this way God made Jesus a high priest, a priest like Melchizedek.

## Warning Against Falling Away

11We have much to say about this, but it is hard to explain because you are so slow to understand. 12By now you should be teachers, but you need someone to teach you again the first lessons of God's message. You still need the teaching that is like milk. You are not ready for solid food. 13Anyone who lives on milk is still a baby and knows nothing about right

teaching. 14But solid food is for those who are grown up. They have practiced in order to know the difference between good and evil.

6 So let us go on to grown-up teaching. Let us not go back over the beginning lessons we learned about Christ. We should not again start teaching about faith in God and about turning away from those acts that lead to death. 2We should not return to the teaching about baptisms," about laying on of hands," about the raising of the dead and eternal judgment. 3And we will go on to grown-up teaching if God allows.

4Some people cannot be brought back again to a changed life. They were once in God's light, and enjoyed heaven's gift, and shared in the Holy Spirit. 5They found out how good God's word is, and they received the powers of his new world. 6But they fell away from

# relationships

"The wrong things the sinful self does are clear: being sexually unfaithful, not being pure, taking part in sexual sins" (Galatians 5:19). Let's be honest: Sex feels good. Touching and being touched by someone you love is incredible. But it's tons more incredible when you can do it totally guilt-free; and according to God's standards, that's only when you are married. Never let anyone pressure you into sexual activity of any kind. That's not love—it's selfishness.

**5:4 Aaron** Aaron was Moses' brother and the first Jewish high priest. **5:6 Melchizedek** A priest and king who lived in the time of Abraham. (Read Genesis 14:17-24.) **6:2 baptisms** The word here may refer to Christian baptism, or it may refer to the Jewish ceremonial washings. **6:2 laying on of hands** The laying on of hands had many purposes, including the giving of a blessing, power, or authority.

Christ. It is impossible to bring them back to a changed life again, because they are nailing the Son of God to a cross again and are shaming him in front of others.

⁷Some people are like land that gets plenty of rain. The land produces a good crop for those who work it, and it receives God's blessings. ⁸Other people are like land that grows thorns and weeds and is worthless. It is in danger of being cursed by God and will be destroyed by fire.

⁹Dear friends, we are saying this to you, but we really expect better things from you that will lead to your salvation. ¹⁰God is fair; he will not forget the work you did and the love you showed for him by helping his people. And he will remember that you are still helping them. ¹¹We want each of you to go on with the same hard work all your lives so you will surely get what you hope for. ¹²We do not want you to become lazy. Be like those who through faith and patience will receive what God has promised.

¹³God made a promise to Abraham. And as there is no one greater than God, he used himself when he swore to Abraham, ¹⁴saying, "I will surely bless you and give you many descendants."ⁿ ¹⁵Abraham waited patiently for this to happen, and he received what God promised.

¹⁶People always use the name of someone greater than themselves when they swear. The oath proves that what they say is true, and this ends all arguing. ¹⁷God wanted to prove that his promise was true to those who would get what he promised. And he wanted them to understand clearly that his purposes never change, so he made an oath. ¹⁸These two things cannot change: God cannot lie when he makes a promise, and he cannot lie when he makes an oath. These things encourage us who came to God for safety. They give us strength to hold on to the hope we have been given. ¹⁹We have this hope as an anchor for the soul, sure and strong. It enters behind the curtain in the Most Holy Place in heaven, ²⁰where Jesus has gone ahead of us and for us. He has become the high priest forever, a priest like Melchizedek.ⁿ

## THE PRIEST MELCHIZEDEK

7 Melchizedekⁿ was the king of Salem and a priest for God Most High. He met Abraham when Abraham was coming back after defeating the kings. When they met, Melchizedek blessed Abraham, ²and Abraham gave him a tenth of everything he had brought back from the battle. First, Melchizedek's name means "king of goodness," and he is king of Salem, which means "king of peace." ³No one knows who Melchizedek's father or mother was,ⁿ where he came from, when he was born, or when he died. Melchizedek is like the Son of God; he continues being a priest forever.

⁴You can see how great Melchizedek was. Abraham, the great father, gave him a tenth of everything that he won in battle. ⁵Now the law says that those in the tribe of Levi who become priests must collect a tenth from the people— their own people—even though the priests and the people are from the family of Abraham. ⁶Melchizedek was not from the tribe of Levi, but he collected a tenth from Abraham. And he blessed Abraham, the man who had God's promises. ⁷Now everyone knows that the more important person blesses the less important person. ⁸Priests receive a tenth, even though they are only men who live and then die. But Melchizedek, who received a tenth from Abraham, continues living, as the Scripture says. ⁹We might even say that Levi, who receives a tenth, also paid it when Abraham paid Melchizedek a tenth. ¹⁰Levi was not yet born, but he was in the body of his ancestor when Melchizedek met Abraham.

¹¹The people were given the lawⁿ based on a system of priests from the tribe of Levi, but they could not be made perfect through that system. So there was a need for another priest to come, a priest like Melchizedek, not Aaron. ¹²And when a different kind of priest comes, the law must be changed, too. ¹³We are saying these things about Christ, who belonged to a different tribe. No one from that tribe ever served as a priest at the altar. ¹⁴It is clear that our Lord came from the tribe of Judah, and Moses said nothing about priests belonging to that tribe.

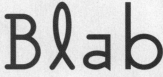

**Q:** My parents got divorced and all their friends have, too. I don't think marriage can really last a lifetime. Can it?

**A:** Marriages are designed to last a lifetime. Lots of them still do. If half of all marriages fail, that still means there is half that don't. Make a habit of talking to older Christians who have been married a long time. Ask them what things helped keep their marriage together. Pray that God will help you be able to trust in marriage again.

**Q:** My parents have bounced me back and forth for so many years that I have a hard time trusting any adults. How can I know who to trust?

**A:** Proverbs 3:5 says you can trust in the Lord with all your heart. Ask him for discernment in all your relationships, which means the ability to tell what's for real and what isn't. If you can't get past your trust issues on your own, give counseling a try.

**Q:** I am adopted and I really want to meet my birthparents. My parents and I haven't discussed this, because I don't want to hurt their feelings. How can I find my birth mom?

**A:** It will hurt your parents more if you look for her behind their backs. Ask them about her; tell them you are old enough to know. See if they will help you look for her, and reassure them that you will always consider them your parents and love them.

**6:14** "I . . . descendants." Quotation from Genesis 22:17.   **6:20; 7:1 Melchizedek** A priest and king who lived in the time of Abraham. (Read Genesis 14:17-24.)   **7:3 No . . . was** Literally, "Melchizedek was without father, without mother, without genealogy."   **7:11 The . . . law** This refers to the people of Israel who were given the Law of Moses.

# Quiz

# WHICH WOMAN OF THE BIBLE DO YOU MOST RESEMBLE?

**RATE YOURSELF FROM 1 (NOT ME AT ALL) TO 10 (DEFINITELY ME) ON EACH OF THE FOLLOWING DESCRIPTIONS:**

1. Even when things in my life are hard, I can always remain hopeful that they will work out.

2. I am good at pointing out the positive qualities and gifts in others.

3. I am really interested in pursuing a career in business.

4. I am extremely loyal to my friends and family, no matter what the circumstances.

5. If an argument arises among my friends, it seems that I'm always the peacemaker.

6. My favorite time with God is when I am singing or listening to praise and worship music.

7. I have to stand up for someone who is being made fun of or mistreated.

8. I am often hosting parties or inviting people over to hang out at my place.

9. I am good at encouraging others.

10. When I need something, I'm not afraid to ask for help.

11. People often come to me to talk about their problems.

12. Whenever I have a problem, I am faithful to keep praying about it until God answers or shows me direction.

13. It's easy for me to trust in God's promises.

14. I enjoy being in positions of leadership.

**WHAT'S YOUR SCORE?**
**ADD TOGETHER YOUR RATINGS FROM QUESTIONS:**

A. 1 and 12: _____
B. 4 and 10: _____
C. 3 and 8: _____
D. 5 and 11: _____
E. 6 and 13: _____
F. 2 and 9: _____
G. 7 and 14: _____

**IF YOUR BIGGEST SCORE FALLS UNDER...**

A, then you resemble **Hannah.** Check out her story in 1 Samuel 1 and 2.

B, then you're a **Ruth.** Check out her story in the Book of Ruth.

C, then you are a lot like **Lydia.** Check out her story in Acts 16.

D, then you're a **Deborah.** Check out her story in Judges 4 and 5.

E, then you are a lot like **Anna.** Check out her story in Luke 2.

F, then you resemble **Elizabeth.** Check out her story in Luke 1.

G, then you are a lot like **Esther.** Check out her story in the Book of Esther.

## JESUS IS LIKE MELCHIZEDEK

[15]And this becomes even more clear when we see that another priest comes who is like Melchizedek.[n] [16]He was not made a priest by human rules and laws but through the power of his life, which continues forever. [17]It is said about him,

"You are a priest forever,
a priest like Melchizedek."    *Psalm 110:4*

## "NOW A BETTER HOPE HAS BEEN GIVEN TO US, AND WITH THIS HOPE WE CAN COME NEAR TO GOD."

[18]The old rule is now set aside, because it was weak and useless. [19]The law of Moses could not make anything perfect. But now a better hope has been given to us, and with this hope we can come near to God. [20]It is important that God did this with an oath. Others became priests without an oath, [21]but Christ became a priest with God's oath. God said:

"The Lord has made a promise
and will not change his mind.
'You are a priest forever.' "    *Psalm 110:4*

[22]This means that Jesus is the guarantee of a better agreement[n] from God to his people.

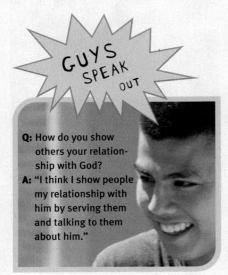

GUYS SPEAK OUT

**Q:** How do you show others your relationship with God?

**A:** "I think I show people my relationship with him by serving them and talking to them about him."

[23]When one of the other priests died, he could not continue being a priest. So there were many priests. [24]But because Jesus lives forever, he will never stop serving as priest. [25]So he is able always to save those who come to God through him because he always lives, asking God to help them.

[26]Jesus is the kind of high priest we need. He is holy, sinless, pure, not influenced by sinners, and he is raised above the heavens. [27]He is not like the other priests who had to offer sacrifices every day, first for their own sins, and then for the sins of the people. Christ offered his sacrifice only once and for all time when he offered himself. [28]The law chooses high priests who are people with weaknesses, but the word of God's oath came later than the law. It made God's Son to be the high priest, and that Son has been made perfect forever.

## JESUS IS OUR HIGH PRIEST

8 Here is the point of what we are saying: We have a high priest who sits on the right side of God's throne in heaven. [2]Our high priest serves in the Most Holy Place, the true place of worship that was made by God, not by humans.

[3]Every high priest has the work of offering gifts and sacrifices to God. So our high priest must also offer something to God. [4]If our high priest were now living on earth, he would not be a priest, because there are already priests here who follow the law by offering gifts to God. [5]The work they do as priests is only a copy and a shadow of what is in heaven. This is why God warned Moses when he was ready to build the Holy Tent: "Be very careful to make everything by the plan I showed you on the mountain."[n] [6]But the priestly work that has been given to Jesus is much greater than the work that was given to the other priests. In the same way, the new agreement that Jesus brought from God to his people is much greater than the old one. And the new agreement is based on promises of better things.

[7]If there had been nothing wrong with the first agreement,[n] there would have been no

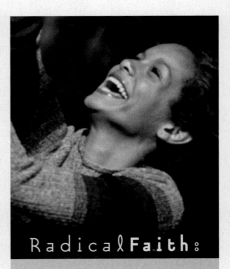

Radical Faith:

## Hebrews 7:18-19

God gave the law to the Israelites in the Old Testament to help them understand his purity and what his holiness requires. The law couldn't save people, but was meant to help people understand how sinful they are before God (Romans 3:20) and that only through Christ can they be saved (Galatians 3:24). Following the rules can never make anyone righteous—you have to be right on the inside, not just the outside, to be righteous. We can't keep all the rules because our hearts aren't pure. It takes more than just trying to do good things to become right before God. Hebrews 7:19 refers to "a better hope" that brings people "near to God," and that hope is Jesus Christ. Being saved from the pain and death of sin, becoming right before God, and getting connected to God all comes through Jesus alone. His sacrifice provides a way for you to be forgiven of every sin and for you to have his righteousness replace your sinfulness. Because of Jesus, you can be renewed and made pure in your heart. Being accepted by God comes through your acceptance of Jesus—not because you do all the right things.

**7:15 Melchizedek** A priest and king who lived in the time of Abraham. (Read Genesis 14:17-24.)    **7:22 agreement** God gives a contract or agreement to his people. For the Jews, this agreement was the Law of Moses. But now God has given a better agreement to his people through Christ.    **8:5 "Be . . . mountain."** Quotation from Exodus 25:40.    **8:7 first agreement** The contract God gave the Jewish people when he gave them the Law of Moses.

337

need for a second agreement. ⁸But God found something wrong with his people. He says:

"Look, the time is coming, says the Lord,
when I will make a new agreement
with the people of Israel
and the people of Judah.
⁹It will not be like the agreement
I made with their ancestors
when I took them by the hand
to bring them out of Egypt.
But they broke that agreement,
and I turned away from them, says the Lord.
¹⁰This is the agreement I will make
with the people of Israel at that time,
says the Lord.
I will put my teachings in their minds
and write them on their hearts.
I will be their God,
and they will be my people.
¹¹People will no longer have to teach their neighbors and relatives
to know the Lord,
because all people will know me,
from the least to the most important.
¹²I will forgive them for the wicked things they did,
and I will not remember their sins anymore." *Jeremiah 31:31-34*

¹³God called this a new agreement, so he has made the first agreement old. And anything that is old and worn out is ready to disappear.

## THE OLD AGREEMENT

9 The first agreement" had rules for worship and a man-made place for worship. ²The Holy Tent was set up for this. The first area in the Tent was called the Holy Place. In it were the lamp and the table with the bread that was made holy for God. ³Behind the second curtain was a room called the Most Holy Place. ⁴In it was a golden altar for burning incense and the Ark covered with gold that held the old agreement. Inside this Ark was a golden jar of manna, Aaron's rod that once grew leaves, and the stone tablets of the old agreement. ⁵Above the Ark were the creatures that showed God's glory, whose wings reached over the lid. But we cannot tell everything about these things now.

⁶When everything in the Tent was made ready in this way, the priests went into the first room every day to worship. ⁷But only the high priest could go into the second room, and he did that only once a year. He could never enter the inner room without taking blood with him, which he offered to God for himself and for sins the people did without knowing they did them. ⁸The Holy Spirit uses this to show that the way into the Most Holy Place was not open while the system of the old Holy Tent was still being used. ⁹This is an example for the present time. It shows that the gifts and sacrifices offered cannot make the conscience of the worshiper perfect. ¹⁰These gifts and sacrifices were only about food and drink and spe-

cial washings. They were rules for the body, to be followed until the time of God's new way.

## THE NEW AGREEMENT

¹¹But when Christ came as the high priest of the good things we now have, he entered the

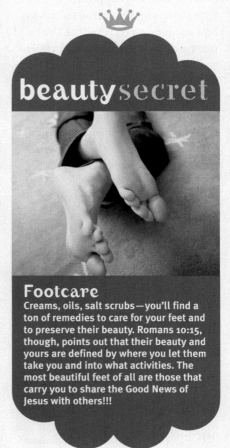

**beauty**secret

**Footcare**
Creams, oils, salt scrubs—you'll find a ton of remedies to care for your feet and to preserve their beauty. Romans 10:15, though, points out that their beauty and yours are defined by where you let them take you and into what activities. The most beautiful feet of all are those that carry you to share the Good News of Jesus with others!!!

 **9:1 first agreement** The contract God gave the Jewish people when he gave them the Law of Moses.

338

# November

**1** This is Good Nutrition Month, so try eating a salad every night with dinner.

**2**

**3** Take a day of rest. Enjoy yourself.

**4** Pray for a person of influence: It's P. Diddy's B-Day.

**5**

**6** The second week of November is World Kindness Week. Try to do something kind every day!

**7** Surprise your parents by cleaning the bathrooms in your house.

**8**

**9** Do some extra chores to save money for Christmas shopping.

**10**

**11** Veterans Day. Call someone who has served in a war. Thank the person for protecting our country.

**12**

**13**

**14** Surprise your mom with an extra long hug.

**15** Read Colossians 2. Tell a friend about what you learned.

**16** Spend time with someone who isn't particularly popular today.

**17**

**18** Try something new.

**19**

**20**

**21**

**22** Prepare for Thanksgiving by writing down five things you are thankful for.

**23**

**24**

**25** Pray for a person of influence: Amy Grant is having a birthday.

**26**

**27** Read Matthew 5–7. Try to live out what you read.

**28** Pray for our political leaders.

**29**

**30** Pray for a person of influence: It's Clay Aiken's birthday.

Thanksgiving is the fourth Thursday in November. Share your good fortune with others.

## Hebrews 10:10, 14

Usually you become better at something because you work at it—like becoming really good at basketball because you practice or gaining respect from others when you succeed at things. Something that is important about God's relationship with you is that he doesn't care about what you can do; he makes you holy and perfect without your earning it. Hebrews 10:10 says that you *are made* holy—you can't make yourself holy. Your role is to place your faith in Christ's sacrifice to make up for your ungodliness. Then you're seen as perfect in God's view because Jesus' one sacrifice is enough to cover the blame of all your sins (check out Hebrews 9:12-14). It was a huge concept for Jews to grasp that God would give permanent forgiveness for sins based on Jesus' one sacrifice. They were used to repetitive animal sacrifices that would bring temporary forgiveness of sins. But Jesus shook all that up. When verse 14 says you're "being made holy," it means you're still a work in progress—God's always working and preparing you for his special purposes on earth. You are acceptable and wonderful in God's eyes—and not because you earned it yourself, but because of your faith in Christ.

greater and more perfect tent. It is not made by humans and does not belong to this world. [12]Christ entered the Most Holy Place only once—and for all time. He did not take with him the blood of goats and calves. His sacrifice was his own blood, and by it he set us free from sin forever. [13]The blood of goats and bulls and the ashes of a cow are sprinkled on the people who are unclean, and this makes their bodies clean again. [14]How much more is done by the blood of Christ. He offered himself through the eternal Spirit[n] as a perfect sacrifice to God. His blood will make our consciences pure from useless acts so we may serve the living God.

[15]For this reason Christ brings a new agreement from God to his people. Those who are called by God can now receive the blessings he has promised, blessings that will last forever. They can have those things because Christ died so that the people who lived under the first agreement could be set free from sin.

[16]When there is a will,[n] it must be proven that the one who wrote that will is dead. [17]A will means nothing while the person is alive; it can be used only after the person dies. [18]This is why even the first agreement could not begin without blood to show death. [19]First, Moses told all the people every command in the law. Next he took the blood of calves and mixed it with water. Then he used red wool and a branch of the hyssop plant to sprinkle it on the book of the law and on all the people. [20]He said, "This is the blood that begins the Agreement that God commanded you to obey."[n] [21]In the same way, Moses sprinkled the blood on the Holy Tent and over all the things used in worship. [22]The law says that almost everything must be made clean by blood, and sins cannot be forgiven without blood to show death.

### CHRIST'S DEATH TAKES AWAY SINS

[23]So the copies of the real things in heaven had to be made clean by animal sacrifices. But the real things in heaven need much better sacrifices. [24]Christ did not go into the Most Holy Place made by humans, which is only a copy of the real one. He went into heaven itself and is there now before God to help us. [25]The high priest enters the Most Holy Place once every year with blood that is not his own. But Christ did not offer himself many times. [26]Then he would have had to suffer many times since the world was made. But Christ came only once and for all time at just the right time to take away all sin by sacrificing himself. [27]Just as everyone must die once and be judged, [28]so Christ was offered as a sacrifice one time to take away the sins of many people. And he will come a second time, not to offer himself for sin, but to bring salvation to those who are waiting for him.

## "CHRIST CAME ONLY ONCE AND FOR ALL TIME AT JUST THE RIGHT TIME TO TAKE AWAY ALL SIN BY SACRIFICING HIMSELF."

10 The law is only an unclear picture of the good things coming in the future; it is not the real thing. The people under the law offer the same sacrifices every year, but these sacrifices can never make perfect those who come near to worship God. [2]If the law could make them perfect, the sacrifices would have already stopped. The worshipers would be made clean, and they would no longer have a sense of sin. [3]But these sacrifices remind them of their sins every year, [4]because it is impossible for the blood of bulls and goats to take away sins.

[5]So when Christ came into the world, he said:

"You do not want sacrifices and offerings,
but you have prepared a body for me.
[6]You do not ask for burnt offerings
and offerings to take away sins.

**9:14 Spirit** This refers to the Holy Spirit, to Christ's own spirit, or to the spiritual and eternal nature of his sacrifice.   **9:16 will** A legal document that shows how a person's money and property are to be distributed at the time of death. This is the same word in Greek as "agreement" in verse 15.   **9:20 "This . . . obey."** Quotation from Exodus 24:8.

7Then I said, 'Look, I have come.

It is written about me in the book.

God, I have come to do what you want.' "

*Psalm 40:6-8*

8In this Scripture he first said, "You do not want sacrifices and offerings. You do not ask for burnt offerings and offerings to take away sins." (These are all sacrifices that the law commands.) 9Then he said, "Look, I have come to do what you want." God ends the first system of sacrifices so he can set up the new system. 10And because of this, we are made holy through the sacrifice Christ made in his body once and for all time.

11Every day the priests stand and do their religious service, often offering the same sacrifices. Those sacrifices can never take away sins. 12But after Christ offered one sacrifice for sins, forever, he sat down at the right side of God. 13And now Christ waits there for his enemies to be put under his power. 14With one sacrifice he made perfect forever those who are being made holy.

15The Holy Spirit also tells us about this. First he says:

16"This is the agreement" I will make

with them at that time, says the Lord.

I will put my teachings in their hearts

and write them on their minds."

*Jeremiah 31:33*

**Q:** What will you look for in a wife?

**A:** "Hmmm . . . a good, Christian woman (good-looking is also okay)."

17Then he says:

"Their sins and the evil things they do—

I will not remember anymore."

*Jeremiah 31:34*

18Now when these have been forgiven, there is no more need for a sacrifice for sins.

## CONTINUE TO TRUST GOD

19So, brothers and sisters, we are completely free to enter the Most Holy Place without fear because of the blood of Jesus' death. 20We can enter through a new and living way that Jesus opened for us. It leads through the curtain —Christ's body. 21And since we have a great priest over God's house, 22let us come near to God with a sincere heart and a sure faith, because we have been made free from a guilty conscience, and our bodies have been washed with pure water. 23Let us hold firmly to the hope that we have confessed, because we can trust God to do what he promised.

## "LET US THINK ABOUT EACH OTHER AND HELP EACH OTHER TO SHOW LOVE AND DO GOOD DEEDS."

24Let us think about each other and help each other to show love and do good deeds. 25You should not stay away from the church meetings, as some are doing, but you should meet together and encourage each other. Do this even more as you see the day" coming.

26If we decide to go on sinning after we have learned the truth, there is no longer any sacrifice for sins. 27There is nothing but fear in waiting for the judgment and the terrible fire that will destroy all those who live against God. 28Anyone who refused to obey the law of Moses was found guilty from the proof given by two or three witnesses. He was put to death without mercy. 29So what do you think should be done to those who do not respect the Son of God, who look at the blood of the agreement that made them holy as no different from oth-

## Hebrews 10:17-23

Do you ever feel that receiving salvation through God's grace alone may not really be enough? It sounds so easy. Just believe that Jesus Christ is the Son of God and that he died for your sins, and that by accepting that, you are forgiven of your sins and receive the gift of eternal life. You may say, "Shouldn't you have to do other things on top of all that? Read the Bible every day? Be nice to your little brother or sister? Pray every day and always attend church? There has to be more."

Here's a little secret: All that extra stuff is great and it pleases God, but it doesn't guarantee your salvation. God doesn't want us to live in fear and doubt of our salvation. We can be sure and confident that God doesn't add extra provisions to his promise of salvation or give us new requirements to catch up on every so often. God is always up front and honest—never sneaky. So believe it! It's that easy.

**10:16 agreement** God gives a contract or agreement to his people. For the Jews, this agreement was the Law of Moses. But now God has given a better agreement to his people through Christ. **10:25 day** The day Christ will come to judge all people and take his people to live with him.

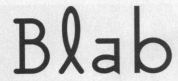

**Q:** I want a baby. I really, really want one. They are so cute and fun. I think I'm ready to be a mom. Is this wrong?

**A:** Maternal feelings often develop in your teens, but that doesn't mean it would be the best plan for your life to have a baby right now. Offer your babysitting services to couples with infants to satisfy your baby craving, and pray that you will have patience until the right time comes.

**Q:** I am having a hard time forgiving myself for something I did last year. I have asked God to forgive me, and I know he has, but I can't seem to stop thinking about it. What can I do?

**A:** Are you thinking about it because you still haven't confessed to other people involved and asked them for forgiveness, too? Would doing so help them and you? Sometimes we can't let go of the past because there are still things that need to be taken care of. If that is the case, rectify it. If not, and you are just beating yourself up over something God has forgiven and forgotten, ask him to release you from this unnecessary guilt.

**Q:** I had a really bad fight with my friend. How can I patch things up with her?

**A:** Go to her and say not only "I'm sorry," but also "Will you forgive me?" Go with a broken and humble heart. Many times, a true apology is all in the tone of voice. Ask her how you can restore your friendship. If she is still mad, give her time to cool off, and pray for her.

ers' blood, who insult the Spirit of God's grace? Surely they should have a much worse punishment. ³⁰We know that God said, "I will punish those who do wrong; I will repay them." And he also said, "The Lord will judge his people." ³¹It is a terrible thing to fall into the hands of the living God.

³²Remember those days in the past when you first learned the truth. You had a hard struggle with many sufferings, but you continued strong. ³³Sometimes you were hurt and attacked before crowds of people, and sometimes you shared with those who were being treated that way. ³⁴You helped the prisoners. You even had joy when all that you owned was taken from you, because you knew you had something better and more lasting.

³⁵So do not lose the courage you had in the past, which has a great reward. ³⁶You must hold on, so you can do what God wants and receive what he has promised. ³⁷For in a very short time,

"The One who is coming will come
    and will not be delayed.
³⁸The person who is right with me
    will live by trusting in me.
But if he turns back with fear,
    I will not be pleased with him."

*Habakkuk 2:3-4*

³⁹But we are not those who turn back and are lost. We are people who have faith and are saved.

## WHAT IS FAITH?

**11** Faith means being sure of the things we hope for and knowing that something is real even if we do not see it. ²Faith is the reason we remember great people who lived in the past.

³It is by faith we understand that the whole world was made by God's command so what we see was made by something that cannot be seen.

⁴It was by faith that Abel offered God a better sacrifice than Cain did. God said he was pleased with the gifts Abel offered and called Abel a good man because of his faith. Abel died, but through his faith he is still speaking.

⁵It was by faith that Enoch was taken to heaven so he would not die. He could not be found, because God had taken him away. Before he was taken, the Scripture says that he was a man who truly pleased God. ⁶Without faith no one can please God. Anyone who comes to God must believe that he is real and that he rewards those who truly want to find him.

⁷It was by faith that Noah heard God's warnings about things he could not yet see. He obeyed God and built a large boat to save his family. By his faith, Noah showed that the world was wrong, and he became one of those who are made right with God through faith.

> ## "FAITH MEANS BEING SURE OF THE THINGS WE HOPE FOR AND KNOWING THAT SOMETHING IS REAL EVEN IF WE DO NOT SEE IT."

⁸It was by faith Abraham obeyed God's call to go to another place God promised to give him. He left his own country, not knowing where he was to go. ⁹It was by faith that he lived like a foreigner in the country God promised to give him. He lived in tents with Isaac and Jacob, who had received that same promise from God. ¹⁰Abraham was waiting for the city" that has real foundations—the city planned and built by God.

¹¹He was too old to have children, and Sarah could not have children. It was by faith that Abraham was made able to become a father, because he trusted God to do what he had promised. ¹²This man was so old he was almost dead, but from him came as many descendants as there are stars in the sky. Like the sand on the seashore, they could not be counted.

¹³All these great people died in faith. They did not get the things that God promised his

**notes**  **10:30** "I . . . them." Quotation from Deuteronomy 32:35.  **10:30** "The Lord . . . people." Quotation from Deuteronomy 32:36; Psalm 135:14.  **11:10 city** The spiritual "city" where God's people live with him. Also called "the heavenly Jerusalem." (See Hebrews 12:22.)

people, but they saw them coming far in the future and were glad. They said they were like visitors and strangers on earth. ¹⁴When people say such things, they show they are looking for a country that will be their own. ¹⁵If they had been thinking about the country they had left, they could have gone back. ¹⁶But they were waiting for a better country—a heavenly country. So God is not ashamed to be called their God, because he has prepared a city for them.

¹⁷It was by faith that Abraham, when God tested him, offered his son Isaac as a sacrifice. God made the promises to Abraham, but Abraham was ready to offer his own son as a sacrifice. ¹⁸God had said, "The descendants I promised you will be from Isaac."ⁿ ¹⁹Abraham believed that God could raise the dead, and really, it was as if Abraham got Isaac back from death.

²⁰It was by faith that Isaac blessed the future of Jacob and Esau. ²¹It was by faith that Jacob, as he was dying, blessed each one of Joseph's sons. Then he worshiped as he leaned on the top of his walking stick.

²²It was by faith that Joseph, while he was dying, spoke about the Israelites leaving Egypt and gave instructions about what to do with his body.

²³It was by faith that Moses' parents hid him for three months after he was born. They saw that Moses was a beautiful baby, and they were not afraid to disobey the king's order.

²⁴It was by faith that Moses, when he grew up, refused to be called the son of the king of Egypt's daughter. ²⁵He chose to suffer with God's people instead of enjoying sin for a short time. ²⁶He thought it was better to suffer for the Christ than to have all the treasures of Egypt, because he was looking for God's reward. ²⁷It was by faith that Moses left Egypt and was not afraid of the king's anger. Moses continued strong as if he could see the God that no one can see. ²⁸It was by faith that Moses prepared the Passover and spread the blood on the doors so the one who brings death would not kill the firstborn sons of Israel.

BIBLE BIOS

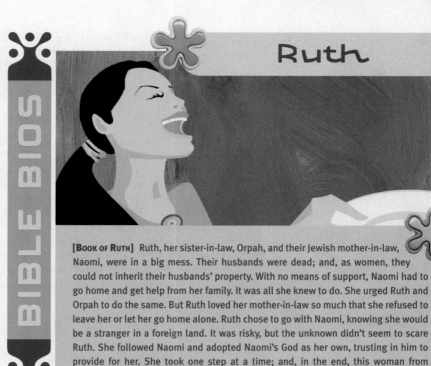

## Ruth

**[BOOK OF RUTH]** Ruth, her sister-in-law, Orpah, and their Jewish mother-in-law, Naomi, were in a big mess. Their husbands were dead; and, as women, they could not inherit their husbands' property. With no means of support, Naomi had to go home and get help from her family. It was all she knew to do. She urged Ruth and Orpah to do the same. But Ruth loved her mother-in-law so much that she refused to leave her or let her go home alone. Ruth chose to go with Naomi, knowing she would be a stranger in a foreign land. It was risky, but the unknown didn't seem to scare Ruth. She followed Naomi and adopted Naomi's God as her own, trusting in him to provide for her. She took one step at a time; and, in the end, this woman from Moab—this non-Israelite—became great-grandmother to King David and part of Jesus' family tree! What an awesome honor for a brave, unselfish risk taker.

²⁹It was by faith that the people crossed the Red Sea as if it were dry land. But when the Egyptians tried it, they were drowned.

³⁰It was by faith that the walls of Jericho fell after the people had marched around them for seven days.

³¹It was by faith that Rahab, the prostitute, welcomed the spies and was not killed with those who refused to obey God.

³²Do I need to give more examples? I do not have time to tell you about Gideon, Barak, Samson, Jephthah, David, Samuel, and the prophets. ³³Through their faith they defeated kingdoms. They did what was right, received God's promises, and shut the mouths of lions. ³⁴They stopped great fires and were saved from being killed with swords. They were weak, and yet were made strong. They were powerful in battle and defeated other armies. ³⁵Women received their dead relatives raised back to life. Others were tortured and refused to accept their freedom so they could be raised from the dead to a better life. ³⁶Some were laughed at

and beaten. Others were put in chains and thrown into prison. ³⁷They were stoned to death, they were cut in half, and they were killed with swords. Some wore the skins of sheep and goats. They were poor, abused, and treated badly. ³⁸The world was not good enough for them! They wandered in deserts and mountains, living in caves and holes in the earth.

³⁹All these people are known for their faith, but none of them received what God had promised. ⁴⁰God planned to give us something better so that they would be made perfect, but only together with us.

## FOLLOW JESUS' EXAMPLE

**12** We have around us many people whose lives tell us what faith means. So let us run the race that is before us and never give up. We should remove from our lives anything that would get in the way and the sin that so easily holds us back. ²Let us look only to Jesus, the One who began our faith

 **11:18** "The descendants . . . Isaac." Quotation from Genesis 21:12.

343

and who makes it perfect. He suffered death on the cross. But he accepted the shame as if it were nothing because of the joy that God put before him. And now he is sitting at the right side of God's throne. ³Think about Jesus' example. He held on while wicked people were doing evil things to him. So do not get tired and stop trying.

### GOD IS LIKE A FATHER

⁴You are struggling against sin, but your struggles have not yet caused you to be killed. ⁵You have forgotten the encouraging words that call you his children:

> "My child, don't think the Lord's discipline
> is worth nothing,
> and don't stop trying when he corrects
> you.
> ⁶The Lord disciplines those he loves,
> and he punishes everyone he accepts as
> his child."                    *Proverbs 3:11-12*

⁷So hold on through your sufferings, because they are like a father's discipline. God is treating you as children. All children are disciplined by their fathers. ⁸If you are never disciplined (and every child must be disciplined), you are not true children. ⁹We have all had fathers here on earth who disciplined us, and we respected them. So it is even more important that we accept discipline from the Father of our spirits so we will have life. ¹⁰Our fathers on earth disciplined us for a short time in the way they thought was best. But God disciplines us to help us, so we can become holy as he is. ¹¹We do not enjoy being disciplined. It is painful, but later, after we have learned from it, we have peace, because we start living in the right way.

## "KEEP ON LOVING EACH OTHER AS BROTHERS AND SISTERS."

### BE CAREFUL HOW YOU LIVE

¹²You have become weak, so make yourselves strong again. ¹³Live in the right way so that you will be saved and your weakness will not cause you to be lost.

¹⁴Try to live in peace with all people, and try to live free from sin. Anyone whose life is not holy will never see the Lord. ¹⁵Be careful that no one fails to receive God's grace and begins to cause trouble among you. A person like that can ruin many of you. ¹⁶Be careful that no one takes part in sexual sin or is like Esau and never thinks about God. As the oldest son, Esau would have received everything from his father, but he sold all that for a single meal. ¹⁷You remember that after Esau did this, he wanted to get his father's blessing, but his father refused. Esau could find no way to change what he had done, even though he wanted the blessing so much that he cried.

¹⁸You have not come to a mountain that can be touched and that is burning with fire. You have not come to darkness, sadness, and storms. ¹⁹You have not come to the noise of a trumpet or to the sound of a voice like the one the people of Israel heard and begged not to hear another word. ²⁰They did not want to hear the command: "If anything, even an animal, touches the mountain, it must be put to death with stones."ⁿ ²¹What they saw was so terrible that Moses said, "I am shaking with fear."ⁿ

²²But you have come to Mount Zion,ⁿ to the city of the living God, the heavenly Jerusalem. You have come to thousands of angels gathered together with joy. ²³You have come to the meeting of God's firstbornⁿ children whose names are written in heaven. You have come to God, the judge of all people, and to the spirits of good people who have been made perfect.

**12:20** "If . . . stones." Quotation from Exodus 19:12-13.    **12:21** "I . . . fear." Quotation from Deuteronomy 9:19.    **12:22 Mount Zion** Another name for Jerusalem, here meaning the spiritual city of God's people.    **12:23 firstborn** The first son born in a Jewish family was given the most important place in the family and received special blessings. All of God's children are like that.

²⁴You have come to Jesus, the One who brought the new agreement from God to his people, and you have come to the sprinkled blood" that has a better message than the blood of Abel."

²⁵So be careful and do not refuse to listen when God speaks. Others refused to listen to him when he warned them on earth, and they did not escape. So it will be worse for us if we refuse to listen to God who warns us from heaven. ²⁶When he spoke before, his voice shook the earth, but now he has promised, "Once again I will shake not only the earth but also the heavens."" ²⁷The words "once again" clearly show us that everything that was made—things that can be shaken—will be destroyed. Only the things that cannot be shaken will remain.

²⁸So let us be thankful, because we have a kingdom that cannot be shaken. We should worship God in a way that pleases him with respect and fear, ²⁹because our God is like a fire that burns things up.

**13** Keep on loving each other as brothers and sisters. ²Remember to welcome strangers, because some who have done this have welcomed angels without knowing it. ³Remember those who are in prison as if you were in prison with them. Remember those who are suffering as if you were suffering with them.

⁴Marriage should be honored by everyone, and husband and wife should keep their marriage pure. God will judge as guilty those who take part in sexual sins. ⁵Keep your lives free from the love of money, and be satisfied with what you have. God has said,

"I will never leave you;
   I will never forget you." *Deuteronomy 31:6*

⁶So we can be sure when we say,

"I will not be afraid, because the Lord is my helper.
   People can't do anything to me."

*Psalm 118:6*

⁷Remember your leaders who taught God's message to you. Remember how they lived and died, and copy their faith. ⁸Jesus Christ is the same yesterday, today, and forever.

⁹Do not let all kinds of strange teachings

## Bible Basics

Jesus taught people during his three years of ministry by telling a lot of stories. We call the stories **parables**, and many describe them as "stories that teach a lesson by comparing two things." When Jesus wanted to teach a new idea, communicate a moral lesson, or reveal a spiritual truth, he planted the idea within the framework of a story his audience would all be able to relate to. For example, in one parable known as "The Son Who Left Home" (Luke 15:11-32), Jesus taught about forgiveness and reconciliation by telling a story about a son who turned his back on his family, partied his inheritance away, then realized how foolish he was and came humbly back home to his dad. Many of the parables spoke about farming and sheep tending, as the area where Jesus preached was primarily poor and rural. Jesus' parables are found in Matthew, Mark, and Luke.

## *Music Reviews*

GROUP: **KUTLESS**   ALBUM: **SEA OF FACES**

*Sea of Faces* is this band's sophomore effort, and it confidently shows no fear that their second album might not be as good as the first. Kutless cuts back on the screaming and rap that made appearances on the first album and adds more melodic riffs and catchy hooks that keep this project rockin' and rollin' along. The title track quickly became a Christian radio favorite, and you can expect more to follow, like the blistering "Treason" and "Let You In" and the quieter "All Alone."

**WHY IT ROCKS: KUTLESS AVOIDS THE SOPHOMORE SLUMP WITH SPIRITUAL SONGS THAT STIR THE SOUL AND ROCK THE PARTY.**

**12:24 sprinkled blood** The blood of Jesus' death.   **12:24 Abel** The son of Adam and Eve, who was killed by his brother Cain (Genesis 4:8).   **12:26 "Once . . . heavens."** Quotation from Haggai 2:6, 21.

## Radical Faith:

### Hebrews 12:1-2

God hasn't put you on earth to just sit around and wait for heaven. Heaven's definitely something to look forward to; but every moment that you're breathing, you are on a mission to live out what God wants. And you should get rid of whatever gets in the way of that purpose. You've got to downsize, if not remove, anything that receives so much of your attention that it drains your hunger for God. What slows you down, robs your time, or soaks up your devotion and affection? Whether you need to change direction completely or need strength to stay on track, God is the One to turn to. Let him be the passion of your life. Verse 2 encourages you to "look only to Jesus." Plant yourself in the Word—live in it, day in and day out. Grow in your understanding of Jesus and what his heart is like. Growing closer to him and living in obedience to him are choices you have to make every day. Don't dwell only on yourself or your circumstances, but pray for strength and courage. Jesus will strengthen and lead you. Keep your eyes glued to him.

lead you into the wrong way. Your hearts should be strengthened by God's grace, not by obeying rules about foods, which do not help those who obey them.

[10]We have a sacrifice, but the priests who serve in the Holy Tent cannot eat from it. [11]The high priest carries the blood of animals into the Most Holy Place where he offers this blood for sins. But the bodies of the animals are burned outside the camp. [12]So Jesus also suffered outside the city to make his people holy with his own blood. [13]So let us go to Jesus outside the camp, holding on as he did when we are abused.

[14]Here on earth we do not have a city that lasts forever, but we are looking for the city that we will have in the future. [15]So through Jesus let us always offer to God our sacrifice of praise, coming from lips that speak his name. [16]Do not forget to do good to others, and share with them, because such sacrifices please God.

[17]Obey your leaders and act under their authority. They are watching over you, because they are responsible for your souls. Obey them so that they will do this work with joy, not sadness. It will not help you to make their work hard.

[18]Pray for us. We are sure that we have a clear conscience, because we always want to do the right thing. [19]I especially beg you to pray so that God will send me back to you soon.

[20-21]I pray that the God of peace will give you every good thing you need so you can do what he wants. God raised from the dead our Lord Jesus, the Great Shepherd of the sheep, because of the blood of his death. His blood began the eternal agreement that God made with his people. I pray that God will do in us what pleases him, through Jesus Christ, and to him be glory forever and ever. Amen.

[22]My brothers and sisters, I beg you to listen patiently to this message I have written to encourage you, because it is not very long. [23]I want you to know that our brother Timothy has been let out of prison. If he arrives soon, we will both come to see you.

[24]Greet all your leaders and all of God's people. Those from Italy send greetings to you.

[25]Grace be with you all.

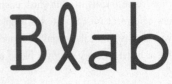

**Q:** I always blurt out without thinking. What are some ways that I can learn to think before I speak?

**A:** Copy down all the Bible verses you can find about the tongue and put them where you will see them often. Memorize some, and ask God to work in your life in this area. Develop a habit of counting to ten mentally before you open your mouth. This new habit should help you think before you blurt.

**Q:** My mom says girls should not call guys. I think she's old-fashioned. Who is right?

**A:** You both are. In this day of cell phones and instant messaging, guys and girls communicate back and forth much more freely than in the past. But mom is right when it comes to guys you're crushing on. Guys are created to be the pursuers. They want to come after you. Putting yourself in their face all the time by calling them is a definite turn-off and can be downright pushy. As a general rule, guys will respect you more if they do the calling.

**Q:** My mom gave me a cell phone to use when I am visiting my dad and stepmom, but my dad says he doesn't want me to have a phone. What do I do?

**A:** Thank your mom for the phone, but let her know about the rules at dad's house. If mom still insists that you use it, tell your dad and ask him to take it up with her. Or decide with dad where he wants you to keep the phone at his house, so he knows you aren't trying to break his rules.

**V**isualize a screen door on a submarine. The late Christian artist Rich Mullins used this word-picture to show the uselessness of faithless works, but the idea behind his words could have been pulled straight from the heart of James. While Paul is passionate about teaching people how to be made right with God through faith, James reminds us that we should produce good deeds to back up our faith.

# James

### Faith in Action

This short letter by James packs quite a punch. It's full of strong words and powerful images that really sink into your soul. In just five chapters, James offers insight into temptation, pure religion, respect for all people, caring for widows and orphans, controlling our speech, not judging others, the power of prayer, and greed. He wants us to understand that when we truly encounter God, we'll want to serve him in practical, tangible ways. People who love God desire to share that with everyone. James tells us exactly how we can do that.

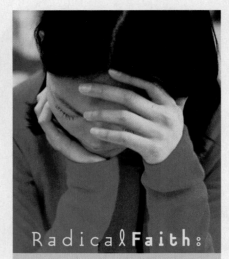

## Radical Faith:

# James 1:2-4

Imagine that you get a letter from a friend, and it starts something like this: "You're going to be having hard times soon, but count yourself blessed." Not such a great letter, right? You'd probably be pretty confused and worried. But that's exactly how this letter from James begins. James isn't meaning to come off cold; he's just telling the truth. You want to grow in your faith and get closer with God, right? Well, in order for you to grow, sometimes trials have to come to test your faith. And when you rely on your faith in those times, your faith becomes stronger. We tend to try to do things on our own when there are no trials in sight. But things of lasting worth and great value don't always come when things are comfortable. They come when you patiently and relentlessly trudge through the hardest days. James says to "be full of joy" when you're suffering because it'll bring all that really matters into perspective. You'll be closer to God. You'll be more like God and reflect his love. James is right! You can find joy in what comes from the hard stuff, because God is in the process of blessing you with the good stuff.

1 From James, a servant of God and of the Lord Jesus Christ.

To all of God's people who are scattered everywhere in the world:

Greetings.

## FAITH AND WISDOM

[2]My brothers and sisters,[n] when you have many kinds of troubles, you should be full of joy, [3]because you know that these troubles test your faith, and this will give you patience. [4]Let your patience show itself perfectly in what you do. Then you will be perfect and complete and will have everything you need. [5]But if any of you needs wisdom, you should ask God for it. He is generous and enjoys giving to all people, so he will give you wisdom. [6]But when you ask God, you must believe and not doubt. Anyone who doubts is like a wave in the sea, blown up and down by the wind. [7-8]Such doubters are thinking two different things at the same time, and they cannot decide about anything they do. They should not think they will receive anything from the Lord.

## TRUE RICHES

[9]Believers who are poor should be proud, because God has made them spiritually rich. [10]Those who are rich should be proud, because God has shown them that they are spiritually poor. The rich will die like a wild flower in the grass. [11]The sun rises with burning heat and dries up the plants. The flower falls off, and its beauty is gone. In the same way the rich will die while they are still taking care of business.

## TEMPTATION IS NOT FROM GOD

[12]When people are tempted and still continue strong, they should be happy. After they have proved their faith, God will reward them with life forever. God promised this to all those who love him. [13]When people are tempted, they should not say, "God is tempting me." Evil cannot tempt God, and God himself does not tempt anyone. [14]But people are tempted when their own evil desire leads them away and traps them. [15]This desire leads to sin, and then the sin grows and brings death.

## Promises:

# James 1:5

You have to make a lot of decisions and solve a lot of problems in your life from day to day. And sometimes they aren't easy problems. What to wear today? Easy. What to wear today for your school picture that will be forever burned into yearbook history? Harder.

But what happens when you're faced with a really serious problem that could involve other people and may have great consequences in your life? You can hopefully find a good friend or a trusted adult to confide in and one who will give you good advice. But better than that, you can pray and ask God for wisdom to help you in any given situation. Being completely holy, just, and omnipotent (look it up), God has more wisdom than anyone here on earth could ever have. And better yet, he loves giving his wisdom to us when we ask for it. Could you have a better confidant and advice-giver than God? No way. Go to him today with your problems—big ones or small ones—and pray that he would give you wisdom and discernment to make good decisions in your life.

notes    **1:2 brothers and sisters** Although the Greek text says "brothers" here and throughout this book, James's words were meant for the entire church, including men and women.

[16]My dear brothers and sisters, do not be fooled about this. [17]Every good action and every perfect gift is from God. These good gifts come down from the Creator of the sun, moon, and stars, who does not change like their shifting shadows. [18]God decided to give us life through the word of truth so we might be the most important of all the things he made.

### LISTENING AND OBEYING

[19]My dear brothers and sisters, always be willing to listen and slow to speak. Do not become angry easily, [20]because anger will not help you live the right kind of life God wants. [21]So put out of your life every evil thing and every kind of wrong. Then in gentleness accept God's teaching that is planted in your hearts, which can save you.

## relationships

"Where jealousy and selfishness are, there will be confusion and every kind of evil" (James 3:16). Remember that verse from 1 Corinthians 13 that says that love is not jealous? James 3:16 tells you exactly what happens when envy enters your relationships. Do you act ugly when other girls talk to your boyfriend? How does your guy treat you if he sees a guy talking to you? If either of you has a jealous streak that causes you to be angry or hateful, take it up with the Lord.

[22]Do what God's teaching says; when you only listen and do nothing, you are fooling yourselves. [23]Those who hear God's teaching and do nothing are like people who look at themselves in a mirror. [24]They see their faces and then go away and quickly forget what they looked like. [25]But the truly happy people are those who carefully study God's perfect law that makes people free, and they continue to study it. They do not forget what they heard, but they obey what God's teaching says. Those who do this will be made happy.

## "DO NOT BECOME ANGRY EASILY, BECAUSE ANGER WILL NOT HELP YOU LIVE THE RIGHT KIND OF LIFE GOD WANTS."

### THE TRUE WAY TO WORSHIP GOD

[26]People who think they are religious but say things they should not say are just fooling themselves. Their "religion" is worth nothing. [27]Religion that God accepts as pure and without fault is this: caring for orphans or widows who need help, and keeping yourself free from the world's evil influence.

### LOVE ALL PEOPLE

2 My dear brothers and sisters, as believers in our glorious Lord Jesus Christ, never think some people are more important than others. [2]Suppose someone comes into your church meeting wearing nice clothes and a gold ring. At the same time a poor person comes in wearing old, dirty clothes. [3]You show special attention to the one wearing nice clothes and say, "Please, sit here in this good seat." But you say to the poor person, "Stand over there," or, "Sit on the floor by my feet." [4]What are you doing? You are making some people more important than others, and with evil thoughts you are deciding that one person is better.

## Promises

# James 1:17

What do you think are some of the best things in life? You can probably think of lots. Good friends. Laughter. Discounts at your favorite store. Football games in the fall. Love. Jumping on a trampoline. A great pair of jeans. Eating cookie dough. Getting asked out by that special guy. The way your grandmother's kitchen smells. Waves crashing on a sunny beach.

We like to think about the good things in life, don't we? Several years ago, a book called *14,000 Things to Be Happy About* was published. The book is simply full of lists of things that make the author happy on a day-to-day basis, such as "free kittens," "knowing the absolutely right way to do something," "finger paintings," and about 13,997 other random items. It's good to think about things that make us happy. And when we do, we can thank God, who is the giver of them and of all good things. He loves for us to be happy and to appreciate his creation. Thank God right now for the things in your life that make you happy; and as you go about your day, remember him and how much he loves you! You make him happy because you are his creation.

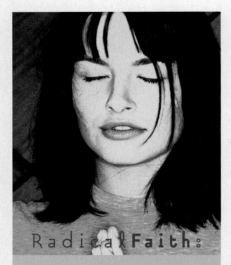

# Radical Faith:

## James 4:7-8

"Give yourselves completely to God." Completely? How about just enough so you feel like a good person? Or just a little, so you don't feel like a weirdo compared to some of your friends? Well OK, let's say you do just that. You give some of yourself to God and give the rest to your cool image, to your friends, or to having fun. Meanwhile, there's an enemy in the picture. Peter says he "goes around like a roaring lion looking for someone to eat" (1 Peter 5:8). Would you want to be near a roaring lion and only partly protected by God? Um, no thanks. You may easily find yourself bombarded by the devil's evil schemes (that are meant to hurt you) and surrounded by temptations to turn away from God. Refuse to give in to the enemy. Draw near to God—give yourself entirely to him—and he will fill you with his goodness and power. Resist the messages and impulses you encounter that are not from God, and the devil can't do much to defeat you. Use Scripture to fight him off. Jesus did that in Luke 4. God's power is greater than Satan's. It's your choice. Tell the devil to get lost.

5Listen, my dear brothers and sisters! God chose the poor in the world to be rich with faith and to receive the kingdom God promised to those who love him. 6But you show no respect to the poor. The rich are always trying to control your lives. They are the ones who take you to court. 7And they are the ones who speak against Jesus, who owns you.

8This royal law is found in the Scriptures: "Love your neighbor as you love yourself."[n] If you obey this law, you are doing right. 9But if you treat one person as being more important than another, you are sinning. You are guilty of breaking God's law. 10A person who follows all of God's law but fails to obey even one command is guilty of breaking all the commands in that law. 11The same God who said, "You must not be guilty of adultery,"[n] also said, "You must not murder anyone."[n] So if you do not take part in adultery but you murder someone, you are guilty of breaking all of God's law. 12In everything you say and do, remember that you will be judged by the law that makes people free. 13So you must show mercy to others, or God will not show mercy to you when he judges you. But the person who shows mercy can stand without fear at the judgment.

## FAITH AND GOOD WORKS

14My brothers and sisters, if people say they have faith, but do nothing, their faith is worth nothing. Can faith like that save them? 15A brother or sister in Christ might need clothes or food. 16If you say to that person, "God be with you! I hope you stay warm and get plenty to eat," but you do not give what that person needs, your words are worth nothing. 17In the same way, faith that is alone—that does nothing—is dead.

18Someone might say, "You have faith, but I have deeds." Show me your faith without doing anything, and I will show you my faith by what I do. 19You believe there is one God. Good! But the demons believe that, too, and they tremble with fear.

20You foolish person! Must you be shown that faith that does nothing is worth nothing? 21Abraham, our ancestor, was made right with God by what he did when he offered his son Isaac on the altar. 22So you see that Abraham's faith and the things he did worked together. His faith was made perfect by what he did. 23This shows the full meaning of the Scripture that says: "Abraham believed God, and God accepted Abraham's faith, and that faith made him right with God."[n] And Abraham was called God's friend.[n] 24So you see that people are made right with God by what they do, not by faith only.

25Another example is Rahab, a prostitute, who was made right with God by something she did. She welcomed the spies into her home and helped them escape by a different road.

26Just as a person's body that does not have a spirit is dead, so faith that does nothing is dead!

## beauty secret

### Laughter

It's said that laughter is the best medicine—and it's really true. Whether you're with a group of friends or with strangers, look for ways to make people laugh. Your lightheartedness will spread joy to others and allow the beauty of God to shine through you.

notes: **2:8 "Love . . . yourself."** Quotation from Leviticus 19:18. **2:11 "You . . . adultery."** Quotation from Exodus 20:14 and Deuteronomy 5:18. **2:11 "You . . . anyone."** Quotation from Exodus 20:13 and Deuteronomy 5:17. **2:23 "Abraham . . . God."** Quotation from Genesis 15:6. **2:23 God's friend** These words about Abraham are found in 2 Chronicles 20:7 and Isaiah 41:8.

## CONTROLLING THE THINGS WE SAY

3 My brothers and sisters, not many of you should become teachers, because you know that we who teach will be judged more strictly. ²We all make many mistakes. If people never said anything wrong, they would be perfect and able to control their entire selves, too. ³When we put bits into the mouths of horses to make them obey us, we can control their whole bodies. ⁴Also a ship is very big, and it is pushed by strong winds. But a very small rudder controls that big ship, making it go wherever the pilot wants. ⁵It is the same with the tongue. It is a small part of the body, but it brags about great things.

A big forest fire can be started with only a little flame. ⁶And the tongue is like a fire. It is a whole world of evil among the parts of our bodies. The tongue spreads its evil through the whole body. The tongue is set on fire by hell, and it starts a fire that influences all of life. ⁷People can tame every kind of wild animal, bird, reptile, and fish, and they have tamed them, ⁸but no one can tame the tongue. It is wild and evil and full of deadly poison. ⁹We use our tongues to praise our Lord and Father, but then we curse people, whom God made like himself. ¹⁰Praises and curses come from the same mouth! My brothers and sisters, this should not happen. ¹¹Do good and bad water flow from the same spring? ¹²My brothers and sisters, can a fig tree make olives, or can a grapevine make figs? No! And a well full of salty water cannot give good water.

## TRUE WISDOM

¹³Are there those among you who are truly wise and understanding? Then they should show it by living right and doing good things with a gentleness that comes from wisdom. ¹⁴But if you are selfish and have bitter jealousy in your hearts, do not brag. Your bragging is a lie that hides the truth. ¹⁵That kind of "wisdom" does not come from God but from the world. It is not spiritual; it is from the devil. ¹⁶Where jealousy and selfishness are, there will be confusion and every kind of evil. ¹⁷But the wisdom that comes from God is first of all pure, then peaceful, gentle, and easy to please. This wisdom is always ready to help those who are troubled and

## BIBLE BIOS

# Sarah

[GENESIS 11–23] Sarah was desperate. Well past the baby-bearing years and without any children, she was worried that God wasn't holding up his end of the deal. After all, her husband Abraham was supposed to be the father of a great nation. So Sarah decided to try to help God out. She sent her maid, Hagar, to sleep with Abraham, and *voilà!* Ishmael was born. God came back to Sarah—who was then ninety years old—and he assured her that he was still faithful. Sarah laughed out loud at the thought. But God made good on his promise; and she gave birth to Isaac, whose Hebrew name sounds the same as the word for "he laughed." No doubt God had a sense of humor too, proving to Sarah that what seems impossible—and even what we've grown tired of hoping for—is more than possible with him.

# LEARN I+ & LIVE I+

**James 1:27**
**Learn It:** You worship God when you care for widows and orphans and when you keep yourself free from the world's influence.
**Live It:** Consider adopting a Compassion child. Check out www.compassion.com for more information.

**James 3:6**
**Learn It:** The tongue can spread bad things like a wildfire. It starts a fire that influences all of life.
**Live It:** Pray daily that God will help you control your tongue, and take a few seconds to think before you speak.

**James 5:16**
**Learn It:** Confess your sins to each other, and pray for each other.
**Live It:** Ask a trusted friend to be your accountability partner. Tell that friend when you mess up, and pray about it together.

## top 10
### random ways to give yourself a break

**10** Go to bed early.

**9** Light pretty candles.

**8** Go for a walk and observe nature around you.

**7** Give your worries to God.

**6** Work out for 30 minutes daily.

**5** Schedule a day off to play.

**4** Have someone massage your shoulders or scalp.

**3** Inhale and exhale deeply ten times.

**2** Get your nails done.

**1** Take a picnic to a park or beach.

to do good for others. It is always fair and honest. [18]People who work for peace in a peaceful way plant a good crop of right-living.

## "COME NEAR TO GOD, AND GOD WILL COME NEAR TO YOU."

### GIVE YOURSELVES TO GOD

4 Do you know where your fights and arguments come from? They come from the selfish desires that war within you. [2]You want things, but you do not have them. So you are ready to kill and are jealous of other people, but you still cannot get what you want. So you argue and fight. You do not get what you want, because you do not ask God. [3]Or when you ask, you do not receive because the reason you ask is wrong. You want things so you can use them for your own pleasures.

[4]So, you are not loyal to God! You should know that loving the world is the same as hating God. Anyone who wants to be a friend of the world becomes God's enemy. [5]Do you think the Scripture means nothing that says, "The Spirit that God made to live in us wants us for himself alone"? [6]But God gives us even more grace, as the Scripture says,

"God is against the proud,
but he gives grace to the humble."

*Proverbs 3:34*

[7]So give yourselves completely to God. Stand against the devil, and the devil will run from you. [8]Come near to God, and God will come near to you. You sinners, clean sin out of your lives. You who are trying to follow God and the world at the same time, make your thinking pure. [9]Be sad, cry, and weep! Change your laughter into crying and your joy into sadness. [10]Don't be too proud in the Lord's presence, and he will make you great.

### YOU ARE NOT THE JUDGE

[11]Brothers and sisters, do not tell evil lies about each other. If you speak against your fel-

low believers or judge them, you are judging and speaking against the law they follow. And when you are judging the law, you are no longer a follower of the law. You have become a judge. [12]God is the only Lawmaker and Judge. He is the only One who can save and destroy. So it is not right for you to judge your neighbor.

### LET GOD PLAN YOUR LIFE

[13]Some of you say, "Today or tomorrow we will go to some city. We will stay there a year, do business, and make money." [14]But you do not know what will happen tomorrow! Your life is like a mist. You can see it for a short time, but then it goes away. [15]So you should say, "If the Lord wants, we will live and do this or that." [16]But now you are proud and you brag. All of this bragging is wrong. [17]Anyone who knows the right thing to do, but does not do it, is sinning.

### A WARNING TO THE RICH

5 You rich people, listen! Cry and be very sad because of the troubles that are coming to you. [2]Your riches have rotted, and your clothes have been eaten by moths. [3]Your gold and silver have rusted, and that rust will be a proof that you were wrong. It will eat your bodies like fire. You saved your treasure for the last days. [4]The pay you did not give the work-

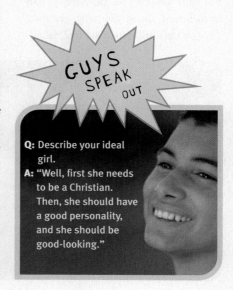

### GUYS SPEAK OUT

**Q:** Describe your ideal girl.
**A:** "Well, first she needs to be a Christian. Then, she should have a good personality, and she should be good-looking."

**notes** 4:5 "The Spirit . . . alone?" These words may be from Exodus 20:5.

ers who mowed your fields cries out against you, and the cries of the workers have been heard by the Lord All-Powerful. [5]Your life on earth was full of rich living and pleasing yourselves with everything you wanted. You made yourselves fat, like an animal ready to be killed. [6]You have judged guilty and then murdered innocent people, who were not against you.

## Be Patient

[7]Brothers and sisters, be patient until the Lord comes again. A farmer patiently waits for his valuable crop to grow from the earth and for it to receive the autumn and spring rains. [8]You, too, must be patient. Do not give up hope, because the Lord is coming soon. [9]Brothers and sisters, do not complain against each other or you will be judged guilty. And the Judge is ready to come! [10]Brothers and sisters, follow the example of the prophets who spoke for the Lord. They suffered many hard things, but they were patient. [11]We say they are happy because they did not give up. You have heard about Job's patience, and you know the Lord's purpose for him in the end. You know the Lord is full of mercy and is kind.

## Be Careful What You Say

[12]My brothers and sisters, above all, do not use an oath when you make a promise. Don't use the name of heaven, earth, or anything else to prove what you say. When you mean yes, say only yes, and when you mean no, say only no so you will not be judged guilty.

## The Power of Prayer

[13]Anyone who is having troubles should pray. Anyone who is happy should sing praises. [14]Anyone who is sick should call the church's elders. They should pray for and pour oil on the person[n] in the name of the Lord. [15]And the prayer that is said with faith will make the sick person well; the Lord will heal that person. And if the person has sinned, the sins will be forgiven. [16]Confess your sins to each other and pray for each other so God can heal you. When a believing person prays, great things happen. [17]Elijah was a human being just like us. He prayed that it would not rain, and it did not rain on the land for three and a half years! [18]Then Elijah prayed again, and the rain came

**DIDYA KNOW**

**THE TOP 5 WORRIES OF TEEN GIRLS: 1) BEING ATTACKED WITH A WEAPON, 2) BEING FORCED TO DO SOMETHING SEXUAL, 3) GETTING A DISEASE, 4) GETTING IN A CAR ACCIDENT, AND 5) BEING GOSSIPED ABOUT.** WWW.HARRISINTERACTIVE.COM

down from the sky, and the land produced crops again.

## Saving a Soul

[19]My brothers and sisters, if one of you wanders away from the truth, and someone helps that person come back, [20]remember this: Anyone who brings a sinner back from the wrong way will save that sinner's soul from death and will cause many sins to be forgiven.

**5:14 pour oil on the person** Oil was used in the name of the Lord as a sign that the person was now set apart for God's special attention and care.

# Peter, one of the original 12 followers

of Christ, was often considered the spokesman for the group. Jesus himself gave Peter (originally known as Simon) his name, which means "stone" or "rock." Peter was a strong, committed believer, always ready to defend Jesus, whether with words or with a sword. This passion, although sometimes misguided, fueled Peter's faith and made his ministry successful.

# 1 Peter

## Encouragement for Persecuted Believers

This first letter from Peter in Rome was to believers in Asia Minor. Fires in Rome (possibly set by its own emperor, Nero) had devastated the Roman culture, destroying temples, shrines, and homes. Nero, sensing the resentment of the people was mounting, chose Christians as his scapegoat, blaming them for setting the fires. It didn't take long for hostility toward believers to rise to unbearable levels, so Peter was inspired to write this letter to teach fellow Christians how to live victoriously in the midst of persecution.

And how do we as Christians deal with animosity? Peter's answer is to focus on Christ as our model. Jesus, who suffered every pain and grief that has ever been known to man, maintained grace, dignity, and mercy in the midst of his abuse and humiliation on the cross. He is our role model—especially when we're facing persecution.

1 From Peter, an apostle of Jesus Christ.

To God's chosen people who are away from their homes and are scattered all around the countries of Pontus, Galatia, Cappadocia, Asia, and Bithynia. ²God planned long ago to choose you by making you his holy people, which is the Spirit's work. God wanted you to obey him and to be made clean by the blood of the death of Jesus Christ.

Grace and peace be yours more and more.

## we Have a Living Hope

³Praise be to the God and Father of our Lord Jesus Christ. In God's great mercy he has caused us to be born again into a living hope, because Jesus Christ rose from the dead. ⁴Now we hope for the blessings God has for his children. These blessings, which cannot be destroyed or be spoiled or lose their beauty, are kept in heaven for you. ⁵God's power protects you through your faith until salvation is shown to you at the end of time. ⁶This makes you very happy, even though now for a short time different kinds of troubles may make you sad. ⁷These troubles come to prove that your faith is pure. This purity of faith is worth more than gold, which can be proved to be pure by fire but will ruin. But the purity of your faith will bring you praise and glory and honor when Jesus Christ is shown to you. ⁸You have not seen Christ, but still you love him. You cannot see him now, but you believe in him. So you are filled with a joy that cannot be explained, a joy full of glory. ⁹And you are receiving the goal of your faith—the salvation of your souls.

¹⁰The prophets searched carefully and tried to learn about this salvation. They prophesied about the grace that was coming to you. ¹¹The Spirit of Christ was in the prophets, telling in advance about the sufferings of Christ and about the glory that would follow those sufferings. The prophets tried to learn about what the Spirit was showing them, when those things would happen, and what the world would be like at that time. ¹²It was shown them that their service was not for themselves but for you, when they told about the truths you have now heard. Those who preached the Good News to you told you those things with the help of the Holy Spirit who was sent from heaven—things into which angels desire to look.

## a Call to Holy Living

¹³So prepare your minds for service and have self-control. All your hope should be for the gift of grace that will be yours when Jesus Christ is shown to you. ¹⁴Now that you are obedient children of God do not live as you did in the past. You did not understand, so you did the evil things you wanted. ¹⁵But be holy in all you do, just as God, the One who called you, is holy. ¹⁶It is written in the Scriptures: "You must be holy, because I am holy."ⁿ

## "SO WHILE YOU ARE HERE ON EARTH, YOU SHOULD LIVE WITH RESPECT FOR GOD."

¹⁷You pray to God and call him Father, and he judges each person's work equally. So while you are here on earth, you should live with respect for God. ¹⁸You know that in the past you were living in a worthless way, a way passed down from the people who lived before you. But you were saved from that useless life. You were bought, not with something that ruins like gold or silver, ¹⁹but with the precious blood of Christ, who was like a pure and perfect lamb. ²⁰Christ was chosen before the world was made, but he was shown to the world in these last times for your sake. ²¹Through Christ you believe in God, who raised Christ from the dead and gave him glory. So your faith and your hope are in God.

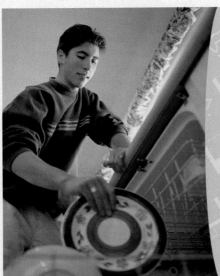

## ⊙ ➡ CHECK IT OUT

### MAKE A DIFFERENCE DAY

For more than a decade, volunteers have been joining together on the fourth Saturday of October to make a difference in their local communities on *USA Weekend Magazine's* Make A Difference Day.

Make A Difference Day is the most encompassing national day of helping others and is a celebration of neighbors helping neighbors. In 2003, 3 million people cared enough about their local friends and neighbors to volunteer on that day and accomplish thousands of projects in hundreds of towns.

Projects can be big or small—for a neighborhood or a single neighbor. Past projects have included delivering winter coats and pairs of gloves, giving hats to young cancer patients, cleaning and improving homes in a local neighborhood, and building a new playground. Look around your community and see what needs to be done.

*Get involved by visiting* **www.usaweekend.com/diffday/**.

**1:16** "You must be . . . holy." Quotation from Leviticus 11:45; 19:2; 20:7.

# Blab

**Q:** My mom wants me to end my relationship with my dad when I am 18. She says he is abusive, but I have never really seen that. She has sort of given me an ultimatum—him or her. I love both my parents. What do I do?

**A:** Sounds like your mom has a real control issue and maybe fears that you love your dad more. Do not let anyone bully or threaten you into doing the wrong thing, and dissing your dad is definitely wrong. Pray that God will give you the right words to say to your mom to reassure her that you will always love her. Tell her you need to have a relationship with her and your dad. Be loving, but firm.

**Q:** My extended family is always fighting, and holidays are a nightmare. We're all supposed to get together at Thanksgiving, and I don't think I can take it. What should I do?

**A:** Be the peacemaker. You may not be able to control everyone else, but you can control yourself. And you can help steer relatives who don't get along away from each other. Pray for grace before any stressful family occasion.

**Q:** I have been in foster care for most of my life, and I find it really hard to get close to people. I want to learn to have lasting relationships, but I have never really seen one. How can I learn?

**A:** Talk to your youth pastor, pastor, or a counselor about your concerns. See if they can find healthy families and married couples that you can spend time with. Ask questions, and read good books about relationships. Pray that God will help you let down your guard.

22Now that you have made your souls pure by obeying the truth, you can have true love for your Christian brothers and sisters.ⁿ So love each other deeply with all your heart. 23You have been born again, and this new life did not come from something that dies, but from something that cannot die. You were born again through God's living message that continues forever. 24The Scripture says,

> "All people are like the grass,
> and all their glory is like the flowers of
> the field.
> The grass dies and the flowers fall,
> 25 but the word of the Lord will live
> forever."          *Isaiah 40:6-8*

And this is the word that was preached to you.

## JESUS IS THE LIVING STONE

2 So then, rid yourselves of all evil, all lying, hypocrisy, jealousy, and evil speech. 2As newborn babies want milk, you should want the pure and simple teaching. By it you can grow up and be saved, 3because you have already examined and seen how good the Lord is.

4Come to the Lord Jesus, the "stone"ⁿ that lives. The people of the world did not want this stone, but he was the stone God chose, and he was precious. 5You also are like living stones, so let yourselves be used to build a spiritual temple—to be holy priests who offer spiritual sacrifices to God. He will accept those sacrifices through Jesus Christ. 6The Scripture says:

> "I will put a stone in the ground in
> Jerusalem.
> Everything will be built on this
> important and precious rock.
> Anyone who trusts in him
> will never be disappointed."    *Isaiah 28:16*

7This stone is worth much to you who believe. But to the people who do not believe,

> "the stone that the builders rejected
> has become the cornerstone."
>           *Psalm 118:22*

8Also, he is

> "a stone that causes people to stumble,
> a rock that makes them fall."    *Isaiah 8:14*

## Radical Faith:

# 1 Peter 3:8-9

What do you do when someone is mean, belittling, or cold toward you? Or when someone's actions really bother you or make you jealous? Remember what God is like, and let his character shape your response. "He is kind even to people who are ungrateful and full of sin. Show mercy, just as your Father shows mercy" (Luke 6:35-36). You have been shown miraculous mercy from God, so why wouldn't you give grace to other people? Give what God gave to you when you didn't deserve it. Give love, acceptance, warmth, and kindness to the girl at school you don't like or who doesn't like you. To "bless" someone literally translates to mean to "speak well" of someone—saying kind things toward the people who are the furthest thing from friendly to you. Jesus even goes beyond being nice toward people who hurt you and says to pray for them, too (Matthew 5:44). Pray for the people you feel negativity toward—even when it's hard—because they're valuable to God. He loves them and they are works-in-progress, just like you. If you're having a really hard time with this issue, be honest with God. Let him help you manage your feelings and handle your behavior toward others his way.

**1:22 brothers and sisters** Although the Greek text says "brothers" here and throughout this book, Peter's words were meant for the entire church, including men and women.   **2:4 "stone"** The most important stone in God's spiritual temple or house (his people).

# LEARN I+ & LIVE I+

**1 Peter 2:11**
**Learn It:** Christians are like foreigners and strangers in the world. Avoid evil things your body wants that will hurt your soul.
**Live It:** The next time you do not feel like you fit in, keep this verse in mind.

**1 Peter 3:9**
**Learn It:** Do not insult someone who insults you or pay them back when they hurt you.
**Live It:** Pray for those who are mean to you, and count to ten before you answer any insults they throw at you.

**2 Peter 2:1**
**Learn It:** There will be false teachers who teach things that are wrong.
**Live It:** Be careful that the spiritual leaders you follow make it their practice to follow God's Word without adding to or subtracting from it.

They stumble because they do not obey what God says, which is what God planned to happen to them.

⁹But you are a chosen people, royal priests, a holy nation, a people for God's own possession. You were chosen to tell about the wonderful acts of God, who called you out of darkness into his wonderful light. ¹⁰At one time you were not a people, but now you are God's people. In the past you had never received mercy, but now you have received God's mercy.

## LIVE FOR GOD

¹¹Dear friends, you are like foreigners and strangers in this world. I beg you to avoid the evil things your bodies want to do that fight against your soul. ¹²People who do not believe are living all around you and might say that you are doing wrong. Live such good lives that they will see the good things you do and will give glory to God on the day when Christ comes again.

## YIELD TO EVERY HUMAN AUTHORITY

¹³For the Lord's sake, yield to the people who have authority in this world: the king, who is the highest authority, ¹⁴and the leaders who are sent by him to punish those who do

# Changed Lives

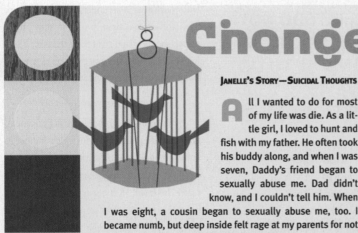

### JANELLE'S STORY—SUICIDAL THOUGHTS

All I wanted to do for most of my life was die. As a little girl, I loved to hunt and fish with my father. He often took his buddy along, and when I was seven, Daddy's friend began to sexually abuse me. Dad didn't know, and I couldn't tell him. When I was eight, a cousin began to sexually abuse me, too. I became numb, but deep inside felt rage at my parents for not knowing what was happening to me. By the time I was nine, I began to push my family away. I became obsessed with death and thoughts of suicide. I read everything I could find about death, even obituaries in the newspaper, and tried overdosing on many occasions. I stuck it out through high school, and on the night I turned 18, I sneaked out and moved in with my best friend's family. My parents were angry, and my mother told everyone in town that I was a wild child. I enrolled in Christian college because I had a scholarship there and because my best friend was going there, but my troubles were not over. I tried to kill myself again. Again, I failed. I began drinking heavily and decided to try one more time to die. Then, my roommate asked me to go to a Christian concert, and I went along. I heard about a Christian ministry that offered hope to young women like me. I was like, "Yeah, right," but I was intrigued enough to fill out an application. To my surprise, I was accepted right away, which foiled my suicide plans. When I got there, I began to experience real love for the first time. Slowly, I began to trust. I tested my boundaries, but they still loved me. That helped me heal. I began to devour God's Word and really committed my life to him. I realized how much he loved me. Now I work as a residential supervisor in the program, so that I can share my story with other girls like me.

*To find help in overcoming suicidal thoughts visit www.aacc.net, www.newlife.com, or www.christianprogramsforteens.com. For information about residential care for females, visit mercyministries.com. (Names have been changed for the sake of privacy. Janelle tells her story after going through biblically based counseling with Mercy Ministries.)*

# Music Reviews

**GROUP:** THIRD DAY

**ALBUM:** THIRD DAY (CLASSIC HIT)

This Atlanta-based rock band took years to become an "overnight" sensation, combining singer Mac Powell's distinctive vocals with the band's sizzling, Southern-style rock 'n' roll. This 1996 debut album holds up well, with heavy-hitters "Consuming Fire" (the first song the guys ever wrote together) and "Blackbird," as well as beautiful ballads "Thief" and "Praise Song." One of the highlights of the album is still "Love Song," a delicate tune that portrays Jesus singing about his awesome love for us.

**WHY IT ROCKS: GREAT GUITARS AND SOUTHERN FLAVOR FROM GUYS WHO LOVE GOD—MMM, MMM GOOD!**

wrong and to praise those who do right. ¹⁵It is God's desire that by doing good you should stop foolish people from saying stupid things about you. ¹⁶Live as free people, but do not use your freedom as an excuse to do evil. Live as servants of God. ¹⁷Show respect for all people: Love the brothers and sisters of God's family, respect God, honor the king.

## FOLLOW CHRIST'S example

¹⁸Slaves, yield to the authority of your masters with all respect, not only those who are good and kind, but also those who are dishonest. ¹⁹A person might have to suffer even when it is unfair, but if he thinks of God and stands the pain, God is pleased. ²⁰If you are beaten for doing wrong, there is no reason to praise you for being patient in your punishment. But if you suffer for doing good, and you are patient, then God is pleased. ²¹This is what you were called to do, because Christ suffered for you and gave you an example to follow. So you should do as he did.

²²"He had never sinned,
and he had never lied."        *Isaiah 53:9*

²³People insulted Christ, but he did not insult them in return. Christ suffered, but he did not threaten. He let God, the One who judges rightly, take care of him. ²⁴Christ carried our sins in his body on the cross so we would stop living for sin and start living for what is right. And you are healed because of his wounds. ²⁵You were like sheep that wandered away, but now you have come back to the Shepherd and Protector of your souls.

> ## "LIVE AS FREE PEOPLE, BUT DO NOT USE YOUR FREEDOM AS AN EXCUSE TO DO EVIL. LIVE AS SERVANTS OF GOD."

## WIVES AND HUSBANDS

**3** In the same way, you wives should yield to your husbands. Then, if some husbands do not obey God's teaching, they will be persuaded to believe without anyone's saying a word to them. They will be persuaded by the way their wives live. ²Your husbands will see the pure lives you live with your respect for God. ³It is not fancy hair, gold jewelry, or fine clothes that should make you beautiful. ⁴No, your beauty should come from within you—the beauty of a gentle and quiet spirit that will never be destroyed and is very precious to God. ⁵In this same way the holy women who lived long ago and followed God made themselves beautiful, yielding to their own husbands. ⁶Sarah obeyed Abraham, her husband, and called him her master. And you women are true children of Sarah if you always do what is right and are not afraid.

⁷In the same way, you husbands should live with your wives in an understanding way, since they are weaker than you. But show them respect, because God gives them the same blessing he gives you—the grace that gives true life. Do this so that nothing will stop your prayers.

## SUFFERING FOR DOING RIGHT

⁸Finally, all of you should be in agreement, understanding each other, loving each other as family, being kind and humble. ⁹Do not do wrong to repay a wrong, and do not insult to repay an insult. But repay with a blessing, because you yourselves were called to do this so that you might receive a blessing. ¹⁰The Scripture says,

"A person must do these things
    to enjoy life and have many happy days.
He must not say evil things,
    and he must not tell lies.
¹¹He must stop doing evil and do good.
    He must look for peace and work for it.
¹²The Lord sees the good people
    and listens to their prayers.

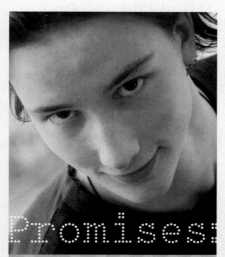

## Promises:

## 1 Peter 5:7

Got troubles? What would our lives be like if our worries and stresses were actually physical objects that we had to carry around all day? Picture this: It's time to get ready for the day and you start to pack your backpack. As you're picking up your textbooks, you see a brick sitting on your bed that contains the worry you have over your big algebra test today. You pick it up and reluctantly place it in the backpack. There are more bricks, too—ones of self-consciousness over your outfit, fear of not fitting in, and anger at your mom. All these go into the backpack, too. Now your bag is so heavy that you can barely lift it, but you strap it on anyway and head out, slowed down by all the weight.

Often, we carry our burdens and our worries around all day in our minds. They aren't physically heavy, but mentally they can weigh you down and even make you feel depressed. God doesn't desire that kind of life for us. When we ask, he will take the bricks out, one by one, and carry them himself. It's just one of the ways that he cares for us.

But the Lord is against
those who do evil." *Psalm 34:12-16*

[13]If you are trying hard to do good, no one can really hurt you. [14]But even if you suffer for doing right, you are blessed.

"Don't be afraid of what they fear;
do not dread those things." *Isaiah 8:12-13*

[15]But respect Christ as the holy Lord in your hearts. Always be ready to answer everyone who asks you to explain about the hope you have, [16]but answer in a gentle way and with respect. Keep a clear conscience so that those who speak evil of your good life in Christ will be made ashamed. [17]It is better to suffer for doing good than for doing wrong if that is what God wants. [18]Christ himself suffered for sins once. He was not guilty, but he suffered for those who are guilty to bring you to God. His body was killed, but he was made alive in the spirit. [19]And in the spirit he went and preached to the spirits in prison [20]who refused to obey God long ago in the time of Noah. God was waiting patiently for them while Noah was building the boat. Only a few people—eight in all—were saved by water. [21]And that water is like baptism that now saves you—not the washing of dirt from the body, but the promise made to God from a good conscience. And this is because Jesus Christ was raised from the dead. [22]Now Jesus has gone into heaven and is at God's right side ruling over angels, authorities, and powers.

## change your lives

4 Since Christ suffered while he was in his body, strengthen yourselves with the same way of thinking Christ had. The person who has suffered in the body is finished with sin. [2]Strengthen yourselves so that you will live here on earth doing what God wants, not the evil things people want. [3]In the past you wasted too much time doing what nonbelievers enjoy. You were guilty of sexual sins, evil desires, drunkenness, wild and drunken parties, and hateful idol worship. [4]Nonbelievers think it is strange that you do not do the many wild and wasteful things they do, so they insult you. [5]But they will have to explain

this to God, who is ready to judge the living and the dead. [6]For this reason the Good News was preached to those who are now dead. Even though they were judged like all people, the Good News was preached to them so they could live in the spirit as God lives.

## use God's gifts wisely

[7]The time is near when all things will end. So think clearly and control yourselves so you will be able to pray. [8]Most importantly, love each other deeply, because love will cause many sins to be forgiven. [9]Open your homes to each other, without complaining. [10]Each of you has received a gift to use to serve others. Be good servants of God's various gifts of grace. [11]Anyone who speaks should speak words from God. Anyone who serves should serve with the strength God

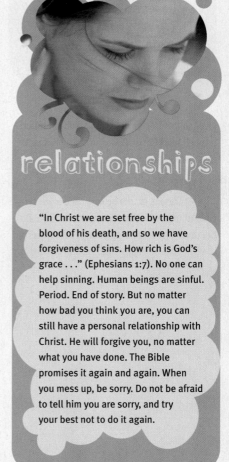

## relationships

"In Christ we are set free by the blood of his death, and so we have forgiveness of sins. How rich is God's grace . . ." (Ephesians 1:7). No one can help sinning. Human beings are sinful. Period. End of story. But no matter how bad you think you are, you can still have a personal relationship with Christ. He will forgive you, no matter what you have done. The Bible promises it again and again. When you mess up, be sorry. Do not be afraid to tell him you are sorry, and try your best not to do it again.

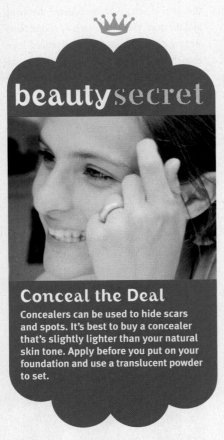

# beautysecret

## Conceal the Deal

Concealers can be used to hide scars and spots. It's best to buy a concealer that's slightly lighter than your natural skin tone. Apply before you put on your foundation and use a translucent powder to set.

Christ's sufferings so that you will be happy and full of joy when Christ comes again in glory. ¹⁴When people insult you because you follow Christ, you are blessed, because the glorious Spirit, the Spirit of God, is with you. ¹⁵Do not suffer for murder, theft, or any other crime, nor because you trouble other people. ¹⁶But if you suffer because you are a Christian, do not be ashamed. Praise God because you wear that name. ¹⁷It is time for judgment to begin with God's family. And if that judging begins with us, what will happen to those people who do not obey the Good News of God?

¹⁸"If it is very hard for a good person to be saved,

the wicked person and the sinner will surely be lost!'"

¹⁹So those who suffer as God wants should trust their souls to the faithful Creator as they continue to do what is right.

## THE FLOCK OF GOD

5 Now I have something to say to the elders in your group. I also am an elder. I have seen Christ's sufferings, and I will share in the glory that will be shown to us. I beg you to ²shepherd God's flock, for whom you are responsible. Watch over them because you want to, not because you are forced. That is how God wants it. Do it because you are happy to serve, not because you want money. ³Do not be like a ruler over people you are responsible for, but be good examples to them. ⁴Then when Christ, the Chief Shepherd, comes, you will get a glorious crown that will never lose its beauty.

⁵In the same way, younger people should be willing to be under older people. And all of you should be very humble with each other.

"God is against the proud,

but he gives grace to the humble."

*Proverbs 3:34*

⁶Be humble under God's powerful hand so he will lift you up when the right time comes. ⁷Give all your worries to him, because he cares about you.

⁸Control yourselves and be careful! The devil, your enemy, goes around like a roaring lion looking for someone to eat. ⁹Refuse to give in to him, by standing strong in your faith. You know that your Christian family all over the world is having the same kinds of suffering.

¹⁰And after you suffer for a short time, God, who gives all grace, will make everything right. He will make you strong and support you and keep you from falling. He called you to share in his glory in Christ, a glory that will continue forever. ¹¹All power is his forever and ever. Amen.

## FINAL GREETINGS

¹²I wrote this short letter with the help of Silas, who I know is a faithful brother in Christ. I wrote to encourage you and to tell you that this is the true grace of God. Stand strong in that grace.

¹³The church in Babylon, who was chosen like you, sends you greetings. Mark, my son in Christ, also greets you. ¹⁴Give each other a kiss of Christian love when you meet.

Peace to all of you who are in Christ.

gives so that in everything God will be praised through Jesus Christ. Power and glory belong to him forever and ever. Amen.

## SUFFERING AS A CHRISTIAN

¹²My friends, do not be surprised at the terrible trouble which now comes to test you. Do not think that something strange is happening to you. ¹³But be happy that you are sharing in

notes    **4:18 "If . . . lost!"** Quotation from Proverbs 11:31 in the Septuagint, the Greek version of the Old Testament.

360

# h *ave you ever known someone*

you just couldn't trust? Maybe they'd tell you half of the truth, but you could never tell when you were getting the whole truth? A lot of teachers were coming into churches in Asia Minor telling portions of the truth, but mixing it with false teaching.

# 2 Peter

## Beware of False Teachers

Since his first letter, Peter had become progressively more troubled by the false teachers who were penetrating the churches. Exposing their wrong teachings, Peter has stern words about the false prophets. Peter gets right to the point, coming out waving the truth like a banner.

Why the urgency? Many scholars believe that Peter wrote this second letter from prison, while awaiting his own death. This explanation seems reasonable, since Peter was crucified shortly after its writing. (According to some accounts, he was crucified upside down, because he felt unworthy to die the same way as Jesus did.) So, in a way, this is Peter's "last will and testament" —his last opportunity to warn believers of the dangers in the false teachings they were hearing.

In his closing chapter, Peter gives a final admonition for believers to be ready for the return of Christ. It's a reminder that still holds true today.

## Radical Faith:

## 2 Peter 1:3-4

Does it ever seem like you don't have what it takes to please God? To live a life without sin, to serve him, and to unconditionally love others is a tall order to fill. And to have a character, heart, and mind like God's is virtually impossible. But no matter how inadequate you may feel, Peter makes it clear that you *can* share in being like God. How? Through God's power, not yours. His grace enables you to be more like him. Your role is to be submissive to his Spirit and to willingly accept everything he offers. God will teach you more and lead you further every day. His Word reveals what he's about and how his ways work. He has given you special gifts to use for serving him. And he's given you his Spirit who makes it all happen. Paul talks about how when believers are changed to be more like God, this brings God even more glory (2 Corinthians 3:18). You reflect the glory of God to others. When you feel like you don't have what it takes to live right.and love others as God does, remember that the ability to be godly doesn't come from you—it comes from God being in you.

1 From Simon Peter, a servant and apostle of Jesus Christ.

To you who have received a faith as valuable as ours, because our God and Savior Jesus Christ does what is right.

²Grace and peace be given to you more and more, because you truly know God and Jesus our Lord.

### GOD HAS GIVEN US BLESSINGS

³Jesus has the power of God, by which he has given us everything we need to live and to serve God. We have these things because we know him. Jesus called us by his glory and goodness. ⁴Through these he gave us the very great and precious promises. With these gifts you can share in being like God, and the world will not ruin you with its evil desires.

⁵Because you have these blessings, do your best to add these things to your lives: to your faith, add goodness; and to your goodness, add knowledge; ⁶and to your knowledge, add self-control; and to your self-control, add patience; and to your patience, add service for God; ⁷and to your service for God, add kindness for your brothers and sisters in Christ; and to this kindness, add love. ⁸If all these things are in you and are growing, they will help you to be useful and productive in your knowledge of our Lord Jesus Christ. ⁹But anyone who does not have these things cannot see clearly. He is blind and has forgotten that he was made clean from his past sins.

¹⁰My brothers and sisters," try hard to be certain that you really are called and chosen by God. If you do all these things, you will never fall. ¹¹And you will be given a very great welcome into the eternal kingdom of our Lord and Savior Jesus Christ.

¹²You know these things, and you are very strong in the truth, but I will always help you remember them. ¹³I think it is right for me to help you remember as long as I am in this body. ¹⁴I know I must soon leave this body, as our Lord Jesus Christ has shown me. ¹⁵I will try my best so that you may be able to remember these things even after I am gone.

### WE SAW CHRIST'S GLORY

¹⁶When we told you about the powerful coming of our Lord Jesus Christ, we were not telling just smart stories that someone invented. But we saw the greatness of Jesus with our own eyes. ¹⁷Jesus heard the voice of God, the Greatest Glory, when he received honor and glory from God the Father. The voice said, "This is my Son, whom I love, and I am very pleased with him." ¹⁸We heard that voice from heaven while we were with Jesus on the holy mountain.

## "THERE USED TO BE FALSE PROPHETS AMONG GOD'S PEOPLE, JUST AS YOU WILL HAVE SOME FALSE TEACHERS IN YOUR GROUP."

¹⁹This makes us more sure about the message the prophets gave. It is good for you to follow closely what they said as you would follow a light shining in a dark place, until the day begins and the morning star rises in your hearts. ²⁰Most of all, you must understand this: No prophecy in the Scriptures ever comes from the prophet's own interpretation. ²¹No prophecy ever came from what a person wanted to say, but people led by the Holy Spirit spoke words from God.

### FALSE TEACHERS

2 There used to be false prophets among God's people, just as you will have some false teachers in your group. They will secretly teach things that are wrong—teachings that will cause people to be lost. They will even refuse to accept the Master, Jesus, who bought their freedom. So they will bring quick ruin on themselves. ²Many will follow their evil ways and say evil things about the way of truth. ³Those false teachers only want your money, so they will use you by telling you lies. Their judgment spoken against them long ago is still coming, and their ruin is certain.

---

**1:10 brothers and sisters** Although the Greek text reads "brothers" here and throughout this book, Peter's words were meant for the entire church, including men and women.

4When angels sinned, God did not let them go free without punishment. He sent them to hell and put them in caves of darkness where they are being held for judgment. 5And God punished the world long ago when he brought a flood to the world that was full of people who were against him. But God saved Noah, who preached about being right with God, and seven other people with him. 6And God also destroyed the evil cities of Sodom and Gomorrah" by burning them until they were ashes. He made those cities an example of what will happen to those who are against God. 7But he saved Lot from those cities. Lot, a good man, was troubled because of the filthy lives of evil people. 8(Lot was a good man, but because he lived with evil people every day, his good heart was hurt by the evil things he saw and heard.) 9So the Lord knows how to save those who serve him when troubles come. He will hold evil people and punish them, while waiting for the Judgment Day. 10That punishment is especially for those who live by doing the evil things their sinful selves want and who hate authority.

These false teachers are bold and do anything they want. They are not afraid to speak against the angels. 11But even the angels, who are much stronger and more powerful than false teachers, do not accuse them with insults before the Lord. 12But these people speak against things they do not understand. They

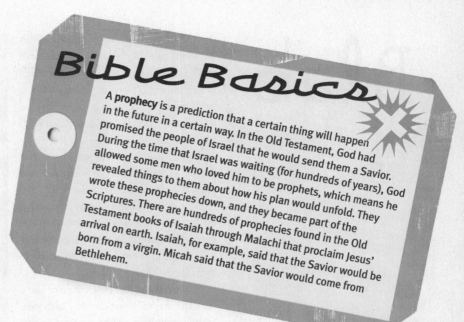

# Bible Basics

A **prophecy** is a prediction that a certain thing will happen in the future in a certain way. In the Old Testament, God had promised the people of Israel that he would send them a Savior. During the time that Israel was waiting (for hundreds of years), God allowed some men who loved him to be prophets, which means he revealed things to them about how his plan would unfold. They wrote these prophecies down, and they became part of the Scriptures. There are hundreds of prophecies found in the Old Testament books of Isaiah through Malachi that proclaim Jesus' arrival on earth. Isaiah, for example, said that the Savior would be born from a virgin. Micah said that the Savior would come from Bethlehem.

are like animals that act without thinking, animals born to be caught and killed. And, like animals, these false teachers will be destroyed. 13They have caused many people to suffer, so they themselves will suffer. That is their pay for what they have done. They take pleasure in openly doing evil, so they are like dirty spots and stains among you. They delight in trickery while eating meals with you. 14Every time they look at a woman they want her, and their desire for sin is never satisfied. They lead weak people into the trap of sin, and they have taught their hearts to be greedy. God will punish them! 15These false teachers left the right road and lost their way, following the way Balaam went. Balaam was the son of Beor, who loved being paid for doing wrong. 16But a donkey, which cannot talk, told Balaam he was sinning. It spoke with a man's voice and stopped the prophet's crazy thinking.

17Those false teachers are like springs without water and clouds blown by a storm. A place in the blackest darkness has been kept for them. 18They brag with words that mean nothing. By their evil desires they lead people into the trap of sin—people who are just beginning to escape from others who live in error. 19They promise them freedom, but they themselves are not free. They are slaves of things that will be destroyed.

For people are slaves of anything that controls them. 20They were made free from the evil in the world by knowing our Lord and Savior Jesus Christ. But if they return to evil things and those things control them, then it is worse for them than it was before. 21Yes, it would be better for them to have never known the right way than to know it and to turn away from the holy teaching that was given to them. 22What they did is like this true saying: "A dog goes back to what it has thrown up,"" and, "After a pig is washed, it goes back and rolls in the mud."

## JESUS WILL COME AGAIN

3 My friends, this is the second letter I have written you to help your honest minds remember. 2I want you to think about the words the holy prophets spoke in the past, and remember the command our Lord and Savior gave us through your apostles. 3It is most important for you to understand what will happen in the last days. People will laugh at you. They will live doing the evil things they want to do. 4They will say, "Jesus promised to come again. Where is he? Our fathers have died, but the world continues the way it has been since it was made." 5But they do not want to remember what happened long ago. By the word of God heaven was made, and the earth

notes **2:6 Sodom and Gomorrah** Two cities God destroyed because the people were so evil. **2:22 "A dog . . . up"** Quotation from Proverbs 26:11.

# Blab

**Q:** My parents just said they are having another baby, and I am totally grossed out. First of all, now I know for sure that they still do it. Second, they're going to be, like, ancient when this kid grows up. How can I be happy for them?

**A:** Ask God for help. After all, a baby is exciting and a blessing. Be grateful that your parents are still in love when so many parents are divorced. Help your mom plan so that you can feel part of things. Offer to babysit when your new brother or sister arrives.

**Q:** I constantly forget things and lose things, and it makes everyone mad at me. How can I do better?

**A:** People probably get upset because you cost them time or money, or they think you are unappreciative when you lose or forget things. It also costs you a great deal. Discipline yourself to write to-do lists and refer to them often. Get in the habit of writing down everything you will need for the next day. Try not to get rushed, and pray that God will help you be more responsible.

**Q:** I have known for a long time that I am gay, but I know the Bible says it is wrong. Still, I can't make these feelings go away. What can I do?

**A:** The Bible is very clear that homosexuality is a sin. Some people's gay feelings never go away, but you can choose not to act on them. Still, this is very serious. You need to find a trusted counselor to talk about this issue right away.

was made from water and with water. 6Then the world was flooded and destroyed with water. 7And that same word of God is keeping heaven and earth that we now have in order to be destroyed by fire. They are being kept for the Judgment Day and the destruction of all who are against God.

8But do not forget this one thing, dear friends: To the Lord one day is as a thousand years, and a thousand years is as one day. 9The Lord is not slow in doing what he promised—the way some people understand slowness. But God is being patient with you. He does not want anyone to be lost, but he wants all people to change their hearts and lives.

10But the day of the Lord will come like a thief. The skies will disappear with a loud noise. Everything in them will be destroyed by fire, and the earth and everything in it will be burned up.ⁿ 11In that way everything will be destroyed. So what kind of people should you be? You should live holy lives and serve God, 12as you wait for and look forward to the coming of the day of God. When that day comes, the skies will be destroyed with fire, and everything in them will melt with heat. 13But God made a promise to us, and we are waiting for a new heaven and a new earth where goodness lives.

14Dear friends, since you are waiting for this to happen, do your best to be without sin and without fault. Try to be at peace with God. 15Remember that we are saved because our Lord is patient. Our dear brother Paul told you the same thing when he wrote to you with the wisdom that God gave him. 16He writes about this in all his letters. Some things in Paul's letters are hard to understand, and people who are ignorant and weak in faith explain these things falsely. They also falsely explain the other Scriptures, but they are destroying themselves by doing this.

17Dear friends, since you already know about this, be careful. Do not let those evil people lead you away by the wrong they do. Be careful so you will not fall from your strong faith. 18But grow in the grace and knowledge of our Lord and Savior Jesus Christ. Glory be to him now and forever! Amen.

## Promises:

# 2 Peter 3:9

Think about all the common phrases we use to describe *time*: Time is relevant. Time is short. Time is money. Time is precious.

Time is an elusive creature, and many people value it in different ways. "Well, time isn't that important to me," you may say. "I'm a laid-back person who rarely gets in a hurry." Uh-huh. Remember that the next time you are standing in a long line that never seems to end or waiting for your Internet browser to load. We live in an impatient culture that heavily relies on high-speed Internet, PDAs, and lots of other shortcuts and conveniences to make our days move as quickly as possible.

The early Christians were impatient, too. They believed Jesus when he said that he would return to earth to rule, and they wanted him to come—sooner than later. Peter encouraged the restless group by reminding them that God's timing is very different from ours and that he would return when he knew the time was right. Today, thousands of years later, Christ still hasn't returned, but we can trust that one day he will return and that his timing will be perfect.

notes    **3:10 will be burned up** Many Greek copies say, "will be found." One copy says, "will disappear."

# December

**1**
It's World AIDS Day. Learn more about what you can do at www.data.org.

**2**

**3**

**4**
Pray for your brother or sister today. Ask God to bless them in a fresh, new way.

**5**

**6**

**7**
Read Luke 2. Reflect on Christ's birth.

**8**

**9**

**10**

**11**
Make homemade cards for relatives, friends, and classmates.

**12**

**13**
Go sledding. Take along a younger cousin or neighbor.

**14**

**15**
love

**16**
Anniversary of the Boston Tea Party. Have your own tea party in remembrance.

**17**

**18**
Pray for a person of influence: It's Steven Spielberg's birthday.

**19**

**20**

**21**
Finish up that last-minute Christmas shopping!

**22**
It's the first day of winter. Enjoy the coolest season of the year.

**23**

**24**
Christmas Eve. Celebrate this time with your family.

**25**
Christmas Day. Think about your favorite family traditions. What makes them so special?

**26**

**27**

**28**
Take advantage of all the after-Christmas sales.

**29**
Think about what New Year's resolutions you want to make for the upcoming year.

**30**

**31**
New Year's Eve. Throw a party. Enjoy the friends God has blessed you with!

We should love each other, because love comes from God.
—1 John 4:7

# John, Jesus' dear friend and one

of the "Sons of Thunder," writes this first of three letters in advanced age. (That's a nice way of saying John is an old man.) Writing as a father in intimate conversation with his child, this letter is tender and conversational. John doesn't offer a lot of outright instruction. Instead, his letter is full of spiritual litmus tests—ways to determine if a teaching is true and pure.

# 1 John

### God Is Love

The writer of 1 John mentions four different reasons he is writing. He wants to add to the believers' joy, guard them against sin, warn them about false teachers, and strengthen their faith. His desire is to assure believers of eternal life.

John wants believers to know that God's character calls for both holy living and loving fellow followers of Christ. In fact, he notes that one of the distinguishing marks of being a believer is loving your brothers and sisters in Christ. John is quick to remind readers that love makes itself real, not just in words but in sacrifice.

The overwhelming theme of 1 John is summed up in one sentence: "Whoever does not love does not know God, because God is love" (4:8, emphasis added). Thus, John tells us how to love God, our neighbors, and ourselves. It's truly a love letter.

## Radical Faith:

# 1 John 1:9

So you messed up. Like *really* messed up. You did what you knew you weren't supposed to do, you're in trouble for it, and you feel awful about it. And you feel really alone—not to mention unacceptable and ashamed. You want to please God, but how in the world do you get back on track? Do it God's way. Jesus offered his life as a sacrifice to pay for every one of your mistakes. He created a way to make your conscience "pure from useless acts so [you] may serve the living God" (Hebrews 9:14). Confession is admitting to God the reality of where you are. Repentance is saying that you don't want to stay there and that you want to be somewhere else. God creates the bridge between those two spots. Confession means stopping in your tracks and turning to face God. Repentance is connecting with him and moving forward with him in his direction. Go to God and be honest. Read through Psalm 51. Use it as the basis for your prayers. Remember that you can't really be close to him when sin is in your heart. Ask God to breathe new life into you, to transform you, and to help you. He will.

1 We write you now about what has always existed, which we have heard, we have seen with our own eyes, we have looked at, and we have touched with our hands. We write to you about the Word[n] that gives life. [2]He who gives life was shown to us. We saw him and can give proof about it. And now we announce to you that he has life that continues forever. He was with God the Father and was shown to us. [3]We announce to you what we have seen and heard, because we want you also to have fellowship with us. Our fellowship is with God the Father and with his Son, Jesus Christ. [4]We write this to you so you can be full of joy with us.

## GOD FORGIVES OUR SINS

[5]Here is the message we have heard from Christ and now announce to you: God is light,[n] and in him there is no darkness at all. [6]So if we say we have fellowship with God, but we continue living in darkness, we are liars and do not follow the truth. [7]But if we live in the light, as God is in the light, we can share fellowship with each other. Then the blood of Jesus, God's Son, cleanses us from every sin.

[8]If we say we have no sin, we are fooling ourselves, and the truth is not in us. [9]But if we confess our sins, he will forgive our sins, because we can trust God to do what is right. He will cleanse us from all the wrongs we have done. [10]If we say we have not sinned, we make God a liar, and we do not accept God's teaching.

## JESUS IS OUR HELPER

2 My dear children, I write this letter to you so you will not sin. But if anyone does sin, we have a helper in the presence of the Father—Jesus Christ, the One who does what is right. [2]He is the way our sins are taken away, and not only our sins but the sins of all people.

[3]We can be sure that we know God if we obey his commands. [4]Anyone who says, "I know God," but does not obey God's commands is a liar, and the truth is not in that person. [5]But if someone obeys God's teaching, then in that person God's love has truly

reached its goal. This is how we can be sure we are living in God: [6]Whoever says that he lives in God must live as Jesus lived.

## THE COMMAND TO LOVE OTHERS

[7]My dear friends, I am not writing a new command to you but an old command you have had from the beginning. It is the teaching you have already heard. [8]But also I am writing a new command to you, and you can see its truth in Jesus and in you, because the darkness is passing away, and the true light is already shining.

[9]Anyone who says, "I am in the light,"[n] but hates a brother or sister,[n] is still in the darkness. [10]Whoever loves a brother or sister lives in the light and will not cause anyone to stumble in his faith. [11]But whoever hates a brother or sister is in darkness, lives in darkness, and does not know where to go, because the darkness has made that person blind.

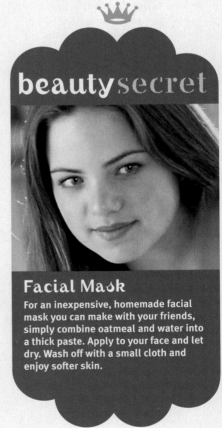

# beauty secret

## Facial Mask

For an inexpensive, homemade facial mask you can make with your friends, simply combine oatmeal and water into a thick paste. Apply to your face and let dry. Wash off with a small cloth and enjoy softer skin.

---

**1:1 Word** The Greek word is "logos," meaning any kind of communication. Here, it means Christ, who was the way God told people about himself. **1:5 light** Here, it is used as a symbol of God's goodness or truth. **2:9 light** Here, it is used as a symbol of God's goodness or truth. **2:9 brother or sister** Although the Greek text says "brother" here and throughout this book, the writer's words were meant for the entire church, including men and women.

Promises:

# 1 John 3:19-20

Have you ever followed your heart and ended up somewhere you didn't want to be? Many people believe that the heart—representative of our essence, our soul—is the greatest tool we have for guidance in our lives. Follow your heart, they say. And our hearts, in this sense, are wonderful in a lot of ways. They allow us to love, to feel joy and sorrow, to be excited, to be inspired.

But our hearts can also harbor things that aren't so nice or helpful, such as hate, anger, and selfish desires. Sometimes the heart can mislead us and take us places where we don't want to go—places where we may get into trouble or hurt others. God knows our hearts and their desires. And he knows that often they aren't the best guides. That's why he wants us to pray to him and ask for guidance and wisdom. He offers them freely and will never deceive us. Thank him today that he is bigger than our hearts and our flimsy efforts to guide ourselves. Thank him for his patience and love.

¹²I write to you, dear children,
  because your sins are forgiven through
  Christ.
¹³I write to you, parents,
  because you know the One who existed
  from the beginning.
 I write to you, young people,
  because you have defeated the Evil One.
¹⁴I write to you, children,
  because you know the Father.
 I write to you, parents,
  because you know the One who existed
  from the beginning.
 I write to you, young people,
  because you are strong;
  the teaching of God lives in you,
  and you have defeated the Evil One.

¹⁵Do not love the world or the things in the world. If you love the world, the love of the Father is not in you. ¹⁶These are the ways of the world: wanting to please our sinful selves, wanting the sinful things we see, and being too proud of what we have. None of these come from the Father, but all of them come from the world. ¹⁷The world and everything that people want in it are passing away, but the person who does what God wants lives forever.

## REJECT THE enemies OF CHRIST

¹⁸My dear children, these are the last days. You have heard that the enemy of Christ is coming, and now many enemies of Christ are already here. This is how we know that these are the last days. ¹⁹These enemies of Christ were in our fellowship, but they left us. They never really belonged to us; if they had been a part of us, they would have stayed with us. But they left, and this shows that none of them really belonged to us.

²⁰You have the gift" that the Holy One gave you, so you all know the truth. ²¹I do not write to you because you do not know the truth but because you do know the truth. And you know that no lie comes from the truth.

²²Who is the liar? It is the person who does not accept Jesus as the Christ. This is the enemy of Christ: the person who does not accept the Father and his Son. ²³Whoever does not accept the Son does not have the Father. But whoever confesses the Son has the Father, too.

²⁴Be sure you continue to follow the teaching you heard from the beginning. If you continue to follow what you heard from the beginning, you will stay in the Son and in the Father. ²⁵And this is what the Son promised to us—life forever.

²⁶I am writing this letter about those people who are trying to lead you the wrong way. ²⁷Christ gave you a special gift that is still in you, so you do not need any other teacher. His gift teaches you about everything, and it is true, not false. So continue to live in Christ, as his gift taught you.

## "WHEN OUR HEARTS MAKE US FEEL GUILTY, WE CAN STILL HAVE PEACE BEFORE GOD."

²⁸Yes, my dear children, live in him so that when Christ comes back, we can be without fear and not be ashamed in his presence. ²⁹If you know that Christ is all that is right, you know that all who do right are God's children.

## we are GOD'S CHILDREN

3 The Father has loved us so much that we are called children of God. And we really are his children. The reason the people in the world do not know us is that they have not known him. ²Dear friends, now we are children of God, and we have not yet been shown what we will be in the future. But we know that when Christ comes again, we will be like him, because we will see him as he really is. ³Christ is pure, and all who have this hope in Christ keep themselves pure like Christ.

⁴The person who sins breaks God's law. Yes, sin is living against God's law. ⁵You know that Christ came to take away sins and that there is no sin in Christ. ⁶So anyone who lives in Christ does not go on sinning. Anyone who goes on sinning has never really understood Christ and has never known him.

notes  **2:20 gift** This might mean the Holy Spirit, or it might mean teaching or truth as in verse 24.

# LEARN I+ & LIVE I+

**1 John 2:11**
**Learn It:** If you hate your brother or sister, you live in darkness.
**Live It:** If you still have bitterness or hate in your heart for someone, you must deal with it so that God can shine through you. Do you need to ask someone for forgiveness?

**1 John 3:18**
**Learn It:** We must love not only by our words, but also by our actions.
**Live It:** Cook dinner for your family tonight. Be extra nice to your brother or sister. Show someone you care by doing something kind for them.

**2 John 4**
**Learn It:** John was happy to learn that some children (or church members) were following Christ.
**Live It:** Write a note to two of your Christian friends. Encourage them for staying strong in the faith.

⁷Dear children, do not let anyone lead you the wrong way. Christ is all that is right. So to be like Christ a person must do what is right. ⁸The devil has been sinning since the beginning, so anyone who continues to sin belongs to the devil. The Son of God came for this purpose: to destroy the devil's work.

⁹Those who are God's children do not continue sinning, because the new life from God remains in them. They are not able to go on sinning, because they have become children of God. ¹⁰So we can see who God's children are and who the devil's children are: Those who do not do what is right are not God's children, and those who do not love their brothers and sisters are not God's children.

## WE MUST LOVE EACH OTHER

¹¹This is the teaching you have heard from the beginning: We must love each other. ¹²Do not be like Cain who belonged to the Evil One and killed his brother. And why did he kill him? Because the things Cain did were evil, and the things his brother did were good.

¹³Brothers and sisters, do not be surprised when the people of the world hate you. ¹⁴We know we have left death and have come into life because we love each other. Whoever does not love is still dead. ¹⁵Everyone who hates a brother or sister is a murderer," and you know that no murderers have eternal life in them. ¹⁶This is how we know what real love is: Jesus gave his life for us. So we should give our lives for our brothers and sisters. ¹⁷Suppose someone has enough to live and sees a brother or sister in need, but does not help. Then God's love is not living in that person. ¹⁸My children, we should love people not only with words and talk, but by our actions and true caring.

¹⁹⁻²⁰This is the way we know that we belong to the way of truth. When our hearts make us feel guilty, we can still have peace before God.

# CHECK IT OUT

## NATIONAL CENTER FOR MISSING & EXPLOITED CHILDREN

The National Center for Missing and Exploited Children (NCMEC) was first started in 1984 to help families and professionals nationwide in their attempts to prevent children from being abducted, endangered, and sexually exploited.

NCMEC serves as a clearinghouse of information about missing and exploited children and distributes photographs and descriptions of missing children worldwide. It operates a CyberTipline that the public can use to report Internet-related child sexual exploitation. Among other services, the organization also helps individuals and law-enforcement agencies in the prevention, investigation, prosecution, and treatment of cases involving missing and exploited children.

You can help protect kids by posting banners and links to NCMEC on your website, sign up for email alerts about missing kids, or link to a local chapter to find out about volunteer opportunities and internships.

*Get involved by visiting* **www.missingkids.com.**

 **3:15 Everyone . . . murderer** If one person hates a brother or sister, then in the heart that person has killed that brother or sister. Jesus taught about this sin to his followers (Matthew 5:21-26).

God is greater than our hearts, and he knows everything. 21My dear friends, if our hearts do not make us feel guilty, we can come without fear into God's presence. 22And God gives us what we ask for because we obey God's commands and do what pleases him. 23This is what God commands: that we believe in his Son, Jesus Christ, and that we love each other, just as he commanded. 24The people who obey God's commands live in God, and God lives in them. We know that God lives in us because of the Spirit God gave us.

## warning against false teachers

4 My dear friends, many false prophets have gone out into the world. So do not believe every spirit, but test the spirits to see if they are from God. 2This is how you can know God's Spirit: Every spirit who confesses that Jesus Christ came to earth as a human is from God. 3And every spirit who refuses to say this about Jesus is not from God. It is the spirit of the enemy of Christ, which you have heard is coming, and now he is already in the world.

4My dear children, you belong to God and have defeated them; because God's Spirit, who is in you, is greater than the devil, who is in the world. 5And they belong to the world, so what they say is from the world, and the world listens to them. 6But we belong to God, and those who know God listen to us. But those who are not from God do not listen to us. That is how we know the Spirit that is true and the spirit that is false.

## love comes from god

7Dear friends, we should love each other, because love comes from God. Everyone who loves has become God's child and knows God. 8Whoever does not love does not know God, because God is love. 9This is how God showed his love to us: He sent his one and only Son into the world so that we could have life through him. 10This is what real love is: It is not our love for God; it is God's love for us in

# Tabitha

[ACTS 9:36-43] Tabitha was the kind of woman who understood how important small kindnesses could be. While anyone looking on would consider her a widow of modest means, all those who knew Tabitha were amazed by her generosity. Small, simple kindnesses were as common to her as breathing. So when Tabitha died unexpectedly, her entire community was heartbroken. She was irreplaceable to them. Jesus' followers were also among the grief-stricken. They placed Tabitha's body in an upper room and sent word for Peter to come. When Peter arrived, he prayed. And God must have thought Tabitha was irreplaceable, too. He brought this woman back to life, back to community who loved her so much.

# Music Reviews

| GROUP: | ALBUM: |
|---|---|
| CCM TOP 100 GREATEST SONGS | IN CHRISTIAN MUSIC, VOLS. 1-4 |

25 selections from

CCM TOP 100

GREATEST SONGS IN CHRISTIAN MUSIC

VOLUME 1

OK, all you music fans who want great Christian music but don't know where to dive in, here's the perfect package for you. *CCM Magazine* and Creative Trust Workshop have teamed up to release what they think are the top 100 songs of all time in modern Christian music on four discs of 25 songs each. Volume One is off to a strong start with a variety of groups and musical styles from the 1970s forward, ranging from The Imperials old-school "Praise the Lord" to Third Day's "Consuming Fire." Rich Mullins is here with "Awesome God," and Amy Grant sings "Lead Me On"—and that just scratches the surface.

**WHY IT ROCKS: CHRISTIAN MUSIC'S BEST OF THE PAST AND PRESENT ARE ALL TOGETHER IN ONE PLACE.**

sending his Son to be the way to take away our sins.

¹¹Dear friends, if God loved us that much we also should love each other. ¹²No one has ever seen God, but if we love each other, God lives in us, and his love is made perfect in us.

¹³We know that we live in God and he lives in us, because he gave us his Spirit. ¹⁴We have seen and can testify that the Father sent his Son to be the Savior of the world. ¹⁵Whoever confesses that Jesus is the Son of God has God living inside, and that person lives in God. ¹⁶And so we know the love that God has for us, and we trust that love.

God is love. Those who live in love live in God, and God lives in them. ¹⁷This is how love is made perfect in us: that we can be without fear on the day God judges us, because in this world we are like him. ¹⁸Where God's love is, there is no fear, because God's perfect love drives out fear. It is punishment that makes a person fear, so love is not made perfect in the person who fears.

¹⁹We love because God first loved us. ²⁰If people say, "I love God," but hate their brothers or sisters, they are liars. Those who do not love their brothers and sisters, whom they have seen, cannot love God, whom they have never seen. ²¹And God gave us this command: Those who love God must also love their brothers and sisters.

## FAITH IN THE SON OF GOD

5 Everyone who believes that Jesus is the Christ is God's child, and whoever loves the Father also loves the Father's children. ²This is how we know we love God's children: when we love God and obey his commands. ³Loving God means obeying his commands. And God's commands are not too hard for us, ⁴because everyone who is a child of God conquers the world. And this is the victory that conquers the world—our faith. ⁵So the one who wins against the world is the person who believes that Jesus is the Son of God.

⁶Jesus Christ is the One who came by water" and blood." He did not come by water only, but by water and blood. And the Spirit

## Radical Faith:

# 1 John 5:3-5

When you love someone, it shows. If something is in your heart, it will come through in your actions. God has expressed his love to you by making you his child. He provided a way through Jesus to make you holy like him. He's also expressed his love to you by revealing the best way to live—in his ways and in his presence. When you're in him, you're able to conquer anything in this world. And that means the hard things you face don't have to control you. Nothing has to take you down. If you have put your faith in Jesus for forgiveness of your sins, you have received his Spirit. His commands are a safe haven that protects you from harm, nurtures your relationship with him, and helps you grow in godliness. All of that is critical. Jesus said that obeying his teachings would bring rest and care (Matthew 11:28-30). John said that your faith in God and his power can bring more strength than this world can imagine (1 John 5:4). You live because he lives; trust and follow him. He's shown extreme goodness, power, and love to you. Love him back by following his every word.

## Promises:

# 1 John 5:14-15

Does it ever feel ridiculous to you to pray to a God you can't see? Has anyone ever told you that you are putting too much stock in a useless religion? It's hard for those who don't believe—and sometimes even for those who do—to fully understand the concept of a relationship with God. Most people understand the concept of *religion*, but they don't get the fact that God isn't interested in empty routine or tradition—he wants a relationship with you! In Hosea 6:6, God says, "I want faithful love more than I want animal sacrifices. I want people to know me more than I want burnt offerings."

And the cool thing is that the more we get to know God, the more our desires become his desires and the more our heart becomes like his heart. We will begin to want the things that he wants for us. When we pray and ask for guidance and direction, he will answer us and guide us. He hears us, he loves us, and he wants us to know him more.

 **5:6 water** This probably means the water of Jesus' baptism. **5:6 blood** This probably means the blood of Jesus' death.

# Quiz

# WHAT'S YOUR servant style?

**YOUR BEST FRIEND JUST BROKE UP WITH HER BOYFRIEND AND IS HAVING A HARD TIME. TO CHEER HER UP, YOU:**

A. Grab a couple of her fave magazines and treats and go spend the day with her.
B. Head over to her house with your manicure set, prepared to give her a pick-me-up pedicure.
C. Take her to her favorite coffee shop for a latté and lots of time to listen.
D. Gather a group of friends and take her out for a fun night of miniature golf.

**YOU RECENTLY LEARNED ABOUT THE DEVASTATING AIDS CRISIS THAT IS AFFECTING AFRICA. YOU WANT TO DO SOMETHING TO HELP, SO YOU:**

A. Decide to organize a fund-raiser to raise money for the cause.

B. Get with a local group who are sending Christmas gifts to African children and help them pack up gifts.
C. Volunteer to write encouraging letters to the patients.
D. Hop a plane with a group who is going to build homes for orphans in Africa.

**WHEN FACED WITH A TASK TO ACCOMPLISH, YOUR MOTTO IS:**

A. Get organized.
B. Tackle the biggest need first.
C. Consider everyone involved.
D. Get moving.

**A COMMUNITY NEARBY IS DEVASTATED BY A TERRIBLE STORM. YOU:**

A. Start a drive at your school to collect food and clothing for those who lost their homes.

B. Help sort through and separate the donations to be sent to the victims.
C. Get with your mom to make dinner for some of the affected families.
D. Visit the community and physically help sort through the wreckage.

**YOUR MOM JUST STARTED A NEW JOB AND IS STRESSED TO THE MAX. YOU REALIZE SHE NEEDS SOME HELP, SO YOU:**

A. Make a chore chart for you and your siblings to pick up the slack.
B. Pick up the living room before she gets home so she walks into a neat space.
C. Offer to make dinner so the family can sit down together for a peaceful meal.
D. Put your rubber gloves on and go all Mr. Clean on the nasty dinner dishes so mom doesn't have to worry about it.

**IF YOU ANSWERED MOSTLY As, YOU'RE AN ORGANIZING DIVA!**
You are putting your leadership skills to good use. Whether it's setting up a bake sale or collecting canned goods, you know how to get people moving.

**IF YOU ANSWERED MOSTLY Bs, YOU'RE A HELPING HAND!**
You are always ready to pitch in whenever needed. You are a hard worker and thoughtful to boot. People really appreciate your willingness to help out.

**IF YOU ANSWERED MOSTLY Cs, YOU'RE A TRUSTY COMPANION!**
People are your main concern, so you are always there for someone, ready to listen. You like personal interaction more than anything, so you're great to have around to comfort and encourage others.

**IF YOU ANSWERED MOSTLY Ds, YOU'RE AN ACTION STAR!**
Never one to take the quiet path, you are itching to get in and get your hands dirty. Your enthusiasm and willingness to help others are extraordinary.

says that this is true, because the Spirit is the truth. ⁷So there are three witnesses that tell us about Jesus: ⁸the Spirit, the water, and the blood; and these three witnesses agree. ⁹We believe people when they say something is true. But what God says is more important, and he has told us the truth about his own Son. ¹⁰Anyone who believes in the Son of God has the truth that God told us. Anyone who does not believe makes God a liar, because that person does not believe what God told us about his Son. ¹¹This is what God told us: God has given us eternal life, and this life is in his Son. ¹²Whoever has the Son has life, but whoever does not have the Son of God does not have life.

## We Have Eternal Life Now

¹³I write this letter to you who believe in the Son of God so you will know you have eternal life. ¹⁴And this is the boldness we have in God's presence: that if we ask God for anything that agrees with what he wants, he hears us. ¹⁵If we know he hears us every time we ask him, we know we have what we ask from him.

¹⁶If anyone sees a brother or sister sinning (sin that does not lead to eternal death), that person should pray, and God will give the sinner life. I am talking about people whose sin does not lead to eternal death. There is sin that leads to death. I do not mean that a person should pray about that sin. ¹⁷Doing wrong is always sin, but there is sin that does not lead to eternal death.

¹⁸We know that those who are God's children do not continue to sin. The Son of God keeps them safe, and the Evil One cannot touch them. ¹⁹We know that we belong to God, but the Evil One controls the whole world. ²⁰We also know that the Son of God has come and has given us understanding so that we can know the True One. And our lives are in the True One and in his Son, Jesus Christ. He is the true God and the eternal life.

²¹So, dear children, keep yourselves away from gods.

ADOLESCENTS WITH TATTOOS AND/OR BODY PIERCINGS WERE MORE LIKELY TO HAVE ENGAGED IN RISK-TAKING BEHAVIORS SUCH AS DRUG USE, SEXUAL ACTIVITY, AND SUICIDE. WWW.PEDIATRICS.AAPUBLICATIONS.ORG

*t*his book begins with "From the Elder." That's easy enough—we have no reason to doubt that the Elder is John. "To the chosen lady and her children." Huh? Excuse me? Who is this chosen lady? Chosen by whom? For what? The truth is, we really don't know to whom this letter is addressed. The "chosen lady" could be figurative language, symbolizing a church, with "her children" being its members. She could also be a specific woman with children—thus making her the only woman in the New Testament to whom a book is addressed.

# 2 John
## Don't Welcome False Teachers into Your Midst

Much of the content in this letter is similar to 1 John, only more concise. John could be summing up in this personal letter what he wrote to the churches of Asia Minor in his earlier letter.

John does, however, go a step further here. Beyond just warning the reader about false teachers, he advises her not to even welcome these teachers into her home. Hospitality was a big deal in biblical times. Without modern forms of transportation and hotels on every corner, people relied on the hospitality of others when they traveled. But John's admonition is that if you welcome such a person, you actually share in the evil work they do (verse 11).

One chapter. Thirteen verses. Short letter. Big message.

¹From the Elder."

To the chosen lady" and her children:

I love all of you in the truth," and all those who know the truth love you. ²We love you because of the truth that lives in us and will be with us forever.

³Grace, mercy, and peace from God the Father and his Son, Jesus Christ, will be with us in truth and love.

⁴I was very happy to learn that some of your children are following the way of truth, as the Father commanded us. ⁵And now, dear lady, this is not a new command but is the same command we have had from the beginning. I ask you that we all love each other. ⁶And love means living the way God commanded us to live. As you have heard from the beginning, his command is this: Live a life of love.

⁷Many false teachers are in the world now who do not confess that Jesus Christ came to earth as a human. Anyone who does not confess this is a false teacher and an enemy of Christ. ⁸Be careful yourselves that you do not lose everything you have worked for, but that you receive your full reward.

⁹Anyone who goes beyond Christ's teaching and does not continue to follow only his teaching does not have God. But whoever continues to follow the teaching of Christ has both the Father and the Son. ¹⁰If someone comes to you and does not bring this teaching, do not welcome or accept that person into your house. ¹¹If you welcome such a person, you share in the evil work.

¹²I have many things to write to you, but I do not want to use paper and ink. Instead, I hope to come to you and talk face to face so we can be full of joy. ¹³The children of your chosen sister" greet you.

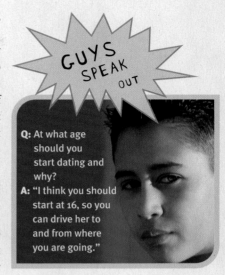

**GUYS SPEAK OUT**

**Q:** At what age should you start dating and why?
**A:** "I think you should start at 16, so you can drive her to and from where you are going."

**DIDYA KNOW**

**NEARLY ONE IN FOUR TEENS PERSONALLY KNOWS SOMEONE WHO WAS SEXUALLY ABUSED AS A CHILD OR TEENAGER.**

WWW.STOPCHILDABUSENOW.ORG

**notes** **1 Elder** "Elder" means an older person. It can also mean a special leader in the church (as in Titus 1:5). **1 lady** This might mean a woman, or in this letter it might mean a church. If it is a church, then "her children" would be the people of the church. **1 truth** The truth or "Good News" about Jesus Christ that joins all believers together. **13 sister** Sister of the "lady" in verse 1. This might be another woman or another church.

## Here's a common scenario:

A young missionary couple on furlough (a leave of absence) visit your church one Sunday evening. They have a rather long slide presentation of their work in Paraguay. Orphaned children . . . a new well they helped dig . . . a dilapidated church that needs repairs. They share of the miracles they've witnessed and the tragedies, as well. They close by asking for financial and prayer support. Sound familiar? Maybe you've been to a service like this. And maybe you were even moved in spirit. But were you moved to action?

# 3 John
## Support Those in Christian Ministry

John's third letter is to an individual named Gaius. We don't know much about Gaius except that he welcomed complete strangers into his home because they were believers in Christ. It seems that John had written ahead to a church, asking for hospitality for traveling ministers, but Diotrephes, who considered himself the church's leader, refused to welcome them. Gaius, however, was warm and generous.

John uses this letter to thank Gaius, but he also succeeds in teaching us about opening our hearts and homes to those who are in the service of the Lord.

376

¹From the Elder.″

To my dear friend Gaius, whom I love in the truth:″

²My dear friend, I know your soul is doing fine, and I pray that you are doing well in every way and that your health is good. ³I was very happy when some brothers and sisters″ came and told me about the truth in your life and how you are following the way of truth. ⁴Nothing gives me greater joy than to hear that my children are following the way of truth.

⁵My dear friend, it is good that you help the brothers and sisters, even those you do not know. ⁶They told the church about your love. Please help them to continue their trip in a way worthy of God. ⁷They started out in service to Christ, and they have been accepting nothing from nonbelievers. ⁸So we should help such people; when we do, we share in their work for the truth.

⁹I wrote something to the church, but Diotrephes, who loves to be their leader, will not listen to us. ¹⁰So if I come, I will talk about what Diotrephes is doing, about how he lies and says evil things about us. But more than that, he refuses to accept the other brothers and sisters; he even stops those who do want to accept them and puts them out of the church.

¹¹My dear friend, do not follow what is bad; follow what is good. The one who does good belongs to God. But the one who does evil has never known God.

¹²Everyone says good things about Demetrius, and the truth agrees with what they say. We also speak well of him, and you know what we say is true.

¹³I have many things I want to write you, but I do not want to use pen and ink. ¹⁴I hope to see you soon and talk face to face. ¹⁵Peace to you. The friends here greet you. Please greet each friend there by name.

# beauty secret

## Food and Acne

Lots of people say that what you eat—including French fries and chocolate—can give you zits, but scientists haven't been able to find any substantial link between food and acne. A healthy diet is still important for your body; but if your acne just won't go away, see a doctor or dermatologist.

# relationships

Friends who love God protect each other from sexual temptation. Song of Solomon 8:9 says, "If she is a door, we will protect her with cedar boards." Boarding someone up behind a locked door may be extreme, but the bottom line is that good friends should stick together on the issue of being pure and keeping their virginity. Whether you're dating or hanging out with a guy, it's a good idea to stay in groups as much as possible. Keep each other accountable. It's much easier to be strong when you know others are staying strong, too.

---

**notes** **1 Elder** "Elder" means an older person. It can also mean a special leader in the church (as in Titus 1:5). **1 truth** The truth or "Good News" about Jesus Christ that joins all believers together. **3 brothers and sisters** Although the Greek text says "brothers" here and throughout this book, the writer's words were meant for the entire church, including men and women.

**i**t is thought that our author Jude may have been a brother of James, which would have also made him a brother of Jesus. Although he had previously rejected Jesus' claim to be the Messiah—wouldn't you have a hard time believing your brother or sister was God?—he became a believer after Christ's resurrection.

# Jude
## Be Wary of Those Who Distort the Truth

At the time that this letter was written, it's estimated that all of the original twelve followers of Jesus had been martyred (killed for their faith) except for John. The Christian faith was at what seemed like an all-time low. False teachers and powerful spiritual warfare were at work, trying to dilute and distort the truth of Jesus' resurrection from the dead.

Jude mounts a rigorous defense of this truth. He makes a clear distinction between having normal, human doubts and rejecting God's authority. He encourages solid believers to nurture the immature ones but to firmly reject the sin of others. Jude wrote this letter to the church to clear up any deceptions and remind believers that what we do really does matter to God.

The final verse is a perfect segue into the final New Testament book, Revelation. "To him be glory, greatness, power, and authority," indeed!

## RadicalFaith:

# Jude 14-15

You weren't alive when Jesus came to earth the first time, but you might be when he comes the second time. When he comes again, Jesus is going to be seen in all his glory—there will be no questioning of his power when he returns (Matthew 24:30-31). God has given you secret insight into what's coming up, and you can't afford to ignore it. Daniel had a vision in which everyone was standing before God and facing judgment (Daniel 7:9-10). Jude said that God will "judge every person." That means you. That means everyone you know. There will be judgment for every action and for every word spoken (Matthew 12:36). If you've put your faith in Christ, God's mercy covers every mistake you've committed and every flaw you have. Christ's righteousness makes you clean and forgiven in God's eyes. But, according to Scripture, that doesn't necessarily mean that you won't somehow be held accountable for how you used your abilities, your opportunities, and your time while on earth. If the Day of Judgment were today, what would God say about you? What are you doing to lead others to Christ? Pray about how you can help others know God. Be faithful, and God will honor your commitment to him.

[1]From Jude, a servant of Jesus Christ and a brother of James.

To all who have been called by God. God the Father loves you, and you have been kept safe in Jesus Christ:

[2]Mercy, peace, and love be yours richly.

### GOD WILL PUNISH SINNERS

[3]Dear friends, I wanted very much to write you about the salvation we all share. But I felt the need to write you about something else: I want to encourage you to fight hard for the faith that was given the holy people of God once and for all time. [4]Some people have secretly entered your group. Long ago the prophets wrote about these people who will be judged guilty. They are against God and have changed the grace of our God into a reason for sexual sin. They also refuse to accept Jesus Christ, our only Master and Lord.

[5]I want to remind you of some things you already know: Remember that the Lord saved his people by bringing them out of the land of Egypt. But later he destroyed all those who did not believe. [6]And remember the angels who did not keep their place of power but left their proper home. The Lord has kept these angels in darkness, bound with everlasting chains, to be judged on the great day. [7]Also remember the cities of Sodom and Gomorrah" and the other towns around them. In the same way they were full of sexual sin and people who desired sexual relations that God does not allow. They suffer the punishment of eternal fire, as an example for all to see.

[8]It is the same with these people who have entered your group. They are guided by dreams and make themselves filthy with sin. They reject God's authority and speak against the angels. [9]Not even the archangel" Michael, when he argued with the devil about who would have the body of Moses, dared to judge the devil guilty. Instead, he said, "The Lord punish you." [10]But these people speak against things they do not understand. And what they do know, by

## Promises!

# Jude 24

Temptation. It's as old as Eve and the forbidden fruit, consuming humankind relentlessly for thousands of years. Paul struggled with it. Even Jesus was tempted by Satan in the desert. It's no news to you that dealing with temptation can be hard. As soon as you vow not to do something, suddenly it's right there in front of your face, daring you to ignore it.

So what can you do in the face of temptation? You've probably heard the phrase "There's always a way out"; it's often used when referring to dealing with temptation. And it's true—God can always help you to be strong and not to fall. God is not affected by temptation, so you can pray that he will help you to stand firm in the face of a hard situation. He gives you another tool, as well—your good sense. Another sure way to overcome temptation is to remove yourself from places, situations, and people that you know will cause you to struggle. God understands the battle and he hasn't left you hanging out there alone. Use the tools he has given you to be victorious today!

**7 Sodom and Gomorrah** Two cities God destroyed because they were so evil.  **9 archangel** The leader among God's angels or messengers.

feeling, as dumb animals know things, are the very things that destroy them. [11]It will be terrible for them. They have followed the way of Cain, and for money they have given themselves to doing the wrong that Balaam did. They have fought against God as Korah did, and like Korah, they surely will be destroyed. [12]They are like dirty spots in your special Christian meals you share. They eat with you and have no fear, caring only for themselves. They are clouds without rain, which the wind blows around. They are autumn trees without fruit that are pulled out of the ground. So they are twice dead. [13]They are like wild waves of the sea, tossing up their own shameful actions like foam. They are like stars that wander in the sky. A place in the blackest darkness has been kept for them forever.

[14]Enoch, the seventh descendant from Adam, said about these people: "Look, the Lord is coming with many thousands of his holy angels to [15]judge every person. He is coming to punish all who are against God for all the evil they have done against him. And he will punish the sinners who are against God for all the evil they have said against him."

[16]These people complain and blame others, doing the evil things they want to do. They brag about themselves, and they flatter others to get what they want.

## A WARNING AND THINGS TO DO

[17]Dear friends, remember what the apostles of our Lord Jesus Christ said before. [18]They said to you, "In the last times there will be people who laugh about God, following their own evil desires which are against God." [19]These are the people who divide you, people whose thoughts are only of this world, who do not have the Spirit.

[20]But dear friends, use your most holy faith to build yourselves up, praying in the Holy Spirit. [21]Keep yourselves in God's love as you wait for the Lord Jesus Christ with his mercy to give you life forever.

[22]Show mercy to some people who have doubts. [23]Take others out of the fire, and save them. Show mercy mixed with fear to others, hating even their clothes which are dirty from sin.

## PRAISE GOD

[24]God is strong and can help you not to fall. He can bring you before his glory without any wrong in you and can give you great joy. [25]He is the only God, the One who saves us. To him be glory, greatness, power, and authority through Jesus Christ our Lord for all time past, now, and forever. Amen.

**a** lamb with seven horns and seven eyes. Locusts that sting like scorpions. A dragon with seven heads and ten horns. At first glance, the Book of Revelation can seem more like a horror movie than a book from the Bible. Actually, Revelation details John's bizarre—but completely cool—vision on the isle of Patmos.

# Revelation

## The Big Finish

So what does it all mean? Bible scholars still debate about whether John's wild revelation is a portrayal of actual futuristic events or if it's meant to be symbolic. Only God can know for sure. But what we do know is that, at some point, God will put an end to the sin, devastation, and chaos that we humans have allowed Satan to cultivate in the world. And each of us will be held accountable for our own faith, attitudes, and actions on earth.

It's pretty amazing that God would use John, "the follower Jesus loved," to deliver his final love letter to us. Yes, Revelation really is a love letter for those who have put our trust and faith in Christ. Not only does God share his promises for the future of his bride—that's us, his followers—but Revelation also assures a blessing for all those who read it, hear it, and do what it says (1:3).

**top 10**

random ways to get close to God

**10** Admire his creation.

Memorize Bible verses. **9**

**8** Attend church and youth group.

Start a Bible study. **7**

**6** Spend time with others who love him.

Be faithful in giving. **5**

**4** Sing praises out loud.

Ask him for help when you need it. **3**

**2** Talk to him like you would a friend.

Read his word — a lot. **1**

## JOHN TELLS ABOUT THIS BOOK

1 This is the revelation" of Jesus Christ, which God gave to him, to show his servants what must soon happen. And Jesus sent his angel to show it to his servant John, [2]who has told everything he has seen. It is the word of God; it is the message from Jesus Christ. [3]Happy is the one who reads the words of God's message, and happy are the people who hear this message and do what is written in it. The time is near when all of this will happen.

## JESUS' MESSAGE TO THE CHURCHES

[4]From John.

To the seven churches in the country of Asia:

Grace and peace to you from the One who is and was and is coming, and from the seven spirits before his throne, [5]and from Jesus Christ. Jesus is the faithful witness, the first among those raised from the dead. He is the ruler of the kings of the earth.

He is the One who loves us, who made us free from our sins with the blood of his death. [6]He made us to be a kingdom of priests who serve God his Father. To Jesus Christ be glory and power forever and ever! Amen.

[7]Look, Jesus is coming with the clouds, and everyone will see him, even those who stabbed him. And all peoples of the earth will cry loudly because of him. Yes, this will happen! Amen.

[8]The Lord God says, "I am the Alpha and the Omega." I am the One who is and was and is coming. I am the Almighty."

[9]I, John, am your brother. All of us share with Christ in suffering, in the kingdom, and in patience to continue. I was on the island of Patmos," because I had preached the word of God and the message about Jesus. [10]On the Lord's day I was in the Spirit, and I heard a loud voice behind me that sounded like a trumpet. [11]The voice said, "Write what you see in a book and send it to the seven churches: to Ephesus, Smyrna, Pergamum, Thyatira, Sardis, Philadelphia, and Laodicea."

[12]I turned to see who was talking to me.

When I turned, I saw seven golden lampstands [13]and someone among the lampstands who was "like a Son of Man." He was dressed in a long robe and had a gold band around his chest. [14]His head and hair were white like wool, as white as snow, and his eyes were like flames of fire. [15]His feet were like bronze that glows hot in a furnace, and his voice was like the noise of flooding water. [16]He held seven stars in his right hand, and a sharp double-edged sword came out of his mouth. He looked like the sun shining at its brightest time.

[17]When I saw him, I fell down at his feet like a dead man. He put his right hand on me and said, "Do not be afraid. I am the First and the Last. [18]I am the One who lives; I was dead, but look, I am alive forever and ever! And I hold the keys to death and to the place of the dead. [19]So write the things you see, what is now and what will happen later. [20]Here is the secret of the seven stars that you saw in my right hand and the seven golden lampstands: The seven lampstands are the seven churches, and the seven stars are the angels of the seven churches.

## TO THE CHURCH IN EPHESUS

2 "Write this to the angel of the church in Ephesus:

"The One who holds the seven stars in his right hand and walks among the seven golden lampstands says this: [2]I know what you do, how you work hard and never give up. I know you do not put up with the false teachings of evil people. You have tested those who say they are apostles but really are not, and you found they are liars. [3]You have patience and have suffered troubles for my name and have not given up.

[4]"But I have this against you: You have left the love you had in the beginning. [5]So remember where you were before you fell. Change your hearts and do what you did at first. If you do not change, I will come to you and will take away your lampstand from its place. [6]But there is something you do that is right: You hate what the Nicolaitans" do, as much as I.

[7]"Every person who has ears should listen

1:1 **revelation** Making known truth that has been hidden.  1:8 **Alpha and the Omega** The first and last letters of the Greek alphabet. This means "the beginning and the end."  1:9 **Patmos** A small island in the Aegean Sea, near the coast of Asia Minor (modern Turkey).  1:13 **"like . . . Man"** "Son of Man" is a name Jesus called himself.  2:6 **Nicolaitans** This is the name of a religious group that followed false beliefs and ideas.

to what the Spirit says to the churches. To those who win the victory I will give the right to eat the fruit from the tree of life, which is in the garden of God.

## TO THE CHURCH IN SMYRNA

8"Write this to the angel of the church in Smyrna:

"The One who is the First and the Last, who died and came to life again, says this: 9I know your troubles and that you are poor, but really you are rich! I know the bad things some people say about you. They say they are Jews, but they are not true Jews. They are a synagogue that belongs to Satan. 10Do not be afraid of what you are about to suffer. I tell you, the devil will put some of you in prison to test you, and you will suffer for ten days. But be faithful, even if you have to die, and I will give you the crown of life.

11"Everyone who has ears should listen to what the Spirit says to the churches. Those who win the victory will not be hurt by the second death.

## TO THE CHURCH IN PERGAMUM

12"Write this to the angel of the church in Pergamum:

"The One who has the sharp, double-edged sword says this: 13I know where you live. It is where Satan has his throne. But you are true to me. You did not refuse to tell about your faith in me even during the time of Antipas, my faithful witness who was killed in your city, where Satan lives.

14"But I have a few things against you: You have some there who follow the teaching of Balaam. He taught Balak how to cause the people of Israel to sin by eating food offered to idols and by taking part in sexual sins. 15You also have some who follow the teaching of the Nicolaitans." 16So change your hearts and lives. If you do not, I will come to you quickly and fight against them with the sword that comes out of my mouth.

17"Everyone who has ears should listen to what the Spirit says to the churches.

## Bible Basics

Christ told several stories about sheep, making the analogy that people are the sheep and he (God) is the shepherd. A shepherd tends his sheep by feeding them, leading them to water, keeping them safe, making sure they don't wander away, and getting them out of trouble. That's a lot of what God does for us humans he created. He provides for us, sustains us, protects us from harm, nudges us if we are straying from our relationship with him, and rescues us when we call out to him—no matter what kind of mess we have made. Sheep are not very smart on their own. They need a shepherd or they will die. Likewise, we need Christ as our **Great Shepherd**, or we will die spiritually and face an eternity separated from our creator.

## → CHECK IT OUT

### SALVATION ARMY

The Salvation Army is an evangelical part of the universal Christian Church that provides aid and preaches the gospel to people in more than 100 countries around the world. The Salvation Army began in 1865 when William Booth, a London minister, gave up his pulpit and decided to hit the streets and take the gospel message where it would reach the poor, the homeless, and the hungry. Today, the Salvation Army continues Booth's intention through its mission statement, which says: "Its message is based on the Bible. Its ministry is motivated by the love of God. Its mission is to preach the gospel of Jesus Christ and to meet human needs in His name without discrimination."

From improving the nutrition of people in a rural town in the Democratic People's Republic of Korea to helping hurricane victims in Florida, the Salvation Army is still fulfilling its mission. Volunteers can donate items to local thrift stores, donate money to bell ringers at Christmas, and volunteer in many capacities.

*Get involved by visiting* www.salvationarmy.org.

notes  **2:15 Nicolaitans** This is the name of a religious group that followed false beliefs and ideas.

# LEARN I+ & LIVE I+

**3 John 11**
**Learn It:** Do not follow what is bad; follow good.
**Live It:** Look for a role model—whether it's a sports hero, celebrity, or youth worker—who loves God and makes it obvious to everyone.

**Jude 23**
**Learn It:** Take people out of the fire of God's wrath and save them, but hate even their clothes that are dirty from sin.
**Live It:** Keep sharing the Good News with unsaved friends, but be very wary of falling in with the wrong things they are doing.

**Revelation 3:19**
**Learn It:** God corrects and punishes the ones he loves.
**Live It:** When you have sinned, recognize that there is complete forgiveness, but there may still be painful consequences to discourage your sinning again.

"I will give some of the hidden manna to everyone who wins the victory. I will also give to each one who wins the victory a white stone with a new name written on it. No one knows this new name except the one who receives it.

## TO THE CHURCH IN THYATIRA

18"Write this to the angel of the church in Thyatira:

"The Son of God, who has eyes that blaze like fire and feet like shining bronze, says this: 19I know what you do. I know about your love, your faith, your service, and your patience. I know that you are doing more now than you did at first.

## DIDYA KNOW

**58% OF TEEN GUYS SAY TATTOOS AND 54% SAY PIERCINGS ARE NOT SEXY.** *ELLEGIRL*

20"But I have this against you: You let that woman Jezebel spread false teachings. She says she is a prophetess, but by her teaching she leads my people to take part in sexual sins and to eat food that is offered to idols. 21I have given her time to change her heart and turn away from her sin, but she does not want to change. 22So I will throw her on a bed of suffering. And all those who take part in adultery with her will suffer greatly if they do not turn away from the wrongs she does. 23I will also kill her followers. Then all the churches will know I am the One who searches hearts and minds, and I will repay each of you for what you have done.

24"But others of you in Thyatira have not followed her teaching and have not learned what some call Satan's deep secrets. I say to you that I will not put any other load on you. 25Only continue in your loyalty until I come.

26"I will give power over the nations to everyone who wins the victory and continues to be obedient to me until the end.

27'You will rule over them with an iron rod, as when pottery is broken into pieces.'

*Psalm 2:9*

28This is the same power I received from my Father. I will also give him the morning star. 29Everyone who has ears should listen to what the Spirit says to the churches.

## TO THE CHURCH IN SARDIS

3 "Write this to the angel of the church in Sardis:

"The One who has the seven spirits and the seven stars says this: I know what you do. People say that you are alive, but really you are dead. 2Wake up! Make yourselves stronger before what you have left dies completely. I have found that what you are doing is less than what my God wants. 3So do not forget what you have received and heard. Obey it, and change your hearts and lives. So you must wake up, or I will come like a thief, and you will not know when I will come to you. 4But you have a few there in Sardis who have kept their clothes unstained, so they will walk with me and will wear white clothes, because they are worthy. 5Those who win the victory will be dressed in white clothes like them. And I will not erase their names from the book of life, but I will say they belong to me before my Father and before his angels. 6Everyone who has ears should listen to what the Spirit says to the churches.

## TO THE CHURCH IN PHILADELPHIA

7"Write this to the angel of the church in Philadelphia:

"This is what the One who is holy and true, who holds the key of David, says. When he opens a door, no one can close it. And when he closes it, no one can open it. 8I know what you do. I have put an open door before you, which no one can close. I know you have a little strength, but you have obeyed my teaching and were not afraid to speak my name. 9Those in the synagogue that belongs to Satan say they are Jews, but they are not true Jews; they are liars. I will make them come before you and bow at your feet, and they will know that I have loved you. ¹⁰You have obeyed my teaching about not giving up your faith. So I will keep you from the time of trouble that will come to the whole world to test those who live on earth.

¹¹"I am coming soon. Continue strong in your faith so no one will take away your crown. ¹²I will make those who win the victory pillars in the temple of my God, and they will never have to leave it. I will write on them the name of my God and the name of the city of my God, the new Jerusalem,ⁿ that comes down out of heaven from my God. I will also write on them my new name. ¹³Everyone who has ears should listen to what the Spirit says to the churches.

## TO THE CHURCH IN LAODICEA

¹⁴"Write this to the angel of the church in Laodicea:

"The Amen,ⁿ the faithful and true witness, the beginning of all God has made, says this: ¹⁵I know what you do, that you are not hot or cold. I wish that you were hot or cold! ¹⁶But because you are lukewarm—neither hot, nor cold—I am ready to spit you out of my mouth. ¹⁷You say, 'I am rich, and I have become wealthy and do not need anything.' But you do not know that you are really miserable, pitiful, poor, blind, and naked. ¹⁸I advise you to buy from me gold made pure in fire so you can be truly rich. Buy from me white clothes so you can be clothed and so you can cover your shameful nakedness. Buy from me medicine to put on your eyes so you can truly see.

¹⁹"I correct and punish those whom I love. So be eager to do right, and change your hearts and lives. ²⁰Here I am! I stand at the door and knock. If you hear my voice and open the door, I will come in and eat with you, and you will eat with me.

²¹"Those who win the victory will sit with me on my throne in the same way that I won the victory and sat down with my Father on his throne. ²²Everyone who has ears should listen to what the Spirit says to the churches."

## JOHN SEES HEAVEN

**4** After the vision of these things I looked, and there before me was an open door in heaven. And the same voice that spoke to me before, that sounded like a trumpet, said, "Come up here, and I will show you what must happen after this." ²Immediately I was in the Spirit, and before me was a throne in heaven, and someone was sitting on it. ³The One who sat on the throne looked like precious stones, like jasper and carnelian. All around the throne was a rainbow the color of an emerald. ⁴Around the throne there were twenty-four other thrones with twenty-four elders sitting on them. They were dressed in white and had golden crowns on their heads. ⁵Lightning flashes and noises and thundering came from the throne. Before the throne seven lamps were burning, which are the seven spirits of God. ⁶Also before the throne there was something that looked like a sea of glass, clear like crystal.

In the center and around the throne were four living creatures with eyes all over them, in front and in back. ⁷The first living creature was like a lion. The second was like a calf. The third had a face like a man. The fourth was like a flying eagle. ⁸Each of these four living creatures had six wings and was covered all over with eyes, inside and out. Day and night they never stop saying:

"Holy, holy, holy is the Lord God Almighty.
He was, he is, and he is coming."

⁹These living creatures give glory, honor, and thanks to the One who sits on the throne, who lives forever and ever. ¹⁰Then the twenty-four elders bow down before the One who sits on the throne, and they worship him who lives forever and ever. They put their crowns down before the throne and say:

¹¹"You are worthy, our Lord and God,
to receive glory and honor and power,
because you made all things.
Everything existed and was made,
because you wanted it."

**5** Then I saw a scroll in the right hand of the One sitting on the throne. The scroll had writing on both sides and was kept closed

## RadicalFaith:

# Revelation 4:8-11

Everything on earth is just the way it is because God made it that way. He has control and authority over it all. Everything that you think is beautiful and lovely, God created. He is wonderful. He loves us intensely. Because of his great love, he delights in being close to you. And God is holy. That means he is set apart from everything else; nothing else is as good as he is. It means that he's absolutely perfect and absolutely pure. It means that every living creature will eventually bow in awe before God and cry out praises to him. In heaven, nothing will blur your vision of how powerful, wonderful, loving, and holy he is; and you will want to do nothing but look at him and offer praise to him. You will be completely satisfied and overwhelmed by the desire to worship God. You were designed for worshiping God in heaven and on earth. Live out that role on earth, knowing you'll be doing the same thing in eternity.

**3:12 Jerusalem** This name is used to mean the spiritual city God built for his people. See Revelation 21–22. **3:14 Amen** Used here as a name for Jesus; it means to agree fully that something is true.

with seven seals. [2]And I saw a powerful angel calling in a loud voice, "Who is worthy to break the seals and open the scroll?" [3]But there was no one in heaven or on earth or under the earth who could open the scroll or look inside it. [4]I cried hard because there was no one who was worthy to open the scroll or look inside. [5]But one of the elders said to me, "Do not cry! The Lion[n] from the tribe of Judah, David's descendant, has won the victory so that he is able to open the scroll and its seven seals."

[6]Then I saw a Lamb standing in the center of the throne and in the middle of the four living creatures and the elders. The Lamb looked as if he had been killed. He had seven horns and seven eyes, which are the seven spirits of God that were sent into all the world. [7]The Lamb came and took the scroll from the right hand of the One sitting on the throne. [8]When he took the scroll, the four living creatures and the twenty-four elders bowed down before the Lamb. Each one of them had a harp and golden bowls full of incense, which are the prayers of God's holy people. [9]And they all sang a new song to the Lamb:

"You are worthy to take the scroll
    and to open its seals,
because you were killed,
    and with the blood of your death you
        bought people for God
    from every tribe, language, people, and
        nation.
[10]You made them to be a kingdom of priests
        for our God,
    and they will rule on the earth."

[11]Then I looked, and I heard the voices of many angels around the throne, and the four living creatures, and the elders. There were thousands and thousands of angels, [12]saying in a loud voice:

"The Lamb who was killed is worthy
to receive power, wealth, wisdom, and
    strength,
honor, glory, and praise!"

[13]Then I heard all creatures in heaven and on earth and under the earth and in the sea saying:

"To the One who sits on the throne
    and to the Lamb
be praise and honor and glory and power
    forever and ever."

[14]The four living creatures said, "Amen," and the elders bowed down and worshiped.

6 Then I watched while the Lamb opened the first of the seven seals. I heard one of the four living creatures say with a voice like thunder, "Come!" [2]I looked, and there before me was a white horse. The rider on the horse held a bow, and he was given a crown, and he rode out, determined to win the victory.

[3]When the Lamb opened the second seal, I heard the second living creature say, "Come!" [4]Then another horse came out, a red one. Its rider was given power to take away peace from the earth and to make people kill each other, and he was given a big sword.

[5]When the Lamb opened the third seal, I heard the third living creature say, "Come!" I looked, and there before me was a black horse, and its rider held a pair of scales in his hand. [6]Then I heard something that sounded like a voice coming from the middle of the four living creatures. The voice said, "A quart of wheat for a day's pay, and three quarts of barley for a day's pay, and do not damage the olive oil and wine!"

[7]When the Lamb opened the fourth seal, I heard the voice of the fourth living creature say, "Come!" [8]I looked, and there before me was a pale horse. Its rider was named death, and Hades[n] was following close behind him. They were given power over a fourth of the earth to kill people by war, by starvation, by disease, and by the wild animals of the earth.

[9]When the Lamb opened the fifth seal, I saw under the altar the souls of those who had been killed because they were faithful to the word of God and to the message they had received. [10]These souls shouted in a loud voice, "Holy and true Lord, how long until you judge the people of the earth and punish them for killing us?" [11]Then each one of them was given a white robe and was told to wait a short time longer. There were still some of their fellow servants and brothers and sisters[n] in the service of Christ who must be killed as they were. They had to wait until all of this was finished.

[12]Then I watched while the Lamb opened the sixth seal, and there was a great earthquake. The sun became black like rough black cloth, and the whole moon became red like blood. [13]And the stars in the sky fell to the earth like figs falling from a fig tree when the wind blows. [14]The sky disappeared as a scroll when it is rolled up, and every mountain and island was moved from its place.

[15]Then the kings of the earth, the rulers, the generals, the rich people, the powerful people, the slaves, and the free people hid themselves in caves and in the rocks on the mountains. [16]They called to the mountains and the rocks, "Fall on us. Hide us from the face of the One who sits on the throne and from the anger of

## beautysecret

### Nail Polish

You can use a variety of colors—and a combination of colors—to spruce up your nails.

If your nail polish becomes too thick or hard to use, add a few drops of nail polish remover to thin it. Store your nail polish in the refrigerator for long-lasting use.

5:5 **Lion** Here refers to Christ.   6:8 **Hades** The unseen world of the dead.   6:11 **brothers and sisters** Although the Greek text says "brothers" here and throughout this book, both men and women would have been included.

386

the Lamb! 17The great day for their anger has come, and who can stand against it?"

## THE 144,000 PEOPLE OF ISRAEL

7 After the vision of these things I saw four angels standing at the four corners of the earth. The angels were holding the four winds of the earth to keep them from blowing on the land or on the sea or on any tree. 2Then I saw another angel coming up from the east who had the seal of the living God. And he called out in a loud voice to the four angels to whom God had given power to harm the earth and the sea. 3He said to them, "Do not harm the land or the sea or the trees until we mark with a sign the foreheads of the people who serve our God." 4Then I heard how many peo-ple were marked with the sign. There were one hundred forty-four thousand from every tribe of the people of Israel.

5From the tribe of Judah twelve thousand
    were marked with the sign,
from the tribe of Reuben twelve thousand,
from the tribe of Gad twelve thousand,
6from the tribe of Asher twelve thousand,
from the tribe of Naphtali twelve thousand,
from the tribe of Manasseh twelve
    thousand,
7from the tribe of Simeon twelve thousand,
from the tribe of Levi twelve thousand,
from the tribe of Issachar twelve thousand,
8from the tribe of Zebulun twelve thousand,
from the tribe of Joseph twelve thousand,
and from the tribe of Benjamin twelve
    thousand were marked with the sign.

## THE GREAT CROWD WORSHIPS GOD

9After the vision of these things I looked, and there was a great number of people, so many that no one could count them. They were from every nation, tribe, people, and language of the earth. They were all standing before the throne and before the Lamb, wearing white robes and holding palm branches in their hands. 10They were shouting in a loud voice, "Salvation belongs to our God, who sits on the throne, and to the Lamb." 11All the angels were standing around the throne and the elders and the four living creatures. They all bowed down on their faces before the throne and worshiped God, 12saying, "Amen! Praise, glory, wisdom, thanks, honor, power, and strength belong to our God forever and ever. Amen!"

13Then one of the elders asked me, "Who are these people dressed in white robes? Where did they come from?"

14I answered, "You know, sir."

And the elder said to me, "These are the people who have come out of the great dis-tress. They have washed their robes" and made them white in the blood of the Lamb. 15Because of this, they are before the throne of God. They worship him day and night in his temple. And the One who sits on the throne will be present with them. 16Those people will

## relationships

When your sister, brother, or friend does something you know they shouldn't, do you go tell someone to get them in trouble? Matthew 18:15 says, "If your fellow believer sins against you, go and tell him in private what he did wrong." Yep, you have to talk to that person first. If they don't listen, the Bible says get some friends together and try talking to the person again. If they still refuse to change, then you can tell someone in authority. Make sure your goal is to help them and not to hurt them.

## Radical Faith:

# Revelation 7:15-17

Picture how you feel when you haven't eaten all day and you finally get to eat. Think about the last time you were up all night and then finally got to go to sleep. Remember a time when you were in the "safe zone" in a game of tag and you could relax because you knew no one could get to you. Those feelings are a microscopic version of what heaven will be like. You will never be dissatisfied or be in pain. You won't have to worry about getting tired. You'll be far away from anything that can hurt you. All the sadness, loss, and frustration in your earthly life will be completely gone. You will be with your Shepherd—your protector who knows and loves you. You will know true, deep, satisfying life. You will be overcome with God's love, intensity, holiness, and beauty. Nothing can compare to what God's glory will be like. There is peace in knowing that all the pain you experience on earth will come to an end. But even greater is the joy that comes from knowing you will remain in God's presence and glory for eternity.

 **notes** 7:14 **washed their robes** This means they believed in Jesus so that their sins could be forgiven by Christ's blood.

# Music Reviews

**GROUP:** OUT OF EDEN

**ALBUM:** THIS IS YOUR LIFE (CLASSIC HIT)

Sisters Lisa and Danielle Kimmey and Andrea Kimmey-Baca were the first group signed to the record label Gotee, which was started by dc talk member tobyMac and a few friends over a decade ago. *This Is Your Life* is Out Of Eden's fourth album since they started back in 1994. The Kimmey sisters pump on urban tracks like the bold proclamation of faith "Different Now" and the worshipful "Praise You."

**WHY IT ROCKS: LISA KIMMEY WRITES SONGS THAT GO DEEP, WITH PLENTY OF DANCE BEATS AND URBAN SENSIBILITIES THAT MAKE THIS DISC A HIT.**

never be hungry again, and they will never be thirsty again. The sun will not hurt them, and no heat will burn them, <sup>17</sup>because the Lamb at the center of the throne will be their shepherd. He will lead them to springs of water that give life. And God will wipe away every tear from their eyes."

## THE SEVENTH SEAL

8 When the Lamb opened the seventh seal, there was silence in heaven for about half an hour. <sup>2</sup>And I saw the seven angels who stand before God and to whom were given seven trumpets.

<sup>3</sup>Another angel came and stood at the altar, holding a golden pan for incense. He was given much incense to offer with the prayers of all God's holy people. The angel put this offering on the golden altar before the throne. <sup>4</sup>The smoke from the incense went up from the angel's hand to God with the prayers of God's people. <sup>5</sup>Then the angel filled the incense pan with fire from the altar and threw it on the earth, and there were flashes of lightning, thunder and loud noises, and an earthquake.

## THE SEVEN ANGELS AND TRUMPETS

<sup>6</sup>Then the seven angels who had the seven trumpets prepared to blow them.

<sup>7</sup>The first angel blew his trumpet, and hail and fire mixed with blood were poured down on the earth. And a third of the earth, and all the green grass, and a third of the trees were burned up.

<sup>8</sup>Then the second angel blew his trumpet, and something that looked like a big mountain, burning with fire, was thrown into the sea. And a third of the sea became blood, <sup>9</sup>a third of the living things in the sea died, and a third of the ships were destroyed.

<sup>10</sup>Then the third angel blew his trumpet, and a large star, burning like a torch, fell from the sky. It fell on a third of the rivers and on the springs of water. <sup>11</sup>The name of the star is Wormwood." And a third of all the water became bitter, and many people died from drinking the water that was bitter.

<sup>12</sup>Then the fourth angel blew his trumpet, and a third of the sun, and a third of the moon, and a third of the stars were struck. So a third of them became dark, and a third of the day was without light, and also the night.

<sup>13</sup>While I watched, I heard an eagle that was flying high in the air cry out in a loud voice, "Trouble! Trouble! Trouble for those who live on the earth because of the remaining sounds of the trumpets that the other three angels are about to blow!"

9 Then the fifth angel blew his trumpet, and I saw a star fall from the sky to the earth. The star was given the key to the deep hole that leads to the bottomless pit. <sup>2</sup>Then it opened up the hole that leads to the bottomless pit, and smoke came up from the hole like smoke from a big furnace. Then the sun and sky became dark because of the smoke from the hole. <sup>3</sup>Then locusts came down to the earth out of the smoke, and they were given the power to sting like scorpions." <sup>4</sup>They were told not to harm the grass on the earth or any plant or tree. They could harm only the people who did not have the sign of God on their foreheads. <sup>5</sup>These locusts were not given the power to kill anyone, but to cause pain to the people for five months. And the pain they felt was like the pain a scorpion gives when it stings someone. <sup>6</sup>During those days people will look for a way to die, but they will not find it. They will want to die, but death will run away from them.

<sup>7</sup>The locusts looked like horses prepared for battle. On their heads they wore what looked like crowns of gold, and their faces looked like human faces. <sup>8</sup>Their hair was like women's hair, and their teeth were like lions' teeth. <sup>9</sup>Their chests looked like iron breastplates, and the sound of their wings was like

**8:11 Wormwood** Name of a very bitter plant; used here to give the idea of bitter sorrow. **9:3 scorpions** A scorpion is an insect that stings with a bad poison.

the noise of many horses and chariots hurrying into battle. [10]The locusts had tails with stingers like scorpions, and in their tails was their power to hurt people for five months. [11]The locusts had a king who was the angel of the bottomless pit. His name in the Hebrew language is Abaddon and in the Greek language is Apollyon."

[12]The first trouble is past; there are still two other troubles that will come.

[13]Then the sixth angel blew his trumpet, and I heard a voice coming from the horns on the golden altar that is before God. [14]The voice said to the sixth angel who had the trumpet, "Free the four angels who are tied at the great river Euphrates." [15]And they let loose the four angels who had been kept ready for this hour and day and month and year so they could kill a third of all people on the earth. [16]I heard how many troops on horses were in their army—two hundred million.

[17]The horses and their riders I saw in the vision looked like this: They had breastplates that were fiery red, dark blue, and yellow like sulfur. The heads of the horses looked like heads of lions, with fire, smoke, and sulfur coming out of their mouths. [18]A third of all the people on earth were killed by these three terrible disasters coming out of the horses' mouths: the fire, the smoke, and the sulfur. [19]The horses' power was in their mouths and in their tails; their tails were like snakes with heads, and with them they hurt people.

[20]The other people who were not killed by these terrible disasters still did not change their hearts and turn away from what they had made with their own hands. They did not stop worshiping demons and idols made of gold, silver, bronze, stone, and wood—things that cannot see or hear or walk. [21]These people did not change their hearts and turn away from murder or evil magic, from their sexual sins or stealing.

## THE ANGEL AND THE SMALL SCROLL

**10** Then I saw another powerful angel coming down from heaven dressed

# Tamar

**[2 SAMUEL 13]** The story of King David's daughter, Tamar, is a perfect case study for Dysfunctional Family 101. Her half brother, Amnon, tricked her into being alone with him and made a lewd sexual advance toward her. When she rejected his disgusting offer, Amnon raped her. And while Tamar needed her father's help the most, David did nothing to punish Amnon. But Tamar's brother, Absalom, became so angry that he murdered Amnon two years later after having talked Tamar into keeping quiet about the rape. Instead of finding the immediate family support and encouragement she really needed to cope with such a terrible crime, Tamar was manipulated by the men in her life.

in a cloud with a rainbow over his head. His face was like the sun, and his legs were like pillars of fire. [2]The angel was holding a small scroll open in his hand. He put his right foot on the sea and his left foot on the land. [3]Then he shouted loudly like the roaring of a lion. And when he shouted, the voices of seven thunders spoke. [4]When the seven thunders spoke, I started to write. But I heard a voice from heaven say, "Keep hidden what the seven thunders said, and do not write them down."

[5]Then the angel I saw standing on the sea and on the land raised his right hand to heaven, [6]and he made a promise by the power of the One who lives forever and ever. He is the One who made the skies and all that is in them, the earth and all that is in it, and the sea and all that is in it. The angel promised, "There will be no more waiting! [7]In the days when the seventh angel is ready to blow his trumpet, God's secret will be finished. This secret is the Good News God told to his servants, the prophets."

[8]Then I heard the same voice from heaven again, saying to me: "Go and take the open

scroll that is in the hand of the angel that is standing on the sea and on the land."

[9]So I went to the angel and told him to give me the small scroll. And he said to me, "Take the scroll and eat it. It will be sour in your stomach, but in your mouth it will be sweet as honey." [10]So I took the small scroll from the angel's hand and ate it. In my mouth it tasted sweet as honey, but after I ate it, it was sour in my stomach. [11]Then I was told, "You must prophesy again about many peoples, nations, languages, and kings."

## THE TWO WITNESSES

**11** I was given a measuring stick like a rod, and I was told, "Go and measure the temple of God and the altar, and count the people worshiping there. [2]But do not measure the yard outside the temple. Leave it alone, because it has been given to those who are not God's people. And they will trample on the holy city for forty-two months. [3]And I will give power to my two witnesses to prophesy for one thousand two hundred sixty days, and they

**notes** 9:11 **Abaddon, Apollyon** Both names mean "Destroyer."

# Blab

**Q:** I sinned and a friend of mine saw me. Now I am afraid she will never believe my faith is real. Have I blown my chance to witness?

**A:** When you sin, it gives you an opportunity to share with your friend what grace means and why people need God in the first place. You are not perfect, and God does not expect you to be. Tell your friend you were wrong and that you have asked God to forgive you. Then show her that you won't do it again. This will make an even bigger impression on her than if your friend just saw you trying to be perfect all the time.

**Q:** I always thought sin was dark, evil, and bad. But really, a lot of the things that are sin are fun. Does God just want to take away our fun with his rules?

**A:** Sin can be great fun. Sex feels good; getting a buzz makes you feel giddy. Even stealing can give you a head rush. If sin weren't fun, no one would do it. No one would mess up, and then what would we need God for? The problem with sin is its nasty consequences. They are painful and lead to self-destruction without God.

**Q:** What is fasting? Should I do it?

**A:** Fasting means giving up something for God. Traditionally, it means giving up food, like Jesus did when he went into the desert. When your body is still growing, fasting from food may not be the best plan. Check with your parents and your doctor first.

will be dressed in rough cloth to show their sadness."

[4] These two witnesses are the two olive trees and the two lampstands that stand before the Lord of the earth. [5] And if anyone tries to hurt them, fire comes from their mouths and kills their enemies. And if anyone tries to hurt them in whatever way, in that same way that person will die. [6] These witnesses have the power to stop the sky from raining during the time they are prophesying. And they have power to make the waters become blood, and they have power to send every kind of trouble to the earth as many times as they want.

[7] When the two witnesses have finished telling their message, the beast that comes up from the bottomless pit will fight a war against them. He will defeat them and kill them. [8] The bodies of the two witnesses will lie in the street of the great city where the Lord was killed. This city is named Sodom[n] and Egypt, which has a spiritual meaning. [9] Those from every race of people, tribe, language, and nation will look at the bodies of the two witnesses for three and one-half days, and they will refuse to bury them. [10] People who live on the earth will rejoice and be happy because these two are dead. They will send each other gifts, because these two prophets brought much suffering to those who live on the earth.

[11] But after three and one-half days, God put the breath of life into the two prophets again. They stood on their feet, and everyone who saw them became very afraid. [12] Then the two prophets heard a loud voice from heaven saying, "Come up here!" And they went up into heaven in a cloud as their enemies watched.

[13] In the same hour there was a great earthquake, and a tenth of the city was destroyed. Seven thousand people were killed in the earthquake, and those who did not die were very afraid and gave glory to the God of heaven.

[14] The second trouble is finished. Pay attention: The third trouble is coming soon.

## THE SEVENTH TRUMPET

[15] Then the seventh angel blew his trumpet. And there were loud voices in heaven, saying:

"The power to rule the world
now belongs to our Lord and his Christ,
and he will rule forever and ever."

[16] Then the twenty-four elders, who sit on their thrones before God, bowed down on their faces and worshiped God. [17] They said:

"We give thanks to you, Lord God
Almighty,
who is and who was,
because you have used your great power
and have begun to rule!
[18] The people of the world were angry,
but your anger has come.
The time has come to judge the dead,
and to reward your servants the prophets
and your holy people,
all who respect you, great and small.
The time has come to destroy those who
destroy the earth!"

[19] Then God's temple in heaven was opened. The Ark that holds the agreement God gave to his people could be seen in his temple. Then there were flashes of lightning, noises, thunder, an earthquake, and a great hailstorm.

## THE WOMAN AND THE DRAGON

**12** And then a great wonder appeared in heaven: A woman was clothed with the sun, and the moon was under her feet, and a crown of twelve stars was on her head. [2] She was pregnant and cried out with pain, because she was about to give birth. [3] Then another wonder appeared in heaven: There was a giant red dragon with seven heads and seven crowns on each head. He also had ten horns. [4] His tail swept a third of the stars out of the sky and threw them down to the earth. He stood in front of the woman who was ready to give birth so he could eat her baby as soon as it was born. [5] Then the woman gave birth to a son who will rule all the nations with an iron rod. And her child was taken up to God and to his throne. [6] The woman ran away into the desert to a place God prepared for her where she would be taken care of for one thousand two hundred sixty days.

[7] Then there was a war in heaven. Michael[n] and his angels fought against the dragon, and

**notes**    **11:8 Sodom** City that God destroyed because the people were so evil.    **12:7 Michael** The archangel—leader among God's angels or messengers (Jude 9).

390

the dragon and his angels fought back. [8]But the dragon was not strong enough, and he and his angels lost their place in heaven. [9]The giant dragon was thrown down out of heaven. (He is that old snake called the devil or Satan, who tricks the whole world.) The dragon with his angels was thrown down to the earth.

[10]Then I heard a loud voice in heaven saying:

"The salvation and the power and the
    kingdom of our God
    and the authority of his Christ have now
    come.
The accuser of our brothers and sisters,
    who accused them day and night before
    our God,
    has been thrown down.
[11]And our brothers and sisters defeated him
    by the blood of the Lamb's death
    and by the message they preached.
They did not love their lives so much
    that they were afraid of death.
[12]So rejoice, you heavens
    and all who live there!
But it will be terrible for the earth and the
    sea,
    because the devil has come down to
    you!
He is filled with anger,
    because he knows he does not have
    much time."

## "THIS MEANS THAT GOD'S HOLY PEOPLE MUST HAVE PATIENCE AND FAITH."

[13]When the dragon saw he had been thrown down to the earth, he hunted for the woman who had given birth to the son. [14]But the woman was given the two wings of a great eagle so she could fly to the place prepared for her in the desert. There she would be taken care of for three and one-half years, away from the snake. [15]Then the snake poured water out of its mouth like a river toward the woman so the flood would carry her away. [16]But the earth helped the woman by opening its mouth and swallowing the river that came from the mouth of the dragon. [17]Then the dragon was very angry at the woman, and he went off to make war against all her other children—those who obey God's commands and who have the message Jesus taught.

[18]And the dragon stood on the seashore.

### THE TWO BEASTS

**13** Then I saw a beast coming up out of the sea. It had ten horns and seven heads, and there was a crown on each horn. A name against God was written on each head. [2]This beast looked like a leopard, with feet like a bear's feet and a mouth like a lion's mouth. And the dragon gave the beast all of his power and his throne and great authority. [3]One of the heads of the beast looked as if it had been killed by a wound, but this death wound was healed. Then the whole world was amazed and followed the beast. [4]People worshiped the dragon because he had given his power to the beast. And they also worshiped the beast, asking, "Who is like the beast? Who can make war against it?"

[5]The beast was allowed to say proud words and words against God, and it was allowed to use its power for forty-two months. [6]It used its mouth to speak against God, against God's name, against the place where God lives, and against all those who live in heaven. [7]It was given power to make war against God's holy people and to defeat them. It was given power over every tribe, people, language, and nation. [8]And all who live on earth will worship the beast—all the people since the beginning of the world whose names are not written in the Lamb's book of life. The Lamb is the One who was killed.

[9]Anyone who has ears should listen:
[10]If you are to be a prisoner,
    then you will be a prisoner.
If you are to be killed with the sword,
    then you will be killed with the sword.

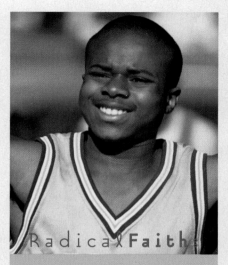

Radical Faith

## Revelation 11:15

Don't you love it when you're on the winning team? When you're on the side that holds the reigning championship crown? When you're devoted to God, you have something even better to look forward to for all of eternity. God will bring justice to every inch of his creation, and he will reign as king on the throne forever. Everyone will acknowledge that only he is perfect, good, all-powerful, and right. Everyone will bow before him, and those who doubted will be ashamed (Isaiah 45:23-24). Daniel had a glimpse of Jesus reigning with God in the future: "He was given authority, glory, and the strength of a king. People of every tribe, nation, and language will serve him. His rule will last forever, and his kingdom will never be destroyed" (Daniel 7:14). God is so powerful, so perfect, so beautiful, so holy . . . so much more than anyone can put into words or imagine. But you can be sure that one day you will see his face and join all the heavenly beings who cry out their worship to him. You'll want more than anything just to give him glory and honor. You'll get to share in the glory of the One who will reign forever!

# Promises:

# Revelation
## 12:10-12

No matter what some people may debate, the devil (a.k.a. Satan or Lucifer) is real. He loves to tempt, lure, and otherwise assert control over human beings until they do things that are immoral, wrong, and hurtful. Basically, he wants all of us, especially Christians, to turn away from God and to doubt his goodness. In C. S. Lewis's *The Screwtape Letters*, a fictional senior demon, Screwtape, mentors his nephew, Wormwood, on the best ways to make humans fall into temptation. Screwtape coaches Wormwood on various subjects, such as war, prayer, anxiety, laughter, and gluttony, and shows him how to push humans away from God, constantly referring to God as the "Enemy."

Revelation is full of fanciful-sounding scripture involving all sorts of weird creatures and surreal events. It can be hard to follow and comprehend. But what it all boils down to is this: God will be victorious over all the earth, and Satan will be defeated and lose all of his power over us. God will reign forever and bring restoration and healing to his people. What a joyful and powerful way to end the Bible. Our God reigns!

This means that God's holy people must have patience and faith.

[11]Then I saw another beast coming up out of the earth. It had two horns like a lamb, but it spoke like a dragon. [12]This beast stands before the first beast and uses the same power the first beast has. By this power it makes everyone living on earth worship the first beast, who had the death wound that was healed. [13]And the second beast does great miracles so that it even makes fire come down from heaven to earth while people are watching. [14]It fools those who live on earth by the miracles it has been given the power to do. It does these miracles to serve the first beast. The second beast orders people to make an idol to honor the first beast, the one that was wounded by the deadly sword but sprang to life again. [15]The second beast was given power to give life to the idol of the first one so that the idol could speak. And the second beast was given power to command all who will not worship the image of the beast to be killed. [16]The second beast also forced all people, small and great, rich and poor, free and slave, to have a mark on their right hand or on their forehead. [17]No one could buy or sell without this mark, which is the name of the beast or the number of its name. [18]This takes wisdom. Let the one who has understanding find the meaning of the number, which is the number of a person. Its number is six hundred sixty-six.

## THE SONG OF THE SAVED

14 Then I looked, and there before me was the Lamb standing on Mount Zion." With him were one hundred forty-four thousand people who had his name and his Father's name written on their foreheads. [2]And I heard a sound from heaven like the noise of flooding water and like the sound of loud thunder. The sound I heard was like people playing harps. [3]And they sang a new song before the throne and before the four living creatures and the elders. No one could learn the new song except the one hundred forty-four thousand who had been bought from the earth. [4]These are the ones who did not do sinful things with women, because they kept themselves pure. They follow the Lamb every place he goes. These one hundred forty-four thousand were bought from among the people of the earth as people to be offered to God and the Lamb. [5]They were not guilty of telling lies; they are without fault.

## THE THREE ANGELS

[6]Then I saw another angel flying high in the air. He had the eternal Good News to preach to those who live on earth—to every nation, tribe, language, and people. [7]He preached in a loud voice, "Fear God and give him praise, because the time has come for God to judge all people. So worship God who made the heavens, and the earth, and the sea, and the springs of water."

[8]Then the second angel followed the first angel and said, "Ruined, ruined is the great city of Babylon! She made all the nations drink the wine of the anger of her adultery."

# beautysecret

## Lotions

Using different lotions can help keep your skin soft and healthy. Keep a small bottle of lotion in your purse—with the cap closed tightly—and another one in your bathroom. Apply lotion after your shower and even when you're away from home. Your skin will thank you!

14:1 **Mount Zion** Another name for Jerusalem; here meaning the spiritual city of God's people.

## CHECK IT OUT

### PREGNANCY CENTERS.ORG

Pregnancy Centers.org offers visitors a network of crisis pregnancy centers around the United States and Canada to help girls make decisions for life when they are faced with an unexpected or unwanted pregnancy. Trained phone consultants are available 24 hours a day to take calls and emails and to potentially save the lives of unborn children. Crisis pregnancy centers offer free pregnancy tests, counseling, assistance to pregnant teens and women, ultrasounds, and other services.

Volunteers can also visit the site and type in their zip code to find a list of crisis pregnancy centers in their area. By contacting a local center and offering your help, you can volunteer for a number of jobs, from training to be a phone counselor to walking in local walkathon fund-raisers.

Donations of baby items are always needed, and you can also get educated about other ways that you can spread the message of abstinence until marriage and the right to life campaigns.

*Get involved by visiting* **www.pregnancycenters.org.**

⁹Then a third angel followed the first two angels, saying in a loud voice: "If anyone worships the beast and his idol and gets the beast's mark on the forehead or on the hand, ¹⁰that one also will drink the wine of God's anger, which is prepared with all its strength in the cup of his anger. And that person will be put in pain with burning sulfur before the holy angels and the Lamb. ¹¹And the smoke from their burning pain will rise forever and ever. There will be no rest, day or night, for those who worship the beast and his idol or who get the mark of his name." ¹²This means God's holy people must be patient. They must obey God's commands and keep their faith in Jesus.

¹³Then I heard a voice from heaven saying, "Write this: Happy are the dead who die from now on in the Lord."

The Spirit says, "Yes, they will rest from their hard work, and the reward of all they have done stays with them."

### THE EARTH IS HARVESTED

¹⁴Then I looked, and there before me was a white cloud, and sitting on the white cloud was One who looked like a Son of Man." He had a gold crown on his head and a sharp sickle" in his hand. ¹⁵Then another angel came out of the temple and called out in a loud voice to the One who was sitting on the cloud, "Take your sickle and harvest from the earth, because the time to harvest has come, and the fruit of the earth is ripe." ¹⁶So the One who was sitting on the cloud swung his sickle over the earth, and the earth was harvested.

¹⁷Then another angel came out of the temple in heaven, and he also had a sharp sickle. ¹⁸And then another angel, who has power over the fire, came from the altar. This angel called to the angel with the sharp sickle, saying, "Take your sharp sickle and gather the bunches of grapes from the earth's vine, because its grapes are ripe." ¹⁹Then the angel swung his sickle over the earth. He gathered the earth's grapes and threw them into the great winepress of God's anger. ²⁰They were trampled in the winepress outside the city, and blood flowed out of the winepress as high as horses' bridles for a distance of about one hundred eighty miles.

### THE LAST TROUBLES

**15** Then I saw another wonder in heaven that was great and amazing. There were seven angels bringing seven disasters. These are the last disasters, because after them, God's anger is finished.

²I saw what looked like a sea of glass mixed with fire. All of those who had won the victory over the beast and his idol and over the number of his name were standing by the sea of glass. They had harps that God had given them. ³They sang the song of Moses, the servant of God, and the song of the Lamb:

"You do great and wonderful things,

*Psalm 111:2*

Lord God Almighty. *Amos 3:13*

Everything the Lord does is right and true,

*Psalm 145:17*

King of the nations.

⁴Everyone will respect you, Lord, *Jeremiah 10:7*

and will honor you.

Only you are holy.

All the nations will come

and worship you, *Psalm 86:9-10*

because the right things you have done

are now made known." *Deuteronomy 32:4*

⁵After this I saw that the temple (the Tent of the Agreement) in heaven was opened. ⁶And the seven angels bringing the seven disasters came out of the temple. They were dressed in clean, shining linen and wore golden bands tied around their chests. ⁷Then one of the four living creatures gave to the seven angels seven golden bowls filled with the anger of God, who lives

---

**notes**   **14:14 Son of Man** "Son of Man" is a name Jesus called himself.   **14:14 sickle** A farming tool with a curved blade. It was used to harvest grain.

Radical Faith:

## Revelation 16:5-7

The writer of Proverbs 2:8 says this about God's character: "He makes sure that justice is done." Pictures of God's judgment throughout Scripture can make you tremble—and they should. His punishment may appear fierce, but he is always correct. God cannot be unjust in his judgments; to be unjust goes against his character. One day everyone and everything will bow before God, worship him, and declare that he brings perfect justice. God will bring consequences to all that is evil because he is just. Every choice you make in your life will be seen. "Nothing in all the world can be hidden from God. Everything is clear and lies open before him, and to him we must explain the way we have lived" (Hebrews 4:13). There is nothing kept from God; he sees every thought and every action. You will be held accountable to him for all that you do and all that you are. The time of judgment will come unexpectedly, and it will come like a thief (2 Peter 3:10). Until then, the truth remains that anyone who calls on the name of the Lord will be saved (Acts 2:21). Those who have given their lives to Christ will be covered with God's righteousness.

forever and ever. [8]The temple was filled with smoke from the glory and the power of God, and no one could enter the temple until the seven disasters of the seven angels were finished.

### THE BOWLS OF GOD'S ANGER

16 Then I heard a loud voice from the temple saying to the seven angels, "Go and pour out the seven bowls of God's anger on the earth."

[2]The first angel left and poured out his bowl on the land. Then ugly and painful sores came upon all those who had the mark of the beast and who worshiped his idol.

[3]The second angel poured out his bowl on the sea, and it became blood like that of a dead man, and every living thing in the sea died.

[4]The third angel poured out his bowl on the rivers and the springs of water, and they became blood. [5]Then I heard the angel of the waters saying:

"Holy One, you are the One who is and who was.

You are right to decide to punish these evil people.

[6]They have poured out the blood of your holy people and your prophets.

So now you have given them blood to drink as they deserve."

[7]And I heard a voice coming from the altar saying:

"Yes, Lord God Almighty,

the way you punish evil people is right and fair."

[8]The fourth angel poured out his bowl on the sun, and he was given power to burn the people with fire. [9]They were burned by the great heat, and they cursed the name of God, who had control over these disasters. But the people refused to change their hearts and lives and give glory to God.

[10]The fifth angel poured out his bowl on the throne of the beast, and darkness covered its kingdom. People gnawed their tongues because of the pain. [11]They also cursed the God of heaven because of their pain and the sores they had, but they refused to change their hearts and turn away from the evil things they did.

[12]The sixth angel poured out his bowl on the great river Euphrates so that the water in the river was dried up to prepare the way for the kings from the east to come. [13]Then I saw three evil spirits that looked like frogs coming out of the mouth of the dragon, out of the mouth of the beast, and out of the mouth of the false prophet. [14]These evil spirits are the spirits of demons, which have power to do miracles. They go out to the kings of the whole world to gather them together for the battle on the great day of God Almighty.

[15]"Listen! I will come as a thief comes! Happy are those who stay awake and keep their clothes on so that they will not walk around naked and have people see their shame."

[16]Then the evil spirits gathered the kings together to the place that is called Armageddon in the Hebrew language.

[17]The seventh angel poured out his bowl into the air. Then a loud voice came out of the temple from the throne, saying, "It is finished!" [18]Then there were flashes of lightning, noises, thunder, and a big earthquake—the worst earthquake that has ever happened since people have been on earth. [19]The great city split into three parts, and the cities of the nations were destroyed. And God remembered the sins of Babylon the Great, so he gave that city the cup filled with the wine of his terrible anger. [20]Then every island ran away, and mountains disappeared. [21]Giant hailstones, each weighing about a hundred pounds, fell from the sky upon people. People cursed God for the disaster of the hail, because this disaster was so terrible.

### THE WOMAN ON THE ANIMAL

17 Then one of the seven angels who had the seven bowls came and spoke to me. He said, "Come, and I will show you the punishment that will be given to the great prostitute, the one sitting over many waters. [2]The kings of the earth sinned sexually with her, and the people of the earth became drunk from the wine of her sexual sin."

[3]Then the angel carried me away by the Spirit to the desert. There I saw a woman sitting

on a red beast. It was covered with names against God written on it, and it had seven heads and ten horns. ⁴The woman was dressed in purple and red and was shining with the gold, precious jewels, and pearls she was wearing. She had a golden cup in her hand, a cup filled with evil things and the uncleanness of her sexual sin. ⁵On her forehead a title was written that was secret. This is what was written:

THE GREAT BABYLON
MOTHER OF PROSTITUTES
AND OF THE EVIL THINGS OF THE EARTH

⁶Then I saw that the woman was drunk with the blood of God's holy people and with the blood of those who were killed because of their faith in Jesus.

When I saw the woman, I was very amazed. ⁷Then the angel said to me, "Why are you amazed? I will tell you the secret of this woman and the beast she rides—the one with seven heads and ten horns. ⁸The beast you saw was once alive but is not alive now. But soon it will come up out of the bottomless pit and go away to be destroyed. There are people who live on earth whose names have not been written in the book of life since the beginning of the world. They will be amazed when they see the beast, because he was once alive, is not alive now, but will come again.

## "THE LAMB WILL DEFEAT THEM, BECAUSE HE IS LORD OF LORDS AND KING OF KINGS."

⁹"You need a wise mind to understand this. The seven heads on the beast are seven mountains where the woman sits. ¹⁰And they are seven kings. Five of the kings have already been destroyed, one of the kings lives now, and another has not yet come. When he comes, he must stay a short time. ¹¹The beast that was once alive, but is not alive now, is also an

eighth king. He belongs to the first seven kings, and he will go away to be destroyed.

¹²"The ten horns you saw are ten kings who have not yet begun to rule, but they will receive power to rule with the beast for one hour. ¹³All ten of these kings have the same purpose, and they will give their power and authority to the beast. ¹⁴They will make war against the Lamb, but the Lamb will defeat them, because he is Lord of lords and King of kings. He will defeat them with his called, chosen, and faithful followers."

¹⁵Then the angel said to me, "The waters that you saw, where the prostitute sits, are peoples, races, nations, and languages. ¹⁶The ten horns and the beast you saw will hate the prostitute. They will take everything she has and leave her naked. They will eat her body and burn her with fire. ¹⁷God made the ten horns want to carry out his purpose by agreeing to give the beast their power to rule, until what God has said comes about. ¹⁸The woman you saw is the great city that rules over the kings of the earth."

### BABYLON IS DESTROYED

**18** After the vision of these things, I saw another angel coming down from heaven. This angel had great power, and his glory made the earth bright. ²He shouted in a powerful voice:

"Ruined, ruined is the great city of
     Babylon!
   She has become a home for demons
 and a prison for every evil spirit,
     and a prison for every unclean bird and
       unclean beast.
³She has been ruined, because all the
       peoples of the earth
   have drunk the wine of the desire of her
       sexual sin.
 She has been ruined also because the kings
       of the earth
   have sinned sexually with her,
 and the merchants of the earth
   have grown rich from the great wealth of
       her luxury."

⁴Then I heard another voice from heaven saying:

**top 10**

random scriptures to memorize

**10** Ephesians 6:11-17

Philippians 4:13 **9**

**8** Romans 3:23

Galatians 5:22-23 **7**

**6** 1 Corinthians 13:4-7

Proverbs 31 **5**

**4** Psalm 139

Joshua 1:9 **3**

**2** John 3:16

Psalm 23 **1**

# Music Reviews

| GROUP: | ALBUM: |
|---|---|
| VARIOUS | HIP HOPE HITS 2005 |

THE HOTTEST POSITIVE HIP HOP OF THE YEAR

For rap and hip hop fans that also happen to consider themselves Christians, *Hip Hope Hits 2005* is a breath of fresh beats. Now you can enjoy sweet rhymes and mixes with a positive message from Christian music's most talented urban artists—all on one collection. The new GRITS single "Hittin' Curves" and tobyMac's exclusive remake of the little-known and wonderfully offbeat "Ill-M-I" (by Soul Junk on his unique 2000 offering titled *1956*) alone make this project worth the price. Throw in the fact that it also contains cuts by John Reuben, Verbs, DJ Maj, LA Symphony, Ill Harmonics, T-Bone, Pigeon John, 4th Avenue Jones, and Souljahz, and you can't go wrong.

**WHY IT ROCKS: HOT HIP HOP AND ROCKIN' RAPS INCORPORATE EAST COAST AND WEST COAST STYLES.**

"Come out of that city, my people,
so that you will not share in her sins,
so that you will not receive the disasters
that will come to her.
5Her sins have piled up as high as the sky,
and God has not forgotten the wrongs
she has done.
6Give that city the same as she gave to
others.
Pay her back twice as much as she did.
Prepare wine for her that is twice as strong
as the wine she prepared for others.
7She gave herself much glory and rich
living.
Give her that much suffering and sadness.
She says to herself, 'I am a queen sitting on
my throne.
I am not a widow; I will never be sad.'
8So these disasters will come to her in one
day:
death, and crying, and great hunger,
and she will be destroyed by fire,
because the Lord God who judges her is
powerful."
9The kings of the earth who sinned sexually with her and shared her wealth will see the smoke from her burning. Then they will cry and be sad because of her death. 10They will be afraid of her suffering and stand far away and say:

"Terrible! How terrible for you, great city,
powerful city of Babylon,
because your punishment has come in one
hour!"
11And the merchants of the earth will cry and be sad about her, because now there is no one to buy their cargoes— 12cargoes of gold, silver, jewels, pearls, fine linen, purple cloth, silk, red cloth; all kinds of citron wood and all kinds of things made from ivory, expensive wood, bronze, iron, and marble; 13cinnamon, spice, incense, myrrh, frankincense, wine, olive oil, fine flour, wheat, cattle, sheep, horses, carriages, slaves, and human lives.
14The merchants will say,
"Babylon, the good things you wanted are
gone from you.
All your rich and fancy things have
disappeared.
You will never have them again."
15The merchants who became rich from selling to her will be afraid of her suffering and will stand far away. They will cry and be sad 16and say:
"Terrible! How terrible for the great city!
She was dressed in fine linen, purple
and red cloth,
and she was shining with gold, precious
jewels, and pearls!
17All these riches have been destroyed in one
hour!"

Every sea captain, every passenger, the sailors, and all those who earn their living from the sea stood far away from Babylon. 18As they saw the smoke from her burning, they cried out loudly, "There was never a city like this great city!" 19And they threw dust on their heads and cried out, weeping and being sad. They said:
"Terrible! How terrible for the great
city!
All the people who had ships on the sea
became rich because of her wealth!
But she has been destroyed in one hour!
20Be happy because of this, heaven!
Be happy, God's holy people and
apostles and prophets!
God has punished her because of what she
did to you."
21Then a powerful angel picked up a large stone, like one used for grinding grain, and threw it into the sea. He said:
"In the same way, the great city of Babylon
will be thrown down,
and it will never be found again.
22The music of people playing harps and
other instruments, flutes, and
trumpets,
will never be heard in you again.
No workman doing any job
will ever be found in you again.

The sound of grinding grain
will never be heard in you again.
23The light of a lamp
will never shine in you again,
and the voices of a bridegroom and
bride
will never be heard in you again.
Your merchants were the world's great
people,
and all the nations were tricked by your
magic.
24You are guilty of the death of the prophets
and God's holy people
and all who have been killed on earth."

## People in Heaven Praise God

**19** After this vision and announcement I heard what sounded like a great many people in heaven saying:

"Hallelujah!"

Salvation, glory, and power belong to our
God,
2   because his judgments are true and right.

He has punished the prostitute
who made the earth evil with her sexual
sin.
He has paid her back for the death of his
servants."

3Again they said:

"Hallelujah!

She is burning, and her smoke will rise
forever and ever."

4Then the twenty-four elders and the four living creatures bowed down and worshiped God, who sits on the throne. They said:

"Amen, Hallelujah!"

5Then a voice came from the throne, saying:

"Praise our God, all you who serve him
and all you who honor him, both small
and great!"

6Then I heard what sounded like a great many people, like the noise of flooding water, and like the noise of loud thunder. The people were saying:

"Hallelujah!

Our Lord God, the Almighty, rules.
7Let us rejoice and be happy
and give God glory,
because the wedding of the Lamb has
come,
and the Lamb's bride has made herself
ready.
8Fine linen, bright and clean, was given to
her to wear."

(The fine linen means the good things done by God's holy people.)

9And the angel said to me, "Write this: Happy are those who have been invited to the wedding meal of the Lamb!" And the angel said, "These are the true words of God."

10Then I bowed down at the angel's feet to worship him, but he said to me, "Do not worship me! I am a servant like you and your brothers and sisters who have the message of Jesus. Worship God, because the message about Jesus is the spirit that gives all prophecy."

# Changed Lives

### Megan's Story—Eating Disorders

On the outside, I was smart and talented. My parents loved each other and loved me. But inside, I lived in fear that I just wasn't good enough. I was the middle sister of three girls, and one of my sisters and I were always in unspoken competition. My mother became worried about my weight and started taking me to weight loss programs in the sixth grade. The weight issue just added more pressure. When I was 16, I developed a full-fledged eating disorder. I was put in an eating disorders treatment program, and learned all the "tricks" from the other patients. When I got home, I simply stopped eating, surviving for the next six months on little more than coffee and celery. I lost 100 pounds, and everyone thought it was great that I had so much will power. Eventually, I started eating again but was so afraid of gaining weight back that I threw up or took huge doses of laxatives every time I ate. I even shoplifted laxatives with a friend. When I started college, the behavior continued. One time, I blacked out in

the shower after taking ninety laxatives. I woke up in the floor in my own vomit. For the next two years, I was in and out of college and became more and more sick. I threw up ten times a day and took thirty to sixty laxatives at a time. I was always broke from my junk food binges. I constantly sabotaged myself, to the point that I finally had to receive electroshock therapy. A roommate who was a Christian finally confronted me about my bulimia, and I broke down. I was ready for change, so I applied to a Christian program that specialized in helping girls with eating disorders. I learned how much God really loved me and that he said I was made in "an amazing and wonderful way" (Psalm 139:14). He delivered me from my dependence on medications and helped me learn not to abuse food. I finished my degree, completed a Master's degree, and wrote my thesis on eating disorders. Now I work in the program that helped save my life, and I love helping other girls who feel hopeless like I did.

*For more information on overcoming eating disorders, visit www.minirthacademy.com or www.remuda-ranch.com. For information about residential care for females, visit www.mercy-ministries.com. (Names have been changed for the sake of privacy. Megan tells her story after going through biblically based counseling with Mercy Ministries.)*

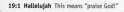

**notes** 19:1 **Hallelujah** This means "praise God!"

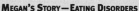

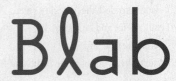

**Q:** Does it matter to God whether I go to a Christian school or public school?

**A:** No. There are advantages and disadvantages to both. Christian schools give you a better foundation in God's Word, because they not only teach you Bible as a subject but also teach every other subject from a biblical worldview. However, public schools may offer a wider variety of academics and give you more opportunities to share your faith. The choice is up to your parents, you, and God. Ask him for strength wherever you go.

**Q:** I am home schooled, and I feel different because of it. Is it wrong to want to be the same as everyone else?

**A:** It's normal to want to fit in, but appreciate your unique opportunities. Think of it this way: if every single food tasted exactly the same, eating would be pretty boring. In the same way, God designed a life for you that is different from anyone else's, and home schooling is just one aspect of that. Enjoy it.

**Q:** I see other people get things that I want, and I always feel jealous. How can I stop feeling that way?

**A:** The Bible says in the Ten Commandments that you should not covet, which means to want other people's things. Ask God to line up your desires with his, so that you will want the things he wants for you. Pray that you will not get too caught up in material things. Go one step further and clean out your room, getting rid of things you really don't need.

## THE RIDER ON THE WHITE HORSE

[11]Then I saw heaven opened, and there before me was a white horse. The rider on the horse is called Faithful and True, and he is right when he judges and makes war. [12]His eyes are like burning fire, and on his head are many crowns. He has a name written on him, which no one but himself knows. [13]He is dressed in a robe dipped in blood, and his name is the Word of God. [14]The armies of heaven, dressed in fine linen, white and clean, were following him on white horses. [15]Out of the rider's mouth comes a sharp sword that he will use to defeat the nations, and he will rule them with a rod of iron. He will crush out the wine in the winepress of the terrible anger of God the Almighty. [16]On his robe and on his upper leg was written this name: KING OF KINGS AND LORD OF LORDS.

[17]Then I saw an angel standing in the sun, and he called with a loud voice to all the birds flying in the sky: "Come and gather together for the great feast of God [18]so that you can eat the bodies of kings, generals, mighty people, horses and their riders, and the bodies of all people—free, slave, small, and great."

[19]Then I saw the beast and the kings of the earth. Their armies were gathered together to make war against the rider on the horse and his army. [20]But the beast was captured and with him the false prophet who did the miracles for the beast. The false prophet had used these miracles to trick those who had the mark of the beast and worshiped his idol. The false prophet and the beast were thrown alive into the lake of fire that burns with sulfur. [21]And their armies were killed with the sword that came out of the mouth of the rider on the horse, and all the birds ate the bodies until they were full.

## THE THOUSAND YEARS

**20** I saw an angel coming down from heaven. He had the key to the bottomless pit and a large chain in his hand. [2]The angel grabbed the dragon, that old snake who is the devil and Satan, and tied him up for a thousand years. [3]Then he threw him into the bottomless pit, closed it, and locked it over him. The angel did this so he could not trick the people of the earth anymore until the thousand years were ended. After a thousand years he must be set free for a short time.

[4]Then I saw some thrones and people sitting on them who had been given the power to judge. And I saw the souls of those who had been killed because they were faithful to the message of Jesus and the message from God. They had not worshiped the beast or his idol, and they had not received the mark of the beast on their foreheads or on their hands. They came back to life and ruled with Christ for a thousand years. [5](The others that were dead did not live again until the thousand years were ended.) This is the first raising of the dead. [6]Happy and holy are those who share in this first raising of the dead. The second death has no power over them. They will be priests for God and for Christ and will rule with him for a thousand years.

[7]When the thousand years are over, Satan will be set free from his prison. [8]Then he will go out to trick the nations in all the earth—Gog and Magog—to gather them for battle. There are so many people they will be like sand on the seashore. [9]And Satan's army marched across the earth and gathered around the camp of God's people and the city God loves. But fire came down from heaven and burned them up. [10]And Satan, who tricked them, was thrown into the lake of burning sulfur with the beast and the false prophet. There they will be punished day and night forever and ever.

## PEOPLE OF THE WORLD ARE JUDGED

[11]Then I saw a great white throne and the One who was sitting on it. Earth and sky ran away from him and disappeared. [12]And I saw the dead, great and small, standing before the throne. Then books were opened, and the book of life was opened. The dead were judged by what they had done, which was written in the books. [13]The sea gave up the dead who were in it, and Death and Hades" gave up the dead who

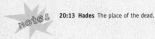

were in them. Each person was judged by what he had done. ¹⁴And Death and Hades were thrown into the lake of fire. The lake of fire is the second death. ¹⁵And anyone whose name was not found written in the book of life was thrown into the lake of fire.

## THE NEW JERUSALEM

21 Then I saw a new heaven and a new earth. The first heaven and the first earth had disappeared, and there was no sea anymore. ²And I saw the holy city, the new Jerusalem," coming down out of heaven from God. It was prepared like a bride dressed for her husband. ³And I heard a loud voice from the throne, saying, "Now God's presence is with people, and he will live with them, and they will be his people. God himself will be with them and will be their God. ⁴He will wipe away every tear from their eyes, and there will be no more death, sadness, crying, or pain, because all the old ways are gone."

⁵The One who was sitting on the throne said, "Look! I am making everything new!" Then he said, "Write this, because these words are true and can be trusted."

⁶The One on the throne said to me, "It is finished. I am the Alpha and the Omega," the Beginning and the End. I will give free water from the spring of the water of life to anyone who is thirsty. ⁷Those who win the victory will receive this, and I will be their God, and they will be my children. ⁸But cowards, those who refuse to believe, who do evil things, who kill, who sin sexually, who do evil magic, who worship idols, and who tell lies—all these will have a place in the lake of burning sulfur. This is the second death."

⁹Then one of the seven angels who had the seven bowls full of the seven last troubles came to me, saying, "Come with me, and I will show you the bride, the wife of the Lamb." ¹⁰And the angel carried me away by the Spirit to a very large and high mountain. He showed me the holy city, Jerusalem, coming down out of heaven from God. ¹¹It was shining with the glory of God and was bright like a very expensive jewel, like a jasper, clear as crystal. ¹²The

city had a great high wall with twelve gates with twelve angels at the gates, and on each gate was written the name of one of the twelve tribes of Israel. ¹³There were three gates on the east, three on the north, three on the south, and three on the west. ¹⁴The walls of the city were built on twelve foundation stones, and on the stones were written the names of the twelve apostles of the Lamb.

¹⁵The angel who talked with me had a measuring rod made of gold to measure the city, its gates, and its wall. ¹⁶The city was built in a square, and its length was equal to its width. The angel measured the city with the rod. The city was twelve thousand stadia" long, twelve thousand stadia wide, and twelve thousand stadia high. ¹⁷The angel also measured the wall. It was one hundred forty-four cubits" high, by human measurements, which the angel was using. ¹⁸The wall was made of jasper, and the city was made of pure gold, as pure as glass. ¹⁹The foundation stones of the city walls were decorated with every kind of jewel. The first foundation was jasper, the second was sapphire, the third was chalcedony, the fourth was emerald, ²⁰the fifth was onyx, the sixth was carnelian, the seventh was chrysolite, the eighth was beryl, the ninth was topaz, the tenth was chrysoprase, the eleventh was jacinth, and the twelfth was amethyst. ²¹The twelve gates were twelve pearls, each gate having been made from a single pearl. And the street of the city was made of pure gold as clear as glass.

²²I did not see a temple in the city, because the Lord God Almighty and the Lamb are the city's temple. ²³The city does not need the sun or the moon to shine on it, because the glory of God is its light, and the Lamb is the city's lamp. ²⁴By its light the people of the world will walk, and the kings of the earth will bring their glory into it. ²⁵The city's gates will never be shut on any day, because there is no night there. ²⁶The glory and the honor of the nations will be brought into it. ²⁷Nothing unclean and no one who does shameful things or tells lies will ever go into it. Only those whose names

Radical Faith:

## Revelation 21:3-5

We can't know everything about what heaven will be like, but what we do know about it from Scripture is stunning. God is going to make everything new—a new heaven, a new earth, and a new you. In heaven, there will be no more night—just glorious brightness all the time. All the light will come shining from God himself (Revelation 22:5). His very presence will fill and complete and satisfy and overwhelm everything. Your heart will be restored and healed in every sense. All the sadness and pain that you've ever known will be swept out of you. All that was ever wrong will be made right. You'll be free of suffering and completely satisfied. You will know absolute peace, and it will be everlasting. You'll have a new body that is perfect and complete. Even if we can't know exactly how heaven will be, we can know that it will be precious, brilliant, glorious, magnificent, perfect, complete, and beautiful. God is keeping the rest a surprise. Put your hope in him, and worship him now as you joyfully anticipate the beauty and glory of what's to come.

**21:2 new Jerusalem** The spiritual city where God's people live with him.   **21:6 Alpha and the Omega** The first and last letters of the Greek alphabet. This means "the beginning and the end."   **21:16 stadia** One stadion was a distance of about two hundred yards; about one-eighth of a Roman mile.   **21:17 cubits** A cubit is about half a yard, the length from the elbow to the tip of the little finger.

## relationships

"Do not be fooled: 'Bad friends will ruin good habits'" (1 Corinthians 15:33). Choose your friends carefully. Be friendly to everyone, but be careful to develop deep friendships with others who love Christ and who will be loyal to you. Good friends build you up and encourage you to do the right thing. If a friend talks you into betraying your boyfriend, deceiving your parents, or dumping your schoolwork, that's not a healthy friendship. Stick close to real friends who challenge and encourage you.

are written in the Lamb's book of life will enter the city.

**22** Then the angel showed me the river of the water of life. It was shining like crystal and was flowing from the throne of God and of the Lamb ²down the middle of the street of the city. The tree of life was on each side of the river. It produces fruit twelve times a year, once each month. The leaves of the tree are for the healing of all the nations. ³Nothing that God judges guilty will be in that city. The throne of God and of the Lamb will be there, and God's servants will worship him. ⁴They will see his face, and his name will be written on their foreheads. ⁵There will never be night again. They will not need the light of a lamp or the light of the sun, because the Lord God will give them light. And they will rule as kings forever and ever.

⁶The angel said to me, "These words can be trusted and are true." The Lord, the God of the spirits of the prophets, sent his angel to show his servants the things that must happen soon.

⁷"Listen! I am coming soon! Happy is the one who obeys the words of prophecy in this book."

⁸I, John, am the one who heard and saw these things. When I heard and saw them, I bowed down to worship at the feet of the angel who showed these things to me. ⁹But the angel said to me, "Do not worship me! I am a servant like you, your brothers the prophets, and all those who obey the words in this book. Worship God!"

¹⁰Then the angel told me, "Do not keep secret the words of prophecy in this book, because the time is near for all this to happen. ¹¹Let whoever is doing evil continue to do evil. Let whoever is unclean continue to be unclean. Let whoever is doing right continue to do right. Let whoever is holy continue to be holy."

¹²"Listen! I am coming soon! I will bring my reward with me, and I will repay each one of you for what you have done. ¹³I am the Alpha and the Omega," the First and the Last, the Beginning and the End.

¹⁴"Happy are those who wash their robes" so that they will receive the right to eat the fruit from the tree of life and may go through the gates into the city. ¹⁵Outside the city are the evil people, those who do evil magic, who sin sexually, who murder, who worship idols, and who love lies and tell lies.

¹⁶"I, Jesus, have sent my angel to tell you these things for the churches. I am the descendant from the family of David, and I am the bright morning star."

## "LISTEN! I AM COMING SOON! HAPPY IS THE ONE WHO OBEYS THE WORDS OF PROPHECY IN THIS BOOK."

¹⁷The Spirit and the bride say, "Come!" Let the one who hears this say, "Come!" Let whoever is thirsty come; whoever wishes may have the water of life as a free gift.

¹⁸I warn everyone who hears the words of the prophecy of this book: If anyone adds anything to these words, God will add to that person the disasters written about in this book. ¹⁹And if anyone takes away from the words of this book of prophecy, God will take away that one's share of the tree of life and of the holy city, which are written about in this book.

²⁰Jesus, the One who says these things are true, says, "Yes, I am coming soon."

Amen. Come, Lord Jesus!

²¹The grace of the Lord Jesus be with all. Amen.

**22:13 Alpha and the Omega** The first and last letters of the Greek alphabet. This means "the beginning and the end." **22:14 wash their robes** This means they believed and obeyed Jesus so that their sins could be forgiven by Christ's blood. The "washing" may refer to baptism (Acts 22:16).

But I say to you, love your enemies. Pray for those who hurt you. If you do this, you will be true children of your Father in heaven. He causes the sun to rise on good people and on evil people, and he sends rain to those who do right and to those who do wrong.

—Matthew 5:44-45

Don't judge other people, or you will be judged. You will be judged in the same way that you judge others, and the amount you give to others will be given to you. Why do you notice the little piece of dust in your friend's eye, but you don't notice the big piece of wood in your own eye?

—Matthew 7:1-3

Ask, and God will give to you. Search, and you will find. Knock, and the door will open for you. Yes, everyone who asks will receive. Everyone who searches will find. And everyone who knocks will have the door opened.

—Matthew 7:7-8

Jesus said to his followers, "Go everywhere in the world, and tell the Good News to everyone."

—Mark 16:15

Jesus said to all of them, "If people want to follow me, they must give up the things they want. They must be willing to give up their lives daily to follow me. Those who want to save their lives will give up true life. But those who give up their lives for me will have true life."

—Luke 9:23-24

Then Jesus said, "Whoever accepts this little child in my name accepts me. And whoever accepts me accepts the One who sent me, because whoever is least among you all is really the greatest."

—Luke 9:48

God loved the world so much that he gave his one and only Son so that whoever believes in him may not be lost, but have eternal life.

—John 3:16

But Jesus said, "I tell you the truth, the Son can do nothing alone. The Son does only what he sees the Father doing, because the Son does whatever the Father does."

—John 5:19

Jesus said to her, "I am the resurrection and the life. Those who believe in me will have life even if they die. And everyone who lives and believes in me will never die."

—John 11:25-26

I am the vine, and you are the branches. If any remain in me and I remain in them, they produce much fruit. But without me they can do nothing.

—John 15:5

You were made free from sin, and now you are slaves to goodness.

—Romans 6:18

Yes, I am sure that neither death, nor life, nor angels, nor ruling spirits, nothing now, nothing in the future, no powers, nothing above us, nothing below us, nor anything else in the whole world will ever be able to separate us from the love of God that is in Christ Jesus our Lord.

—Romans 8:38-39

Do not change yourselves to be like the people of this world, but be changed within by a new way of thinking. Then you will be able to decide what God wants for you; you will know what is good and pleasing to him and what is perfect.

—Romans 12:2

Love is patient and kind. Love is not jealous, it does not brag, and it is not proud.

—1 Corinthians 13:4

Be alert. Continue strong in the faith. Have courage, and be strong. Do everything in love.

—1 Corinthians 16:13-14

If anyone belongs to Christ, there is a new creation. The old things have gone; everything is made new!

—2 Corinthians 5:17

But the Spirit produces the fruit of love, joy, peace, patience, kindness, goodness, faithfulness, gentleness, self-control. There is no law that says these things are wrong.

—Galatians 5:22-23

God has made us what we are. In Christ Jesus, God made us to do good works, which God planned in advance for us to live our lives doing.

—Ephesians 2:10

Now you who are not Jewish are not foreigners or strangers any longer, but are citizens together with God's holy people. You belong to God's family.

—Ephesians 2:19

Do not worry about anything, but pray and ask God for everything you need, always giving thanks. And God's peace, which is so great we cannot understand it, will keep your hearts and minds in Christ Jesus.

—Philippians 4:6-7

Brothers and sisters, think about the things that are good and worthy of praise. Think about the things that are true and honorable and right and pure and beautiful and respected.

—Philippians 4:8

I can do all things through Christ, because he gives me strength.

—Philippians 4:13

Do not let anyone treat you as if you are unimportant because you are young. Instead, be an example to the believers with your words, your actions, your love, your faith, and your pure life.

—1 Timothy 4:12

God did not give us a spirit that makes us afraid but a spirit of power and love and self-control.

—2 Timothy 1:7

But run away from the evil young people like to do. Try hard to live right and to have faith, love, and peace, together with those who trust in the Lord from pure hearts.

—2 Timothy 2:22

We all share in Christ if we keep till the end the sure faith we had in the beginning.

—Hebrews 3:14

Faith means being sure of the things we hope for and knowing that something is real even if we do not see it.

—Hebrews 11:1

You also are like living stones, so let yourselves be used to build a spiritual temple—to be holy priests who offer spiritual sacrifices to God. He will accept those sacrifices through Jesus Christ.

—1 Peter 2:5

But you are a chosen people, royal priests, a holy nation, a people for God's own possession. You were chosen to tell about the wonderful acts of God, who called you out of darkness into his wonderful light.

—1 Peter 2:9

Here I am! I stand at the door and knock. If you hear my voice and open the door, I will come in and eat with you, and you will eat with me.

—Revelation 3:20

# my Prayer Requests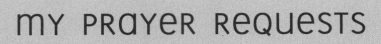

Date/Prayer Requests

_____

_____

_____

_____

_____

_____

_____

_____

_____

_____

_____

_____

_____

_____

_____

_____

_____

_____

Date Prayer Answered

_____

_____

_____

_____

_____

_____

_____

_____

_____

_____

_____

_____

_____

_____

_____

_____

_____

_____